Beginning
SharePoint® 2007
Administration

Windows® SharePoint® Services 3.0 and
Microsoft® Office SharePoint® Server 2007

Göran Husman

BICENTENNIAL
1807
WILEY
2007
BICENTENNIAL

John Wiley and Sons

Beginning SharePoint® 2007 Administration:
Windows® SharePoint® Services 3.0 and Microsoft® Office SharePoint® Server 2007

Published by
Wiley Publishing, Inc.
10475 Crosspoint Boulevard
Indianapolis, IN 46256
www.wiley.com

Copyright @ 2007 by Wiley Publishing, Inc., Indianapolis, Indiana

Published simultaneously in Canada

ISBN: 978-0-4701- 2529-8

Manufactured in the United States of America

10 9 8 7 6 5 4 3 2

Library of Congress Cataloging-in-Publication Data:
Husman, Göran.
  Beginning SharePoint 2007 administration : comp services / Göran Husman.
    p. cm.
  Includes index.
  ISBN 978-0-470-12529-8 (paper/website)
  1. Intranets (Computer networks) 2. Web servers. 3. Web portals. I. Title.
  TK5105.875.I6H867 2007
  004.6'8—dc22

                              2007013699

For general information on our other products and services please contact our Customer Care Department
within the United States at (800) 762-2974, outside the United States at (317) 572-3993 or fax (317) 572-4002.

Trademarks: Wiley, the Wiley logo, Wrox, the Wrox logo, Wrox Programmer to Programmer, and related
trade dress are trademarks or registered trademarks of John Wiley & Sons, Inc. and/or its affiliates, in the
United States and other countries, and may not be used without written permission. Microsoft, SharePoint,
and Windows are registered trademarks of Microsoft Corporation in the United States and/or other countries. All other trademarks are the property of their respective owners. Wiley Publishing, Inc., is not associated with any product or vendor mentioned in this book.

Wiley also publishes its books in a variety of electronic formats. Some content that appears in print may not
be available in electronic books.

I dedicate this book to all my kids—you are the true joy in my life!

About the Author

Göran Husman is a true computer nerd who started his career as a computer programmer in 1978. After working as a C and Fortran developer for a medical university and later a large telecom company, he started his own consulting company in 1989. Due to market demands he soon switched his focus from UNIX to the MS environment and from developing code to implementing large e-mail systems and building information systems. Göran has also been hired as a computer trainer since the beginning of 1980. In 1993 he became one of the first certified MS Certified Trainers (MCT) in Sweden, and he has regularly conducted MS courses ever since. He is also certified by Microsoft as an MCP (with the number 2888) and an MSCE. His great engagement in e-mail systems awarded him status as Sweden's first MS Exchange MVP (Most Valuable Professional) by Microsoft. He switched his focus to MS SharePoint in 2003, and in January 2006 Microsoft awarded him status as Sweden's first SharePoint Portal Server MVP, which was renewed in January 2007. Göran has written a large amount of training material for the Swedish market over the years, and in 2001 his book *Exchange 2000 Server on Site* was released in the United States. In 2006 his book *Beginning SharePoint Administration* was released by Wrox. He is also frequently a speaker at conferences and seminars. Today Göran divides his time between consulting contracts, training, leading his company Human Data, and from time to time writing books. Oh, and he is also the proud father of six great kids from the ages of 6 to 28, which may be his greatest achievement in life.

Credits

Senior Acquisitions Editor
Jim Minatel

Development Editor
Kelly Talbot

Technical Editor
Phred Menyhert

Production Editor
Eric Charbonneau

Copy Editor
Foxxe Editorial Services

Editorial Manager
Mary Beth Wakefield

Production Manager
Tim Tate

Vice President and Executive Group Publisher
Richard Swadley

Vice President and Executive Publisher
Joseph B. Wikert

Compositor
Robin Kibby, Happenstance Type-O-Rama

Proofreader
Jen Larsen

Indexer
Johnna VanHoose Dinse

Anniversary Logo Design
Richard Pacifico

Acknowledgments

When I finished my last book about SharePoint 2003, my wife was assuring me that she would not accept another book — amazingly enough, she actually did accept that I was going to write this book after all, and I am forever grateful for her understanding and patience. Being a computer widow is not easy. But now I have promised her to stay away from book projects, at least for some time. I just wonder how long I can keep this promise….

There are a lot of other people who I really want to thank for helping me write this book. First is Jim Minatel, the Senior Acquisitions Editor at Wrox, who was brave enough to give me the chance to write this second book about SharePoint. I also want to thank my great agent Neil J. Salkind at Studio B, who convinced me to write this book. There are also some people at Wrox who have done a heroic job: Kelly Talbot, my Development Editor, who had to correct my bad grammar and sometimes totally confused descriptions (thanks Kelly—I really appreciate all your assistance!). Then I want to thank Phred Menyhert, my Technical Editor, for his great job of scrutinizing the technical part of the book. I was constantly amazed at his sharp eye for detail and for his highly technical skills. I am solely responsible for the content of this book, but all the invaluable tips from Phred helped me write a book that is full of clear and valuable descriptions on how to perform important tasks in SharePoint.

During the writing of this book, I also got numerous tips and tricks from my colleagues, employees, and fellow SharePoint nerds on the Internet. I want to thank them all: Michael Jansson, Gustaf Westerlund, and John Selnes, plus all the great SharePoint MVP fellows. You are all great guys, and your SharePoint expertise is outstanding!

Finally I want to thank my beloved wife Marina for her support and understanding. I know this hasn't always been easy, but sometimes a nerd's got to do what a nerd's got to do. This is simply the life of a computer widow.

And to my fantastic kids, Anna, Thomas, Marielle, Alex, Beatrice, and Johan—I love you all!

Contents

Contents

Contents

Contents

Contents

Contents

Introduction

When I first started planning for this book, I took some time to think about the challenges that face a beginning SharePoint 2007 administrator. The many SharePoint courses I have conducted as a SharePoint trainer have given me a good understanding of these challenges. All my SharePoint consulting has also been very helpful, because theory is one thing, but real-world experience is another. I also remember my own frustration and the numerous questions I had when I was trying to learn what SharePoint 2007 was all about. I have written the book that I wished I had when I started to work with SharePoint. My hope is that you will find it full of practical and easy-to-follow instructions that will help you get your SharePoint environment up and running in no time.

The goal of this book is to be your practical guide when building your SharePoint 2007 environment. I have tried to be very clear and focus on the steps that you must understand to build a production environment. Because SharePoint is a very broad subject with lots of details, I had to make sure that the book contains information that you most likely will need to know, such as how to install SharePoint, how to administrate it, how to customize it, and how to perform backup and restore procedures.

But administration is not the only important aspect of SharePoint. I know that most beginning SharePoint administrators also want to know what SharePoint is and what it can be used for. As the administrator, you will most likely be consulted by your users when they want to know how to get the most out of SharePoint 2007. That is why the book also contains several chapters on how to use the features of SharePoint.

Finally, the book has several references and tips for smart add-ons and utilities that will enhance the functionality of SharePoint, such as better navigation, integration with other systems, and workflow solutions. The book describes many free utilities and commercial third-party products. It also shows you where to find new utilities, because there is almost no other Microsoft product that has as many related new products and utilities constantly showing up.

Who This Book Is For

This book is intended for the beginning SharePoint administrator and for the administrator who has been working with SharePoint 2007 for some time but wants to know more about how it works. It will also help you understand the differences between SharePoint 2003 and SharePoint 2007 and help you find the arguments for upgrading. The book assumes that you have a basic understanding of the MS Windows 2003 operating system, including the Active Directory, as well as web applications in general. There is no need to be an expert in these areas, because the book explains everything you must know, but as always it helps to know the environment a product lives in. The book's main focus is planning, installation, configuration, and administration, but it also covers the basic information about customizing SharePoint—for example, how to create templates, how to build your own Site Definition, and how to use SharePoint Designer for extending the look and feel of SharePoint.

The book covers the differences between MS Office SharePoint Server 2007 (MOSS) and Windows SharePoint Services 3.0 (WSS) and helps you decide whether you need only WSS or if you should also implement MOSS. Regardless of your choice, the book describes how to use that environment in an optimal way. If you already have a SharePoint installation up and running, you can either skip Chapter 2 for WSS installation and Chapter 4 for MOSS installation, or you can explore them to get a better understanding of how your SharePoint environment was set up.

What This Book Covers

This book covers Windows SharePoint Service 3.0 (WSS) and MS Office SharePoint Server 2007 (MOSS). It does not describe how to migrate from earlier versions of these products, because that task must be very carefully tailored to your specific needs. It will help you install and configure a SharePoint environment for most types of organizations, both small and large. The book takes a very practical point of view. It is meant to be read from the beginning to the end, although you should also be able to use it as a reference book. It focuses on typical scenarios and tasks that a SharePoint administrator will face, such as configuring an intranet, setting up document management, and project management.

This book also covers how to use SharePoint 2007 together with MS Office, including Office 2007, and especially MS Outlook 2007. It shows you how these products work together to address typical situations for information workers (users working with projects, document management, and meetings).

You will also find an introduction to SharePoint Designer 2007 and how to use it for extending and customizing SharePoint sites; for example, how to customize master pages and page layout files, and create workflows.

How This Book Is Structured

The book begins with an introductory chapter to give you a sense of what SharePoint 2007 can do. It then continues with four more chapters of detailed instructions on how to install and configure WSS and MOSS, along with explanations of what you must think about when selecting the type of MS SQL database for your SharePoint server. These chapters include information that describes how to configure specific features of WSS and SPS, such as how to control what the users can do in SharePoint, how to work with intranet news pages, and how to set up Active Directory synchronization. In Chapter 5 you will also find information on how to customize MOSS, including how to change the colors, menus, and logos, how to configure SharePoint to accept incoming e-mail, and how to work with a records repository.

The remaining chapters are independent of each other, so you can read whatever interests you, but the book is written to encourage reading from beginning to end. Some of the content is hard to understand if you have skipped previous chapters, so I suggest that you read it from the beginning and skip parts that do not interest you at the time. Later, if you find that you need to understand those parts, you can go back to them then.

Chapter 6 describes the different site templates, including both MOSS and WSS site templates. It also describes how to use My Sites in an optimal way. You will also find an introduction to the web content management feature that now comes with SharePoint 2007.

Chapter 7 shows you the many ways that SharePoint integrates with other MS Office products, especially Office 2007. It also discusses the differences between Office 2007 and previous Office versions, including MS Outlook and MS InfoPath.

Chapter 8 focuses on advanced administration, mainly for the MOSS environment, such as managing the search feature, creating audience groups, managing user security, handling site definitions, creating templates, and more. Even if you are mainly focusing on WSS, you will still find some interesting information here about important MOSS features and how using MOSS differs from using WSS.

Chapter 9 shows you how the web content management features work in MOSS 2007. It also explains the difference between a page and a web site and how to configure them.

In Chapter 10 you will find a lot of tips on how to use SharePoint with MS Office for better file and document management. The chapter covers the ways you can configure and customize document libraries, such as activating version history, custom properties, and custom views. It also explains what Document Workspaces are used for and how to achieve workflow functionality in SharePoint 2007.

Chapter 11 shows you a practical way of building an intranet with either WSS or MOSS and how they differ from each other. This chapter summarizes a lot of features described in the earlier chapters, and will help you understand how to use SharePoint 2007.

Chapter 12 describes how to customize SharePoint sites without using a tool such as SharePoint Designer; for example you will learn how to create your own site definitions, how to create a custom CSS file, and how to customize the navigation in SharePoint 2007.

Chapter 13 describes how to use SharePoint Designer 2007 for customizing SharePoint sites and extending their functionality. You do not need any previous SharePoint Designer or FrontPage 2003 knowledge to get important information from this chapter.

Chapter 14 finally discusses one of the most important tasks for a SharePoint administrator: how to make backups and perform restores of your SharePoint environment. Sooner than you may think, this SharePoint server will become business critical, because it will contain lots of important documents, lists, and contacts. You don't want to lose that information. Make sure to read Chapter 14 to understand how to restore your SharePoint environment.

What You Need to Use This Book

This book is full of practical step-by-step instructions. To get the most out of this book, you should run SharePoint so that you can test these instructions. If you don't have a SharePoint environment, the book tells you how to find either the full WSS version or the evaluation version of MOSS and install it. You will also need a Windows 2003 server up and running, preferably in an Active Directory domain, to install SharePoint. A tip is to use an MS Virtual PC 2007 or VMware environment for building your test environment.

Some of these instructions and examples require you to run other programs, such as MS Office 2007, MS Outlook 2007, MS InfoPath 2007, and SharePoint Designer 2007. You can follow many, but not all, of the instructions if you have earlier versions of MS Office, such as Office 2003.

Conventions

To help you get the most from the text and keep track of what's happening, we've used a number of conventions throughout the book.

Try It Out

The *Try It Out* is an exercise you should work through, following the text in the book.

1. They usually consist of a set of steps.
2. Each step has a number.
3. Follow the steps through with your copy of the database.

> **Boxes like this one hold important, not-to-be forgotten information that is directly relevant to the surrounding text.**

Tips, hints, tricks, and asides to the current discussion are offset and placed in italics like this.

As for styles in the text:

We *highlight* new terms and important words when we introduce them.

We show keyboard strokes like this: Ctrl+A.

We show URLs and code within the text like this: `persistence properties`.

We present code in two different ways:

```
In code examples we highlight new and important code with a gray background.
```

```
The gray highlighting is not used for code that's less important in the
present context, or has been shown before.
```

Source Code

As you work through the examples in this book, you may choose either to type in all the code manually or to use the source code files that accompany the book. All of the source code used in this book is available for download at www.wrox.com. Once at the site, simply locate the book's title (either by using the Search box or by using one of the title lists) and click the Download Code link on the book's detail page to obtain all the source code for the book.

> Because many books have similar titles, you may find it easiest to search by ISBN; this book's ISBN is 978-0-4701-2529-8.

Once you download the code, just decompress it with your favorite compression tool. Alternately, you can go to the main Wrox code download page at www.wrox.com/dynamic/books/download.aspx to see the code available for this book and all other Wrox books.

Errata

We make every effort to ensure that there are no errors in the text or in the code. However, no one is perfect, and mistakes do occur. If you find an error in one of our books, such as a spelling mistake or faulty piece of code, we would be very grateful for your feedback. By sending in errata you may save another reader hours of frustration and at the same time you will be helping us provide even higher-quality information. w

To find the errata page for this book, go to www.wrox.com and locate the title using the Search box or one of the title lists. Then, on the book details page, click the Book Errata link. On this page you can view all errata that has been submitted for this book and posted by Wrox editors. A complete book list including links to each book's errata is also available at www.wrox.com/misc-pages/booklist.shtml.

If you don't spot "your" error on the Book Errata page, go to www.wrox.com/contact/techsupport.shtml and complete the form there to send us the error you have found. We'll check the information and, if appropriate, post a message to the book's errata page and fix the problem in subsequent editions of the book.

p2p.wrox.com

For author and peer discussion, join the P2P forums at p2p.wrox.com. The forums are a web-based system for you to post messages relating to Wrox books and related technologies and interact with other readers and technology users. The forums offer a subscription feature to e-mail you topics of interest of your choosing when new posts are made to the forums. Wrox authors, editors, other industry experts, and your fellow readers are present on these forums.

Introduction

At http://p2p.wrox.com you will find a number of different forums that will help you not only as you read this book but also as you develop your own applications. To join the forums, just follow these steps:

1. Go to p2p.wrox.com and click the Register link.

2. Read the terms of use and click Agree.

3. Complete the required information to join as well as any optional information you wish to provide, and click Submit.

4. You will receive an e-mail with information describing how to verify your account and complete the joining process.

> *You can read messages in the forums without joining P2P but in order to post your own messages, you must join.*

Once you join, you can post new messages and respond to messages other users post. You can read messages at any time on the Web. If you would like to have new messages from a particular forum e-mailed to you, click the Subscribe to this Forum icon by the forum name in the forum listing.

For more information about how to use the Wrox P2P, be sure to read the P2P FAQs for answers to questions about how the forum software works as well as many common questions specific to P2P and Wrox books. To read the FAQs, click the FAQ link on any P2P page.

Introduction to Microsoft SharePoint 2007

I am extremely happy you are reading this book. It tells me that you are planning to install SharePoint 2007 or at least are curious about it. Congratulations! This is a very good move! This is the third generation of SharePoint, and it is so much better than its predecessors. In fact, at the TechEd 2006 conference I heard a Microsoft representative talk about how they build a new software application: "First we do a lot of planning, analysis and of course guessing at what the customer wants in such a product; this results in version 1.0. Of course, we quickly realize that we missed a number of things, so we learn from that, rebuild the product, and then release version 2.0. This version will most likely also miss some important features, which our customers tell us in a very frank and honest way. So, we sit down again, add the missing features, plus a lot more, and fix weaknesses, and then we release version 3.0. And this time we usually get it right!"

If we apply that logic to the different SharePoint versions, we see that in 2001 Microsoft released version 1.0 of SharePoint Team Services and SharePoint Portal Server 2001. In 2003 Microsoft released version 2.0, which was known as Windows SharePoint Services and SharePoint Portal Server 2003. Finally, in late 2006 they released version 3.0, which is known as Windows SharePoint Services and Microsoft Office SharePoint Server. If you ask someone who has been working with all these versions, they will tell you that Microsoft's story about software versions is indeed true; version 3.0 of SharePoint, also known as "SharePoint 2007," is a fantastic application. It has almost everything you would want in such a program. I love it, and I am sure you will it too!

So what is SharePoint 2007, and what can it do for you? That is the subject for this book. You will learn step by step how to install, configure, and maintain a SharePoint environment, regardless of the size of your company. You will also learn how to take advantage of all the cool features it includes, such as extended integration with products like MS Word and MS Outlook. And, hopefully, you will find this book easy to understand, and sometimes even fun to read. The objective in this chapter is to show you why SharePoint is such an interesting product and to give you some ideas of what you can do after installing it.

What Is SharePoint?

SharePoint helps you gather information together, regardless of what type it is. It may be MS Word documents or any other type of file, but it may also be information that you usually store in other types of applications, such as contact lists, team calendars, product databases, project planning, or news lists. SharePoint also helps you find information, even when you don't know where it is stored, and SharePoint helps you keep track of updated information. In other words, SharePoint does not invent any new information type; instead, it helps you get the right information when you need it without spending lots of time looking for it. Even more importantly, all this information is easily shared among users, such as project teams, departments, or even entire organizations.

Microsoft has performed a thorough analysis of how people use their computers in most types of organizations. Microsoft has a very good understanding of what types of problems these users have and what things that need to be changed or removed in order to help the users work more effectively. One of Microsoft's findings indicates that people tend to become frustrated when they need help from the administrator or Help desk to do even simple things, such as creating a place in the network for sharing information within a team or adding a new team member. Users want to have more power to do what they want, when they want, and exactly how they want. This concept is sometimes referred to as self-service and is a new trend in the computer business. For example, you can find applications that allow the user to reset her password, change her properties in the Active Directory (AD), and so on.

SharePoint is built around this concept, and the main idea is to allow the ordinary user to create web sites for projects and other activities without any support from the server administrator or Help desk. This requires some training for the SharePoint user, but SharePoint is straightforward and easy to learn. Your role, as the SharePoint Server administrator, is to install, maintain, and configure SharePoint. You are also the person people will contact when they need help understanding how do things in SharePoint, such as creating sites and managing lists of information. That's why this book tells you how to do these things and gives you tips and hints to make things easier for you and your users. I am sure that you will like it for your own personal use, too — SharePoint is simply a fantastic application with enormous potential, if you know how to use it correctly!

It is actually hard to describe what SharePoint is in just a few words, but let's give it a try. Using this application, you can build a web-based environment that includes the following, and more:

- ❑   A public Internet site
- ❑   An intranet portal for the organization and each department
- ❑   An extranet portal for your customers and partners
- ❑   A team site for your sales department
- ❑   A project site for the development team
- ❑   A document management system that is compliant with Sarbanes-Oxley (SOX) and ISO-9000
- ❑   A personal site for each user where they can store personal data and create links to their team sites
- ❑   A digital dashboard for storing business intelligence data such as key performance indicators
- ❑   A place to search and locate any type of information, regardless of where it is stored
- ❑   A record management system for storing legal information in a secure way

The list goes on and on. Since SharePoint is such a flexible and powerful application, it is almost only your own imagination that limits what you can do with it. It is also very fun to work with, since it is so easy to build an impressive solution with it. Microsoft has most certainly created a killer application — again! Figure 1-1 shows a typical SharePoint 2007 site, just to give you an idea about how it looks.

Figure 1-1

The History of SharePoint

In order to understand how to install and manage SharePoint, you need to know its history. This will help you understand not only where it comes from but also some abbreviations that are used in SharePoint 2007.

Around 2000, Microsoft unveiled an application called a Digital Dashboard. This web-based application used a new concept called web parts, which are rectangular areas on a web page that display some type of information, such as a list of contacts, links, or documents. This was innovative because the user could now arrange the web parts on the web page herself, without any help from an HTML programmer.

In 2001, Microsoft released its first two SharePoint products. One was SharePoint Team Services (STS), and the other was SharePoint Portal Server (SPS). Only a few organizations implemented these products, which was a pity since they offered a number of advanced collaboration features, especially for MS Office users. STS was a free web-based product used for collaboration. You could use it to share contacts, calendar events, and documents within teams and small departments. The information was stored in an MS SQL database. It was a nice application, but it did not have any document-management features, and it was not built for creating intranet solutions for larger organizations.

SPS was a separate product, initially made as an MS Exchange 2000 public folder application (under the beta name Tahoe). However, during the beta phase of Tahoe, Microsoft got a loud and clear message from the customers: "Do not mess with our Exchange system!" So Microsoft finally released the SPS using a built-in MS Exchange 2000 server database (which made more than one SharePoint administrator wonder why on earth the SharePoint server event log contained messages from the Exchange Information Store). This new SPS had built-in document-management features, such as document versioning, checkout/checkin, and document workflow. It also had a good search engine that allowed the user to find information, regardless of where it was stored. One serious problem with SPS 2001 was the quality of its performance and the limited number of documents it could manage. And it did not have some of the nice collaboration features that STS had. In fact, the two products were competing with each other, to some extent, which is not a good way of convincing the customer to invest in SharePoint technology. Also, SPS was not free like STS, but licensed per server and per user.

In October 2003, Microsoft released its second generation of SharePoint. The old STS, now renamed Windows SharePoint Services (WSS), was basically a fancier version of STS (internally, Microsoft referred to it as STS version 2). SPS kept its name, SharePoint Portal Server, but that was about all that was kept from the previous SPS version. No longer did SPS have its own MS Exchange database, and no longer was SPS a separate product! Now it was an add-on to the WSS application. Finally, Microsoft had one integrated SharePoint solution, completely based on the MS SQL Server database.

Still, there were some annoying things about the SharePoint 2003 editions. Although they now looked very similar, they did not behave in a similar way. For example, the permission settings for lists in WSS was different from the same type of lists in SPS, and while SPS was security-trimmed (users only saw what they were allowed to see), WSS was not.

At the end of 2006, Microsoft released the third generation of SharePoint. WSS kept its name, and the version number changed to WSS 3.0. WSS still was a free add-on for Windows 2003 Server and used an MS SQL–based server to store its content. Its bigger brother SPS was now renamed MS Office SharePoint Server (MOSS), but it was still an optional add-on to WSS and was using the same MS SQL database as WSS. The MOSS server was available in different editions and with optional services, such as MOSS 2007 Standard and MOSS 2007 Enterprise, plus Office Forms Server and Office SharePoint Server 2007 for Search.

The important things you should remember from this section are:

❑   STS is the old name for WSS and is still used in SharePoint 2007 in some places, such as the administrative tool `tsadm.exe` and the folder sts storing the site definition for WSS sites.

❑   MOSS has replaced SPS.

❑   MOSS comes in Standard and Enterprise editions and has optional servers.

❑   MS SQL Server is used by MOSS and WSS 3.0.

> **This book describes the features and functionality of both WSS 3.0 and MOSS 2007, which are also known as SharePoint Products and Technology (SPPT) 2007.**

Differences between WSS and MOSS

When thinking of WSS and MOSS, the important thing to understand is that WSS is the foundation and MOSS is an optional add-on. In fact, you cannot install MOSS by itself. If you try to do this, you will be requested to install WSS first. So, the question is: What differs between WSS and MOSS? If you have never seen SharePoint before, some of these answers might be hard to understand. Give it a try anyhow. The following chapters further flesh out the following points.

Windows SharePoint Services 3.0

WSS 3.0 has the following characteristics:

- ❑ It is a web-based application.
- ❑ It stores all information in an MS SQL database.
- ❑ It displays information using web parts.
- ❑ It has good document-management features.
- ❑ It has a number of list types that you can use for storing all kinds of information.
- ❑ It allows you to build workflow solutions that start when a document is changed.
- ❑ It is perfect for simple, but effective, intranet solutions.
- ❑ It is ideal for collaboration on project data, meetings, social events, and the like.
- ❑ It has its own index and search engine.
- ❑ Its lists and libraries can operate as RSS Feeds.
- ❑ It comes with site temples for creating Wiki and Blog sites.
- ❑ It is a free add-on to MS Windows 2003 Server (any edition).

In other words, WSS is the perfect place to collect information for your projects, your customers, and your meetings. You can move all documents from your file system into WSS and by doing so get access to the powerful document-management features it offers. It is also a very good solution when you need local intranets for teams or departments. And all this is free when you run Windows 2003 Server!

But there are things that WSS does not offer. The following are just a few examples:

- ❑ There is no support for indexing and searching information outside the WSS.
- ❑ It has no advanced intranet features, such as targeted information and content management.
- ❑ It has no advanced document management features, such as document policies.
- ❑ It has no record management of legal and other important documents.
- ❑ It cannot display InfoPath forms in a web browser.
- ❑ It cannot display MS Excel spreadsheets as web parts.
- ❑ It comes with less than 10 web parts.
- ❑ It cannot read and write to and from external databases.

This is where MOSS comes in.

MS Office SharePoint Server 2007

MOSS 2007 uses the same types of sites as WSS 3.0 but adds a lot of functionality to WSS 3.0, making it possible to do the following:

- ❑ Use global search functionality to find any type of information regardless of type and location.

- ❑ Target information to one or more user groups.

- ❑ Import user data from Active Directory.

- ❑ Use advanced content management for public Internet sites or portal sites.

- ❑ Use the RSS web part to list information fetched from RSS feeds.

- ❑ Display and use InfoPath forms with a web client, using the Forms Service.

- ❑ Display MS Excel spreadsheets and charts in a web part, using Excel Services.

- ❑ Search, display and edit content in external databases, such as SAP, using Business Data Catalog.

- ❑ Give each SharePoint user a personal web site, for both private and public use.

These characteristics make MOSS a very good solution for building public Internet sites or global intranets that are smart enough to show the right information to the right people. MOSS is also a good solution when you want to build a site for displaying business data, such as MS Excel spreadsheets, forms, and key performance indicators (KPIs)

What You Need to Run SharePoint

This section provides general information about what you need to install and run SharePoint, both WSS and MOSS. It also has general guidelines on the hardware configuration and some tips for building a test environment. Chapter 2 provides the exact steps on how to do the actual installation of a WSS 3.0 only environment. Chapter 4 provides the installation steps for a MOSS 2007 environment.

Software Requirements

Because SharePoint is a web application, you need to have a web server. The only web server that supports SharePoint is Internet Information Server version 6 (and later versions), which runs on Windows 2003 Server and later generations of Windows Server. You can use any edition of Windows 2003 Server, including the cheaper Web Edition.

You need to install the Windows component ASP.NET web platform, as described in Chapter 2, plus upgrade it to support ASP.NET 2.0, including Windows Workflow Foundation (Win WF). If you want SharePoint to act as a mail server, thus allowing users to send mail to its lists, you must also install the Windows component SMTP. All of this is covered in detail in Chapters 2 and 4.

The last, but not least, component you need is an MS SQL–based database. You have two choices: Microsoft SQL Server 2005 Express, which comes free with SharePoint 2007 or the full MS SQL 2000/2005 Server. These two choices give you different features, as listed in the following table:

Feature	SQL Server Express	MS SQL 2000/2005
Limited database size	Yes (4 GB max — but see comment in the text below)	No
Can run on a separate server	No	Yes
Includes management tools	No	Yes
License type	Free	Per CPU or per user

However, the story is a bit more complicated than this! If you install a pure WSS 3.0 environment, you will have a special version of SQL Server Express referred to as the Embedded SQL Server Express. This version does not have any size limitations, which means that you can run WSS 3.0 using this embedded database edition in a production environment — and both of these are free when running on Windows 2003 Server! But if you install MOSS, you get the 4 GB size-limited version of SQL Server Express. This means that you cannot use MOSS with SQL Server Express in a production environment due to the limitation; rather, you must use the MS SQL 2000/2005 Server.

There is one more important difference regarding SQL Server Express and SQL 2000/2005 Server: The former must be installed on the same server as SharePoint (WSS or MOSS), while MS SQL 2000/2005 gives you an option of choosing what server to use for storing all the data. Only by using the full SQL 2000/2005 Server can you keep SharePoint and the database on separate servers, which provides improved performance and scalability. This is known in SharePoint terms as a small server farm configuration.

Hardware Requirements

In addition to all the software requirements, the server hardware must also be configured properly. For a test environment, you can get by with 1 GB of memory and at least 10 GB of free disk space. This type of requirement is easily met by using virtual server software, such as MS Virtual PC. The CPU type is not important in a test environment, but in a production environment you will want a high-speed single or multiple-CPU configuration. You learn more about this in Chapters 2 and 4.

Building a Test Environment

Using a virtual server, such as MS Virtual PC, makes it possible to build and test SharePoint on your ordinary MS Windows XP client. It also makes it possible to test and play with different configurations and scenarios. And if (or, more likely, when) things go wrong, you can simply use the undo feature of MS Virtual PC. Another nice option with virtual servers is to make a copy of the virtual server environment and, if necessary, restore that copy in the event that your test environment becomes messed up beyond repair!

I recommend that you use a virtual server for testing everything detailed in this book. It will make it much easier for you in case something goes wrong, and you won't have to worry about testing and playing around. Once you know how SharePoint works, you can then go on to use your own production environment.

Integrating with MS Office

Given that you are reading this book, the chance that you use MS Office for creating documents, spreadsheets, and presentations is rather high. Therefore, this section is important for you. SharePoint will not change the way you are working with Office documents, but it will enhance the functionality, making many things a lot easier than they are without using SharePoint. What features you can expect to have depends on what version of MS Office you are using.

The story is this: MS Office 2007 was released together with SharePoint 2007 at the end of 2006. They were built to be integrated, just like the previous SharePoint 2003 and Office 2003. If you use Office 2003 along with SharePoint 2007, you will get a lot of the functionality in SharePoint 2007, but not everything. Using older MS Office versions, such as 2000 or XP, will allow such a user to read and save documents to SharePoint 2007, but nothing more. The reason is that these older versions of MS Office do not know about SharePoint, so they lack this integration capability. Do not expect Microsoft to release an update for any version previous of MS Office 2007, and frankly if you've seen what Office 2007 can do, you'll want to upgrade — it is both much easier to work with and has a lot of new features.

The following list gives you an idea about what to expect when running Office 2000/XP versions with SharePoint 2007:

❑ **File Save Integration:** Microsoft Office 2000 integrates with Windows SharePoint Services. Users can open and save files stored on SharePoint sites. They can also receive alerts in Outlook 2000.

❑ **Basic Data Integration:** Microsoft Office XP provides for data integration with SharePoint sites. Users can view properties and metadata for files stored on SharePoint sites. They can also export list data to Microsoft Excel 2002.

❑ **Contextual Integration**: SharePoint integrates fully into the business tasks that users perform every day with Microsoft Office 2003 Editions.

Microsoft produced a white paper describing Office integration with SharePoint 2007 called "Fair, Good, Better, Best." Fair is what you get with Office 2000, good means the functionality achieved by MS Office XP, better is what you get with MS Office 2003, and best requires you to run Office 2007. Note that there is no technical problem in using SharePoint in a mixed MS Office environment, but it will place an extra burden on the Help desk and the support team, since each version will support different SharePoint 2007 features. A more detailed comparison of the four MS Office versions is presented in the following table (including new SharePoint 2007 features in the second half of the list):

Feature	Office Version	
Save and open files from SharePoint sites	Office 2000:	Yes
	Office XP:	Yes
	Office 2003:	Yes, enhanced (Office plus FrontPage, InfoPath, OneNote, Microsoft Project, Publisher, Visio)
	Office 2007:	Like Office 2003, plus SharePoint Designer
Create new documents in web browser	Office 2000:	No
	Office XP:	Yes (Excel, FrontPage, PowerPoint, Word)
	Office 2003:	Yes (Excel, FrontPage, InfoPath, PowerPoint, Microsoft Project, Publisher, Word)
	Office 2007:	Like Office 2003, plus SharePoint Designer
Collect document columns automatically	Office 2000:	No
	Office XP:	No
	Office 2003:	Yes
	Office 2007:	Yes
Change document columns in both Office and the web browser	Office 2000:	Data stored, but not displayed
	Office XP:	Yes
	Office 2003:	Yes, enhanced (Excel, FrontPage, InfoPath, PowerPoint, Visio, Word)
	Office 2007:	Like Office 2003, plus SharePoint Designer

Feature	Office Version	
Track document versions	Office 2000:	No. Use web browser to view and manage document versions.
	Office XP:	No. Use web browser to view and manage document versions.
	Office 2003:	Enhanced (Excel, PowerPoint, Visio, Word)
	Office 2007:	Like Office 2003, and can also compare document versions very easily
Check out and check in documents	Office 2000:	No. Use web browser to manually check out and check in documents.
	Office XP:	No. Use web browser to manually check out and check in documents.
	Office 2003:	Yes, enhanced (Excel, PowerPoint, Visio, Word). Use web browser to manually check out and check in other types of documents.
	Office 2007:	Like Office 2003
Upload multiple documents	Office 2000:	No
	Office XP:	No
	Office 2003:	Yes
	Office 2007:	Yes
Use inline discussions	Office 2000:	Yes
	Office XP:	Yes
	Office 2003:	Yes
	Office 2007:	Yes

Feature	Office Version	
Create document workspace	Office 2000:	No
	Office XP:	No
	Office 2003:	Yes
	Office 2007:	Yes
Create meeting workspace	Office 2000:	No
	Office XP:	No
	Office 2003:	Yes, with Outlook 2003
	Office 2007:	Yes, with Outlook 2007
Synchronize calendar, tasks, and contact list in SharePoint sites	Office 2000:	No
	Office XP:	No
	Office 2003:	Yes, but only from SharePoint to Outlook 2003
	Office 2007:	Yes, two-way synchronization with Outlook 2007
Alert integration with Outlook	Office 2000:	No
	Office XP:	No
	Office 2003:	Yes
	Office 2007:	Yes
Display lists as RSS information	Office 2000:	No
	Office XP:	No
	Office 2003:	Yes
	Office 2007:	Yes

Feature	Office Version	
Using Excel services	Office 2000:	No
	Office XP:	No
	Office 2003:	Yes, can publish to SharePoint site from Excel
	Office 2007:	Yes, same as Office 2003
Access to business data catalog	Office 2000:	No
	Office XP:	No
	Office 2003:	No
	Office 2007:	Yes, allows Office 2007 documents to display content in external data sources, using SharePoint 2007 lists
InfoPath forms services	Office 2000:	Yes
	Office XP:	Yes
	Office 2003:	Yes
	Office 2007:	Yes
InfoPath forms in Office clients	Office 2000:	No
	Office XP:	No
	Office 2003:	No
	Office 2007:	Yes
Document information panel	Office 2000:	No
	Office XP:	No
	Office 2003:	No
	Office 2007:	Yes, can display and modify document properties in customizable InfoPath-based forms in Office clients

Feature	Office Version	
Access to workflows	Office 2000:	No
	Office XP:	No
	Office 2003:	No
	Office 2007:	Yes, can start and complete workflow tasks from within the Office 2007 client
PowerPoint slide libraries	Office 2000:	No
	Office XP:	No
	Office 2003:	No
	Office 2007:	Yes
Use record management	Office 2000:	No
	Office XP:	No
	Office 2003:	No
	Office 2007:	Yes, allows Office 2007 documents to be stored in a record repository
Compose and publish Wikis and blogs using Word	Office 2000:	No
	Office XP:	No
	Office 2003:	No
	Office 2007:	Yes

Built-In Features of SharePoint

So, what features can you expect in SharePoint 2007? The answer depends on what version you implement: MOSS or WSS. Following is a list of everyday scenarios showing you how SharePoint can make things easier for you and your users. Chapter 10 provides more detailed steps on how to create a SharePoint environment that solves these problems.

Alerts (WSS and MOSS)

One feature that both WSS and MOSS offer is something Microsoft refers to as alerts. An alert is a request you create in SharePoint to be notified by e-mail when SharePoint content changes (for example, when a document is updated, a contact is deleted, or a News item is added). Using alerts, you can be sure to keep yourself updated about changes to information that is important to you! SharePoint will send you an e-mail to notify you what has happened. The following information types are examples of what can be watched by alerts:

❑   Complete document libraries, or single documents and files.

❑   Complete picture libraries or single pictures.

❑   Contact lists or single contacts.

❑   Link lists or single links.

❑   News lists or single news items.

❑   Event lists or single events.

Alerts can watch a lot more places and types of information, as you will see in Chapter 10. This is extremely useful — you will no longer miss any important updates!

RSS (WSS and MOSS)

A new feature in SharePoint 2007 is support for the relatively new Really Simple Syndication technique. Using this feature a user can also be notified when new items are added to any type of SharePoint lists, such as document libraries, contacts, news, and tasks lists. This is similar to alerts, but the main difference between them is that alerts send e-mails that will be stored in your Inbox along with other e-mail, while all RSS notifications will be collected in one folder (see Figure 1-2).

File and Document Management (WSS and MOSS)

Today you organize your files by using a folder structure and giving your files descriptive names so that they are easy to find. But you also know that after some time, it gets harder and harder to find the file when you need it. And even worse, you may have several copies of different versions of the same file. How can you be sure you're looking at the right version? If you are looking for a file that somebody else created, it gets even harder because the folder structure may not be as intuitive as you would like it to be and the filenames may not be as descriptive as they should be.

This is where SharePoint comes in. All files and documents in SharePoint are stored in document libraries. This is very similar to a folder in the file system, but on steroids! The document library in SharePoint 2007 has lots of new features compared to previous SharePoint versions, which will help you organize, compose, and find the files you are looking for. The key features are as follows:

❑   **Document Columns:** Add your own columns to describe the files and documents, such as Document Type, Customer Name, Project Name, or Status. These columns can be local for a specific document library or they can be shared between libraries, using a feature called Site Columns.

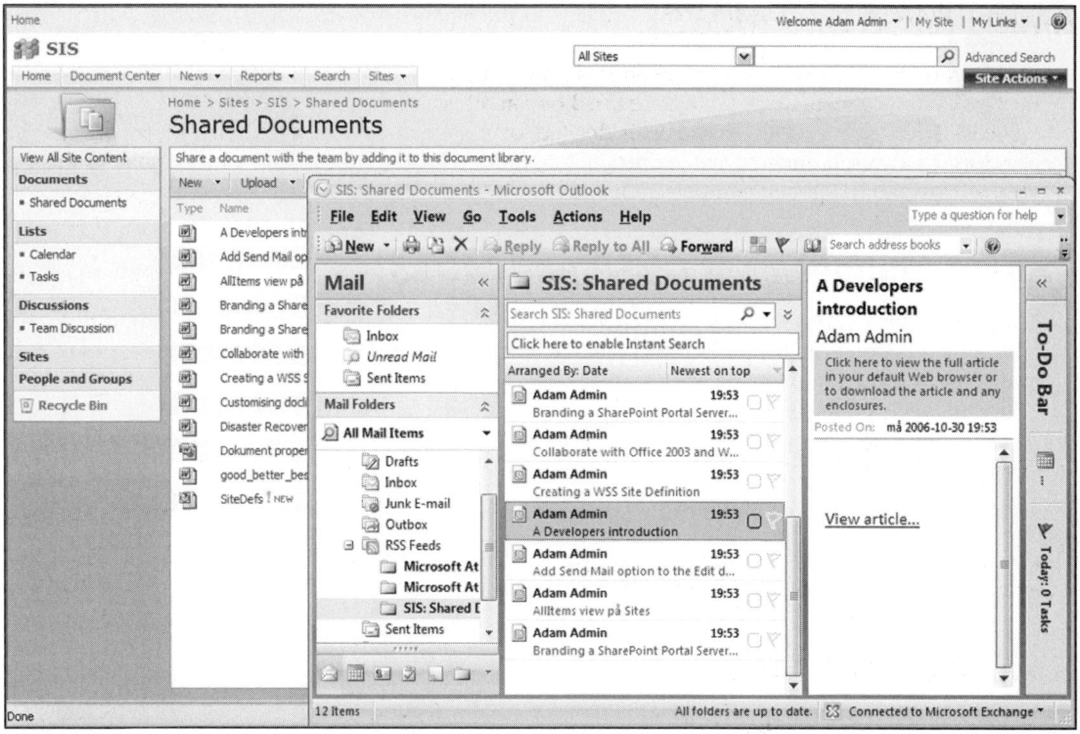

Figure 1-2

❑ **Document Views:** Create your own view of how the files should be presented. For example, you could create a view that shows only documents of the type Contract for the customer Volvo, sorted by its status.

❑ **Document Workflows**: When adding or modifying a document, a workflow can start. For example, this workflow could send an e-mail to some people in your team to collect feedback or to get an approval by your manager before getting published.

❑ **Content Types**: Allows you to create multiple document templates for a document library. A user that creates a new document will be able to choose between these templates. These templates can be based on different file types (such as Word and Excel files), different content, and different workflows, columns, and policies. SharePoint 2003 users have been waiting for this feature for a long time!

❑ **Individual Permissions**: You can set a specific permission for each document if necessary. For example, if you remove the Read permission for a specific document, users will not see it at all.

❑ **Check Out/In:** You can force a user to check out (lock a document) before editing a document. Only when this document later is checked in (unlocked) will the updated version be visible for all users.

These features make it easier for you to name your documents. You no longer need files with names like `Contract_Volvo_version05.doc`. And more importantly, you can force the writers of documents to enter information in these columns when they save their files, which will automatically start the workflow you have defined.

There are many other interesting features in SharePoint related to document management. In this book, you will see and try all of the important features.

Project Management (WSS and MOSS)

Think about how you work with projects. What type of information is related to a standard project? Although it depends on the project, you will find that most projects share the following types of information among the project members:

- ❑ **Gantt Schema**: A list of project tasks, including start and due dates, displayed in a graphical calendar view.
- ❑ **Documents:** Examples include MS Word files, Excel spreadsheets, text files, and PowerPoint presentations.
- ❑ **Members:** A list of all the members in the project.
- ❑ **Calendar:** A list of events, such as meetings, conferences, and project milestones.
- ❑ **Contacts:** A list of external contacts, such as vendors, partners, consultants, and other resources.
- ❑ **Tasks:** A list of things to do, assigned to project members.
- ❑ **e-mail:** Questions, status, and comments regarding the project.

The problem without SharePoint and specific project-management tools is that this information is stored in several places. Documents and files are stored in a file share; members exist in an e-mail distribution list; calendar events, contacts, and tasks are stored in an Outlook public folder; and e-mail is, of course, stored in each member's personal Inbox. Another way to describe this is organized chaos. Each project member needs to know and remember exactly where each type of information is stored. If she does not, valuable time is wasted searching for the information. To make things worse, if a new member joins the project, you must explain to her where everything is stored and how it works. To make sure that the new member understands what has been going on, you must forward a copy of all mail related to this project — if you can find it. The new member then faces the challenging task of reading all this e-mail and understanding what it contains.

I am sure you recognize this situation! To solve this problem, you need something that can store all this information in a single place — or at least make all the information available through a single source. This is exactly what SharePoint does! Here is how you do it:

1. Create a SharePoint web site for the project.

2. Add the members to the site. SharePoint sends the members an e-mail with an invitation and a link to the site. SharePoint may also create a mailing list for this project team to make it easy for you to share e-mail.

3. Create a document library to store all files and documents, and copy any related file to this document library.

4. Create another document library to store all e-mail, and copy all project-related e-mail to this document library. Give this document library an e-mail address, and make that address a member of the project team mailing list.

5. Create a calendar, a task list, and a contact list, and then use these lists for the project data.

6. Create a project task list, and display it as a Gantt schema.

Such a project site could look something similar to Figure 1-3. Chapter 2 gives detailed steps on how to create this type of web site and all its lists and fill it with data. You will also learn how easy it is to design the page to make it easy to use.

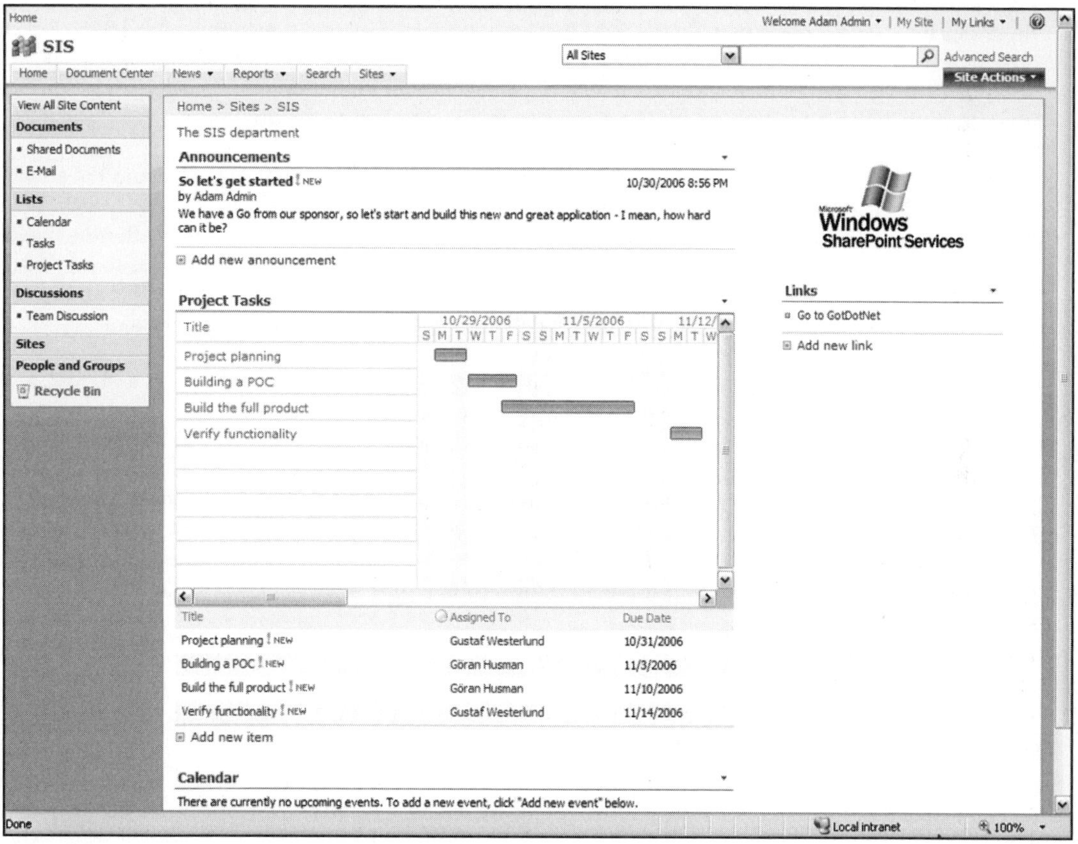

Figure 1-3

Managing Meetings (WSS)

If there is one thing that almost everyone agrees on, it is that most meetings are a huge pain! Why? The usual complaints are that they are a waste of time, boring, and too long; that meeting participants are unprepared; and that it's hard to follow up on tasks and activities after the meeting. That indicates that even a small step forward to make meetings more effective is important. With SharePoint, you will be able to change many tasks related to meetings into something more positive.

In a typical meeting, the meeting organizer uses Outlook to invite participants, as well as to reserve resources such as the conference room. A meeting is an event where the following steps occur:

1. A number of people are invited.

2. The invitees come together.

3. While together, they discuss a number of topics.

4. The discussion results in a number of actions and decisions.

The Typical Meeting Process

Let's look at a typical meeting process. In this example the meeting organizer creates an agenda and describes the meeting objective. (By the way, have you noticed how many meetings don't have a clear objective? Meeting objectives should be brief, clear, and easy for everyone to understand.) The meeting organizer then estimates the length of the meeting and sends an invitation to all participants. Some documents, with information needed for the meeting, may be attached to the invitation.

Later, the actual meeting takes place. Each participant has his own copy of the agenda and the attached documents. Well, actually, some participants forgot the agenda and need to print a copy; somebody else did not see the attached document, so he also needs to print a copy. About 15 minutes after the meeting should have started, everyone is ready to proceed. Because there is no clear indication as to how long each agenda point should take to discuss, the meeting takes 20 minutes longer than expected. This makes some people feel stressed because they have other appointments after this meeting.

During the meeting, someone takes notes about all the activities agreed upon, the tasks assigned, and the decisions made. This information is later listed in the meeting minutes. One more person also takes notes because, after this meeting, she will be the person appointed to check the minutes.

One week later, the meeting minutes are created and checked and sent to all participants by e-mail. A few of these participants actually read the minutes, some just take a quick glance at them, and some do not have time to even open the document. The next time this team has a meeting, only a few participants have read the previous minutes, and many have missed that they were assigned tasks. And the story goes on.

Using SharePoint for Effective Meetings

The preceding story might not be true for every organization, of course, but I am sure you are familiar with the ways meetings can go wrong. So, what can SharePoint do to make this process both more effective and more interesting? Thanks to the integration of Outlook and SharePoint, you can simultaneously send a meeting invitation, book a conference room, and create a meeting workspace, a web site where you can host all information regarding the meeting, including the following:

❑ **Agenda:** A list of all the items you will discuss during the meeting, including who is responsible for each one, how long it will take, and any comments regarding the items.

❑ **Participants:** SharePoint automatically creates a list of all invited participants. This list is automatically updated with the status of each participant so that everyone can see who will come or why someone declined the invitation.

❑ **Tasks:** A list of all the tasks agreed upon during the meeting.

❑ **Decisions:** A list of all the decisions agreed upon during the meeting.

❑ **Document Library:** Contains any document with information that will prepare the participants for the meeting, as well as documents created as a result of the meeting.

All this information is available to each participant directly when they receive the invitation. This means that the participant can see the agenda before it takes place, maybe add some extra items to it, and get access to any document with information related to the meeting. If needed, the participant can add her own documents.

When the actual meeting takes place, you use a video projector that displays the meeting workspace so that everyone can see it. No one needs a printed copy of the meeting agenda because it is listed on the meeting workspace. All documents are listed in the document workspace — if there is a discussion about what a document contains, the organizer can quickly open the document for everyone to see.

Any activities, tasks, or decisions that are agreed upon during the meeting are directly entered into the list. Everyone can see this, so there is no need for anyone to check the meeting minutes afterwards. The effect is that everyone will be involved in whatever decision is made. This makes the meeting more interesting and engaging. Because the agenda clearly states the amount of time it should take to discuss each item, the participants can focus on that subject and try to stay within the estimated time.

Because everything is recorded directly in tasks and decision lists during the meeting, you don't need any meeting minutes at all! If a participant afterwards needs to see what was decided in the meeting, she can simply go back to the meeting in the Outlook calendar and click the link to open the meeting workspace again.

In Chapter 7, you will see how to create a meeting workspace, configure what lists it contains, and fill it with data. You will also see that repeated meetings can be linked to the same meeting workspace, giving you one page for each meeting instance and making it very simple to go back and see what you discussed in a previous meeting.

Keeping Your Organization Updated (MOSS)

For many years now, organizations have used an intranet to make sure that everyone has access to general information, such as company news, information from the Human Resources department, or a list of all employees and their contact information. SharePoint is a great tool to help you create an intranet. With SharePoint, you often refer to the intranet as "the portal site," or simply "the portal."

Using SharePoint for your intranet has many advantages. It is fast, it can support organizations with millions of users, and it has several interesting features, such as the following:

❑ **Content Management:** MOSS has implemented and enhanced all the important features from MS Content Management Server. This allows you to edit web content, such as the intranet home pages and news, with features like check out/check in, approval procedures, version history, and workflows. This is the main feature that most users of SPS 2003 have been waiting for.

❑ **News:** This is a special site in MOSS where some, or all, users create news pages about the company and its customers and partners. This news site is based on the content management features mentioned above.

❑ **Targeting:** Helps you make sure that your news, links, and other information are visible to only a certain group of people, which is also referred to as an "audience."

❑ **Active Directory Synchronization:** Makes it possible to present relevant information about your users, such as e-mail addresses, departments, phone numbers, pictures, descriptions, and so on. SharePoint stores this information in its profile database.

❑ **Document Center:** Allows you to copy documents from a workspace area, such as a project site, to a specific document archive with its own set of permissions, policies, and workflows. For example, say that your teams develop documents, and some of these documents should be published to the intranet. Using a document archive makes it easy for the author to publish the document to that location.

❑ **Report Center:** This is a special site in MOSS where you can create, distribute, and manage important business data.

❑ **Site Directory:** Displays a list of existing web sites, including their names, descriptions, owners, and other properties. This makes it easy for a user to quickly find a specific web site.

❑ **My Site:** A personal site for each user that typically is used for displaying personal information, such as news, links, e-mail, and calendars, as well as document and picture libraries. There is also a public view of this site that displays information about the user, such as e-mail address, phone numbers, department, and a general description.

In addition, you will find that the News pages allow you to define when to display and remove the news from the list. News is not automatically deleted; instead, it is archived and will still be possible to find using the search feature in SharePoint. You can link pictures to your news, and you can make the news item show up in several places, such as on the organization-wide intranet and on a local intranet for a given department.

An intranet based on MOSS will automatically add links to the web sites you create for your projects, meetings, and other shared team sites. These links will show up in the site directory in MOSS, where the user can browse through different categories of sites, such as project sites, team sites and so on. The categories used in this site directory are created by the SharePoint administrator. The intranet also allows you to create any type of list, including document libraries, contacts, and events. If you decide to go with both MOSS and WSS, it is hard to find a good reason why you should use an additional product only for the intranet. Doing this will not only make things harder for you to support and manage (backup and restore), but it will also force your organization to pay two server licenses rather than one.

Now take a look at an intranet scenario. Say that your organization has three departments: Sales, IT, and Human Resources. You also have some special groups: The executive team, a project team, and an external sales force. Your task is to make sure each of them gets the right information, in an easy and intuitive way. Your CEO requires a common intranet where all important information regarding the company, its customers, and its employees are presented. Each department requires its own intranet. The IT folks tell you they are sick and tired of all the sales info, and the sales guys asks you politely if there is a way to filter out everything except the sales-related information. And all of them say they want a fast and easy way to find the right web site where all the information is stored for the projects, meetings, customers, and so on. And by the way, the executive group wants an easy way of finding all contracts, regardless of where they are stored. How do you solve this?

One simple solution would be to do this:

1. Install MOSS and WSS.

2. Create a common intranet portal for the organization.

3. Create a separate page on the intranet for each department, with its own news listing, document libraries, and contact lists. These pages are:

    ❑ Sales

    ❑ IT

    ❑ HR

4. Create these audiences:

    ❑ Sales Team

    ❑ IT Team

    ❑ HR Team

    ❑ Executive Team

    ❑ Project Team

    ❑ External Sales Team

5. Instruct your general news authors how to target their news items to a specific audience so that each audience only sees information targeting their group.

6. Instruct local news authors in the departments on how to create news items only for their own areas.

7. Use the site directory in MOSS to create new web sites for each project, team site, and so on. This ensures that all web sites are listed in the site directory and are therefore easy to find.

8. Create a document library named Contract on the Document Center site. Tell the salespeople that whenever they create a new contract document to make sure that it also is submitted to this document library.

9. Make sure every user has updated information in the Active Directory (AD), such as phone numbers, department, company name, and e-mail address. Then synchronize the AD with SharePoint once every night. Make sure each user profile in SharePoint links to a photo of the user. Instruct everyone that whenever they see a name listed, they can simply click it to get more information about that user.

Finding Your Information Faster (MOSS)

How often do you search for information? I would guess at least once every day. Assume the average user spends 10 minutes every day searching for information. If you have 200 users, this would be about 2000 minutes, or 33 hours per day. You could also put it this way: Your organization pays for 200 employees, but it only gets the efficiency of 196 (4 people times 8 working hours = 32 hours in total per day). What this means is that even small improvements in efficiency may lead to big results. And not just for the owners of the company — the employees will be also happy because they can concentrate on doing their jobs instead of searching for information.

Both WSS 3.0 and MOSS 2007 has its own built-in search and indexing engine; the difference is that WSS will only allow the user to search in SharePoint sites, while MOSS allows the user to search almost anywhere, both in SharePoint and in external sources, such as MS Exchange server and file servers. Because the WSS search functionality is fairly intuitive, this section discusses the search and indexing features of only MOSS.

A number of client-based search tools are available, such as MSN Search and Google Search. At the time of this writing, these tools are not made for searching SharePoint information, so you need to implement MOSS in order to get a real search and index engine. But this is not just any search engine; it is a very sophisticated tool that enables you to search for any type of data in SharePoint, regardless of where it is stored. You can also instruct the index engine to make information outside the SharePoint database searchable, including these content sources:

❑ Every web site in the SharePoint environment (including all MOSS and WSS sites).

❑ Any file server in your IT environment (including older NT 4 and Windows 2000 servers).

❑ Your MS Exchange database (such as all public folders or role-based mailboxes such as Help Desk).

❑ External business and production databases, such as SAP and Oracle.

❑ Any Lotus Notes database you may have.

❑ Other internal web sites (such as your old intranet, your public web site, or similar sites).

❑ External web sites (such as your partner's web site — and why not your competitor's?).

What File Types Can You Search?

Before SharePoint allows you to search, it must index the content sources. So, the question should really be "What file types can MOSS index?" And the answer is: practically anything stored in a computer! You can index MS Office file formats, such as MS Word and MS Excel, and all standard file formats, such as text files, HTML, and RTF files.

What about other common file types, such as PDF, ZIP, and CAD files? In order to explain this, I have to tell you a little more about the indexing process. The process is more complicated than this, but the basic steps are these:

1. When the scheduled task for indexing starts, the index engine looks into every place you have instructed it to look in, also known as Content Sources.

2. When it finds a file, it looks at the file type (for example, DOC).

3. It checks a list in SharePoint where you have specified what file types you want indexed. In this example, DOC is a file type that should be indexed.

4. The index process now needs a program that understands how to read DOC files. Such programs are referred to as Index Filters (IFilters, for short). Every file type needs its own IFilter, including DOC files.

5. The IFilter opens the file and starts scanning it. Whenever it finds some text, it sends it through a filter that removes words that should not be indexed (such as "yes," "no," "one," and "two" and numerals like 1, 2, or 3). The resulting stream of words are then stored in an index file, along with information about the name and location of this file.

6. When all the text in the file is read, the IFilter closes the file, and the process starts again with step 2, looking for next file.

So if you want to make file types like PDF searchable, you need to do two things: Configure SharePoint to look for PDF files and install an IFilter for the PDF file type. The index engine does not include this by default. You may wonder why Microsoft has not added common file types such as PDF or ZIP. The answer is simple: At the time MOSS was released, Adobe owned the PDF format, so Microsoft could not include an IFilter for legal reasons. So, Adobe is making the IFilter for the PDF — and the good news is that Adobe is giving it away for free to encourage people to use the PDF format for storing all kinds of content. In Chapter 8, you learn how to find and install common IFilters, including the PDF version.

What Type of Searching Can You Do?

The default configuration of the SharePoint search engine allows you to search for whole words and their stemmers only. For example, you can search for "write" and you will also find files with "writing" and "wrote." However, if you search for the word "Admin," you will not find "Administrator" because "Admin" is not recognized as a whole word.

You can also search for document properties, also referred to as metadata, such as author, title, and file size. The list of properties is different for different types of documents. For example, if you want to see what properties a standard MS Word document has available, you can do this:

1. Open any Word 2007 file.
2. Choose the Office button ➪ Prepare ➪ Properties.

Now you will see all standard properties for this document, such as Author and Title, in the document property pane directly above the document text. You will also see any custom columns in the document library where this document is stored, since Word and SharePoint automatically synchronize, or propagate, custom columns between them.

All the standard properties on the document property pane are searchable. You can also make combinations, such as searching for documents containing the word "Viking" with the standard attribute "Author" equal to "Göran Husman." This is satisfactory for most search scenarios. But sometimes you want to search for a document that matches your own custom column value. You may recall that you can add any number of columns to a document library, for example "Doc Type" or "Status." As you learn in Chapter 8, even these column properties can be searchable if you configure SharePoint properly.

If your SharePoint search engine has indexed many documents, the search result may give you too many matching documents. If so, you want to limit the search to a given area. This is made possible by configuring search scopes. For example, you can create one search scope for MS Exchange, another for files on the file system, and a third that only shows results from a specific SharePoint site. This reduces the number of search results, but it requires that you know in what search scope your document belongs.

Finally, you can define keyword best bets. This feature helps your users to find frequently requested information. For example, suppose that when you talk with the sales manager, she tells you that members in her team often need access to the product specifications. The problem is that these products have several names. The bestselling product is article X2025A, but most customers refer to this as the "Super Gadget." To add to the problem, the internal name used by the sales team is the "Money Maker." She wants her team to be able to search for any of these terms and still find the product specification for the X2025A. With the keyword best bet feature in SharePoint, this is an easy fix. You simply need to create a list of each alias for the keyword X2025A and then link this keyword to the proper document. When someone later searches for any of these words, that person will find the product specification for X2025A at the top of the search results. Below it, he will find all other documents that match this search criterion.

Accessing SharePoint over the Internet

Very soon after you start working with SharePoint, you will find that it contains more and more of your business-critical data. You also become aware of the fact that you need online access to the SharePoint server in order to work with the documents, projects, and everything else stored in the SharePoint database. So you start thinking, "How do I access this information when I am not at the office?" One way is to use the offline functionality of MS Outlook 2007, which allows a user to make a copy for a document library in an Outlook folder, thus making it possible to read and even update documents while offline. Another answer is: You can make your SharePoint information accessible over the Internet, in a secure way, while still getting good performance. You have to plan this carefully and configure SharePoint and the other modules involved, such as the firewall.

> If the SharePoint server is accessible over the Internet, SharePoint 2007 allows even a mobile phone to connect to a SharePoint list using a special view that only shows text.

How You Do It

Because SharePoint is a web application running on top of IIS 6, it is very easy to make SharePoint accessible from outside your organization. You simply open up your firewall so that it allows connections to the SharePoint server from the outside. But this is not a good solution from a security perspective. This leaves your SharePoint server wide open to the world, and there are lots of threats for this server that could destroy it or even the other servers on your network. Another big problem with this simple solution is that your password and user account could be transferred over the Internet unencrypted, depending on what type of authentication method you use. Someone listening in on your communication could learn your password and be able to log on as you!

A better solution is to install a Secure Socket Layer (SSL) certificate on your IIS 6 and demand that every access to the SharePoint server use SSL-encrypted connections. That is, the user must enter the Uniform Resource Locator (URL) address to the SharePoint server starting with `https://`. The effect of this is that your logon credentials are protected. There is no longer any risk that someone will see your password.

The best solution is to prohibit the external users from accessing the SharePoint server directly from the outside, combined with the SSL-encrypted connection. Instead, your users would access something that looks like the SharePoint server but in reality is a replica. This type of replica is known as an application proxy server. Microsoft has a product for this: the Internet Security and Acceleration Server, also known as the MS ISA server. With this solution, things works like this:

1. The external user connects to the SharePoint web address over the Internet, using an SSL connection such as `https://intranet.filobit.com`. This could be the exact same address for users on the inside, except for the `https://` part (internally, you would use `http://` instead).

2. The user connection is passing through the firewall but is directed to the MS ISA server instead of the real SharePoint server.

3. The MS ISA server looks at the requested URL address, checks its rules, and if everything is okay, connects to that URL and retrieves the SharePoint page. This page is then sent back to the user.

4. The user sees the requested URL and believes he is connected to the real SharePoint server. He clicks a link on that page, and, once again, the MS ISA server gets a request for a new URL, repeating step 3.

The nice thing with this solution is that the user never gets access to anything more than the MS ISA server, which normally is installed on the Demilitarized Zone (DMZ) segment of the network. This segment is where you put all your publicly available servers, such as your public web site. You can use the rules in the MS ISA server to control exactly what the user can see and do. For example, in some organizations, users have different levels of access, depending on where they are situated at the moment. Inside the network, they have full access; on the Internet, they have access to only some part of SharePoint. This is something that only the MS ISA server can help you deploy because SharePoint itself cannot distinguish access to its information in this way. Another bonus effect is that frequently requested web pages are cached on the MS ISA server, meaning that these pages will be displayed more quickly for the users.

Allowing External Partners Access

Now you know the general steps in configuring the SharePoint environment for access over the Internet. But what about partners and other users living outside your organization? If there is a need to give them limited access to your SharePoint server, it can be done! Before you do this, you must understand how SharePoint controls what the user can do with its access control feature.

Every user who wants to access any part of SharePoint must belong to a SharePoint group that defines the exact permission. Some of the default SharePoint groups are these:

❑ **Visitor:** Allows the user to open and read information, including documents, pictures, and list content. The user will not be able to create, modify, or delete information in SharePoint.

❑ **Member:** Allows the user to do everything a Visitor can do, plus create, modify, and delete information, including news, documents, contacts, and so on.

❑ **Owner:** Has full access to the site. Can do everything, including adding and deleting members and changing their access. This group is often referred to as the site administrator group.

> SharePoint groups are not specifically used for intranet scenarios; instead they are used for controlling access to any part of SharePoint, regardless of user access.

First, look at how you can allow access internally. Assume that you have an employee named Anna. She needs access to your intranet, and she will only read information. You add Anna's user account to the SharePoint group Visitors on the intranet portal site. Later, Anna comes back to you and says that she needs both read and write access to a given project site; now you add Anna's user account to the site group Members for this particular project site. Anna now belongs to different SharePoint groups in different parts of the SharePoint environment. Whenever she is accessing SharePoint, it will validate her user account and check what SharePoint group she belongs to.

If you want to allow access to a user outside your organization, it must be possible to authenticate that user. In other words, the external user needs to log on so that SharePoint can see what access he is granted. This will be a problem with external users because they don't have a user account in your network. One simple way to resolve this is to create a local user account for each of these external users. You can assign the user membership in any SharePoint group you like, and you can create rules in the MS ISA server to control exactly what part of SharePoint they can access. The external user must remember to log on with the local account you created. So everyone is happy now, at least for a while.

Problems with This Solution

But this solution is far from perfect. It works, this is true, but what happens if this external person moves to another company? For example, suppose that Michael works for the company ABC. Michael is involved in a project in your organization, Filobit Inc, and needs access to the SharePoint site where all the project information is stored. You create a local user account for Michael, grant him the proper access, and tell him the URL for the project site and that his logon name is `Filobit\Michael`. He starts working on the project, and everything works as expected. One month later, Michael leaves ABC, and starts working for its competitor, XYZ. You don't have an agreement with XYZ, so its employees are not allowed access to your project site. You need to disable the account `Filobit\Michael`. But how will you know that Michael has left his old company, ABC? There is no automatic process that will inform you about this. Hopefully, someone at ABC tells you this, or somebody in the project team gets this information and tells you. Clearly, this situation will be very hard to handle if you have 10 or more external partners. But at the moment, this is how things work.

> A new feature in SharePoint 2007 called Forms Based Authentication allows you to create a logon page for external users and store those external accounts in an SQL Server database, instead of the Active Directory. This feature is beyond the scope of this book, since it requires both programming skills and good understanding of SQL Server; for more information see `http://blogs.msdn.com/sharepoint/archive/2006/08/16/configuring-multiple-authentication-providers-for-sharepoint-2007.aspx`.

ADFS

However, there is some light at the end of the tunnel. Starting with Release 2 of Windows 2003 Server, Microsoft released a feature called Active Directory Federation Service (ADFS). The objective of ADFS is to resolve precisely this type situation (that is, letting two completely separate organizations share access to web applications like SharePoint without the need to create local accounts for the remote organization). The idea is rather simple and easy to understand, but the technique beneath is advanced and worth its own book.

The basic idea of ADFS is to make it possible for an organization to use its own user accounts to get access on a remote web application. For example, assume that you have two companies, A and B. User Bob works for B, and he needs access to a SharePoint site in A. Bob talks to the administrator for the site in A, which then grants the B\Bob account access to the requested site.

The magic in this scenario is managed by adding extra servers to your Active Directory domain, one in each organization. The primary ADFS server is referred to as the federation server and hosts the federation service component. Its primary task is to route incoming requests from the Internet to the web site a user is trying to access. It is also responsible for creating a security token that will be passed on to the web application. The process that validates the external user is the ADFS Web Agent, which runs on the web server (in this case, the SharePoint server).

Most organizations do not want their federation server exposed to the Internet. You can protect it by installing an optional federation proxy server. This proxy relays federation requests from the outside world to your internal federation server, meaning that your federation server is no longer exposed directly to the outside world.

> ADFS is based on the standard Security Assertion Markup Language (SAML), which means that that the external company need not be running MS Windows.

MS Groove

With SharePoint 2007 there is a new type of solution for this situation. Using MS Groove, a project's members are able to share and collaborate on SharePoint lists and libraries, regardless of the project members' organizational membership. It is a very attractive solution for teams and groups of up to 15 members, and Groove will automatically synchronize any updates of these lists and libraries between all members as soon as they get connected to the Internet. The current version of MS Groove has its own user database, so there is no requirement that all members have user accounts in the same Windows domain.

One thing to remember with Groove is that it is an independent application that may be used as a standalone product or synchronized with SharePoint content. It is not a special application made for SharePoint as of today, although this will probably change in the future. In a way, Groove and SharePoint are both offering a shared workplace for teams, although the strength of Groove is its great replication engine that works independently of the users' organizational membership, while SharePoint's strength is all the functionality mentioned earlier in this chapter, including integration with all MS Office products.

> For more information about MS G¡roove look at
> http://www.microsoft.com/office/groove.

Summary

In this chapter you learned the following:

❑ SharePoint is a web-based application that helps users share and collaborate with any type of data and information.

❑ SharePoint lets the ordinary user create sites and document libraries in a secure and controlled manner.

❑ The previous versions of SharePoint were STS (SharePoint Team Services) and SPS 2003 (SharePoint Portal Server). STS was replaced by WSS 3.0 (Windows SharePoint Services), and SPS 2003 was replaced by MOSS 2007.

❑ Moss now comes in several editions, and with optional server modules.

❑ WSS is the base module of SharePoint. It is used to create sites for managing and sharing information, such as projects, customer data, meetings, and local intranets.

❑ MOSS is the optional add-on package. It enhances WSS with several new features, such as Search, Excel Services, and Forms Server, plus new site templates such as Internet Site, Intranet Portal, and Record Management sites.

❑ To install SharePoint, the server needs Windows 2003 Server with IIS and ASP.NET activated.

❑ SharePoint can use two types of SQL databases: MS SQL 2000/2005 Server and SQL Server Express.

❑ SQL Server Express must be installed on the same computer as SharePoint.

❑ MS SQL 2000/2005 Server can be installed on a separate computer if required.

❑ WSS has a special version of SQL Server Express, named Embedded SQL Server Express.

❑ SharePoint 2007 (WSS and MOSS) is best integrated with MS Office 2007.

❑ You can use older versions of MS Office, but you will lose functionality, and the integration with SharePoint 2007 is not as good as with Office 2007.

❑ You can use SharePoint to build intranets for the complete organization, for the department, or for any local groups of teams, if requested.

❑ The index and search functionality MOSS 2007 are very good! It makes it possible to search anywhere and in practically any file type.

❑ WSS 3.0 now comes with its own index and search engine, but it is limited to searching in WSS sites only.

❑ You can use MOSS to index new file types by installing a corresponding IFilter (Index Filter).

❑ You can search for content in both files and properties, such as Author, Title, and Size.

❑ You can configure SharePoint to make your own library columns searchable.

❑ You can define keyword best bets for frequently requested information.

❑ SharePoint requires every user to have an account in order to authenticate. You can use local sever accounts or domain accounts, and thanks to the new pluggable authentication system you can also store accounts in a MS SQL server

- ❑ To allow a secure access to the SharePoint server from the Internet you must use a MS ISA server or similar product.

- ❑ If external users such as partners or customers need access, you must create an account for them in your environment.

- ❑ Another way of allowing users in remote organizations access to your SharePoint server is to install the Active Directory Foundation Service (ADFS).

- ❑ Using MS Groove a project team can share and collaborate on SharePoint list or library, regardless of the team members' organizational membership.

By now, you have a general idea of what SharePoint is and how you can use it. In the next chapter, you learn how to install and configure Windows SharePoint Services 3.0.

Installing Windows SharePoint Services

In this chapter, you learn how to prepare and install the Windows SharePoint Server 3.0 (WSS) system with both types of available database configurations. You also learn how to prepare for the installation and understand the different types of system user accounts involved in this action. After the installation is done, you learn how to check that everything is okay. You also learn basic troubleshooting techniques.

> WSS can run in either an NT 4 or Active Directory domain. It also runs in a workgroup environment (for example, a stand-alone server). The instructions in this chapter use an Active Directory domain.

This chapter is organized by initial sections describing what you are about to do and why, then a step-by-step description on how to do it, and finally some more information on the steps involved, including any tips and tricks based on real-world scenarios.

What Is New in WSS 3.0

This new version of WSS comes with a lot of new features and functionality. It is also faster, but it requires more memory than its predecessor WSS 2.0. It is still a free add-on for any Windows 2003 Server edition, and WSS in itself requires no special client access licenses. Following is a list of the most important changes compared to WSS 2.0:

❑ **Undelete:** Recover deleted list and library items, such as documents, plus complete lists and libraries. Note that undelete does not work on entire sites!

❑ **Item-level security:** Set permission on individual list and library items, such as a contact or a document. You can also set permissions for a folder in a library.

❑ **Send-To:** Send a link to a document, or send a copy of the document to another location.

❑ **Receive e-mail:** Libraries can receive SMTP messages, including their attachments.

❑ **Content types:** Create multiple document templates, each with individual metadata columns, workflows, and policies.

❑ **RSS support:** View all updates of a list or library by using a *Real Simple Syndication* (RSS) feed; see more about this in Chapter 7.

❑ **Gantt support:** Create Gantt charts for any type of list with start and stop dates.

❑ **New Site templates:** Use site templates for wiki and blog sites.

❑ **Surveys:** Take advantage of enhanced features, such as conditional branching and page breaks.

❑ **People and groups:** This new type of column allows you to use any user name or group as metadata.

❑ **Two-way synchronization:** Allows an Outlook 2007 user to take document library offline and to synchronize task lists, contacts, and calendar lists both ways between WSS and Outlook 2007.

❑ **Security trimmed:** WSS now hides links and objects that a user does not have at least Read permission to.

❑ **Workflows:** Any list or library can have one or more workflows associated with it.

❑ **Master Pages:** The look and feel of a WSS page is now controlled by a Master Page, which is an ASP.NET 2.0 feature.

❑ **Tree view:** Display a tree view of your site's content and also any subsite and its content.

❑ **Breadcrumb trails:** At the top of each page is a breadcrumb trail that shows the pages you visited before the current one.

There are actually even more new features in WSS 3.0, but the functionality now is very good. WSS 3.0 will satisfy the needs of many smaller installations that do not require more advanced features such as global searching, Excel services, and Business Data Catalog, which come with MOSS 2007.

Preparing to Install WSS

WSS is the base module of SharePoint 2007, and it can use one of two available database types:

❑ MS SQL Server 2005 Express (embedded)

❑ MS SQL 2000 or 2005 Server

> **Contrary to the standard edition of MS SQL Server 2005 Express, the embedded version has no space limitation.**

SharePoint also needs some user accounts in order to work, and it is your job to decide what accounts are to be used (which is discussed throughout this chapter). You should plan what WSS will be used for and who the users will be. This may affect the structure of your WSS environment.

Although WSS 3.0 is a great product, you should really think twice before making the choice to install it without MOSS. WSS has a lot of benefits, not the least of which is that it comes free with Windows 2003 Server. However, it also has its drawbacks. You should analyze what problems you are trying to solve with SharePoint. If you later decide to upgrade to MOSS, it can be done, but you will have to complete several manual steps in order to make it work. So, the best course of action is to be sure that you have the right version installed from the beginning.

> The first version of WSS, released in 2001, was named SharePoint Team Services (STS). The STS acronym is still used in today's version of WSS. Whenever you see something that begins with "STS" in this book, such as STSADM and STS_Config, think "WSS."

Think about what needs and problems you want to address with your SharePoint installation. Most likely you cannot answer this question on your own. You must talk with your end users because they are the ones who will use SharePoint. Talk with people in your organization and ask questions like the ones in the following table.

Question	People to Ask	Comment
Do you need an intranet for the whole organization?	Top management, people responsible for managing organization-wide information	For a small company with fewer than 50 users, WSS may be sufficient. But if there is a lot of information, MOSS will better suit your needs.
Do you need a local intranet for your department or team?	Middle management, team leaders	WSS is a good choice if the department or team is working with the same type of information.
Do you want to be able to search for information across sites or external to SharePoint?	All types of users	Only MOSS offers global search functionality.
Is searching inside a specific SharePoint site enough for your needs?	All types of users	This is a complementary question to the previous one; if the answer is yes, you could fulfill this need by using WSS and MS SQL Server together.

Question	People to Ask	Comment
Do groups of users need to share and update different types of information?	All types of users	If the answer is yes, this need is fulfilled by WSS.
Do you need a way of presenting more information than just the e-mail addresses and phone numbers for some or all of your users?	Middle management, team leaders, project leaders	MOSS has the My Site feature, which presents much more information about users than the typical Employee List.
Do you need a way to display MS Excel spreadsheets and charts to users without requiring them to have MS Excel?	Information management, middle management, team leaders, project leaders	MOSS alone supports this with the Excel Service.
Do your users need to display and fill out forms with a web browser?	Information management, middle management, team leaders, project leaders	MOSS alone supports this with the Forms Service.
Do you need to display and update data in external data sources, such as SAP and Oracle databases?	Information management, middle management, team leaders, project leaders	MOSS alone supports this with the Business Data Catalog (BDC) feature.

> **In addition to asking these questions, be sure to check how much money a MOSS-based solution will cost and discuss this with whoever is in charge of allocating the money. When you have this conversation, don't forget to also talk about how extra costs can creep into any project, regardless of how much planning is done. Make sure there is an adequate surplus of finances available to deal with unanticipated problems.**

If you get one or more answers that indicate a MOSS solution is preferable, you must think carefully about what version to install. Sometimes, a requested functionality is not worth the investment that MOSS requires, and sometimes it is. You should always have a follow-up question ready when your users, especially the managers, tell you that they need a MOSS-only feature: "Is this feature worth the investment of X number of dollars?" It has happened more than once that these users then say, "No! Let's start with WSS only." If so, let them know that an upgrade later on will take time and money and it is easiest to start with MOSS if this is what they will need in the end — maybe this will change their mind again.

If the results of your investigation suggest a solution based on WSS, you have two database options: if the number of users is less than 1000, you can use a MS SQL Server 2005 Express installed on the same computer as WSS. Else you will need the full MS SQL Server — if you use MS SQL Server, you can also chose between a locally installed database or a remote database server. For example, you could use a MS SQL Server that is used for other applications but has the available resources for your WSS environment.

Types of WSS Configurations

In this section, assume that your SharePoint solution will be based on WSS alone. (To see configurations for the SharePoint solution that includes MOSS, see Chapter 4.) Now you must answer the following question: What database configuration should I use? The following table describes your options.

Database	Local Database Engine	Remote Database Server
MS SQL Server 2005 Express (embedded edition)	Yes	Not supported
MS SQL 2000/2005 Server	Yes	Yes

Each solution has its own pros and cons:

❑ The MS SQL Server 2005 Express database is free, whereas MS SQL Server is not.

❑ A local database engine has the following characteristics:

    ❑ It requires no network communication and therefore is very fast.

    ❑ No extra server is necessary, so it will be easier to install and maintain.

    ❑ However, the hardware requirements are higher when you want to run both WSS and the database on the same server, so you may need extra hardware for this server.

If you are just building a simple test environment, you will most likely be happy with a local MS SQL Server 2005 Express database. In the previous table, the second row describes two more options that you could use with MS SQL Server: one using a local SQL server, and one using a remote SQL server. To make sure that you understand all the different options, following is a summary of each of the three configurations.

Single-Server Configuration with Local MS SQL Server 2005 Express

This is the preferred configuration for a small WSS environment where collaboration, sharing information, and document management are requested. It is free, it even has a basic search capability, and you do not have to pay any extra license for the WSS or MS SQL Server 2005 Express software. You can get this type of configuration up and running within 15 minutes, because most of the settings for getting WSS and the database to communicate with each other are automatically configured. Microsoft refers to this type of configuration as *stand-alone server*, because it has both SharePoint and the database engine on the same physical server.

There are no hard limitations regarding the number of users or the size of the database, although Microsoft recommends not to exceed 1000 users with this database.. It also has all the WSS functionality that you would find in a WSS and MS SQL Server environment

Single-Server Configuration with Local MS SQL 2000/2005 Server

This configuration is perfect for the small organization or department that wants a very good platform for building a basic intranet, for information sharing, and collaboration, as well as basic search capability. The cost is higher than the previous configuration because you need an MS SQL Server, which is not free. But if you already have invested in the MS SQL Server and it has free capacity available, you could install WSS on that same server. This would make a great solution.

> **You need one MS SQL Server *Client Access License* (CAL) for each WSS user. Make sure your current license agreement covers all the WSS users.**

Using this database edition, there are no limitations regarding the number of users or the size of the database,. It has the same type of search capability as when using a SQL Server Express, i.e. a user can start the search from the current site, and all its subsites. However, this search feature will not allow a global search; In other words, if you have a number of sites, you must know exactly in what site collection the information is stored to be able to find it.

A Small Farm: WSS with a Separate MS SQL Server

The last configuration is where you install WSS on one server and MS SQL Server on another server. This is something Microsoft refers to as a *small farm*. This increases the number of users supported, and you have all the functionality of the previously described configuration. Once again, this would not be a free installation because you need the MS SQL Server, but if you have such an installation already somewhere in your IT environment, there may be no extra cost. This depends on the type of license you have for this existing MS SQL Server, as described previously.

There is no added WSS functionality with this solution, aside from the increased number of users supported. However, you could use this configuration with a clustered MS SQL 2005 Server environment, with up to eight nodes, thus giving you both fault tolerance and higher availability.

Hardware Requirements

SharePoint is an application that works best when it gets lots of memory and CPU resources. Version 3.0 of WSS requires about twice as much memory as its predecessor. The reason for this is, of course, that the new WSS version has a lot more features and advanced functionality. A server with 1 GB of memory may support about 100 WSS users, as long as you have the disk capacity to store all the data needed. See the next section for more details.

> **Microsoft recommends that WSS 3.0 be installed on servers based on a 64-bit CPU, because 64-bit CPUS provide a substantial increase in general performance and support a larger memory than 32-bit CPU servers.**

There are several things you must understand when planning your WSS server:

❑   SharePoint is a web application! There is no permanent connection between the client browser and the SharePoint server. Every time you open a link or a document, the browser connects, gets what you requested, and closes the connection immediately after that, regardless of how long the user looks at that information.

❑   The number of users in the organization is not the same as the number of simultaneous users.

❑   Different activities in SharePoint require different resources. For example, displaying a project site normally generates a very light load on the server, whereas indexing the database generates a much higher load.

Calculating the Number of NOPS Required

There is a general, well-proven formula that you can use for calculating the load, or the *normalized operations per second* (NOPS), on the SharePoint server. From that you can estimate the number of supported users, given a certain hardware configuration. The formula requires you to find out or estimate a number of values:

> **The term "normalized" means that the formula takes into account a number of variables that affect the calculated number of operations per second.**

$$\frac{A \times B \times C \times D}{360{,}000 \times E} = \text{normalized operations per second (NOPS)}$$

Given the following estimated data that you must supply:

❑   A = The number of users.

❑   B = The percentage of active users on a typical day.

❑   C = The number of operations per active user per day.

❑   D = The peak factor.

❑   E = The number of working hours per day.

Two of these estimated parameters need to be explained in more detail. The peak factor is a value between 1 and 10, which is used to indicate the peak hours during the work hours. For example, if the organization works from 9 A.M. to 5 P.M., it is a safe bet that most workers start their day by opening their SharePoint environment, because that is where all their information can be found. After that you will probably have an even load. Then directly after lunch, you would get another peak again. A peak factor of 1 means "no peak load at all." A factor of 10 means "a peak load all day." A typical organization would have a peak factor value of 5. If you want to be on the safe side, use the higher value of 7.

The other estimated parameter is the number of operations per active user per day, which has to do with how much your SharePoint environment will be utilized per day. This is also a value between 1 and 10, where 1 means that your users access SharePoint for almost no time at all and 10 means your users work all day with SharePoint. For a typical organization you would get something close to 10 for this value.

Example 1: An Organization with 200 Very Active Users

Your organization has 200 employees (A). The percentage of active users in a typical day is 80 (B). The number of operations per active user is 10 (C). The number of working hours for the organization as a whole is 12 hours (E). You estimate the peak factor (D) to be 10, to be on the safe side. The formula for this organization will look like this:

$$\frac{200 \times 80 \times 10 \times 10}{360,000 \times 12} = 0.37 \text{ NOPS}$$

Example 2: An Organization with 4,500 Normal Users

Your organization has 4,500 employees (A). The percentage of active users in a typical day is 50 (B). The number of operations per active user is 10 (C). The number of working hours for the organization as a whole is 12 hours (E). You estimate the peak factor (D) to be 5. The formula for this organization will look like this:

$$\frac{4,500 \times 50 \times 10 \times 5}{360,000 \times 12} = 2.60 \text{ NOPS}$$

Now you have a good idea of the load your system will generate. The next step is to use this information to calculate the hardware you need. In the following table are some typical configurations and the estimated normalized operations per second they support.

Server Configuration	Estimated NOPS Supported
A single server with both WSS and MS SQL 2005 Server Express, configured with 2 GB of memory and a 2.8-GHz 64-bit CPU	Up to 35 NOPS
One WSS server and one SQL Server, both configured with 2 GB of memory and a dual 2.8-GHz 64-bit CPU	Up to 65 NOPS
One WSS server and one SQL Server, both configured with 2 GB of memory and a dual 3.06-GHz 64-bit CPU	Up to 105 NOPS

From this table you can learn three important things:

1. You don't need a very large server to run WSS for most installations.

2. Separating the WSS server and the MS SQL server improves the NOPS throughput.

3. The CPU is the most important resource; it should have at least 2 GB of memory. Notice the difference between 2.8- and 3.06-GHz CPUs.

The important fact to remember here is that when a server has at least 2 GB of memory, it will support thousands of users, if it is appropriately configured!

Calculating the Disk Space Needed

The disk space that WSS itself requires is less than 50 MB, so the important part is the database where SharePoint will store all its information. The database application requires about 100 MB for its binary files. It does not matter if you are using the SQL Server 2005 Express engine or the MS SQL Server; you still need to follow this simple but important rule:

> **You must always have at least 50 percent free space on your database disk!**

If you don't have at least 50 percent free space on your database disk, you will not be able to perform database maintenance and troubleshooting, since these activities may need to make a copy of the database in order to perform their tasks. So what will require the most space in the database? The answer is simply: Your documents! They will not be compressed, in fact, they will require up to 20% more space in the SQL Server, so a 1-MB Word file will require 1.2 MB of database disk space. The other things you store will, of course, also take some space, but they will most likely not take anywhere near as much space as the files you store. And a SharePoint site itself will require less than 200 KB of database space.

> **Remember that the new file format in MS Office 2007 generates files that are less than 50 percent of the size of previous MS Office file formats!**

So to estimate the disk space needed for your database, start by estimating the number of files it will contain. For example, assume that you estimate that it will contain about 50,000 files and documents, with an average size of 500 KB. In total this will require at least 25 GB. Add to that 5 GB for the other types of information you will store, and you get 30 GB in total. Following the preceding rule, you must have at least a 60-GB disk for the database alone.

Remember that if you implement a *small farm* configuration (one WSS server and one MS SQL server), you only require the 60 GB of disk space on the database server. The WSS server itself requires very little disk space.

Software Requirements

As you may recall from the previous chapter, SharePoint is a web application, and it requires Internet Information Services 6.0 (IIS 6), which in turn requires you to run MS Windows 2003 Server. SharePoint also requires that ASP.NET and its supporting components be installed. The easiest way to get this configuration right for a SharePoint server, with nothing more and nothing less than is needed, is to follow these steps:

1. Log on to your Windows 2003 server as the administrator.
2. Click Start ⇨ Control Panel.
3. Click the Add or Remove Programs ⇨ Windows Component button.
4. Select the Application Server and click on Details.

5. Make sure that everything is cleared, including Internet Information Service (IIS).

6. Check the ASP.NET box, and it will automatically check all the components it needs.

7. Click Next, then Finish to save this configuration.

> Note that if you have Microsoft .NET Framework 2.0 installed on this computer, you may have to use the `aspnet_regiis.exe` tool in order to install WSS 3.0. See this article for more information: `http://msdn2.microsoft.com/en-us/library/k6h9cz8h(VS.80).aspx`.

Remember that you can use any edition of Windows 2003 Server for the WSS installation. However, if you choose the Web Edition of Windows 2003 Server, it must be connected to a separate MS SQL Server, since that edition of Windows Server does not support local databases.

The IIS Virtual Server

In the good old days, each web application required its own physical web server, clearly not the most economical solution. Microsoft solved this by allowing its IIS to create and manage virtual web servers (for example, the default web site). In this approach, each web application running on top of IIS 6 needs its own virtual server. This will make it possible to run several web applications on the same physical server. In order to make it possible to separate each virtual server, they must differ in at least one of the following: the IP number, the port number, or the host header name.

But that solution created a new problem: If one web application crashed, it also killed all other web applications running on the same IIS. Microsoft's solution was to invent the *application pool*, which gives a private virtual address space and security context for each web application. One virtual web server is linked to one application pool. However, each application pool can be linked to more than one virtual server, thus sharing address space and security context.

> IIS 6 supports up to 9 virtual IIS servers with individual application pools or 99 virtual IIS servers sharing the same application pool.

When installing SharePoint, you need to be sure about these two things:

1. What virtual IIS server SharePoint will be installed on.

2. What user account the linked application pool will use.

The application pool security context can be either a built-in account, typically the network service, or a standard user account. Whatever account you choose, it must have permissions to read and write to and from the SQL database. Make sure that the user account is granted permission as a database creator and security administrator in MS SQL Server.

> Sharing the same application pool among several virtual IIS servers makes it possible for the other web applications to access the SQL database! Microsoft recommends that you use a separate application pool for the virtual IIS server that WSS will run in.

Besides the application pool used by the virtual IIS web server for the WSS sites, there will also be a separate application pool for the web-based Central Administration tool that comes with SharePoint. This must be a separate application pool. It cannot share the same application pool as the WSS virtual server.

Before SharePoint can use a virtual web server in IIS, it must be extended with new functionality. This is known as a "web application" in SharePoint 2007. The SharePoint administrator creates the web application when needed, using the SharePoint Central Administration tool by either selecting an existing virtual web server in IIS or creating a new virtual web server, which will then be extended. Each web application can then be used to host one or more site collections, as described in more detail later in this chapter.

Minimum and Recommended Configurations

To summarize the previous hardware and software requirement sections, you can use the following table, which lists Microsoft's minimum and recommended configurations. Remember that for a pilot installation you will actually get away with slightly less than the given minimum memory size in the following table.

Item	Minimum Requirement	MS Recommends
Operating system	Any edition of Microsoft Windows Server 2003	Any edition of Microsoft Windows Server 2003
CPU	1 CPU running at 2.5 GHz	2 CPUs running at least 3 GHz
RAM	1 GB	2 GB or more
Disk space	Minimum 3 GB of free disk space	Minimum 10 GB of free disk space
File system	NTFS	NTFS
IIS version	6.0 with ASP.NET (in Worker Process Isolation Mode)	6.0 with ASP.NET (in Worker Process Isolation Mode)
Database engine	SQL Server 2005 Express or SQL Server 2000 with Service Pack 3a	A separate SQL Server 2005 and its latest service pack
Internet browser	IE 6.0 with the latest service pack	IE 7 with the latest service pack

> WSS will work in a stand-alone computer or in a Active Directory domain member. If AD domain users must have access to this WSS environment, you must make this computer a member of that Active Directory.

Installing WSS

By now, you have the necessary information to start the installation of WSS. The following section describes the exact steps required to install WSS in all three combinations possible. Before you start following these steps, make sure that nobody is using this server for anything else, at least not during the installation. If you have other applications installed on the same server, make a backup before you start. That way you will be prepared in the unlikely event that something goes wrong and the server gets messed up beyond repair!

During the installation of WSS, the setup program will create a web application for its web-based Central Administration tool named *SharePoint Central Administration v3*, configured to use a randomly selected TCP port over 1023. This web application will be connected to a new application pool with the same name as the web application

The Config and Content Databases

There are two types of databases that WSS will use: the configuration database and the content database. During the installation of WSS, you or the setup program will create these, depending on how complex the installation scenario is. These two database types contain the following information:

- ❑ **Configuration Database:** Contains all the configurations for this SharePoint environment. It is shared among all WSS servers (if more than one) and the SQL databases (if more than one). There is always only one configuration database, regardless of the number of WSS and SQL databases. For WSS installations using the MS SQL Server (not SQL Server 2005 Express), you will name this configuration database; the default name is SharePoint_Config.

- ❑ **Content Database:** This database contains all data and information that belongs to the WSS web sites, such as news lists, document libraries, and the web site itself. It also includes management data, such as user names and permission settings. Initially, you have one single content database, but you can create as many as you need. Large organizations may have more than a thousand content databases. The first WSS content database will get the default name WSS_Content. You will name any new content database that you add.

In the following sections, you will find all three possible configurations of WSS. Each configuration is completely described, including detailed steps on how to perform this type of installation. Many of these steps are identical in two or all of the installation scenarios. I recommend that you focus on the type of installation that is most interesting to you at this moment. Later on, you can come back to this chapter when you need to perform another type of installation.

Installing a Single Server with the SQL Server 2005 Express

Installing a WSS using a MS SQL Server 2005 Express database is very straightforward and easy. You can do it within 10 minutes without much hassle. Follow the steps in the next Try It Out to install both the WSS application and the database on the same server.

Try It Out   Install WSS and SQL Express on a Single Server

1. Log on as an administrator to the Windows 2003 server you will use for your WSS and MS SQL Server 2005 Express installation.

2. Make sure that Windows 2003 Server has the latest service packs and security patches installed by going to Start ➪ All Programs ➪ Windows Update.

3. Download and run the .NET Framework 3.0 package from Microsoft's web site, which will add Windows Workflow Foundation and ASP.NET 2.0 as core features of Windows 2003 Server:

   a. Go to www.microsoft.com/downloads and enter **dotnetfx3setup.exe** in the search field.

   b. From the resulting files click Microsoft .NET Framework 3.0 Redistributable Package to open its download page.

   c. Before you download this file, make sure to select the language of your Windows 2003 Server; by default it will be English.

   d. You can now click Download to start the download a "bootstrap file" (a file that will start the download of the actual package) or you can scroll down on this page, and click either X86 Redist Package (32-bits Windows Server; 50 MB) or X64 Redist Package (64-bits Windows Server; 90 MB) to download the full setup file.

   e. When downloaded, run this file to install the .NET Framework 3.0. Select the option "I have read and ACCEPT the terms of the License Agreement" (if you do), and click Install. This will start the setup, which will take several minutes to complete, depending on your hardware. When done you will get a message that the setup has been completed successfully.

4. Download the latest version of WSS from Microsoft's web site:

   a. Go to www.microsoft.com/downloads and enter **Sharepoint.exe** in the search field.

   b. From the results click either the Windows SharePoint Services 3.0 for a 32-bit Windows Server or the Windows SharePoint Services 3.0 x64 for a 64-bit Windows Server.

   c. Make sure to select the default language you need for your WSS 3.0 installation, using the Change Language menu on this page. (Note that in this example we assume that it will be an English version!) Then click Download to start the actual download (77 MB for the 32-bit version or 85 MB for the 64-bit version).

5. Verify that you have ASP.NET installed, as previously described in the section "Software Requirements."

6. Start the installation by running the `SharePoint.exe` file you downloaded:

    a. The first dialog page is about the license agreement. If you accept the terms, select "I accept the terms of this agreement" and click Continue.

    b. The next page is important. Click Basic to use the SQL Server 2005 Express database that comes with WSS 3.0. If you instead click Advanced, you will want to use an MS SQL Server database, as shown in Figure 2-1. In this example, however, be sure to click Basic.

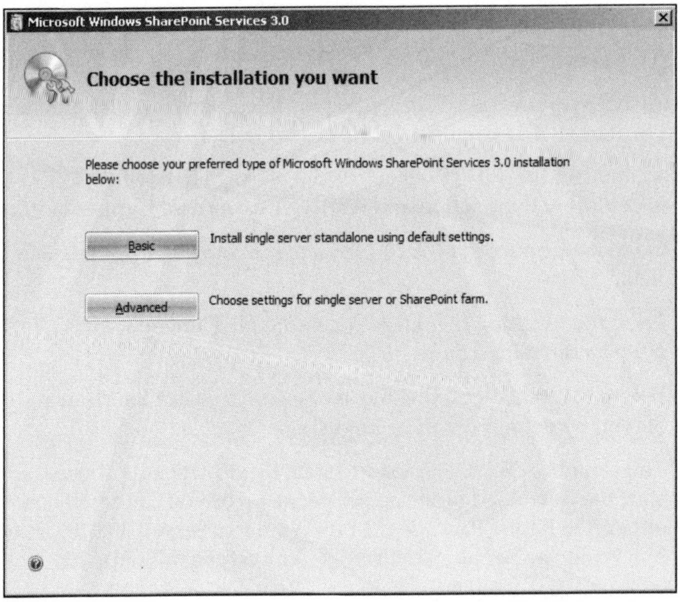

Figure 2-1

    c. The installation takes a few minutes; when completed you will see a page where the option Run the SharePoint Product and Technologies Configuration Wizard now is pre-selected. Click Close to close the setup program, and start the Configuration Wizard.

7. The Configuration Wizard will set up the configuration needed to run WSS, such as creating the Central Administration tool and the web application needed to host the first site collection. It is important that you run this wizard. Follow these steps:

    a. On the Welcome to SharePoint Products and Technologies page, click Next.

    b. You will get a dialog box that informs you that the IIS and other related services will be started or reset during the configuration. Click Yes to continue. The configuration wizard now starts and performs a variety of tasks. It will take 5–15 minutes to complete, depending on the server hardware.

    c. When completed, you will (hopefully) see the message "Configuration Successful." Click Finish and the site created by the Configuration Wizard will open (see Figure 2-2). This site is now ready to be used.

Figure 2-2

Checking the Installation

Before going on, it is a good idea to investigate what new things were installed on the server:

1. Start by opening the IIS manager: Start ➪ Administration Tools ➪ Internet Information Service (IIS) Manager.

2. Expand the server node and then the Web Sites node. Note that you have three IIS virtual servers here:

   ❑ **Default Web Site:** This site is stopped, since another virtual server using TCP port 80 will be used. The reason for this is increased security; the files and locations for the default web site are well known and therefore are an easy target for malicious code like viruses.

   ❑ **SharePoint – 80:** A new virtual server created by the Configuration Wizard, which listens on TCP port 80. It is used by SharePoint for all user web sites, such as project sites, team sites, and so on.

   ❑ **SharePoint Central Administration v3:** Used by SharePoint for the administration web site.

3. Right-click virtual server SharePoint – 80, and select Properties.

4. Switch to the Home Directory tab; note what application pool name this virtual server is using. The default is SharePoint – 80. Close the properties for this virtual server.

5. Expand the Application Pools node in the left-hand column of the IIS Manager.

6. Right-click the application pool SharePoint – 80 (used by the virtual server SharePoint – 80) and switch to the Identity tab. Note what security account this application pool is using. By default, it is the predefined Network Service.

Do the same with the virtual server for the SharePoint Central Administration web site:

1. Right-click on its node.

2. Check the Home Directory tab to see its application pool (which should be the SharePoint Central Administration v3).

3. Open the properties for that application pool, and check that its security account on the Identity page also is the same predefined Network Service account.

> This security account is granted access to the SQL Server 2005 Express database and is used by WSS whenever it needs to read or write to or from databases.

To summarize this, WSS uses two virtual IIS servers: one for the web sites that your SharePoint users utilize and one for the central administration of SharePoint. These two virtual servers use separate application pools. Both these application pools use the same security account.

Installing a Single Server with a Local MS SQL Database

You may recall that previous sections mentioned that the SQL Server 2005 Express should only be used for organizations up to 1000 users, and that this database must be installed on the same computer as SharePoint itself. This is a strong reason for selecting the full MS SQL Server (2000 or 2005) for larger organizations. That database edition also has powerful management tools for configuration, security settings, and backup procedures.

The following sections describe how to install both the WSS application and a MS SQL Server database on the same server. Note that for the MS SQL 2000 version you must install Service Pack 3a or later before using it for WSS. You can also use MS SQL 2005 Server as the database server for WSS 3.0.

The following example assumes that you have an MS SQL 2000 Server installed and running on the server where you will install WSS 3.0. Make sure that you have MS SQL Server installed and running before performing the following steps. In order to get the indexing and search functionality to work in WSS, you must also make sure that MS SQL Server has the Full-Text Search option installed.

| Try It Out | Install WSS and MS SQL on a Single Server |

1. Log on as an administrator to the Windows 2003 server you will use for your WSS and MS SQL Server 2005 Express installation.

2. Make sure that Windows 2003 Server has the latest service packs and security patches installed by going to Start ➪ All Programs ➪ Windows Update.

3. Download and run the .NET Framework 3.0 package from Microsoft's web site, which will add Windows Workflow Foundation and ASP.NET 2.0 as core features of Windows 2003 Server:

    a. Go to `www.microsoft.com/downloads` and enter **dotnetfx3setup.exe** in the search field.

    b. From the resulting files click Microsoft .NET Framework 3.0 Redistributable Package to open its download page.

    c. Before you download this file, make sure to select the language of your Windows 2003 Server; by default it will be English.

    d. You can now click Download to start the download a "bootstrap file" (a file that will start the download of the actual package) or you can scroll down on this page, and click either X86 Redist Package (32-bits Windows Server; 50 MB) or X64 Redist Package (64-bits Windows Server; 90 MB) to download the full setup file.

    e. When downloaded, run this file to install the .NET Framework 3.0; select the option "I have read and ACCEPT the terms of the License Agreement" (if you do), and click Install. This will start the setup, which will take several minutes to complete, depending on your hardware. When done you will get a message that the setup has been completed successfully.

4. Download the latest version of WSS from Microsoft's web site:

    a. Go to `www.microsoft.com/downloads` and enter **Sharepoint.exe** in the search field.

    b. From the results click either the Windows SharePoint Services 3.0 for a 32-bit Windows Server or the Windows SharePoint Services 3.0 x64 for a 64-bit Windows Server.

    c. Make sure to select the default language you need for your WSS 3.0 installation, using the Change Language menu on this page. (Note in this example we assume that it will be the English version!) Then click Download to start the actual download (77 MB for the 32-bit version or 85 MB for the 64-bit version).

5. Verify that you have ASP.NET installed, as previously described in the section "Software Requirements."

6. Start the installation by running the `SharePoint.exe` file you downloaded:

    a. The first dialog page is about the license agreement. If you accept the terms, select "I accept the terms of this agreement" and click Continue.

    b. The next page is important. Click Advanced to prepare WSS to use a SQL Server database (see Figure 2-1).

    c. On the Server Type page, select the option Web Front End. Switch to the tab Data Location, and select the disk and folder where the WSS files will be stored. Remember that best practice is to install any application, such as WSS, in a disk other than C: because that is the default disk used by the Windows Server to store the system page file. When you are done, click Install Now to start the actual installation.

    d. The installation takes a few minutes. When it is completed, you will see a page where the option Run the SharePoint Product and Technologies Configuration Wizard is now preselected. Click Close to close the setup program, and start the Configuration Wizard.

7. The Configuration Wizard will set up the configuration needed to run WSS, such as creating the Central Administration tool and the web application needed to host the first site collection. It is important that you run this wizard. Follow these steps:

a. On the Welcome to SharePoint Products and Technologies page, click Next.

b. You will get a dialog box that informs you that the IIS and other related services will be started or reset during the configuration. Click Yes to continue. The Configuration Wizard starts.

c. On the Connect to a server farm page, select the option "No, I want to create a new server farm." The other option, "Yes, I want to connect to an existing server farm," is used when you install the next WSS server and want to join the same farm as the first server. But for now, make sure to select No here, then click Next.

d. On the page Specify Configuration Database Settings (see Figure 2-3), enter the server database's name, which in this example is the same server as the WSS server (for example srv1). Accept the default database name, `SharePoint_Config`. In the section Specify Database Access Account, you must enter an existing user account, plus its password, which SharePoint will use when communicating with MS SQL Server. In this example, you will use the existing account `Filobit\WSS_service`. Click Next when ready.

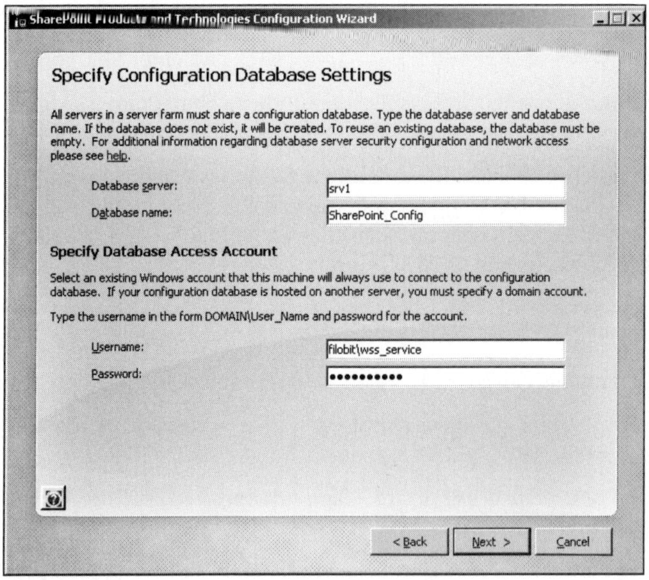

Figure 2-3

e. On the page Configure SharePoint Central Administration web application, you can accept the default TCP port number, but I recommend that you set a port number that is easy to remember, such as 5000. Accept the default NTLM as the authentication provider. Click Next to continue.

f. On the page Completing the SharePoint Products and Technologies Configuration Wizard, you will see a summary of the settings you have selected. If they are okay, then click Next to start the Configuration Wizard.

> **If you want to enable Active Directory Account Creation Mode for this WSS installation, click Advanced, enable this mode, and configure its settings. You will learn more about this in Chapter 3.**

g. The Configuration Wizard now starts and performs a variety of tasks. it will take 5–15 minutes to complete, depending on the server hardware.

h. When it is completed, you will (hopefully) see the message "Configuration Successful." Click Finish and the Central Administration tool will open (see Figure 2-4). The installation of SharePoint is now done, and the next step is to complete the configuration of WSS and then create your first web site.

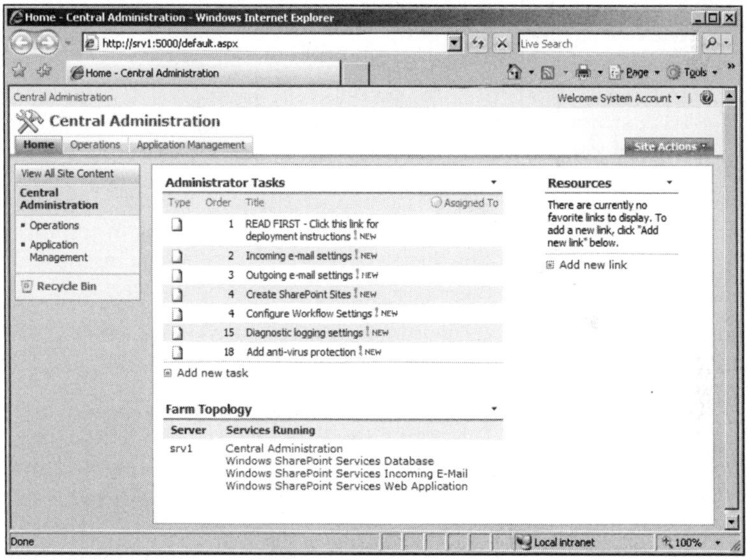

Figure 2-4

When you choose the Advanced installation mode, you get more control over the installation than with Basic installation. However, you also have to answer more questions, such as what database you want to use, what user account WSS will use when communicating with the SQL Server, and so on. Even when the Configuration Wizard is completed, you will still have to configure some more settings, such as outgoing e-mail settings. This is why the Central Administration tool displays a list of administrative tasks, as shown in Figure 2-4.

Another difference between these two installation options is that Advanced mode will not automatically create any site. At first, you may think that this is disturbing, but in fact it is not. This will give you a chance to select the type of site you want for your first site. Although all WSS sites have the same code base, they can look very different. For example, one site may be perfect for sharing information within a team or group, while another site may be suitable for storing meeting details. The difference between these sites is in the site template. Every time you create a new site, you will also select a specific site template for that site, and that gives the site its initial look and feel. You can then modify that initial design to make it suit your needs. WSS 3.0 comes with a number of site templates, and you will later learn more about all these templates.

Let's look at the administrative tasks listed in Figure 2-4. Their purpose is to guide you through the steps necessary to get a fully functional WSS environment. Following is a short description of each of them, but you will learn more about them in Chapter 3:

- ❏ **READ FIRST – Click this link for deployment instructions:** Open this task, and click on its link, Read the Quick Start Guide, which explains most of the administrative actions and tasks available in WSS 3.0. This guide can also be displayed by clicking on the blue question mark icon at the top-right part of any page in the Central Administrative tool and then clicking Getting Started ➪ Quick Start Guide.

- ❏ **Incoming e-mail:** This administrative task will contain a link to the Operations page and its link Configure Incoming e-mail Settings, where you configure if and how SharePoint will receive incoming e-mail. You can choose to open that configuration page in either way shown. This task is only necessary to complete if you want to activate this WSS feature.

- ❏ **Outgoing e-mail settings:** This administrative task contains a link to the Operations page and its link Outgoing e-mail settings. Use this configuration page to define outgoing e-mail settings.

- ❏ **Create SharePoint Sites:** This administrative task contains a link to the Application Management page and its link Create or Extend Web Application. This is the first step you must take when creating the first WSS site. It also contains the second step, which is to create a site collection.

- ❏ **Configure Workflow Settings:** This administrative task contains a link to the Application Management page and its link Workflow Settings. Use this link to control whether user-defined workflows are enabled and whether workflows will send e-mail notifications to users who are assigned tasks but do not have access to the site running this workflow.

- ❏ **Diagnostic logging settings:** This administrative task contains a link to the Operations page and its link Diagnostic Logging. Use this configuration page to control the settings for diagnostic logging.

- ❏ **Add anti-virus protection:** This administrative task contains a link to the Operations page and its Antivirus link. Use this configuration page to define the antivirus settings. Note that you must purchase a SharePoint aware antivirus solution before this page is useful to configure.

To create the first WSS site, you must complete at least one of these administrative tasks: the Create SharePoint Sites. The general steps for creating the first site are these: Create a web application, then create a site collection, and select the site template for the first site. This is exactly what the Configuration Wizard did to create the Central Administrative tool, when you first ran it after the initial installation. Creating a user web site is no different from creating the Central Administrative web site! The steps for creating the first web site are described in detail in Chapter 3.

Installing a Single Server Using a Remote MS SQL Database

Most of the steps in this configuration are similar or identical to the previous configuration with a local MS SQL Server. The reasons for using a remote MS SQL Server are these:

- ❏ **Increased performance:** The WSS server can handle many more users.

- ❏ **Fault tolerance:** It is possible to connect WSS to an MS SQL cluster.

- ❏ **Better economy:** You can use a previously installed MS SQL Server.

The following sections describe how to install WSS 3.0 on one computer named SRV1 and connect to an existing MS SQL database on a server named DC1. Both of these servers are members of the domain `Filobit`.

Make sure that you have the MS SQL Server installed and running on DC1 before performing the following steps. To get the indexing and search functionality to work in WSS, you must also make sure that the MS SQL Server has the Full-Text Search option installed.

Try It Out   Install WSS and MS SQL on Separate Servers

1.   Log on as an administrator to the Windows 2003 server you will use for your WSS and MS SQL Server 2005 Express installation.

2.   Make sure Windows 2003 Server has the latest service packs and security patches installed by going to Start ⇨ All Programs ⇨ Windows Update.

3.   Download and run the .NET Framework 3.0 package from Microsoft's web site, which will add Windows Workflow Foundation and ASP.NET 2.0 as core features of Windows 2003 Server:

   a.   Go to www.microsoft.com/downloads and enter **dotnetfx3setup.exe** in the search field.

   b.   From the resulting files click Microsoft .NET Framework 3.0 Redistributable Package to open its download page.

   c.   Before you download this file, make sure to select the language of your Windows 2003 Server. By default it will be English.

   d.   You can now click Download to start the download a bootstrap file, (a file that will start the download of the actual package), or you can scroll down on this page, and click either X86 Redist Package (32-bits Windows Server; 50 MB) or X64 Redist Package (64-bits Windows Server; 90 MB) to download the full setup file.

   e.   When it is downloaded, run this file to install .NET Framework 3.0. Select the option "I have read and ACCEPT the terms of the License Agreement" (if you do), and click Install. This will start the setup, which will take several minutes to complete, depending on your hardware. When it is done, you will get a message saying that the setup has completed successfully.

4.   Download the latest version of WSS from Microsoft's web site:

   a.   Go to www.microsoft.com/downloads and enter **Sharepoint.exe** in the search field.

   b.   From the results click either the Windows SharePoint Services 3.0 for a 32-bit Windows Server or the Windows SharePoint Services 3.0 x64 for a 64-bit Windows Server.

   c.   Make sure to select the default language you need for your WSS 3.0 installation, using the Change Language menu on this page. (Note that in this example, we assume that it will be English!) Then click Download to start the actual download (77 MB for the 32-bit version or 85 MB for the 64-bit version).

5.   Verify that you have ASP.NET installed, as previously described in the section "Software Requirements."

6. Start the installation by running the `SharePoint.exe` file you downloaded:

    a. The first dialog page is about the license agreement. If you accept the terms, select "I accept the terms of this agreement" and click Continue.

    b. The next page is important. Click Advanced to prepare WSS for using a SQL Server database. (See Figure 2-1).

    c. On the Server Type page, select the option Web Front End. Switch to the Data Location tan, and select the disk and folder where the WSS files will be stored. Remember that best practice is to install any application, such as WSS, on a disk other than C: because that is the default disk used by the Windows Server to store the system page file. When done, click Install Now to start the actual installation.

    d. The installation takes a few minutes. When it is completed, you will see a page where the option Run the SharePoint Product and Technologies Configuration Wizard is prese-lected. Click Close to close the setup program, and start the Configuration Wizard.

7. The Configuration Wizard will set up the configuration needed to run WSS, such as creating the Central Administration tool and the web application needed to host the first site collection. It is important that you run this wizard. Follow these steps:

    a. On the Welcome to SharePoint Products and Technologies page, click Next.

    b. You will get a dialog box that informs you that the IIS and other related services will be started or reset during the configuration. Click Yes to continue. The Configuration Wizard starts.

    c. On the Connect to a server farm page, select the option "No, I want to create a new server farm." The other option, "Yes, I want to connect to an existing server farm," is used when you install the next WSS server and want to join the same farm as the first server. But for now, make sure to select No here, then click Next.

    d. On the page Specify Configuration Database Settings (see Figure 2-3), enter the server database's name, which in this example is the server DC1. Accept the default database name `SharePoint_Config`. In the section Specify Database Access Account, you should enter an existing domain user account (although you can also use the built-in account Network Service), plus its password, which SharePoint will use when communicating with MS SQL Server. Note that this account must be granted the SQL Server permissions Security Administrators and Database Creators, as described in step 8 below. In this exam-ple, you will use the existing account `Filobit\WSS_service`. Click Next when ready.

    e. On the page Configure SharePoint Central Administration Web Application, you can accept the default TCP port number, but I recommend that you set a port number that is easy to remember, such as 5000. Accept the default NTLM as the authentication provider. Click Next to continue.

    f. On the page Completing the SharePoint Products and Technologies Configuration Wizard, you will see a summary of the settings you have selected. If they are okay, then click Next to start the Configuration Wizard.

> If you want to enable Active Directory Account Creation Mode for this WSS installation, first click Advanced, enable this mode, and configure its settings. You will learn more about this in Chapter 3.

    g. The Configuration Wizard now starts and performs a variety of tasks. It will take 5–15 minutes to complete, depending on your server hardware.

    h. When completed, you will (hopefully) see the message "Configuration Successful." Click Finish, and the Central Administration tool will open (see Figure 2-4). The installation of SharePoint is now done, and the next step is to complete the configuration of WSS and then create your first web site.

8. The security account you defined in step 7d above must be granted access to MS SQL Server, including built-in accounts like the Network Service account. This is done automatically by SharePoint's Configuration Wizard, but just to let you know how to do this manually, the steps are described here (this example assumes that you are using an MS SQL 2000 Server):

    a. Open the management tool for SQL by navigating to Start ➪ All Programs ➪ Microsoft SQL Server ➪ Enterprise Manager.

    b. Expand the local SQL Server, then expand the Security node.

    c. Right-click Logins and select New Login.

    d. Enter the name and domain for the user you defined for the application pool, as illustrated in Figure 2-5. (For the Network Service account, you must type the full name: NT AUTHORITY\NETWORK SERVICE.)

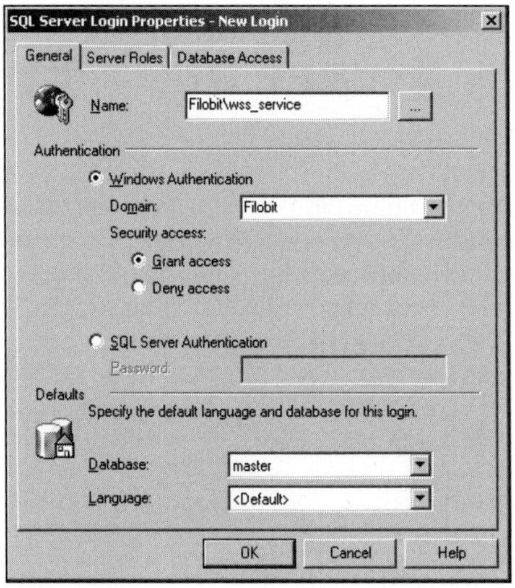

Figure 2-5

e. Switch to the Server Roles tab, and check the two options Security Administrators and Database Creators, as shown in Figure 2-6.

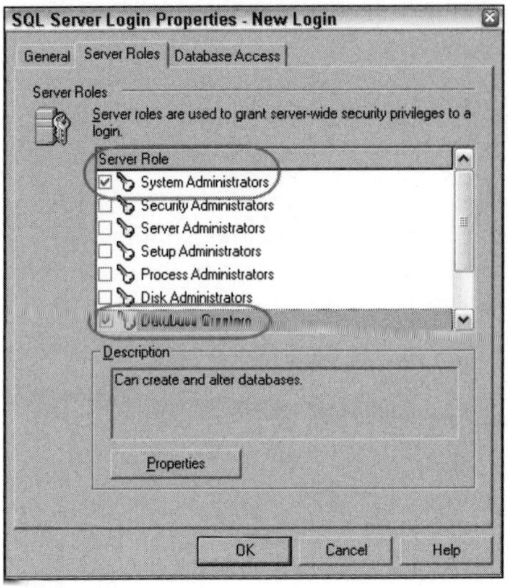

Figure 2-6

f. Click OK to save this. Then close SQL Enterprise Manager.

Upgrading SQL Server 2005 Express to MS SQL Server

Many organizations start investigating what WSS can do by installing WSS using a local SQL Server 2005 Express database. The idea is often to run a pilot project. More often than not, this pilot project then incidentally turns into a production environment, with lots of important data that cannot be discarded. I am sure you don't belong to such an organization, but you probably know somebody else who does, right? Well, you can tell your friend that it is possible to move up from the SQL Server 2005 Express database to the full MS SQL 2000 or 2005 Server, so there is no need to worry.

You have two types of possible upgrade scenarios:

❑ An in-place upgrade of SQL Server 2005 Express to a local MS SQL Server.

❑ Moving from a local SQL Server 2005 Express to a separate MS SQL Server.

The first scenario is straightforward: Simply run the setup program for MS SQL Server to upgrade SQL Server 2005 Express. The other scenario are more complicated, but not impossible. You might remember from earlier sections in this chapter that a remote SQL Server gives you better performance and also makes it possible to build a fault-tolerant MS SQL Server cluster. You will find the steps for each upgrade scenario in the following sections.

Preparing to Upgrade the SQL Server 2005 Express

The first and most important thing to remember is to back up your current WSS data. You are about to perform a very sensitive operation, and if something goes wrong, you must be sure you can go back to the previous version.

If it is a simple server configuration with just the WSS and the SQL Server 2005 Express database, you can of course perform a full Windows 2003 Server backup, including the system state (the local Registry, the IIS Metabase, and the boot files). The other option is to make a backup of the content database alone to make sure that you have all data intact in case the upgrade to MS SQL for some reason does not work as expected.

Doing a Full Server Backup

The first option, doing a full server backup, is always a good idea even if you will do a separate database backup later. This option ensures that you can do a complete restore of the Windows 2003 Server, including the WSS environment and all its data. You can use the backup utility that comes with Windows 2003 Server for this operation, if you want. See the following Try It Out.

Try It Out   Do a Full Server Backup

1. Log on as an administrator to the WSS server. Make sure that no one will use this server during the backup procedure.

2. Choose Start ➪ All Programs ➪ Accessories ➪ System Tools ➪ Backup.

3. This starts the backup program in Wizard mode (unless you previously have unchecked that option), which is fine for your purpose this time. Click Next.

4. Make sure the following page has the following option selected: Backup files and settings. Click Next.

5. On the page What to back up, make sure you select the option All information on this computer. Note that this makes a complete backup of all data on the server. It also creates a system recovery disk that makes it possible to restore all data in case of a major failure. Click Next.

6. On the page Backup Type, Destination and Name, choose where to store this backup file and give it a proper name, such as Full WSS Server Backup. Click Next to go on.

> **You need a diskette to complete this backup operation. With this diskette you can later boot up the server and it will do a complete restore of the server!**

7. On the next page you see a summary of your options. If it is okay, click Finish to close this page and start the backup procedure.

Of course, you can use whatever backup routine you normally run for your computers instead of this procedure. Just make sure that it is a complete backup, including the system state.

There is one drawback to this type of backup procedure: You will only be able to do a complete restore, if necessary. For example, you cannot just restore the WSS content database. That is why the second backup option is interesting.

Doing a File Backup of the WSS Databases

Once again, you have two options for this. You can simply stop the SQL Server 2005 Express database and make a file copy of all the database files, or you can use the STSADM tool that comes along with WSS for backing up parts or the entire content database.

> There are lots of good and very cheap backup management tools for all types of MS SQL databases, including MS SQL Server 2005 Express. For example, check out www.simego.com and www.msde.biz. You can also use a local copy of the MS SQL Enterprise Manager.

Try It Out   Copy All WSS Database Files Manually

To make a simple file copy of the database in SQL Server 2005 Express, do this:

1. Stop the service MSSQLSERVER (choose Start ➪ Administrative Tools ➪ Services).

2. Copy the files in C:\Program Files\Microsoft SQL Server\MSSQL \Data. (There may be more than one database in SQL Server 2005 Express. If you just want to copy the WSS config and content databases, look for all files starting with WSS or SharePoint.)

3. Start the MSSQLSERVER service again.

If you need to restore these database files after a failed MS SQL upgrade procedure, make sure to have a working WSS and SQL Server 2005 Express installation and then copy the WSS and SharePoint files back to the original file location.

Doing a Backup of the Content Database

This method is very fast and selective. You will only back up the content for the WSS environment. The result will be files that can be used to migrate into any WSS or even MOSS environment. The tool you must use here is STSADM.EXE. It is stored deep down in the file system, or to be exact, in this folder:

```
C:\Program Files\Common Files\Microsoft Shared\web server extensions\12\BIN
```

This is a command-based tool that you need to run in a command window. You will often need to access STSADM and other tools in this folder, and instead of entering the full path to these tools every time, it is easier to configure Windows to search in this folder directly. If you are old enough to remember when MS-DOS ruled the computer world, you might remember there is a system variable named PATH. When you enter a program name in a command window, Windows looks for that file in all file paths defined in this variable. The following Try It Out explains how to add the path to STSADM to this system variable.

Try It Out   **Update the PATH System Variable**

1.   Start Windows Explorer and navigate to the path for the STSADM as given previously. Right-click the file path in the Address field and select Copy.

2.   Click Start to see the Windows start menu.

3.   Right-click My Computer, and select Properties.

4.   Switch to the Advanced tab, and click its Environment Variables button.

5.   In the lower pane named System Variables, locate PATH and click Edit.

6.   Go to the end of the current list under Variable value (use the End key or the right arrow on the keyboard). Type in a semicolon (;) as a separator, and paste in the path you copied in step 1. Then click OK three times to save this modification and close all dialog boxes.

7.   Test it by opening a command window (Start ⇨ Run and type **Cmd**), then type **STSADM** in this command window. If you get a long list of options, you did it right. If not, redo the steps above, and be careful to do everything exactly as described.

By now, you have access to STSADM and the other tools in the same folder, regardless of where you are in the folder tree. But before you can perform your backup, you must know how it works. Every web site you create in WSS is either a top site or a subsite. Top sites are the start of a tree with any number of nested subsites, much like a top folder and subfolders in a file system. SharePoint calls this a *site collection*. All site collections are stored in a given content database in SQL Server. STSADM will help you back up a given site collection (a top site and all its subsites).

If you installed WSS using the Basic installation option, a site collection was automatically created containing one top site. In Chapter 3, you will learn how to create new top sites and subsites for each of these top sites. To make it simple, say you only have a site collection consisting of one top site with five subsites. The URL address for this top site is http://srv1, and you want to back up this complete site structure to a file named WSS-back.bak in the folder C:\Bkup. To do this, follow these steps:

Try It Out   **Use STSADM to Back Up a Site Structure**

1.   Log on to the WSS server as an administrator.

2.   Open a command window, type in the following text, and press Enter key:

```
Stsadm -o Backup -url http://srv1 -filename c:\bkup\wss-back.bak
```

3.   When the backup is done, you will see the file wss-back.bak in the folder C:\bkup.

Upgrading WSS to a Local MS SQL 2005 Server

By now, you have your WSS environment backed up. It is time to upgrade your SQL Server 2005 Express database to the full MS SQL 2005 Server. As mentioned before, this is a very straightforward process. Just make sure that no one is using the system before you start to upgrade. Follow the steps in the Try It Out to upgrade the database.

> The following is a quick guide for upgrading to SQL Server 2005. Be sure to follow Microsoft's detailed instructions for upgrading more complex SQL Server scenarios: http://msdn2.microsoft.com/en-us/library/ms143516.aspx.

Try It Out   Upgrade SQL Server 2005 Express to a Local MS SQL 2005 Server

1. Log on to the WSS server as an administrator.

2. Make sure that no one is using the WSS system.

> Important: Make sure that Windows 2003 Server is updated with Service Pack 1 or later if you want to upgrade to MS SQL Server 2005!

3. Mount the MS SQL 2005 Server CD. You automatically see a dialog box where you can start the installation. Stop this installation page, and instead click Start ➪ Run: D:\Setup\Setup SKU-UPDATE=1 directly from the CD (assuming that D: is mapped to the CD). This step is required to upgrade an existing SQL Server Express!

4. On the End User License Agreement page, read the terms, and if you agree, check I accept the licensing terms and conditions, and click Next.

5. On the next page, you will be informed about what will be installed. Click Install to continue. After a short period, during which the setup program checks the installation prerequisites, click Next.

6. After a system configuration check, you will see the page Welcome to the Microsoft SQL Server Installation Wizard. It will show all checks that have been done. They all should be marked with a green check mark. If not, read the message and take the recommended action. Click Next to continue the installation of SQL Server 2005.

7. You will see a page with the server name, company name, and the production key. If necessary, update these values, and click Next.

8. On the page Components to install, check SQL Server Database Services. You may also want to check the option Workstation components, Books Online, and development tools, then click Next.

9. On the page Instance Name, select the option Named instance and enter the name of the WSS SQL instance, usually OFFICESERVERS. (You can also click on Installed instances to see all available SQL server instances.) Click Next.

10. On the page Service Account, enter the user account to be responsible for the SQL Server services, then click Next.

11. On the page Authentication Mode, accept Windows Authentication Mode, and click Next.

12. On the page Collation Settings, accept the default, and click Next.

13. On the page Ready to Install, click Install. The actual installation and upgrade process now starts; wait for it to complete.

14. When the installation is completed, click Next and then Finish.

15. Finally, check for the latest service pack for MS SQL Server 2005 on the MS SQL home page: `http://www.microsoft.com/sql/download`.

16. Check your WSS environment. Make sure it works like before. You should see no differences, except possibly better performance.

Uninstalling WSS

The final section of this chapter is about removing WSS. You can choose to remove just a single site collection, for example used for your team sites, or you can remove a complete WSS installation and all its databases. If the databases remain, you can later reinstall WSS and reconnect to those databases.

Removing a Site Collection but Leaving the Binary Files

This process removes a given site collection in WSS from its web application, but it does not remove the binary files from the server, nor its database files. For example, you may have a test environment using one web application and a production WSS using another web application on the same physical Windows 2003 server, and now you want to copy the site collection between these web applications.

To remove the test environment, follow these steps:

1. Start the SharePoint Central Administration tool.

2. Open the Application Management page.

3. Click Delete site collection in the SharePoint Site Management section.

4. Click the menu next to the site collection, and select Change Site Collection.

5. Select the site collection to be removed. When you are absolutely sure it is the right one, click OK.

6. Click Delete and then OK to permanently delete the web site.

7. Click OK.

You are now free to use the web application for other site collections. If you have another site collection in the same web application, it will continue to work, since the previous steps just deleted one single site collection, not the complete web application.

Removing a Web Application

This process is very similar to the previous process, but it may have bigger consequences: If you remove an existing web application, all its site collections will also be removed. Note that a web application may have any number of site collections, although the default limit is 15,000. To delete a specific web application follow these steps:

1. Start the SharePoint Central Administration tool.

2. Open the Application Management page.

3. Click Delete Web application in the SharePoint Web Application Management section.

4. Make sure to select the right web application using the menu listed on this page.

5. Choose whether you also want to remove the content databases and/or the virtual IIS web server. Click Delete when you are sure that it is the right web application to remove. Then click OK to accept the deletion of the web application.

Removing WSS Completely

A more drastic method is to remove WSS completely from the Windows 2003 server. This does not actually remove the database, be it SQL Server 2005 Express or the MS SQL Server. If you want to remove these database engines, you must do this manually after WSS is uninstalled.

To remove WSS completely from a Windows 2003 server, follow these steps:

1. Select Start ➪ Control Panel ➪ Add or Remove Programs.

2. Click the Microsoft Windows SharePoint Services 3.0 and then click the Remove button.

3. Complete the removal process. WSS is now gone!

4. Check to see if there are other WSS-related applications that also should be removed (for example, any third-party add-ons).

5. If you also want to remove the database engine, locate its name and click Remove.

Note that this will automatically remove both the WSS and the MS SQL 2005 Express database engines at the same time. However, if you used an SQL Server 2000 or 2005 database, it will not uninstall these database servers, and WSS databases will still remain intact.

When you remove WSS, you also remove the virtual IIS server used by the WSS administrative web site, along with its application pool. However, the default web site remains after the installation, along with its application pool.

Summary

In this chapter, you learned the following:

- ❑ STS was the previous version of WSS. You will still today find lots of references to the acronym STS, although it actually refers to WSS.

- ❑ Make sure that you know what SharePoint edition you need: stand-alone WSS or WSS with MOSS.

- ❑ Make sure that you know what database engine you need: SQL Server 2005 Express or MS SQL Server (2000 or 2005).

- ❑ There are three types of WSS configurations:

  - ❑ WSS with a local SQL Server 2005 Express database.

  - ❑ WSS with a local MS SQL Server database.

  - ❑ WSS with a remote MS SQL Server database.

- ❑ Using WSS with SQL Server 2005 Express needs no special Client Access License besides the usual Windows 2003 Server CALs.

- ❑ The term single server means a SharePoint installation with a local database.

- ❑ The term small farm means one SharePoint server and a separate MS SQL server.

- ❑ With at least 1.5 GB of memory, you can actually set up a WSS production environment for at least 200 people.

  - ❑ There is a formula you can use to calculate the number of NOPS (normalized operations per second).

  - ❑ With at least 2 GB of memory, WSS will have the memory for using its internal database buffers in an optimal way.

  - ❑ A single server with WSS and SQL Server 2005 Express on a 2-GB server and a dual 3GHz 64-bit CPU can be used for an organization with up to 20,000 users.

- ❑ It is the documents and files that fill up the main part of the database. The other data types are small in comparison. Make sure to always have at least 50 percent free disk space on the database disk.

- ❑ You need IIS and ASP.NET on a Windows 2003 server to install WSS.

- ❑ Application pools are private virtual areas that the web application uses for its needs. If something goes wrong with the web application, it does not affect applications in other application pools.

- ❑ IIS 6.0 supports up to 9 virtual IIS servers with individual application pools or 99 virtual servers sharing the same application pool.

❑ WSS uses two types of databases: the config and the content databases.

  ❑ The config database stores configuration settings and connections between the WSS and the SQL database server. There is always only one config database. Its default name is `SharePoint_Config`.

  ❑ The content database stores all the data, including all documents, web pages, and more. One content database may support up to 15,000 site collections, and you can have as many content databases as you need. The default name for the first database is `WSS_Content`.

❑ The file `SharePoint.exe` is the complete WSS installation package. It can be downloaded from Microsoft's web site.

  ❑ You can expand the `SharePoint.exe` package, by using the flag `/Extract:<path>`. It results in a number of files, including the true installation file for WSS, named `SETUP.EXE`.

  ❑ By default, WSS always installs into a new virtual IIS Web server, named SharePoint–80 that is created automatically by the Configuration Wizard.

❑ The tool `TSADM.exe` comes with WSS and can be used for many things, including creating site collections, web applications, and application pools.

❑ Each application pool uses a security account that regulates what the web applications using this application pool can do. You can use any user account or built-in accounts such as Network Service.

❑ The application pool security account needs to be a member of the Security Administrators and the Database Creators role in the MS SQL Server.

❑ A web application is a virtual IIS web server that has been extended by SharePoint; each web application can host multiple site collections.

❑ A site collection is the container for user web sites; each site collection consists of one top site, and zero or any number of subsites.

❑ Upgrading a SQL Server 2005 Express database engine to a local MS SQL server is very easy. Simply perform an in-place upgrade.

❑ There are several ways of performing a backup procedure for a SQL Server 2005 Express database. You can use tools like STSADM, install the SQL Server 2005 tools, or purchase third-party backup tools.

❑ To completely uninstall WSS from a computer, use Add or Remove Programs. This will also uninstall the SQL Server 2005 Express installation used by WSS. However, this will not remove any SQL Server 2000/2005 database engines.

❑ To remove the database engine, such as SQL Server 2005 Express or the MS SQL Server, you must use Add or Remove Programs separately.

In the next chapter, you learn more about how to configure Windows SharePoint Services.

Configuring and Managing Windows SharePoint Services

In the previous chapter, you learned about the different installation scenarios available and how to set up WSS to work with either SQL Server 2005 Express or MS SQL Server. In this chapter, you learn more about configuring and managing installed WSS, including how to activate and configure the search feature. In order to successfully manage the WSS environment, you need to understand important concepts in the context of that environment, such as web sites, site collections, and the security model. The objective in this chapter is to give you the knowledge needed to set up the WSS environment so that it will match the needs of your users.

Before you start configuring WSS, check to see if your server has the Internet Explorer Enhanced Security Configuration setting activated, because this may cause a strange problem. You will find this setting in the Windows Components Wizard (see Figure 3-1), accessed via the Add or Remove Programs applet in the Control Panel.

Figure 3-1

If this setting is active, you may have problems performing SharePoint administrative tasks on the WSS server itself, depending on how your Internet Explorer is configured. If the WSS virtual server is defined as something other than the zones Local Sites or Trusted Sites, you will not be able to run scripts or execute code necessary for some parts of the SharePoint administration. The effect will be that on remote clients you can do everything, whereas on the WSS server itself you will experience problems. You can solve this in two ways:

❑ Uninstall Internet Explorer Enhanced Security.

❑ Define the URL to the virtual IIS server that WSS uses as a Trusted Site in Internet Explorer.

The last option is the most secure. By default, your WSS virtual server should be listed as a trusted site. If it isn't, you can adjust that by following these steps:

1. Open Internet Explorer.

2. Go to Tools ➪ Internet Options ➪ Security.

3. Click Trusted Sites and the Sites button.

4. Add the URL address for your virtual server (for example, http://srv1) as a trusted site.

> If the WSS sites don't use SSL encryptions, you must first uncheck "require server verification (https:) for all sites in this zone."

Important Concepts

WSS 3.0 is a web application. It uses web sites and web-related concepts to do its job. Some of these terms and functionality may be well known to you already. But some have very specific meanings in the SharePoint environment. You may recall from previous chapters that WSS is the basic foundation for SharePoint and that there is an optional extension called Microsoft Office SharePoint Server (MOSS). Even if you implement MOSS, you will still need the information in this chapter to understand how the WSS part works, since the basic structure and functionality is based on WSS, regardless of whether it is a WSS site or a MOSS site.

Administration Web Sites and User Web Sites

Windows SharePoint Services has two types of web sites:

❑ The SharePoint Central Administration web site that is used for advanced configuration and management of WSS.

❑ The user web site (also known as team sites, project sites, and meeting workspaces) contains the actual information that is shared between users, such as documents, lists, and images. There can be as many of these web sites as needed.

One important distinction between these two types of web sites is that only a SharePoint administrator will use the Administration web site, whereas everyone may use the user web sites. As you may remember from Chapter 2, these two web sites use two different web applications, that is, they are using different virtual IIS servers:

❑ **SharePoint Central Administration:** Used by the Administration web site and runs in its own application pool (default name: SharePoint Central Administration v3). By default, this web site will use a randomly selected TCP port, but you can set this number manually if you choose anything other than the Basic installation mode.

❑ **SharePoint – 80:** Used by the user web site and runs in a separate application pool (default name: **SharePoint – 80**). Note that the name for this virtual server may be different if you created a separate virtual server for this purpose. The default web site is also frequently used for this type of web site. By default, this web site will use TCP port 80, to make it easy for end users to access it.

If you, for any reason, need to stop all users from accessing the WSS environment, open the IIS Manager tool, right-click SharePoint – 80 (or whatever virtual IIS server the user web site uses), and select Stop. To enable the users to access it, right-click again, and select Start.

The Central Administration Web Site

You have already used the Central Administration web site in Chapter 2. This web site allows the administrator to do more advanced administration and configuration of the WSS environment, such as create new web applications, create site collections, configure the content databases, and define what database server to use. In this chapter, you learn about all the important configuration settings available in this web site and how to make the most out of your WSS environment.

SharePoint has its own security system that makes sure only users with the proper permissions are able to access the Administration web site. As an extra security feature, this web site uses a randomly selected port number, known as the administrative port, which you must know in order to access it. This port number is set automatically for Basic installations, and can be set manually for Advanced installations, when the Configuration Wizard runs after the initial installation. Note that if you set the port number manually, make sure to use a number above 1024, since all numbers below this limit are referred to as "well known ports" that may be used by other applications.

You have several ways of accessing this Administration web site, assuming that you have the proper permission. The easiest way is to use the Windows 2003 startup folder by going to Start ➪ Administrative Tools ➪ SharePoint 3.0 Central Administration. Another way is to open this web site directly by using a browser. This requires that first you know the administrative port. Assuming that the port number is 5000 (as in Figure 3-2), you can open the web site using the URL address `http://localhost:5000`, then the string localhost will be replaced by the server name, as shown in Figure 3-3.

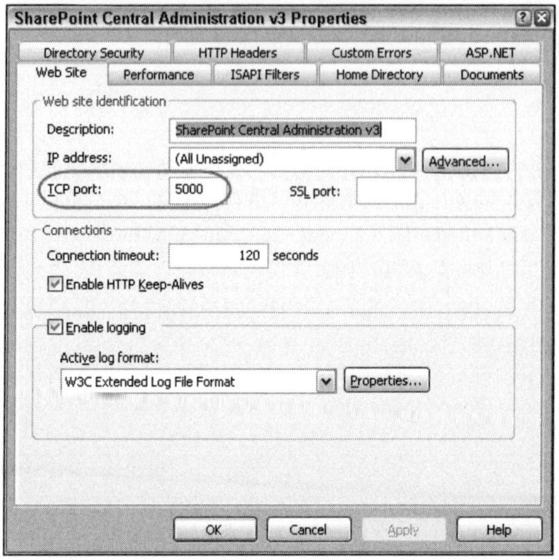

Figure 3-2

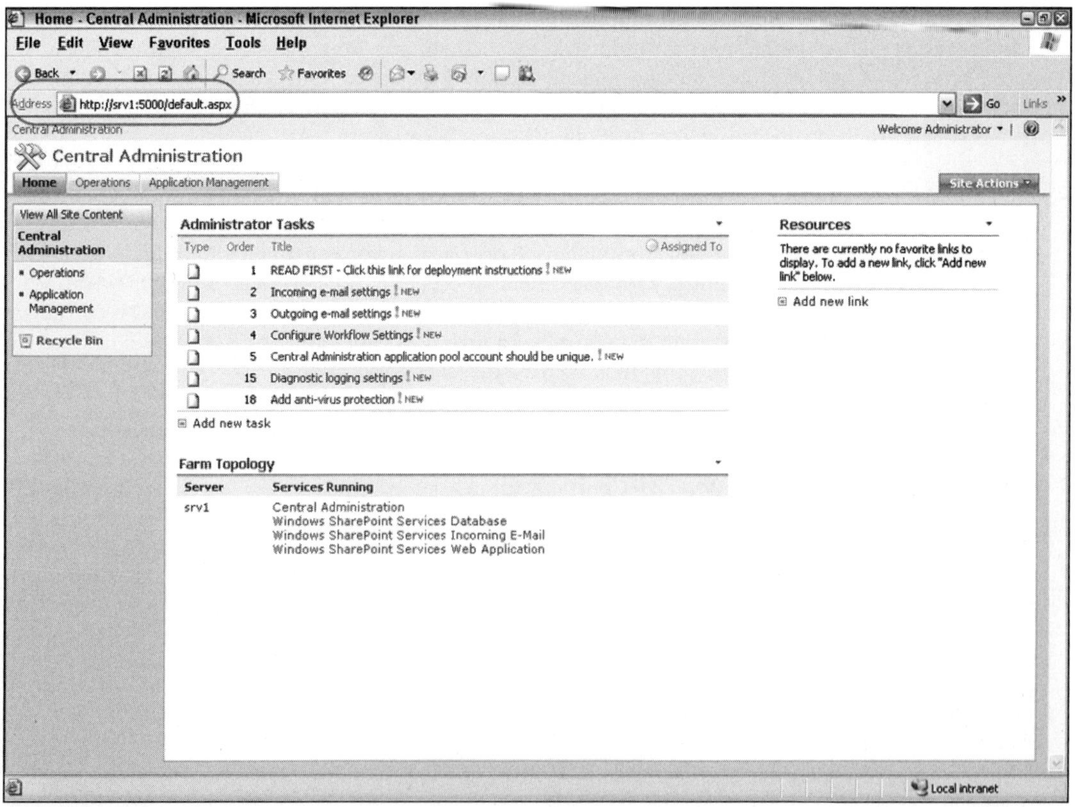

Figure 3-3

Be sure to protect this Administration web site. If a malicious user can access it, that user can remove content or even remove WSS from the virtual IIS server. But to do this, the malicious user would both have to learn the administrative port number and get access to the web site.

> **Even if you use the default Windows Authentication method to access the Central Administration web site, it will not protect the data sent between your web client and SharePoint. Use Secure Socket Layer (SSL) to protect the Central Administration web site if you need to access it over the Internet. If you don't need Internet access to this site, configure your firewall to prohibit access to the TCP port used by the Central Administration tool.**

The User Web Sites

This is where the action is! These web sites are the foundation for creating shared web pages, team collaborations, departmental intranets, project sites, and so on. When you installed WSS using the Basic installation method (as described in Chapter 2), your first user web site was created automatically. It should look like the one in Figure 3-4.

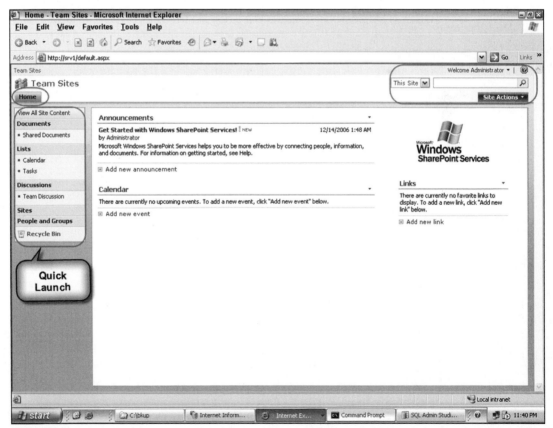

Figure 3-4

The name of this default site, which is ready to be used, is team sites. The only user who can access this site now is the user account you used when installing WSS. But you can grant access to any number of users or groups, each with individual permission settings, if required.

Note the URL address displayed in the Address field of Figure 3-4:

```
http://srv1/default.aspx
```

In this example, the WSS server name is SRV1. De**fault.aspx** is the page displaying the content for this web site. Its suffix `.aspx` indicates that this page is based on ASP.NET code. On the top of the web page are some links to different parts of the web site:

❑   **Home:** Takes you to the start page for this web site (that is, the page displayed in Figure 3-4).

❑   **Welcome <user>:** This is a menu that shows the name of the current user; click on it to display the menu options:

    ❑   **My Settings:** Displays information about the current user, such as the name, picture, department and e-mail address. Use the button Edit Item to change these settings. Use the button My Alerts to add and list all alerts for this site. Use the button My Regional Settings to see the default regional setting inherited from the web site, such as the Locale, Time Zone, and Calendar type. You can change these settings, if necessary.

    ❑   **Sign in as Different User.** Allows you to log out from the current user identity and Log on as another user. This is a very handy feature for the administrator when she want to see how a page looks to another user.

    ❑   **Sign Out:** This will sign out the current user, and close the web browser.

    ❑   **Personalize This Page:** Use this feature when you want to customize the look and feel of the current web page. These changes will only be visible to this user, that is, a personal view of this page. By default users with Read permission will not have this functionality enabled, and thus they will not see this link.

❑   **<Question mark>:** This button will open the Help system for WSS in a separate window.

❑   **<Search field>:** This search functionality is only active if this WSS installation is using SQL Server 2000/2005, with full-text indexing activated. You will find more about WSS searching later in this chapter.

❑   **Site Actions:** This menu will have different options, depending on what site you are looking at, and your permissions. By default, three options are listed here:

    ❑   **Create:** Allows you to create any type of list, library, or page supported by WSS, such as document libraries, contact lists, and issue tracking lists. You can also use this page to create a new subsite under the current site.

    ❑   **Edit Page:** This link will open the current page, for example the `Default.aspx` page, in edit mode. Note that any changes you make here will be visible to all other users of this site. Use this link to modify and add new content to this page, also known as web parts. You will learn more about web pages later. When done, click Exit Edit Mode to save any changes.

    ❑   **Site Settings:** This will open the general configuration settings for the current site (see Figure 3-5). Use this page to add new members to this site, to change its look and feel, to view templates and galleries, and to access many more settings. Note that the top site, that is, the first site in a site collection, will have several settings not available in subsites.

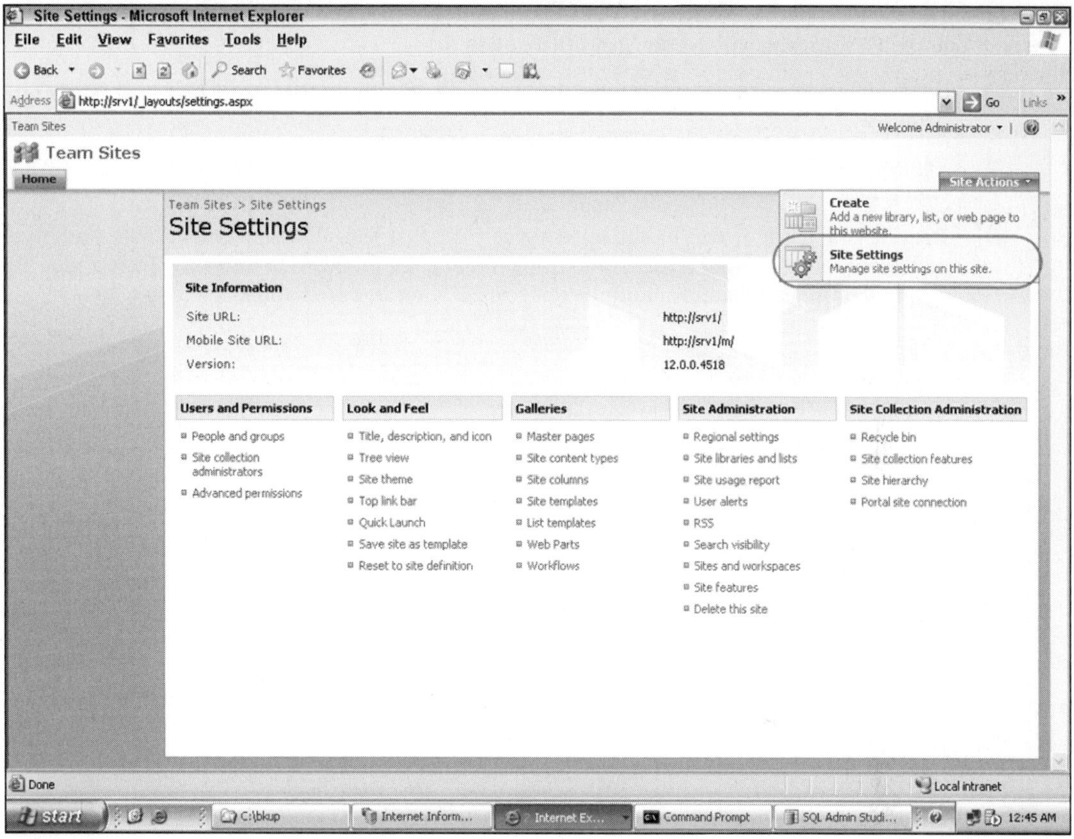

Figure 3-5

Besides the links and buttons at the top of this web site, there are several links in the Quick Launch bar, located by default at the left of the page (see Figure 3-4). The links listed here point to lists and libraries that are configured to be visible on the Quick Launch bar. There may exist more lists and libraries than are listed on the Quick Launch bar. To see them all, click View All Site Content. Note that all headlines in the Quick Launch bar also work as links to a web page that lists all objects of that particular type. For example, click on the headline Documents to display a list of all document libraries. Following are the default links on a team site in the Quick Launch bar (see Figure 3-6):

❑ **View All Site Content:** Shows a web page with all the content for this team site, for example the document libraries, lists, and subsites.

❑ **Pictures:** This is a header for future picture libraries. By default, there are no picture libraries on a team site.

❑ **Documents:** Shows all document, form and wiki page libraries configured to be visible on the Quick Launch bar; by default a team site lists the Shared Documents library.

❑ **Lists:** Shows all lists configured to be visible on the Quick Launch bar; by default a team site lists the Calendar and Tasks lists.

❑ **Discussions:** Shows all discussion lists configured to be visible on the Quick Launch bar; by default a team site will list the Team Discussion list.

❑ **Sites:** Shows all subsites under the current site; by default there is no subsite on a newly created team site.

❑ **People and Groups:** Click on its link to open the page where the permissions for this site are configured.

❑ **Recycle Bin:** Click on this link to open a web page that lists all deleted items, lists, and libraries on this web site. Use the breadcrumb trail on that page to return to the home page again. You will find more information about the Recycle Bin later in this chapter.

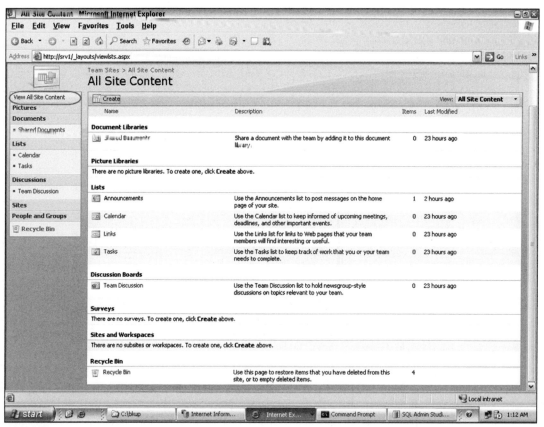

Figure 3-6

Note that if a link, list, library, or menu option is missing, the current user probably does not have permission to view it!

Note that the local administration page for this site (Site Actions ⇨ Site Settings) is not the same as the Central Administration web site mentioned earlier in this chapter. The local Site Settings page is where you configure the current site, for example set the permission settings, change its description, and work with templates, just to mention a few things. This type of administration is covered in detail in Chapters 9, 10, and 11.

> **Whatever web page you are looking at, click Home or use the breadcrumb trail to go back to the start page of the site.**

Top Sites, Subsites, and Site Collections

For each WSS installation, you have at least one top site like the one you just investigated. Under this top site, you can create new sites, referred to as subsites (also known as "Webs"). Each subsite may, in turn, have its own subsite, creating a tree similar to a file system in which the top site is the root. If you need more than one top site, you can create a new one using the WSS administration web site, which creates the root for a new site tree. Figure 3-7 shows an example with two top sites that have several subsites each.

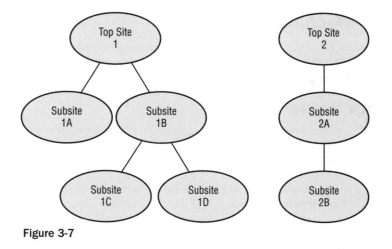

Figure 3-7

Each top site, including any optional subsites, is referred to as a site collection. There can be only one top site in each site collection, but there can be any number of subsites. Some configuration settings are specific to given site collections, such as the following:

- ❏ Inheritance of permission settings.
- ❏ SharePoint groups.
- ❏ Ownership and full access to all subsites.
- ❏ Creation and use of templates for web sites, lists, and web parts.
- ❏ Usage statistics.
- ❏ Site hierarchy.

You can copy some things (such as templates) from one site collection to another, but you should think of each site collection as an isolated island. For example, you could be the administrator in site collection A but still have no access whatsoever to site collection B. This is often exactly what different departments require: "We want our own SharePoint environment, without any possibility that someone belonging to another department can access our information!"

SharePoint uses the term web site for each web within a site collection, so the top site and all its subsites are examples of web sites. Another term you will see for these web sites is workspaces. The only difference between the two is the layout. You still have the same features and administration as with any other web site.

The reason for these two names is interesting. The development team for WSS has used the term "web site" since the beginning, that is, SharePoint Team Services released in 2001. However, when Office 2003 was released, it was designed to be integrated with WSS 2.0. One new feature in MS Office 2003 was that it could create web sites for working with documents, and MS Outlook 2003 could create web sites for meetings. But the MS Office team did not find the term "web site" very descriptive and intuitive, so they chose the new term "workspace" instead. These names are still valid in WSS 3.0 and MS Office 2007. So, whenever you see the term "workspace," understand that it is a web site created by an MS Office client.

The Security Mechanism

SharePoint keeps track of its own security settings. However, you still manage security by controlling how access is granted to different accounts. You need to be concerned with two types of security settings: user web sites and Administration web sites.

Security Settings for User Web Sites

You can grant any individual user account, from a domain or a local server account, access to all or parts of SharePoint. You can also grant access to security groups (domain or local) but not to mail distribution lists, since they are not classified as security objects, that is, they cannot be granted any type of permission.

Each user or group account must be granted some level of permission in order to get any access to SharePoint and its content. Basically, you do this in one of two ways: Make the user a member of a SharePoint group, or add the user or security group account directly to the permission list for the SharePoint object he needs to access. The level of access is controlled by the permission level, which you can think of as a security role. By default all WSS sites have these permission levels defined:

❑ **Limited Access:** This is a special type of security role that a user or group is granted to provide access to a specific list, library, or item, but not the site itself. In WSS 2.0 this was called "Guest." For example, if the user Anna is granted read access to a specific document library but not the site it belongs to, then Anna would get Limited Access to the site. This is handy if you want Anna to be able to open objects in the site, such as this document library, but not have any other access. (For example, she will not be able to see anything else on this site, including its home page.)

❑ **Read:** Can read, copy, and print documents, files, and list content in a user web site. Can also create alerts for lists, libraries, and their content.

❑ **Contribute:** Can do everything that Read allows and can also create, modify, and delete documents, files, and list content. Can add personal views of lists and libraries, plus do a personal customization of the site's home page.

❑ **Design:** Can do everything Contribute allows, plus can customize the design of the home page, for example change the color of the page, add and modify shared web parts, and create new document libraries and lists.

❑ **Full Control:** Has full access to everything, including security settings and local management of the web site. This is the only role that can create subsites. This role is also sometimes referred to as the "site administrator."

Later in this chapter you learn how to change these default site groups as well as create new ones.

Security Settings for the Central Administration Web Site

The previous section described how the user web site works. But how do you modify the inner guts of WSS? You may remember that I said that the account used during the installation will initially also be the only account that can access the Central Administration web site. But this is not completely true!

Assume that Anna is the only user who can access the Administration web site. In other words, she is the SharePoint Goddess. By mistake, you happen to delete her user account. Quickly you try to repair the damage before anyone notices, so you create a new user account, with the exact same name and password. Will Anna still be able to use the Administration web site? No! Because when you created a new account, it got a new Security ID (SID), although with the same name. But SharePoint has granted administrative access to the old SID for Anna, so she cannot get in.

How do you solve this? Well, you can't unless you do a restore of the user account, that is, restore the complete Active Directory database, and this is not an easy task. Is there an easier way? Yes! Your escape route out of this misery is the fact that every user who is a member of the local Administrators group of the WSS server automatically has full and unlimited access to the Central Administration tool! The solution is to add Anna's new account to this group.

The important thing for you to understand that everyone — every user and every member of any domain group — who is a member of the local Administrators group is a SharePoint God or Goddess. And by default, the domain group Domain Admins is always a member of the local Administrator group in every computer in the domain. This results in the fact that every member of Domain Admins has full access to the Central Administration tool. But not to any of the user sites in WSS! This is different from WSS 2.0, where members of the local Administrator group had full access to every site, both administrative and user sites! So, the security is better in WSS 3.0. However, any user who can access the Central Administrator tool can also add themselves as Owners to any user site, so note that only trusted people should be members of the local Administrator group!

Beginning SharePoint Administration

This section describes the most common tasks you will perform as a full administrator for a fresh WSS installation. You also learn the basics of how the security works for sites and content. The objective here is to give you the basic information needed to set up a fully functional WSS environment. At this moment, it does not matter whether you've chosen a SQL Server 2005 Express or MS SQL database, or whether it is a local or remote database engine.

Creating Your First Sites

The first thing you most likely want to do is to create new user sites. After all, this is where all files, lists, and other information will be stored.

If you selected the Basic installation method during the installation of WSS 3.0, you got your first top site and, therefore, the first site collection created automatically. This top site is called Team Sites, and its URL address is `http://srv1/default.aspx` (assuming that the name of the Windows 2003 server is SRV1). The suffix `/default.aspx` is simply the default content page displayed when opening this web site.

> If you chose the Advanced method when installing WSS you have to create the first site collection (that is, the first top site) manually. Later in this chapter you will see how to create a site collection.

You can create a subsite to this team web site by using the following steps:

Try It Out   **Create a Subsite**

1. Log on to any computer in the network as a SharePoint administrator, that is, the user account used when installing WSS, since this is the only user account that has access to the team web site at the moment. Later in this chapter, you will see how to add more users. Start the web browser and open the URL address to your new SharePoint site (for example, `http://srv1`).

2. Click Site Actions ⇨ Create on the top link bar. This gives you a page that shows all types of objects you can create for this web site, including document libraries, contact lists, plus sites and workspaces in the Web Pages section.

3. Click Sites and Workspaces.

4. The next page is a web form where you define the new subsite, as you can see in Figure 3-8. Fill in the following fields:

   a. **Title:** Enter the title for this site. Spaces and any Unicode characters, such as Å and Ü, are okay here. You can change this text later, if necessary.

   b. **Description:** Enter a description of the site. It will be displayed on the web page. You can change this text later.

   c. **URL name:** Enter the web URL address for this site. Note that the prefix is inherited from the parent of this subsite and cannot be changed; in this example, it's `http://srv1/`. Although it is okay to use blank spaces and 8-bit characters here, you should avoid using them to prevent problems or strange URL addresses later on. For example, if you create an URL with the name `http://srv1//räksmörgås`, it will actually be listed as the URL `http://srv1/r%C3%A4ksm%C3%B6rg%C3%A5s`. It is also a good thing to keep the name of this URL as short as possible, while still making it descriptive. This will make it easier for you to later type in this address manually, if you want to.

   d. **Select a template:** In this example, select the team site. There are 10 different site templates, divided into two tabs: Collaboration, and Meetings. Later you will learn how to create new site templates.

    e.   **User Permissions:** By default, this option allows you to inherit the user permissions from the parent web site (that is, the team web site in this case). You can also choose to use unique permission settings for this subsite. The advantage of inherited permissions is that, if you later modify the permission settings for the top site, these new settings will also be used in the subsite. Whatever you choose, you can later switch it to the other option.

    f.   **Navigation:** Select Yes to display this subsite on the Quick Launch bar at the parent site. You can also select to display the name of this subsite on the top link bar of the parent site. These settings will make it easier for users to quickly access this site later.

    g.   **Navigation Inheritance:** Select Yes to make this subsite inherit the same top link bar as its parent site, that is, the team site in this example.

5.   Click Create to start the process to create this site. This is normally complete in a matter of seconds. When it is done the new subsite is displayed.

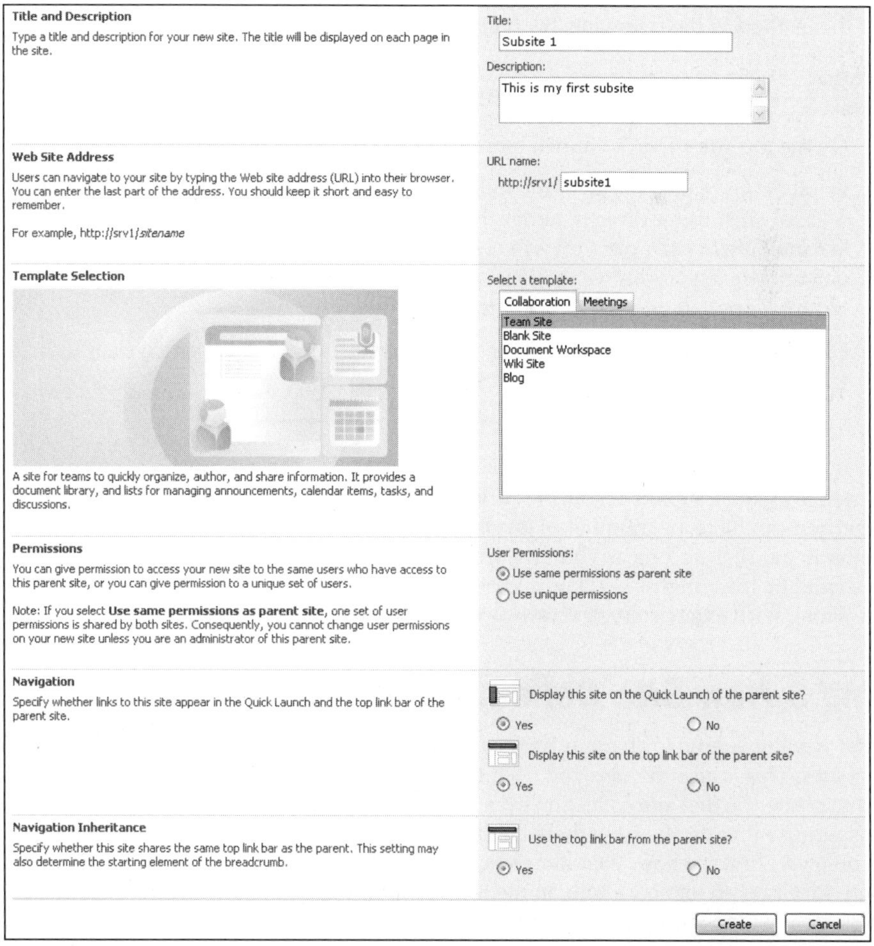

Title and Description Type a title and description for your new site. The title will be displayed on each page in the site.	Title: `Subsite 1` Description: `This is my first subsite`
Web Site Address Users can navigate to your site by typing the Web site address (URL) into their browser. You can enter the last part of the address. You should keep it short and easy to remember. For example, http://srv1/*sitename*	URL name: http://srv1/ `subsite1`
Template Selection	Select a template: **Collaboration** Meetings **Team Site** Blank Site Document Workspace Wiki Site Blog
A site for teams to quickly organize, author, and share information. It provides a document library, and lists for managing announcements, calendar items, tasks, and discussions.	
Permissions You can give permission to access your new site to the same users who have access to this parent site, or you can give permission to a unique set of users. Note: If you select **Use same permissions as parent site**, one set of user permissions is shared by both sites. Consequently, you cannot change user permissions on your new site unless you are an administrator of this parent site.	User Permissions: ◉ Use same permissions as parent site ○ Use unique permissions
Navigation Specify whether links to this site appear in the Quick Launch and the top link bar of the parent site.	Display this site on the Quick Launch of the parent site? ◉ Yes ○ No Display this site on the top link bar of the parent site? ◉ Yes ○ No
Navigation Inheritance Specify whether this site shares the same top link bar as the parent. This setting may also determine the starting element of the breadcrumb.	Use the top link bar from the parent site? ◉ Yes ○ No
	Create Cancel

Figure 3-8

Take a look at this new subsite. Does it not look very similar to the top site? It has the same color, the same web parts, and the same lists. In fact, it should look exactly like the other web site because it is built on the same site template! Look at the breadcrumb trail for this page: It says Team Sites > Subsite 1. From this, you can tell that the current site is a subsite and its parent is the Team Web Site. Another indication that this is a subsite is the URL address: `http://srv1/subsite1` (again, we do not care about the suffix `/default.aspx` because this is the name of the content page you are looking at right now). When you understand how to read the URL address, you can see exactly where in the site tree a given web site is situated.

Click on the breadcrumb trail Team Sites to go back to the parent (and in this case top) site. Look carefully to understand which site you are looking at. Check the URL: `http://srv1`. This is the proof you need that you are at the top site again.

To open the subsite again, you can either click its name on the top menu, that is, Subsites 1, or click the site's name in the Quick Launch bar, under the headline Sites. The reason that this subsite is listed in these two locations is that you selected this option during steps 4f and 4g above.

If you chose not to display the new subsite in the top menu, or the Quick Launch bar, you could still find it using the method in the following Try It Out.

Try It Out   List and Go to Any Subsite

1.   On the top site's Quick Launch bar, click View All Site Content.

2.   Scroll down to the bottom of the following page. Under the section Sites and Workspaces, you will see all subsites directly under this top site, regardless of whether they are listed on the parent site. In this example, you will only see one site here, "Subsite 1." If you hover the mouse cursor over it, you can see its URL address listed on the status row for your web browser: `http://srv1/subsite1`. Click it to go to this subsite now.

3.   Check that you actually are looking at the subsite now. You have two clear indicators of this: the URL address and the breadcrumb trail.

If you need to create a subsite under the current subsite, you do it in exactly the same way you did the first time. You can have any number of levels in your site collections, and each level can have any number of sites in parallel, as long as you give sites in the same level unique URL names. Remember that the names should be meaningful — if your users cannot easily find the site they need at the moment, something is wrong with either your structure or the way these sites are accessed.

Creating a New Site Collection

Now that you know how to create subsites, the next step is to learn to create new site collections, that is, new top sites. This is also the step you need to take in case WSS was installed using the Advanced method to create the first site collection ever for this WSS installation. This is a bit trickier because there is no easy-to-use link for this anywhere on the first site collection, but this problem can also be solved. In this section, you first see how to create a site using the SharePoint 3.0 Central Administration (SCA) tool, and then learn how to display a link on the first top site that will allow anyone with the proper permission to create new top sites.

Before you create a new site collection, you should think about what web application it will use. In Chapter 2, you learned that every site collection must be created in a given web application, and that a web application is an extended virtual IIS server, for example the default web site. When you create the second site collection, you must decide if you will need a new web application or if you can use the same web application as the first site collection. In most situations, you will use the same web applications, but you may want to create a new web application if you need any of these:

❑ **Separate application pool settings:** For every site collection, you will have separate users and administrators, but if you also need a separate Application pool identity, you should create a new web application for this site collection.

❑ **Separate TCP port or host header name:** If you need a separate TCP port number or a separate Host Header name for the new site collection, you should create a new web application.

❑ **Separate security settings:** When creating a new web application, you can define a specific authentication provider (NTLM or Kerberos), whether anonymous access will be activated, and whether Secure Sockets Layer (SSL) should be used.

❑ **Separate database server and name:** If you need to create a new site collection and want it to store its content on a specific SQL server and/or database name, then create a new web application. This may be very handy if you have a distributed organization and want to create a site collection for each location in your organization, with local access to their database. Note that this also requires one SQL server at every location.

❑ **Separate URL:** When you want the URL to be different from that of any other site collection, you must create a separate web application. If not, all new site collections created after the first will get a URL that contains the name of the first site collection. For example, if the first site collection has the URL http://srv1, a second site collection named "newSC" will get the URL http://srv1/sites/newSC.

Creating a Top Site Using the SharePoint Central Admin Tool

Initially, this is the only way of creating a new site collection in WSS. You must be a WSS farm administrator, or a member of the local Administrators group on the WSS server, to do this. Follow these steps to create a new site collection in the same web application as the first site collection:

| Try It Out | Create a New Site Collection Using the SCA Tool |

1. Start the SCA tool (Start ⇨ Administrative Tools ⇨ SharePoint 3.0 Central Administration).

2. Open the Application Management page.

3. Click Create site collection in the SharePoint Site Management section; on the next page, (see Figure 3-9), enter these settings:

   a. Make sure that http://srv1 is selected as the web application; if not, use its menu and select the correct web application for the new site collection.

   b. Enter the title for this new site collection; for example "Site Collection 2." This can later be changed.

   c. Enter the Description for this site collection. This can later be changed.

d. Define the URL for the new top site. This cannot be changed later. When you create a new site collection using the same web application as the first site collection, it will inherit the URL of the first site collection, plus the string "/sites/" as a delimiter. In this example, you will create a new site collection with the URL "top2," so the complete URL address will then be http://sites1/sites/top2. The delimiter "/sites/" is known as a wildcard inclusion URL path. In other words, if you ever find a site with the URL http://srv1/sites/sales, you know that this is a site collection with a top site named "sales," and it was created after the first site collection.

e. **Select a template:** Choose the site template the top site for this new site collection will be built upon; you have 10 different site templates by default, divided into two tabs. You cannot select another site template later, but you can modify the selected site template.

f. **Primary Site Collection Administrator:** This can an be changed later. Enter the user account or e-mail address for the owner of this top site. This user will also be the owner of all subsites in this site collection. You cannot prohibit a site collection administrator from accessing to any of the site's subsites, regardless of the permission settings.

g. **Secondary Site Collection Administrator:** This can be changed later. This is an optional owner, who, like the first administrator, also has "divine" access to all sites in this site collection. Enter the user account or e-mail address, if any, for this secondary owner. In Chapter 6, you will see how WSS can help you clean up unused web sites by sending an e-mail to the owners and offering to remove these sites. If you have two owners, the chance is much greater that one of them will read the e-mail and can take the appropriate action.

h. **Quota Template:** This can be changed later. Use this setting to configure a size limit for this complete site collection. If your WSS environment is fresh, you do not have any quota template defined yet. If you want to define one, right-click the Manage Quota Template link on the left to create what you need, and then go back to the first page and click Refresh to see the new template in the pull-down menu.

i. **Site Language:** This is only visible if you have installed a WSS language template pack. This cannot be changed later. By default, you will have only the language of the installed WSS pack (for example, English), but if you install new WSS language template packs, you will be able to select between them here. Later, you learn where to find these language packs and how to install them.

j. Click OK to save your settings.

4. The next page is just a confirmation that the site has been created successfully. If it hasn't, you will see the reason why here. You can click OK to go back to the Central Administration page or click the URL link to open your new top site in a new browser window. This site collection, and its top site, are now ready to be used.

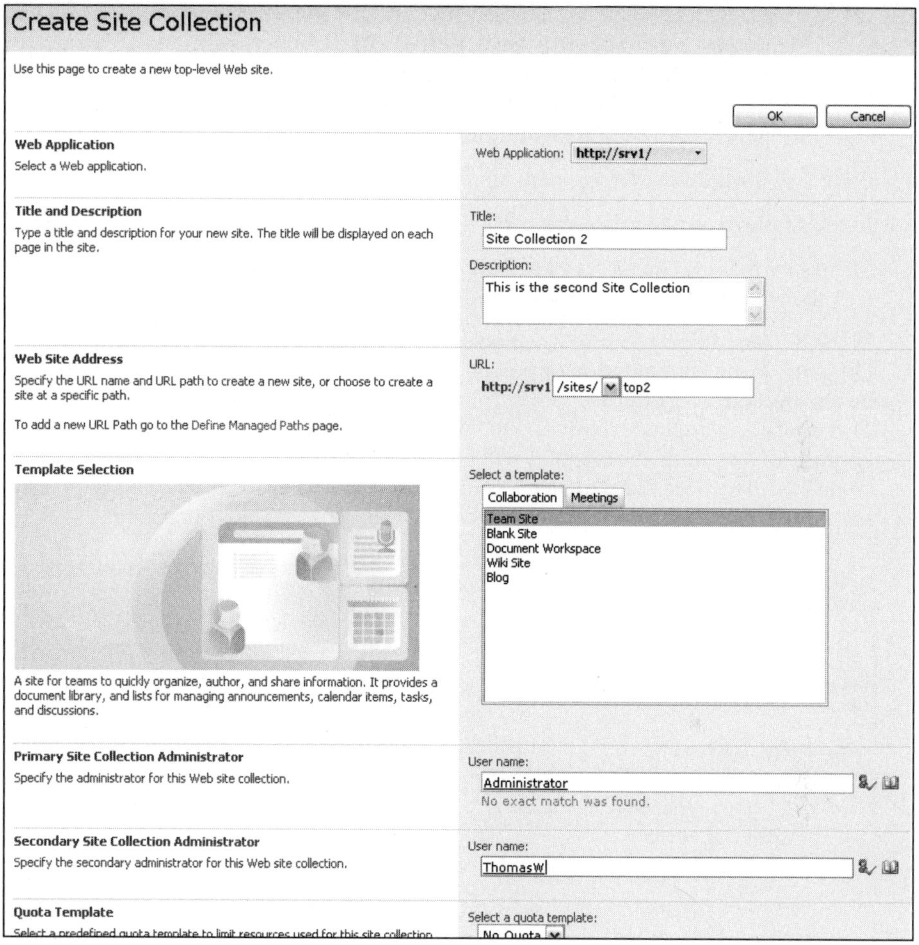

Create Site Collection

Use this page to create a new top-level Web site.

[OK] [Cancel]

Web Application
Select a Web application.

Web Application: **http://srv1/** ▾

Title and Description
Type a title and description for your new site. The title will be displayed on each page in the site.

Title:
Site Collection 2

Description:
This is the second Site Collection

Web Site Address
Specify the URL name and URL path to create a new site, or choose to create a site at a specific path.

To add a new URL Path go to the Define Managed Paths page.

URL:
http://srv1 /sites/ ▾ top2

Template Selection

A site for teams to quickly organize, author, and share information. It provides a document library, and lists for managing announcements, calendar items, tasks, and discussions.

Select a template:

| Collaboration | Meetings |

Team Site
Blank Site
Document Workspace
Wiki Site
Blog

Primary Site Collection Administrator
Specify the administrator for this Web site collection.

User name:
Administrator
No exact match was found.

Secondary Site Collection Administrator
Specify the secondary administrator for this Web site collection.

User name:
ThomasW

Quota Template
Select a predefined quota template to limit resources used for this site collection.

Select a quota template:
No Quota ▾

Figure 3-9

Creating a Top Site Using the WSS User Web Site

If users need an easy way to create new top sites (site collections), without asking you as an administrator to do it for them, it can be done. There is a special configuration setting in WSS called Self-Service Site Creation that regulates this. Note that you can still control which users will be able to create site collections because these users must be granted the Use Self-Service Site Creation permission.

When you activate this self-service feature, you see a new message show up in the Announcement list for the first top site in your WSS environment. This message contains a link to the ASP.NET script that creates the top sites, scsignup.aspx. You can later create your own link to run that script, as you can see in the following Try It Out, where you activate this feature.

Try It Out   **Activate Self-Service Site Creation**

1. Log on as an administrator to the WSS server.

2. Start the SharePoint 3.0 Central Administration tool (SCA).

3. Click the Application Management tab.

4. In the Application Security section, click Self-service site management.

5. Make sure that the correct web application is selected at the top of this page; if not, use its menu and change this value. (See Figure 3-10.)

6. In the Enable Self-Service Site Creation section, select On to activate this feature; the default is Off. The second configuration option on this page is the Require secondary contact box. If this box is checked, every top site will require a secondary owner (that is, another user account). This can be a very good feature if you later turn on the automatic cleanup of unused sites, because all owners of the top sites will get an e-mail from WSS asking whether the site should be deleted. This secondary owner is commonly a role-based user, such as Helpdesk, Support, or something similar. Set this option, and click OK to save and close this page.

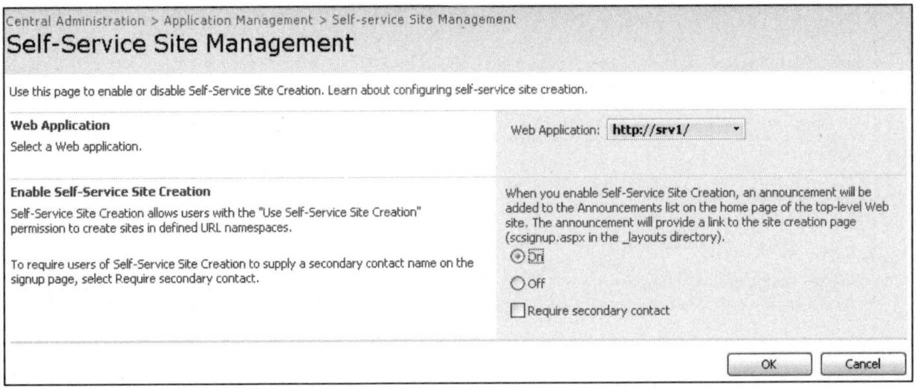

Figure 3-10

The self-service site creation feature is now turned on. Open the first top site in your WSS environment (http://srv1) and check the Announcements list. You should see a new item here, as in Figure 3-11.

The link in this announcement takes you to the web form for creating new top sites. But this is not the best place to store such a link. Later on, there may be many new announcements, and it may be hard to find this one. One easy solution is to create a link in the Links list (see the following Try It Out).

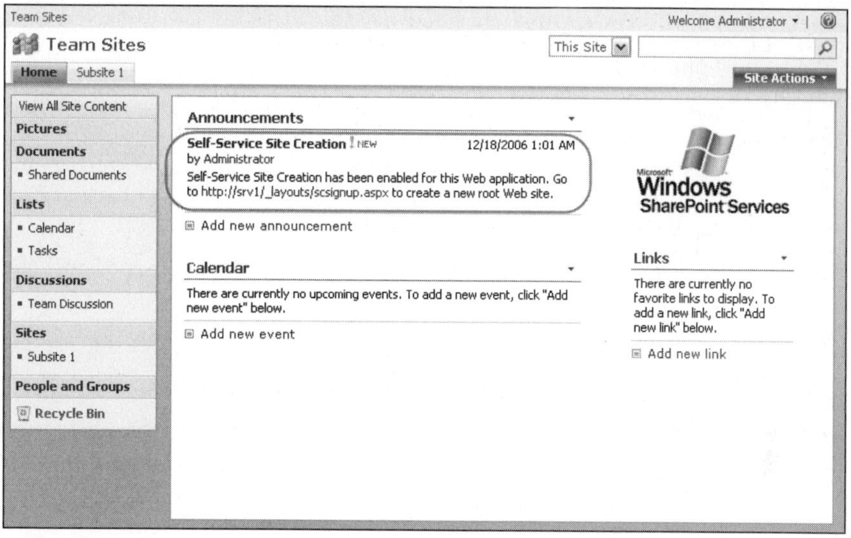

Figure 3-11

Try It Out   Create a Top Site Using the scsignup.aspx Page

1. Go to the home page of your first top site (`http://srv1` in this example).

2. In the new announcement, highlight the complete link `http://srv1/_layouts/scsignup.aspx`; right-click it and select Copy Shortcut.

3. Under the Links list, click Add new link.

4. Right-click the URL box and select Paste. It should now show the previously copied link.

5. Enter a descriptive name for this link in the description box (for example, Create New Top Site, as in Figure 3-12).

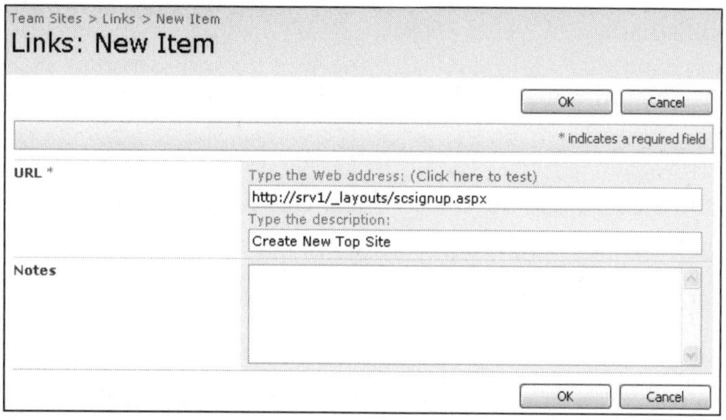

Figure 3-12

6. Click OK. You will now return to the home page for this site.

7. Test the new link by clicking Create New Top Site.

8. You will now see the web form where you create new top sites. Note that it will be slightly different from the one you can activate using the WSS administration tool. For example, the URL address for this top site will always be under the /sites/ path, since you cannot select another web application. Another difference is that you cannot set the Site Collection Administrator. It will automatically be the user who created the site collection.

   a. **Title:** Enter the title for this web site. This title shows up on the home page.

   b. **Description:** Enter a description of this top site.

   c. **URL name:** Enter the URL address for this top site. Note that it automatically has a prefix of http://srv1/sites if your server is named srv1.

   d. **Template Selection:** Select the site template to be used by this new top site.

   e. Click Create to save and close this page. The new site collection, and its top site, will now be created, and then displayed.

Configuring WSS to Use an Outgoing SMTP Mail Server

Before progressing any further, you need to configure WSS to use an SMTP mail server for outgoing e-mail. The receiving mail server can be any server that accepts SMTP messages, for example MS Exchange Server. The reason is that WSS needs to send messages in several different situations, for example:

❏ Error messages to the owner of the site collection.

❏ Warning messages whenever the size of the site collection is near the quota template limit.

❏ Notifications to a user that she has been granted access to a site.

❏ Alert messages to a user that has requested to be notified when a specific document library has been modified.

To set up WSS to use a specific mail server, in this case the local MS Exchange 2003 server, follow the instructions in this Try It Out.

Try It Out   **Configure WSS to Use a Mail Server**

1. Log on as an administrator to the WSS server.

2. Start the SharePoint Central Administration tool.

3. Click Configure default e-mail server settings in the Server Configuration section.

4. In the following web form (see Figure 3-13), enter the e-mail settings.

   a. **Outbound SMTP server:** Enter the full name for the mail server, also known as the Fully Qualified Domain Name (FQDN). Remember that it does not have to be an MS Exchange server; it can be any Simple Mail Transfer Protocol (SMTP) server, remote or local. However, you must make sure that this server allows WSS to send mail to your users; if not, the mail server may need extra configuration settings to allow it to relay messages. This is seldom a problem when using the internal mail servers in your network, but it may be a problem when using external mail servers located at an Internet service provider (ISP).

b. **From address:** The virtual sender of these WSS messages, that is, the address that the receiver of messages from SharePoint will see listed as the sender. Note that this e-mail address does not need to exist! It can be any e-mail address.

c. **Reply-to address:** If a user replies to a WSS message, it will go to this address. This address must exist. Avoid using a personal e-mail address here; instead, use a role-based address, such as helpdesk@filobit.com.

d. **Character set:** Defines what character set WSS will use for its e-mail messages. There is very seldom a reason for changing this from the default 65001 (Unicode UTF-8) unless you have a very old or strange SMTP mail server that will be receiving these messages.

e. Click OK to save these settings.

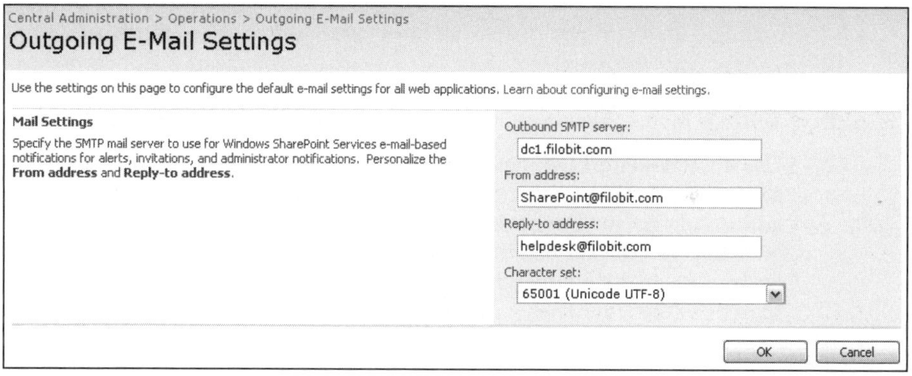

Figure 3-13

Configuring WSS to Accept Incoming SMTP e-mail

A new feature introduced in SharePoint 2007 is that you can configure libraries to accept incoming e-mail messages. To make this work, you must first activate the Windows Component SMTP, since this will allow this Windows 2003 Server to operate as an SMTP server; you can then think of the libraries as mailboxes that accept e-mail, including any attachments. Some examples of when this can be handy are listed below:

❑ Collect all e-mail regarding a specific project in a document library in the project site.

❑ Let users send a help desk request to a document library.

❑ Let customers send their orders to a document library.

To set up WSS to accept incoming SMTP messages follow the steps in the Try It Out.

Try It Out   Configure WSS for Incoming SMTP Messages

1.   Log on as an administrator to the WSS server.

2.   Open the Windows Component, and activate the SMTP service:

    a.   Click Start ➪ Control Panel ➪ Add or Remove Programs.

    b.   Click Add/Remove Windows Component.

    c.   Select the application server, click Details.

    d.   Select Internet Information Service (IIS), and click Details.

    e.   Finally, check the option SMTP Service. Click OK twice, then click Next, and Finish.

    f.   To follow the best practice, you should now run Windows Update to make sure that this server has the latest updates and security patches for the SMTP service.

3.   Open the SharePoint 3.0 Central Administration tool, and switch to the Operations page.

4.   Click Incoming e-mail settings; in the web form (see Figure 3-14), enter these settings:

    a.   **Enable sites on this server to receive e-mail?** Select Yes.

    b.   **Settings mode:** Select Automatic.

    c.   **Use the SharePoint Directory Management Service to create distribution groups and contacts?** Select No this time. This will require that you manually add the e-mail address of each mail-enabled library to your ordinary e-mail servers global address list. Note that you can select Yes here, if you also configure the Directory Management Service. If you do, SharePoint will automatically create a mail-enabled `Contact` object in Active Directory whenever a SharePoint library is mail-enabled.

    d.   **e-mail server display address:** Note this address, since this will be the Fully Qualified Domain Name (FQDN) address for all mail-enabled SharePoint libraries. Since SharePoint will operate as an SMTP server, it must have its own FQDN address, and it will be different from the ordinary address used for all user e-mail addresses in your domain! By default, this FQDN will be the name of this server, plus the domain name. For example, if the server is named SRV1 in the domain FILOBIT.COM, this FQDN name will be `@srv1.filobit.com`. You can change it, but then you must add an Mail Exchanger (MX) record to your Domain Name Server (DNS) for this FQDN.

    e.   **Safe e-mail Servers:** The default setting is Accept mail from all e-mail servers, which will configure the SMTP service to accept e-mail from any SMTP server. For more security, you can enter the FQDN name of the SMTP servers that SharePoint will accept e-mail from.

    f.   Click OK to save and close this web form.

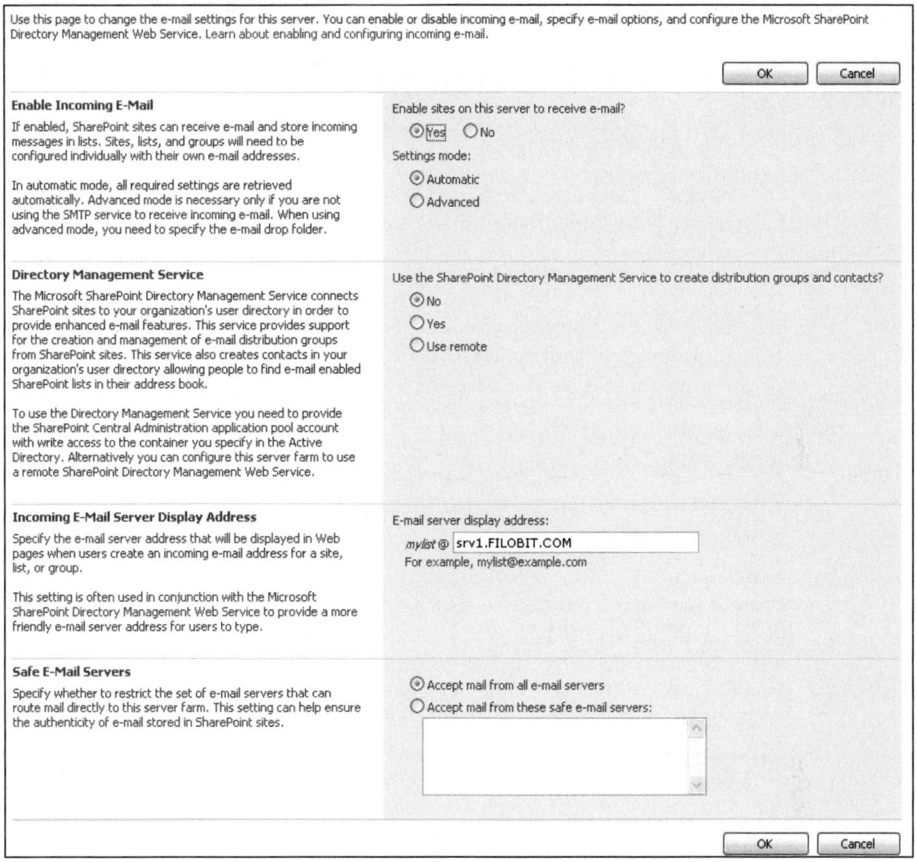

Use this page to change the e-mail settings for this server. You can enable or disable incoming e-mail, specify e-mail options, and configure the Microsoft SharePoint Directory Management Web Service. Learn about enabling and configuring incoming e-mail.

[OK]   [Cancel]

Enable Incoming E-Mail

If enabled, SharePoint sites can receive e-mail and store incoming messages in lists. Sites, lists, and groups will need to be configured individually with their own e-mail addresses.

In automatic mode, all required settings are retrieved automatically. Advanced mode is necessary only if you are not using the SMTP service to receive incoming e-mail. When using advanced mode, you need to specify the e-mail drop folder.

Enable sites on this server to receive e-mail?

⦿ Yes   ○ No

Settings mode:

⦿ Automatic
○ Advanced

Directory Management Service

The Microsoft SharePoint Directory Management Service connects SharePoint sites to your organization's user directory in order to provide enhanced e-mail features. This service provides support for the creation and management of e-mail distribution groups from SharePoint sites. This service also creates contacts in your organization's user directory allowing people to find e-mail enabled SharePoint lists in their address book.

To use the Directory Management Service you need to provide the SharePoint Central Administration application pool account with write access to the container you specify in the Active Directory. Alternatively you can configure this server farm to use a remote SharePoint Directory Management Web Service.

Use the SharePoint Directory Management Service to create distribution groups and contacts?

⦿ No
○ Yes
○ Use remote

Incoming E-Mail Server Display Address

Specify the e-mail server address that will be displayed in Web pages when users create an incoming e-mail address for a site, list, or group.

This setting is often used in conjunction with the Microsoft SharePoint Directory Management Web Service to provide a more friendly e-mail server address for users to type.

E-mail server display address:

mylist @ [srv1.FILOBIT.COM]
For example, mylist@example.com

Safe E-Mail Servers

Specify whether to restrict the set of e-mail servers that can route mail directly to this server farm. This setting can help ensure the authenticity of e-mail stored in SharePoint sites.

⦿ Accept mail from all e-mail servers
○ Accept mail from these safe e-mail servers:

[OK]   [Cancel]

Figure 3-14

5. The final steps are to mail-enable the document libraries, plus add their SMTP address to the global address list in your ordinary mail system. Open a SharePoint site based on the Team Site template (for example, `http://srv1`); it contains a document library that you can test this e-mail feature with. Then enter these values in the form (see Figure 3-15):

a. Click on the document library Shared Documents to open it.

b. Click Settings ➪ Document Library Settings ➪ Incoming e-mail settings.

c. **Allow this document library to receive e-mail?** Select Yes, and then enter the mail address for this library. Note that the FQDN address is preconfigured and cannot be modified. Use a naming convention for all mail-enabled SharePoint libraries to make it easier for you later to identify that a given e-mail address belongs to a SharePoint library.

    d. **e-mail Attachments:** Select how SharePoint should treat any mail attachment and whether saved attachments will be overwritten by new messages with the same file name. There are three different options for incoming attachments:

      ❑ Save all attachments in root folder: This will mix any attachment with the rest of the content for this library.

      ❑ Save all attachments in folder grouped by e-mail subject: This will create a new folder in this document library for every e-mail subject; all e-mail attachments with this subject will be saved in this folder. This is a good option if you want to organize attachments, based on the e-mail's subject.

      ❑ Save all attachments in folders grouped by e-mail sender: This option is very similar to the previous option, except it will organize the attachments in folders, based on the e-mail's sender address.

    e. **Save original e-mail?** Select Yes if you want to save the body of the actual message as a separate file. Select No if you just want to save the e-mail attachments.

    f. **Save meeting invitations?** Select Yes to save any message with a meeting invitation sent to this library.

    g. **e-mail security policy:** Select Accept e-mail messages based on document library permissions to ensure that only e-mail sent by users with permission to add content to this library will be accepted. If you select Accept e-mail messages from any sender, then it will accept any message, including e-mail spam.

    h. Click OK to save and close this web form.

Figure 3-15

6. If you configured SharePoint not to use the Directory Management Service in step 4c above, then you must add the e-mail address of each mail-enabled library manually in Active Directory (AD). You do this by creating a Contact object in AD, with the SMTP address for the library. For example, say you mail-enabled a document library and gave it the SMTP address `TeamSite-DocLib1@srv1.filobit.com`, then do this to add its address to the global address list in Active Directory:

    a. Log on as a domain administrator to a domain controller, and open the Active Directory Users and Computers (ADUC) tool.

    b. Select the Organizational Unit (OU) where you want to create the `Contact` object, for example Users.

    c. Right-click on the OU, and select New ⇨ Contact.

    d. Enter a descriptive name in the form. The Display name will be listed in the global address list, so give it a descriptive name, then click Next.

    e. Accept the default, Create an Exchange e-mail address. This will, in fact, not create a mailbox in Exchange, but rather add an SMTP address for this Contact to the Global Catalog in Active Directory, thus making this address show up in Outlook users' global address list. To define the address for this Contact, click Modify ⇨ SMTP Address and click OK, then enter the SMTP address for the mail-enabled document library. In this example, enter **TeamSite-DocLib1@srv1.filobit.com**, and click OK. Then click Next and Finish.

    f. Now you have to wait for the Remote Update Service in the Exchange Server to run, before this address shows up in the global address list. This process run every 60 seconds, but you can also force it to run, using the Exchange System Manager if you are impatient. To see if the process has finished, you can open the newly created `Contact` object in the ADUC tool, and see if its e-mail address is listed or not.

    > **If the MS Outlook client is configured for cached mode, then it will not see the newly created Contact show up in the global address list (GAL) until MS Outlook has downloaded the updated GAL. You can force this update by selecting Tools ⇨ Send/Receive ⇨ Download Address Book.**

7. All is now set to start sending e-mail to this document library. Start MS Outlook, and create an e-mail to this recipient (that should show up in the GAL in Outlook) with at least one attachment; enter a subject and some text in the message body, then click Send.

8. Open the receiving document library in SharePoint and wait for this attachment to show up; it will usually take a minute or two. Note that if you configured the library to only accept e-mail from users with permissions to add items to this list, you must send the test message as such a user! In Figure 3-16, the library has received one attachment that is stored in a folder named after the e-mail's subject, or in this case "Test 1."

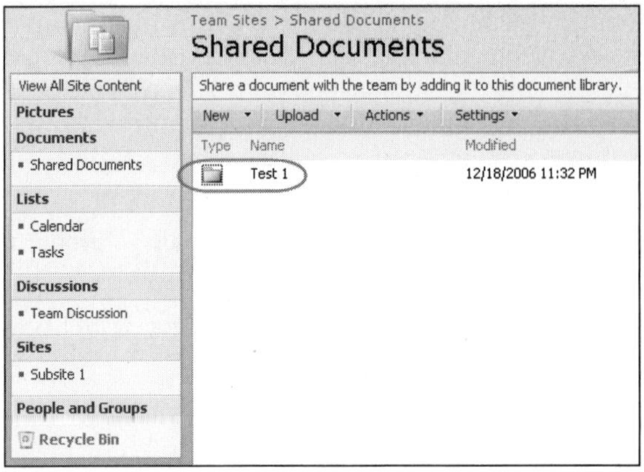

Figure 3-16

Managing Access Control of Web Sites

By now, you know how to create sites. The next logical step is to learn to configure the access to these sites. This is something the creator of the site normally will do without any assistance from the SharePoint administrator.

You may remember from previous sections that any security object, such as local or domain user accounts or security groups, may be granted access to WSS sites. Usually, this is achieved by adding these users or groups to a SharePoint group, such as the Team Site Members. These objects must be associated with a Permission Level role, such as the Read or the Contribute role. For example, say you have two users: MarielleS (Filobit\MarielleS and AlexS (Filobit\AlexS). You want to add them as a visitor (Read access) and a member (Contribute access), respectively. You can do this by making them members of a SharePoint group with the matching permissions, or you can grant these user accounts the corresponding permission level directly (such as "Team Site Visitors" for visitor [read] access and "Team Site Members" for member [contribute] access). Best practice is to use SharePoint groups when possible; follow these steps to add these users to you first top site, in this example named Team Site:

Try It Out   Add Users to Your Web Site

1. Log on as an administrator to any computer with network access to the WSS server.

2. Open Internet Explorer and open the team site by entering the URL http://srv1.

3. Click People and Groups in the Quick Launch bar to open the permissions page for this site.

4. Click the New button, and enter the first name, MarielleS (or Filobit\MarielleS), in the User/Groups field. Next use the menu in the Give Permissions section to select "Team Sites Visitors." Note that SharePoint on the same page allows you to send an e-mail to Marielle, to inform her about the new permission, including a link to this site. See Figure 3-17. Click OK to save and close this form, and send the e-mail.

5. Click the New button to add the second user, AlexS, this time to the group "Team Site Members," which will grant Alex permissions corresponding to a contributor, then enter some text in the message body, and click OK.

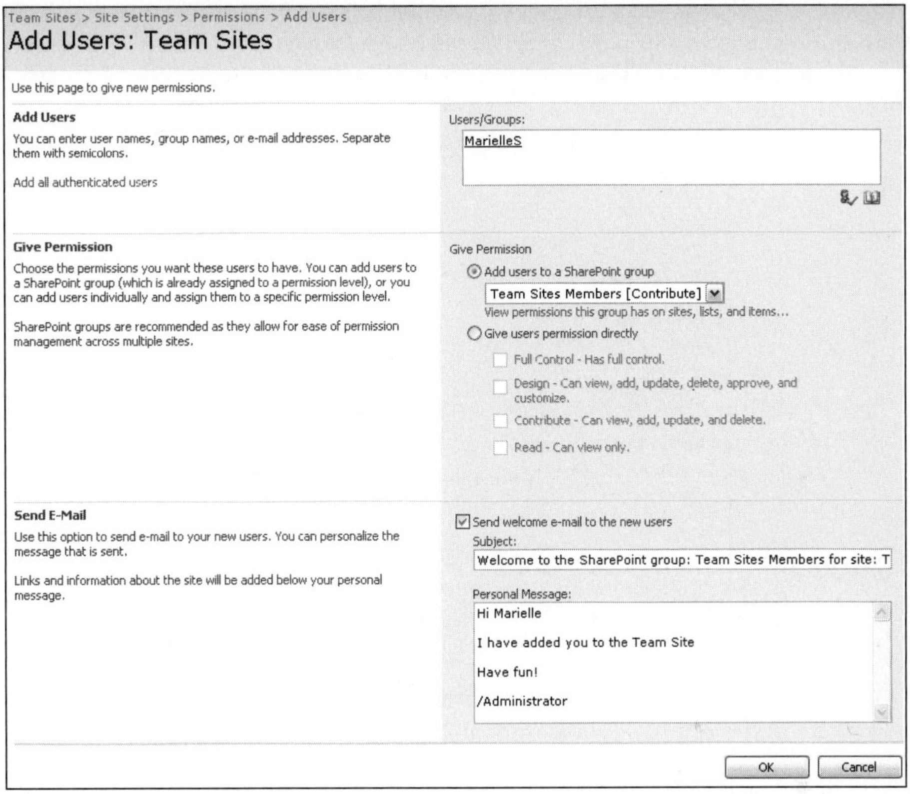

Team Sites > Site Settings > Permissions > Add Users

Add Users: Team Sites

Use this page to give new permissions.

Add Users

You can enter user names, group names, or e-mail addresses. Separate them with semicolons.

Add all authenticated users

Users/Groups:

MarielleS

Give Permission

Choose the permissions you want these users to have. You can add users to a SharePoint group (which is already assigned to a permission level), or you can add users individually and assign them to a specific permission level.

SharePoint groups are recommended as they allow for ease of permission management across multiple sites.

Give Permission

⦿ Add users to a SharePoint group

[Team Sites Members [Contribute] ▾]

View permissions this group has on sites, lists, and items...

○ Give users permission directly

☐ Full Control - Has full control.

☐ Design - Can view, add, update, delete, approve, and customize.

☐ Contribute - Can view, add, update, and delete.

☐ Read - Can view only.

Send E-Mail

Use this option to send e-mail to your new users. You can personalize the message that is sent.

Links and information about the site will be added below your personal message.

☑ Send welcome e-mail to the new users

Subject:

[Welcome to the SharePoint group: Team Sites Members for site: T]

Personal Message:

Hi Marielle

I have added you to the Team Site

Have fun!

/Administrator

[OK] [Cancel]

Figure 3-17

6. These two users now have access to the team site; Marielle with Read access, and Alex with Contribute access. To see the membership, click on the name for each SharePoint group in the Quick Launch bar, that is, Team Sites Member, and Team Sites Visitor. You can also click the link All People, and it will show a list of all users with access to this site, including some of their properties, such as their Picture, Name, About Me, Job Title, and Department.

7. If you need to change the permission for any given user, you can in either of these ways, depending of how they are granted access:

    ❑   **To change the membership of a SharePoint group:** There is no way to reconfigure the membership directly, so you must first remove the user from the old SharePoint group, then add the user to the new SharePoint group.

    ❑   **To change the permission granted for a user or group added directly to a site, that is, with no membership in a SharePoint group:** Click Site Permissions in the Quick Launch bar displayed when looking at the People and Groups page. Next, check the check box for the user to be modified, and click Actions ➪ Edit User Permissions, then select the new permission and click OK.

Alternatively, instead of entering the user accounts manually (as described in steps 4 and 5), you can click the Address Book button on the same page; you can search for names and groups, including built-in groups such as Authenticated Users, in the Active Directory and add them to SharePoint (see Figure 3-18).

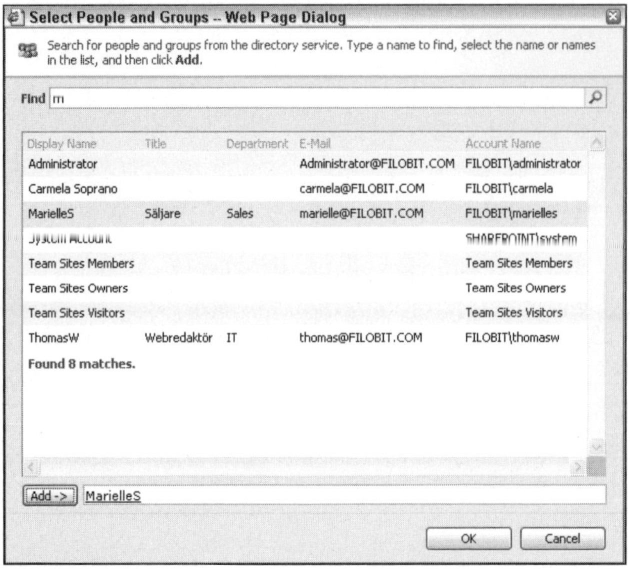

Figure 3-18

In previous SharePoint versions, you could select a Distribution List, and SharePoint would then expand that list and enter its members instead. This is no longer possible in WSS 3.0.

More Advanced WSS Administration

Now you know the basics of sites and how to control them. In this section, you learn the details about site groups, anonymous access, site templates, and how to activate the search feature in WSS.

SharePoint Groups

Previously, you learned that a user must be associated with a Permission Level role before he can access anything in SharePoint. The default Permission Levels are Read, Contribute, Design, and Full Control. The easiest way to grant a user permissions is to use any of the three SharePoint groups that automatically are created for each new SharePoint site configured to use its own security settings (i.e., each site that does not inherit its permissions from a parent site). The name for these SharePoint groups will start with the name of the site they belongs to, for example, if the site is named "ABC," the SharePoint groups will start with "ABC." Although these groups have been mentioned earlier, they are listed here as well, in this example for a site named "ABC":

❑ **ABC Visitors:** This SharePoint group is associated with the Permission Level Read. Any member of this group can view, copy and print content in list and libraries, including previous versions, if any.

❑ **ABC Members:** This SharePoint group is associated with the Permission Level Contribute. Members of this group can also add, modify, and delete lists and library content.

❑ **ABC Owners:** This SharePoint group is associated with the Permission Level Full Control. Members of this group have full access to this site, and all its content, corresponding to a local site administrator.

> **Not only are these SharePoint groups convenient for granting users access, but they also have some magic functionality when used in MOSS and its My Site. More about that in Chapter 5.**

When necessary you can create new SharePoint groups. For example, if you need a group of users that can read content but also create subsites, none of the three default groups will allow that. But before you start creating this new group, you must first create a new Permission Level role that matches the permission you need, that is, Read plus Create Site, in this example. The following Try It Out demonstrates how you do this.

Try It Out   Create New Permission Level Role

1. Log on as a SharePoint administrator and open the top site in this site collection.

2. Click People and Groups in the Quick Launch bar to display the Permission configuration page.

3. Click Site Permissions in the Quick Launch bar.

4. Click Settings ➪ Permission Levels. This will display all existing Permission Level roles.

5. You could now click Add a Permission Level and start defining the new permission level role needed. However, a smarter way is to copy the settings for the Read role and modify its detailed permission settings. So, click Read to open that role's detailed permissions. Scroll down to the end of that page, and click Copy Permission Level.

6. Enter a name for this Permission Level role, for example Super Reader. Next, enter a short description to explain the permissions for this role, then check the permission Create Subsites (under the headline Site Permissions). Click Create at the bottom of this page to save and close the form. The new permission level is now listed along the others, as shown in Figure 3-19.

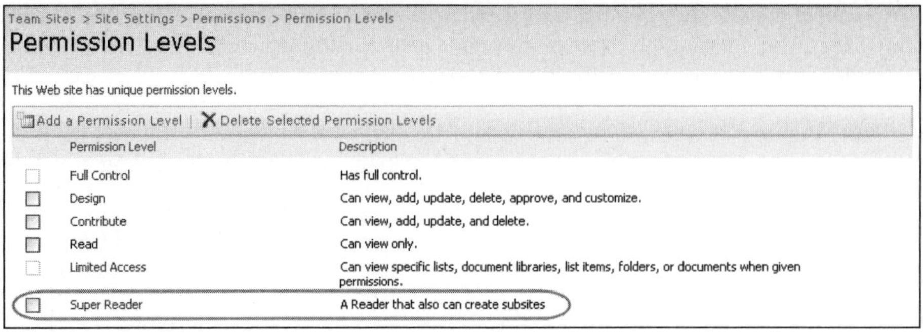

Figure 3-19

Now you have the permission level you need for the new SharePoint group, so the next step is to create the new SharePoint group that will be associated with the Super Reader role, as explained in the following Try It Out.

Try It Out   Create New SharePoint Groups

1. Log on as a SharePoint administrator, and open the site where you want to create the new SharePoint groups, for example `http://srv1`.

2. Click People and Groups in the Quick Launch bar, click next to the New button (but not on it) to open its menu, and then select New Group.

3. On the web form, enter these settings (see Figure 3-20):

    a. **Name:** Enter the name for this group, for example Team Site Super Readers. Try to use a descriptive name. A good idea is to use the same prefix as the default group's.

    b. **About Me:** Enter a description of this group.

    c. **Group Owner:** Define who can change the settings for this group, including its membership. By default, it will be the user who created the group.

    d. **Group Settings:** This section allows you to define who can view the membership of this group and who can edit its membership.

    e. **Membership Requests:** This section allows you to define whether users can request to join and leave this group. The default setting is No. If you set this option to Yes, you can also define what e-mail address any request will be sent to. This could also be a mail group, such as `Support@filobit.com`.

    f. **Give Group Permission to this Site:** In this section, you will see the newly created permission level Super Reader. Check it, and click Create.

4. This new SharePoint group is now listed along the other groups on the People and Groups page. You can now start adding users and security groups to it. Initially, it will only contain one member — the user that created the group.

5. **Optional:** If you need to modify the permission level for this particular group, select the group so that its members is displayed, then use the menu Settings ➪ Group Settings, and you will see the same configuration form as when you created this group. Make whatever modification is needed, and then click OK. Notice that this page also has a button for deleting this group.

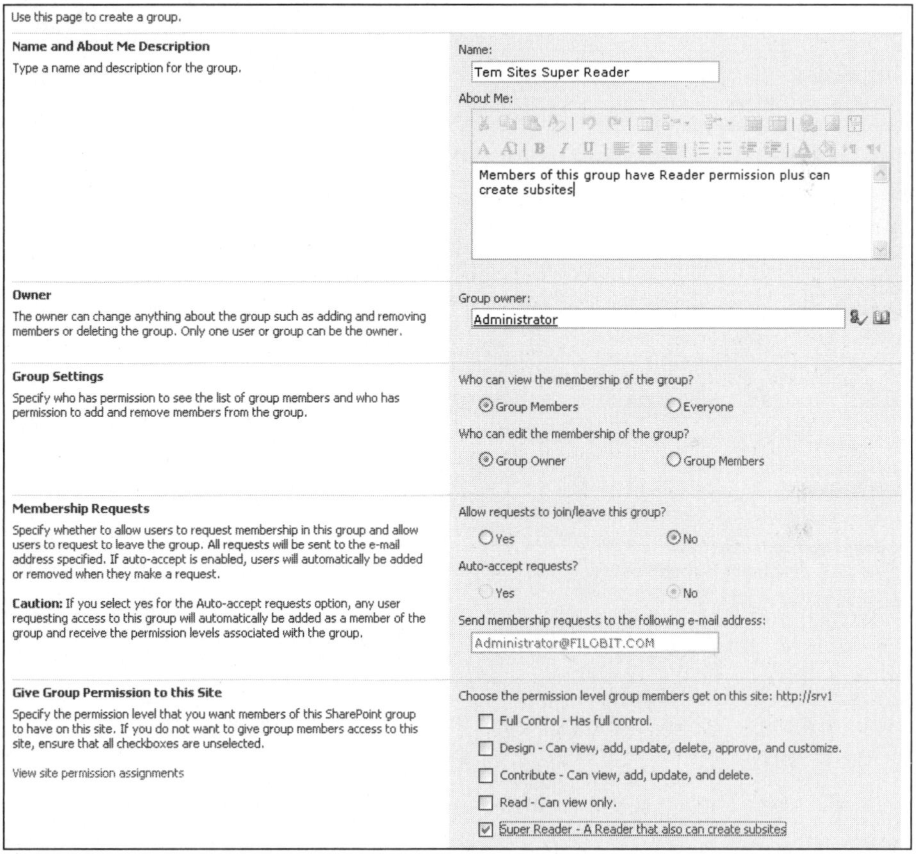

Use this page to create a group.

Name and About Me Description
Type a name and description for the group.

Name:

Tem Sites Super Reader

About Me:

Members of this group have Reader permission plus can create subsites

Owner
The owner can change anything about the group such as adding and removing members or deleting the group. Only one user or group can be the owner.

Group owner:

Administrator

Group Settings
Specify who has permission to see the list of group members and who has permission to add and remove members from the group.

Who can view the membership of the group?
◉ Group Members   ○ Everyone

Who can edit the membership of the group?
◉ Group Owner   ○ Group Members

Membership Requests
Specify whether to allow users to request membership in this group and allow users to request to leave the group. All requests will be sent to the e-mail address specified. If auto-accept is enabled, users will automatically be added or removed when they make a request.

Caution: If you select yes for the Auto-accept requests option, any user requesting access to this group will automatically be added as a member of the group and receive the permission levels associated with the group.

Allow requests to join/leave this group?
○ Yes   ◉ No

Auto-accept requests?
○ Yes   ◉ No

Send membership requests to the following e-mail address:

Administrator@FILOBIT.COM

Give Group Permission to this Site
Specify the permission level that you want members of this SharePoint group to have on this site. If you do not want to give group members access to this site, ensure that all checkboxes are unselected.

View site permission assignments

Choose the permission level group members get on this site: http://srv1

☐ Full Control - Has full control.

☐ Design - Can view, add, update, delete, approve, and customize.

☐ Contribute - Can view, add, update, and delete.

☐ Read - Can view only.

☑ Super Reader - A Reader that also can create subsites

Figure 3-20

In the following tables, you can see all the default permission levels and their exact settings. Knowing this information can be useful if you start changing these site groups and want to restore the default settings. Unfortunately, there is no such thing as a Restore Default button, so be careful if you need to change these settings.

Permission Level: Read	Description
View Items	View items in lists, view documents in document libraries, view web discussion comments, and set up e-mail alerts for lists.
Open Items	View the source of documents with server side file handlers, for example open files and documents in a library.
View Versions	View past versions of a list item or document.
Create Alerts	Create e-mail alerts.
View Application Pages	View forms, views, and application pages. Enumerate lists.
Use Self-Service Site Creation	Create a web site using Self-Service Site Creation.
View Pages	View pages in the current web site.
Browse User Information	View information about users of the web site.
Use Remote Interfaces	Use SOAP, WebDAV, or SharePoint Designer interfaces to access the web site.
Use Client Integration Features	Use features that launch client applications. Without this permission, users will have to work on documents locally and upload their changes.
Open	Allows users to open a web site, list, or folder in order to access items inside that container.

Permission Level: Design	Description
Manage Lists	Create and delete lists, add or remove columns in a list, and add or remove public views of a list.
Override Check Out	Discard or check in a document that is checked out to another user.
Add Items	Add items to lists, documents to document libraries, and web discussion comments.
Edit Items	Edit items in lists, edit documents in document libraries, edit web discussion comments in documents, and customize web part pages in document libraries.
Delete Items	Delete items from a list, documents from a document library, and web discussion comments from documents.
View Items	View items in lists, view documents in document libraries, view web discussion comments, and set up e-mail alerts for lists.
Approve Items	Approve a minor version of a list item or document.
Open Items	View the source of documents with server-side file handlers, for example open files and documents in a library.
View Versions	View past versions of a list item or document.
Delete Versions	Delete past versions of a list item or document.
Create Alerts	Create e-mail alerts.
View Application Pages	View forms, views, and application pages. Enumerate lists.
Add and Customize Pages	Add, change, or delete HTML pages or web part pages, and edit the web site using a Windows SharePoint Services–compatible editor.
Apply Themes and Borders	Apply a theme or borders to the entire web site.
Apply Style Sheets	Apply a style sheet (.css file) to the web site.
Browse Directories	Browse directories in a web site, for example document libraries.
View Pages	View pages in a web site.
Browse User Information	View information about users of the web site.
Use Remote Interfaces	Use SOAP, WebDAV, or SharePoint Designer interfaces to access the web site.

Continued

Permission Level: Design	Description
Use Client Integration Features	Use features that launch client applications. Without this permission, users will have to work on documents locally and upload their changes.
Open	Allows users to open a web site, list, or folder in order to access items inside that container.
Edit Personal User Information	Allows a user to change his or her own user information, such as adding a picture.
Manage Personal Views	Create, change, and delete personal views of lists.
Add/Remove Personal Web Parts	Add or remove personal web parts on a web part page.
Update Personal Web Parts	Update web parts to display personalized information.

Permission Level: Full Control	Description
Manage Lists	Create and delete lists, add or remove columns in a list, and add or remove public views of a list.
Override Check Out	Discard or check in a document that is checked out to another user.
Add Items	Add items to lists, documents to document libraries, and web discussion comments.
Edit Items	Edit items in lists, edit documents in document libraries, edit web discussion comments in documents, and customize web part pages in document libraries.
Delete Items	Delete items from a list, documents from a document library, and web discussion comments from documents.
View Items	View items in lists, view documents in document libraries, view web discussion comments, and set up e-mail alerts for lists.
Approve Items	Approve a minor version of a list item or document.
Open Items	View the source of documents with server-side file handlers, for example open files and documents in a library.
View Versions	View past versions of a list item or document.

Permission Level: Full Control	Description
Delete Versions	Delete past versions of a list item or document.
Create Alerts	Create e-mail alerts.
View Application Pages	View forms, views, and application pages. Enumerate lists.
Manage Permissions	Create and change permission levels on the web site and assign permissions to users and groups.
View Usage Data	View reports on web site usage.
Create Subsites	Create subsites such as team sites, Meeting Workspace sites, and Document Workspace sites.
Manage Web Sites	Grants the ability to perform all administration tasks for the web site as well as manage content.
Add and Customize Pages	Add, change, or delete HTML pages or web part pages, and edit the web site using a Windows SharePoint Services–compatible editor.
Apply Themes and Borders	Apply a theme or borders to the entire web site.
Apply Style Sheets	Apply a style sheet (.css file) to the web site.
Create Groups	Create a group of users that can be used anywhere within the site collection.
Browse Directories	Browse directories in a web site, for example document libraries.
View Pages	View pages in a web site.
Enumerate Permissions	Enumerate permissions on the web site, list, folder, document, or list item.
Browse User Information	View information about users of the web site.
Manage Alerts	Manage alerts for all users of the web site.
Use Remote Interfaces	Use SOAP, WebDAV, or SharePoint Designer interfaces to access the web site.
Use Client Integration Features	Use features that launch client applications. Without this permission, users will have to work on documents locally and upload their changes.
Open	Allows users to open a web site, list, or folder in order to access items inside that container.

Continued

Permission Level: Full Control	Description
Edit Personal User Information	Allows a user to change his or her own user information, such as adding a picture.
Manage Personal Views	Create, change, and delete personal views of lists.
Add/Remove Personal Web Parts	Add or remove personal web parts on a web part page.
Update Personal Web Parts	Update web parts to display personalized information.

Taking some time to study the preceding tables will help you understand what permission level a SharePoint group, user, or security group should be associated with. Also notice that only the Full Control permission level is allowed to create new subsites in an existing top site. It is common for organizations to request that users with the permission level Contribute be able to create subsites. This is easy to fix: Simply modify the Contribute permission level and add the right Create Subsite to it.

However, this might not be such a brilliant idea, after all. Imagine that six months after this modification, a new SharePoint administrator joins your team. She notices that several users can create subsites, although they are just granted the Contribute permission level. Because she knows that this level should not have the right to do this, she starts to troubleshoot the WSS environment. You get the idea, right? Changing default and well-known permission level roles is just asking for confusion later. Or worse, imagine some administrator adding the Add Item ability to the Read permission level! This would then give users with Read level the ability to also create new items, such as documents and contacts, although the name Read clearly implies read access only. This could easily confuse administrators later on. Best practice is instead to create a new permission level. Fortunately, there is a way to copy existing permission level settings, as described in the previous Try It Out, "Create New Permission Level Role," so adding a new permission level role is an easy task.

Anonymous Access

In some situations, you need to allow anonymous users access to a web site. You should think hard about this before you open up SharePoint — or anything else, for that matter — to everyone. Or perhaps you want to open WSS to all users in your organization, which is different from opening it up to anonymous users. In the following section, you will find the steps on how to perform both of these configurations.

Opening WSS Sites for Every User in Your Organization

The important thing to understand here is that you can grant access to all users who log on; that is, they all have logged on using user accounts in Active Directory and have been authenticated. This is not the same as opening the SharePoint environment to anonymous access! Windows Server has several special groups; one of these groups is called Everyone, and another is called Authenticated Users. The difference between them is that the Authenticated Users group contains only members who have actually logged on, using an ordinary user account, whereas the group Everyone also contains any type of connected session that does not require explicit log on, also known as a NULL session. In other words, it is safer to grant the group Authenticated Users access to SharePoint, and you should think hard before you give the group Everyone access. To add the Authenticated Users group access, follow the instructions in the Try It Out.

Try It Out   **Open WSS to All Authenticated Users**

1.   Log on as the WSS administrator.

2.   Open the web site you want to open to all authenticated users. Note that this setting will only affect the current site (and all subsites that inherit permission settings from it). This setting can be used on every web site that has unique permission settings, not just the top site.

3.   Choose People and Group. Since you want to allow all authenticated users Read access, you can simply add the security group Authenticated Users as a member of the SharePoint group Visitors. Click on the *<Site Name>* Visitors group listed in the Quick Launch bar. Remember that all WSS sites automatically have this group created when configured for local permissions, instead of inheriting permissions from its parent site.

4.   Click New.

5.   On the following web form (see Figure 3-21), click the link Add all authenticated users (to the right), and the security group Authenticated Users will automatically show up in the Users/Groups field. Clear the check box Send welcome e-mail to the new users, since the Authenticated Users group is not mail-enabled.

6.   Click OK to save and close this page.

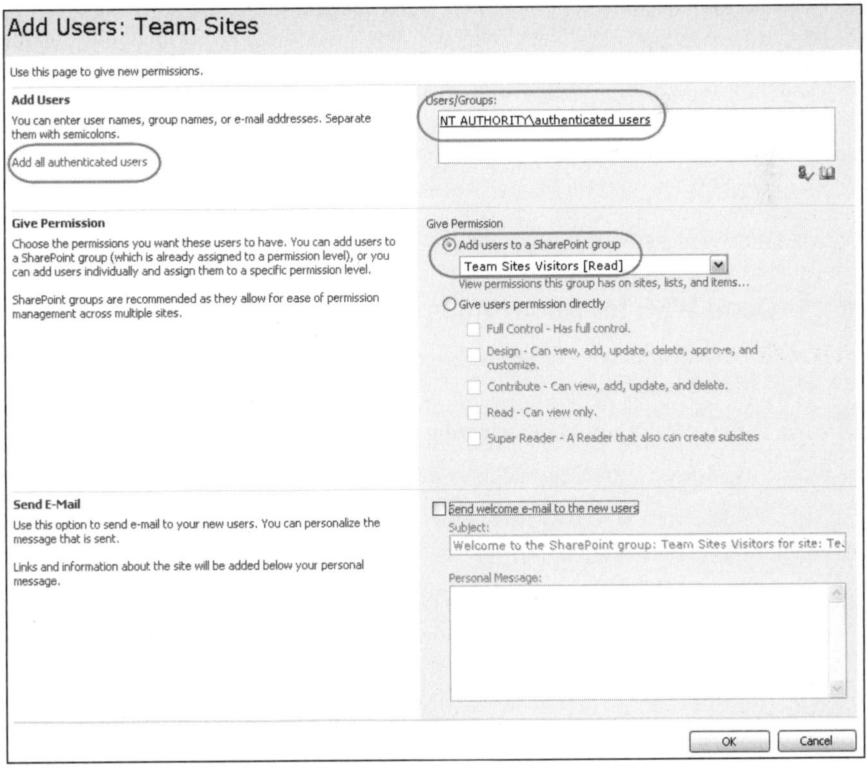

Figure 3-21

Once again, this is a safe method if you want to open a WSS site to everyone in your organization — you can be sure no one outside the organization will be able to access this site.

Opening WSS Sites for Anonymous Access

But if you want to allow everyone access, regardless if they are internal or external users, the previous method will not work. A typical example is when you want to open a WSS site to everyone on the Internet. Most likely, such a WSS environment will not contain sensitive information or anything not meant for public access. There are three typical scenarios when exposing a WSS server to the Internet:

❑ **Connect the WSS server directly to the Internet:** Bad idea! It will not survive for long before someone hacks it. Do not connect any server directly to the Internet!

❑ **Protect the WSS server behind a firewall:** Better idea. Many organizations find this an acceptable solution — if the firewall is properly configured. Typically such a WSS server will be connected to the Demilitarized Zone (DMZ) network segment.

❑ **Protect the WSS behind an MS ISA server, which in turn may be protected by the ordinary firewall:** This is a very good — and safe — solution that will satisfy even high-security requirements. Users on the Internet will never access the WSS directly; they will instead be directed to the MS ISA server, which in turn connects to the WSS server, grabs the information the user requests, and sends it back to the user.

The WSS server in the last scenario is so well protected that you may choose to allow external access to all or parts of the same WSS server you use for internal access. For example, your users could access the WSS site when they are working from home, or your partners may access WSS as a extranet, perhaps placing orders and looking up internal prices. It is up to you whether you want a separate WSS server for this or you accept to run a single server for all WSS information, including Internet access, internal users, and extranet users.

If you need to open all or parts of WSS for anonymous access, follow the steps in the next Try It Out.

Try It Out   Open WSS for Anonymous Access

1. Log on as an administrator to the WSS server, and open the SharePoint 3.0 Central Administration tool.

2. Switch to the Application Management page.

3. Click on the Authentication providers in the Application Security section. On the web page, do this:

    a. Make sure the web application is the one used by your WSS site collection; for example `http://srv1`.

    b. Click Default zone. This will open a new web form.

    c. In the Anonymous Access section, check Enable anonymous access.

    d. Click Save to close and save this form.

The actions you just took were to open the web application `http://srv1` to anonymous access. For this to work, the corresponding virtual IIS web server (e.g., the default web site) must also be configured to allow anonymous access. In previous SharePoint versions, this was a manual step, but in WSS 3.0 it was automatically performed by the Central Administration tool. If you want to check the virtual IIS server, then do this:

4. Open the Internet Information Service (IIS) Manager, then:

    a. Right-click the virtual IIS server used by WSS (for example, Default Web Site), and select Properties.

    b. Switch to the Directory Security tab.

    c. In the Authentication and access control section, click the Edit button.

    d. Note that the setting Enable anonymous access is selected. Observe that the account IUSR_SRV1 (assuming that the server is named SRV1) is listed in the User name box. This account will be used by IIS whenever someone tries to access anything in this virtual IIS web server. If you prefer, you can use your own account instead. The IURS_SRV1 user is a member of the built-in Active Directory group Guest but is not a member of Authenticated Users.

    e. Click OK if you modified any of these settings; otherwise, click Cancel.

    f. Close the IIS Manager. You do not need to reset IIS!

> If you later uncheck the Enable anonymous access setting as described in step 4, it will also disable anonymous settings in the virtual IIS web site.

5. Open the WSS web site you want to open to anonymous access (for example, `http://srv1`).

6. Click People and Groups ➪ Site Permissions ➪ Settings ➪ Anonymous Access. You will see a web form like the one in Figure 3-22.

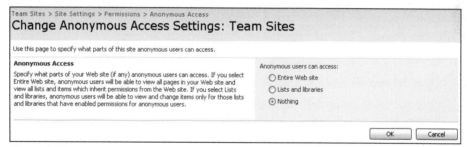

Figure 3-22

7. Select what rights the anonymous users will have on this site. You have the following options:

    ❏ **Entire Web site:** Anyone can access every part of this particular WSS site, including all lists and libraries and their contents. Warning: this will also open any subsite that inherit its permissions from this site to anonymous access.

    ❏ **Lists and libraries:** Anyone can access any list or library on this WSS site that has explicitly enabled anonymous access. They cannot view the pages in this web site, such as the home page, so users must have a direct link that opens the particular list or library that they are allowed to view.

    ❏ **Nothing:** The default choice. Nothing is accessible to anonymous users.

8. Click OK to save and close this web folder. This setting will immediately be active.

If you opened the complete site to anonymous access, then open a new web browser to test how it works, (you may have to log out from Windows first, to clear any cached credentials). Notice that you will be able to view any part of this WSS site now, but you cannot add or change any settings, since you are accessing the site anonymously. Therefore, SharePoint cannot see what permission your user account normally would have. But there is a new link named Sign In in the upper-right corner of the home page for this site (see Figure 3-23). Click on it to log on, and then your normal permission level will become active.

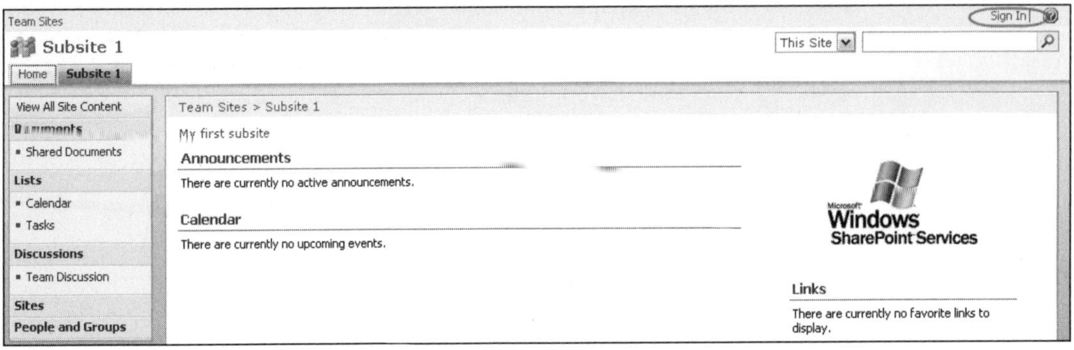

Figure 3-23

To make this discussion about anonymous access complete, you need to know how to open specific lists for anonymous access. The second option in step 7 above, Lists and libraries, allows anonymous users to view, modify, or add information in any list that you open to anonymous access. If you selected that option, then follow the steps in the next Try It Out to open a list or library for anonymous access.

Try It Out   Open a List or Library to Anonymous Access

1. Log on as a site owner or SharePoint administrator.

2. Open the web site that is opened for anonymous access, using the Lists and libraries option.

3. Open the list or library to be accessed by anonymous users, for example the Shared Documents library.

4. Click Settings ➪ Document Library Settings, then click Permissions for this document library.

5. Click Actions ➪ Edit Permissions. You must now first stop the inheritance of the parent's permissions before this list can be opened for anonymous access. Click OK to accept the option to stop the inheritance of permissions.

6. Click Settings ➪ Anonymous Access.

7. Set the type of access anonymous users will have in this particular list (or library):

   ❑ **In Lists:** Anonymous users can be granted Full Access (that is, they can view, add, modify, and delete items.

   ❑ **In Libraries:** Anonymous users can be granted View Items access only.

8. Click OK to save and close this page. These settings will become effective immediately.

Working with Custom Site Templates

By now you have a rather good understanding of the basics in WSS. You know how to create sites and subsites, add users and groups, create custom SharePoint groups and permission level roles, and enable anonymous access. But there is more — a lot more!

Wouldn't it be nice to control exactly what new sites look like right from the beginning? For example, assume that you have been asked to create 10 web sites for an upcoming project and that they all must look the same. You know that the look and feel of each web site can be designed by adding and modifying web parts on the site's home page, and you want happy users, so you start working on the design. After some time, you have created the first web site and it looks good. You check with the future users of these sites, and they are happy, too. Now you only have nine more web sites to create, with the exact same layouts and web parts, and then you are done.

But wait — there is a smarter way of doing this. The work process looks like this:

1. Create the first web site. Make sure that it really looks like the users expect it to!

2. Save the site as a site template.

3. Create the second web site, using this new site template.

That's all there is to it — Now it is very easy to create as many new sites with this template as needed!

Creating Custom Site Templates

You can take any existing web site, including a subsite, and save it as a custom site template. A template can also contain actual data, such as documents and list content. You can create as many site templates as you need. All site templates can be used anywhere in this site collection. If you want to use a site template in another site collection, you can do this by exporting the template from the content database to a file in a file system, and then importing that file back to the database into the other site collection.

However, there are some important limitations:

❑ You cannot modify an existing template. You can, however, delete the old template and create a new one with the same name and description.

❑ Any site that has been created using a custom template will not be affected if the template is recreated. Make sure that the template is perfect before you create new web sites based on it.

❑ Site templates are language-dependent. If you create a site template from a Swedish web site, it cannot be used when creating English web sites. (In fact, it will not even be visible for sites based on languages other than the template's language.)

❑ The content included in the site template cannot be larger than 500 MB.

> **The Canadian company KWizCom offers a free language type converter for SharePoint templates. Using this, you could take an English site template and convert its language type, for example, to German. Note that you still need to change the text labels manually. Download this excellent tool from this address:** www.kwizcom.com.

Only top site administrators and full SharePoint administrators can create and apply custom templates. If you want to create a template using a subsite, you must be an administrator on both the current subsite and the top site. All custom templates are stored as STP files, which is a SharePoint-specific file format for templates. These STP files are stored in the content database, not in the ordinary file system, but you can export them to the file system. These templates are all collected into something SharePoint calls a site template gallery, where you can view, import, and delete custom sites. There is only one site template gallery per site collection, and it is only available from the top site of this site collection. To create a custom site template, follow the steps in the next Try It Out.

Try It Out   **Create a Custom Site Template**

1.   Log on as the owner of the site you want to create a site template from, then open that site.

2.   Design the look and feel of this site. Make sure that you have created all the lists, document libraries, and web parts you need for this site template. When you (and especially the future users of these sites) are happy with the look and feel of this site, save it as a site template like this: Click Site Actions ➪ Site Settings.

3.   In the Look and Feel section, click Save site as template. You will see web form requesting information about this new template (see Figure 3-24).

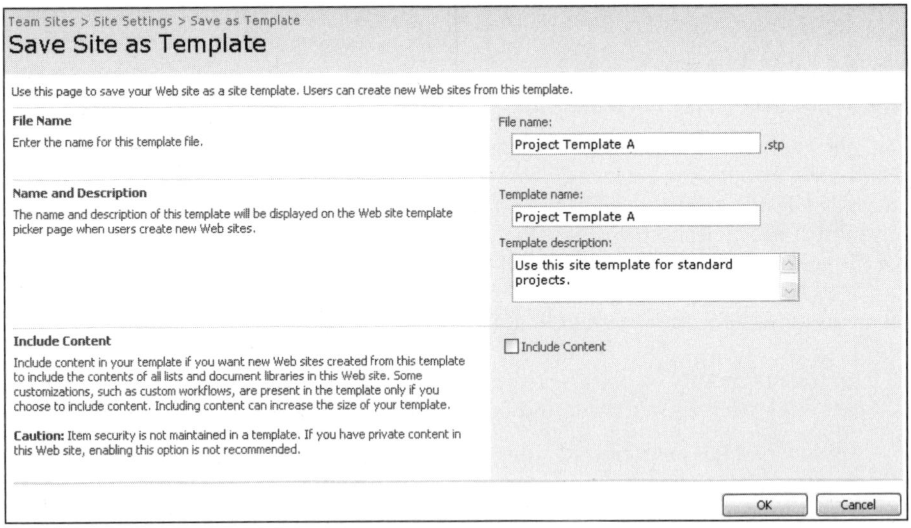

Team Sites > Site Settings > Save as Template

Save Site as Template

Use this page to save your Web site as a site template. Users can create new Web sites from this template.

File Name Enter the name for this template file.	File name: [Project Template A] .stp
Name and Description The name and description of this template will be displayed on the Web site template picker page when users create new Web sites.	Template name: [Project Template A] Template description: [Use this site template for standard projects.]
Include Content Include content in your template if you want new Web sites created from this template to include the contents of all lists and document libraries in this Web site. Some customizations, such as custom workflows, are present in the template only if you choose to include content. Including content can increase the size of your template. **Caution:** Item security is not maintained in a template. If you have private content in this Web site, enabling this option is not recommended.	☐ Include Content

[OK]   [Cancel]

Figure 3-24

4.   Fill in the template information:

❑   **File name:** Enter the name of the template file. (As mentioned previously, it will not be stored in the file system but in the SQL database!)

❑   **Template name:** Enter a short description for the template. This will be listed along with all other templates later.

❑ **Template description:** Enter more information about the template (for example, what it is used for, who should use it, and what it contains). This information will also be visible on the template list.

❑ **Include content:** Use this check box if you want to store current content in the site template. Note that the maximum size for this content is 500 MB.

❑ Click OK to save and close the web form.

5. The next page shows you whether the template was successfully created or not. If it was successful, you see a link to the site template gallery. If you want to list all site templates now, click that link. If not, you can click OK to close the page.

> **If you want to return to the site template gallery, open the top site first, then click Site Actions ⇨ Site Settings ⇨ Site templates in the Galleries section.**
>
> **If you cannot successfully create the site template, check that you have administrative rights for both the top site in this site collection and the current site!**

Now you must test it to make sure it works:

1. Make sure that you are logged on as a user with owner permissions for the current site, enabling you to create a new subsite. Note that this can be anywhere in the site collection tree; it does not have to be under the site you used to create this custom template!

2. Choose Site Actions ⇨ Create ⇨ Sites and Workspaces in the Web Pages section.

3. Enter the following on this form:

   a. **Title:** Enter the title for this new site.

   b. **Description:** Enter a description for this new site.

   c. **URL name:** Enter the URL name for this new site.

   d. **Select a language:** (This option is only available if you have installed WSS language packs.) If you have installed any WSS language packs, then select the correct language. (Remember that site templates are language-dependent!)

   e. **Select a template:** Select the Custom tab, and it will list all the site templates available for the selected language. Select the newly created site template.

   f. **Permissions:** Select the type of user permissions you want (either Use same permissions as parent site or Use unique permissions).

   g. **Navigation:** Select if you want this site to be listed on the Quick Launch bar of the parent site, or not.

   h. **Navigation Inheritance:** Select if you want to use the same top link menu bar as the parent site.

   i. Finally, click Create to save and close the page. After the site is created, it will automatically open.

4.   Inspect the new site. Make sure that everything looks the same as the template: the same lists and libraries, the same color scheme, and the same web parts and layout. The only things that should differ are the title, description, and URL for the site, as well as the permission settings.

Copying Custom Site Templates to Other Site Collections

You now know how to create and use the site templates. Suppose that you show your template to your colleague, who is the owner of a separate site collection, and he is so impressed that he demands a copy of your site template! The question is how do you copy the template to the other site collection? As you may recall from the earlier discussion about site collections, a template can only be used within the site collection in which it was created. But you can export a template; the general steps are:

1.   Go to the site template gallery where the template is located.

2.   Save the template to a file on the file system.

3.   Go to the template gallery for the other site collection.

4.   Import that file to that gallery.

The detailed steps are also quite straightforward and easy. To copy your site template, just follow the steps in the next Try It Out.

Try It Out   **Copy a Site Template to Another Site Collection**

1.   Log on as an administrator for the first site collection.

2.   Open the top site where the site template is currently stored.

3.   Choose Site Actions ⇨ Site Settings.

4.   Click Site templates in the Galleries section. You will see a list of all custom site templates for the site collection.

5.   Click the name for the site template you want to copy (for example, IT-Projects).

6.   Choose to Save this file, and select a folder to save the file in. Keep the filename (IT-Projects.stp) unless you want to change it, and click the Save button. Then click Close to close the dialog box.

7.   Open the top site in the other site collection. Make sure that you are logged on as an administrator for the second site collection.

8.   Choose Site Actions ⇨ Site Settings, and click Site templates. You now see all custom site templates for the site collection.

9.   Click Upload to import the template from the file system to that site collection. Use the Browse button to select the template file you saved in step 6; click Open and then Save and OK. The template has now been copied to that site collection.

10. Test it by creating a new subsite in that site collection using the copied template. Everything should look exactly as it did in the first site collection.

Adding a Site Template to the Global Site Template Gallery

The templates you have been working with up to this point have all been limited to a given site collection. But what happens when you create a new top site, and thus a new site collection? How do you make your own site templates available when creating a new top site?

Doing this is actually something that requires extra help, because WSS does not allow you to do it with the ordinary web-based administrator tool. Once again, you must call upon the STSADM.EXE tool you used for backups and restore. If you followed the instructions in Chapter 2 on how to add the path to this tool to the system environment path, you will find this to be very easy to do.

Try It Out   **Add Site Templates Using STSADM**

1. Log on to the WSS server as a SharePoint administrator.

2. Start up a command prompt (Start ⇨ Run, then enter **Cmd** and press Enter).

3. Use steps 1 to 6 of "Try It Out: Copy a Site Template to Another Site Collection" to save the site template you want to add to the global site template gallery. For this example, you can assume that the file is c:\tmp\it-project.stp.

4. Type the following command, and press Enter:

```
STSADM -o addtemplate -filename c:\tmp\it-projekt.stp -title "My Template" ↵
-description "This is a global site template imported using stsadm"
```

> If you get a list of all available options for STSADM now, you have misspelled something. Check your spelling and repeat this step.

5. You must now reset the IIS. While still at the command prompt, type **IISRESET**, and press Enter.

6. When the command is finished, test by creating a new site collection, using this template for the top site. Go to http://srv1 (or whatever your first top site is called), and use its previously added link to create a new site collection. You should see the new site template My Template on the Custom tab in the Template Selection section in the list of templates.

How Custom Site Templates Really Work

While you still have the command prompt window open, you can try some more things. For example, if you want to see what global site templates are installed, type this command:

```
STSADM -O enumtemplates
```

It will show all custom site templates that you have added manually. But what about those default site templates, such as the Team Site and the Blank Site? They are listed along with your own templates when creating the new site, but they are not listed here by STSADM. Well, they are a bit special. You will not see them listed here because they are part of the actual site definition. When you created your custom templates, you actually told WSS to save the modifications to the site that differed from its basic site definition — nothing more. In other words, the template file you copied to the file system before is not a complete site definition! For example, if you try importing this file into another WSS installation that for some reason does not have the same basic site definition, it will fail!

In Chapter 6, you learn how to create your own site definitions. Using that technique, you will be able to make modifications to a site definition, and all existing web sites, based on this site definition, will be updated.

Importing Custom Site Templates from External Sources

As you have seen, creating custom site templates and exporting them to other WSS environments is easy. It will work as long as the receiving WSS server has the same basic site definition installed, based on the same WSS language pack. This is something you could use, for example, to make nice templates to distribute to others.

Microsoft has made 40 ready-to-use site templates that it gives away for free. These are known internally at Microsoft as the "Fab40"or the Fabulous Forty. These are really good, and you are free to modify them as you wish. Microsoft does not actually call them custom site templates but Application templates for WSS. The easiest way to find them is by going to www.microsoft.com and searching for "Application templates for Windows SharePoint Service 3.0." Or you can try this direct link: www.microsoft.com/technet/windowsserver/sharepoint/wssapps/v3templates.mspx.

Here, you will find 40 site templates. Note that some are multi-language, but most of them are for US-English sites only, but these can be converted to any language, using the previously mentioned tool from www.kwizcom.com. A few of them are described here to help give you an understanding of what they contain:

❑ **Absence Request and Vacation Schedule Management:** Use this web site to make vacation requests, see when your team members are away, and find links to job sites if you want to help others.

❑ **Board of Directors:** Use this web site to track tasks required by the board, keep member information, manage a calendar of meetings and activities, and store mission and business meeting minutes.

❑ **Classroom Management:** A teacher can use this web site to store all information regarding a single class, such as lesson plans, assignments, tasks, and grading.

❑ **Helpdesk:** Use this web site to assist the help desk or customer support in managing requests from customers and to improve team communication. It contains an issue tracker, a document library for storing scripts, Knowledge Base articles, how-to guides, and more.

❑ **Project Tracking Workspace:** Use this web site as a central place to store all information regarding a project. It will help the project manager and the team to collaborate and keep track of issues, tasks, and deadlines.

❑ **Compliance Process Support Site:** Use this web site to assist in your compliance process, for example for the Sarbanes-Oxley Act, and ISO 9000 certifications.

Using these templates is easy, but remember that they are based on the default site definition, using the English language (language code: 1033). If you want to use these templates, you must create an English web site for several of these Fab40 templates, while others are available in multiple languages.

Removing User Accounts

As you know by now, all users must be members of site groups in order to access any part of SharePoint. In most organizations, these domain user accounts are stored in the Active Directory. This section describes what happens when these user accounts are deleted from the AD. You might assume that SharePoint automatically cleans up when someone is removed from the AD. But if you do, you are wrong!

A related situation occurs when someone moves from one department to another, making it necessary for his or her rights to be updated accordingly. In the following sections are some of the most common scenarios in which a user account would need to be removed and how you should act in each situation.

Removing Single User Accounts

Say that the owner of user account `Filobit\Michael` has decided to leave the company. He has been a very active user in WSS and has been granted access with different types of permission levels to different parts of the SharePoint environment. For example, he is a member of the Visitor SharePoint group in two site collections; he is also the owner of one site collection and an administrator of five subsites. Now you remove his user account from the Active Directory — what happens next?

Because SharePoint is not directly dependent on the AD or even Windows NT, there is no automatic synchronization between SharePoint and the AD. If you remove a user account in the AD, the only thing that will happen in the AD is that the user account will no longer be able to be used for accessing SharePoint. But the name of this account will still be listed everywhere, which is annoying. But think again. Assume that SharePoint removed an account, as soon as it was deleted from the Active Directory. If it did so, this name would suddenly be removed from all sites and workspaces that this user had been using! In fact, SharePoint cannot just clear a user automatically; it could remove important information. So you have to do it yourself, if you need to remove this name.

One way of clearing a user name is to remove this account in every place it is listed. But unless you have a very small WSS environment, doing this is a very labor-intensive task. To easily remove a user from every location in a given site connection, just follow the steps in the next Try It Out.

Try It Out   **Remove a User Account from a Site Collection**

1. Log on as the site collection administrator.
2. Open the top site for this site collection.
3. Click People and Groups and then All People.
4. Check the user to be removed from this site collection, then click Actions ⇨ Delete Users from Site Collection. Click OK when asked if you really want to delete this user. This user is now removed from every instance in this site collection, including any SharePoint groups.

> **If a user account is renamed instead of removed, you must run the STSADM tool to update all existing permissions to use the new user account name instead! Open a command prompt and run** `stsadm -o migrateuser -oldlogin <name> -newlogin <name> -ignoresidhistory`.

Okay, that was easy. But what do you do if there are lots of site collections? Well, you will not like this answer: You must remove the user account from each site collection individually.

Removing a Domain Security Group

This is no different from how you remove a user account. The method previously described to remove a user will also work when removing security groups.

Removing the Owner of a Site Collection

This is a bit tricky because the ownership of site collections does not necessarily show up in the ordinary lists where users and groups are displayed with their site group membership. So, you must first list the actual site collection administrators, replace that owner's name, and then remove the user account from the site collection. You might remember that there can be up to two owners of a site collection. You can see the ownership by following the steps in the next Try It Out.

Try It Out   **List Owners of a Site Collection**

1. Log on as the site collection administrator.

2. Open the SharePoint 3.0 Central Administration tool.

3. Open the Application Management page.

4. In the SharePoint Site Management section: click Site collection administrators.

5. On the following page (see Figure 3-25) make sure that the right web application is displayed; to know that you must know the URL of your site collection. Note the two name fields on this page: Primary Site Collection Administrator and Secondary Site Collection Administrator. Every site collection must at least have a primary site collection administrator.

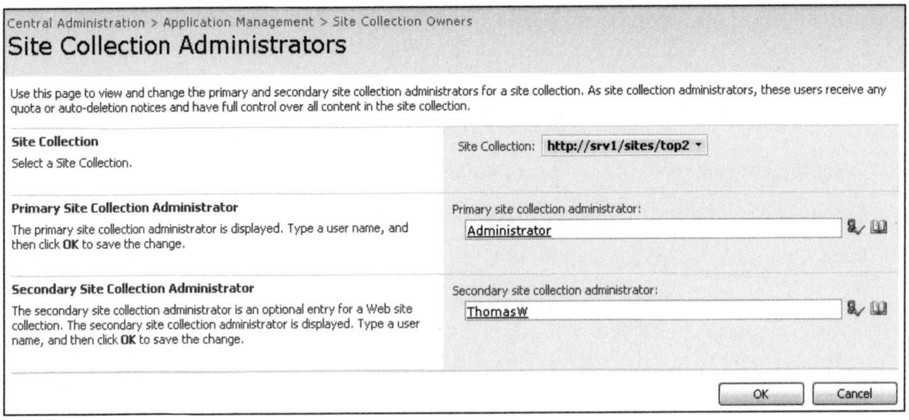

Figure 3-25

Now that you know the names for this site collection, the next step is to replace the site collection administrator's name with a new user name, and then remove that old administrator account from the site collection.

Try It Out — Remove a Site Administrator Account from the Site Collection

1. Start by replacing the old site collection administrator (in the form presented in step 5 above), with the new administrator, then click OK.

2. After removing a site collection administrator, he or she will still be listed as a user in this site collection. The next step, therefore, is to remove that user account from this site collection. Open the top site in that site collection.

3. Click People and Groups, then click All People.

4. Check the user account of the old site collection administrator, and click Actions ➪ Delete Users from Site Collection. Then click OK to accept to delete the user.

> **You cannot remove a site collection administrator from the site collection's user list. You must always first remove the role of site collection administrator first!**

Summary

In this chapter, you learned the following:

❑ Be careful with the Internet Explorer Enhanced Security. It can give you trouble if your browser does not recognize WSS as a trusted or local site.

❑ SharePoint uses two types of sites: administrative sites and user sites.

❑ The administrative site is used only by SharePoint administrators (that is, members of the Local Administrators group of the WSS server or members of the Site Collection Administrators list, defined in the Central Administration tool

❑ The user sites are where the users create team sites, meeting workspaces, project sites, and so on.

❑ Every WSS site has a home page. This is where the user accesses the lists and libraries.

  ❑ The home page contains one or more web parts.

  ❑ A web part is a window inside the home page that displays information. This information may come from a different part of this site, from a different site, or even from an external database.

❑ Sites are organized in site trees. On top is the top site; below are its subsites.

  ❑ The top site, including all its subsites, is referred to as a site collection.

  ❑ Many features (such as permission inheritance, ownership, templates, and more) are limited to one given site collection.

❑ The term workspace means the same thing as the term web site.

❑ SharePoint uses local server or domain user accounts and security group accounts to grant permissions.

❑ Each permission role is controlled by a Permission Level, such as Read, Contribute, and so on.

  ❑ You can create your own permission level for a site collection.

  ❑ If you cannot create groups in the Active Directory, you can create SharePoint groups to be used anywhere in SharePoint.

❑ To create a new top site, you can use the SharePoint Central Administration tool.

❑ You can also configure WSS to enable self-service site creation, which displays a link to a page where you can create top sites using the user web site instead of the administrator tool.

❑ By default, only a user with membership in the *<site name>* Owner can create subsites.

❑ You must configure WSS to communicate with any SMTP server before alerts, errors, and other messages can be sent from WSS.

❑ SharePoint can accept e-mail messages into libraries. This requires that the Windows Component SMTP Service be installed locally on the SharePoint server.

❑ You can enable anonymous access to all or part of WSS.

❑ MS ISA Server is easy to configure to make itself look like a SharePoint server for the users. It will grab whatever information the user requests and send it back to the user.

❑ Creating custom site templates makes it easier to create several sites with the exact same look and feel.

  ❑ You can save content along with the site template, as long as it is less than 500 MB in size.

  ❑ A site template will only be visible within its own site collection.

  ❑ Site templates are always built for a given language. You cannot use French templates for a German site, for example, unless you use the STP Language Converter tool.

  ❑ You can copy site templates to other site collections by saving the template to a file.

  ❑ You can add site templates to the global template gallery using the STSADM tool.

  ❑ Custom site templates are not complete templates. They just contain elements that differ from a given site definition.

  ❑ If you create many sites using a site template and later want to change the template, changing it will not affect existing sites.

❑ When a user account is removed from the Active Directory, it will not automatically be removed from SharePoint.

❏ You can remove a user account from a complete site collection, but there is no feature to remove the user from all site collections at once.

❏ You cannot remove a user account from the site collection if it is defined as a site collection administrator.

❏ You can use the SharePoint Central Administration tool and its site collection administrators to control and modify the owner for a given site collection.

Now you know how to create sites and do general administration of WSS. In the next chapter, you learn how to install and configure Microsoft Office SharePoint Server, or MOSS 2007.

Installing MS Office SharePoint Server 2007

In this chapter, you will learn how to install MS Office SharePoint Server (MOSS) with both types of available database configurations. You will also learn how to prepare for the installation and to understand the different types of system user accounts involved in this activity. After the installation is completed, you will learn how to check that everything is okay and some basic troubleshooting tips.

This chapter is organized into initial sections that explains what you are about to do and why, followed by a step-by-step description showing how to do it, and finally some more information, including any tips and tricks based on real-world scenarios.

Preparing for MOSS

In Chapter 2, you learned how to install the stand-alone version of Windows SharePoint Services (WSS 3.0). When installing MOSS you also install WSS, and the administration you learned to do in Chapter 3 is still valid. When running a MOSS environment, it is common to refer to the WSS part as the team sites, and this name is also used in this and following chapters. The procedure to install MOSS is very similar, but there are several important differences, such as the following:

❑ More system user accounts to define and plan for.

❑ Two more types of databases.

❑ New SharePoint service roles.

❑ A different type of SQL Server 2005 Express database.

The effect is that you must plan more carefully when installing MOSS compared to WSS. But you also gain many new and enhanced features, which enable you to build better solutions for sharing information among users in teams, departments, and complete organizations, and for more effective personal use.

In Chapter 2, you saw that WSS is the foundation for MOSS. It is simply impossible to install MOSS without WSS, and the setup program does it for you, so your SharePoint environment consists of one or more MOSS portal sites and any number of WSS sites. Everything you learned about WSS in the previous chapter is still valid when running MOSS and WSS together, including the option of running MOSS in a nondomain environment.

Just as with WSS, you can choose between two database types: Microsoft SQL Server 2005 Express (SQL Express), and MS SQL 2000 or 2005 Server. One thing you must learn right away is that the SQL Express version that comes with the stand-alone version of WSS is not the same as the SQL Express version that comes along with MOSS! The difference is that the WSS version of SQL Express, also known as Embedded SQL Express, is unlimited in size, while the SQL Express that comes with MOSS is limited to 4 GB of data. This is very confusing, and one can only speculate about the reason behind this decision. Maybe Microsoft thinks that if you invest in MOSS, you should also invest in the full SQL Server database engine.

MOSS Standard or Enterprise Edition?

There are two editions of MOSS: Standard, and Enterprise; they differ in functionality and price. You can upgrade from Standard Edition to Enterprise, but not the other way around. So, you'd better think twice about which edition your organization needs. Some of the most important features that are unique to MOSS compared to WSS 3.0, and the differences between the Standard and Enterprise Editions are listed in the following table.

Feature/Function	Description	Standard	Enterprise
Site Manager	A module that gives the administrator a hierarchical view of the complete SharePoint environment. The administrator can create new sites, including lists and libraries, and list all documents awaiting approval, plus a lot more.	Yes	Yes
Social Networking Web Part	Used in personal sites (My Site) to show other people that you have something in common, such as being members of the same group or having the same boss.	Yes	Yes
Personal Site (My Site)	Used for two purposes: by the user as a personal web site, for personal documents, pictures, calendar, and the like, and also to display public information about the user, such as a name, a picture, a department, a phone number, shared documents, and so on.	Yes	Yes
Site Directory	A directory of all sites; makes it easier for users to find a given site.	Yes	Yes

Feature/Function	Description	Standard	Enterprise
User Profile	Stores properties about users; can import properties from Active Directory.	Yes	Yes
Audit Targeting	Allows the content author to target information to a specific group of people; for example, to show IT-related information only to computer nerds.	Yes	Yes
Portal Site Templates	Used to build portal sites, based on Publishing Pages, also known as web content management controlled web pages.	Yes	Yes
Roll-up Web Parts	Shows information stored in other locations that is related to the current user, for example tasks assigned to me.	Yes	Yes
Colleagues and Membership Web Part	Shows what memberships you and another user have in common.	Yes	Yes
Enterprise Search	Allows the user to search in over 200 file types in almost any content source, plus search for properties.	Yes	Yes
People Search	Allows the user to search for people based on properties such as names, department, company, skills, title, and more.	Yes	Yes
Business Data Search	Allows the user to search in external data sources connected to SharePoint using the Business Data Catalog, such as databases, SAP, line-of-business systems, and the like.	No	Yes
Retention and Audit Policy	Controls documents and information retention and auditing.	Yes	Yes
Policies, Audit and Compliance	Makes it possible to support compliance with SOX, ISO, HIPAA.	Yes	Yes
Slide Libraries	Allows the user to store single PPT pages individually, regardless of what PPT presentation they belong to, and then select the pages needed to create a new presentation.	Yes	Yes
Site Variations	Makes it possible to create a web site that adjusts its language for content, depending on the current user.	Yes	Yes

Continued

Feature/Function	Description	Standard	Enterprise
Brower-based Forms	Allows the user to open and use InfoPath forms in a web browser.	No	Yes
Browser-based Excel sheets	Allows the user to open and use Excel spreadsheets and diagrams in a web browser.	No	Yes
Share Excel sheets	Stores Excel spreadsheets and diagrams in SharePoint's Excel Services.	No	Yes
Data Connection Libraries	Defined connection to external data sources, that will allow MS Office 2007 applications to share and use these data sources.	No	Yes
Business Data Catalog (BDC)	Allows the user to configure connections to external data sources, then use that data in SharePoint lists and Web Parts.	No	Yes
Business Data Web Parts	Specially designed Web Parts for displaying external data retrieved by the BDC.	No	Yes
Report Center	A special web site for managing report libraries, data connection libraries, and spreadsheets, typically used for Business Intelligence.	No	Yes
Key Performance Indicators (KPI)	KPIs are used for communicate goals and status to drive results. Using the KPI Web Part, a user can create a KPI list within a Web Part page, without writing code.	No	Yes
Filter Web Parts	Used to filter information presented in other Web Parts.	No	Yes

When Do You Need MOSS?

Since WSS comes free with Windows 2003 Server and MOSS is not free, you must evaluate the needs of your users. In Chapter 2 you have a more complete list, but the following table lists some of the more common arguments for using MOSS. If you have one or more of these needs, then you must install MOSS. These questions should probably be answered by users in your organization. Make sure to explain to them why it is so important that they think hard before answering these questions.

Question	People to Ask	Comment
Do you need an intranet that allows you to target information to certain groups?	Top management, people responsible for managing organization-wide information.	Only MOSS allows audience targeting of Web Parts, news items, and lists of information.
Do you need an easy and fast way to navigate a web site regardless of its location?	Subject matter experts, project leaders, power users, end users.	MOSS offers the Site Directory to meet this need. You can build similar functionality in WSS, but it requires much more work.
Do you want to be able to search for information stored both inside and outside SharePoint?	All types of users.	Only MOSS offers global search functionality.
Do you need a way of presenting more information than just the e-mail address and phone number for some or all of your users?	Middle management, team leaders, project leaders.	MOSS has its "My Site" feature, which presents much more information about users than the typical "Employee List."
Is there a need to integrate non-Microsoft applications into the SharePoint environment?	Top management, people responsible for managing organization-wide information.	MOSS has a feature called "Single Sign-On," which allows you to write code that displays information stored in other applications, such as SAP.
Is there a need to be compliant with special regulations such as SOX or HIPAA?	Top management, the legal department, information managers.	MOSS has support for compliance, policies, and auditing of documents and other types of information.
Is there a need to let users fill in forms, using a web browser?	Top management, people responsible for managing organization-wide information.	MOSS Enterprise Edition has the Forms Service, which will meet this need.
Is there a need to share Excel spreadsheets among users, without disclosing the formulas, and use these spreadsheets with a web browser?	Top management, people responsible for managing organization-wide information.	MOSS Enterprise Edition has Excel Services, which meets this need.
Is there a need to connect SharePoint to an external data source, for example an Oracle a database, or a SAP system?	Top management, sales managers, HR managers.	MOSS Enterprise Edition has the Business Data Catalog feature, which will meet this need.

Continued

119

The license model for MOSS is based on the MOSS edition, the number of MOSS servers and the number of MOSS users, that is, Client Access Licenses (CAL). If a user is just reading information, she still needs one MOSS CAL. The exact cost for MOSS installation depends on the type of software agreement you have with Microsoft and the number of users. If you have many users, you will pay less per user license than if you have a few users. You need to contact your license distributor to get the exact price.

MOSS allows you to choose between the free, but limited, SQL Express database and the full and unlimited MS SQL 2000 or 2005 Server. Since the SQL Express size limit of 4 GB is so low, in practice you must choose the full MS SQL Server for a production environment. Note that there does not have to be an exclusive MS SQL server for MOSS; if you have an existing MS SQL server and it has available capacity, you can use it.

Three Database Combinations

There are two types of databases and two types of locations possible. However, one of these options is not supported, so there are in total three types of configurations. The following table describes the options you have for MOSS and its database engine:

SQL	Local Database Engine	Remote Database Server
SQL Express	Yes	Not supported
MS SQL 2000/2005 Server	Yes	Yes

Even though SQL Express comes free with MOSS, it is very hard to imagine this combination in a production environment, due to the 4 GB size limitation of SQL Express. Still, it may be relevant in some cases, and you will find more information about how to install it in the next section.

Single-Server Configuration with a Local SQL Express

This is an installation of both MOSS (including WSS) and SQL Express on the same computer. Microsoft sometimes refers to this configuration as a stand-alone server. The typical scenario for this kind of configuration is a pilot project or an evaluation of SharePoint. You should think twice before using this configuration in a production environment, due to the limitations of the SQL Express database.

> **Avoid installing SQL Express on an Active Directory domain controller, since they will conflict! Microsoft has released a fix for this:** StandaloneDCWorkaround.msi. **Without this fix, an error stating "The trial period for this product has expired" will be displayed.**

MOSS has its own search and index module that is independent of the MS SQL database engine. Even when using the SQL Express database, you have access to the advanced search features in the portal site.

Single-Server Configuration with a Local MS SQL Server

This configuration is known as the single-server configuration and is perfect for the small- to medium-sized organization. It is also a very good solution for larger departments or subsidiaries of larger companies that need a very good intranet solution with advanced search capabilities, as well as a team collaboration platform. The cost is higher than the previous configuration, since it requires both a MOSS license and an MS SQL Server license.

> **You need one MOSS Client Access License (CAL) and one MS SQL Server 2000/2005 CAL for each MOSS user.**

This database engine allows you to build a MOSS solution for many thousands of users, since there are no size limitations. Note that you do not need to activate the full-text search feature in MS SQL Server, since MOSS has its own search engine and does not rely on MS SQL Server for searching.

A Small Farm: MOSS with a Separate MS SQL Server

As with WSS alone, you can choose to install MOSS, including WSS, on one server and MS SQL Server 2000/2005 on another server. Microsoft calls this a small farm, just like the combination of one WSS and one MS SQL on two separate servers. The term farm simply means that you have two or more servers, regardless of the type of SharePoint installation.

Using a farm offers the following main advantages:

❑ Better performance (it can support more users).

❑ Capability to build clustered SQL servers (requires the Enterprise Edition of MS SQL Server).

It is possible to build MOSS solutions with more than one MOSS server for load balancing and fault tolerance. Microsoft calls such installations medium or large farms, depending on how many SharePoint servers you use. To understand how these medium and large farms work, you must learn about the different roles in MOSS, known as the front-end server roles, and what databases MOSS is using.

The Databases in MOSS

Since MOSS is more advanced than WSS, it also needs more types of databases to perform its tasks. Two of these types are the same as in a WSS environment, and the others are exclusive to MOSS installations. When installing MOSS using the Basic mode, each database name will have a suffix based on a Globally Unique Identifier (GUID) string, which is a 32-character-long string. If you install MOSS using the Advanced mode, you will be able to set these names manually:

❑ **Configuration database:** (Used by WSS and MOSS.) Contains SharePoint configuration settings, such as front-end and back-end servers, mail servers, and portal site names. The name for this database is `SharePoint_Config`.

❑ **Content database:** (Used by WSS and MOSS.) Contains the actual data, stored in the portal site and the team sites. Default name prefix: `WSS_Content`.

❑ **Shared Services database:** (Used by MOSS.) Used to store information about the Shared Service provided; its default name is SharedServices1_DB.

❑ **Shared Services Search database:** (Used by MOSS.) Stores search index and related content in the database SharedServices1Search_DB.

❑ **Shared Services Content:** (Used by MOSS.) Stores general information for the Shared Services Provider instances in the database SharedServices_Content.

❑ **Administrative Content:** (Used by MOSS.) Stores content related to central administration in the database file SharePoint_AdminContent.

You may create a new content database when needed, but the other types must exist in one copy only. Besides these databases, you may create one more, when installing the Single Sign-On function in MOSS. That database will be named by the administrator (for example, SSO for single sign-on).

The Front-End and Back-End Roles

MOSS has more built-in functionality than WSS. To accomplish this, MOSS is divided into four different services, known as front-end roles. These roles are:

❑ Web Service

❑ Search Service

❑ Index Service

❑ Help Search Service

❑ Excel Calculation Service

❑ Document Conversion Services

All these service roles can be configured to run on one single MOSS server or separated into several servers. Besides these front-end service roles, there is also the back-end server, which simply means the server that runs the SQL database engine. This can actually be the same physical server as the front-end server; if so, you have a single-server configuration.

By dividing the MOSS functionality into different roles, you can build solutions that match your requirements. For example, small and medium organizations with up to 10,000 users may be satisfied with a small farm consisting of one front-end server running all MOSS roles and one back-end server running MS SQL. Another organization may require fault tolerance and build a solution with multiple front-end servers running the Web and Search service, one more front-end server running the Index, Excel and Conversion services, plus a clustered SQL-environment as the back-end server.

In previous versions of SharePoint, only a limited number of configurations were supported, usually referred to as small, medium and large farms. This is no longer the case in SharePoint 2007, so you have the freedom now to configure whatever combination of front-end and back-end servers you wish to for your SharePoint environment.

The Web Service Role

This front-end role actually runs on both MOSS and stand-alone WSS installations. It is responsible for answering any request from users who connect to the SharePoint server. In other words, this role shows the user the web site pages and content. This Web role will constantly read and write to and from the back-end server to do whatever the user requests.

The basic action in any web application is very simple: A web client requests a web page by entering a URL address or clicking a link. This is known as a GET request and results in a connection to the web server, asking the web server to find the requested page and send it back using the HTML format. After that, the session between the client and the server is disconnected. When the user clicks another link, a new connection is established. After the new page is sent back to the client, the session is disconnected again. There is nothing that requires that the exact same web server be used for all the connected sessions from a web client. If you have another web server with access to the same information, it may answer the next connection from this web client. This is known as a stateless connection.

SharePoint's Web role uses stateless connections. If you install the Web role on several servers, it is possible to divide the client load among them. But you need to solve two problems first. One is to make sure all that web servers have access to the same information. This is done by using a common back-end database for all of them. The second thing is that all of these web servers must look like one single SharePoint server; otherwise, the web clients must select a particular web server to communicate with. By using the Windows Server 2003 Network Load Balancing (NLB) service, you will resolve the second issue. The NLB service is a feature in Windows Server 2003 that allows up to 32 physical web servers to share a virtual server name; to the client all these servers will look like one. This is known as a web farm (or a web cluster). However, SharePoint only supports up to eight servers running the Web service role.

To summarize: Use the NLB service when you need to create a web farm with two or more SharePoint servers running the Web role. It will automatically direct a new client session to the Web role that is available with the least load. If a Web role server goes down, clients will be directed to another Web role server. The result is both load balancing and fault tolerance.

The Search Service Role

This SharePoint role exists only for MOSS installations; WSS alone does not have this. This role is also referred to as the "Search Query" role. The responsibility of this role is to answer to search queries entered by the client. For example, when a user searches for the phrase "Viking," this happens:

1. The user enters the phrase in the search field in MOSS.

2. This request is received by the Web service.

3. The Web service sends the request to the Search service.

4. The Search service looks for this phrase in its indexing files.

5. The result (no match or a list of matching documents, files, and pages) is returned in Extensible Markup Language (XML) format to the Web service.

6. The Web service converts the result to HTML and sends this information back to the client.

This raises several questions: What are index files, where do they come from, and where are they stored? The answers are: An index file is a type of list that consists of thousands of words, with a pointer to all the content sources, that is, files, documents, list items, and pages, where these words will be found.

These index files are created by the Index service and replicated to each server running the Search service. These index file are stored locally on the server running the Search service, by default in the folder C:\Program Files\Microsoft Office Servers\12.0\Data\Office Server\Applications. By default, there is one single index, regardless of the content source.

> **Use the command** `stsadm -o editssp` **to change the location of the index files.**

You can install more than one MOSS server running the Search service. Since this service is using local index files, it is not dependent on other servers or roles to do its job. It is possible to combine the Search service with other services, such as the Web and Index service. This makes it possible to use the Search role on the same server that is running the Web role, even in web farm scenarios, as long as each Search role server has identical copies of the index files. That would result in load balancing and fault tolerance for the search feature in MOSS.

> **To configure more than one search server in your farm, you cannot configure your index server as a search server.**

The Index Service Role

This SharePoint service is also exclusive to MOSS installations. The Index service is responsible for building the index files by crawling through content sources. The actual crawling process is not performed by the Index server, but one or more of the front-end web servers.The SharePoint administrator configures what content sources this service will index, and how often. The index files created by the crawling process are automatically copied by the Index service to all search servers, in case you have a configuration with a separate index and search servers. You can configure this role to index the following content sources:

❑ Any file server in your network.

❑ Your MS Exchange server (including public folders).

❑ Any Lotus Notes database.

❑ Any other web application internally.

❑ Any external web site on the Internet.

❑ External data sources, using the Business Data Catalog.

For example, you can configure the Index service to scan and index all files and documents on your file server, all public folders in your MS Exchange server, your partner's public web sites, and your Oracle database. When the users later search for information, they will find it, as long as it is stored in any of these content sources, including any part of the SharePoint database.

The Index service is very resource-intensive in terms of CPU and disk access. Separating this service from the Web and Search services will allow you to support many more users in the SharePoint environment. The indexing activity can be split among several SharePoint servers. There is no fault tolerance built into this role, so if one index server or the front-end web server that does the actual crawling goes down, no other will take over the indexing crawling that server is configured to do. You can load balance by dividing the content sources to be indexed among the index servers.

> **Only one index server can crawl a given content source.**

The WSS Help Search Service Role

This help Search service is available for both WSS and MOSS installations; its responsibility is to index SharePoint's help files and thus make them searchable. Note that this service will not index the user content of a WSS server, only the help content!

The Excel Calculation Service Role

This is only available for MOSS Enterprise installations. This is classified as an application service in SharePoint, and its purpose is to enable users to access MS Excel spreadsheets from within SharePoint sites; these spreadsheets may be stored in document libraries, or outside SharePoint. This service can be installed on multiple SharePoint servers, to achieve fault tolerance and load balancing.

The Document Conversion Service Role

This is another application service in SharePoint. Its purpose is to make it possible to convert documents from one format to another, for example from InfoPath forms to HTML, or a MS Word .doc file to HTML.

Medium and Large Farms

Previously in this chapter, you learned that a configuration with one MOSS server and one MS SQL server is referred to as a small farm and is designed to support up to 10,000 users. If you need to support more users or to ensure high availability, you need to build configurations with more than one MOSS server and maybe even more MS SQL servers.

The first option is to build a medium farm, which will support up to 50,000 users, depending on the configuration. Starting with SharePoint 2007, you can design any combination of SharePoint servers, for example:

- ❑ A typical medium farm configuration with three SharePoint servers:
  - ❑ Two MOSS front-end servers with both the Web and the Search role.
  - ❑ One MOSS front-end server with both the index and all application services.
  - ❑ One or more MS SQL back-end servers.
- ❑ A medium farm in a clustered environment:
  - ❑ A Windows 2003 cluster with two nodes, running active/passive mode. Each node runs the MOSS front-end Web and Search roles, plus the back-end MS SQL Server.
  - ❑ One MOSS front-end server with both the index and all application services.

You can also build a large farm configuration that can support more than a million users, depending on the exact configuration and the hardware settings for the servers, for example:

❑ Two to eight servers running MOSS assigned the Web role.

❑ Two to four servers running MOSS assigned the Search role.

❑ One to four servers running MOSS assigned the Index role, plus all application services.

❑ Two or more servers running as a clustered MS SQL server.

Hardware Requirements

MOSS is similar to WSS when it comes to hardware requirements, although the memory requirements for a MOSS server are higher, due to the extra features available, such as the search functionality, Excel Services, and the Business Data Catalog. As long as there is at least 2 GB of memory, the speed and the number of CPUs will affect performance most. Just as with WSS, if you want to set up a demo environment or do a simple pilot installation, you will get far with 1 GB of memory and a single-CPU server. But be careful — there has been more than one pilot installation that suddenly came to be regarded as a production environment. If you suspect that this could happen to you, I recommend installing the pilot project on a server that meets the requirements for the production environment or is easy to upgrade with more CPUs and memory.

Important things to keep in mind when planning the production environment include the following:

❑ SharePoint is a web application! There is no permanent connection between the client browser and the SharePoint server. Every time a user opens a link or a document, the browser connects, gets what the user requested, and closes the connection immediately after that, regardless of how long the user looks at that information. The result is that users who are not actively using MOSS are not consuming resources on the server. Make sure that this connection is fast enough to handle all simultaneously connected users.

❑ The number of users in the organization is not the same as the number of simultaneous users. Typically, less than 10 percent of the total number of users are requesting information in SharePoint at any given time.

❑ Different activities in SharePoint require different resources; for example, displaying a project site normally generates a very light load on the server, while indexing the database generates a much higher load. Make sure to schedule CPU-intensive tasks, such as indexing off-hours.

Calculating the Number of NOPS Required

You may recall the exact figures for calculating the normalized operations per second (NOPS) from Chapter 2, but here is the formula again for calculating the load on the SharePoint portal server. The term "normalized" means that the formula takes into account a number of variables, listed below. This information is used for estimating the number of supported users, given a hardware configuration:

$$\frac{A \times B \times C \times D = \text{number of normalized operations per second (NOPS)}}{360,000 \times E}$$

Given the following estimated data that you must supply:

❑ A = The number of users

❑ B = The percentage of active users in a typical day

❑ C = The number of operations per active user per day (1–10, typically 8)

❑ D = Peak factor (1–10, typically 5)

❑ E = The number of working hours per day

For more details about these parameters, see Chapter 2.

Example: An Organization with 15,000 Normal Users

Your organization has 15,000 employees (A). The percentage of active users in a typical day is 50 (B). The number of operations per active user is 7 (C). The number of working hours for the organization as a whole is 12 hours (E). You estimate the peak factor (D) to 10. The formula for this organization will look like this:

$$\frac{15,000 \times 50 \times 7 \times 10}{360,000 \times 12} = 12 \text{ normalized operations per second (NOPS)}$$

Now you have a good idea of the load your system will generate. The next step is to use this information to calculate the hardware you need. In this table are some typical configurations and the estimated number of normalized operations per second they support.

Server Configuration	Estimated NOPS Supported
Small farm: One MOSS server and one SQL server, both configured with 2 GB memory and a dual 2.8 GHz CPU	65 NOPS
Small farm: One MOSS server and one SQL server, both configured with 2 GB memory and a dual 3.06 GHz CPU	105 NOPS
Medium farm: Two web and search servers, one index and job plus 1 MS SQL server with 2 GB memory and 2 x 3.06 CPU	110 NOPS

As you can see from the preceding table, for a typical organization there is no need to install anything other than a small farm, if only the performance is important! Notice that increasing the CPU speed makes a dramatic improvement of the number of NOPS supported.

Calculating the Disk Space Needed

When planning for the required disk space, you do not have to worry about the MOSS binary files, since they are small compared to other files. More important are the index and database files. Remember that with MOSS you get the free SQL Express database that is limited to 4 GB in size. Very few MOSS installations have less data than this limit, so you will normally end up using MS SQL Server. Regardless of the database type, you still need to follow this important rule:

> **You must always have at least 50 percent free space on your database disk!**

The reason for this is that some database troubleshooting utilities need to make a copy of the database to perform their tasks. If you don't have the required space, you may get into a situation where you cannot fix a problem.

There is no difference between MOSS and WSS when it comes to estimating the required volume of data for your SharePoint environment. The documents, files, and pictures are responsible for more than 90 percent of the total database volume. To estimate the disk space needed for your database, start by estimating the number of files it will contain. For example, assume that you estimate it will contain about 100,000 files and documents, with an average of 400 KB; in total this will require 40 GB. Add to that 10 GB for the other types of information you will store, and you get 50 GB in total. Following the rule, you must have at least a 100 GB disk for the database files alone.

> **The new XML-based file format used in MS Office 2007 will reduce the file sizes to 50 percent, or less, compared to previous file formats. This is just one important reason to use MS Office 2007 in your organization, and there are many more.**

Software Requirements

Since MOSS is a web application, it requires Internet Information Services 6.0 (IIS 6), running on MS Windows 2003 Server. MOSS also requires that ASP.NET and its supporting components be installed. The easiest way to get this configuration right for a SharePoint server is to follow the steps in this Try It Out.

Try It Out   Prepare Windows 2003 for MOSS 2003

1. Log on to your Windows 2003 server as the administrator.

2. Click Start ⇨ Control Panel.

3. Click on the button Add/Remove Windows Component.

4. Select the Application Server and click on Details.

5. Make sure that everything is cleared, including the Internet Information Service (IIS).

6. Set the ASP.NET check box, and it will automatically check all the components it needs, which happens to be the exact components needed by MOSS.

7. Click OK to save this configuration.

8. The next step is to install the .NET Framework 3.0 package, which will install ASP.NET 2.0 and Windows Workflow Foundation on this server:

    a. Go to www.microsoft.com/downloads and enter **dotnetfx3setup.exe** in the search field.

    b. Among the resulting files, click on Microsoft .NET Framework 3.0 Redistributable Package to open its download page.

    c. Before you download this file, make sure to select the language of your Windows 2003 Server; by default it will be English.

    d. You can now click Download to start the downloading of a "bootstrap file," that is, a small file that will start the downloading of the actual package, or you can scroll down this page and click either X86 Redist Package (32-bits Windows Server; 50 MB) or X64 Redist Package (64-bits Windows Server; 90 MB) to download the full setup file.

    e. When downloaded, run this file to install the .NET Framework 3.0; select the option I have read and ACCEPT the terms of the License Agreement (if you do), and click Install. This will start the setup, which will take several minutes to complete, depending on your hardware. When it is done, you will get a message stating that the setup has completed successfully.

You may use any edition of Windows 2003 Server for a MOSS installation. However, the Windows 2003 Server Web Edition does not allow a local database installation; in that case, you must use a remote MS SQL server.

The IIS Virtual Server

In Chapter 2, you got the background on the development of Internet Information Server (IIS), its virtual web servers, and their application pools, but here is a quick recap:

❑ A web application is a virtual IIS web server that has been extended by SharePoint's Central Administration tool.

❑ Each virtual IIS web server is running within an application pool, which will control the memory, system resources, and user identity used by its virtual IIS web server, and its site collection.

❑ A site collection is created whenever a new top site is created; you can then create any number of nested subsites under this top site. Site collections are used to host SharePoint-based web sites, for example an intranet, with its subsites, or a public Internet site. Another example of a site collection is the SharePoint Central Administration tool.

❑ Every site collection must be stored within a web application.

❑ One web application can be used by multiple site collections.

In other words, when you need to create a new top site in SharePoint, you create a site collection; this site collection must be stored within a web application. To create a web application, you will extend an existing virtual IIS server. All of this is done using the Central Administration tool.

MS Office SharePoint Server has the same requirements as WSS in this respect. But where WSS started with two web applications (extended virtual IIS web servers), MOSS will create up to five different web applications during its installation, as you will see in the list below. Each of these web applications will be using a virtual IIS server with its application pool. All of this will be created during the installation and initial configuration of MOSS:

❑ **The user web site:** By default will create a new virtual IIS server named SharePoint - 80 and an application pool with the same name.

❑ **The administrative site:** By default uses the SharePoint Central Administration v3 site and an application pool with the same name.

Each web application can host multiple site collections, but only the top site in each site collection can be used for a portal site or public Internet site. An alternative is to create a separate web application for each portal site or Internet site. IIS supports up to nine virtual IIS servers with individual application pools. Since the administrative web sites share some virtual IIS servers as well as application pools, this server can have up to five portal sites with individual application pools. You can also use one single application pool that is shared with up to 99 virtual IIS servers.

When installing MOSS you will be able to create and select the web applications for the administrative site collections. The next step is then to create a web application for the site collection to be used by the user web site, typically the intranet site. You need to be sure about these two things regarding the user web site:

❑ Which web application will be used by the user site collection? Be sure to use one that is using a virtual IIS web site with TCP port 80, to make it easy for users to open this site collection.

❑ What user account will be used as the security account for this application pool?

Each application pool uses a setting called Security Account, which defines the security context for the application pool and its web sites. This can either be a built-in account (typically the Network Service) or a standard user account. Make sure that the selected account is granted the permission Database Creators and the Security Administrators in MS SQL Server. If you select a Basic MOSS installation, this is done for you automatically.

> **When using a separate MS SQL Server, select a domain user account as the application pool security account, since it is easier to grant it MS SQL roles.**

The application pool security account is just one of many examples of service accounts (i.e., user accounts used for specific services). In general, you should avoid creating a lot of service accounts, since the more you have, the harder they are to manage. Because the same service account can be used by several application pools, you should create a separate user account, for example SP_Service, and use it as the security account for multiple application pools used by SharePoint's site collections.

> **Use a separate service account for the application pool used by the Central Administration web application.**

The remaining application pools can usually share the same service account, unless you have very specific security requirements.

Service Accounts Used by MOSS

MOSS is more advanced than WSS and therefore needs more service accounts. Depending on how complex your SharePoint installation is, you might need more or fewer service accounts. You should create these accounts before starting the installation, but remember that you can use the same user account for more than one service if you want to keep the number of service accounts to a minimum.

> Avoid using the standard Administrator account as a service account, since you need to update each MOSS service every time you change the password.

During the installation of MOSS, you need two or more of the following service accounts, depending on the type of SharePoint configuration. For example, the single-server MOSS installation with an SQL Express database only requires the Default Content Access Account to create the portal; the rest are preconfigured but may be changed later. Some of these service accounts are requested when you activate special features later, even for a single-server installation of MOSS. Use the following table as a reference for some of these service accounts in a MOSS installation and configuration.

Service Account	Description	Recommendations
Application Pool Security Account	This account defines the security context for the web server connected to the application pool. It is also used when MOSS communicates with the database server. It must be a member of the Security Administrator and Database Creators role in MS SQL Server.	For single-server installations, use the Network Service account. For MOSS farms, use a domain user account for these application pools, such as `sp_appservice`.
Default Content Access Account	This account is used when the Index role crawls locations outside SharePoint's databases. This account must have Read access in these locations to do its job, but you can configure SharePoint to use a special user account for given locations.	Use an account with Read access to most of the locations that will be indexed; for example, `sp_CA_account`.
Configuration Database Account	This account is used by MOSS when communicating with the configuration database. You can use a local account or a domain account. It must be a member of the local server's Power User group or the local Administrators group.	This account will only be requested when using a full version of MS SQL Server. In most installations, it is okay to use the same account that is used for the Application Pool security account.

Minimum and Recommended Configurations

The following table provides a summary of the previous hardware and software requirement sections; it lists Microsoft's minimum and recommended configurations. Remember that for a pilot installation you can actually get away with even less than the given minimum memory size listed in the following table.

Item	Minimum Requirement	MS Recommends
Operating System	Any edition of Microsoft Windows Server 2003	Any edition of Microsoft Windows Server 2003
CPU	1 CPU running at 2.5 GHz	2 CPUs running at least 3 GHz
RAM	1 GB	2 GB
Disk space	3 GB	3 GB plus free space for the web sites
File System	NTFS	NTFS
IIS version	6.0 with ASP.NET (in Worker Process Isolation Mode)	6.0 with ASP.NET (in Worker Process Isolation Mode)
Database engine	SQL Express	A separate SQL 2000 server with SP3, or SQL Server 2005 and its latest service pack
Internet Browser	IE 5.01 with SP2 or later	IE 6 with the latest service pack, or later IE versions

Installing MOSS

By now, you have the necessary information to start the installation of MOSS. The following section describes the exact steps required to install Microsoft Office SharePoint Server 2007. If you have other web applications installed on the same server, please make a backup before you start, to be prepared for the unlikely possibility that something goes wrong and the server gets messed up beyond repair!

When installing MOSS in Advanced mode, you have a choice of which web application to use for the portal and team sites. When you select the virtual IIS server for this web application, it is automatically extended, and you do not need to do this manually.

> **In the following sections are three complete sets of step-by-step instructions on how to install MOSS. You only have to read the description for the particular type of installation you are about to do. To get the MOSS 2007 installation CD, you typically order it from your favorite software vendor.**

Installing on a Stand-Alone Server with SQL Express

Installing a MOSS using a local SQL Express database is very straightforward and easy. You can do it within 10 minutes without much hassle. Remember that you cannot perform this type of installation on a domain controller, since it will not allow the SQL Express database! Follow the steps in the Try It Out to install both the MOSS application and the SQL Express database on the same server.

Try It Out   **Install MOSS and SQL Express on a Stand-Alone Server**

1. Log on as an administrator to the Windows 2003 server you will use for your MOSS and SQL Express installation.

2. Make sure that Windows 2003 Server has the latest service packs and security patches installed by going to Start ⇨ All Programs ⇨ Windows Update.

3. Verify that you have ASP.NET, and the .NET Framework 3.0 package installed on this server, as previously described in the "Software Requirements" section.

4. Start the installation by mounting the MOSS CD-ROM. You can also choose to start it via SETUP.EXE on the CD-ROM directly.

5. The first page asks about the product key. Note that this key will decide if you are installing Standard or Enterprise edition of MOSS. If you install the Standard Edition, you can later upgrade to Enterprise, but not the other way around! Enter the product key and click Continue.

> **Microsoft provides free product keys for a 180-day trial period. One product key is for the MOSS Standard Edition, and one is for the Enterprise Edition. This installation can later be converted to a fully licensed MOSS server simply by entering a real production key. If you do so, everything stored in the servers is retained, and there is no need for a reinstallation of MOSS.**

6. On the next page, choose the type of installation you want. Since you will be installing a stand-alone server, click Basic. The installation now starts and runs from 5 to 15 minutes, depending on the server hardware.

7. After the installation, you will be prompted to run the SharePoint Product and Technologies Configuration Wizard. Click Close to close the installation program and start the Configuration Wizard.

8. On the welcome page, click Next, then click Yes to accept that the IIS will be restarted during the configuration. This process now starts, and takes about 5 to 15 minutes, depending on the server hardware.

9. When the configuration is completed, click Finish. The intranet portal that the Configuration Wizard created automatically for you is now displayed and ready to be used (see Figure 4-1).

Figure 4-1

After the Installation of the Stand-Alone Server

There are many things to do directly after the installation, but some of these need immediate attention, and other things will be taken care of when appropriate. For a single-server installation of MOSS, you should now do these two things:

❑ Download and install the latest service pack for MOSS and WSS. You start by installing the WSS service pack and then the MOSS service pack. Good places to start looking for these service packs are www.microsoft.com/technet/windowsserver/sharepoint for WSS and www.microsoft.com/office/sharepoint for MOSS. You may also find these service packs using Microsoft Update.

❑ Do a full backup of the MOSS server environment with the backup utility that comes with MOSS (see the end of this chapter) or your ordinary backup program, if it is SharePoint-aware.

Checking the New Folder and Applications

The portal site is now up and running, and you will very soon check it out. But first take a look at what has changed in the Windows 2003 server. You have several new file directories used by MOSS and the underlying WSS environment:

❑ `C:\Program Files\Common Files\Microsoft Shared\web server extensions\12:` (Where 12 is the internal version number of MOSS.) This folder has several new directories, including a Bin directory where several tools for WSS are stored. All these files and folders are identical to a pure WSS installation.

❑ `C:\Program Files\Microsoft Office Servers\12.0`: This location has several folders and files specific for the MOSS application. There is a Bin directory that contains all the DLL files for MOSS. In the Data folder you will find index files, and in the Log folder are installation log files and other log files that you can view from within the MOSS administrative tool.

❑ `C:\Program Files\Microsoft Microsoft Office Servers\12.0\Data\MSSQL`: This folder structure stores the SQL Express information; the Data folder stores the actual SQL database files; the Log folder stores the MS SQL transaction log files and error log files.

There are also two new application links listed in the Start ➪ All Programs ➪ Microsoft Office Server node. By default you will see these links there:

❑ **SharePoint 3.0 Central Administration:** This is the administrative tool for SharePoint. This is simply a link to the web site in the virtual IIS server "SharePoint Central Administration."

❑ **SharePoint Products and Technologies Configuration Wizard:** This is the online help manual for SharePoint. You can also find help inside the user portal site almost anywhere.

> **You can also start both of these two tools from Start ➪ Administrative Tools.**

Checking the New Virtual IIS Server Settings

Finally, you will find that a number of web applications (such as virtual IIS web servers) that have been both created and extended by the installation program and the Configuration Wizard. Since MOSS is much more advanced than WSS, you will find more web applications in the IIS Web Sites node. To see them, open the IIS manager: Start ➪ Administration Tools ➪ Internet Information Service (IIS) Manager. Then expand the node Web Sites. Note that you have a number of IIS virtual web servers there:

❑ **SharePoint Central Administration v3:** Used by SharePoint for the administration web site. This virtual server was created during the initial phase of the MOSS installation, before the portal site was created.

❑ **SharePoint – 80:** This is the virtual server that hosts the site collection used by the portal site.

❑ **SharePoint – nnn:** (nnn = a randomly created TCP port number). This virtual server is used by the Shared Service Provider, and its first instance, `SharedServices1`; you will learn more about the Shared Service Provider later in this chapter

❑ **Office Server Web Services:** This is a general service for enabling MOSS and other Office Server applications to use the Web service technique to retrieve or store data from SharePoint's database.

Right-click on SharePoint – 80 and select Properties. Switch to the Home Directory tab. Note the application pool name this virtual server is using; by default it will be SharePoint – 80, the same name as the virtual IIS server itself. The other virtual IIS server, SharePoint Central Administration v3, will by default use the application pool SharePoint Central Administration v3. Expand the node Application Pools (located directly above the Web Sites node), right-click on either of the two application pools mentioned above, and switch to the Identity tab. Note that the security account this application pool is using is the built-in Network Service account, which is fine since this installation is using a local SQL Express database.

To summarize: MOSS uses four virtual IIS servers for a stand-alone installation, one for the web sites that your SharePoint users utilize and three others for the administration of SharePoint. All of these virtual servers use separate application pools. But all these application pools use the same security account, that is, Network Service.

> The following section describes how to install MOSS using the MS SQL Server database, instead of the SQL Express database; You can skip this section if it does not match your required installation procedure. However, if you want to know how to install MOSS in advanced mode using the full SQL Server product, be sure to read the following section.

Installing a MOSS Using the MS SQL Database

One of the most common installation scenarios for small- and medium-sized organizations is a MOSS that uses a MS SQL Server; this SQL server may be installed on the SharePoint server, i.e., a single server, or a remote server, i.e., a small farm. Many of the following steps are identical to the previous installation scenario using a local SQL Express database, except for these important things:

❑   You need to install MS SQL Server before installing MOSS. If you are using SQL Server 2000, you must install Service Pack 3a or later. If you are using SQL Server 2005, install Service Pack 2 or later.

❑   You will need to define more service accounts. An example is the user account that MOSS will use when communicating with the MS SQL server (also used as the Application Pool Identity account).

> SQL Server 2000 runs with just 64 MB of memory, while SQL Server 2005 needs at least 192 MB. For a stand-alone server, you may want to use the old SQL Server 2000, due to its lower memory requirements.

If this is the first time you install MOSS, you may need some assistance on how to set up SQL Server as well. Follow these steps to install both MS SQL 2000 + SP3a and MOSS 2007 on the same server:

Try It Out   **Install MS SQL Server 2000 and Service Pack 4**

1.   Log on as an administrator on the Windows 2003 server you will use for your MOSS and MS SQL installation.

2.   Make sure that Windows 2003 Server has the latest service packs and security patches installed by going to Start ➪ All Programs ➪ Windows Update.

3.   Verify that you have ASP.NET and the .NET Framework 3.0 package is installed, as described in the "Software Requirements" section in this chapter.

4.   Mount the CD with the MS SQL 2000 Server. On the Welcome page, click Next.

5.   **Computer name page:** Select Local Computer, and click Next.

6.   **Installation Selection page:** Select Create a new instance of SQL Server, or install Client Tools, then click Next.

7. **User Information page:** Enter the registered owner of the SQL 2000 license, and click Next.

8. **Software license agreement page:** Read the agreement and if you accept it, click Yes to continue.

9. **Installation Definition page:** Select Server and Client Tools, and click Next.

10. **Instance page:** Make sure that the Default option is checked, and click Next.

11. **Setup Type page:** Choose the option Typical, and click Next.

12. **Service Account page:** Accept the default option, "Use the same account for each service. Auto start SQL Server Service." Then select the user account that will be used by the SQL services. For a local installation you can select the option Use the Local System account. If you select another account, make sure that it is a member of the computer's local Power Users group or the local Administrators group. Click Next to continue.

13. **Authentication Mode page:** Accept the default, Windows Authentication Mode, and click Next.

14. **Start Copying Files page:** Click Next to continue.

15. **Choose License Mode page:** Select the type of license you have, then click Continue to start the actual installation.

16. **Setup Complete page:** Click Finish to complete the installation of MS SQL Server 2000.

17. The next step is to install the service pack for MS SQL Server 2000. SharePoint requires at least Service Pack 3a, but you should install Service Pack 4 or later. You can get this service pack from the following URL: `www.microsoft.com/technet/prodtechnol/sql/2005/downloads`. Look for the latest service pack for MS SQL Server 2000. Download it and expand it, then start the installation file `Setup.bat`.

18. **Welcome page:** Click Next.

19. **Software License Agreement page:** Read it and if you accept it, click Yes to continue.

20. **Instance Name page:** Click Next.

21. **Connect to Server page:** Accept the default option, "The Windows account information I use to log on to my computer with (Windows authentication)," and click Next.

22. **SA Password Warning page:** Enter a password for the SQL account SA. Make sure to store it in a safe place. Then click OK.

23. **SQL Server 2000 Service Pack 4 Setup page:** Check the option "Upgrade Microsoft Search and apply SQL Server 2000 SP4 (required)," then click Continue.

24. **Error Reporting page:** If you want to activate this feature, check this box. Click OK.

25. **Start Copying Files page:** Click Next. This step will take several minutes to complete.

26. When the installation is done, you will see a dialog box reminding you to make a backup. Click OK and then Finish to complete the installation of the service pack.

> **The SQL Server service MSSQLSERVER has not started at this point. You may have to start it manually or restart the server before installing MOSS.**

This concludes the MS SQL Server 2000 installation. Since you are configuring a single-server installation, the next step will be to install MOSS on the same server. During this installation you will be asked about several service accounts for SharePoint. One of these is the configuration database administration user account. In previous versions of SharePoint, you had to manually grant this account the proper permission to the SQL Server, that is, Security Administrators and Database Creators; this is now done automatically by SharePoint's Configuration Wizard. If you later want to check this manually, follow the steps in the Try It Out below. But remember that at this stage you have not installed MOSS, so you will not find any MOSS service accounts yet.

Try It Out   **Checking Accounts Given Permissions to SQL**

1.   Log on as an administrator to the MS SQL server.

2.   Start the SQL management tool by going to Start ➪ All Programs ➪ Microsoft SQL Server ➪ Enterprise Manager.

3.   Expand the nodes: Microsoft SQL Servers ➪ SQL Server Group ➪ (local) (Windows NT).

> **A red dot at the server icon (in the system tray) indicates that the SQL Server service is not yet started. If you see this red dot, right-click on the server node and select Start now.**

4.   Expand the Security node, and click Logins to see all accounts given permissions to the SQL server. Double-click on the user account you want to check, and open the Server Role tab to see its given permissions. Then click OK to save and close it.

5.   Close the SQL Server Enterprise Manager.

SQL Server 2000 is now ready for the MOSS server. Follow the steps in the next Try It Out to install MOSS.

Try It Out   **Install MOSS 2007 Using a SQL Server**

1.   Log on as an administrator to the Windows 2003 server you will use for your MOSS and SQL Express installation.

2.   Make sure that Windows 2003 Server has the latest service packs and security patches installed by going to Start ➪ All Programs ➪ Windows Update.

3.   Verify that you have ASP.NET and the .NET Framework 3.0 package installed on this server, as previously described in the "Software Requirements" section.

4.   Start the installation by mounting the MOSS CD-ROM. You can also choose to start by using SETUP.EXE on the CD-ROM directly.

5.   The first page asks about the product key. Note that this key will indicate if you are installing the Standard or Enterprise Edition of MOSS. If you install the Standard Edition, you can later upgrade to Enterprise, but not the other way around! Enter the product key and click Continue.

> Microsoft provides free product keys for a 180-day trial period. One product key is for the MOSS Standard Edition and one is for the Enterprise Edition. This installation can later be converted to a fully licensed MOSS server simply by entering a real product key. If you do so, everything stored in the server is retained, and there is no need for a reinstallation of MOSS.

6. On the next page, choose the type of installation you want; since you will install a single-server configuration, click Advanced. Next, you can choose from three types of installations:

   ❑ **Complete:** Installs all components on the same server. You can later add more servers to form a SharePoint farm. This requires a preinstalled version SQL Server.

   ❑ **Web Front End:** Installs only the components necessary to display Web content in HTML to the users. You can later add more servers to form a SharePoint farm. This requires a preinstalled SQL Server.

   ❑ **Stand-alone:** Installs all components, plus the SQL Express database on this computer; that is, it performs the same type of installation as Basic, but allows the administrator to configure more settings, such as the file locations. You cannot add servers later to this setup.

7. Select Complete installation, then switch to the File Location tab and choose where the SharePoint files will be installed. For the best performance, use a physical disk other than the Windows boot disk. Click Install Now when all the settings are okay, and you are ready to start the installation.

8. After the installation, you will be prompted to run the SharePoint Product and Technologies Configuration Wizard. Click Close to close the installation program and start the Configuration Wizard.

9. On the Welcome page, click Next, then click Yes to agree that the IIS will be restarted during the configuration. This process now starts, and takes about 5 to 15 minutes, depending on the server hardware.

10. On the Connect to a server farm page, you can choose between connect to an existing SharePoint farm or create a new one. Since this is the first server you are installing, you must select No, I want to create a new server farm, and then click Next.

11. On the Specify Configuration Database Settings page (see Figure 4-2), you can define which SQL server this SharePoint server will use, plus the name of the configuration database, and the database access user account. Enter the name of the database server (i.e., the local server for a stand-alone installation or a separate server for a small farm). Accept the default name for the configuration database, then enter the user account that SharePoint will use whenever it communicates with the SQL Server. Click Next to continue.

> The user account defined as the Database Access Account will automatically be granted permissions as Security Admins and Database Creators in the SQL Server, by the Configuration Wizard.

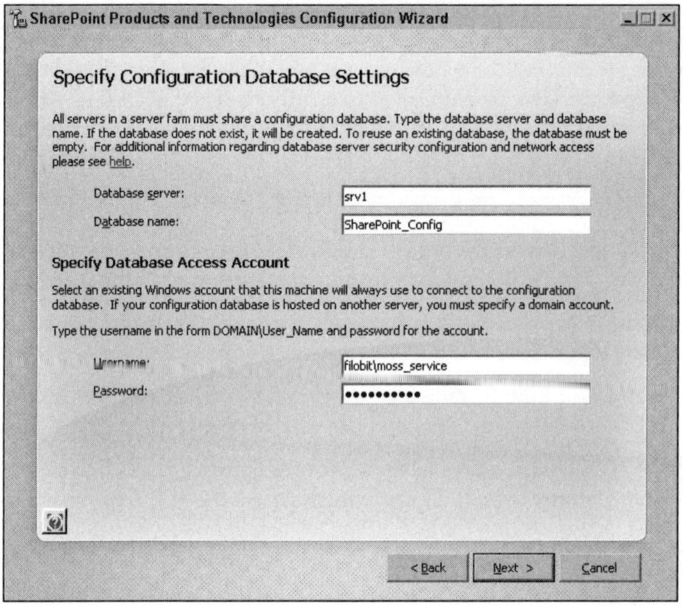

Figure 4-2

12. On the Configure SharePoint Central Administration Web Application page, you will define the TCP port number used by the web application (i.e., an extended virtual IIS server) that will host the Central Administration tool. By default, this TCP port number is randomly chosen, but a good tip is to set this number to something easier to remember, for example 5000. You must also choose the type of authentication provider. Unless you have configured the Kerberos settings in your Windows domain, select NTLM, and click Next to continue to next page.

13. On the Completing the SharePoint Products and Technologies Configuration Wizard page, you will see a summary of your chosen settings. If something is wrong, then click Back and correct the error. If all is okay, click Next to start the configuration process, which will create the Central Administration tool, and the virtual IIS servers and applications pools, just to mention a few things.

14. When the Configuration Wizard is completed, click Finish to close this page. Next, the Central Administration tool will open.

15. The installation and basic configuration is completed, but you will need to perform several more steps before the new SharePoint server has a user site up and running. Just look at the text in red on the left side of this page, saying "Server Farm Configuration Not Complete!" To assist you, SharePoint displays a task list on the home page of its Central Administration tool, which you should follow in the given order. Start by clicking on READ FIRST for deployment instructions. On the page with the task details is a description of this task and what you are supposed to do next. Click the link in the Action field, to see the Quick Start Guide. Next click Delete Item and then Yes to remove this item from the task list.

16. The next task is Initial deployment: Add servers to farm. This task should take you to the Operations page, and its link Servers in farm. If it does not; simply open the Operations page and click the Servers in farm link manually. On that page you will see a summary of all SharePoint servers in the farm, and it will consist of just one single server for now, since this is the first server in the farm. This server is also running several services, such as the Central Administration service, the Windows SharePoint Services database, and Windows SharePoint Services web application. At this time, there is nothing to change on this page, so click Home on the top menu bar to return to the task list, then delete this task, as described in the previous step.

17. The next task is Initial deployment: Assign services to servers. This task will take you to the Operations page, and its Services on server link. Here, you can see a list of all services for the farm. Select the Single Server or Web Server for small server farms option at the top of the page (see Figure 4-3), then look at the list of services below. If there is any service with the comment Required on Farm that is not running, click the Start link in the Action column. By default, none of these services is running:

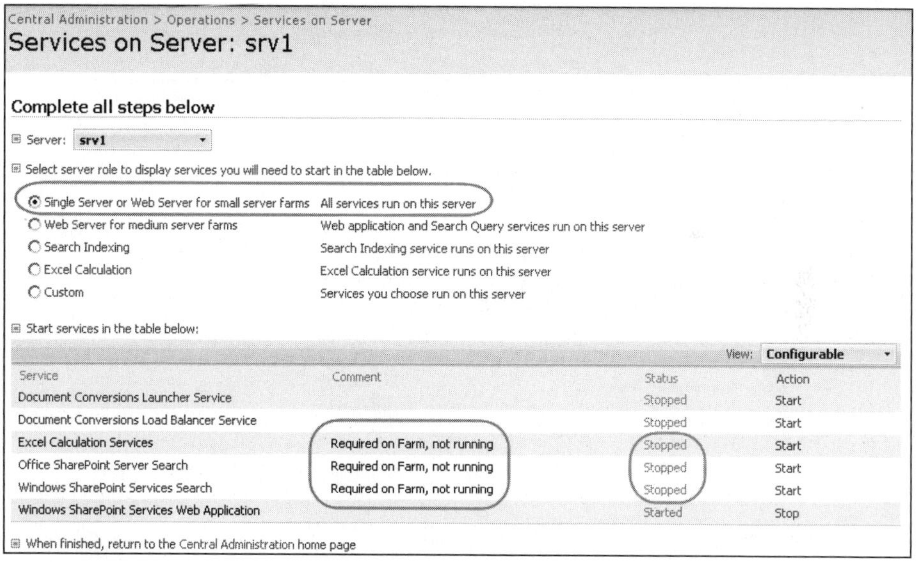

Figure 4-3

a. Click Start for the Excel Calculation Services.

b. Click Start for the Office SharePoint Server Search. This will open a new page (see Figure 4-4) where you can configure the search settings. You can choose if this server will be running the indexing service and/or the Search Query service. Check both of these options to have this server run both indexing and search queries. This is the way that you define what SharePoint role a specific server have when there is more than one SharePoint server in this farm. Add an e-mail address that will receive any messages about the Search service. Next, enter the user name and password for the Farm Search Service Account. This account will be used by the Windows 2003 Office Search Service. For a simple installation of MOSS, you can use the same account here as for the other service accounts (`sp_service`). You can see the file location for the index files listed here, but you cannot change it. Select indexer performance if necessary, or keep the default setting, Partly reduced. Finally, you can select one particular server that will be responsible for running the indexing process. Since this is a very CPU-intensive task, it may be a good idea to have a separate server dedicated to index crawling. Click Start to save and close this page.

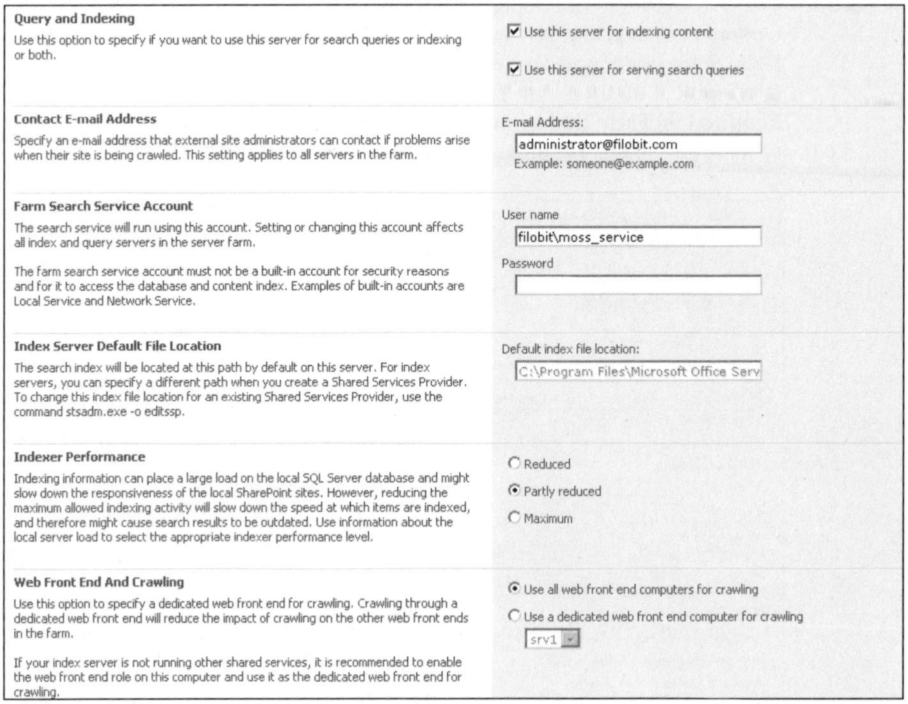

Query and Indexing
Use this option to specify if you want to use this server for search queries or indexing or both.

☑ Use this server for indexing content

☑ Use this server for serving search queries

Contact E-mail Address
Specify an e-mail address that external site administrators can contact if problems arise when their site is being crawled. This setting applies to all servers in the farm.

E-mail Address:
`administrator@filobit.com`
Example: someone@example.com

Farm Search Service Account
The search service will run using this account. Setting or changing this account affects all index and query servers in the server farm.

The farm search service account must not be a built-in account for security reasons and for it to access the database and content index. Examples of built-in accounts are Local Service and Network Service.

User name
`filobit\moss_service`
Password

Index Server Default File Location
The search index will be located at this path by default on this server. For index servers, you can specify a different path when you create a Shared Services Provider. To change this index file location for an existing Shared Services Provider, use the command stsadm.exe -o editssp.

Default index file location:
`C:\Program Files\Microsoft Office Serv`

Indexer Performance
Indexing information can place a large load on the local SQL Server database and might slow down the responsiveness of the local SharePoint sites. However, reducing the maximum allowed indexing activity will slow down the speed at which items are indexed, and therefore might cause search results to be outdated. Use information about the local server load to select the appropriate indexer performance level.

○ Reduced
◉ Partly reduced
○ Maximum

Web Front End And Crawling
Use this option to specify a dedicated web front end for crawling. Crawling through a dedicated web front end will reduce the impact of crawling on the other web front ends in the farm.

If your index server is not running other shared services, it is recommended to enable the web front end role on this computer and use it as the dedicated web front end for crawling.

◉ Use all web front end computers for crawling
○ Use a dedicated web front end computer for crawling
 `srv1`

Figure 4-4

c. Click Start for the Windows SharePoint Services Search. This is also a long configuration page (see Figure 4-5). Use this page to configure how WSS Search will index the help files (but not the WSS content) in SharePoint. Enter a user name to be used as the service account, plus its password. Do not use built-in accounts for this setting. For simple installations, you can use the same account here as for other services (such as `sp_service`)! Then enter a user name and password to be used as the Content Access Account (which account this service will use when indexing content). Accept the default database server name and its database table name, and then define how often this content will be indexed; the default is once every five minutes. Click Start when ready.

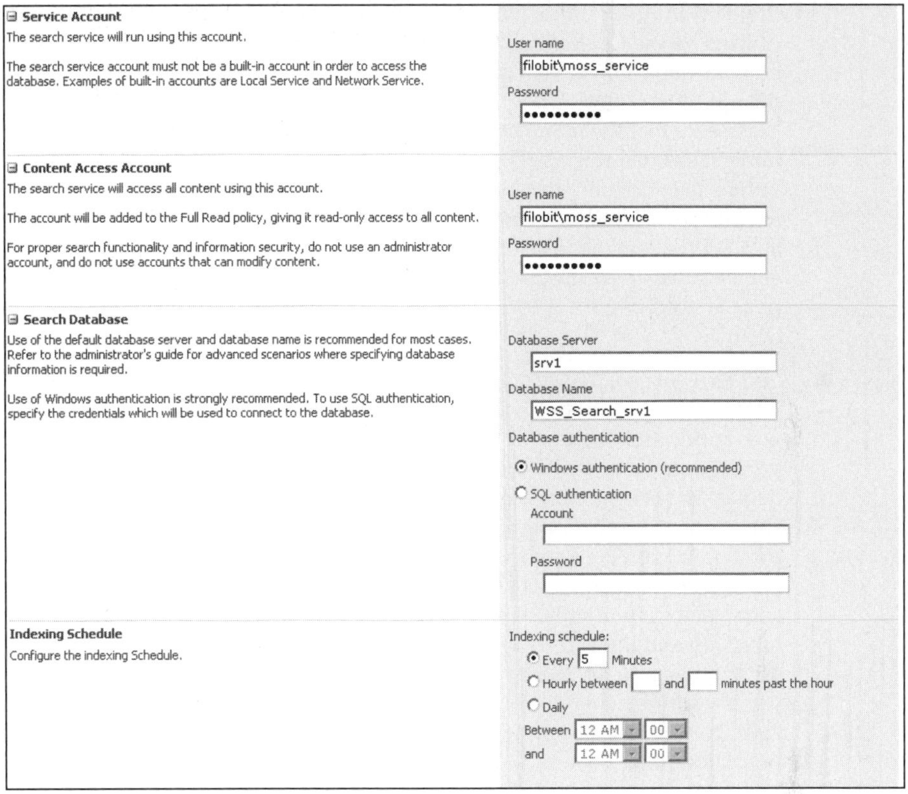

Figure 4-5

18. The Services on Server opens again. Notice that there is no service marked as "Required on Farm not running" any more. Although there are some services not yet started, at this time you do not need them. Later, you will come back to this page again. Click Home to return to the Administrators task list. Delete this task now.

19. The final task is to create a Shared Service Provider (SSP). You will learn more about this SSP in Chapter 5, but for now, open this task, and click its Action link, Configure server farm's shared services. On the next page, you will configure a number of settings:

> During the following procedure, you will start with one web page, then temporarily switch to another page to create web applications, then go back to the first page again. This may happen several times, depending on your configuration.

a. **SSP Name:** Note the name of this SSP: SharedServices1. Here, you configure the web application that the SSP will use. Click Create a new Web Application. A second page will now show up; this page is very long with lots of settings. Use it to define the new web application for the SSP. Start by changing the Port number to something like 5001 (if you want to continue with the same number series you used for the web application utilized by the Central Administration tool). Notice that the Description name for the new IIS web site will change to reflect the TCP port number chosen. Accept the other default settings, but further down on this page you will see an Application Pool section. Make sure that the name here also contains the TCP port number, to make it easy to understand that this application pool is connected to the virtual IIS web site above. Enter a user account and its password, to be used by the application pool; for example, `sp_service`. Note that this account will automatically be granted permission to the SQL Server database as Security Admins and Database Creators. Then click OK to save and close this page. You will now be back at the previous page, the SSP configuration page. If you see a warning stating "You must specify a value for this required field," it can be ignored, since you have not yet completed this page.

b. You have just created the web application for the SSP itself. The next step is to define what web application users' personal sites, My Site, will use. You can create a separate web application for the My Site or use an existing web application. To create a new web application, click Create a new Web application. This opens the web page where you define the new web application. In the IIS Web Site section, select Create a new IIS web site, and set the port number to something easy to remember, for example 6000. Then in the Application Pool section, select Create new application pool;" notice that the name of this application pool is identical to that of the virtual IIS web site above. This is smart, since it will make it easier to understand which application pool is used by which virtual IIS web site. Next select Configurable, and enter the user account for the application pool. In most installations, you will do fine with the same user account that you used for the SSP application pool you created in step a above. Click OK to close and save the web application creation page. Once again, you are taken back to the SSP configuration page.

> Note that if you want to use the same web application for both the portal web site and My Site, then you must create the web application and the site collection for the portal site before you define what web application My Site will have!

c. The next section on this SSP configuration page is SSP Service Credentials. Enter the user name and password that this service will use for interservice communications and for running SSP-scoped timer jobs. You can use the same user account that you used for steps a and b above.

d. Note the database names to be used for the SSP Database, and the Search Database; accept the settings for these two sections.

e. Note the name of the listed index server. If you have more than one index server you could choose which one that will crawl the content for all web applications associated with this SSP. Here, you can set the exact file location to be used for the index files.

f. If you want to configure Secure Socket Layer (SSL) to be used when communicating with Web services for this SSP, select Yes in this section; otherwise, select No. Be sure that you have installed the necessary SSL certificate before you activate SSL.

g. Click OK to save and start creating this Shared Service Provider. This step may take several minutes, depending on your server hardware.

Let's summarize what you have at this stage: MOSS is installed, using Advanced installation mode. You have configured the required services, such as the search service, and you have just completed the installation and configuration of a Shared Service Provider instance, named SharedServices1, which among several other things, also contains the users' My Site configuration. The next time you open the home page in Central Administration, there is no longer a warning that your server is not yet configured. Instead of the previous Administrator's Tasks list with 4 items, you know see a new list with 10 new items. In Chapter 5, you will learn more about these tasks items, but for now you can let them be.

Just to make sure that your SharePoint installation really works, let's create the first portal web site. If you tried the Basic installation mode described earlier, you may remember that it automatically created a portal site for you. So, why not create the same portal site manually this time? It is simple, just follow the steps below:

1. Open the SharePoint Central Administration tool, then switch to the Application Manager page.

2. Just like any SharePoint site, user web sites, such as the portal site, must have a web application that hosts its site collection. First, you create the web application:

   a. Click Create or extend web application in the SharePoint Web Application Management section.

   b. Click Create a new Web application. (You will recognize the next page from when you created the Shared Service Provider.)

   c. In the IIS Web Site section, you define what virtual IIS server this new web application will use. Since it will later be used to create a user site, you really need to have a virtual IIS web site using TCP port 80. So, either select "Use an existing IIS web site" and select Default Web Site, or create a new IIS web site using port 80 (make sure to stop or remove the default web site, in this case).

   d. In the Application Pool section, you define what application pool the virtual IIS web site will use. You can use one that SharePoint is already using, but the best practice is to create a separate application pool for the users' web site: Click Create new application pool and enter the user account for this application pool. As before, it is okay in most situations to use the same account that you used for the other SharePoint application pools.

   e. In the Database Name and Authentication section, you will see the default database name for this web application. Since this will be the database used for storing user web sites, it should have a name that is easy to recognize. Change it to anything meaningful to you; for example, WSS_ Content. Click OK to save and close this page and create the new web application.

3. After creating a web application, the next step is to create the site collection, and thus also its top site. The exact look and feel of this new site is dependent on the site template you choose. Since the purpose of this exercise is to create the same portal site structure that the Basic installation mode did, you will choose the Collaboration Portal site template, as described next:

   a. Make sure that the Application Management page is open, then click Create site collection, in the SharePoint Site Management section.

   b. Check that the web application listed at the top of this web form is the one you just created in step 2 above; if not, click on the current name, and select Change Web Application.

   c. Enter the Title for this new portal site, and enter a description.

   d. Notice the URL; you will use it to open this portal.

   e. In the Template Selection section, open the Publishing tab, and select Collaboration Portal.

   f. In the Primary Site Collection Administrator section, enter the user account that will be the full administrator for this site collection.

   g. In the Secondary Site Collection Administrator section, enter the user account that will be a secondary administrator for this site collection, if any.

   h. Click OK to close this page and start creating this site collection. Note that the Collaboration Portal site template is rather complex, and therefore it will take some time to complete this step. When it is done, you will have one top site, and five subsites, each based on the advanced content management functionality that SharePoint calls a Publishing Page.

   i. When done, click the link on the next page to open the new collaboration portal site. It should look similar to Figure 4-1 earlier in this chapter.

After the Installation of MOSS Using the MS SQL Server

Two things you should do immediately after the installation of MOSS 2003 has completed:

❑ Download and install the latest service pack for MOSS and WSS, if any.

❑ Do a full backup of the SharePoint Portal Server environment with the backup utility that comes with MOSS (see the end of this chapter for a quick guide) or with your ordinary backup program, if it is SharePoint-aware.

Checking the New Folder and Applications

The portal site is now up and running. Take a look at what has changed in the Windows 2003 server. You have several new file directories used by MOSS and the underlying WSS environment. For example, you will find that a number of newly created web applications, for example, a virtual IIS server that has been both created and extended by the installation program and the Configuration Wizard. Since MOSS is much more advanced than WSS, you will find more web applications in the IIS Web Sites node. To see them, open the IIS manager: Start ➪ Administration Tools ➪ Internet Information Service (IIS) Manager. Then expand the node Web Sites. Note that you have a number of IIS virtual servers here, usually with names like these:

❑ **SharePoint Central Administration v3:** Used by SharePoint for the administration web site. This virtual IIS web server was created during the initial phase of the MOSS installation, before the portal site was created.

❑ **Default Web Site:** This is the virtual IIS web server that is used by the Collaboration Portal site collection.

❑ **SharePoint – *nnn*:** (*nnn* = the TCP port number selected by you.) This virtual IIS web server is used by the Shared Service Provider and its first instance, SharedServices1.

❑ **SharePoint – *nnn*:** (*nnn* = the TCP port number selected by you.) This virtual IIS web server is used by the My Site site collection, unless you chose to install My Site on an existing web application.

❑ **Office Server Web Services:** This is a general service that enables MOSS and other Office Server applications to use Web service techniques to retrieve or store data from SharePoint's database.

Right-click on the virtual IIS server SharePoint Central Administration v3, and open its properties. It will, by default, use the application pool SharePoint Central Administration v3. Expand the Application Pools node (located directly above the Web Sites node), right-click on either of the two application pools mentioned above, and switch to the Identity tab. Note that the security account that this application pool is using is the user account chosen by you when you installed MOSS. This user account is also granted permission to the SQL Server 2000 database.

To summarize this type of installation: MOSS uses up to five virtual IIS web servers for an Advanced installation, one for the web sites that your SharePoint users utilize and up to four others for the administration of SharePoint. All of these virtual servers use separate application pools, and each of them can have its own security account, or you can configure them to use the same account.

Backing Up MOSS 2007

The obvious thing to do after a successful installation is to back up the SharePoint server. You will read a lot more about backing up and restoring in Chapter 14. However, since you have just completed a MOSS installation, you are probably anxious to know how to protect your work with a backup, so the basics of backing up MOSS are covered here.

With MOSS 2007 come two backup programs: One is the `stsadm.exe` utility, and one is a backup procedure included in SharePoint's Central Administration tool. Using the latter, you can quickly create a full backup of your new MOSS environment, including both user web sites and administrative web sites. In previous versions of SharePoint, you needed to have SQL Client Tools installed on the SharePoint server in order to perform backup and restore, but this is not necessary in SharePoint 2007. To use the Central Administration backup procedure, make sure that the following accounts have Write permission to the file backup location:

❑ The database server's SQL service account.

❑ The WSS Timer service account (the same account as the Central Administration application pool account: `sp_appservice`).

❑ The user account used by the Central Administration application pool.

Follow the steps in the Try It Out below to back up your new MOSS server.

Do a Backup of Your MOSS Server

1. Log on to the MOSS server as an administrator.

2. Select a shared disk resource where you can store the backup files; for example, `\\DC1\SPBackup`. Make sure that the accounts in the bulleted list above have Write permission to that share.

> When you create a new file share in Windows 2003, it will by default set the permission for the group Everyone = Read. This will prohibit even administrators from writing to that share. Add the user accounts in the bulleted list above with Write permissions, or enable the group Everyone to have Full permission.

3. Start SharePoint's Central Administration tool: Start ➪ All Programs ➪ Microsoft Office Server ➪ SharePoint 3.0 Central Administration.

4. Switch to the Operations page.

5. In the Backup and Restore section, click Perform a backup. This will display a web form where you define what to back up (see Figure 4-6). Note that the smallest object you can back up is a web application (one or more site collections belonging to that web application). You can also make a backup of the complete farm, as described here:

a. Check the Farm check box. This will ensure that the complete farm is backed up.

b. Click Continue to Backup Options.

c. On the following page, make sure to select Type of backup = Full. Set the backup location where the backup files will be stored; for example, \\srv1\bkup. Note that an estimate of the volume to be backed up is listed here. When ready, click OK.

d. The backup process now starts, and a status page is displayed (see Figure 4-7). When the backup is completed, this page sets the property Phase = Completed.

Central Administration > Operations > Perform a Backup

Perform a Backup - Step 1 of 2: Select Component to Backup

Select the items you want to backup now. To start a backup, click **Continue to Backup Options**. To see a list of previous backups, click **View History** and provide a path for backup history location.

▶ Continue to Backup Options | 🔎 View History

Select	Component	Type	Description
☐	⊟ Farm	Farm	Content and configuration data for the entire server farm.
	SharePoint_Config	Configuration Database	Configuration data for the entire server farm.
☐	⊟ Windows SharePoint Services Web Application	Windows SharePoint Services Web Application	Collection of Web Applications
☐	⊟ SharePoint - 5002	Web Application	Content and configuration data for this Web application.
☐	WSS_Content_3167843c5360476987c10666fd3bc4ed	Content Database	Content for the Web Application.
☐	⊟ SharePoint - 80	Web Application	Content and configuration data for this Web application.
☐	WSS_Content_68811b525f6c4434ba360214165f1df0	Content Database	Content for the Web Application.
	⊟ WSS_Administration	Central Administration	Collection of Web Applications
	⊟ Web Application	Web Application	Content and configuration data for this Web application.
☐	SharePoint_AdminContent_649bc7cb-6626-4314-be73-cb6dd9c56c41	Content Database	Content for the Web Application.
☐	⊟ SharedServices1	Shared Services Provider	Database and Configuration Settings for this Shared Services Provider
	⊟ SharePoint - 5001	Web Application	Content and configuration data for this Web application.
☐	WSS_Content	Content Database	Content for the Web Application.
	SharedServices1_DB	Shared Service Provider Database	Stores Configuration Settings for this Shared Services Provider
	UserProfileApplication	User Profile Application	User Profile Application
	SessionStateSharedApplication	Session State	Session State
	⊟ Shared Search Index	Search index files for SharedServices1	Search index file for the Shared Services Provider
	SharedServices1_Search_DB	Search database for SharedServices1	Search database containing the property store and the crawler history
☐	Global Search Settings	Search object in configuration database	Crawler impact rules for the farm
☐	⊟ Windows SharePoint Services Help Search	Index files and Databases	Search instances for Windows SharePoint Services
	⊟ Search instance	Index files on SRV1	Search index files on the search server
	WSS_Search_SRV1	Search database for SRV1	Search database for the search server

Figure 4-6

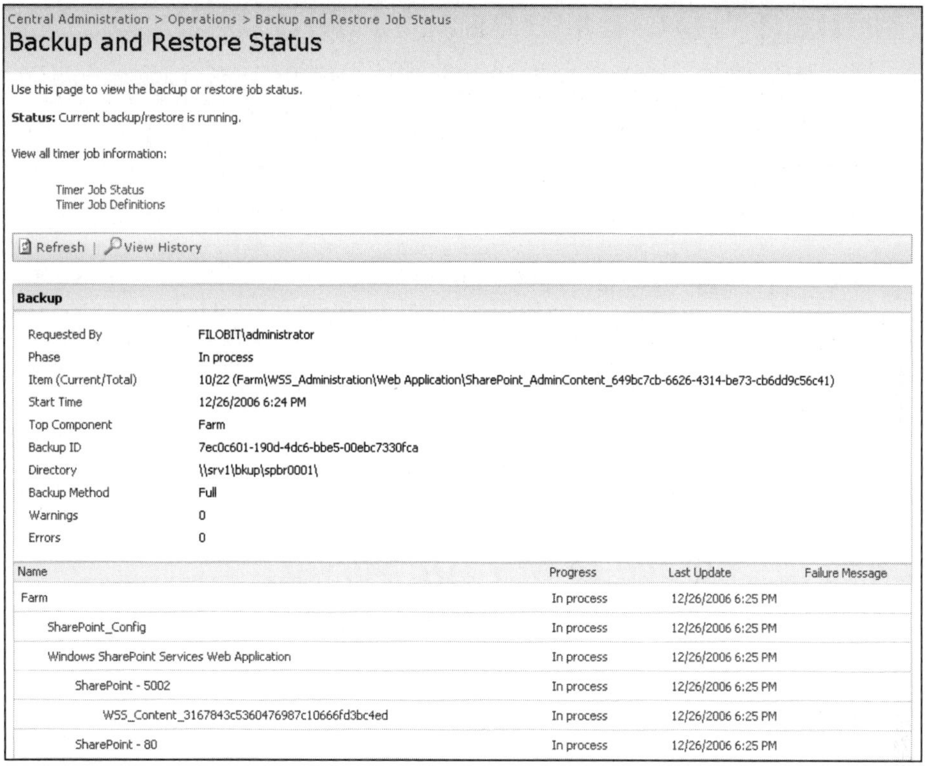

Central Administration > Operations > Backup and Restore Job Status

Backup and Restore Status

Use this page to view the backup or restore job status.

Status: Current backup/restore is running.

View all timer job information:

Timer Job Status
Timer Job Definitions

 Refresh | View History

Backup

Requested By	FILOBIT\administrator
Phase	In process
Item (Current/Total)	10/22 (Farm\WSS_Administration\Web Application\SharePoint_AdminContent_649bc7cb-6626-4314-be73-cb6dd9c56c41)
Start Time	12/26/2006 6:24 PM
Top Component	Farm
Backup ID	7ec0c601-190d-4dc6-bbe5-00ebc7330fca
Directory	\\srv1\bkup\spbr0001\
Backup Method	Full
Warnings	0
Errors	0

Name	Progress	Last Update	Failure Message
Farm	In process	12/26/2006 6:25 PM	
SharePoint_Config	In process	12/26/2006 6:25 PM	
Windows SharePoint Services Web Application	In process	12/26/2006 6:25 PM	
SharePoint - 5002	In process	12/26/2006 6:25 PM	
WSS_Content_3167843c5360476987c10666fd3bc4ed	In process	12/26/2006 6:25 PM	
SharePoint - 80	In process	12/26/2006 6:25 PM	

Figure 4-7

6. Open the file location where the backup files are stored. You will see a file named
`spbrtoc.xml`. This is a manifest file that describes all the backups stored in this folder; without
this file you cannot perform a restore, so be sure to protect it! Note that this location also contains a subfolder named `spbrnnnn`, where *nnnn* is a index starting with 0000 that increases by
one every time you run a new backup process. Inside that folder are a large number of files containing the content that is backed up.

Now you have a complete backup of all data, including any index files and user profile data. You do not
need to run a SQL backup. You have everything you need to perform a full restore if you lose data.

> **Running this type of backup will not back up the file structure of SharePoint, IIS
> settings, or domain user accounts. In order to restore data with this backup, you
> must have a MOSS installation with the same settings as when you ran the backup
> process. Otherwise, you may not be able to restore everything! A simple way to do
> this is to run a full file backup on the MOSS server, including "System State,"
> which will also back up the IIS Metabase and the Registry database on the server.**

Upgrading SQL Express to MS SQL Server

If for any reason you choose to install MOSS 2007 with a local SQL Express database and later find that you need to upgrade it to MS SQL 2000/2005 Server, you have two choices:

❑ Perform an in-place upgrade of SQL Express to a local MS SQL server. This is easy.

❑ Move from SQL Express to a separate MS SQL server. This is a complicated process.

> There is a quick guide for an in-place upgrade to SQL Server 2005. Be sure to follow Microsoft's detailed instructions for upgrading more complex SQL Server scenarios. The guide can be found at: `http://msdn2.microsoft.com/en-us/library/ms143516.aspx`.

This section describes the first option only: an in-place upgrade. If you want to move from a local database to a remote database server, you must check for a migration guide in Microsoft's Knowledge Base.

Preparing to Upgrade to MS SQL Server

The most important thing to do before starting the upgrade process is to back up your current MOSS database. You are about to perform a very sensitive operation, and if something goes wrong, you must be sure you can go back to the previous version. The previous section described how to back up your database.

During this upgrade process, no one can use the MOSS server. Make sure to pick a time when no one is using the server. Since the SQL Express version that comes with MOSS only allows up to 4 GB of data, this upgrade process should be fairly quick, depending on your server hardware, but plan for at least two hours to be on the safe side.

Upgrading MOSS to a Local MS SQL Server

As mentioned before, this is a very straightforward process. Make sure that no one is using the system before you start to upgrade, because they may lose information during this process. The best practice is to schedule this upgrade process at a specific time and date and inform all affected users when this will happen. Note that you can only upgrade SQL Express to SQL Server 2005 (any edition) but not to SQL Server 2000. If you upgrade SQL Express to SQL Server 2005, you cannot use the graphical installation mode. You must run the `Setup.exe` program with the command switch `/SKUUPGRADE=1`.

Try It Out   **Upgrade SQL Express to MS SQL Server 2005**

1. Log on to the MOSS server as an administrator.

2. Make sure that no one is using MOSS.

3. Click Start ➪ Run ➪ Browse, and locate the `Setup.exe` program for SQL Server 2005. At the end of this line, add `SKUUPGRADE=1` (see Figure 4-8) and click OK.

Figure 4-8

4. On the End User License Agreement page, read the license text, and if you agree, check I accept the licensing term and conditions and click Next.

5. The setup program will now load a number of components required for the SQL Server setup; wait until it is finished. When it is done, click Next.

6. On the Welcome page, click Next. A system configuration check is now performed; it should complete without any warnings or errors. If not, read the message and correct the problem. Click Next to continue.

7. On the Registration Information page, check that the server name is correct, and click Next.

8. On the Components to install page, check the option SQL Server Database Services, and click Next.

9. On the Instance Name page, make sure to use the option Default instance to upgrade the current SQL Express. If you have more instances installed on the SQL Express, then click the button Installed Instances to get a list of these instances. Then click OK and make sure that the option Named Instance = OFFICESERVERS (which is the default name that SharePoint uses for Basic installations of MOSS) is selected. When you're ready, click Next.

10. On the Existing components page, check the option SQL Server Database Services (which is your SQL Express installation), then click Next.

11. On the Upgrade Logon Information page, make sure that Windows Authentication Mode is selected, then click Next.

12. On the Ready to Install page, click Install to start the actual installation. This will take 5–60 minutes, depending on the size of the SQL Express database and the hardware configuration of the server.

13. When the setup is complete, make sure that there are no errors or warnings. Click Next, and then Finish.

Open a web browser, and check the MOSS environment. Make sure that it works like before. You should see no differences, except possibly better performance. Open the MS SQL Server Enterprise Manager and take a look at the databases for the local server. You should see the same databases as before, using the same instance name.

> **Do not remove the SQL Express database from the MOSS Server! It is used by the upgraded MS SQL Server and contains the actual databases.**

Post-Installation Tasks

The first thing to do after an installation or upgrade is to test SharePoint. Log on as an administrator, start Internet Explorer, enter the URL for the MOSS portal, then open the Central Administration tool and make sure that everything works as before.

You may recall from earlier in this chapter that there are several databases used by MOSS. Microsoft does not want you to modify them in any way other than running SharePoint's web sites and the Central Administration tool. However, there is some interesting information hidden in these databases, as described in the following sections.

The Configuration Database

The purpose of the configuration database is to store SharePoint's configuration settings, such as what front-end servers exist, their role, and what back-end server is used. There is only one single configuration database for all SharePoint servers in the farm. It coordinates how all the SharePoint servers know each other and their roles.

If you need to expand the SharePoint farm with a new front-end server, you install MOSS on it and during the configuration you tell it to connect to the existing SharePoint farm, which is the same as saying the server will use an existing configuration database. This concept is very similar to the way that a new Windows 2003 domain controller is added to an existing Windows domain. If you need to remove a SharePoint server, you simply disconnect it from the configuration database.

The default name of this SQL database is `SharePoint_Config` (possibly with a GUID string at the end of the name, which is typical for a Basic installation of MOSS). This database contains a lot of interesting information regarding your SharePoint environment. For example, you can look into the tables of the configuration database to see what portal site it belongs, as explained in the following Try It Out.

> **Never change the SQL tables unless specifically instructed to do so by Microsoft Support. If you make a mistake, it most likely will corrupt the database!**

Try It Out   Check the Configuration Database Tables

1. After the MOSS is installed, log on as a SQL administrator.

2. Open the SQL Server Manager Studio. Tip: If you don't have this management tool, then look at SQL Admin Studio from www.simego.com, which also works fine with SQL Express databases.

3. Expand the folders in this tool until you see the `SharePoint_Config` database.

4. Click on Tables to see all tables in this database.

5. Right-click on the table SiteMap, and select Open Table.

6. This will open the table. Look for the column named Path, which lists the default URL address to user and administrative web sites in this farm.

7. There are several interesting tables to look at here, but do not change anything!

> Remember, never change the SQL tables unless instructed to do so by Microsoft Support. If you make a mistake, it can corrupt the database!

The Content Database

All data stored in the SharePoint portal site or any of its WSS sites is contained in the content database. By default the name for this database is `WSS_Content`.

This database will grow as your SharePoint environment is used by users. It is possible to create more than one content database; the first one is by default limited to 15,000 site collections. You will not hit that limit immediately in most organizations. Note that it is the number of site collections that counts, that is, the top sites only, not their subsites, if any. In reality that could mean 10 or 100 times more sites in total, all stored in the same content database. All sites belonging to the same site collection must reside in the same content database; it is not possible to split a large site collection over several content databases!

If you have more than one MS SQL server, you can create new content databases on these other SQL servers. This works well when you have a distributed organization, and the network connections between the different locations are low bandwidth (for example, less than 1024 Kb/s). If you use a locally placed SharePoint server and a local SQL server with content databases, the performance is much better for the user who needs to work with documents and other information in the WSS sites. Previously, this was a complex task to complete, but in SharePoint 2007 it is easy, as long as you can accept that these remote users have their own site collection:

1. Create a new web application. Now you can select what SQL server and database this web application will use. Make sure to use a SQL server near the user's location.

2. Create a site collection in this web application for these remote users.

3. Instruct the remote users to use that site collection when possible.

If you must have one single site collection for all users, then there is no way of distributing the SharePoint database using standard Microsoft tools. As third-party vendors explore the possibilities presented by SharePoint 2007, they will develop more solutions to meet this and other needs.

The User Profile Database

SharePoint Portal Server can run in a Windows NT 4 or Windows 2000/2003 domain environment. If you have been in the IT business for some time, you may remember that the information about user accounts in Windows NT 4 was sparse, to say the least. It just contained the user account name and a description, but no information about departments, phone numbers, e-mail addresses, and so on. Since one of the primary objectives in SharePoint is to make it easier for users to find information, SharePoint needs to store a lot of properties about each user. Microsoft resolved this by creating a specific User Profile database. To see what user profiles are stored in this database, use a SQL database management tool (see the previous section about the configuration database), then expand the `SharedService1_DB` database, right-click on the table UserProfileFull, and select Open Table.

This database is exclusive to MOSS; you do not find it in a pure WSS environment. Unlike the previous SharePoint version, these user profiles are now stored in the database used by the Shared Service Provider, by default named `SharedServices1_DB` (possibly with a GUID suffix if MOSS was installed in Basic mode). A large organization may have several hundred megabytes in this database, but it still will be a very small database compared to the content database.

The information in this database may be entered manually by the SharePoint administrator and to some extent by the user, or it can be automatically imported if the users belong to an Active Directory domain. The latter option requires that the Active Directory be updated with all the user properties you want to import into the user profile.

In the next chapter, you will get all the details about how to configure this importing process and how to control what properties to import from the Active Directory. You will also learn how to define what properties the users are allowed to change.

The user profile also stores information about SharePoint's audiences. This term refers to groups of SharePoint users, like all Salespeople, or all Brain Surgeons, or New Employees. You can filter the information displayed on the portal site to only show information targeted to the audience group. In the next chapter, you will learn how to create and manage audiences.

More MOSS Databases

Besides the more common databases mentioned above, there are several more. Their purpose is to store information related to specific tasks or functions in SharePoint, such as searching or system tables. These databases are:

❑ **SharedServices1_Search _DB:** Stores the settings regarding MOSS indexing and searching.

❑ **SharedServices_Content:** Stores system tables, lists, and variables used by the Shared Service Provider.

❑ **SharePoint_AdminContent:** Stores content in the Central Administration tool.

❑ **WSS_Search:** Stores information used by the WSS Search feature, that is, the system searching the help system.

> **Once again: Do no change any of these databases, unless instructed to do so by Microsoft Support!**

Uninstalling MOSS

The final section of this chapter is about removing MOSS. Remember that when you install MOSS, you also install WSS. Unlike the earlier SharePoint 2003, now both MOSS and WSS will be removed when you uninstall MOSS. You can choose to remove just MOSS and WSS, or MOSS, WSS, and the databases. If the databases remain, you can later reinstall MOSS and WSS and reconnect to these databases.

Uninstalling the Portal Site but Leaving MOSS Intact

This removes the MOSS portal site and its team sites from a given web application, but it does not remove the binary files from the server. For example, you may have a test environment using a separate web application, and you might also have a production MOSS using another web application on the same physical Windows 2003 server.

To remove the test environment, follow these steps:

1. Start SharePoint's Central Administration tool: Start ⇨ Administrative Tools ⇨ SharePoint 3.0 Central Administration.

2. Switch to the Application Management page, then click Delete site collection, in the SharePoint Site Management section.

3. Next to the label Site Collection, click on No Selection, then Change Site Collection, and select the site collection used by the portal site, then click OK.

4. On the next page, make sure that you have selected the correct site collection, then click Delete.

5. Optional: If you want to remove the web application as well, then select the Delete Web Application link on the Application Management page. Just make sure that there are no other site collections using that web application.

All binary files for MOSS and WSS are still there. You can now create a new portal using the same web application (unless you deleted it) or another one. If you want to do this, look at the earlier sections in this chapter where the steps for creating portal sites are described.

Removing MOSS Completely

A more drastic method is to remove MOSS completely from the Windows 2003 server. If this MOSS installation were using a SQL Express database, this would also be deleted, but if it was a preinstalled SQL Server, it would not be removed. If you want to remove a remaining database engine, you must do this separately after you uninstall MOSS.

To remove MOSS and WSS binary files completely from a Windows 2003 Server, follow these steps:

1. Start Add or Remove Programs in the Control Panel.

2. Locate Microsoft Office SharePoint Server 2007 and click the Remove button, and then Yes to confirm that you want to uninstall MOSS. Note that you may also get a second warning stating that you will delete sites. Click OK to accept this.

3. On the Maintenance Mode Options page, select the option Remove the server components of Microsoft Office SharePoint Portal Server 2003, and click Next.

4. When the removal process is done, you click Close to finish this program, then click OK to do a system reboot.

5. If this is a Basic installation of MOSS, then the removal of SQL Express 2005 now starts automatically. If this is an Advanced installation of MOSS, then the database binary files will not be affected; however, the databases MOSS has created on this SQL server will be removed during the removal of MOSS.

6. When the installation is completed, click Close, then click Yes to reboot the server.

When you remove MOSS, you also remove the virtual IIS web servers used by SharePoint's web applications, along with their corresponding application pools. The default web site, however, remains after the installation, along with its application pool.

Summary

In this chapter, you learned that:

❑ MOSS is more advanced (and, therefore, more complicated to install) than WSS.

❑ MOSS has a different type of SQL Express database compared to WSS, which is limited to 4 GB.

❑ MOSS features:

  ❑ Targeting of information on the portal site.

  ❑ Global searching, both inside SharePoint and outside.

  ❑ My Site is used both as a personal web site for the user and to describe the user's properties, such as the e-mail address, phone numbers, department, picture, and much more.

❑ The license model for MOSS is based on the edition selected, Standard or Enterprise; the number of MOSS servers; and number of client access licenses (CAL) that can access MOSS.

❑ Even if you only read information in the portal site, you will need a separate CAL.

❑ MOSS can use MS SQL Server 2005 or 2000.

❑ MOSS can use a local or remote database. A local database can be either SQL Express or MS SQL Server 2000/2005.

❑ You learned the following definitions:

  ❑ **Stand-alone:** MOSS with a local SQL Express.

  ❑ **Single-Server:** MOSS with a local MS SQL Server 2000/2005.

  ❑ **Front-End Server:** A server that has MOSS binaries installed and running one or more of the MOSS roles.

  ❑ **Back-End Server:** A server running MS SQL, used by MOSS for storing data.

  ❑ **Small farm:** MOSS with a remote server running MS SQL Server 2000/2005.

  ❑ **Large and medium farm:** A MOSS configuration with two or more MOSS servers running one or more roles, such as the Web, Index and Search roles.

  ❑ **The Web service:** The service responsible for contact with the user client.

- ❑ **The Search service:** The service responsible for answering any search queries from the client.

- ❑ **The Index service:** The service responsible for crawling through and indexing information.

❑ There are seven different databases in MOSS, used either for administrative purposes or for storing content in user web sites.

- ❑ If you implement the Single Sign-On feature of MOSS, it creates one more database type.

- ❑ There may be any number of content databases, but only one each of the other types.

❑ Hardware requirements for MOSS are higher than for WSS.

❑ You can use the formula for calculating the normalized operations per second (NOPS) to find out the load for a given user population was covered.

❑ Even a small farm may support up to 10,000 users in a typical organization, as long as the hardware is properly configured.

❑ You should make sure that the SQL Server always has at least 50 percent free disk space for its maintenance utilities.

❑ MOSS requires ASP.NET 2.0 and Windows Workflow Foundation with the .NET 3.0 Framework.

❑ MOSS uses several more web applications, virtual IIS web sites, than WSS.

❑ The security account for the application pool is used when communicating with the database.

❑ There are a number of service accounts that you can define during the installation of MOSS, such as:

- ❑ The application pool security account.

- ❑ The default content access account.

- ❑ The configuration database user account.

❑ A Basic installation of MOSS is very easy and fast to perform; it does not ask about the application pool security account or the configuration database user account.

❑ The installation of MOSS must be followed by an installation of the latest service pack.

❑ Some of the new file directories created during the MOSS installation are:

- ❑ `C:\Program Files\Common Files\Microsoft Shared\web server extensions\12`: This is the general file structure for all site definitions and features of MOSS and/or WSS.

- ❑ `C:\Program Files\Microsoft Office Servers\12.0`: This location has several folders and files specific to SharePoint 2007, including the search index.

- ❑ `C:\Program Files\Microsoft Microsoft Office Servers\12.0\Data\MSSQL`: This folder structure stores the SQL Express content.

❑ You can use the SharePoint Central Administration tool for complete backups of all data including all portal sites, all team sites, and index files.

❑ You can upgrade a local SQL Express database to MS SQL Server 2005. This is a straightforward process.

❑ It is possible to migrate from a local SQL Express database to a remote version of MS SQL Server, but it is a complicated process. Check Microsoft's Knowledge Base for more details on this procedure.

❑ You can uninstall MOSS in several ways:

❑ Remove the portal site but not the binaries.

❑ Remove the binaries but not the databases (must be an Advanced installation of MOSS).

❑ Remove everything.

❑ When removing SharePoint completely, you must start by removing MOSS, which also removes WSS, and then the database, if you used a local database.

In the next chapter, you will learn more about managing and configuring this new MOSS environment.

Configuring and Managing MOSS 2007

In this chapter, you learn how to configure and manage the MS Office SharePoint Server 2007. You learn about configuring shared services, global searching, how to import user properties from the Active Directory, and how to target information for different groups of users. Even if you do not plan to implement MOSS at this time, this chapter may still interest you because it describes the features that are specific to MOSS, as opposed to the pure WSS environment. This will help you understand the differences, and when using WSS with MOSS is a better choice than using WSS alone.

Basic Configuration

In Chapter 4, you learned how to install MOSS 2007, and to create a site collection containing a collaboration portal site. You may recall that SharePoint's Central Administration tool, right after the installation of MOSS, displayed a list of four administrative tasks that you had to complete in order to set up the basic configuration:

- ❑ **READ FIRST: Click this link for deployment instructions:** A link to the Quick Guide for administrators.

- ❑ **Initial deployment: Add servers to farm:** This task will take you to the Operators page and its link: Servers in farm. This page displayed all servers in this farm, both SharePoint front-end servers, and SQL Server 2000/2005 back-end servers.

- ❑ **Initial deployment: Assign services to servers:** This task will take you to the Operators page and its link: Services on server; here you configure what services will run on what SharePoint server. This is also the page where you start and stop these services.

- ❑ **Configure server farm's shared services:** This task will open the Shared Services Administration page, where you can create the first shared service provider (SSP), including search, user profile import, audiences, and Excel services.

After completing all four of these tasks, MOSS is ready to be used for creating user web sites. However, there are a lot of new configuration tasks that you may or may not need to complete, in order to activate optional features in MOSS. And this is what you will learn in this chapter. Some of these optional configurations most frequently used in MOSS installations are these:

❑ **Outgoing e-mail settings:** Before MOSS can send e-mail to recipients, you must configure how this SMTP-based communication will take place. For example, MOSS will send e-mail to users that request alert messages when something changes, such as when a new document is added to a document library.

❑ **Incoming e-mail settings:** This will make MOSS work as a receiving SMTP server, accepting mail to configured document libraries, in effect working as mailboxes.

❑ **Global search:** This configures what MOSS will index and what users can search for.

❑ **Active Directory Import:** This configures MOSS to regularly import user properties from the Active Directory into a User Profile database.

❑ **Audience Targeting:** Define groups of users that will be able to view specific content, such as Web Parts, news items, and documents.

❑ **Excel Trusted Locations:** MOSS Enterprise Edition comes with a specific Excel Service that can work as a repository for Excel spreadsheets and graphs, which users can view and work with, using only a web browser. To make this work, the administrator must point out where these Excel files can be stored.

There are actually a lot more settings and configurations available for a MOSS server, which you will see in the next section.

Advanced Administration

The previous list contains just a few of the settings that an administrator has to know about, in order to get the most out of a MOSS environment. In fact, there are more settings available than this book can cover, but you will learn all the important ones here. Remember that MOSS is a very advanced product that also easily can be expanded by adding new features or connecting to other systems. Even so, MOSS is easy to manage and configure, as long as you take it step by step and know what you are doing.

Two Important Tasks to Start With

After all the four tasks in the basic configuration part are completed, you will see a new list of administrator tasks show up on the Central Administrations Home page (if not, press F5 to refresh your web browser). You may remember that directly after the installation of MOSS, text in red said "Server Farm Configuration Not Complete!" Now this text is gone, but still there are most likely some other settings to configure before opening MOSS to all users. Note that in most installation scenarios you do not have to perform all the administrative tasks in this list, nor do you need to follow it in order. In fact, you usually do not follow this order. To help you configure SharePoint 2007 in a proper way, this chapter will present typical tasks to perform and in a more logical order. The complete list of the new administrator tasks is shown in the following table.

No	Task	Description
1.	Incoming e-mail settings	Enable SharePoint to accept incoming SMTP messages, and store them in mail-enabled document libraries.
2.	Outgoing e-mail settings	Enable SharePoint to send SMTP messages to users and administrators.
3.	Configure Workflow Settings	Define how Workflow processes will operate.
4.	Configure Session Throttles for InfoPath Form Services	Define settings for InfoPath, such as timeouts, if browser-enabled or not, and the like.
5.	Add/Change Excel Services Trusted Locations	Define what document library and other locations that are trusted for the Excel files used by Excel Services.
6.	Service level settings for `SharedServices1`	Open the general configuration page for this SSP instance.
7.	Check services enabled in this farm	List any warnings or errors regarding important services. Will also show if this is a trial installation.
8.	Diagnostic logging settings	Configure several logging settings, including error reports and trace loggings.
9.	Enable SSO in the farm	Single Sign-On is used to access non-Microsoft applications.
10.	Add anti-virus protection	When you have purchased an antivirus solution for SharePoint, use this link to configure it.

> If you have the task "Central Administration application pool account should be unique" listed, then you are using the same user account for both the Central Administration application pool and some other web application (probably your user portal). Best practice is to have a separate account for Central Administration; be sure to use the Action link in this task to change the application pool account for the *other* web application!

Although the previous list of tasks is long, you can start with just a two of them to get MOSS in shape to create portal sites with the fundamental features. Some of the tasks you should start with are not even listed on the Administrator Tasks list. You are supposed to know them anyhow. Do not despair! This section will show you how to configure these initial tasks, and many MOSS installations will be satisfied with just these tasks for a long time.

The First Important Task: Outgoing SMTP e-mail

This task is necessary if you want SharePoint to be able to send e-mail. A typical example of this is when a site owner adds a new member to his site, this member will get an e-mail from SharePoint, saying that the person has access, with a link to this site. Another example is when SharePoint discovers some problems and wants to send an error message by e-mail to the administrator. A third example is when a user has created an alert for a document library that sends an e-mail every time a new document is added or an existing document is modified or deleted.

This feature is available for both pure WSS installations and MOSS installations. It is not dependent on the SMTP service in Windows 2003 Server (or IIS to be more specific); SharePoint 2007 has the code to send SMTP messages built into its core features. Note that you do not need MS Exchange Server to make this feature work. Any SMTP mail server that accept e-mail from the SharePoint server will do fine (but some other cool features such as Inbox Web Parts will not work unless you have MS Exchange). To configure this feature, follow the steps in the Try It Out below.

Try It Out   Enable Outgoing SMTP e-mail

1. Log on as the administrator, and start the SharePoint 3.0 Central Administration tool. Switch to the Operations page (or use the Action link in this Administrator tasks item property).

2. Click Outgoing e-mail settings, in the Topology and Services section.

3. In the following web form, enter these values:

   a. **Outbound SMTP server:** Enter the full name to the mail server, for example `dc1.filobit.com`.

   b. **From address:** Enter any mail address you want listed as the sender of the e-mail; note that this address does not need to exist! You can enter any mail address you like here, but choose one that reminds the recipient that the mail comes from SharePoint; for example, `SharePoint@filobit.com`.

   c. **Reply-to address:** This must be an existing e-mail address. If a recipient of SharePoint's e-mail sends a reply, it will be delivered to this address.

   d. **Character set:** Define the character set to be used by SharePoint's SMTP service. Unless you have a very good reason, keep the default setting, that is, 65001 (Unicode UTF-8). However, if you cannot read the e-mail sent from SharePoint, you may need to change this setting. Talk with your mail administrator in this case and ask what character set he or she recommends.

   e. Click OK to save and close this page.

The Second Important Task: Defining the Index Schedule

This task is not listed above in the Administrative tasks, although it is necessary to complete if you want to activate the search feature in MOSS. You may recall that searching and indexing are features managed by the Shared Service Provider (SSP), by default named `SharedServices1`, that you created during the basic configuration steps. So in order to configure search and indexing, you must open the configuration page for `SharedServices1`.

The task you must complete is to define a schedule for the indexing service; by default, MOSS is configured to index its own databases, but there is no schedule set. In other words, you cannot search in MOSS at this moment. This task is simple, just follow the steps in the Try It Out below to set up how often the index service will run.

Define the Indexing Schedule

1. Log on as the administrator; start the SharePoint 3.0 Central Administration tool.

2. Click on the link `SharedServices1` on the Quick Launch bar, to open the configuration page for this SSP.

3. Click Search settings under the section Search.

4. Click Content sources and crawl schedules.

5. If the column values for Next Full Crawl and Next Incremental Crawl both are set to None for "Local Office SharePoint Server sites," then you need to set this schedule now:

   a. Open the quick menu for the "Local Office SharePoint Server sites," and select Edit.

   b. In the Crawl Schedules section, click Create Schedule under Full Crawl and define the schedule (see Figure 5-1). Tip: it is often enough to do a full crawl once every week or maybe even every month.

   c. Click Create Schedule under Incremental Crawl and define a schedule. This should normally take place rather often. For Basic mode installations of MOSS, this value is set to once every 20 minutes. Set a value that suits your organization, but remember that this is a very resource-intensive activity, so make sure you have enough hardware to avoid that users experience SharePoint as slow due to this reason.

   d. To make sure your index is up to date, check the option Start full crawl of this content sources, then click OK.

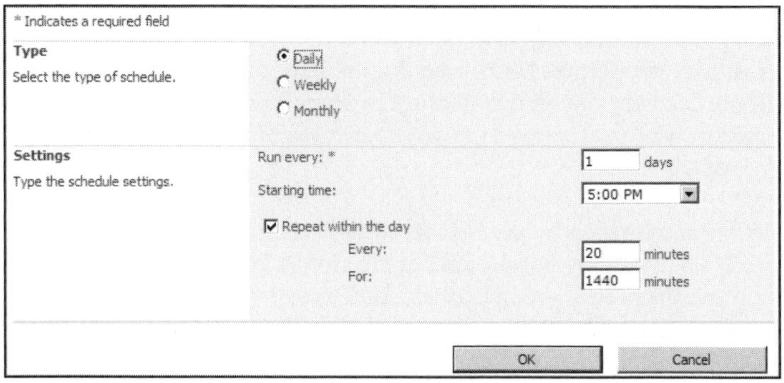

Figure 5-1

At this stage, your MOSS server is ready to allow you to create any type of user site, such as portal sites, and team sites. The content in all of them will regularly be indexed, so users can search for information. Users can also create e-mail based alerts to monitor documents, libraries, and lists for updates.

Other Common Tasks in SharePoint's Central Administration Tool

When you want to add more functionality to your MOSS environment, you must complete some configuration. Typical functionality that you want is to be able to search for users, and to allow users to use My Sites for both personal use and to publish information about themselves to other users in the organization. Another often requested feature is that SharePoint should be able to store e-mail related to a project or similar activities. As discussed earlier, these common tasks do not appear in the Administrators Task list in the Central Administration tool; instead they are organized based on how they are commonly implemented in a typical MOSS environment. Below are more detailed steps on how to add these features to MOSS.

Configuring User Profiles

Each user account in Active Directory can be granted access to a SharePoint web site. Each of these users also may have a number of properties registered in Active Directory, such as an e-mail address, department name, a company name, and a phone number. A very common request in intranet sites is a list of employees, so a user can search for a specific employee. Instead of creating a simple list of employees in SharePoint, you can activate a User Profile database, which stores the name of each user, including their properties; some are retrieved from Active Directory, and some are manually updated by the user or the administrator.

The User Profile database is managed by the SSP, that is, SharedServices1. By default, it will not contain any user names, besides the administrative account, so the first question is if you want to add each user account and corresponding properties manually or if you want to import this information from an external source, such as the Active Directory. In most cases, the latter is preferred, since the Active Directory is already used for storing properties about users, and you probably want to store just one master directory of user properties. MOSS can import that information from Active Directory on a regular basis, typically once every day. A new feature in SharePoint 2007 compared to previous versions is that MOSS can import user properties from any Lightweight Directory Access Protocol (LDAP) source, not only from Active Directory.

Since the user profile is managed by the SSP, its content is also stored in one of the SSP databases: SharedServices1_DB. Exactly what properties are stored for each user is defined in the User Profile settings; some of these properties are imported, some are manually updated. An administrator can add, modify, or delete these user properties at any time, including configuring which of them will be mapped to an Active Directory property, that is, imported from AD.

You will find more information, including the exact configuration steps for activating the User Profile database in Chapter 8, but the following Try It Out provides a quick guide on how to force a manual import of all users from an Active Directory domain named Filobit.

Try It Out   Configure the User Profile Import

1. Log on as the administrator, and start the SharePoint 3.0 Central Administration tool.

2. Click on the SSP link SharedServices1 (assuming that you have accepted the default name).

3. On the next configuration page, click User profiles and properties in the User Profiles and My Sites section.

4. Verify that the Import source is Current domain (FILOBIT), then click the Start full import link. Wait for some time until Profile import status = Idle (a large number of users takes several minutes, or even hours, to import); click Refresh or wait for the automatic refresh to take place.

5. When all users are imported, you will find the number of user profiles imported listed at the top of the page. Click the link View user profile to see a list of these imported users. Use the quick menu for any of these users, and select Edit to view the user's properties.

If the import process fails, the problem is probably that the default Content Access Account does not have the requested permissions to read Active Directory. If this is the case, change the account by clicking on the Search Settings link in the SSP instance, then click Default content access account. Make sure to enter a user account with Read permissions in the Active Directory. Note that local accounts such as Local Service do not have this permission!

The information in the user profile is searchable, but first MOSS must index it; to speed up this process you can force a manual update, as shown in the following Try It Out.

Try It Out   Force a Full Crawl

1. Open the SharePoint 3.0 Central Administration tool and SharedServices1.

2. Click Search settings in the Search section.

3. Click Content sources and crawl schedules.

4. Use the quick menu for Local Office SharePoint Server sites, and select Start Full Crawl.

5. Wait for this crawl to complete; click Refresh or wait for the automatic refresh of this page.

When the crawl process has completed, all the new information in the user profile is updated. Now you can start searching for some of these user properties, for example the Department property. Open the portal web site, and click Search, click the tab People, and then Search Options. A form is now displayed where you can enter what you are searching for (see Figure 5-2). Enter a value in the Department field you know exists in the user profile, and click on the Search icon. You should now see a list of users matching this search criterion.

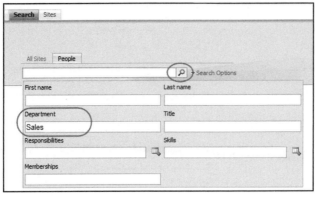

Figure 5-2

Configuring My Sites

This feature is related to the User Profile database, since it will expose many, or possibly all, of a user's properties stored in this database to other users by means of a shared My Site. But My Site is also a private web site for the user, or site collection really. The user can, and should, use this web site instead of a home directory on a file server, or even storing files locally, since it is easier for the user to retrieve this information from any computer that can access the SharePoint server, including over the Internet. The details about My Sites are described in Chapter 6, but here is a short summary since you probably want to get a basic understanding of this feature right now.

All users with at least Read access to SharePoint will be able to create their personal web site simply by clicking on the link My Site at the top right of SharePoint's user web site. When they do so, SharePoint will create the personal site through the service account used by the application pool of the web application where the portal site is created. The user does not need any special permission to create My Site. However, in some situations, such as when installing MOSS using the Basic installation mode, this service account may not get the proper permission. If this happens, the user sees the error message in Figure 5-3.

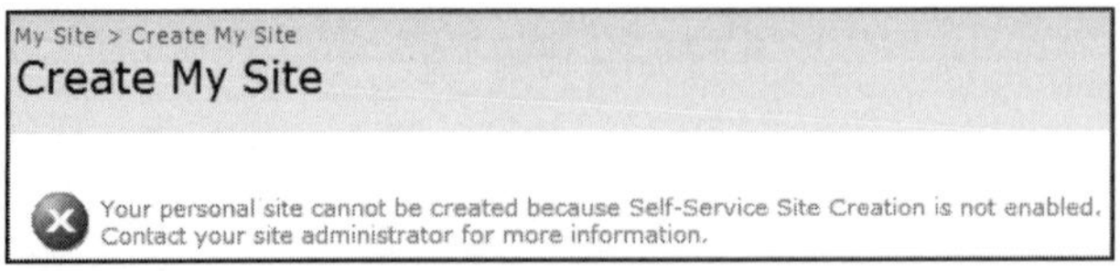

My Site > Create My Site
Create My Site

Your personal site cannot be created because Self-Service Site Creation is not enabled. Contact your site administrator for more information.

Figure 5-3

This error message is actually misleading; the problems has nothing to do with the "self-service site creation" feature; it is simply due to the fact that the service account for the application pool is not allowed to create a site collection for this user. To correct this, follow the steps in the Try It Out below.

Try It Out   Set Permissions for Creating My Site

1. Log on as an administrator for the MOSS server.

2. Start the Internet Information Service (IIS) Manager.

3. Open the properties for the virtual IIS web server, used by the MOSS user web site (e.g., `SharePoint - 80`). Switch to the Home Directory tab and check what application pool it uses, then click Cancel to close this property window.

4. Right-click the application pool identified in step 3, and select Properties. Switch to the Identity page; memorize what user account is used here. Click Cancel to close the property page.

5. Open the general settings for the server object. For example, click Start, right-click on My Computer, and select Manage, then expand the System Tools ➪ Local Users and Groups ➪ Groups. Double-click on the group Administrators, click Add, and add the account identified in step 4, then click OK.

6. Reset the IIS: Open Start ➪ Run and type **IISRESET**, then press the Enter key.

7. Log out and log in as a normal user. Open the web site, for example, `http://srv1`, then click My Site to create this personal web site.

After My Site is created, take a look at the user properties it displays. Click Details in the My Profile section in the Quick Launch bar. Note that some properties are already set; these come from the User Profile database. Also note that you can set some properties yourself, such as About Me, Responsibilities, and others. Whatever you enter here will be stored in the User Profile database when you click Save and Close. Now, click the My Profile tab, and you will see most, but not all, of your properties displayed. This My Profile page is available to all users, by default, although some of its information may be visible only to certain groups, such as My Colleagues. To see how this is controlled, click on Details again, and note the column to the far right of each property line. For example, the property Mobile phone is only visible to the group My Colleagues, while the Fax property is visible to Everyone.

So, how do you define who your colleagues are? Simple, just click on the link Colleague in the Quick Launch bar, and then click Add Colleagues. Next, enter the names of your colleagues in the Type Names field, select who will see these names by using the menu Show these colleagues to, and finally select the group the new colleague will be listed under; the default is General, but you can also choose Peers or create a new group name (see Figure 5-4). Now open the My Home page, and click Show Colleagues to see them all. This list of colleagues is also displayed on the My Profile page.

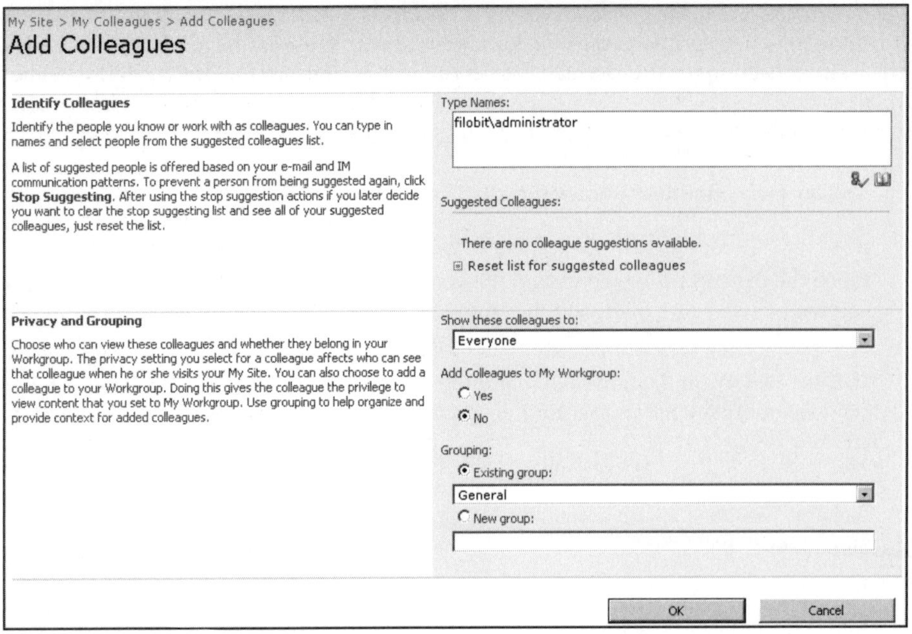

My Site > My Colleagues > Add Colleagues

Add Colleagues

Identify Colleagues

Identify the people you know or work with as colleagues. You can type in names and select people from the suggested colleagues list.

A list of suggested people is offered based on your e-mail and IM communication patterns. To prevent a person from being suggested again, click **Stop Suggesting**. After using the stop suggestion actions if you later decide you want to clear the stop suggesting list and see all of your suggested colleagues, just reset the list.

Privacy and Grouping

Choose who can view these colleagues and whether they belong in your Workgroup. The privacy setting you select for a colleague affects who can see that colleague when he or she visits your My Site. You can also choose to add a colleague to your Workgroup. Doing this gives the colleague the privilege to view content that you set to My Workgroup. Use grouping to help organize and provide context for added colleagues.

Type Names:

filobit\administrator

Suggested Colleagues:

There are no colleague suggestions available.

☐ Reset list for suggested colleagues

Show these colleagues to:

Everyone

Add Colleagues to My Workgroup:

○ Yes
● No

Grouping:

● Existing group:

General

○ New group:

OK   Cancel

Figure 5-4

By default, My Site will not contain a link back to the portal home site. The administrator can define a default link that will automatically be added to each new (but not existing) My Site. To do this, open the URL http:<address_to_MySite>/_layouts/settings.aspx, *then open the link Portal site connection, and enter a name and the URL to the portal home site.*

Enabling Incoming e-mail

This is a new feature in SharePoint 2007 and works for both pure WSS installations and those with MOSS. It is listed as Task 1 in the Administrators Task list. It solves a longstanding problem: How can you collect e-mail related to a specific activity, together with the rest of the information stored in a SharePoint web site? The typical scenario is when you work on a project and use e-mail to communicate with the other project members, and possibly also with external people, such as consultants. By mail-enabling a document library in the project web site, you can forward important e-mail to that document library, or you can add the mail address for this library to the mail group for that projects.

In order to make it possible for SharePoint to receive e-mail, you must install the SMTP service in this Windows 2003 server. SharePoint will then use this SMTP service to accept incoming e-mails and store them in mail-enabled document libraries that in effect work as mailboxes. The important thing to remember is that SharePoint works as an independent SMTP server and that any mail server can send e-mail to it. When you accept that, it is not hard to understand that SharePoint needs its own mail domain, which will be different from the "normal" mail server in your organization. For example, if the mail domain used by your normal mail server is @filobit.com, then SharePoint will add its server name to that domain: @srv1.filobit.com (assuming that the server name is srv1).

As long as your SharePoint server will accept e-mail from internal users only, you will not need to configure a mail exchanger (MX) record in your DNS server, since the name of the domain is also the fully qualified domain name (FQDN) for this server; that is, your normal mail servers will be able to find SharePoint whenever there is an e-mail sent to one of its document libraries. However, if you want SharePoint to be able to accept e-mail from external users as well, you have two choices:

❑ **Create an MX Record for SharePoint:** This will make SharePoint's mail domain `@srv.filobit.com` public, and anyone can now locate this mail server. But this does not mean that SharePoint will accept e-mail from anyone on the Internet; it would be devastating if any of SharePoint's mail addresses became known to a spammer.

❑ **Create an mail address in the normal mail system:** For example, if your mail server is MS Exchange, then you would create a mail-enabled contact with one primary e-mail address that matches exactly the e-mail address for a given document library. The same contact will then get a second mail address using the default mail domain (e.g., @filobit.com), and an external user can then send an e-mail to that address; MS Exchange will receive it, and then immediately forward it to SharePoint and its document library.

Enabling Incoming e-mail with Manually Created e-mail Addresses

The first step is to enable the SMP service for the Windows 2003 server, then configure SharePoint to enable incoming e-mail, and finally mail-enable the document library that will accept e-mail. Follow the steps in the Try It Out below to set up incoming e-mail.

Try It Out   Enable Incoming e-mail

1. Log on as an administrator for the MOSS server.

2. Make sure that the SMTP service is installed on the Windows 2003 server:

   a. Click Start ⇨ Control Panel ⇨ Add or Remove Programs.

   b. Click AddRemove Windows Components in the left bar.

   c. Select Application Server, and click Details.

   d. Select Internet Information Services (IIS), and click Details.

   e. Near the end of this list, check SMTP Service and click OK twice, then click Next. If requested, mount a CD with the Windows 2003 Server setup files.

   f. Close the Add or Remove Program applet.

3. Configure SharePoint to enable incoming e-mail:

   a. Start the SharePoint 3.0 Central Administration tool.

   b. Switch to the Operations page.

   c. Click Incoming e-mail settings.

   d. In the Enable Incoming e-mail section, select Yes. Accept the other default settings; memorize the mail domain listed in the Incoming e-mail Server Display Address section.

   e. Click OK to save and close the web form.

    4.   Mail-enable a document library:

        a.   Open the web site containing the document library you want to mail-enable.

        b.   Click on the document library you want to mail-enable, for example Shared Documents.

        c.   Click Settings ⇨ Document Library Settings.

        d.   Click Incoming e-mail settings, and fill in the form (see Figure 5-5).

        e.   Select Yes in the Incoming e-mail section.

        f.   Enter the mail address for the library. Tip: use a naming standard that makes it easy to understand what web site and document library this address points to. For example, if your site is named Project X, you could enter this address: **ProjectX-DocLib1@srv1 .filobit.com**.

        g.   In the e-mail Attachments section, select how mail attachments should be saved: save all in the root folder; create a subfolder per subject and store the attachments there; or create a subfolder per sender, and save the attachments there. You can also define if you want to overwrite existing files with the same name or not; if not, a number will be added to each file name.

        If you select the option to save e-mail to folders named after the subject, then all e-mail must contain a subject. If not, SharePoint will use the message ID number as the subject name!

        h.   In the section e-mail Message, choose if you want to save the actual mail message or not. If you do not choose to save the message (as an .eml file), only the attachments will be saved, according to your settings in step g above.

        i.   In the e-mail Meeting Invitations section, choose if you want to save incoming meeting invitations or not. If you just want this library to store incoming attachments, you probably do not want to save these invitations.

        j.   In the e-mail Security section, select which senders this library will accept e-mail from. The default is to accept e-mail only from users with Write permissions to the library. Note that if you instead choose the option Accept e-mail messages from any sender, then this library may be attacked by spam mail!

        k.   Click OK to save and close this form.

        If you test the incoming e-mail functionality, and no mail or attachments show up within a few minutes, then check that your user account has permission to write to that document library!

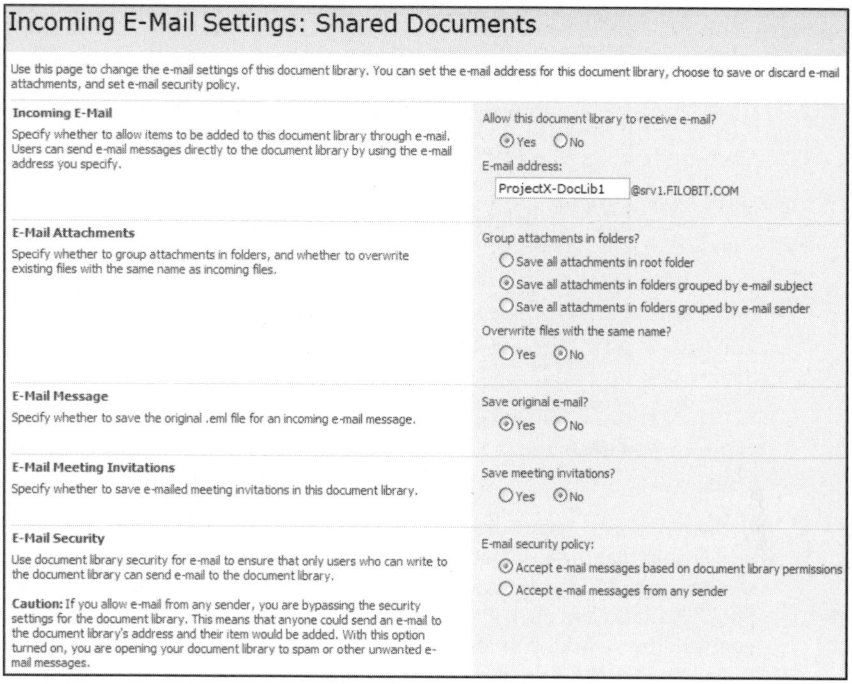

Incoming E-Mail Settings: Shared Documents

Use this page to change the e-mail settings of this document library. You can set the e-mail address for this document library, choose to save or discard e-mail attachments, and set e-mail security policy.

Incoming E-Mail

Specify whether to allow items to be added to this document library through e-mail. Users can send e-mail messages directly to the document library by using the e-mail address you specify.

Allow this document library to receive e-mail?
- ⦿ Yes ○ No

E-mail address:
`ProjectX-DocLib1` @srv1.FILOBIT.COM

E-Mail Attachments

Specify whether to group attachments in folders, and whether to overwrite existing files with the same name as incoming files.

Group attachments in folders?
- ○ Save all attachments in root folder
- ⦿ Save all attachments in folders grouped by e-mail subject
- ○ Save all attachments in folders grouped by e-mail sender

Overwrite files with the same name?
- ○ Yes ⦿ No

E-Mail Message

Specify whether to save the original .eml file for an incoming e-mail message.

Save original e-mail?
- ⦿ Yes ○ No

E-Mail Meeting Invitations

Specify whether to save e-mailed meeting invitations in this document library.

Save meeting invitations?
- ○ Yes ⦿ No

E-Mail Security

Use document library security for e-mail to ensure that only users who can write to the document library can send e-mail to the document library.

Caution: If you allow e-mail from any sender, you are bypassing the security settings for the document library. This means that anyone could send an e-mail to the document library's address and their item would be added. With this option turned on, you are opening your document library to spam or other unwanted e-mail messages.

E-mail security policy:
- ⦿ Accept e-mail messages based on document library permissions
- ○ Accept e-mail messages from any sender

Figure 5-5

5. Make the mail address to this mail-enabled library show up in the users' global address list (GAL) in Outlook. To do this you need to create a `Contact` object in Active Directory with the same mail address as the library. These steps assume that you are using MS Exchange 2000/2003 as your normal mail system!

a. Log on as a Domain Administrator to a Windows 2003 domain controller in your Active Directory domain.

b. Start Active Directory users and computers (ADUC), which you will find in Start ⇨ Administrative Tools.

c. Select the Organizational Unit (OU) where you want to create the new contact; for example, to make this Users, right-click on Users and select New ⇨ Contact.

d. In the form that appears, enter a name for the Contact; pay attention to the Display name, since this is what will be visible in the GAL. You can skip the First name and Last name, but you must enter something in the Full name and Display name. It is okay to enter the same name in these two fields (see Figure 5-6), then click Next.

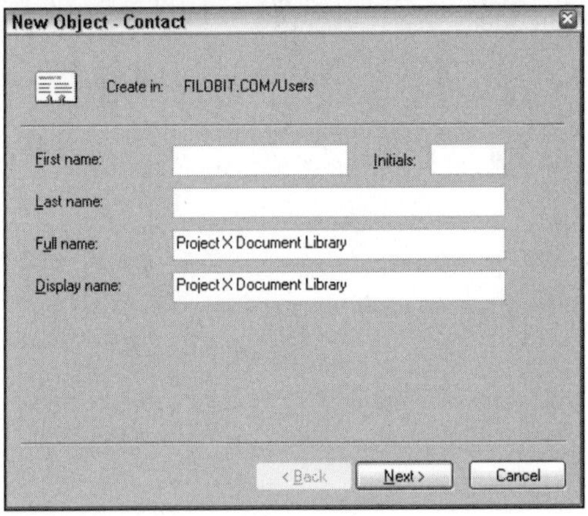

Figure 5-6

    e.   In the next form, make sure that Create an Exchange e-mail address is checked. This will ensure that the Contact will show up in the GAL. Note that this will *not* create a mailbox in the Exchange server! To define the mail address click Modify, then select SMTP Address and click OK. Now enter the same mail address you defined to the mail-enabled library in step 4f above, then click OK. Next, you see a summary of these settings (see Figure 5-7). Click Next to continue, and then Finish on the final page.

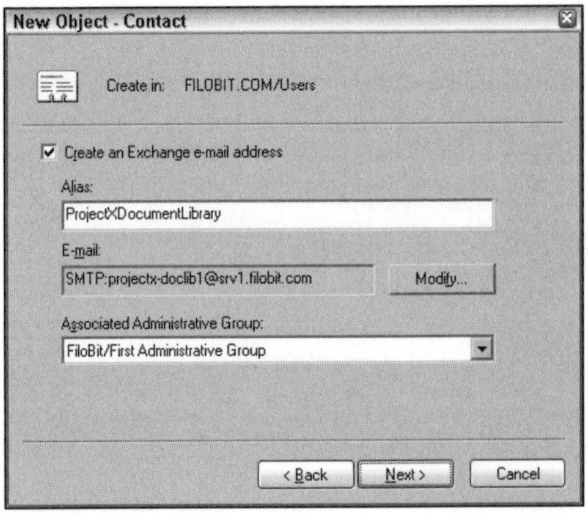

Figure 5-7

6.   Optional: The new contact will show up in Outlooks GAL within one minute. (You may have to download the new address list in Outlook if you run in cached mode.) You may want to give the contact a secondary SMTP address, to allow external users to send mail to that library.

    Remember that you must then also select the option Accept e-mail messages from any sender in step 4j above!

    a.   Open the ADUC again, and locate the contact you just created.

    b.   Right-click on that contact, and select Properties.

   c.   Switch to the e-mail Addresses.

   d.   Click New.

   e.   Click SMTP address, and then OK. Note that you can add any type of alternative address you need for the `Contact` object.

   f.   Enter an alternative SMTP address in the e-mail address field; for example, `Project-X@filobit.com` (assuming that `@filobit.com` is the mail domain for the Exchange server).

   g.   Click OK. Now you will see all e-mail addresses that the `Contact` object has (see Figure 5-8). This means that you can send e-mail to the contact using any of these mail addresses, including the X400 address. When Exchange receives this mail, it will forward them directly to the mail server responsible for the mail domain `@srv1.filobit.com`, that is, the SharePoint server. You can now tell anyone outside your organization to send important e-mail regarding Project X to this address: `Project-X@filobit.com`.

   h.   Click OK again, to close the properties for the contact.

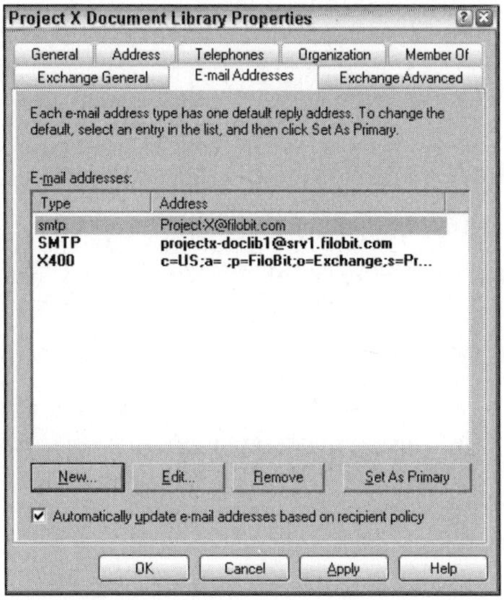

Figure 5-8

Now open Outlook, and create an e-mail: Click on the To button, and select the display address Project X Document Library. Then enter a subject, add some text in the body and add an attachment. When you are ready, click Send. Next, open the document library in SharePoint and wait for the e-mail and attachment to show up.

For more control over the mail traffic between the Exchange server and SharePoint, you can create an SMPT Connector in Exchange for this connection.

Enabling Auto-Created e-mail Addresses

The example above assumed that you wanted to create the e-mail address for the document library manually, but SharePoint has a special module that can do this automatically: SharePoint Directory Management Service. For this to work, you need to do two things:

❑   Enable the Application Pool account write access to Active Directory.

❑   Configure the SharePoint Directory Management Service.

Before SharePoint can create an mail-enabled contact object in Active Directory, it must have permission to write in Active Directory. One easy way to ensure this is to make sure that SharePoint's account is a member of the Active Directory group Domain Admins. But the question is what user account are we talking about? The answer is the user account listed as the security account for the application pool, used by the Central Administration web site. Instead of making this user account a member of Domain Admins, it is possible to grant this account the specific permissions needed to write to the organizational unit where the mail-enabled contact will be created.

The second thing listed on the bulleted list above is to enable and configure the SharePoint Directory Management Service (SDMS). This is done on the web form where you enable incoming e-mail. For example, say you have a SharePoint server named SRV1 and an Active Directory domain named FILO-BIT.COM, and you want all auto-created contacts to be stored in the organizational unit SP2007. The following Try It Out shows how you would do this.

Try It Out   **Enable SharePoint Directory Management Service**

1.   Log on as an administrator to the MOSS server.

2.   Make sure that the organizational unit SP2007 exists and that the application pool account has permission to write to that OU.

3.   Open the Central Administration tool ➪ Operations ➪ Incoming e-mail settings.

4.   In the Directory Management Service section, select Yes, and you will see several new settings show up. To follow the example above, fill in these values (see Figure 5-9):

In order to make it easier for you to read, the information you enter in step a and b below are in capital letters; you can also use small letters if you want.

a.   **Active Directory container where new distribution groups and contacts will be created:** OU=SP2007, DC=FILOBIT, DC=COM.

b.   **SMTP mail server for incoming mail:** @SRV1.FILOBIT.COM.

c.   **Accept messages from authenticated users only:** Yes.

d.   **Allow creating of distribution groups from SharePoint sites?:** Yes.

e.   **Distribution group request approval settings:** This is a multivalue setting that asks what needs to be approved by an administrator before taking effect. The default settings are Create new distribution group and Delete distribution group. In other words,

SharePoint will try to create or delete a distribution group when a site is created or deleted, but an administrator must approve this first. See the section "Approve/reject distribution group" below for more information on that. In this example, you can accept the defaults.

5. This concludes the configuration of the SharePoint Directory Management Service. Click OK to save and close this page.

Now, follow the steps described earlier to mail-enable a document library, and then check in ADUC to verify that a new contact with this e-mail address has been created. This method of auto-creating contacts is, of course, much handier than the first method described, but you should select the one most suitable for your organization.

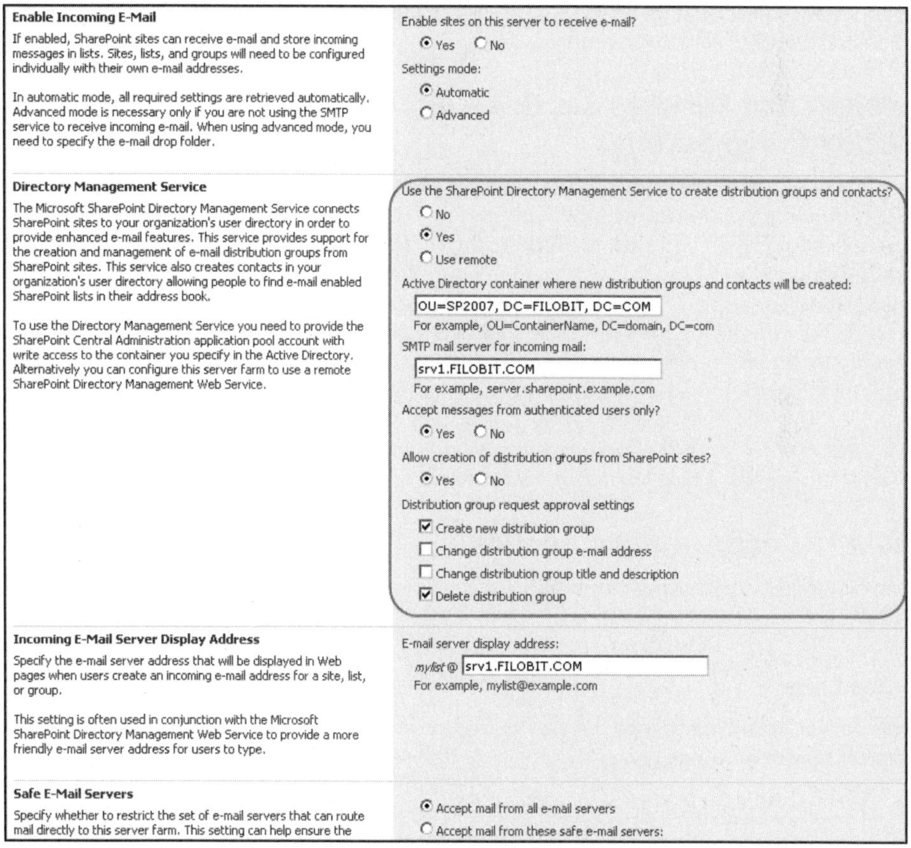

Figure 5-9

This concludes the most common administrative tasks for a typical MOSS 2007 installation. You may want to configure more settings and activate more features, as described in the following section.

The Operations Page

The administrative tasks and configuration options you have completed so far have added a lot of functionality to the MOSS server. But there are also a lot more configuration options in SharePoint's Central Administration tool that you may need in some situations. This tool contains two main pages: Operations and Application Management. The Operations page contains links to general settings and configuration options for the SharePoint server, while the Application Management page contains links for creating and managing tasks related to applications, such as site collections, web applications, and authentication providers. The most commonly used links on the Operations page are described in the following sections, and some of the links on the Application Management page will be described later in this chapter. Many other chapters will cover parts of these links when discussing specific application tasks, such as creating portal sites in Chapter 6.

Open the Central Administration tool, and switch to the Operations page: You have already seen a number of settings on this page, such as Servers in farm, Outgoing e-mail settings, and Incoming e-mail settings, and here is a quick guide to the rest of the settings on this page commonly used for a typical MOSS installation.

The Topology and Services Section's Approve/Reject Distribution Group Settings

When you create a new web site, with its own permission groups, SharePoint can automatically create a mail distribution group for the members in this site. That group will then show up in the Distribution Groups list shown when you click the link Approve/Reject Distribution Groups on the Operations page. If the administrator approves this group, then SharePoint will create a distribution group with that name in Active Directory and add all users to it who are listed as site members. After that, the distribution group will show up in Outlook's GALs so that users can start sending e-mail to that group. This is a very handy feature for project groups and other teams who have their own team site, where it is often required that there be a mail distribution group containing all the members of the site.

> Note that in order to get this working, you must first enable the directory management feature in SharePoint. See the section "Enable Incoming e-mail" earlier in this chapter.

The Security Configurations Section

You can control security settings from here for service accounts, antivirus protection, blocking file types, SSO, and more.

Service Accounts

Use this page to view and change the service account used by specific services and application pools. The type of service accounts you can change are these (see Figure 5-10):

❑ Document Conversion Launcher Service (Windows service).

❑ Document Conversion Load Balancer Service (Windows service).

❑ Single Sign-On Service (Windows service).

❑ The User Web Application Pool (Web application pool ➪ Windows SharePoint Services Web Application).

❑   The SSP Application Pool (Web application pool ⇨ Windows SharePoint Services Web
    Application).

❑   The My Site Application Pool (Web application pool ⇨ Windows SharePoint Services Web
    Application).

An alternative would be to change these accounts directly; for example, changing the application pool
security accounts using IIS Manager. But this does not always work, since SharePoint stores these
accounts in its configuration database. In other words, use this page if possible; if not, then try changing
the account manually.

*Note that you cannot use this page to change the service account used by the Central Administration
application pool.*

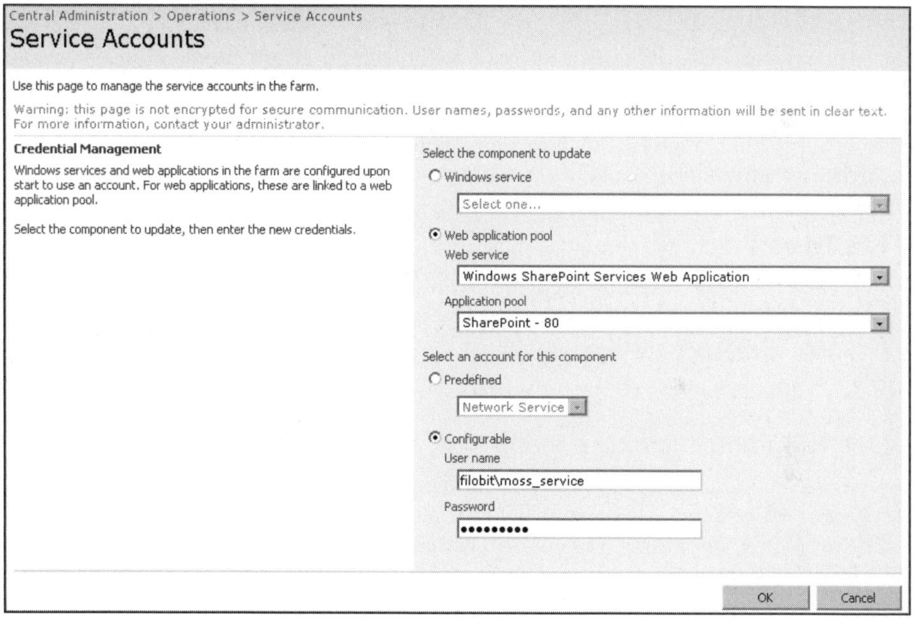

Figure 5-10

Information Rights Management

Use this page to configure Information Rights Management (IRM), which is a complementary service for
MS Office products and MS SharePoint. With IRM a user can define in very fine detail what other users
can do with a specific document or e-mail. For example, a document's author can say that only two people can read the document, but they can do nothing else, such as print or save it. Note that these permissions will be valid regardless of how a user gets hold of the document, including its having been sent as
an e-mail attachment to someone outside the organization.

By default, this page is not active until you install the IRM client with Service Pack 2 or later. You can
find more information about this feature in Chapter 8.

Antivirus

Use this page to configure your SharePoint-aware antivirus application. Note that even if this page looks like it is doing something, it will, in fact, not do anything until you install an antivirus application for SharePoint. Some examples of such products are:

❑ **Forefront Security for SharePoint:** This is a Microsoft product that previously was called Antigen for SharePoint. Check for more information on it at `www.microsoft.com/fore-front/serversecurity/sharepoint/download.mspx`.

❑ **PortalProtect for SharePoint:** This is a product made by Trend Micro. Look for more information on it at `www.trendmicro.com/en/products/file-server/ppsp/evaluate/overview.htm`.

❑ **Antivirus for Microsoft SharePoint:** This product is made by Symantec. Look for more information on it at
`www.symantec.com/enterprise/products/overview.jsp?pcid=1008&pvid=829_1`.

At first, you may think that antivirus protection for SharePoint is unnecessary, since your users have a client-based antivirus application. But think again; you would never run a file server without a virus protection, right? And SharePoint will, at least in part, replace your file servers. So it should have the same level of protection. Plan for the virus protection in SharePoint from the beginning; do not wait until you have a virus-infected file stored in any of SharePoint's document libraries!

Blocked File Types

This section is very important, since it governs what file types SharePoint will accept for storage in any of its libraries, such as document libraries. By default it contains a list of 89 file types, such as `.exe` and `.url`. This page is used for both WSS and MOSS installations, so you will find more information about this in Chapter 8.

Updating the Farm Administrator's Group

Use this page to configure what users will be farm administrators, that is, administrator with full control of the complete MOSS farm. Although this setting also applies to pure WSS installations, it is especially interesting for MOSS, since these types of installations tend to be more complex and have more people involved in the management and administration of the SharePoint farm.

A farm administrator has full access to all settings in the farm. By default, they will not be able to view any content, such as a site or a document library, unless specifically given the permission (i.e., the same rules apply to farm administrators as to ordinary users). But a farm administrator can take ownership of any content and site, if necessary; for example, when they need to fix a problem or assist a site owner.

By default, this farm administrator group contains the user account used by the application pool for the Central Administration tool, plus the user account used to install SharePoint 2007. There is no default group for assisting administrators with limited access, but you could create a SharePoint Group and give it view permissions only, using the steps in the following Try It Out.

> *This SharePoint Group will only get view access to the Home page of Central Administration, not to the Operations or Application Management page!*

Try It Out   **Create a View-Only Administrator**

1. Log on as an administrator for the MOSS server, and start the Central Administration tool.

2. Open the Operations page, and click Update farm administrator's group.

3. Next to the New button, click the black arrow to open its menu, then click New Group.

4. On the web form that appears, enter these values:

   a. **Name:** View-Only Admins.

   b. **About Me:** "This group is for users who will have view-only access to SharePoint's Central Administration tool."

   c. **Group owner:** Accept the default value.

   d. **Group Settings:** Accept the default values.

   e. **Membership Requests:** Accept the default values.

   f. **Give Group Permission to this Site:** Check Read – Can view only.

   g. **e-mail Distribution List:** Accept the default value.

   h. **Archive e-mail:** Accept the default value.

   i. Click Create. The group is now created.

5. The group now contains only the owner account; click New to add users or groups as members of this SharePoint Group.

Since you cannot easily create a group with limited administrative access, you must be very cautious with whom you want as a member of the farm administrator group. Although these administrators cannot see information unless given the permission, they can take ownership and add themselves as members to whatever content exists in SharePoint (exactly as they can with files stored in a file server). Think "Top Management's secret SharePoint workspace," and you'll understand what I mean.

Information Management Policy Configuration

This is a setting exclusive to MOSS installations; its purpose is to let you control what parts of the information management policies you want to be active. These policies will be listed as default configuration options in libraries and lists that will enable one or more policy features. The owner of these lists and libraries may chose any of these preconfigured policies, or choose to define a custom policy. By default, all four of these policies are enabled; if any of these is disabled, then that policy will not be available for any list or library:

❑ **Labels:** This feature will generate labels inserted into MS Office 2007 documents. These labels will show up when the document is printed. The information in these labels are also searchable.

❑ **Auditing:** This feature will audit any user activity on documents and list items, such as when a user reads a document or modifies a list item. This information is stored in the audit log, described later in this chapter.

❑ **Expiration:** This feature lets a user start an action or workflow at a given time; for example, 6 months after a document was created it should be moved to another library.

❑ **Barcodes:** This feature will generate a unique identifier in an MS Office 2007 document. They can also be used to search for documents.

Use this page to disable, or decommission as SharePoint calls it, any of these policy features; this will affect all lists and libraries in MOSS. Note that if a policy feature is already applied, the feature will remain active, but all new sites and libraries will not have that feature available. Click on the policy name to open the web form where the policy is decommissioned or activated.

Two of these policy features also let you configure their settings: Expiration and Barcodes (see Figures 5-11 and 5-12).

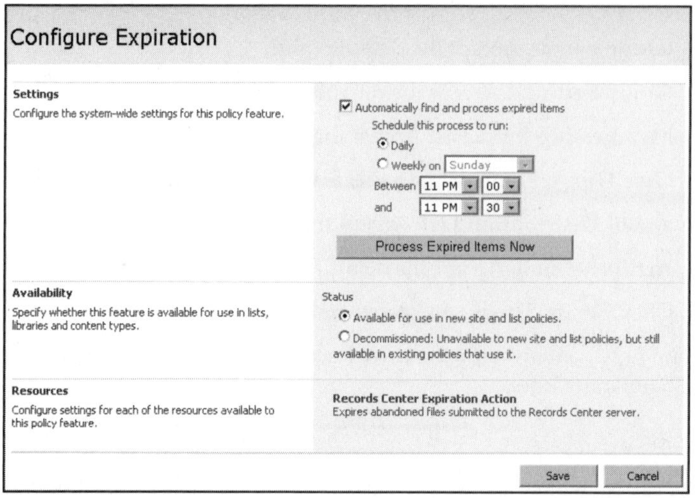

Figure 5-11

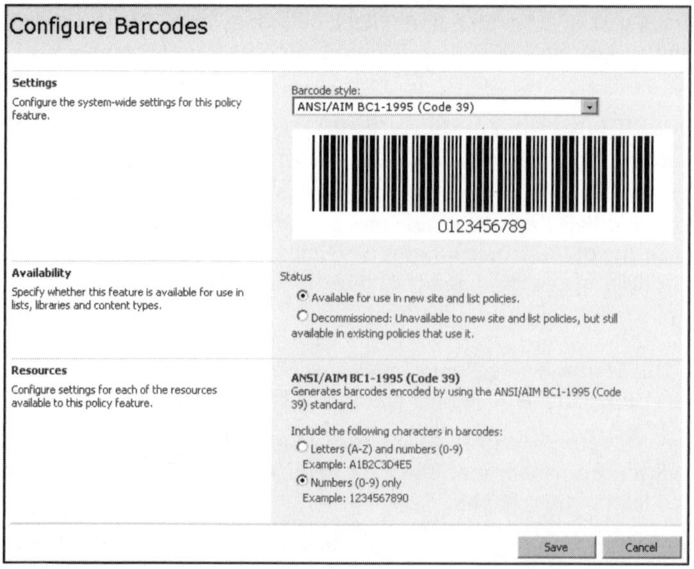

Figure 5-12

Managing Settings for Single Sign-On

This is an exclusive setting for MOSS; its purpose is to configure how the feature Single Sign-On (SSO) works in MOSS. This SSO feature is never used in standard MOSS features; in fact, it is not even installed by default. It is typically used when you have a need to retrieve information from a non-Microsoft application, such as SAP, and use this information in SharePoint. Since these non-Microsoft applications use a proprietary system for authenticating users, it will be a problem when SharePoint needs to access its information. The solution to this is to create a separate SSO database in SharePoint with the user account and password to access specific external content. A SharePoint application can then use the SSO database and the SSO feature to get access to that content.

For example, say that you want to show each user information about their salary on their personal My Site and that information is stored in a SAP system. To read this, you need to log on as a SAP user with the proper permission. If you were the programmer who was supposed to fix this, then you would need not only to create a Web Part that displays the salary information but also to add code to your Web Part so that it knows how to log on to the SAP system. The account used to log on is most likely a sensitive account that must not get into the wrong hands, so not only must your Web Part contain the user account to be used to log on, but it must also store this information in a highly secure way.

All of this is taken care of by the SSO feature: its database with user accounts and passwords to external systems are encrypted, and therefore protected. SSO also contains the code necessary to log on to the external system, so that your Web Part only needs to know how to use the SSO feature. There is also a specific administration tool for SSO, for managing these logon accounts and their passwords. This also means that the programmer does not need to know the logon account; the programmer only needs to know how to activate the SSO features.

The Logging and Reporting Section's Information Management Policy Usage Reports Settings

This MOSS-specific configuration page lets the administrator define how often information management policy reports will be created and where they will be stored. These policies were described earlier in this section, but as a quick reminder here they are again: Labels, Auditing, Expiration, and Barcodes. Most commonly the information related to the Auditing policy will be used when SharePoint creates the policy usage reports. These reports are XML files and will by default be opened in MS Excel 2007.

For example, say that you have enabled auditing policies for a document library named ABC. Your boss asks for a usage report for ABC. If this is a one-time request, you can create the report when necessary, but if your boss wants a regularly created usage report, then you can schedule when to create it. Follow the steps in the Try It Out below to configure the policy usage reports.

Try It Out   **Configure Scheduled Policy Usage Reports**

1. Log on as an administrator to the MOSS server, and start the Central Administration tool.

2. Open the Operations page, and click Information management policy usage reports.

3. Make sure that the page shows the web application used by the SharePoint site; for example, `SharePoint - 80`. If it doesn't, click on the current web application's name, and select Change Web Application, then select the right web application.

4. Complete the rest of the web form (see Figure 5-13):

    a. In the Schedule Recurring Reports section, check Enable recurring policy usage reports.

b. Enter the schedule when SharePoint will create these usage reports; for example, Daily between 6:00 and 7:00 am.

You must define the Report File Location before you can click the Create the Reports Now button! Use this button whenever you need to generate a usage report immediately.

c. In the Report File Location section, enter the path to a document library where the usage reports will be stored. You can also click Check URL and browse to a library, then copy that URL and return to the form. In this example, you will save the reports in the `/docs/documents` library, `http://srv1/docs/documents`.

d. In the Report Template section, choose if you want to use the default report template or if you have a custom-made report template. To create a custom template, use MS InfoPath 2007. For more information on how to do this, go to `msdn.microsoft.com` and search for "SharePoint 2007 policy report template."

e. Click OK when ready.

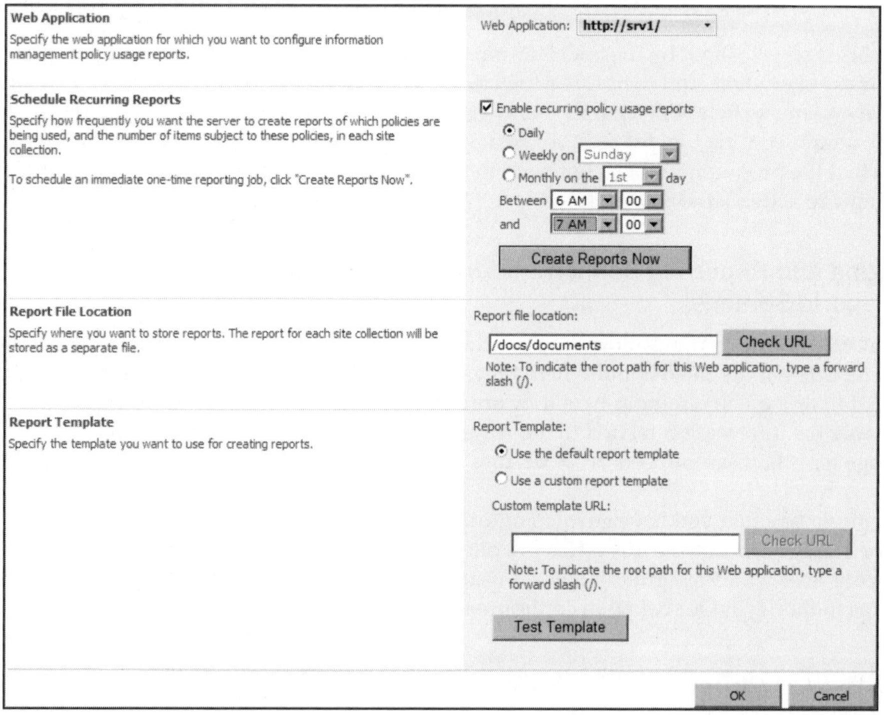

Figure 5-13

These reports will be stored in the document library listed in step c above. Note that any user with Read access to that library will be able to read these reports, so make sure to store them in a proper location to be certain that only authorized users can see them.

The Upgrade and Migration Section

From here, you can manage settings for converting editions, including converting the license type.

Microsoft Content Management Server

This section is used to create migration profiles, when migrating from MS Content Management Server 2002 (MS CMS 2002) to MS Office SharePoint Server 2007. This will help you migrate *content* from MS CSM to MOSS, but not *code*, that is, CMS applications. To get more information about this type of migration, go to `http://msdn2.microsoft.com/en-us/library/aa480225.aspx`.

Enable Enterprise Features

If you installed MS Office SharePoint Server 2007 Standard edition and later want to upgrade to the Enterprise Edition of MOSS, you need to purchase an Enterprise license key and enter this key on the Convert License Type page (see next section), then you can use the Enable Enterprise Features page to enable Enterprise features.

> *You cannot convert from Enterprise Edition to Standard Edition! This require a reinstallation of MOSS.*

Convert License Type

This page is related to the Enable Enterprise Features page; it is used when you want to convert a Standard Edition of MOSS to an Enterprise Edition. Note that you must have a valid MOSS Enterprise product key in order to convert the license type.

Enable Features in Existing Sites

This page is also related to the conversion of a Standard Edition of MOSS to an Enterprise Edition. If you have used the Standard Edition of MOSS for some time, you have a number of sites that are limited to Standard features. If you later convert the license type to Enterprise Edition, all new sites will have the full functionality that Enterprise offers, but the old sites will still only have Standard features. Use this page to enable Enterprise features on those old standard sites.

The Global Configuration Section

This section has several important settings for configuring your entire system.

Master Site Directory Settings

With MOSS comes a special site template called Sites, which works as a site directory. The idea for this directory is to make it easier for users to find a specific web site, for example a project team site. By default, only subsites created in the current site collection show up in this site directory; any sites in other site collections will not show up here.

This page allows you to specify that all new site collections (their top sites, but not their subsites) can be (but don't need to be) listed in a specific site directory. Most MOSS installations will only use a single site directory, but if you have more than one, then plan which of them that will be used to store other site collections, since there can only be one master site directory.

Try It Out   **Enable a Master Site Directory**

1.   Log on as an administrator for the MOSS server, and start the Central Administration tool.

2.   Open the Operations page, and click Master site directory settings.

3.   On the following page, enter these settings (see also Figure 5-14):

   a.   In the Site Directory Location section, enter the full URL to the master directory. Note that if the first site collection created is based on the Collaboration Portal site template, then the site directory will be named /sitedirectory, and it will be located directly under the top web site. For example, if the URL of the top site is http://srv1, then the full URL of the master directory will be http://srv1/sitedirectory/. Click on the link Click here to test if the URL you have entered really points to the site directory.

   b.   In the Site Creation Metadata section, check Enforce listing new sites in Site Directory to make all new top sites to be listed in the directory. Then choose if you want to force these sites and site collections to contain none, one, or all metadata defined in this site directory. If you select one or all site categories (i.e., metadata), then you must select one, or all, metadata when you create a new site collection.

   c.   Click OK to save and close the page.

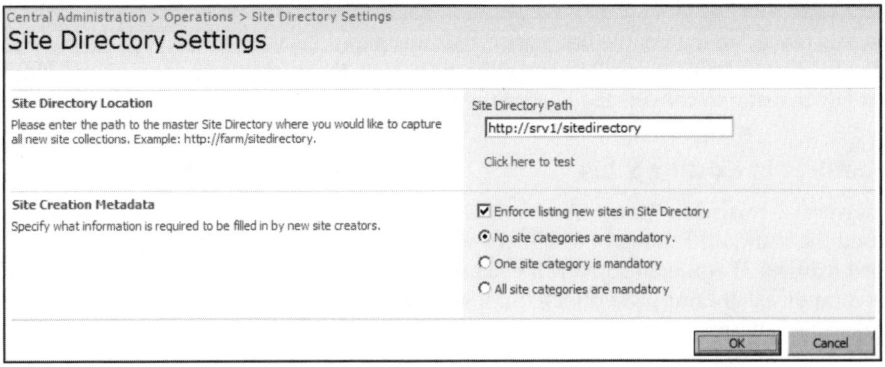

Figure 5-14

The next time you create a site collection (i.e., a new top site), you will also be able to set the metadata for that site, exactly as you will do when creating subsites in the first site collection.

Even after enabling the Master Site Directory, all secondary site collections will not automatically contain a link back to the first site collection. Fix that by clicking Site Actions ➪ Site Settings ➪ Portal site connection on the secondary top site, then enter the full URL to the top site in the first site collection.

Site Directory Link Scan

The site directory will soon be a valuable resource for users looking for a specific SharePoint site. But when you delete a site, its link will still be listed in the site directory. Since it does not point to any valid location, it is now referred to as a "broken link."

On the Site Directory Link Scan page, MOSS has a special feature that can check the site directory for broken links. You just enter the URL to the site directory. But what URL is that? Well, it is not the same URL as you entered earlier; this time you must point all the way down to the list where all site links are stored, including the list view you want to check. For example, if your site directory was created by the Collaboration Portal site template, the complete URL to enter is `http://srv1/SiteDirectory/SitesList/AllItems.aspx`, assuming that the top site is `http://srv1`. Just enter this URL in the Site directory view URL's field, and click OK. If it was the wrong URL, you will receive an error message. If it was correct, a test of all links is now performed and then this page is closed, regardless of whether a broken link was found or not. This may not be the most intuitive user interface, but this is how it works today; it may change in a future service pack. To find out if there were any broken links, you must now open the list with the site link and switch to the Broken Links view, as described in the following Try It Out.

Try It Out   Look for Broken Links

1. Log on as an administrator for the MOSS server, and start the Central Administration tool.

2. Switch to the Operations page, then in the Global Configuration section click Site directory links scan, and enter these settings:

   a. Enter the URL to the list view for the site links; for example, `http://srv1/SiteDirectory/SitesList/AllItems.aspx` (note that this page will remember any previously typed URL that points to a valid site list).

   b. If you also want to update the site directory with modified site titles and descriptions, check the setting Update title and description of links in the site directory automatically.

   c. Click OK to save and close the page.

3. Go to the URL in step 2a. This will open the site list in the site directory.

4. Change the View to Broken Sites. Any site link listed here is broken; either remove the link, or update it by using its quick menu, and selecting Edit Item.

   By default, it will take up to 24 hours before a broken link will be discovered. The reason is that SharePoint runs a process that updates the site directory once per night (01.00 am). You can speed up this process by using the `Stsadm.exe` *tool. For example, to run the site directory update process once every five minutes, open a command prompt and enter this string:* `stsadm -o setsitedirectoryscanschedule -schedule "every 5 minutes between 0 and 59"`.

Quiesce Farm

In some situations you need to take down a SharePoint server, but it may be hard to find a time when the server is not being used. The brutal way, of course, is simply to shut it down, but you may not be so popular among the user community if you do this. The strange phrase "Quiesce farm" is exactly what you need. It will prohibit all new sessions but let the current sessions run for a configurable time, for example 30 minutes, before it stops all SharePoint actions. In other words, *quiesce* means to gracefully shut down a process, such as SharePoint. It can also be used to gracefully stop InfoPath forms from being used, as you will see later in this chapter.

Conclusion for the Operations Page

As you have seen, the Operations page contains a lot of links to general configuration settings. As a SharePoint server administrator, you must learn to use these features, or at least know what they do and when you may need them. If you are wondering about the backup and restore section on this page, it will be covered in detail in Chapter 14. This concludes the description of the Operations page, and the following section will describe commonly used links on the Application Management page.

The Application Management Page

Open the Central Administration tool, and switch to the Application Management page: You have already used a number of settings on this page, such as Create Web applications, and Create site collections. Here is a quick guide to the rest of these settings commonly used in a MOSS installation. Note that Chapter 8 will cover the settings on this page that apply to both WSS and MOSS installations!

The Search Section's Manage Search Service Settings

This page shows the current settings for the Search service in MOSS, such as the server name; contact e-mail address, which is used by the administrator if there are questions about the search feature; and which SSP is hosting the Search service. It also contains links to configuration settings related to the search feature (see also Figure 5-15).

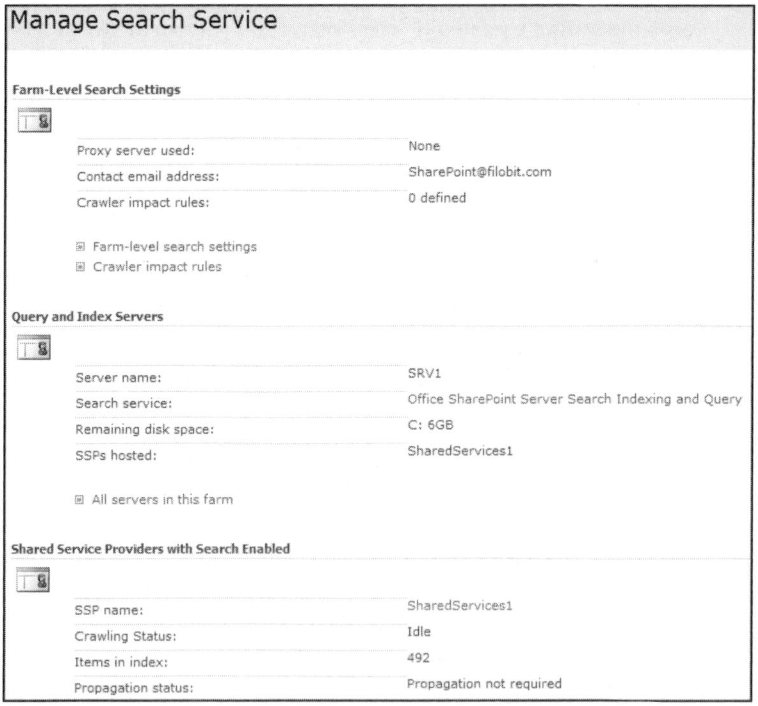

Manage Search Service

Farm-Level Search Settings

Proxy server used:	None
Contact email address:	SharePoint@filobit.com
Crawler impact rules:	0 defined

☒ Farm-level search settings
☒ Crawler impact rules

Query and Index Servers

Server name:	SRV1
Search service:	Office SharePoint Server Search Indexing and Query
Remaining disk space:	C: 6GB
SSPs hosted:	SharedServices1

☒ All servers in this farm

Shared Service Providers with Search Enabled

SSP name:	SharedServices1
Crawling Status:	Idle
Items in index:	492
Propagation status:	Propagation not required

Figure 5-15

The InfoPath Forms Services Section

This section in Application Management has five links, all related to the InfoPath Form Service. Following is a short description of what each of these links is used for:

- **Manage form templates:** Use this page to list and manage all InfoPath forms templates uploaded to the InfoPath Forms Service. Use the quick menu for each template to:

    - View properties for the form template, such as the version, last modification date, and status.

    - Activate this form template for a site collection.

    - Deactivate this form template from a site collection.

    - Quiesce a form template (i.e., prohibit any new instance of this template from being created but allow the instances currently running to be completed).

    - Remove the form template.

    The word quiesce has been chosen by Microsoft to describe a process in which a feature prohibits new sessions but allows all current sessions to continue to run for a period of time that you define.

- **Configure InfoPath Forms Services:** Use this page to configure the settings for the Forms Service, such as:

    - Define if InfoPath forms should be browser-enabled or not.

    - Data Connection Timeouts (default: 10,000 seconds).

    - Data Connection Response Site (default: 1,500 kilobytes).

- **For HTTP data connections:** Force the data connection to use SSL when authenticating by Basic Authentication, or Digest Authentication (default: Yes).

- **Authentication to data sources:** You can allow embedded SQL authentication (default: No).

- **Cross-Domain Access for User Form Templates:** You can allow cross-domain access for user form templates that use connection settings in a data connection file (default: No).

    - Configure Thresholds, that is, the number of postbacks per form session state (default: 75), and the number of actions per postback (default: 200).

    - Configure Form Session State, that is, that active sessions should be terminated after 1,440 minutes, and the maximum size of form session state (default 4096 kilobytes) and that Session State Service should store form session states.

- **Upload Form Template:** Use this feature to upload a new or updated form to the InfoPath Forms Service. Use the check box if you want to overwrite any existing copy of this form. This page also allows you to define what to do with currently opened forms that are about to be updated:

    - Allow existing browser-based form filling sessions to complete using the current version of the form template, or

    - Terminate existing browser-based form filling sessions. Any data in those sessions will be lost.

❑ **Manage Data Connection Files:** Use this page to upload a data connection to external content; this connection can then be used by the InfoPath Form. By default, there are no data connections uploaded.

❑ **Manage the Web Service Proxy:** Use this page to enable the Web service proxy for data connections between the InfoPath forms and Web services. You can also enable the Web service proxy for data connections in user forms.

You will learn more about creating InfoPath forms, and how to use the InfoPath Forms Service, in Chapter 7.

The Office SharePoint Server Shared Services Section

This section in the Application Management page is all about the Shared Service Provider (SSP). You may recall that you created an SSP named SharedServices1 in Chapter 4, and this SSP is responsible for many interesting features, such as user profile import, creating audience groups, and configuring global searching. These features are covered in Chapter 8, but here is a quick summary of the links and configuration pages related to the SSP:

❑ **Create or configure this farm's shared services:** Use this page to create and manage instances of SSP, such as SharedService1. Note that you can also open this page by clicking the Shared Services Administration link in the Quick Launch bar to the left on this page.

❑ **Grant or configure shared services between farms:** Use this page to configure how shared services will work in a multi-farm environment. You may remember that one SharePoint farm will automatically share its SSP instances, but if there is more than one farm, you must use this page to configure the system so that the SSP in one farm can be used in other farms.

❑ **Check services enabled in this farm:** This is not directly related to the SSP, but its page will show a list of services that have some type of problem. In other words, if you see a service listed on this page, there may be something the administrator must do. Note that if you have installed an evaluation copy of MOSS, then you will see a service saying: The trial installation on server SRV1 will expire on *<date>*, plus a description of the impact it will have when this trial period has ended. This list may also show a recommended action for how to solve a problem; for example, how to convert the trial version to a full MOSS installation.

❑ **Configure session state:** This is a setting that will affect the web client. If this setting is on, then SharePoint will remember who you are when you move from one site to another. If the Session State is disabled, users may have to enter their logon credentials when moving to a new part or feature of MOSS. The default setting is enabled. This page also allows you to set a timeout period for a user session; the default is 60 minutes. If a user is inactive longer than that, he or she may need to log on again, depending on if he or she is working from the inside of your network or from the Internet.

The External Service Connections Section's Records Center

A records center is an advanced MOSS feature that works like a stand-alone SharePoint document repository; it could be a separate SharePoint server or a subsite in a site collection. A Records Center is used when an organization needs to move or copy important records, such as records about employees, or important projects, to a safe place where no unauthorized personnel will be able to view or modify them. This configuration page is used to define the URL to the Records Center server, which must have been installed previously.

Before activating the records center, an organization must devise a strategy for how to use this records center; for example, what records should it store, what policies will be applied to these records, who should be able to send records to the repository, and who should be able to view and manage these records? These are important questions that are usually answered by management teams, compliance officers, and information workers. Best practice is to create one document library for each record content type, and avoid mixing content types in the same library; these libraries will store the records.

The next step is to create a Records Center site, preferably on a separate SharePoint server, or at least on a separate Web application (such as an extended IIS web server). You should use a separate SQL Server database to store the content of a records center if the security requirements are very high. In the following example, you will create a site collection in a separate web application and in a new site collection, which will be okay for organizations with moderate security requirements. Follow the steps in the Try It Out below to create a Records Center site in a newly created web application named RecordsCenter, using the TCP port 80 and the host header name RecordCenter.

Try It Out   **Create a Records Center Site**

1.   Log on as an administrator for the MOSS server, and start SharePoint's Central Administration tool.

2.   Switch to the Application Management page.

3.   Click Create or extend Web application, then click Create a new Web application, and give it the description **RecordsCenter**, the TCP port of **80**, and the Host Header name **RecordsCenter**. Also create a separate application pool named **RecordsCenter**, using the account Filobit\sp_service. Click OK to save and close the form. For more information about creating web applications, see Chapter 4.

4.   Since you defined a Host Header name for the Web application in step 3, you must now add this name as an alias record in the DNS:

   a.   Log on to an Active Directory domain controller. Start the DNS by clicking Start ⇨ Administrative tools ⇨ DNS, expand the Forward Lookup Zone, right-click on the domain name (in this example Filobit.com), and select New Alias (CNAME).

   b.   In the form that appears, enter **RecordsCenter** as the alias name, click the Browse button, and locate the SharePoint server name (in this example SRV1), then click OK twice.

   c.   Test your work by opening a command prompt window, and typing **ping recordscenter**; the reply should be the IP number for SRV1.

5.   Switch to the Application Management page again. Click Create Site Collection (in the SharePoint Site Management section). This will create a new site collection for the records center site.

6.   On the web form that appears (see Figure 5-16), enter these settings:

   a.   Click on the Web application, and change it to **RecordsCenter**.

   b.   **Title:** Records Center.

   c.   **Description:** Filobit Record Repository.

   d.   **URL name:** http://recordscenter.

   e.   **Select a template:** Switch to the Enterprise tab, and select Records Center.

   f.   **Primary Site Collection Administrator:** Filobit\Administrator.

   g.   Leave the rest of these settings as they are. Click Create.

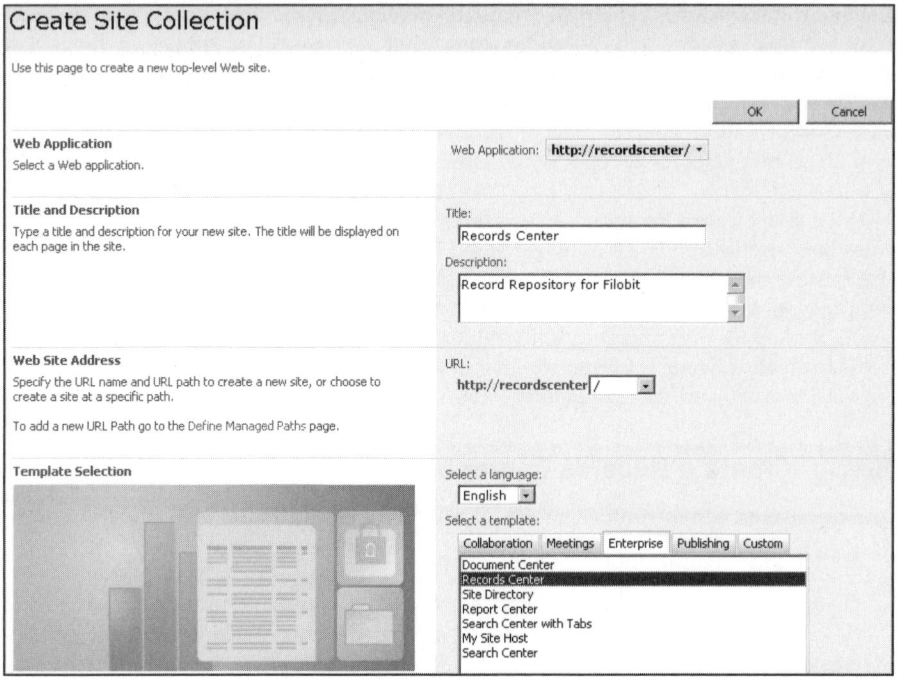

Figure 5-16

The Records Center site is created and displayed. The next step is to configure it properly for the type of records management your organization requires. After that you must configure how an incoming document will be routed to the right library. Start by creating the document library that will store the records. Click Site Actions ➪ Create ➪ Document Library. Give it a name, for example, Financial Reports, and click Create.

The next step is to configure the record routing for the records center site. This is a list of items that defines where an incoming document will be stored. For example, assume that you have five different document libraries, all storing different types of records. Since the user will never manually store the document in a specific library in the records center, you need another process that does that for you. This is what the Record Routing list is used for. By default, there is one document library named Unclassified Records.

7. Create a new Record Routing entry like this: While still in the Records Center site, click on the Record Routing list in the Quick Launch bar, then click New and enter this information (see Figure 5-17):

   a. **Title:** Financial Reports. This must match the title of the document content type.

   b. **Description:** "Store all financial reports in the document library Financial Reports."

   c. **Location:** Financial Reports. This must match the name of the document library where the record documents will be stored.

d. **Alias:** Enter any alias for the default content type, that is, "Title" above. For example, if you also want to route documents based on the content type `Budget` to the same library, then enter Budget here. If you have more than one name, separate them with a slash (/).

e. **Default:** Set this check box if you want the location in step c to receive any documents that do not match any record routing rule.

f. Click OK to save and close the page.

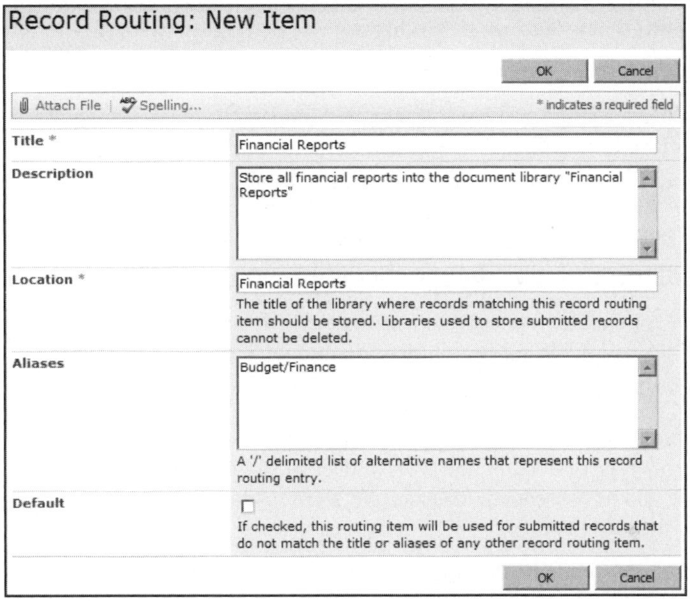

Record Routing: New Item

| | OK | Cancel |

📎 Attach File | 🔤 Spelling... * indicates a required field

Title *   Financial Reports

Description   Store all financial reports into the document library "Financial Reports"

Location *   Financial Reports

The title of the library where records matching this record routing item should be stored. Libraries used to store submitted records cannot be deleted.

Aliases   Budget/Finance

A '/' delimited list of alternative names that represent this record routing entry.

Default   ☐

If checked, this routing item will be used for submitted records that do not match the title or aliases of any other record routing item.

| | OK | Cancel |

Figure 5-17

8. You must now enable the application pool account used by the Web application hosting your user portal, for example "SharePoint – 80," access to the Records Center site. In this particular case, it will not be necessary, since you are using the same account (Filobit\sp_service) for both the user portal and the records center:

a. Use the Internet Information Service (IIS) Manager, and look up what user account that application pool is using (as described earlier several times); in our example it will be Filobit\sp_service.

b. Open the Records Center site.

c. Click People and Groups in the Quick Launch bar.

d. Click the Groups headline in the Quick Launch bar. This will list all groups.

e. Click on the group Records Center Web Service Submitter for RecordsCenter. The application pool account must be a member of this group in order to have write permission to the document libraries in the records center.

f. This group is empty initially; click Add and enter the user name, including the domain name, for the user that the application pool is using as its security account.

g. Close this configuration page.

The Records Center site is now ready to be used. Next you must create a Content Type, i.e. a defined type of document, with a name that exact matches the Title in step 6b above. After that, you must activate this content type in all these document libraries where users are supposed to create financial reports, budgets and financial documents:

9. Open the top site where the users create their documents; for example, `http://srv1`, then click Site Actions ➪ Site Settings ➪ Modify All Site Settings, and modify the following settings:

   a. Click Site Content Types in the Galleries section.

   b. Click Create, and enter the name Financial Reports. Remember that it must match the Title in step 6b.

   c. In the Parent Content Type section, choose Document Content Types and Documents.

   d. Accept the option to put this site content type into the Custom Content Types.

   e. Click OK to save and close this new content type.

   f. Optional: If you want to use a specific document template, click Advanced settings and upload the Word template or document to be used as a template for this content type.

   g. Optional: If you need any custom columns, then add them in the Columns section.

10. When the content type is created, it must be associated with the user's document library, used for storing this type of documents: Open a user site with the document library with which this content type will be associated; for example, the subsite Finance: `http://srv1/sitedirectory/finance`; then do this:

   a. Click on the document library.

   b. Click Settings ➪ Document Library Settings.

   c. Click Advanced settings, select `Allow management of content type = Yes`, then click OK.

   d. A new section named Content Types is displayed; click Add from existing site content types.

   e. Locate the content type Financial Reports, click Add, then OK. This content type is associated with this document library and is ready to be used.

   f. It is now time to add some test documents. Open the document you just added the content type to, then click the black arrow next to the New button to open its menu. Note that you now have two content types: Document and Financial Reports. Select Documents this time, and create a Word file with some text, save it in this document library, and close Word. Then use the menu again, but this time select the Financial Reports type; enter some text, and save the document.

You now have two new documents in this library, one based on the default document content type, and the other based on the Financial Reports type. The only thing that remains is to configure SharePoint to activate the Web service that will assist all users when they want to send a document to the records center:

11. Open the Central Administration tool, switch to the Application Management page, click on the Records center, then enter these settings (see Figure 5-18):

    a. Select Connect to a Records Center.

    b. URL: `http://recordscenter/_vti_bin/officialfile.asmx` (where `http://recordscenter` is the URL to the records center site you created earlier, and the last part of this URL points to the Web service for this site.

    c. Display name: Records Center. This is the name that your users will see in the documents' Send To menus.

    d. Click OK to save and close this page.

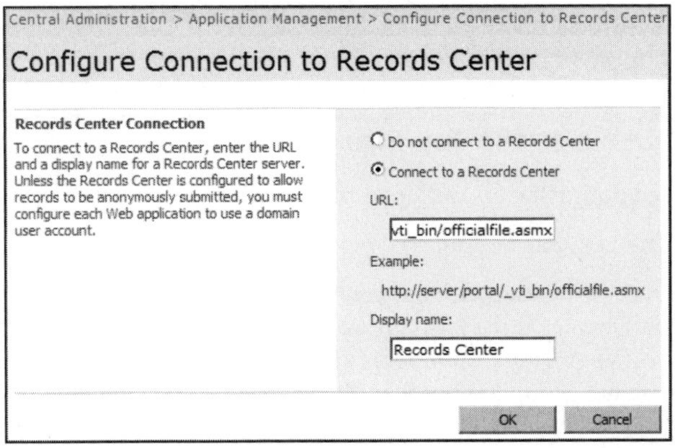

Central Administration > Application Management > Configure Connection to Records Center

Configure Connection to Records Center

Records Center Connection

To connect to a Records Center, enter the URL and a display name for a Records Center server. Unless the Records Center is configured to allow records to be anonymously submitted, you must configure each Web application to use a domain user account.

    ○ Do not connect to a Records Center
    ◉ Connect to a Records Center

    URL:

    `vti_bin/officialfile.asmx`

    Example:

    http://server/portal/_vti_bin/officialfile.asmx

    Display name:

    `Records Center`

    [OK] [Cancel]

Figure 5-18

12. Time to test the records center. Open the document library where you created the two documents in step 11f. Use the quick menu for the first document (based on the default content type), and select Send to ⇨ Records Center. If all went well, you should now see a page saying Operation Completed Successfully. Click OK to go back.

13. Repeat this for the second document. Both of these documents are now sent to the Records Center site.

14. Open the Records Center site; Open the Unclassified Records document library. It contains a folder with a name based on the date and time when it was created; open that folder and your first document will be stored there. Then open the Financial Records library; your second document should be stored there.

Managing Access to the Portal Site

You use almost, but not exactly, the same procedures to manage users in the portal site as in the WSS site. You can allow access to users and security groups in the Active Directory domain or the SharePoint server's local account database. Each user must be granted a permission level (directly or as a member of a SharePoint Group) in order to get access to any part of the portal site. Remember that the home site is the top-level site in the site collection that constitutes the portal site. Any permission settings for that top site will, by default, be inherited by all subsites, such as News, Reports, and Sites, and possibly by their subsites, if any.

Managing Users and Groups

When you create a new top site (and thus a new site collection), you must also define its primary site collection administrator. At that point this person (and you, as a SharePoint server administrator) is the only one with access to this site collection. To add users to the site, you follow the same steps as when adding users to a WSS site, as described in Chapter 3; be sure to read that chapter too, so you are sure how the permission system works for WSS 3.0 sites in SharePoint 2007. To add a user or an Active Directory group, you perform the steps in the following Try It Out. This can be done from any computer, as long as you have administrative rights on the top site.

Try It Out	Add Users to the Top Site

1. Log on as the administrator, and open the top site.

2. Click Site Actions ⇨ Site Settings ⇨ People and Groups.

3. Select the SharePoint Group that the new user will belong to. You may remember from Chapter 3 that SharePoint creates three local groups that have the name of the top site as a prefix, then a suffix: Visitors (View only), Members (View, Add, Modify), and Owners (Full Access). In this example, select the group that ends with Member, then click New.

   a. In the Users/Group field, enter the user's name, or e-mail address. If you add more than one name, separate them with a semicolon (;).

   b. In the Give Permission section, make sure that the selected SharePoint Group is correct. If it is not the correct SharePoint Group, then use its menu to change the group. Note that you can also grant the user a permission level directly, such as Full Control, Design, or Contribute.

   c. At the end of this web form, check the Send welcome e-mail to the new users option, if you want to send an e-mail to inform the users about their new permission with a link to this web site.

   d. Click OK to save and close the page.

4. Verify that it works; log in as the new user and check that it works. Note that SharePoint's security trimmed feature is active, so if this new user is missing some link, such as Site Actions, or cannot see everything that you know exists on this site, it is because he or she does not have the proper permission to do so.

If there are any subsites that inherit their permissions from this site, the new user will now have the same permissions to those subsites as he or she does to this site. If this is not what you want, you can break the inheritance like this as shown in the following Try It Out.

Break the Permission Inheritance

1. Log on as the administrator, and open the subsite where you want to break the permissions inheritance.

2. Click People and Groups in the Quick Launch bar.

3. Click Site Permissions in the Quick Launch bar.

4. Click Actions ⇨ Edit Permissions, then click OK to accept the warning about breaking the permissions inheritance.

5. Now you can add, modify or delete any existing user account or SharePoint Group.

6. Optional: If you want to restore the inheritance of permissions, click Actions ⇨ Inherit Permissions. All customized permissions will be replaced with the inherited permissions.

SharePoint Groups

In Chapter 3, you learned that a user must be associated with a Permission Level role before he or she can access anything in SharePoint. In WSS 3.0 the default permission levels were Read, Contribute, Design, and Full Control. MOSS adds some more Permission levels: Manage Hierarchy, Approve, and Restricted Read. As in WSS, the easiest way to grant a user permissions is to use any of the three default SharePoint Groups that automatically are created for each new SharePoint site configured to use its own security settings (that does not inherit its permissions from a parent site). The name for these SharePoint Groups will start with the name of the site they belong to. For example, if the site is named ABC, the SharePoint Groups' name will start with ABC. MOSS will add more default SharePoint Groups besides these three. All of them are listed here, for a site named ABC:

❑ **ABC Visitors:** This SharePoint Group is associated with the permission level Read: Any member of this group can view, copy, and print content in lists and libraries, including previous versions, if any.

❑ **ABC Members:** This SharePoint Group is associated with the permission level Contribute. Members of this group can also add, modify, and delete lists and library content.

❑ **ABC Owners:** This SharePoint Group is associated with the permission level Full Control. Members of this group have full access to this site, and all its content.

❑ **Approvers:** This SharePoint Group can edit and approve pages, lists, items, and documents.

❑ **Designers:** This SharePoint Group can edit lists, libraries, and pages in a site. It can also create Master Pages, and page layouts in the Master Page Gallery, and it can modify the Cascading Style Sheets (CSS) files.

❑ **Hierarchy Managers:** This SharePoint Group can create sites, lists, list items, and libraries.

❑ **Quick Deploy Users:** This SharePoint Group can schedule Quick Deploy jobs.

❑ **Restricted Readers:** This SharePoint Group can view pages, libraries, and lists, but not their version history.

❑   **Style Resource Readers:** This SharePoint Group can read, but not change, the Master Page Gallery. By default, all authenticated users are members of this group.

❑   **Viewers:** This SharePoint Group can view pages, list items, and documents. If the document has server rendering available, members of this group can only view the document using the server rendering.

Note that members of a site's "Members" SharePoint Group will automatically see all documents and tasks belonging to them in their My Site. For example, if Anna belongs to the ABC Members group in the site ABC, then her My Site will show all documents she has edited and all tasks she has been assigned in the ABC site.

Removing User Accounts

As described several times, all users must be granted a permission level, either directly or as a member of a SharePoint Group, in order to access any part of SharePoint. This is true both for WSS and for MOSS sites. In most organizations, these domain user accounts are stored in the Active Directory. This section describes what happens when these user accounts are deleted from the AD. You might assume that SharePoint automatically cleans up when someone is removed from the AD. But if you do, you are wrong! Think about it: One of your users has been active in several important projects now she has left the company. Do you really want to remove all references to that user? In many situations, the answer is no. So, SharePoint requires the administrator to manually remove the user account when necessary. The good news is that it is easy; just follow the instructions below. There are two ways to delete a user from SharePoint. One is where you remove the user account from all sites in a given site collection. For example, you might want to have a user's Active Directory account still be valid, but remove all access from SharePoint. The other way is to remove all information about a user from the User Profile database. Let's start with the first method as shown in the following Try It Out.

Try It Out   **Remove a User Account from a Site Collection**

1.   Open the top site in the site collection from where the user account should be removed.

2.   Click Site Actions ➪ Site Settings ➪ People And Groups. If the top site is based on a WSS template, you can also click the link "People And Groups" in the Quick Launch bar.

3.   Click the All People link in the Quick Launch bar.

4.   Select the user(s) to be removed, click the Actions menu, and then click Delete Users from Site Collection.

5.   You will now see a warning: "You are about to delete the following users from this site collection. The users will be deleted, and will not have access to any site within the site collection," followed by the name(s) to be deleted. Double-check that this is what you want to do, then click OK to complete the delete operation.

The procedure above will remove the permissions, but not the properties for the user, from the User Profile database. Follow the procedure in the Try It Out below to remove the user from the User Profile database.

Try It Out   **Remove a User from the User Profile Database**

1. Log on as an administrator, and open SharePoint's Central Administration tool.

2. In the Quick Launch bar, click in the shared service provider link, by default, named `SharedServices1`.

3. In the User Profiles and My Sites section, click User profiles and properties.

4. Click View user profiles.

5. In the toolbar, change the view to Profiles Missing from Import. Now, all deleted user accounts are listed. Check the user profiles to be removed from SharePoint, and click Delete on the toolbar.

A related situation occurs when someone is changing the logon account name in the Active Directory (for example, when changing her last name due to marriage). Doing this will not update the user account information in SharePoint unless you follow the steps in the Try It Out below (in this example, a user has changed his logon name from `Filobit\tony` to `Filobit\Antony`):

Try It Out   **Update User Account Information in SharePoint**

1. Log on to the SharePoint server as an administrator.

2. Open a command prompt.

3. Enter the following command (see Chapter 3 about updating the environment variable path to include the path to the file folder storing the STSADM utility):

```
STSADM -o migrateuser -oldlogin filobit\tony -newlogin filobit\antony -
ignoresidhistory
```

If you just want to remove a user from a particular SharePoint Group, you can also use the STSADM utility. For example, to remove the user `Filobit\Adam` *from the SharePoint Group "Home Members" in the site collection* `http://srv1,` *open a command prompt window and enter* `STSADM -o deleteuser -url http://srv1 -userlogin Filobit\adam -group "Home Members"`.

Anonymous Access

Just as in WSS, a MOSS site can be opened for anonymous access. The steps to do this are identical to how this is done in a WSS site, so be sure to read Chapter 3 to see more about these anonymous access settings.

Summary

In this chapter, you learned the following:

❏ After the initial installation of MOSS, there are three final steps that you must do to prepare the new SharePoint server. They are referred to as "administrator tasks."

❏ When these tasks are completed, you will see a new list of administrative tasks.

❏ Not all of these tasks in the new list must be completed, but be sure to configure outgoing e-mail settings and schedule the indexing of SharePoint's databases.

❏ The Central Administration tool is organized into two pages: Operations and Application Management.

❏ Enable incoming e-mail settings if SharePoint should be able to accept incoming e-mail.

❏ Configure User Profile import if you want SharePoint to store user properties.

❏ Define a link to the portal site before you start creating all My Sites.

❏ Create the records center using a separate web application or a separate SharePoint server.

❏ In order to enable creation of My Sites, the user account used by the application pool hosting the Central Administration tool must be a member of the local Administrators group on the SharePoint server.

❏ Be sure to use the Service Account area of the Operations page when you need to update a service account; for example, for an application pool or a SharePoint service.

❏ Do not forget to install antivirus programs that work directly with SharePoint's database!

❏ Single Sign-On is used by programmers and applications to get access to external data sources.

❏ Use information management policy settings, to get full control over documents, during their lifetime.

❏ Granting access to the MOSS site is done exactly as in WSS; the difference is that MOSS has more preconfigured SharePoint Groups.

❏ Use the Master Site Directory Setting to ensure that all new top sites can be listed in the master site directory.

❏ SharePoint has a feature that scans for broken site links in the master site directory.

❏ There are a number of configuration pages related to InfoPath Forms Services; make sure that you know how to use them, to get the most out of the Forms Service.

❏ Anonymous access in MOSS is configured exactly as in WSS sites — be sure that you understand how this works before opening a site to anonymous access. Read more about this in Chapter 3.

In the next chapter, you learn more about creating web sites.

6

Building Web Sites

So far you have seen how to install both WSS and MOSS, and in last chapter you learned how to configure the portal site in MOSS. But the fun does not stop there. There are lots of other interesting things you can do in your new SharePoint environment, and they all build on WSS sites.

This chapter will tell you a lot more about creating sites for both MOSS and WSS. Before you read this chapter, you should have a pretty good understanding of the basic administration. Be sure to read Chapters 3 and 5 before reading this chapter because this will make it much easier to understand the information presented here.

WSS Sites

The web sites you create with WSS 3.0 are similar to the ones in WSS 2.0, but there are important differences! They now have a lot of new features that only were found in SPS 2003 before. For example, you can do a global search that is security trimmed (users only see objects they are allowed to see), and its content can be filtered using audiences. This means that a user now has a much more consistent experience when moving from a WSS site to a MOSS site because the sites behave in the same way. It is true that MOSS sites have a lot of more advanced features than WSS sites, but the basic features are shared between them both. Following is a list of some of the new features in WSS 3.0 (see Figures 6-1 and 6-2):

❑ **Breadcrumb trails:** You will directly see where in the site hierarchy you are now. You can also click on any of the breadcrumbs to jump back to a previous location (see Figure 6-1).

❑ **Persistent Quick Launch bar:** If you open a list in WSS 3.0, it will still show you the Quick Launch bar. Compare that to WSS 2.0 where the Quick Launch bar was replaced with action links specific to the current list, which made it more cumbersome to quickly open another list or library in that site (see Figure 6-1).

❑ **Navigation:** You can display the subsites under the current site. You can also configure the Quick Launch bar to display a tree view of the site hierarchy that includes all lists and libraries, including any folder, plus all subsites (see Figure 6-1).

❑ **Recycle Bin:** All deleted list items or document items will be stored in a Recycle Bin located at the bottom of the Quick Launch bar. The user who deleted the item can simply open the Recycle Bin and restore this item.

❑ **Outlook 2007 integration:** Using the Outlook 2007 client, a user can create a local copy of SharePoint libraries and lists for offline usage. This is true for most list types, except, for example, Survey lists. The information copied to Outlook 2007 is editable. Any change you make is replicated back to the SharePoint source when your computer goes online (see Figure 6-2).

❑ **RSS Feeds:** Using the Really Simple Syndication (RSS) technique, you can configure Outlook 2007 and Internet Explorer 7.0 to retrieve updates of SharePoint lists. Using RSS, you will always know when a SharePoint list or library is updated, without the need to download each new list item or document to Outlook.

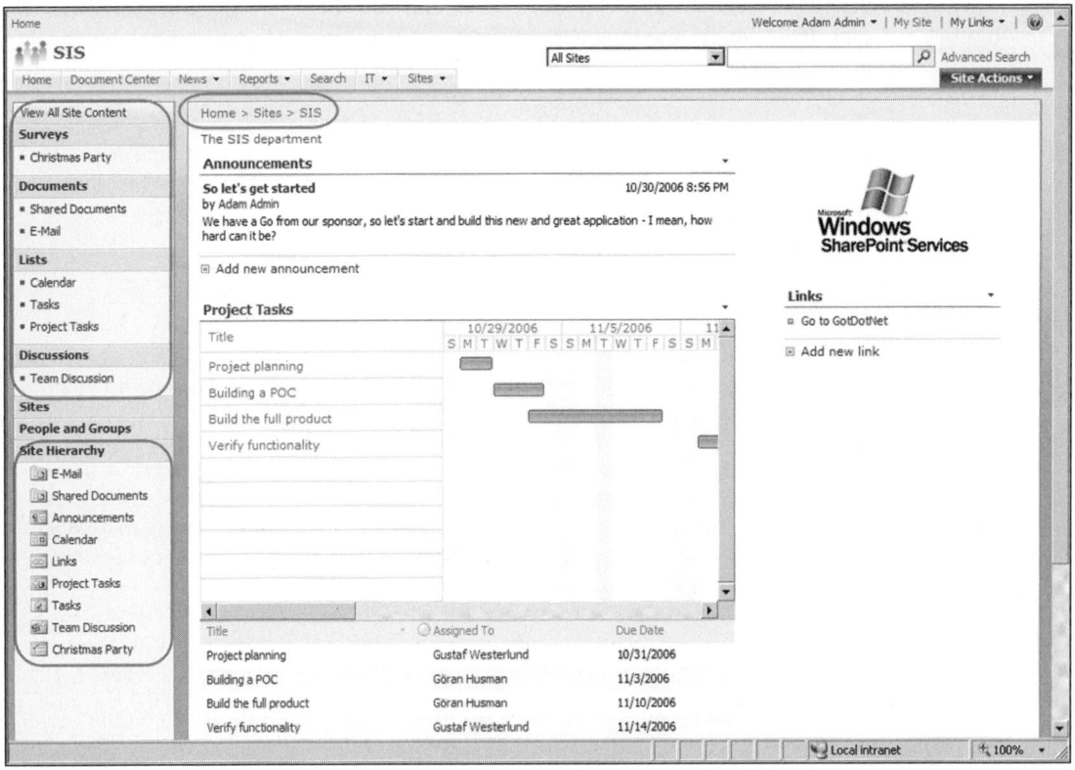

Figure 6-1

Figure 6-2

WSS Default Site Templates

The site templates that are installed by default when deploying a WSS 3.0 server are similar to the ones found in WSS 2.0, except for the many new cool features mentioned above. The idea with WSS is still the same as before: to offer a place where a team can share documents, contacts, and other types of information. True, you can build a simple intranet, using WSS alone, but it will not have the content management features that MOSS offers. But the again, WSS 3.0 is free, and MOSS 2007 is not, so you may be forced to go with WSS for economic reasons. So, let's look at the site templates that come with WSS 3.0:

❑ **Team Site:** This is the standard site template, with some precreated lists and libraries: Shared Documents, Announcements, Calendar, Links, Tasks, and Team Discussions.

❑ **Blank Site:** The same type of site as a team site, except that there are no precreated lists or libraries. The only thing displayed on this "blank site" is an image Web Part that shows the WSS logotype.

❑ **Document Workspace:** This is a special type of site that mostly is used by a team to collaborate on a specific document. Mostly, this type of site is created using the quick menu for a document or directly from within MS Office applications.

❑ **Wiki Site:** This is a new site template for WSS 3.0; use this template to create sites where users can read and add information in a very informal way. Common uses for wiki sites are capturing brainstorming ideas, building a support center knowledge base, and building a general knowledge base. (See Figure 6-3.)

❑ **Blog:** A blog is a site where you share your ideas, comments, and often tips and tricks. Usually, there is a single person who is responsible for a blog site, but it may also be used by teams that want to share information with other users.

❑ **Basic Meeting Workspace:** This type of site is normally used to capture details and information for a meeting. It contains four precreated lists: Objectives, Attendees, Agenda, and Document Library. This type of site is called a workspace, and it is still a common WSS site. This site is most commonly configured when booking a meeting using Outlook 2003 or 2007, although you can create it manually.

❑ **Blank Meeting Workspace:** This is similar to the basic meeting workspace, except that it only has one precreated list: Attendees. Use this template when you want to create all lists manually. The Attendees list is special, since it will automatically be populated by all users invited to an Outlook meeting.

❑ **Decision Meeting Workspace:** This site template contains the following precreated lists: Attendees, Objectives, Agenda, Document Library, Tasks, and Decisions.

❑ **Social Meeting Workspace:** This template has three pages created by default: Home, Discussion, and Photos. This site template also contains these lists: Attendee, Directions, Things to Bring, Discussion Board, and Picture Library. It also displays an image Web Part. This type of site is often used to discuss social events, such as Christmas parties and Birthday celebrations.

❑ **Multipage Meeting Workspace:** This site template is very similar to the social meeting workspace, with its three pages. The difference is the number of lists: This template only has Attendees, Objectives and Agenda. Two of the three pages are empty, and you are supposed to add lists to them.

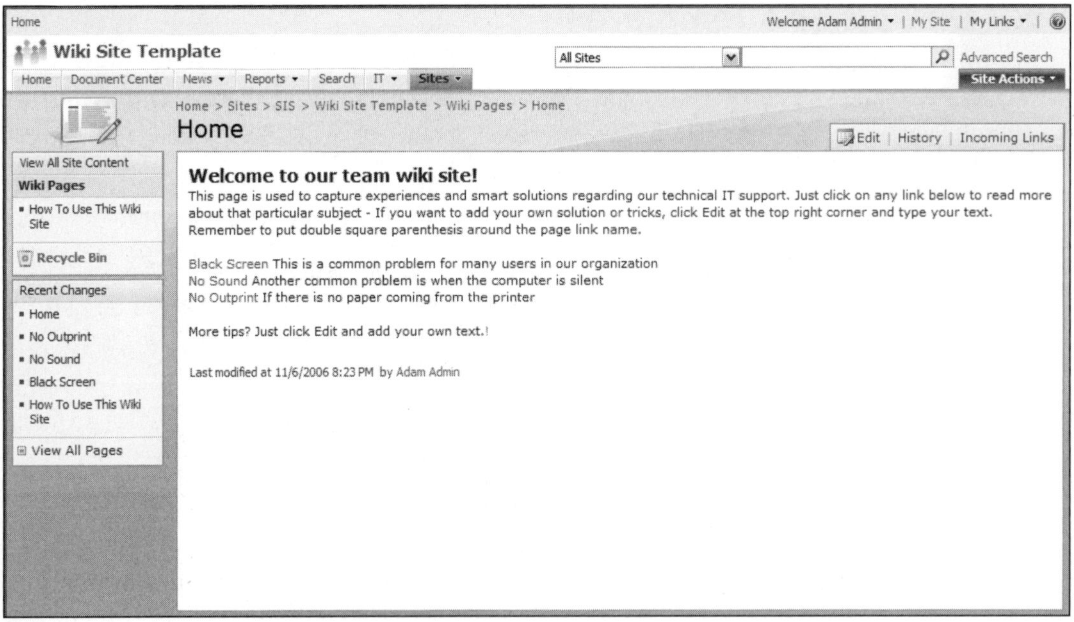

Figure 6-3

WSS Custom Site Templates

All of the default site templates can be modified by a user with the proper permission, for example, an owner or a designer. What you can do depends on how you modify the site. You have two basic choices: using the web browser (e.g., Internet Explorer) or using the SharePoint Designer program. Besides these two options, you can also build your own site definitions, but that is a more advanced topic that you will learn more about in Chapter 12. Following is an introduction to how the default site templates work under the hood:

Whatever changes you make, regardless of whether you use the web browser or SharePoint Designer, will be stored in SharePoint's content database. There will be no files updated outside that database. So how does it work? To begin with, all sites are defined by a number of Active Server Pages (ASP) and Extensible Markup Language (XML) files, stored in the file system on the SharePoint server. For example, every WSS site is defined by the files in this folder:

```
<disk>:\Program Files\Common Files\Microsoft Shared\web server ↵
extensions\12\TEMPLATE\1033\STS
```

STS stands for SharePoint Team Services (from the first version of WSS). Yes, it is curious that Microsoft still sticks with the old abbreviation, but just accept the fact that anytime you see STS, you should think WSS!

There are also a number of files that define the STS site that you will find in the following folder:

```
<disk>:\Program Files\Common Files\Microsoft Shared\web server ↵
extensions\12\TEMPLATE\GLOBAL
```

This last location consists of files that define common characteristics of a number of site definitions, not only STS. In previous versions of SharePoint, every site definition contained its own set of files and a folder you could find in the GLOBAL directory, but in SharePoint 2007 Microsoft has created a global folder structure for them. Only the definitions that are specific to a given site definition will be listed in their own site definition folder.

So, the site definition controls the characteristics of a site. You apply a customization of that site, and that is where site templates comes in. A site template adds the look and feel of the site definition, including pre-created lists and libraries, and colors. But it does not stop there. The navigation elements, the top menus, logotypes, and so on, are defined by something called a Master Page, which is an ASP.NET 2.0 feature. In Chapter 12 you will learn more about how to use Master Pages for your WSS sites. To summarize all this, the way a WSS site looks and works is decided by:

❑ **The site definition files:** Stored in the file system, these define the characteristics of the site, such as what lists that are available, and their features and functionality.

❑ **The site template:** This controls the overall look and feel, including what lists and libraries that will be pre-created.

❑ **The Master Page:** This controls the navigation, the menus, the Quick Launch bar, and the logotype.

And it does not stop here. You can create your own site template by customizing any existing site. So, the question is: Where will your customization be stored? The answer is: in SharePoint's content database! What will it contain? The answer: the differences between the basic site definition and your customizations, no more and no less. If the basic site definition gets deleted, your site will not work, since it only contains the things you changed in the site.

To create your own site template, you simply open an empty site and customize it, and then save it as a template. For example, you can add new listings, change the color theme, and add more Web Parts to the site's home page. The important thing to remember is to start with a site that has the basic functionality you want to use. For example, to customize a site used for meetings, you should start by using a Meeting Workspace template. Use the steps in the following Try It Out to create a site template, based on a Team Site template:

Try It Out   Create a Custom Site Template

1. Log on to the WSS server as an administrator.

2. Use Internet Explorer and open any WSS site, for example: `http://srv1/SiteDirectory/IT`.

3. Click Site Actions ⇨ Create ⇨ Sites and Workspaces.

4. On the next page, enter these values to create a subsite under IT based on the Team Site template, which you then can use for your customization:

   a. **Title:** Site Dummy.

   b. **Description:** Site used to create a custom site template.

   c. **URL name**: Add SiteDummy to the existing URL link, that is: `http://srv1/SiteDirectory/IT/SiteDummy`.

   d. Make sure to select the Team Site template (on the Collaboration tab).

   e. Click Create to save and create the SiteDummy site.

5. The new site is displayed. It is time to customize it. For example, add some lists and a library. Then show them on the site's home page and remove some of the other lists. Finally, change the color by selecting another theme for this site:

   a. Click Site Actions ⇨ Create ⇨ Document Library. Give it the name Protocols, and click Create.

   b. Click Site Actions ⇨ Create ⇨ Contacts. Give it the name Customers, and click Create.

   c. Click Site Actions ⇨ Create ⇨ Project Tasks. Give it the name Project Tasks, and click Create.

   You now have one new document library, and two new lists. Let's show them on the home page for the site:

   d. Click on the breadcrumb link SiteDummy to open the home page for the site. Then select Site Actions ⇨ Edit Page. This page is now open in edit mode.

   e. Remove the Announcements, the Calendar, and the Image Web Part, like this: Click edit on the right side on the Web Part to be deleted, then select Delete and then OK. Note that this will not delete the actual list; it will only remove its Web Part from this page. Repeat this for all three of these Web Parts.

f. Time to add the new lists you created: On the left Web Part zone, click Add a Web Part. Locate and check the Protocols library, the Customers list, and the Project Tasks list, then click Add. All three will now show up. Now, click Exit Edit Mode in the upper-right corner of the page.

The final customization is to change the colors of this site. You will use the Themes feature for this:

g. Click Site Actions ➪ Site Settings ➪ Site theme (in the Look and Feel section), then select Belltown and click Apply. Your site will now have a greenish look.

6. Click on the SiteDummy breadcrumb link to open the home page for this site. Time to save it as a site template: Click Site Actions ➪ Site Settings ➪ Save site as template. Enter the following:

a. **File Name:** GreenTemplate.

b. **Template Name:** Green Template.

c. **Template Description:** My first site template.

d. **Include Content:** For this demo leave it unchecked. You can use this check box if you want to store current content in the site template. Note that the maximum size for this content is now 500 MB. (In WSS 2.0 the limit was 10 MB.)

e. Then click OK to save this template.

The customized site template is now created and ready to be used. So, let's test it by creating a new site and applying this template:

7. Click Site Actions ➪ Create ➪ Sites and Workspaces, then enter these values:

a. **Title:** Test Site.

b. **Description:** Test site.

c. **URL name:** Add test to the existing URL link, that is:
`http://srv1/SiteDirectory/IT/SiteDummy/test.`

d. Make sure to select the Green Template template (on the Custom tab).

e. Click Create to save and create the site. Inspect the new site. Verify that you have the exact same lists, libraries, Web Parts, and colors, as the custom site template. Easy, right?

There are some natural questions now, like these:

❑ "Where can this custom site template be used?" Answer: Everywhere in this site collection!

❑ "What happens if I change the SiteDummy site that was used to create the custom site template?" Answer: Nothing! There is no relation between the site used to create the customized template, and the template itself. And this can, of course, be a problem in some situations, for example when you have created a number of sites based on the customized template and then you need to make a small change, such as adding a list. It can't be done; you will have to update each and every one of those existing sites manually.

❑ "Can I edit the actual site template?" Answer: No. There is no way to change a custom site template once it is created. The only thing you can do if the template is wrong is to create a new one. If you want to use the exact same template name, you must first delete the existing template. You do this by using the Site Template list, as discussed in the next section.

❑ "Can I somehow change existing sites, based on the custom site template?" Answer: No.

❑ "Can existing sites be configured to use another site template?" Answer: No.

So, creating a customized site template is very easy, but it has a drawback, and you must be aware of it!

Moving Custom Site Templates

Creating custom site templates is easy, but they only work within the site collection they were created in. However, you can copy custom site templates between site collections. The trick is to store a copy of the template outside SharePoint, on the file system, then import that file into the other site collection. It works fine, even if you have chosen to store list content in the template (See step 6d above). The general steps are:

1. Go to the top site and open the site template gallery where the template is located.

2. Save the template to a file on the file system.

3. Go to the template gallery for the other site collection.

4. Import that file to the first gallery.

The detailed steps are also quite straightforward and easy. To copy your site template, just follow the steps in the Try It Out below.

Try It Out   Copy a Site Template to Another Site Collection

1. Log on as a site collection administrator.

2. Open the top site where the site template is currently stored.

3. Choose Site Actions ➪ Site Settings ➪ Modify All Site Settings.

4. Click Site templates. You will see a list of all site templates for the site collection. Note: if you don't see this link, you are not on top site of this site collection. If this is the case, click the link Go to top level site settings in the Site Collection Administration section.

5. Click the name for the site collection you want to copy (for example, Green Template).

6. Choose to Save, and select a folder to save the file in. Keep the file name (Green Template.stp) unless you want to change it, and click the Save button. Then click Close to close the dialog box.

7. Open the top site in the other site collection. Make sure that you are logged on as a local administrator for the site.

8. Choose Site Actions ➪ Site Settings ➪ Modify All Site Settings, and then click Site templates. You should now see all templates for this site collection.

9. Click Upload. Use the Browse button to select the template file you saved in step 6; click Open and then OK. In the following form you can change the name, title, and description if necessary. When ready, click OK. The template is now copied to the site collection.

10. Test your work by creating a new subsite in the site collection using the copied template. Everything should look exactly as it did in the first site collection.

Adding a Site Template to the Global Site Template Gallery

The templates you have been working with up to this point have all been limited to a given site collection. But how can you apply your custom site templates when creating a new top site, and thus a new site collection? By default, the new site collection will only show the standard templates. To understand this, you need to know that SharePoint has a global site template gallery. Any site template in that gallery will be available for every site you will create, regardless of whether it is a top site in a new site collection, or a subsite.

To add site templates to that global site template gallery, you will need another tool, because WSS does not allow you to do it with the ordinary web-based administrator tool. Once again, you must call upon STSADM.EXE, which you used before. If you followed the instructions in Chapter 2 on how to add the path to this tool to the system environment path, you will find this very easy to do.

Try It Out   Add Site Templates Using STSADM

1. Log on to the WSS server as a SharePoint administrator.

2. Start up a command prompt (Start ➪ Run, then enter Cmd and press Enter).

3. Use steps 1 to 6 of "Try It Out: Copy a Site Template to Another Site Collection" above to save the site template and add it as a file to the file system. For this example, assume that the file is named c:\tmp\green.stp.

4. Type the following command, and press Enter:

```
STSADM -o AddTemplate -Filename C:\tmp\Green.stp -Title "The Green Template" ↵
-Description "This is a site template copied using Stsadm."
```

> **If you get a list of all available options now, you have misspelled something. Check your spelling, and repeat the steps.**

5. You must now reset the IIS. While still at the command prompt, type **IISReset** and press Enter.

6. When the command is finished, test your work by creating a new top site: Open SharePoint's Central Administration tool, click on the Application Management tab, and then click on Create site collection. You should see the new custom site template in the Custom tab (see Figure 6-4, where the new template is named The Green Template).

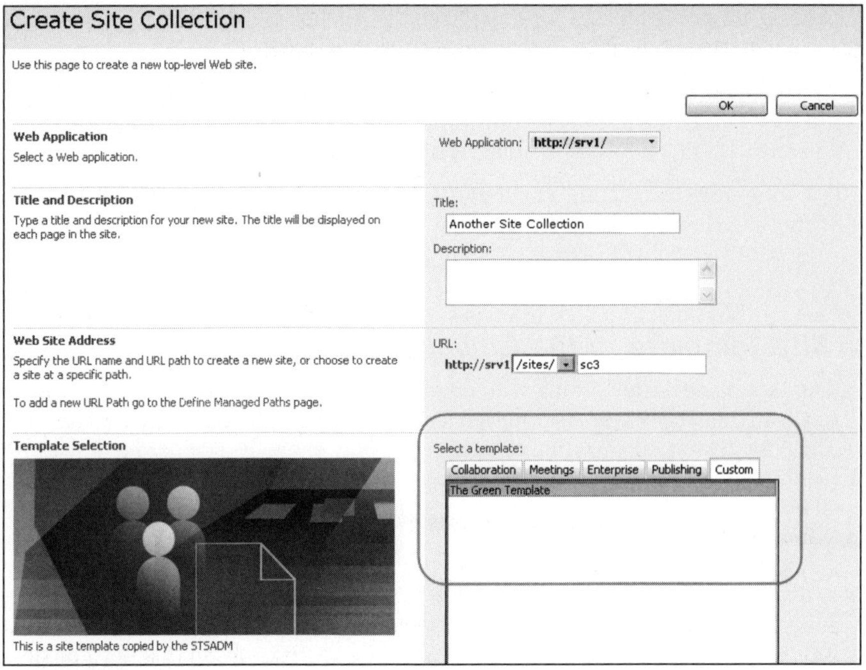

Figure 6-4

Listing a Custom Site Template in the Global Gallery

While you still have the command prompt window open, you can try some more things. For example, if you want to see what global site templates are installed, type this command:

```
STSADM -O EnumTemplates
```

It will show all that you have added manually. But what about those default site templates, such as the Team Site and the Blank Site? They are listed along with your own templates when creating the new site, but they are not listed here. Well, they are a bit special. You will not see them listed here because they are part of the actual site definition. When you created your custom templates, you told WSS to save the modifications of the basic site definition — nothing more. In other words, the template file you copied to the file system is not a complete site definition! For example, if you try importing this file into another WSS installation that for some reason does not have the same site definition, it will fail!

Removing a Custom Site Template from the Global Gallery

You can also remove custom site templates from the global site template gallery. To do this, you will once again use the STSADM tool, as described in the following Try It Out.

Try It Out   **Remove a Site Template Using STSADM**

1. Log on to the WSS server as a SharePoint administrator.

2. Start up a command prompt (Start ➪ Run, then enter Cmd and press Enter).

3. Type the following command and press Enter to delete a site template with the title The Green Template:

    ```
    STSADM –o deletetemplate –Title "The Green Template"
    ```

4. You must now reset the IIS. While still at the command prompt, type **IISReset** and press Enter.

If this was the last custom site template added to the global site template gallery, this process will also remove the Custom tan from the Select a template section (see Figure 6-4).

MOSS Sites

To take advantage of the many interesting and cool features of the sites in a MOSS environment, you need to know more about its functionality and how to use it in an optimal way. The following sections will give you this knowledge. Just remember that this section is about MOSS sites, not WSS sites. If you are running MOSS, you should read all of this information. On the other hand, if you just implement WSS, you should still read this section about MOSS so that you will understand what you are missing!

Comparing MOSS with SPS 2003

In the predecessor of MOSS, you built an intranet portal with a home page and several other pages, such as News, Topics, and Sites. All these pages were referred to as areas, but the truth is that these areas were a special type of WSS site. So, the Home area was the top site, and the other areas were subsites. In other words, the portal site was a site collection, completely separated from any other site collection based on WSS. Any time you created a new WSS site using the Sites area in the portal, you actually created a new WSS site collection. It surely looked like these WSS site collections were organized under the portal site collection, since their URL address indicated that, but they were not. For example, if you had `http://portal` as the URL to the portal site, all its WSS sites got a URL that started with `http://portal/site`. A WSS site collection named Sales would then get the URL `http://portal/sites/sales`, as Figure 6-5 shows.

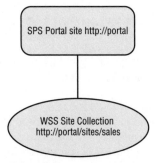

Figure 6-5

So, it was natural to believe that WSS sites should be able to inherit things like permission settings and templates from the portal site collection, but it was not possible. The truth is that both the portal site collection and all WSS site collections were located on the same level. They were all directly organized under the IIS virtual web server (for example, the default web site), and on the same level (see Figure 6-6).

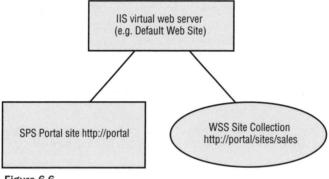

Figure 6-6

The real reason why it was not possible to inherit settings from the portal site is that site collections were, and still are, separate islands of content and settings. In other words, even in MOSS 2007 and WSS 3.0, you still have the exact same structure and therefore the exact same behavior in this respect. For example, you cannot add a user to one site collection and then inherit that user in another site collection. The fact that site collections are isolated from each other is not a bad thing. In fact, this is one of the easiest ways to create a separate SharePoint environment for a group of people that must have its own security settings. For example, say that an organization has two departments: Sales and Research. If these two departments must have their own SharePoint environments while still sharing the same physical SharePoint server, you can create a site collection for each of them. This was also true in the SPS 2003 environment, by the way.

A problem in SPS 2003 was that its areas (or subsites, really) were customized versions of WSS 2.0 sites, so they had a different look and feel than the ordinary WSS 2.0 sites. This is no longer the case in SharePoint 2007. All site collections are based on WSS 3.0! A MOSS site is simply a specific type of site template applied to a WSS site. So, all sites now behave the same way. For example, all sites in SharePoint 2007 are now security trimmed; if a user is not allowed to view a document, a list, or a site, that user will not see it, regardless of whether it is a WSS site or a MOSS site. But the cosmetics are not affected by this new architecture. Each site can, and often has, its own design and menu structure.

If you compare this functionality to SPS 2003 and WSS 2.0, it is a great step forward, since these previous versions not only had different behavior, they also had their own structure, and therefore were customized differently, as the programmer often painfully discovered. As you will see later in Chapter 12, a new feature in SharePoint 2007, called Master Pages, will make it very easy to customize the look and feel of any site, regardless of whether it is a MOSS site or a WSS site. If you later decide that you want to apply a new look to a site, you just redesign its Master Page and the changes will take effect immediately.

To summarize this: The special features of SPS 2003 are now gone. Modified site collection for SPS portal sites, areas, and special customization procedures, compared to WSS 2.0, are no more. In SharePoint 2007, every site is equal in its basic structure, and the main differences between MOSS and WSS 3.0 are the site template applied to them and that MOSS provides a lot more Web Parts than WSS.

MOSS Site Templates

Remember that MOSS is an extension of WSS 3.0, so the site templates that MOSS provides are more advanced than WSS site templates. A default installation of MOSS will offer these site templates, besides all the templates that come with WSS:

❑ **Collaboration Portal (on the Publishing tab):** A site template typically used for creating intranet sites. It also creates a number of subsites, such as a Document Center, a News site, a Reports site, a Search Center, and a Site Directory. This site template is only available when creating a top site (a new site collection).

❑ **Publishing Portal (on the Publishing tab):** A site for Internet-facing web, or an intranet for a large company. This site only contains one subsite: the Press Releases site. This site is also only available when creating a top site.

But there are more site templates that come with MOSS; most of these are the same as the subsites that are automatically created when selecting the Collaboration Portal site template. They can be used when you need to create more News sites, or Document Centers. These site templates include the following:

❑ **Document Center (on the Enterprise tab):** A site template typically used for creating a site containing documents available to all users in the organization.

❑ **Records Center (on the Enterprise tab):** A site template used for creating a site where users can store records. A given Records Manager can use a routing table to control where incoming records are stored. This site contains some special features. For example, once a record is stored, it cannot be changed by the user again.

❑ **Site Directory (on the Enterprise tab):** A site that lists and categorizes links to other SharePoint sites. You can also use it to create links that will be listed by the Tasks and Tools Web Part.

❑ **Report Center (on the Enterprise tab):** A site template used for creating sites that contain reports, presentations, key performance indicators (KPI), and dashboards. Typically, it is used for presenting Business Intelligence information.

❑ **Search Center with Tabs (on the Enterprise tab):** A site used for searching information. This site allows you to create extra tabs beyond the default All Sites and People. You can also customize the search Web Parts and the search result Web Parts on this site.

❑ **My Site Host (on the Enterprise tab):** This site will typically be used to host personal sites for users, also known as My Sites. Note that this site can only be created once per Shared Service Provider.

❑ **Search Center (on the Enterprise tab):** This site template is similar to the Search Center with Tabs, except that it does not have tabs.

> **MOSS sites do not show the link "Save site as template", in the Site Settings page, as described earlier for WSS sites. In order to save a MOSS site as a template add "/_layouts/savetmpl.aspx" at the end of the URL for the site; for example, to save a template from thehttp://srv1/ portal site, enter "http://srv1/_layouts/savetmpl.aspx"**

The Collaboration Portal Site Template

This is probably the most common site template an organization will choose when creating an intranet. It is similar in structure to the old SPS 2003 portal site but with a lot more advanced features. This intranet is built on what SharePoint refers to as "Publishing Pages," which to the user look like a number of tabs. However, in reality, each tab is a subsite under the start page, which is usually named after the company. (See Figure 6-7.)

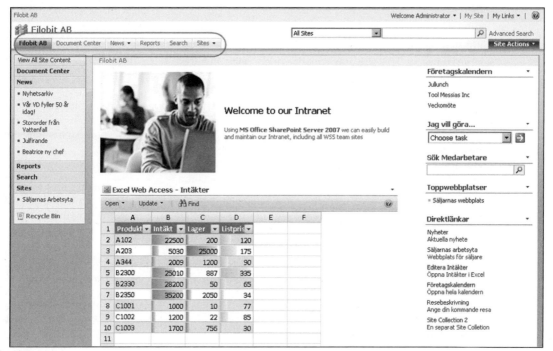

Figure 6-7

All of these sites, such as News, Document Center, and so on, belong to the same site collection, and therefore they can inherit user permissions, list templates, and site templates. You can edit all these sites, just like any site, by using Site Actions ➪ Edit Page. This will open the current page in edit mode. You can then edit the content, pictures, and links, and add, remove, or modify Web Parts on the page. Look at the top of the page on Figure 6-8. You will see that the page was automatically checked out. You need to check in the page and wait for someone with the proper permission to approve it (unless you have the necessary permission to approve and publish the modifications yourself). The page is also under version control. You can revert to a previous version, if the modifications were not good enough. You can also start a workflow (for example, to invite other users to send their comments about the modifications before you make them public).

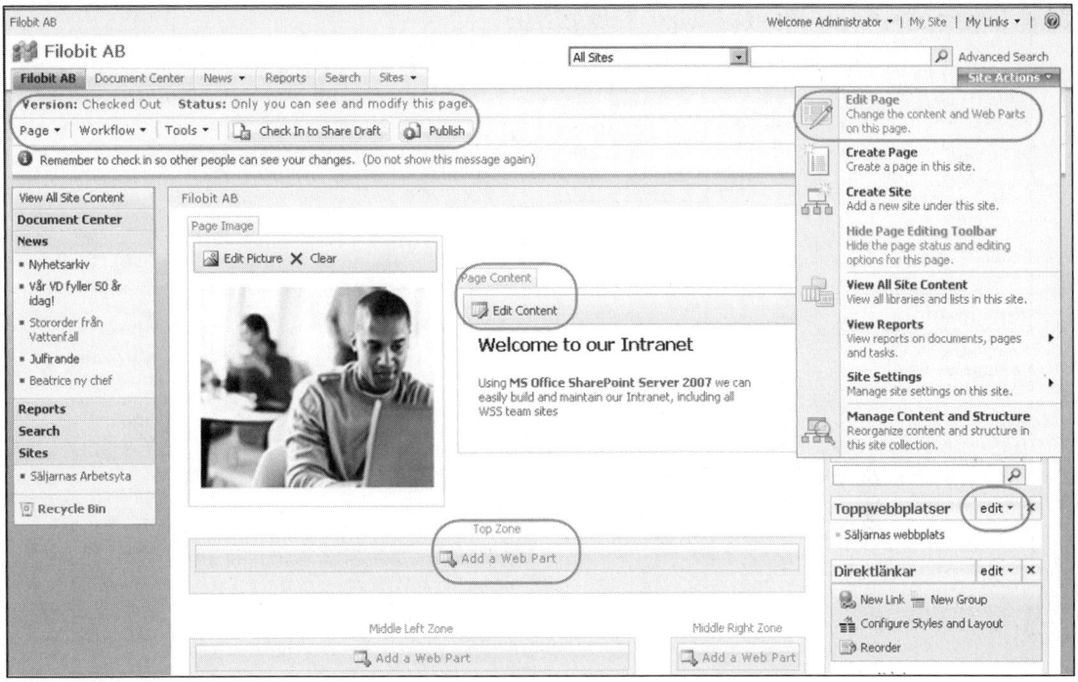

Figure 6-8

The actual page layout is built upon a Publishing Page template, called `DefaultLayout.aspx`, which is stored in a library named Master Page Gallery. You can view and edit this layout by using the SharePoint Designer tool, using this method: Select Site Actions ⇨ Site Settings ⇨ Modify All Site Settings, and click Master pages and page layouts. There you will see a file named `DefaultLayouts.aspx`. Use its quick menu, and select Edit in Microsoft Office SharePoint Designer (SPD), agree that you want to check out this item (see Figure 6-9). Be sure to save your work and then check in this page to see any modifications.

> **Note that MS Office SharePoint Designer is not included in WSS 3.0 or MOSS 2007. It must be purchased and installed separately.**

All these features will make it possible to allow updates of a publicly available intranet page, in a controlled manner, using the Check Out/In, approval, and workflow features. And if anything goes wrong, you can easily revert to the previous version of the page. Most of these features were once only found in a separate product called MS Content Management Server (MS CMS). This product was converted into the Publishing Page features of MOSS 2007 and then extended by all the other cool SharePoint 2007 features, such as workflows.

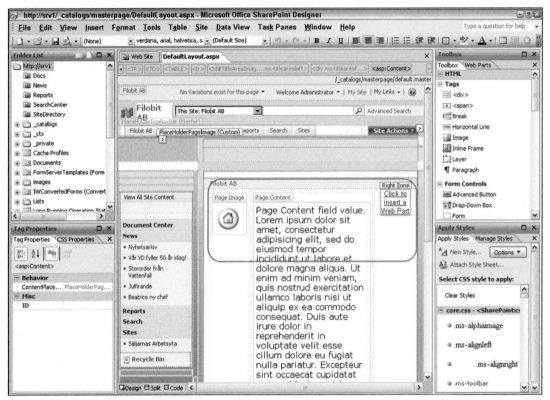

Figure 6-9

The Publishing Portal Site Template

This template is typically used when creating a public Internet web site, or as an intranet for a large organization with several subsidiaries. It is designed to make it easy to enable anonymous access, while still enabling internal users to log on to the web site with more permissions than the anonymous users have. It also has one subsite named Press Releases (see Figure 6-10), which is used to publish news and press releases (what a surprise!).

This start page is built upon a Publishing Page. All the features mentioned for the Collaboration Portal Site Template are also valid for the pages in this site template (such as the start page and the Press Releases page). If you need to edit the layout of the start page, click on Site Actions ⇨ Site Settings ⇨ Modify All Site Settings and click Master pages and page layouts, and then open the file named WelcomeSplash.aspx, as described in the previous section. Note that there is also a direct link to the Master Page Gallery on the start page for this site template.

In order to enable anonymous access to this site, you must perform a number of steps, as described in the Try It Out below. This example assumes that you have created a new site collection using the Publishing Portal site template. (See Chapter 4 for more about site collections.)

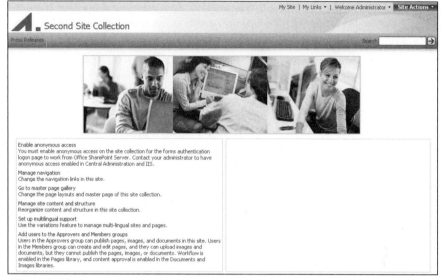

Figure 6-10

Try It Out   Enable Anonymous Access to Internet Site

1. Log on to the MOSS server as a SharePoint administrator.

2. Start SharePoint's Central Administration tool. Open the Application Management page. Click Authentication providers in the Application Security section.

3. Make sure that the web application listed on the right shows the web application used by this Publishing Portal site. If not, click on its menu and switch to the right web application.

4. Click on the zone Default.

5. Check Enable anonymous access, and click Save. Two things will now happen: The virtual IIS server used by this web application will have anonymous access enabled, and the configuration settings for the web application will allow anonymous settings.

6. Open the start page for the Publishing Portal site; click the link Enable anonymous access.

7. Select the type of access that an anonymous user will have: Entire Web site, Lists and libraries, or Nothing (the default setting). (See Figure 6-11.) If you want to open this web site to anyone, select Entire Web Site. Click OK to save your setting.

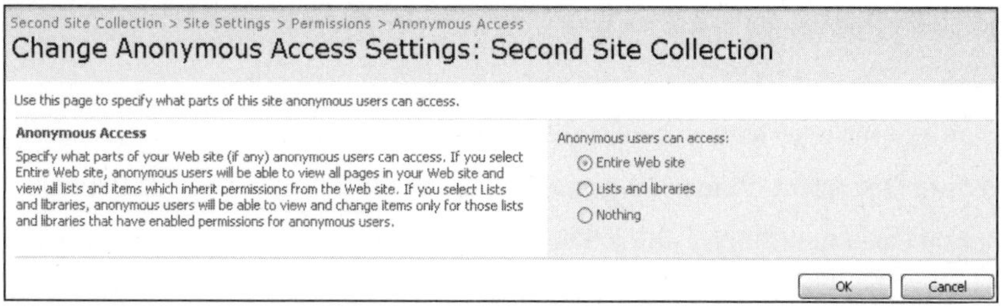

Figure 6-11

8. If you chose Lists and Libraries in the previous step, there are some final steps. You must now configure the list or library to be open for anonymous access. The page you see now is the general page for configuring user permission values:

    a. Click Site Action ⇨ View All Site Content, and select the list or library you want to open for anonymous access (you can also create a new list here), for example the Documents library.

    b. Click Settings ⇨ Document Library Settings.

    c. Click Permissions for the document library. This displays the current permissions for that list.

    d. Click Actions ⇨ Edit Permissions, and click OK to accept to break the inheritance.

    e. Finally, click Settings ⇨ Anonymous Access, and check View Items, then click OK. The content in this library is now open for anyone to read and copy. However, in order for the anonymous user to find this library, you should publish a link to it on a web page that all users can see, such as a public web site.

To add new press releases: Switch to the Press Releases page (or site, really), click Site Actions ⇨ Create Page, enter a name for the page file, and a description, then select any of the article templates listed, and click Create. Next, enter the values for the news page template, and then click Submit for Approval. Note that anytime you create a new page, a workflow will start that prompts for some info about the news article, and then sends an e-mail to each person in the preconfigured SharePoint group Approvers. If you are one of these or a site owner, you can then directly click on the Approve button above your new press release page, then click Approve again, and it will be made public.

The My Sites Template

This is another site template that is exclusive to MOSS; there is no similar functionality in the WSS team site environment. It is an important feature of SharePoint, since its purpose is to help the individual user to work more effectively. You should learn how to make the most out of My Site, in order to understand what you, as an administrator, can do with it, and to educate your users on how to use it. My Site is under the control of the Shared Service Provider in MOSS, and usually has its own web application. Thus, its address may be similar to `http://srv1:5002/personal/<user_name>`, that is, it contains an HTTP port number. Like a coin it has two sides: One is a public view with information about the user, such as an e-mail address, a picture, and skills. This information is either retrieved from the User Profile database, hosted by the Shared Service Provider, or the user himself may be allowed to enter some properties, such as his home phone number. The other side of this coin is a personal view that only the user has access to. Its purpose is to offer the user a private web site, where all the information that is relevant to the user is collected on one place, such as:

❑ **RSS Viewer:** This allows the user to list updates from any RSS source, such as a SharePoint list or an external web site.

❑ **Private Document library:** By default, this can only be accessed by the owner.

❑ **Public Document library and a Shared Picture library:** Its content can be accessed by any portal user; this may be changed.

❑ **My Calendar:** A Web Part that displays an Outlook Web Access view of the user's Outlook calendar.

❑ **My Inbox:** A Web Part that displays the user's Outlook Inbox.

❑ **SharePoint Sites:** A list of the sites that the user works with, and some of their content. Typically, these will be project sites and team sites where the user is a member.

❑ **Colleague Tracker:** This is a Web Part that automatically learns what other users a person is collaborating with. These colleagues will be listed in this Web Part, and the user can directly see if they are online or not (assuming that the user is running MSN instant messaging or has the MS Live Communication Server installed in his network, with the Communicator client).

When a user looks at his My Site, he will see these two sides as two tabs named My Home, which is the personal view, and My Profile, which is the public view. In other words, My Site will make sure the user has access to most of his everyday information, plus access to important information about other users. Your users will love this page, as soon as they understand its meaning and the power they have over it. This site is actually a slightly customized WSS top site, that is, the start of a site collection that the user administrates. All the things you have learned about SharePoint sites will also apply here, except for some small differences. For example, to create a new list you must click the View All Site Content link in the Quick Launch bar, and then Create. The same link can also be used to create subsites under this personal site, for things like small projects, meetings, and personal purposes. Each of these subsites may have its own security setting, exactly like any other site.

The public page of this site is always listed for other users besides the owner. You can look at your public page as well, by clicking the My Profile tab near the left top of the page. It will then show you what details other people will see about you, such as your name, e-mail address, organizational hierarchy, and skills, but also the documents stored in your Shared Documents, what colleagues you have, and any things you and the users who watch your personal site have in common, such as a boss, a membership in a group, or colleagues.

Note that My Site is usually configured to have its own site collection, hosted by its own web application. In other words, these personal sites will not inherit user permissions from the portal or any other site. Any user with a personal site can modify the user permission to its own site collection, for example to allow a colleague to collaborate on documents stored in one of the user's document libraries. Note that MOSS will automatically create a SharePoint group called All People that all users listed in SharePoint will be a member of. This group is used to allow these users access to the public page of your personal site.

Activating My Site

By default all authenticated users, including members of the Visitor site group, will have access to their own My Site, also known as the personal site. This can easily be changed; in Chapter 5 you learned how to manage SharePoint groups. The permissions that control the setting to create and use My Site are Create personal site and Use personal features. These settings are configured in the Shared Service Provider that hosts the My Site feature. If a user is not allowed to view his personal site, he will not see the link My Site on the portal site.

The first time a user clicks the link My Site (in the top-right corner of any standard SharePoint page) a process starts that creates the personal site. During this time a progress bar will be displayed, and when the process is finished the site will open (see Figure 6-12).

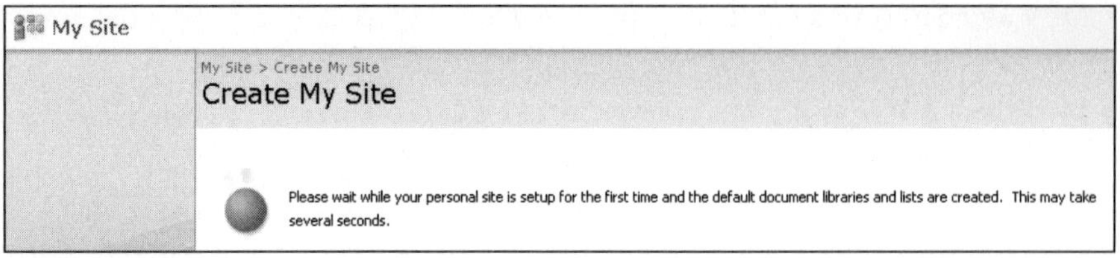

My Site

My Site > Create My Site
Create My Site

Please wait while your personal site is setup for the first time and the default document libraries and lists are created. This may take several seconds.

Figure 6-12

This page contains the information mentioned in the bullet list above, including a Web Part that is not configured yet. Among the first things that will happen is that the user is prompted about creating links from MS Office to this personal site (see Figure 6-13).

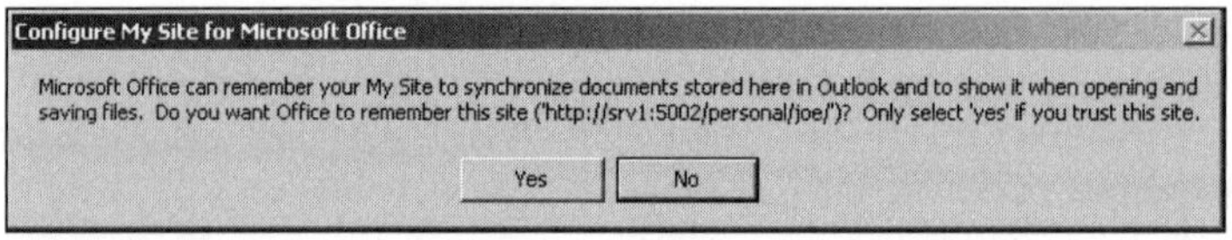

Configure My Site for Microsoft Office

Microsoft Office can remember your My Site to synchronize documents stored here in Outlook and to show it when opening and saving files. Do you want Office to remember this site ('http://srv1:5002/personal/joe/')? Only select 'yes' if you trust this site.

Yes   No

Figure 6-13

You have two options — at least in theory: Yes or No. But if you answer No, you will be prompted again the next time you open My Site. So, give up and answer Yes now. You will actually like what it will do for you! The result will be that all MS Office programs now will display a quick link to the document and image libraries on your personal site, thus making it very easy to save and open documents. See Figure 6-14, where the user Joe Doe's Save As dialog box in MS Office 2007 is displayed:

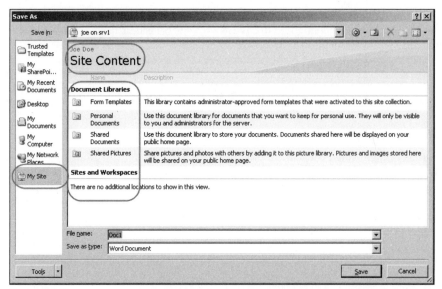

Figure 6-14

Configuring My Site

If you look at a newly created My Site, you will see a My Calendar Web Part that needs to be configured, in case the user wants it. If not, just click the arrow icon on the Web Part menu and select Close. This works with any visible Web Part on this page. But for now, let's configure it to display your Outlook calendar.

> This Web Part will only work with an MS Exchange 2003 or 2007 Server mailbox!

Try It Out   **Configure the My Calendar Web Part**

1. Open My Site as an ordinary portal user.

2. Locate the My Calendar Web Part. Click its link Open the tool pane.

3. The following configuration pane contains two very important settings:

   a. **Mail Server Address:** This must be configured to use the same address that the Outlook Web Access (OWA) client uses for accessing the MS Exchange server. Typically, it looks something like this: `http://mailserver.filobit.com/Exchange` assuming that the fully qualified domain name for that server is `mailserver.filobit.com`. If it does not work, talk with your mail administrator and ask about the OWA address.

   > When using Exchange 2007 mailboxes, this Web Part will enter the mailbox server name automatically.

   b. **Mailbox:** This is the first part of your e-mail address — up to, but not including the @ sign and the mail domain. For example, if your mail address is `Joe@filobit.com`, you will add Joe. SharePoint will automatically suggest your primary e-mail address, so you can just remove the part starting with the @ sign.

   c. **View:** Select the default view for this calendar: Daily or Weekly.

   d. Click OK to save. The calendar Web Part will now display the user's current calendar.

4. As a test, add an appointment for today using MS Outlook, then refresh your personal site page and make sure that you see this appointment in this Web Part, too.

Cool, right? So, why not add a Web Part to display the Outlook box, too? There are in fact a number of Web Parts related to Outlook folders, such as these. Note that most of them require that the user's mailbox is hosted by an Exchange 2003 server:

❑ **My Calendar:** This shows a daily or weekly view of the current user's calendar (Exchange 2003 or later).

❑ **My Inbox:** This shows the Inbox and allows the user to open and reply to messages, but not to create a new message (Exchange 2003 or later).

❑ **My Contacts:** This displays the user's Outlook Contact folder (Exchange 2003 or later).

❑ **My Tasks:** This displays the user's Outlook Tasks folder (Exchange 2003 or later).

❑ **My Mail Folder:** This displays any Outlook folder (Exchange 2000 or later).

This is nice, but it has some drawbacks. For example, the user cannot create new e-mail messages, and it may be cumbersome to add a number of My Mail Folder Web Parts in case the user needs to see several Outlook folders. A better way was introduced in SharePoint 2007. My Page now has a link called OWA Address that will open the full Outlook Web Access client and also will automatically discover the current user's mail server and user account (see Figure 6-15). This allows the user a much richer mail functionality than using the mailbox Web Parts listed above.

Figure 6-15

Note that when the user opens his OWA Address link, he will be redirected to the mail server by a fully qualified domain name (FQDN), for example: `http://dc1.filobit.com/exchange`. This also will automatically classify that link as an Internet zone in most browsers, and the result is that the user must log on every time this OWA Address page is opened for the first time. To resolve this, follow the steps in the Try It Out below.

Try It Out   Configure Auto-Logon to OWA Address

1. Log on as the user, then open the web browser; for example, Internet Explorer 7.

2. Click Tools ⇨ Internet Options/Security, then select the Internet zone, and click Custom Level.

3. Scroll down to the bottom of the Settings list and the Logon section. Select the option Automatic logon with current username and password.

4. Click OK, then Yes, and then OK again to save and close this setting. Note that this must be done for each user, but you can also configure a Group Policy Object setting in Active Directory that sets this for all users.

The My Mail Folder Web Part can also displays Public Folders in Outlook, using a little trick. Although Exchange 2007 is the last version that supports public folders, many organizations still have a lot of information stored there. If you need to display a public folder in SharePoint, you can use this little trick. Configure the My Mail Folder Web Part as described in the Try It Out below. Note that the user must have at least Read access to the public folder for it to be displayed; otherwise, the user will get an error message every time he opens his personal site, because of that Web Part!

For example, say that you have a top-level Public Folder named Projects that all users have access to. To display this public folder in My Site follow the steps in the Try It Out below.

Try It Out   Display a Public Folder with My Mail Folder

1. Log on as the user; open My Site.

2. Click Site Actions ⇨ Edit Page.

3. Select the Web Part zone that you want to add the Web Part to; for example, Middle Right Zone, and click Add a Web Part at the top frame of this zone.

4. Scroll down, and check the My Mail Folder Web Part, then click Add. This Web Part is now added to this zone, but you need to configure it to display the public folder.

5. Click Edit to the left of the My Mail Folder Web Parts menu, and select Modify Shared Web Part to open its configuration pane. Change these settings (assuming that the mail server address is `dc1.filobit.com` and the public folder to be displayed is Projects):

    a. **Mail server address:** `http://dc1.filobit.com/public/projects/?cmd=con-tents&part=1`. This is the trick! This line says that you want to view the Public folder Projects, and that it should be formatted as Content. The part of the line that follows the public folder name must exist (for example, `/?cmd=contents&part=1`); otherwise this Web Part will only display an error!

    b. **Exchange folder name:** You can type anything here, as long as it is not empty. A dot character will do fine.

    c. **Mailbox:** As long as the user have access to that public folder, you do not need any mailbox name here, but again it must not be an empty field, since this will force the Web Part to ask the user for it. You can enter anything here; for example, a dot.

    d. **Title:** `Projects PF`. This setting is in Appearance section.

    e. Click OK to save and close the tool pane for the Web Part.

    > **For more information about formatting the folder content in step 5a, check this blog by KC, a member of the Microsoft Exchange team:** `http://blogs.technet.com/kclemson/archive/2003/11/04/53886.aspx`. **She describes, for example, how to format a calendar folder in a weekly view.**

6. The content of this public folder will be displayed immediately. Log on as a user and make sure that it works as expected.

A common request is to have some of these mail-related Web Parts on other pages than My Site. Yes, you can add them to any site page. For example, the My Mail Folder Web Part described above will also work in a WSS site, as long as all users have at least Read access to that public folder. However, the rest of these mail-related Web Parts require a mailbox name to work, and this will give you a problem. For example, say that you want to list the user's Inbox on the Home area page on the portal. You can add the

My Inbox Web Part, but what mailbox name should it be configured to display? Every user looking at this Web Part has his or her own mailbox name, and the Web Part will not automatically configure its settings dynamically. Do you see the problem? If there were a way to adjust the mailbox name based on the current user, it would work. Since there isn't, do not try to add these types of Web Parts to public site.

In previous versions of SharePoint, you had to add the Web Part My Workspace Sites in order to see any subsites under the current user's personal site. This Web Part still exists, but has been renamed My Workspaces. This Web Part is not really necessary anymore, however, since My Site in SharePoint 2007, by default, will list all sites directly under My Site on its Quick Launch bar, that is, the left pane of this page. If you have several levels of subsites, you may want to use the tree view to be able to see them all. Use the Site Actions ⇨ Site Settings and click Tree view in the Look and Feel section. Check Enable Tree View, and click OK. Your Quick Launch bar will now also have a full tree view of all the subsites, including lists and libraries, under this personal site.

A final Web Part you may want to use for the My Site page is My Workspace Sites. This Web Part will list all sites created directly under the user's personal site. A common default location for sites created using Office and Outlook is My Site. With this Web Part in place, it will be easy for the users to see a list of these team sites and workspaces.

Adding Information to My Site

A SharePoint user will probably use their personal site for storing links to sites, lists, and documents they often work with, making it easier for them to find this information. In SharePoint 2007, there are a lot of options in My Site to assist users with this, such as these (see Figure 6-16):

❑ **My Links:** At the top right of every page in SharePoint 2007 is a list named My Links. Whenever you are at a page you want to easily return to (for example, a site, a list or a library), you can click on My Links and select Add to My Links. This will open a dialog box where the you can define the title and the URL. Just click on My Links again, and point to any of the group names to see a sliding menu displaying all the links for that group.

❑ **SharePoint Sites:** This very powerful Web Part is added by default to My Site as SharePoint Sites. It will display all documents created by you, and all tasks assigned to you, anywhere in the SharePoint environment. By default, it will only display My Site, plus the sites where you are a member of the sites' Member SharePoint group.

❑ **RSS Viewer:** This Web Part will display any Real Simple Syndication (RSS) feed; for example, a publicly available RSS feed, such as www.nasa.gov/rss/breaking_news.rss or any list in SharePoint, since they all support RSS. This is a very good way of keeping track of any updates, without needing to open the source regularly. For more information about RSS, see Chapter 7.

❑ **Colleague Tracker:** This Web Part will automatically discover and list other SharePoint users that you have something in common with. For each of these users, you can take actions, such as scheduling a meeting, sending mail or opening the public view of their My Site.

My Links, SharePoint Sites, and Colleague Tracker are described in more detail below. RSS is discussed in Chapter 7. Note that there are a lot of other Web Parts that you can add to My Site, in order to make it more interesting.

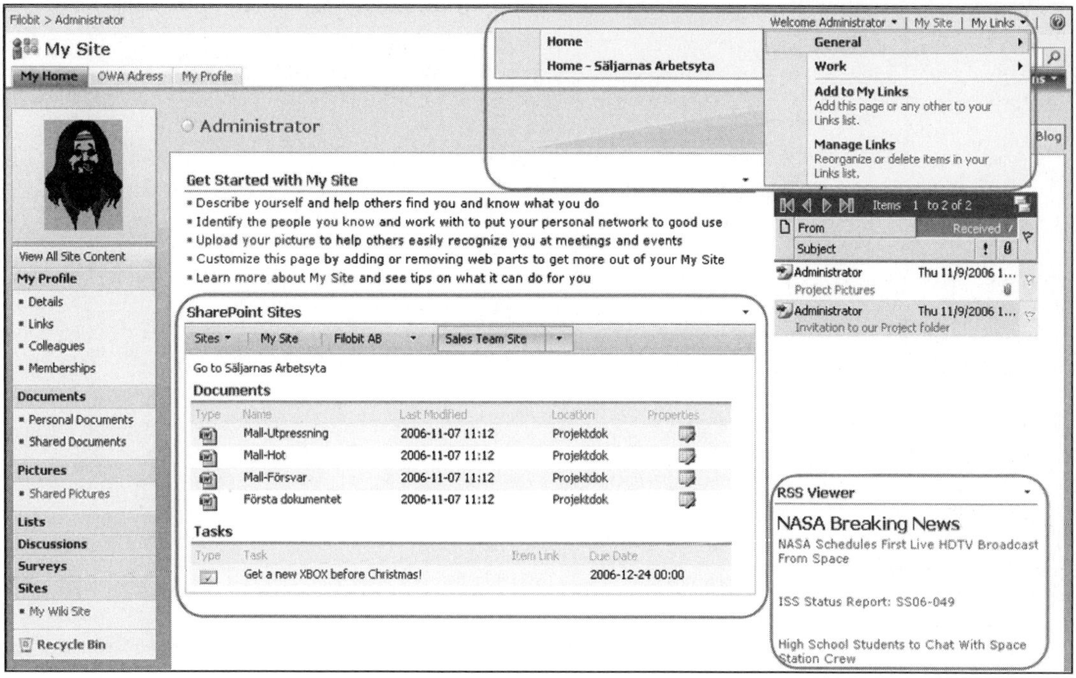

Figure 6-16

The ability to add links anywhere in SharePoint is very powerful and users should be educated on how to use this tool, since it will help them find favorite locations very fast.

Try It Out   Manage My Links

1. Open the portal site; the name of any user with permission to use My Site will do.

2. To add a link to a site, follow these steps:

   a. Open the site you want to store as a link; for example, a project site you often visit.

   b. Click My Links in the top-right corner of the web page, then select Add to My Links.

   c. A dialog box now opens where you can define how to store this link (see Figure 6-17). The link itself is automatically entered in the Address field, and you can now set the title for this link. The Show these links to pull-down menu allows you to choose who can see this link. It can be a private link (i.e., choose Only Me), or you can make it visible to every SharePoint user, or just some; for example, your colleagues. This dialog box also allows you to group links. Select an existing group, such as General, or create a new group. When you have more than one group, these groups will then be displayed as headings when you open the My Links next time. Click OK to save and close the dialog box.

   d. Test the new link. Click My Links and then hover the mouse over the group name you chose in step 2c. All links for this group are now displayed. Select a link and verify that it works.

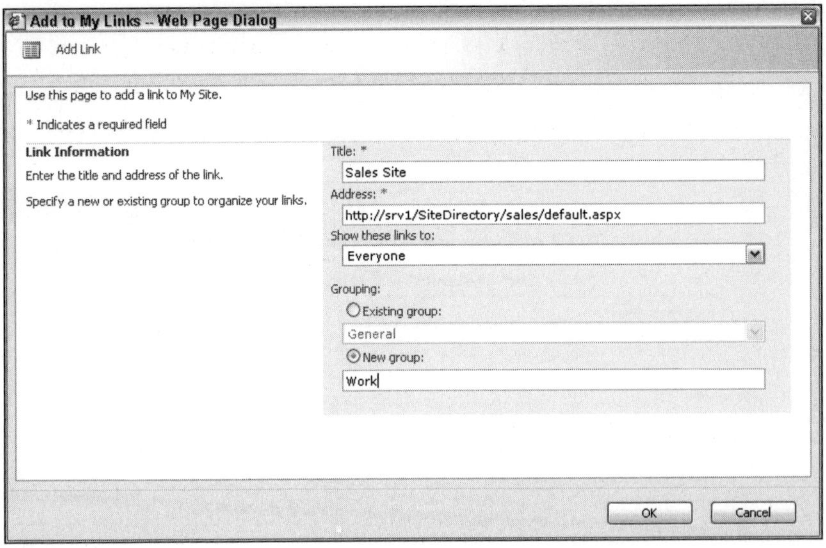

Figure 6-17

3. You can also add a link directly to a list or library, or any SharePoint page, including configuration pages:

   a. Start by opening the list, library or page.

   b. Click My Links, then select Add to My Links.

   c. Fill in the values for the link in the dialog box, as described in step 2c.

4. If you want to change or delete an existing link, do this:

   a. Click My Links, then select Manage Links. This opens a page where all existing links are listed, including what group they belong to.

   b. To modify a link, check the check box for that link, then select Edit Links. This opens the same type of dialog box that you saw when you first created the link. Make whatever modifications are needed, then click OK to save and close the dialog box.

5. To delete an existing link, do this:

   a. Click My Links, then select Manage Links.

   b. Check the check box next to the link you want to delete.

   c. Click Delete, then OK to accept the deletion.

Another very powerful tool displayed on My Site is the SharePoint Sites Web Part. As mentioned before, it will list documents that you created or edited, and tasks assigned to you, in selected sites. By default, it will automatically add the user's My Site, plus up to five other sites where you are a member of that sites <site name> Members group. You can change the number of sites listed from five to any number by opening the configuring pane for this Web Part (Click Site Actions ➪ Edit Page). On the Web Part, click Edit ⇨ Modify Shared Web Part. The Number of tabs to show before More dropdown setting is located in the View section. If there are more sites than the maximum number listed, the first button, Sites, will have a green exclamation mark, indicating that there are more sites available than are displayed on the Web Part. Pull down the Sites menu, and select the new option Membership, which will list the remaining sites. The Web Part may also show a More button if there are more sites that can be displayed.

Try It Out   Manage Sites on the SharePoint Site Web Part

1.   Open My Site.

2.   To manually add a site to this Web Part, you click Sites ⇨ New Site Tab, then enter these values in the Create a new site tab form:

    a.   Select the Type SharePoint site URL and name option.

    b.   **Site URL:** Enter the full URL to the SharePoint site to be listed.

    c.   **Site Name:** If this site is recognized by SharePoint, its name will now automatically be listed. If not, enter the name to be displayed on the menu bar of the Web Part.

    d.   Click Create.

3.   To hide a site listed on this Web Part:

    a.   Click on the arrow to the right of the site button to display its menu, then select Hide.

    b.   The site is removed from the Web Part menu. To view the hidden site, click the Sites button and select the site.

4.   To delete a site listed on this Web Part:

    a.   Click on the arrow to the right of this site button; select Delete from the menu. The button for the site is removed. Note that if this was an automatically listed site, its name will now be moved to the Sites menu.

    b.   To restore this site, you must create it once again, using the New Site Tab described in step 2. Note that if this is an auto-discovered site, you will find its name in the Select site from Membership list in New Site Tab.

The fourth Web Part that, by default, is displayed the on user's My Site is the Colleague Tracker. It will list SharePoint users who have something in common with you, such as users who share a group membership with you or users that you sent mail to. The idea behind this Web Part is to make it easy for you to find other users whom you now and then need to contact. This is an alternative to a global employee list, which many organizations display on their intranet. If the global list contains a lot of people, you will have to search for the user you are interested in. In most cases, you will look for people who belong to the same team as you, or whom you have contacted by e-mail or instant messaging. And this list is probably much smaller than the global address list; this is exactly what the Colleague Tracker is used for. It is similar in concept to the personal address list in MS Outlook.

The relationships that this Web Part looks for when trying to auto-discover users to be listed are described below. Note that only a few of these users will show up directly in this Colleague Tracker list; the rest will be suggestions that you must manually accept:

❏ **Organizational hierarchy:** All users who are defined as someone you report to and all users who report to you . This is the default list of people who will show up in this list.

❏ **Instant Messages Contacts:** All SharePoint users who have contacted you, using either MSN or the MS Communicator client.

❏ **e-mail Contacts:** All SharePoint users you have received mail from.

❏ **Document Editing:** All users who have edited the same document as you.

❏ **Membership:** All users who are members of the same SharePoint groups as you.

If the Web Part has discovered a new user whom you may want to add to this colleague list, a link that says See new colleague suggestions will be displayed. Click the link to see the suggested users. The page that will open up is Add Colleagues. Another way that this can be opened is by clicking on the Colleagues Tracker headline, then clicking Add Colleagues. (See Figure 6-18.)

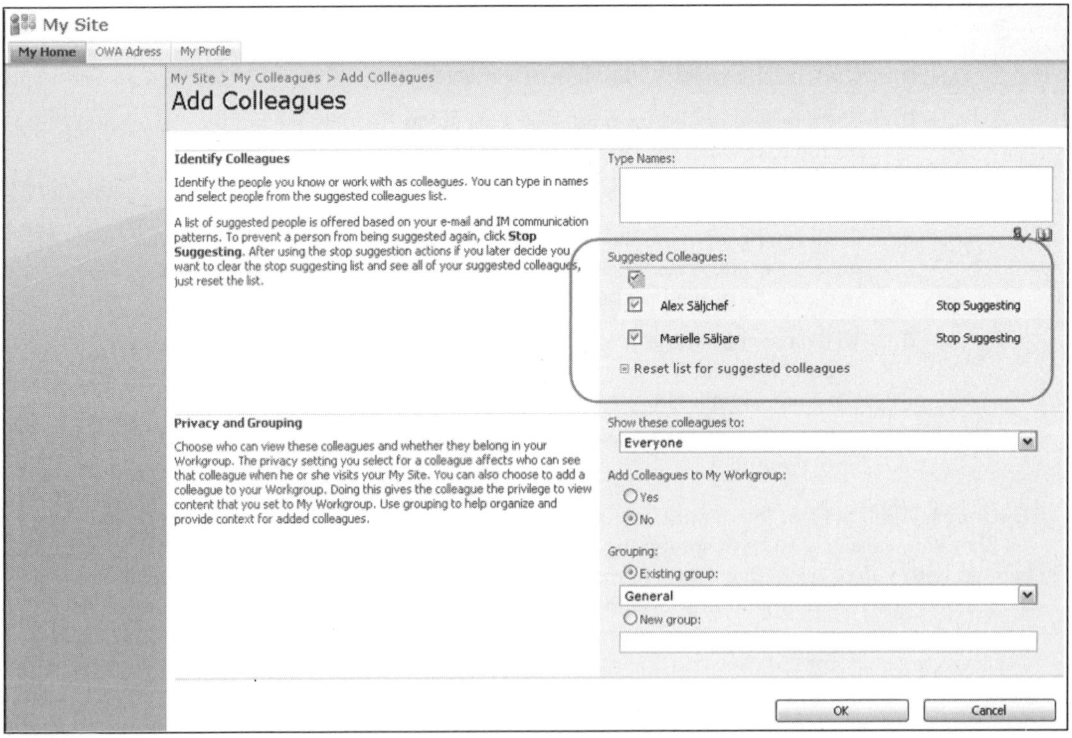

Figure 6-18

On this page, you can also tell SharePoint to stop suggesting a user, or to add users not suggested automatically. Some of these names may be interesting for other users to see, so the public view of the My Site will show all names defined to be shown to everyone. If there are a lot of names, you will want to group them. By default, there is one group named General; on this page you can create new groups when needed.

You may also edit existing names in the Colleagues Tracking list. Simply click the headline Colleague Tracking and all current users are listed. In this form, you can edit these user names; for example, changing who can see them and what group they should be listed under. You can also delete a user from this list by checking the user's check box and clicking Delete. There is also a quick menu for each name with options for editing or deleting the user. Click directly to the right of the name to open this quick menu.

For each user name listed in the Colleague Tracker Web Part in My Site, you may take some action. To see what you can do, click on the presence bullet to the left of the name, to open a menu with these options:

- ❏ **Schedule a Meeting:** This creates a meeting request form in your MS Outlook client, with this name automatically added to the To field.

- ❏ **Office Location:** This displays the defined office location for this user.

- ❏ **View My Site:** This opens the public view of that person's My Site.

- ❏ **Send Mail:** This creates an e-mail with this user as the recipient.

- ❏ **Additional Actions:** This lists other actions, if any.

- ❏ **Add to Outlook Contact:** This adds a user to your personal Outlook contact list.

- ❏ **Outlook Properties:** This displays the properties in Outlook for the user.

Or you can directly click on a user's name to open the public view of his or her My Site.

Do your users need their own blog site? Well, look no further. On My Site there is a personal blog site built in! At the upper right of My Site, you will see the link Create Blog. Click on it, and SharePoint will create the blog for you. It's a separate site, based on the WSS blog site template, discussed earlier in this chapter. You can start adding your blog postings right away by clicking on the Create a post link. The postings in this blog are listed on your personal My Site. On the My Home tab, you will see a list of all headlines of the most recent postings, plus a link to the blog site in the Quick Launch bar, and on My Profile (the public view), the complete content of the most recent blog posts will be displayed.

The Public View of My Site

So far, we have only discussed the personal view of My Site. But there is also a public view of My Site that shows information about the user, plus shared documents, links, blog posts, colleagues, and a list of users with whom the user has things in common. A lot of the information on this public page is retrieved from the User Profile database discussed in Chapter 5. Exactly what other users will see depends on the permissions, set by the owner of the site. In this section, you will learn how to control all these settings for My Site.

It is easy to assume that all users have their own public site, just like the personal view, since it contains personal information. But that is not true. There is only one single website for the public view, and this site is shared among all users. However, its content will depend on which person's public view you are looking at.

The best indication that this is so is that there is no way of configuring the Web Parts for this page, unless you are an administrator. For the typical user, the Site Actions link is hidden. But the administrator can modify this page, either by clicking Site Actions ⇨ Edit Page or by using the SharePoint Designer tool. You will learn more about that in Chapter 13. This public page has several Web Parts and content lists displayed by default:

- ❑ **User Properties:** This is a detailed card with information about this user, such as the name, picture, description, department, title, place in the organizational hierarchy, and contact information.

- ❑ **Memberships:** This is a list of sites this user is a member of.

- ❑ **Documents:** This is a list of documents this user has created or edited in sites where she is a member. This list will only show documents that the user who is currently looking at this site has at least Read permission to.

- ❑ **Colleagues:** This is a list of colleagues that the owner of this site has defined to be visible for the user currently looking at this page.

- ❑ **Links:** This contains any links added by the owner of this site where the option Show these links to is set to a group that the current user looking at this page belongs to.

- ❑ **In Common with:** This Web Part will list all people that you have something in common with, if any.

- ❑ **Shared Documents:** This is a link to the document library that every SharePoint user is granted Read access to, by default.

- ❑ **Private Documents:** A link to the private document library. This library can only be accessed by user with explicit permission. By default, only the owner can view and use the content of this library.

- ❑ **Shared Pictures:** A link to a picture library that every SharePoint user, by default, is granted access to.

You can create new lists and libraries for documents and pictures in your My Site. If these are configured to allow access to anyone except you, their name and content will be possible to read or even update, using the public view of My Site.

Most of the detailed information about the user is retrieved from the User Profile, but not all. For example, a picture of the user, her home phone number and the description. The administrator can also add information manually to the user's profile, or allow users to edit it themselves. If users are allowed to enter this information, the following Try It Out shows how to do it.

Try It Out   **Update Your User Properties on My Site**

1. Open your My Site.

2. Open the My Home page, then click Details in the Quick Launch bar.

3. All fields that you can edit are now displayed. If you see a yellow warning sign next to a field, you should avoid editing that field, since it will be overwritten next time the User Profile is updated, usually every 24 hours. Note that for some fields you can set who sees that particular information. The default information fields you can edit, including the default visibility are:

    a. **About me (visible to: Everyone):** Enter a description, make sure to follow the policy, if any.

    b. **Picture URL (visible to: Everyone):** Click Choose Picture to browse for a picture of yourself on the file system. Note that you cannot browse for a picture stored in a SharePoint list, but you can manually enter the URL to the picture in that list. This picture will then be copied to the local Shared Pictures in your My Site.

    c. **Responsibility (visible to: Everyone):** This field should describe your responsibilities, in one or two words. To see a list of what other users have defined as responsibilities, click the edit icon to the right of this field. The information in this field is also listed as search options on the People search page.

    d. **Skills (visible to: Everyone):** Describe your skills in one or two words. This field also has an edit icon to the right; use it to see what skills other users have defined. This field is also listed as a search option on the People search page.

    e. **Past projects (visible to: Everyone):** Describe your previous or past projects. This will help others to understand what you are working on.

    f. **Interests (visible to: Everyone):** Enter your personal interests here.

    g. **Schools (visible to: Everyone):** Lists the schools you have attended.

    h. **Birthday (visible to: Everyone):** Enter the date for your birthday, for example September 12.

    i. **Assistant (visible to: Everyone):** Enter the name of your assistant, if any, or use the browse button to the right of this field to select a name.

    j. **Mobile phone (visible to: My Colleagues):** Enter your cell phone number.

    k. **Fax (visible to: Everyone):** Enter your fax number.

    l. **Home phone (visible to: My Colleagues):** Enter your home phone number.

    m. Any extra information attributes the administrator may have added to the user profile will be listed here.

4. Click Save and Close.

5. Click My Profile under Select a view, and the result should look something like Figure 6-19.

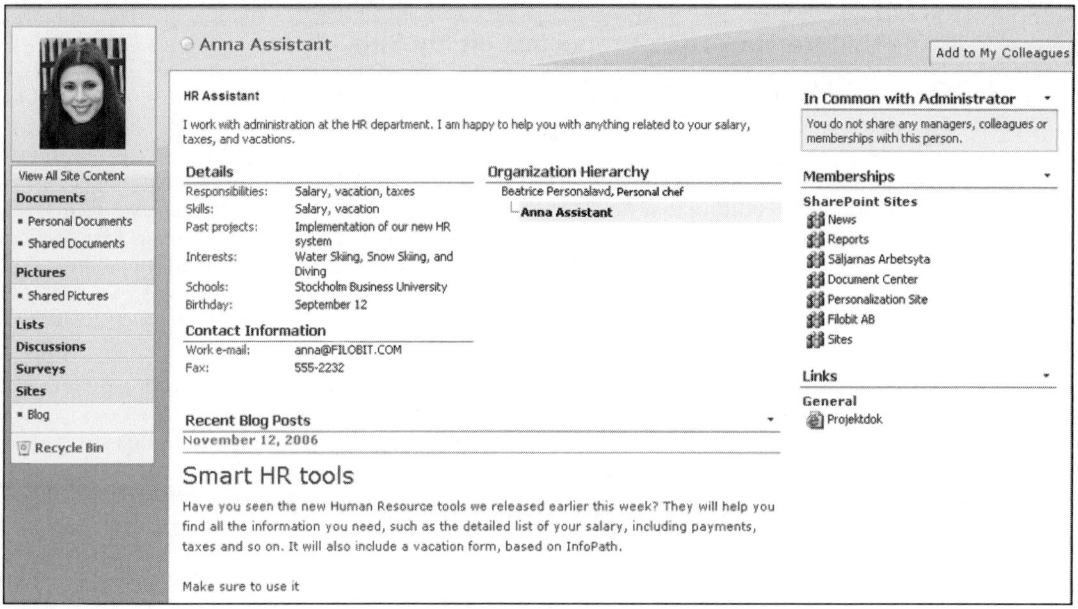

Figure 6-19

Note that every name listed on this page will lead to that person's My Site, which is very handy if you need to get in contact with any of these people. For example, in Figure 6-19 you can see that Anna's boss is Beatrice; to see her My Site just click on her name. Also note that there is a link at the top right of this page called Add to My Colleagues. Use that link if you want to add the person you are looking at right now to your list of colleagues.

Obviously, there is more to My Site than meets the eye. This will make the individual user more effective and reduce the time spent searching for important information, regardless of whether it is business oriented or more personal. If the users start using the document libraries on their My Sites, they may have access to these libraries over the Internet, and from any computer, without any need to configure virtual private networks (VPN). In fact, Microsoft recommends that organizations replace the traditional home directory with the document libraries in the personal site, because it is so easy to use, and you can store any type of information in My Site, not just files.

> **Use MS Outlook 2007 to download a copy of document libraries from the SharePoint server, if you need access to these documents while offline.**

The other great use of My Site is that in all places where you see a name, such as the author of a document, news, or a link, just by clicking this name you can see that user's personal site. Thus, there is no more hunting down the person on a typical employee list on a traditional intranet, or searching Outlook's address list. Just click the name and you will have every piece of information available about this user in a second, such as the e-mail address, phone numbers, responsibilities, and a picture.

Site Permissions

You have already seen in Chapter 3 how to add users and groups to SharePoint groups, such as Visitors and Members to grant permissions to sites. There is an important difference in SharePoint 2007, compared to the previous version, regarding how site permissions work. In SharePoint 2003, there was a very granular set of permissions available in WSS, while the SPS only allowed you to set permission per area page, not on individual lists or libraries. All this is now gone, and WSS 3.0.sites have the exact same type of permissions as the MOSS sites. To view the complete list of rights available for SharePoint 2007 sites, follow the steps in the Try It Out below.

Try It Out   List Available Site Permissions

1. Log on as the administrator, and open a top site, for example the start page on an intranet.

2. Click Site Actions ⇨ Site Settings ⇨ People and Groups

3. Click Site Permissions in the Quick Launch bar.

4. Click the Settings button, then select Permission Levels. This will open a page where all the permission roles are listed, such as Design, Contribute, and Read. These roles are referred to as site permissions. To see exactly what permission an existing site permission has, click its name. You can also create a new Site Permission role here. If you open an existing site permission, you will also find a button that will make an editable copy of that site permission.

5. Regardless of whether you create a new Site Permission or open an existing one, you will see a complete list of the 33 permissions available in SharePoint 2007, as listed in the following table (regardless of site type).

List Permissions	Description
Manage Lists	Create and delete lists, add or remove columns in a list, and add or remove public views of a list.
Override Check Out	Discard or check in a document that is checked out to another user.
Add Items	Add items to lists, add documents to document libraries, and add Web discussion comments.
Edit Items	Edit items in lists, edit documents in document libraries, edit web discussion comments in documents, and customize Web Part pages in document libraries.
Delete Items	Delete items from a list, documents from a document library, and web discussion comments in documents.
View Items	View items in lists, view documents in document libraries, view web discussion comments, and set up e-mail alerts for lists.

Continued

List Permissions	Description
Approve Items	Approve a minor version of a list item or document.
Open Items	View the source of documents with server-side file handlers.
View Versions	View past versions of a list item or document.
Delete Versions	Delete past versions of a list item or document.
Create Alerts	Create e-mail alerts.
View Application Pages	View forms, views, and application pages. Enumerate lists.
Site Permissions	Permission Description
Manage Permissions	Create and change permission levels on the web site and assign permissions to users and groups.
View Usage Data	View reports on web site usage.
Create Subsites	Create subsites such as team sites, Meeting Workspace sites, and Document Workspace sites.
Manage Web Site	Grant the ability to perform all administration tasks for the web site as well as manage content.
Add and Customize Pages	Add, change, or delete HTML pages or Web Part pages, and edit the web site using a Windows SharePoint Services-compatible editor.
Apply Themes and Borders	Apply a theme or borders to the entire web site.
Apply Style Sheets	Apply a style sheet (CSS file) to the web site.
Create Groups	Create a group of users that can be used anywhere within the site collection.
Browse Directories	Enumerate files and folders in a web site using SharePoint Designer and Web DAV interfaces.
Use Self-Service site Creation	Create a web site using Self-Service Site Creation.
View Pages	View pages in a web site.
Enumerate Permissions	Enumerate permissions on the web site, list, folder, document, or list item.

List Permissions	Description
Browse User Information	View information about users of the web site.
Manage Alerts	Manage alerts for all users of the web site.
Use Remote Interfaces	Use SOAP, Web DAV, or SharePoint Designer interfaces to access the web site.
Use Client Integration Features	Use features that launch client applications. Without this permission, users will have to work on documents locally and upload their changes.
Open	Allows users to open a web site and a list of folders in order to access items inside that container.
Edit Personal User Information	Allows a user to change his or her own user information, such as adding a picture.
Personal Permissions	Permission Description
Manage Personal Views	Create, change, and delete personal views of lists.
Add/Remove Personal Web Parts	Add or remove personal Web Parts on a Web Part page.
Update Personal Web Parts	Update Web Parts to display personalized information.

Summary

In this chapter you learned that:

❑ All SharePoint sites you create will have a site template applied.

❑ The is no real difference between WSS sites and MOSS sites, except the type of site templates applied.

❑ The site templates for WSS 3.0 are designed to ease collaboration within teams and groups.

❑ There are two new WSS site templates, not found in the previous version: Wiki and Blog.

❑ When installing MOSS, you get a number of new site templates, most of them based on Publishing Pages.

❑ Publishing Pages are built on MS CMS and extended with new features such as workflows.

❑ Some of the site templates in MOSS can only be applied to top sites, such as the Collaboration Portal.

❑ After a site is created, it has no relation to the site template that was used. It will not react if the site template is modified.

❑ The look and feel of a site's menus, navigation elements, and logotypes are under the control of a Master Page. You can apply a new or modified Master Page anytime to update the look and feel.

❑ My Site is a personal site available for all users. It has two views: a personal view and a public view.

❑ My Site has a public view that lists information and properties for a particular user. Some of this information may be managed by the user.

❑ My Site has special Web Parts for social networking. This will make it easier for users to find colleagues and people they have something in common with.

In the next chapter, you will learn more about the integration between SharePoint sites and MS Office clients.

Office Integration

SharePoint 2007 is a great tool in itself; you can use it straight out of the box to build sites for an intranet, an extranet, public Internet sites, and team sites. It will help users find the information they need, quickly and easily. But the real magic comes when you integrate other products with SharePoint! There are lots of products that can use SharePoint's document libraries directly for storing files and documents, but one product family really shines when it comes to SharePoint integration: MS Office, which most people associate with the typical desktop applications (MS Word, MS Excel, and so on). There are also a lot of other programs that have an excellent integration with SharePoint, especially MS Outlook, MS OneNote, and MS InfoPath. In fact, today it is hard to find any program from Microsoft that does not have some sort of integration with SharePoint 2007; it is safe to say that SharePoint is *the* central information database in a Microsoft-centric IT environment.

This chapter will tell you how this integration works, and what differentiates previous versions of MS Office from the current MS Office 2007 release. You will find a lot of examples and step-by-step instructions on how to use a number of applications together with SharePoint 2007. All of this information is valid for both WSS and MOSS, unless stated otherwise.

> **Entire books are devoted to each MS Office component, and more books are devoted to their integration. This chapter obviously can't cover the breadth and depth of MS Office integration. Instead, the focus is on knowledge and techniques that can be useful with SharePoint administration. Specifically, we will focus on Outlook, InfoPath, and OneNote.**

MS Office Product Suite

The most commonly used product family today, all categories included, is the MS Office product suite. It has been around for more than a decade, but today it is hard to find an organization running anything older than MS Office 2000. The fact is that this product suite works so well that a lot of organizations still use MS Office XP or 2003, while an increasingly number have upgraded to

MS Office 2007. It should come as no surprise that MS Office 2007 has the best integration with SharePoint 2007, and this is by design! A lot of features in SharePoint 2007, such as workflows, simply need an Office version that is built to support that type of functionality; older Office versions will have limited, or no, support for a number of SharePoint 2007 features.

> **In Chapter 1 there is a table that compares the SharePoint functionality among different MS Office versions.**

Do not expect to see any updates released for older MS Office versions that will extend their support for SharePoint 2007. Except for one thing (and this is not really a SharePoint feature): support for the new XML-based file format, introduced in MS Office 2007, through a free add-on named Microsoft Office Compatibility Pack(MOCP). It is important for SharePoint users, since it will allow users with older MS Office programs to work with documents created with MS Office 2007, also for documents stored in a SharePoint document library. To download this MOCP extension of MS Office XP and MS Office 2003, go to www.microsoft.com and search for Office Compatibility Pack, or use this link directly:

```
www.microsoft.com/downloads/details.aspx?familyid=941B3470-3AE9-4AEE-8F43-
C6BB74CD1466&displaylang=en
```

In order to better understand what you can do with these MS Office versions, you need to try some examples. Say that you have a SharePoint 2007 site named IT and that this site contains a document library named Info. To make it more interesting, this Info library has two extra columns: Product and Vendor. It also has been configured to force a checkout procedure, whenever a user needs to update a document. Finally, there is a workflow approval process defined, which will trigger every time a new document is created. In the detailed descriptions below, we assume that you want to use MS Word to work with documents.

MS Office 2000

So let's start with MS Office 2000, and see how that works, according to the example above. This version of Office has a very limited integration with SharePoint 2007. Basically, all you can do is read, write, modify, and delete documents in a SharePoint library:

❑ **Create a document:** The user must create the document in Office 2000, then save the document to the URL that points to the Info library in the IT site. It is not possible to use the New button for the Info library.

❑ **Modify a document:** The user can open a document in the Info library, then modify it, and then save it back.

❑ **Using InfoPath Forms:** There is no MS InfoPath (IP) application in Office 2000, so the only way to open and use IP forms is to configure SharePoint Forms Service to display these forms as web pages.

And that is about it. The conclusion is that a combination of MS Office 2000 and SharePoint 2007 is not the ideal solution. I strongly recommend that anyone using MS Office 2000 upgrade before implementing SharePoint 2007. And remember that Office 2000 is not supported by new service packs or hot fixes anymore. If you have this environment, do yourself a favor and upgrade to Office 2007, okay?

MS Office XP

MS Office XP was released in 2002 and was also known as MS Office 2002. It has some small advantages over MS Office 2000, but not many. Let's see what you can do in this example:

❑ **Create a document:** You must create the document in Office XP, and then save the document to the URL that points to the Info library on the IT site. You can also use the New button on the Info library, which is a difference, compared to Office 2000.

❑ **Modify a document:** You can open a document in the Info library, then modify it, and then save it back.

❑ **Using InfoPath Forms:** There is no MS InfoPath (IP) application in Office XP, so the only way to open and use IP forms is to configure SharePoint Forms Service to display these forms as web pages.

End of story. The conclusion is once again, that a combination of MS Office XP and SharePoint 2007 is not an ideal solution. My recommendation is that anyone using MS Office XP should upgrade before implementing SharePoint 2007. So upgrade, please.

MS Office 2003

Now this is a much better option than any of the two previous Office versions discussed. It was released together with SharePoint 2003 in October 2003; thus, it has a lot of SharePoint functionality built in from start. So, let's see what Office 2003 can do in this example:

❑ **Create a document:** You can either use the New button in the Info library or create the new document in Office 2003, then save the document to the URL that points to the Info library in the IT site.

❑ **Modify a document:** You can open a document in the Info library, then modify it, and then save it back.

❑ **MS Excel synchronization:** With Office 2003, you can export a list from SharePoint to MS Excel 2003, modify its content, and then write the changes back to the SharePoint list.

❑ **MS Access synchronization:** You can export a list or library, and display it as a table in MS Access 2003, and then create and print reports.

❑ **Using InfoPath Forms:** With Office 2003 came the MS InfoPath 2003 client. It is able to open and allow the user to work with IP forms, using either the full IP client or the Forms Server web client. It is also possible to design and develop new IP forms with InfoPath 2003.

❑ **Document management:** In Office 2003, you will find the Task Pane, a special information pane that displays SharePoint-related information directly in the Office 2003 client. For example, you can see and modify the custom columns in the Info library; you can also see the other documents in the same library as that document. There are also links for Check Out/Check In, version history, adding tasks, web links, and creating Document Workspaces in this Task Pane.

❑ **IRM Protection:** With Office 2003, you can use the Information Rights Management (IRM) features to protect Office 2003 documents, and Outlook e-mails. The IRM is built upon the Rights Management Server (RMS), mentioned before in this chapter. Using IRM, the Office 2003 user can define advanced security settings for a document or an e-mail, such as prohibit printing, or forward of e-mail.

❑ **Policy templates:** Office 2003 documents will follow any policy template defined in SharePoint 2007.

It is clear that Office 2003 is a much better client for a SharePoint 2007 environment. If basic SharePoint integration is all you need, then you will get it from Office 2003. But if you want to use all the new features in SharePoint 2007, such as Excel Services, Business Intelligence, RSS feeds, managing documents offline, and two-way synchronization of tasks, contacts, and calendar events, you will still need to upgrade to Office 2007. If this reason is not enough, then maybe this fact is what you need: The new user interface for MS Office 2007 clients is much easier to use compared to Office 2003, especially for users who see Office as just another set of tools they need to use in order to do their jobs — and we all know that they are about 80 percent of a typical organization.

MS Office 2007

This is the crown jewel when it comes to integration between Office clients and SharePoint 2007. It is specially designed with SharePoint 2007 in mind and is so much easier to use, even for features that were available for previous Office versions. The number of applications in the Office 2007 suite is also larger than before, and most, if not all of these can interact with SharePoint 2007 in one way or another. So let's continue our example with the Info library, and the IT web site, to see what you can do with Office 2007:

❑ **Create a document:** You can either use the New button in the Info library or create the new document directly in Office 2007, then save the document to the URL that points to the Info library in the IT site. To help users find the URL, Office 2007 offers several options: a) Use the Office button ➪ Publish ➪ Document Management Server, which lists SharePoint sites known to this user, or b) Use the File ➪ Save dialog box in Office 2007, which is enhanced with a new link called My SharePoint Sites that automatically discovers any sites that the SharePoint administrator publishes using Web services or by local registry entries on the client that are deployed by Group Policy Objects using the Active Directory service.

❑ **Modify a document:** The user can open a document in the Info library, then modify it, and then save it back. In Office 2007, you can also make a local copy of documents in your new SharePoint Drafts folder. The next time you open a locally modified copy while online, Office 2007 will ask if you want to update the server copy with your updated version.

❑ **Excel Services:** With Excel 2007, you can send a spreadsheet or a chart to the Excel Service in MOSS 2007. This allows you to publish Excel info, including formulas and the like, to other groups of people. They will be able to view and enter values but not make a copy of the spreadsheet itself. Thus, this is a very safe way to make advanced formulas and calculations available to others, without the risk that anyone can copy these formulas.

❑ **MS Access two-way synchronization:** You can export a list or library, and display it as a table in MS Access 2003, and then print reports. If you modify the content, you can also write the changes back to the SharePoint list.

❑ **Using InfoPath forms:** Use the MS InfoPath 2007 client to create forms, store them in forms libraries, or send them to the Forms Services in MOSS, or to fill in existing forms. InfoPath 2007 can also create customized versions of Document Information Panels in Office 2007 clients. The forms created by InfoPath 2007 can also be opened with a web browser.

❑ **Document Information Panel:** All Office 2007 Pro Plus or Enterprise applications now have a new panel that displays and allows a user to modify document metadata. This replaces the Task Pane in Office 2003.The Document Information Panels are really InfoPath 2007 forms, which can be customized to meet a special need for a specific type of document. The Document Information Panel will also display information such as whether the document requires a check-out before editing, and any document policy that is applied to this document. (See Figure 7-1.)

Figure 7-1

❑ **Document management:** By using the Office button in Office 2007 and selecting the Server option, a user can do several things, such as perform Check Out/In, view the version history, view workflow tasks, and open Document Management Information, which is similar to the Task Pane in Office 2003. That is, it displays a list of all users with access to a document, allows you to send an e-mail to specified users, creates tasks and links in the site hosting a document, and displays a list of other documents in the current document library.

❑ **Workflows:** Office 2007 applications allow the user to start workflows defined for a document library. The user will also see that a document requires workflow actions.

❑ **IRM protection:** With Office 2007, you can use the Information Rights Management (IRM) features to protect Office 2007 documents and Outlook e-mails. The IRM is built on the Rights Management Server (RMS), mentioned before in this chapter. Using IRM, the Office 2007 user can define advanced security settings for a document or an e-mail, such as prohibit printing or the forwarding of e-mail.

❑ **Policy templates:** Office 2007 documents will follow any policy template defined in SharePoint 2007 for a library.

❑ **Slide library:** You can publish individual PowerPoint 2007 slides to a slide library in SharePoint 2007, then you can pick exactly the slides you need from that library to create a new Power Point 2007 presentation. If the original slide is modified, PowerPoint 2007 will indicate that and allow you to update your presentation.

❑ **Web Content:** With Word 2007, you can create, edit, and publish web content in SharePoint.

❑ **Wiki and Blog:** Directly from Word 2007, you can create posts in wiki and blog sites, hosted by SharePoint 2007.

❑ **Comparing versions:** Office 2007 has a great feature that allows you to compare document versions. For example, look at Figure 7-2; it shows how Word 2007 compares two document versions. Original Document and Revised Document are compared in the middle pane, Compared Document, and all changes are indicated by underlined text. In the left pane, all details about the modifications are listed.

❑ **Barcodes and labels:** With MOSS policies, you can specify that printed copies of a document will contain automatically printed barcodes and text labels; this will only work with Office 2007 applications.

The list speaks for itself. An organization that invests in MOSS should also implement Office 2007. Even if you go for just WSS 3.0, Office 2007 is the best option. You will see a lot of examples, and Try It Out instructions in Chapter 9, on how to use these features in Office 2007.

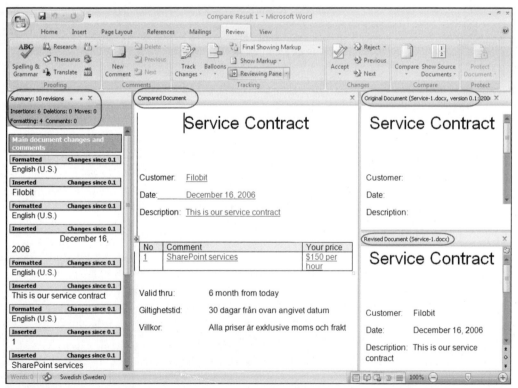

Figure 7-2

The New Generation

This section describes the overall picture of MS Office Server 2007 products. The objective here is to show you what new programs come with the latest generation of Microsoft Office products and to give you a good idea of the new features in SharePoint. Below is a list of the new or updated products that were officially released by early 2007:

- ❑ MS Windows SharePoint Service 2007
- ❑ MS Office SharePoint Server 2007
- ❑ MS Word 2007
- ❑ MS Excel 2007
- ❑ MS PowerPoint 2007
- ❑ MS Access 2007
- ❑ MS Outlook 2007
- ❑ MS Publisher 2007
- ❑ MS InfoPath 2007
- ❑ MS OneNote 2007
- ❑ MS Project Server 2007
- ❑ MS Office Project Portfolio Server 2007
- ❑ MS SharePoint Designer 2007
- ❑ MS Expression Web Designer 2007
- ❑ MS Office Groove 2007
- ❑ MS Visio 2007
- ❑ MS Office Forms Server 2007

There were also several interesting products that were released at the end of 2005 that are totally compatible with the 2007 product line, such as MS SQL Server 2005, MS Dynamics CRM 3.0, MS Communicator, and MS Business Scorecard Manager. As you can see from this list, Microsoft has been very busy the last few years. Their challenge is not only to develop a new version but also to make it integrate with other products and especially SharePoint 2007. So, now it's just up to us to learn all these products. But then again, how hard can it be, right?

One of Microsoft's top priorities for this new version of SharePoint is performance. The goal is to offer even better performance than with SharePoint 2003, and all initial tests indicate that this is the case. As long as you follow the recommended guidelines for building a SharePoint farm (see Chapters 2 and 4), the performance of SharePoint 2007 will greatly surpass what you have today, and this is especially important for large organizations with large farms.

Due to the increased number of products, the number of different MS Office suites has grown to seven. When you want to upgrade to the new Office 2007 version, you have a lot of options to choose between. All of them can use either MS Office SharePoint Server 2007 or MS Windows SharePoint Services 3.0.

However, only MS Office Enterprise, Ultimate, or Professional Pro will enable full integration with SharePoint 2007, since only these editions include MS InfoPath, which is necessary to display the new Document Information Panel for MS Office documents. The new features in SharePoint 2007 are integrated into the Office 2007 products, when appropriate, but you will still be able to use a web browser to take advantage of most of these features if you are running pre–Office 2007 applications.

Application	MS Office Enterprise 2007	MS Office Ultimate	MS Office Professional Pro	MS Office Professional
Excel 2007	Yes	Yes	Yes	Yes
Word 2007	Yes	Yes	Yes	Yes
PowerPoint 2007	Yes	Yes	Yes	Yes
Outlook 2007	Yes	Yes	Yes	Yes
Access 2007	Yes	Yes	Yes	Yes
InfoPath 2007	Yes	Yes	Yes	No
Publisher 2007	Yes	Yes	Yes	Yes
OneNote	Yes	Yes	No	No
Groove 2007	Yes	Yes	No	No
Communicator 2007	Yes	No	Yes	No

The three first packages, MS Office Enterprise 2007, MS Office Ultimate 2007, and MS Office Professional Plus 2007, have extra functionality built in that will allow them to do more in a MOSS 2007 environment; these features are called Enterprise Content Management (ECM) and Rights Management Service (RMS). These extra features will allow a user to publish a spreadsheet directly from MS Excel 2007 to the Excel Services in MOSS 2007. You can also apply special security permissions to a document using RMS, and then store it in a SharePoint document library, for example that this document can only be displayed but not printed or saved. These settings will still be active, even if someone is copying this document to another location or maybe sending it as an e-mail attachment. Using RMS, you can also use a client certificate to electronically sign a document; this information will follow the document wherever it may be stored. If anyone then modifies this document, the Office application will display a warning whenever the document is opened that the electronic signature is invalid, and therefore its content cannot be trusted. To get these RMS features, an administrator must first install the RMS server in your network.

For more information about RMS, check www.microsoft.com/rms. **For more information about ECM, see Chapter 9.**

Besides the four MS Office editions listed in the previous table, there are several other editions available:

❑ Microsoft Office Small Business 2007

❑ Microsoft Office Standard 2007

❑ Microsoft Office Home 2007

❑ Microsoft Office Student 2007

❑ Microsoft Office Basic 2007

As noted earlier in this section, you won't have the full functionality of integration with these products.

Now that you have examined the various Office versions and suites, it is time to move on to some practical and fun things that you can do with Office 2007, starting with Outlook.

MS Outlook

In previous versions of SharePoint, Outlook was simply a handy tool for storing local copies of specific types of SharePoint lists, such as contacts, tasks, and calendar lists. It was great for offline access to these types of SharePoint lists, but it did not allow the user to update them locally and then replicate that modification back to the SharePoint server. But the new Outlook 2007 is very different. It is almost as if this version of Outlook is acting as a SharePoint client, besides being a mail client. It brings so many enhancements to SharePoint users, and for that reason, I recommend that even if, for some reason, you choose not to implement Office 2007, you implement Outlook 2007!

MS Outlook 2003

It is definitely possible to use MS Outlook 2003 with SharePoint 2007. However, it will not have all the new and exciting features that Outlook 2007 offers. Below is list of the standard features that Outlook 2003 offers:

❑ **Task lists:** Outlook allows the user to download a copy of tasks lists for offline usage. These tasks are read-only and changes cannot be replicated back to the SharePoint server, not even with SharePoint 2007.

❑ **Contact lists:** The same thing is true for contact lists. The user can download a read-only copy of a SharePoint contact list, but it cannot be changed in Outlook 2003.

❑ **Calendar lists:** Again, same thing is true; you can only download a read-only copy of SharePoint's calendar lists.

❑ **Alerts:** With Outlook 2003 you can receive and use incoming alert messages sent by SharePoint. You can also view and manage all your alerts defined in SharePoint.

So, Outlook 2003 is good if you are happy with downloading SharePoint lists as read-only copies. But if you need two-way synchronization, then this Outlook version will not do.

MS Outlook 2007

The best Outlook edition available for SharePoint 2007 implementation is Outlook 2007. It has a number of new and exciting features that relate to SharePoint 2007. Note that with SharePoint 2003 you will not have these extra features, even with Outlook 2007! Below is a list of the features available when you combine Outlook 2007 and SharePoint 2007:

❑ **Task lists:** With Outlook 2007, you get full two-way synchronization of task lists in SharePoint. You can view, add, and modify tasks in this list, just like any Outlook task list, and all changes will be replicated back to SharePoint. These tasks will also be displayed along with other Outlook tasks in Calendar view.

❑ **Contact lists:** Another list type that can be replicated from Outlook 2007 to SharePoint 2007. Its content can be updated, including adding new contacts or deleting existing contacts. Any changes will be replicated back to SharePoint. Outlook will, by default, search for users also in these replicated SharePoint contact lists, when a user searches for recipient names.

❑ **Calendar lists:** Use Outlook 2007 for two-way synchronization with Calendar lists in SharePoint. Any changes to this list in Outlook 2007 will be synchronized back to SharePoint within minutes. The copy of this calendar can also be used as an overlay on top of other Outlook calendars. You can also send HTML-formatted copies of replicated SharePoint calendars with this version of Outlook. See Figure 7-3, which shows a SharePoint calendar named SIS. The calendar has been converted to an HTML-formatted e-mail.

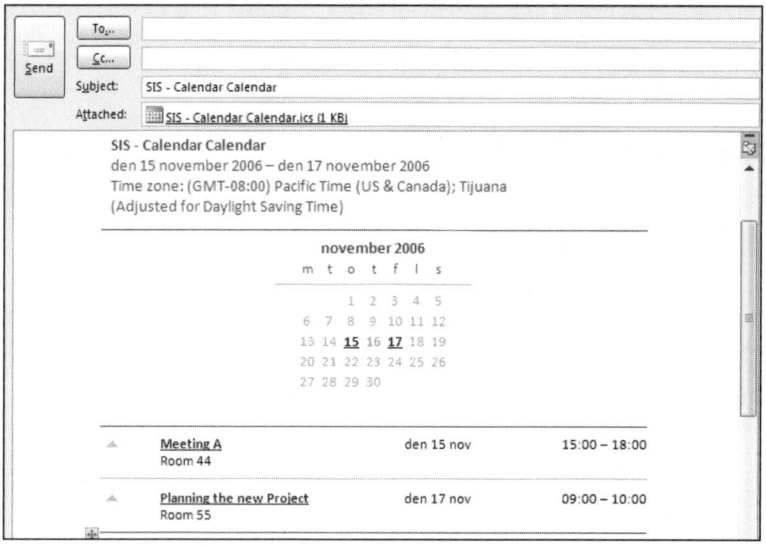

Figure 7-3

❑ **Alerts:** With Outlook 2007, you can receive and use incoming alert messages sent by SharePoint.

❑ **InfoPath forms:** Send forms created by InfoPath 2007 as e-mail. The recipient will see the form directly, and can fill in the form and then return it. These forms may then be stored in a SharePoint library.

❑ **Offline content:** You can download a complete library with documents, images, or forms to an Outlook folder. These downloaded files can be viewed and edited offline. If a document is changed, it will also be stored in the users folder SharePoint Drafts, located in My Documents. The next time this computer goes online, and you open the local copy, SharePoint will ask if you want to upgrade the server copy, that is, the copy stored in the document library in SharePoint.

❑ **Send to:** A new feature in all SharePoint 2007 libraries is that you can use Outlook to send a link to a document, image, or form. The recipient will open the document in read-only mode and can then choose to edit the document, if necessary. This is much smarter than sending complete copies of documents, since you will retain just one single copy of the document, and you will not "litter" your mailbox with large mail attachments.

❑ **Workflow integration:** e-mails with instructions sent by workflows in SharePoint, for example Approve instructions, can be managed directly in Outlook 2007.

❑ **Record Management:** You can forward copies of e-mail directly to SharePoint's Record Management server, where these messages will be stored within a specific record. This requires MS Exchange 2007.

❑ **RSS reader:** Outlook 2007 has built-in support for managing Really Simple Syndication (RSS) feeds. This can be used to display all new items in a SharePoint customer list or documents in a project document library. It can also be used to display information in any standard RSS source, such as news from Internet web sites, or virus warnings from antivirus vendors' web sites.

Offline Content

The list above is extensive, and to see how to use some of the most exciting features, you should try the step-by-step instructions in the Try It Out below. As always, it is easiest to explain how it works by using examples. The user Adam is working at the company Filobit; they recently deployed SharePoint 2007 and MS Office 2003 Professional Plus, which includes MS Outlook 2007 and MS InfoPath 2007. Adam uses the SharePoint site SIS a lot, since it contains the information he needs to do his work. Now and then, Adam is away from the office, so he will be off line, and therefore cut off from the SIS site. But by using the new offline feature in Outlook 2007, he will still be able to view both documents and images offline. The Try It Out shows how Adam does this.

Try It Out   Download SharePoint Libraries to Outlook

1. Log on as Adam.

2. Use Internet Explorer and open the SIS web site, in this example:
   `http://srv1/SiteDirectory/SIS`

3. Open the Shared Documents library, by clicking on its list name in the Quick Launch bar.

4. Click Actions ➪ Connect to Outlook. The first time you do this for a library, Outlook will display a dialog box that ask if you trust this source. Click Yes to continue. If you instead click Advanced, you can define things like the folder name in Outlook, a description, and if you want to follow the default synchronization schedule or not (See Figure 7-4).

5. The list is now displayed in Outlook, under the top folder, SharePoint Lists (see Figure 7-5), and its content is listed. The currently selected document is also listed directly in the Preview Pane, thanks to the new Preview feature in Outlook 2007. To view any of these documents, just select it in the center pane.

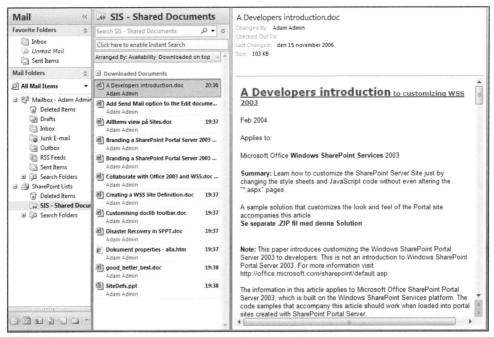

Figure 7-4

Figure 7-5

6. The user Adam now has the information stored in his Outlook client. Later, when he is offline, he reads some of these documents and decides to update one of them. To do this, Adam double-clicks on the document and answers Open when asked if he wants to save, open, or cancel it.

7. The document opens in Word 2007 in Read-only mode. At the top of the document is a statement that says Office Server Document. To modify this document, edit it offline, and save it to the server later, Adam clicks on the Edit Offline button next to that statement.

8. A dialog box is displayed, informing Adam that a copy of this document will be stored in the SharePoint Drafts folder, which will be created if necessary in Adam's My Document. Any modification Adam does to this document will be stored in that SharePoint Drafts folder. Adam clicks OK, and can now start editing this offline copy.

9. When Adam is finished with his editing, he saves and closes Word 2007. The document on Adam's local client is now different than the server copy.

10. The next day, Adam comes to the office. When he gets online with his client, he opens this previously modified document, and then Outlook compares the local copy with the server copy in SharePoint. Since they are different, Outlook now displays a dialog box, asking if he wants to update the server copy (see Figure 7-6). If he clicks Update, all modified documents stored locally in Adam's client will be copied up to the document library on the SharePoint server. Note that if the server copy has been changed during the time Adam has been offline, then Outlook will display another dialog box that informs him about this conflict (see Figure 7-7). If he answers Yes to the question Do you want to view and resolve the conflict in the Document Updates Pane now?, then Word 2007 will start and display the document, including a number of options on how to resolve this conflict (see Figure 7-8).

Figure 7-6

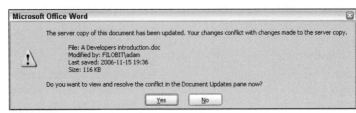

Figure 7-7

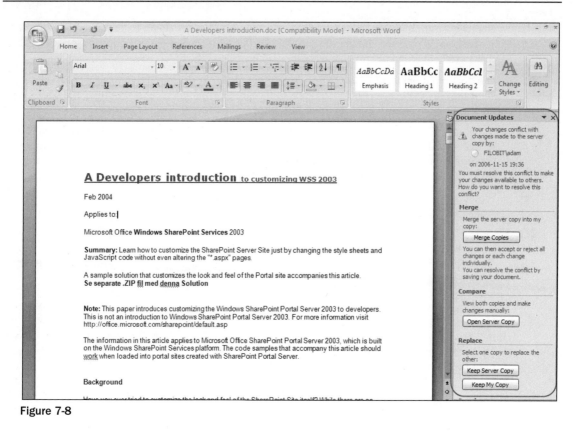

Figure 7-8

To summarize, Outlook 2007 allows the user to take information stored in SharePoint libraries offline. This information may also be edited offline and when the user goes online again, he or she will be offered the opportunity to update the server. If there is a conflict, Outlook 2007 will discover this and give the user several options on how to resolve this.

Using RSS in Outlook

The offline functionality described above is excellent. But sometimes, you do not want to make a copy of a complete library, especially if it contains thousands of documents.. This is where RSS comes in handy, since the information listed in a RSS folder is a short description plus a link to the documents in SharePoint, not the documents themselves. To open a document, just click the link. This requires that you be online and have access to the RSS source, the SharePoint library.

The story behind RSS is this: This XML-based protocol was first released in 1999 by Dan Libby of Netscape. At that time, RSS stood for Rich Site Summary. Its purpose was to create an easy way for a program to subscribe to updates from an information source, for example news headlines published by a news site, such as the *Washington Post* or CNN. The term used here is RSS feed readers (or aggregator), that is, the program that receives the information feed. The RSS release used today is version 2.0, released in 2002, and its abbreviation now stands for Really Simple Syndication. There are actually several versions of RSS available, but the most commonly used is RSS 2.0

Both MS Outlook 2007 and MS Internet Explorer 7.0 have built-in support for RSS 2.0 and can be used as feed readers for any web application that supports RSS 2.0 feeds. Many of the lists and libraries, including News pages, in SharePoint 2007 support RSS feeds, that is, an Outlook 2007 client can set up a RSS feed reader to any SharePoint list. The following steps describe how the user Adam will configure Outlook as a RSS feed reader of the document library Info in the SharePoint site Sales.

Try It Out   **Use RSS to Display List Content in Outlook**

1. Log on as Adam.

2. Open the web site that contains the document library you want to use as a RSS source; for example, `http://srv1/sitedirectory/sales`.

3. Click on the Info document library. Its content will now be listed.

4. Click Actions ⇨ View RSS Feed. This will display a page with info about this RSS feed; that is the source, such as the URL to the feed, and the latest posts in this feed.

5. Click the link subscribe to this RSS feed at the top of this page. If MS Outlook 2007 was not previously started, it will now start. Next, you will see a dialog box, saying Add this RSS Feed to Outlook? It will show the complete URL address; if you click the Advanced button, it will allow you to configure this RSS Feed, including parameters such as these (see Figure 7-9):

    a. **Feed Name:** The name for the folder in Outlook.

    b. **Delivery Location:** The location for the folder in Outlook. By default, all RSS feeds will be collected under the top folder, RSS Feeds.

    c. **Downloads/Automatic download Enclosures for this feed:** Check this box to have enclosures downloaded automatically to the RSS folder in Outlook. This setting will not affect RSS feeds of SharePoint libraries but may be interesting when the RSS feed is a news listing on the Internet.

    d. **Download/Download the full article as an .html attachment to each item:** Check this box if you want the complete posting downloaded to Outlook. If not, only a short description will be downloaded, which will be faster and require less disk space. Note that this setting is not in effect when the RSS feed is a SharePoint library list.

    e. **Update Limit:** This check box is set by default, which makes Outlook's RSS feed reader follow the default download schedule, which is once every hour.

    f. Click OK when you are done with this configuration.

6. Still in the dialog box Add this RSS Feed to Outlook, click Yes to create the feed in Outlook. Immediately, the feed reader will connect to the RSS feed and download all the posts available. In this example, Adam will now see all document names in his new RSS folder in Outlook but not the complete article. To view a document listed in this RSS feed, click View article. That will open the document property web page. To see the document, click its name in the Name field. You can also change RSS posts to include a link directly to the document, as described later in this chapter.

7.   When you are done with this RSS configuration, your web page will still show the RSS configuration link, as described in step 4. Click Back to return to the document library.

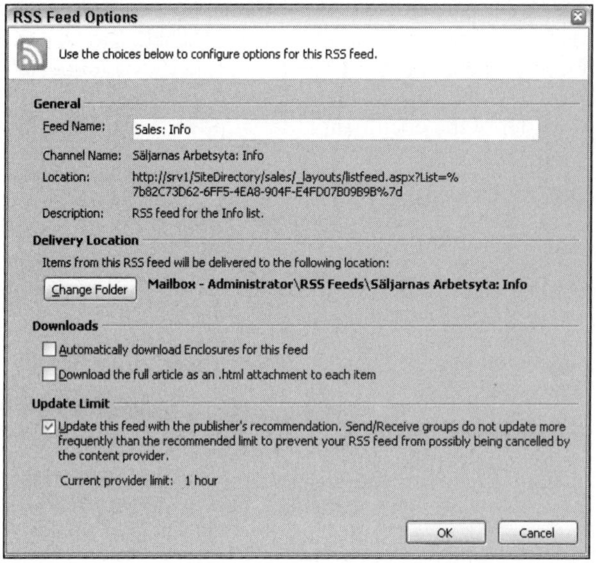

Figure 7-9

You can change an existing RSS feed configuration in Outlook 2007 by opening the Tools menu, then selecting Account Settings. Open the RSS Feeds tab. It will list all existing RSS feeds, and here you can change any of these feeds by selecting them and clicking Change. This will bring up the same configuration dialog box as depicted in Figure 7-9. You can also delete an RSS feed by selecting it and clicking Remove. To create a new feed, click Add, and enter the URL to the RSS source. If you want to change the default folder location in Outlook, click Change Folder, then select another Outlook folder for the RSS feeds. You can also create a new database file that Outlook will use for storing all RSS feeds by clicking New Outlook Data File (see Figure 7-10).

> When creating a new Outlook data file, you should choose the option Office Outlook Personal Folders File (.pst), due to its unlimited size, unless you want to use this PST file later in Outlook XP or earlier editions of Outlook.

All RSS feeds are stored in a local mail database, known as a Personal Store (PST) file. By default, Outlook will create one single PST file that will be used for all information retrieved from SharePoint, including offline synchronization of document libraries, task lists, and RSS feeds. The default size limit for this PST file is referred to as "unlimited," but in reality it is limited to 16 TB (terabytes). The option you have when creating a new PST file is to use the older file format, which is limited to 2 GB. There is no reason to use that older file format, unless you need to copy this PST file to Outlook XP or an older version.

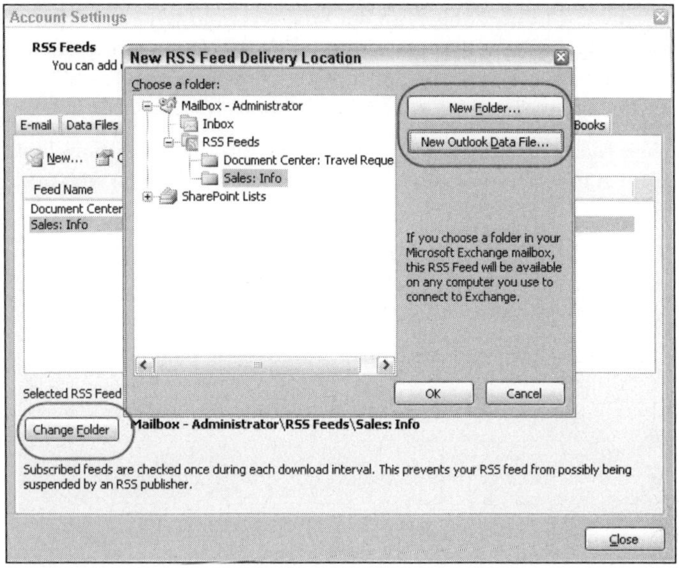

Figure 7-10

There is a master configuration of RSS for the SharePoint farm, which controls if RSS is available or not. Open the Central Administration tool for SharePoint, switch to Application Management, and click Web application general settings in the SharePoint Web Application Management section. There, you will find RSS Settings, which by default will be enabled. If this setting is disabled, then no list or library will have an RSS configuration setting visible. Each site collection also has its RSS configuration, which controls if RSS is enabled or not in this site collection. Almost the same configuration page is also available for each individual site in that site collection, except that these configuration pages cannot control the overall RSS setting for the complete site collection. The following Try It Out contains the steps to configure RSS for a site collection.

Try It Out   **Configure RSS Settings for a Site Collection**

1. Log on as Adam.

2. Open the top site for a site collection; for example, `http://srv1`.

3. Click Site Actions ➪ Site Settings ➪ Modify All Site Settings.

4. Click the link RSS in the Site Administration. This will display the overall configuration settings for this site collection, plus the current top site (see Figure 7-11). Below are the settings available on this page:

   a. **Allow RSS feeds in this site collection:** The default is Yes. This setting will only be visible for the top site in this site collection!

   b. **Allow RSS feeds in this site:** The default is Yes.

   c. **Copyright:** This is an optional text field where you can enter a copyright statement that the RSS feed reader will see.

d. Managing Editor: This is an optional text field where the name for the managing editor of RSS Feeds from this site is listed. The RSS feed reader will be allowed to view this information. The purpose with this field is to inform the RSS feed reader about whom to contact in case there are questions about this RSS.

e. Web Master: Same as for the Managing Editor; this optional text field may be used to inform the RSS feed reader about who the responsible web master is for RSS feeds from this site.

f. Time to Live: This is the preferred synchronization time in minutes for a RSS feed reader that uses any of the lists in this current site as a RSS Feed source. By default, this is set to 60 minutes.

g. Click OK to save and close this configuration page.

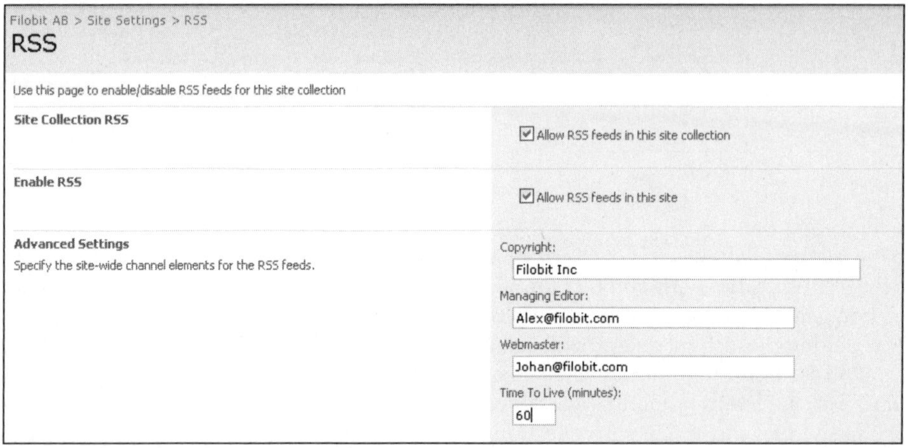

Figure 7-11

Finally, each list and library has its own RSS configuration, which controls if RSS is enabled or not, and what information this RSS feed will send to the feed reader. This is actually the most interesting RSS configuration page, due to all the options it contains. Follow the steps in the Try It Out below to configure the RSS settings for a SharePoint list.

Try It Out   Configure RSS Settings for a SharePoint List

1. Log on as a site owner, and open the site containing the list you want to configure; for example, `http://srv1/SiteDirectory/Sales`.

2. Click on the list or library to be configured; for example, the document library named Info.

3. Click Settings ➪ Document Library Settings ➪ RSS settings. This will open the RSS configuration page for the library (see Figure 7-12). There you will find these settings. Note that not all of these settings will be displayed for all types of feed readers; for example, the Outlook 2007 feed reader will not display the description, nor the image defined in Figure 7-12.

a. Allow RSS feeds for this list: The default is Yes.

b. **Truncate multi-line text fields to 256 characters:** Default is No.

c. **Title:** Enter the default name for the RSS feed, to be used by the RSS feed reader.

d. **Description:** Enter the description for the RSS feed.

e. **Image URL:** Enter the URL for an image that the feed reader can choose to display or not.

f. **Include file enclosures for items in the feed:** The default is No. An enclosure is a way to include links to multimedia content to an RSS feed, such as images, MP3 files, or a link to a document. For example, if you want the RSS feed posts of a document library to include a link directly to the document, then you should set this option to Yes.

g. **Link RSS items directly to their files:** The default is No. This is another way to make the RSS posts contain links to the source document.

h. **Columns:** Choose which columns are to be listed in the RSS posts, including any custom-made columns for this SharePoint list or library.

i. **Item Limit/Maximum items to include:** This will set a limit for how many list items this RSS feed will send to its feed reader; the default is 25 items.

j. **Item Limit/Maximum days to include:** This will set a limit for how old a list item can be; default is 7 days. Older items will not be sent to the feed reader, even if the total number of items does not exceed the maximum number of items to include.

4. Click OK to save and close this configuration page.

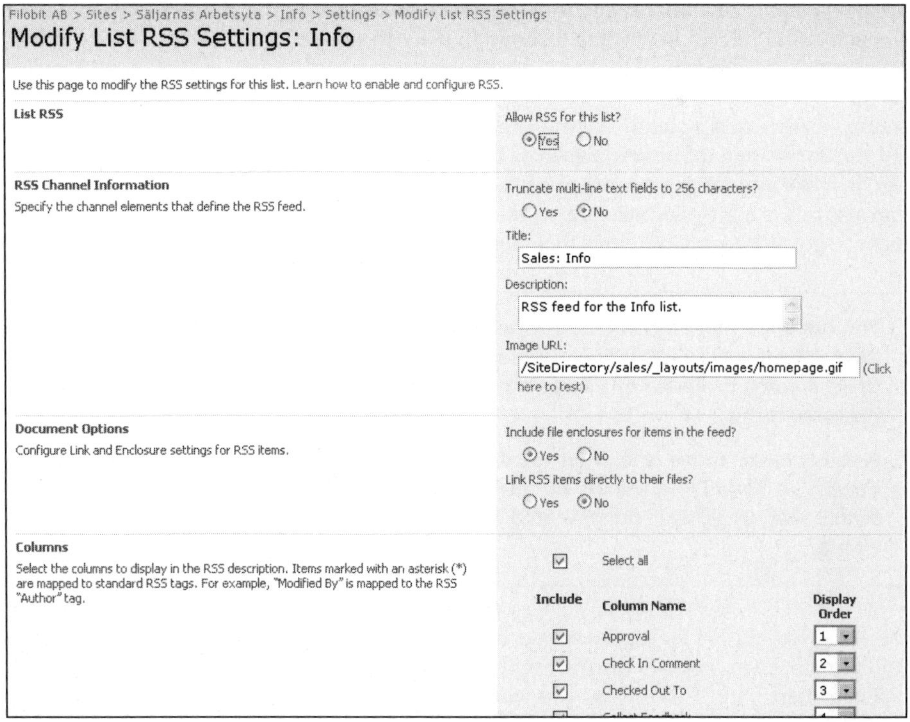

Figure 7-12

As you have seen, there are a lot of places to configure RSS settings. But how do you force an update instead of waiting for the default schedule for a particular RSS feed? The answer is that you do it the same way that you update anything else in MS Outlook. Press the F9 key. However, this alone will not work with RSS feeds, since the Update Limit setting is set by default on the RSS Advanced configuration page, as mentioned at the beginning of this RSS discussion. You may remember that SharePoint lists are, by default, configured to send updates to the RSS feed reader once every 60 minutes. Uncheck the Update Limit for this RSS feed in Outlook, and then press F9 to force an update.

More Effective Meetings with Outlook and SharePoint

It is hardly a secret that traditional meetings often are ineffective and sometimes just plain boring. Why is that? The main reasons are that the preparations for the meeting are bad, those involved in the actual meeting process have problems keeping to the time schedule, the attendees are not prepared, and there are always some members who forgot to bring their meeting invitation. And to make things worse, after the meeting, it can sometimes be hard to find out about decisions and information given out during the meeting. So, in effect, many attendees feel that many meetings are a waste of time.

How can this be improved? One solution is to use SharePoint to keep track of everything about the meetings. But some things, such as sending meeting invitations and keeping track of people's calendars, are handled better by MS Outlook. Both the 2003 and 2007 versions of MS Outlook are fully integrated with SharePoint's meeting functionality, and they are the preferred way of creating meeting invitations and workspaces at the same time. Your users don't have to learn a completely new way of managing these meetings; everything they know about checking the Outlook calendar status for attendees and resources, managing invitations, and moving meetings, is exactly like it was before. However, there are some new features related to creating a common place to store all the meeting details. This place is known as a meeting workspace.

A meeting workspace is a common team site, built on a specific site template. It has a number of precon-figured lists for storing information such as the meeting agenda, decisions, a list of attendees, and a list of tasks. Just like any other team site, it can be modified to suit your needs for this particular meeting. You can also create a series of meeting workspaces that are connected to each other; this will make it very easy to go back to any previous meeting instance to view its details.

> You can use a meeting workspace just as a place to store everything about a meeting, but the best way to use it is to display its content in real time during the meeting, using a video projector or a large monitor. This makes sure that everyone focuses on the same thing.
>
> Another smart move is to enter the decisions and tasks in their lists, and take notes directly in SharePoint during the meeting. This way, all attendees who are still awake will see what is documented and can comment directly if something is wrong.

The following sections list the logical steps for using SharePoint's meeting workspaces for managing meet-ings and using a video projector during the actual meeting. Later you will see the steps for doing this in MS Outlook and SharePoint. This is what you will need to work with meeting workspaces as described:

❑ **Windows SharePoint Services:** MOSS will also do fine.

❑ **MS Outlook 2007 (or 2003):** Earlier Outlook versions are not integrated with SharePoint.

❑ **MS Exchange Server 2007 (or 2003):** To view calendars of the attendees and resources.

If you don't have MS Outlook and MS Exchange, it is still possible to create meeting workspaces, but it is not anywhere near as easy and effective a process as if you have these programs.

Before the Meeting

In this example, you are the meeting organizer who needs to discuss a new project that will start next week. You have five project members, and all of them must participate in this first meeting:

1. You create a meeting agenda, including an estimation of how much time each item will take and who will be responsible for it. The total estimated meeting time seems to be about 60 minutes.

2. Using MS Outlook, you look for a time when all five project members seem to be available.

3. Using MS Outlook, you also look for a conference room that is equipped with a video projector and a network connection and is available for this meeting.

4. You create, but do not yet send, the meeting invitation to all project members, plus the conference room, which happens to be a resource mailbox in this case (but a public folder mailbox will also do fine).

5. Still with the meeting invitation open, you create the meeting workspace in SharePoint.

6. You add a description of the meeting and then send the invitation to the attendees and the resource mailbox.

7. Using your calendar, you open the new meeting workspace and start adding the agenda items, the objective, and some documents that will be discussed during the meeting.

8. All attendees except Bill accept the invitation. Because Bill must be there in order to make decisions, you reschedule this meeting using Outlook. A new invitation is sent out. There is no need to change or update the meeting workspace.

9. Bill sends you an e-mail saying that he needs to add two items to the agenda. You tell him to use the link in his meeting invitation to open its workspace and add these items. Because Bill is an attendee, he is automatically granted the rights to write and update any list in this workspace.

10. Everyone (including you) seems satisfied with the meeting preparations so far. Just relax and await the actual meeting.

During the Meeting

It is time for the meeting. You take your laptop to the conference room and connect it to the network to make sure you can open the meeting workspace. Then, you connect your computer to the video projector. Everything is now ready for your meeting:

1. When all attendees have arrived, you display the meeting workspace using the video projector. You give a quick overview of the meeting workspace so that everyone understands what is displayed.

2. You point your mouse at the list of meeting objectives described on the workspace and tell the attendees what the meeting is all about.

3. You point your mouse at the meeting agenda and show the attendees that each item has a title, a description, the name of the person responsible for each item, and finally how much time each item is supposed to take. Make sure that people understand that they must stick to the estimated time or the meeting will take longer than planned, which is something nobody wants.

4. The first item on the agenda is to greet everyone, welcome them to this meeting, and explain what the meeting is about. You have just done that so you continue with the next item on that list.

5. The next item is to discuss the project plan. Instead of handing out paper, you open the document that describes this plan: Everyone can see this document now, and you can all start discussing this plan.

6. You all agree that Bill should be the project leader. This is entered in the Decision list in the meeting workspace.

7. You go on with the next agenda item. Marina is given the task of ordering new software tools that will be needed during this project. This information is entered in the Task list on the workspace.

8. Marielle comments on the number of project members. She thinks that it will be hard to meet the deadline with just five people. This comment is entered in a list normally used for announcements.

9. For each item on the agenda, a number of decisions, delegated tasks, and comments are made; all of these are entered in their respective lists. When the meeting is over (on time because everyone tried to keep to the expected time slot for each agenda item), you will have full documentation of everything important that happened at the meeting.

10. You end this meeting, reminding all attendees that they can go back to this workspace whenever they need to and read what was said and done.

After the Meeting

Because a meeting normally results in a number of tasks that need to be accomplished in due time, it is interesting to revisit the workspace for some time after the actual meeting. SharePoint stores this information until you actively delete this workspace; if necessary you can reuse this information in later meetings. Following are some typical activities after a meeting:

1. Marina wants to check some details about the task assigned to her, so she looks at her Outlook calendar to find the booking for that meeting, which contains the link to the meeting workspace.

2. Because Bill is the project leader, he also wants to see the complete list of tasks and their due date to check if anybody is behind schedule.

3. The manager for your department says he wants a copy of the meeting minutes. You open the meeting workspace and add the manager as a member of the Visitors SharePoint group, using the built-in feature of SharePoint to send an e-mail to the user who has been granted access to a site. You add some descriptive text in that e-mail and explain that you don't use meeting minutes anymore but instead use SharePoint's workspaces.

4. Marielle wants to find out who the project members are today. She also uses her Outlook calendar and the link in the booking for this meeting to quickly access that meeting workspace and read its list of attendees.

5. One important partner wants to view the details from this meeting. Because he does not have any user account on your network, you cannot ask him to open the workspace for this meeting. And because there are no meeting minutes, you have nothing to send him. Instead you start an MS Live Meeting session, sharing your web browser to display the workspace to this partner. This way, you also can be sure that this partner will not see anything other than what is required.

Integrating Outlook and SharePoint

MS Outlook plays a very important role in managing meetings in SharePoint. It is used to send out invitations and to quickly open the meeting workspace before, during, and after the meeting. MS Outlook is also used to create the meeting workspace, although you can create this workspace from within SharePoint, just like any other team site. Remember that a workspace is just an ordinary team site but uses a special meeting site template.

> Only MS Outlook 2007 and 2003 are integrated with SharePoint. Previous versions of Outlook cannot create a meeting workspace, nor can they see its properties.

In order to create a meeting workspace, the user needs to be assigned the Create Subsites right on the web site that is the parent of the workspace. All users who have a personal web site (My Site) can create meeting workspaces as subsites in their personal web site. By default, only owners of a site have this right. In other words, team sites you have created and personal sites are locations that you can use to create meeting workspaces. Regardless of where the meeting workspace is created, all users who are invited are automatically assigned the right to join that workspace, even if it is created in a personal workspace. Typically, a project manager (who uses a team site for his project information) will create all related meeting workspaces under that project team site, and other users who just need to create an ad hoc meeting workspace will use their own personal site.

> After the workspace site is created, no more meeting workspace or other subsites can be created under that first meeting workspace site!

Managing Integration Features in Outlook

As you can see, Outlook has a lot of features that integrate with WSS 3.0 and MOSS 2007. As an administrator, you may want to control the behavior of this integration. All of these features are stored in the Windows registry settings. These settings can be controlled by the deployment tool that comes with the MS Office 2003 Resource Kit or by the Group Policy Objects (GPOs) in Active Directory.

> Use the GPO templates `Office12.adm` and `Outlk12.adm` to control these SharePoint-related features. See **http://tinyurl.com/y3buyq** for the MS Office 2003 Resource Kit and more information about using these settings.

The following table lists the key registry entries; all of them are in the HKEY_CURRENT_USER \Microsoft\Office\12.0 key.

Key	Value	Type	Description
Common\DWS	PollingInterval	DWORD	The number of minutes before checking for updates of Document Workspace (default 10, allowed values are 1–999).
Common\ MailSettings	DisableSharing Options	DWORD	1 = disable; 0 = enable: Shared Attachments option in Outlook messages.
Common\Security \Trusted Alert Sources	All	DWORD	0 = do not allow; 1 = allow: users to use Outlook to manage all SharePoint alerts (default = 0).
	AllIntranet	DWORD	0 = disallow; 1 = allow: users to use Outlook to manage alerts from all SharePoint sites within Outlook (default = 0).
	AllTrusted	DWORD	0 = do not allow; 1 = allow: users to use Outlook to manage alerts from all intranets (default = 1).
Meetings\ Profile	EntryUI	DWORD	1 = disable; 0 = enable: Meeting Workspaces button on Outlook meeting requests.
	ServerUI	DWORD	2 = disable that user can enter values to server list. If so: publish default, disallow others.
	MRUInternal	String	Set a limit of five servers available for Meeting Workspace sites. See more about this following this table.
Outlook\ Preferences	DisallowSTS	DWORD	1 = disable; 0 = enable: the feature of linking SharePoint contacts and events lists with Outlook.
	STSSyncInterval	DWORD	The number of minutes before the next update process for linked SharePoint contacts and events lists in Outlook (default is 20 minutes). Set any value between 1 and 1430.
SharePoint Tracking\Name#	Name	String	(# = 1-4) The display name of SharePoint site that will be listed in the "Select A Location list."
	URL	String	The URL of SharePoint site to be listed in the Select a Location list.

The settings for the key `SharePointTracking\Name#` and the values `ServerUI` and `MRUInternal` for the `Meetings\Profile` key control what options the user sees listed in the Select a location menu when creating the meeting workspace. The default is to show these sites:

❏ My Site.

❏ Sites listed in the MRUInternal value.

❏ Up to five of the most recently used sites listed in the `SharePointTracking\Name` key.

❏ Up to five of the most recently used sites. This list is built from cookies stored when users visit a site, where they have the Create Subsite right.

❏ "Other," which allows the user to enter any SharePoint URL.

> **You can create up to five** `SharePointTracking\Name#` **(#=0-4) entries to have these sites listed for the user when creating the meeting workspace.**

The five default meeting workspace templates are listed in the following table.

TemplateName	TemplateID
Basic Meeting Workspace	Mps#0
Blank Meeting Workspace	Mps#1
Decision Meeting Workspace	Mps#2
Social Meeting Workspace	Mps#3
Multipage Meeting Workspace	Mps#4

Meeting Workspace Templates

Just like any other WSS site, meeting workspaces are built on a site template. By default, there are five different meeting workspace templates:

❏ **Basic Meeting Workspace:** Contains four lists: Agenda, Attendees, Objectives, and Document Library.

❏ **Blank Meeting Workspace:** Contains no lists or Web Parts.

❏ **Decision Meeting Workspace:** Contains these lists: Agenda, Objectives, Attendees, Document libraries, Tasks, and Decisions.

❏ **Social Meeting Workspace:** Contains three tabs, or pages: Home, Discussions, and Photos. These three pages contain these lists: Attendees, Directions, Things to Bring, Discussions, and Picture Library. You can add new lists to any of these pages. You can also create new pages using the Modify This Workspace link.

❏ **Multipage Meeting Workspace:** Contains three pages: Home, Page 1, and Page 2. The Home page contains the following lists on the Home page: Objectives, Attendees, and Agenda. The other pages are empty until you add one or more lists to them. You can also create new pages, using the Modify This Workspace link.

As with team sites' workspaces, you can save any customized meeting workspace as a site template. This makes it available when creating new meeting workspaces in the same site collection. You may recall from previous discussions that a site collection is all the team sites created under a specific top-level team site, including the top-level site itself.

Creating a Meeting Workspace

Creating a meeting workspace is very easy. This process is fully integrated with the Outlook process to send invitations to users. For example, say that you want to create a meeting workspace for yourself, Anna, and Axel. This workspace should use the basic workspace template and have the name Project ALPHA. Because you are the administrator for the IT team site, you will create it under that site. Use the steps in the Try It Out below to do this.

Try It Out   Create a Basic Meeting Workspace under IT

1. Log on as an administrator for the IT team site.

2. Start MS Outlook and pick a date and time for the meeting with Anna and Axel.

3. On the Outlook Calendar page, choose New ➪ Meeting Request. Enter the attendees, subject, and location like this (see Figure 7-13):

   a. To: Anna Filippa; Axel Pettersson.

   b. Subject: Project ALPHA.

   c. Location: Room 302.

   d. Description: Welcome to our project meeting!

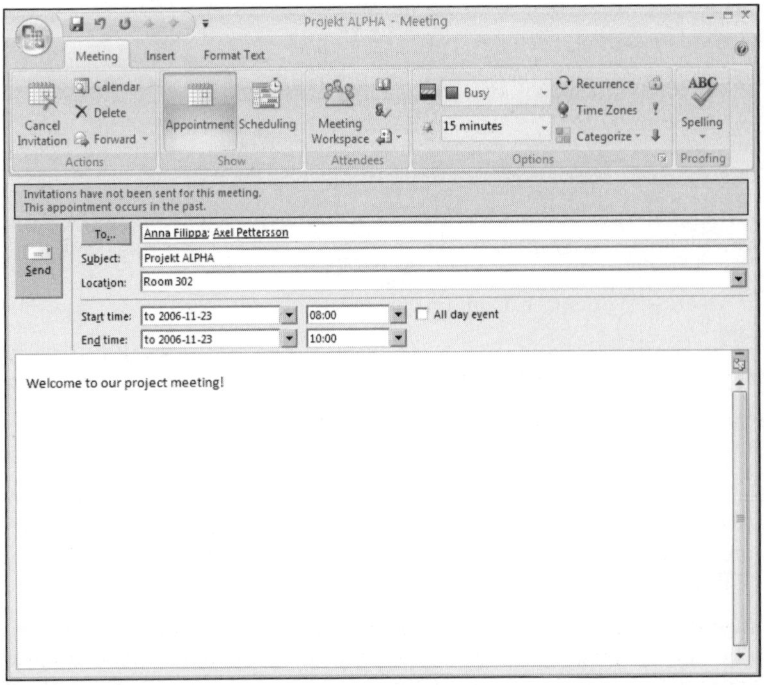

Figure 7-13

4. Normally, you would now click Send, but not this time. Now, you create the meeting workspace! Click the Meeting Workspace button; this opens a new pane at the right of this window (see Figure 7-14).

> If you don't see the Meeting Workspace button, you are creating an appointment instead of a meeting request. Click the Invite Attendees button to change the type.

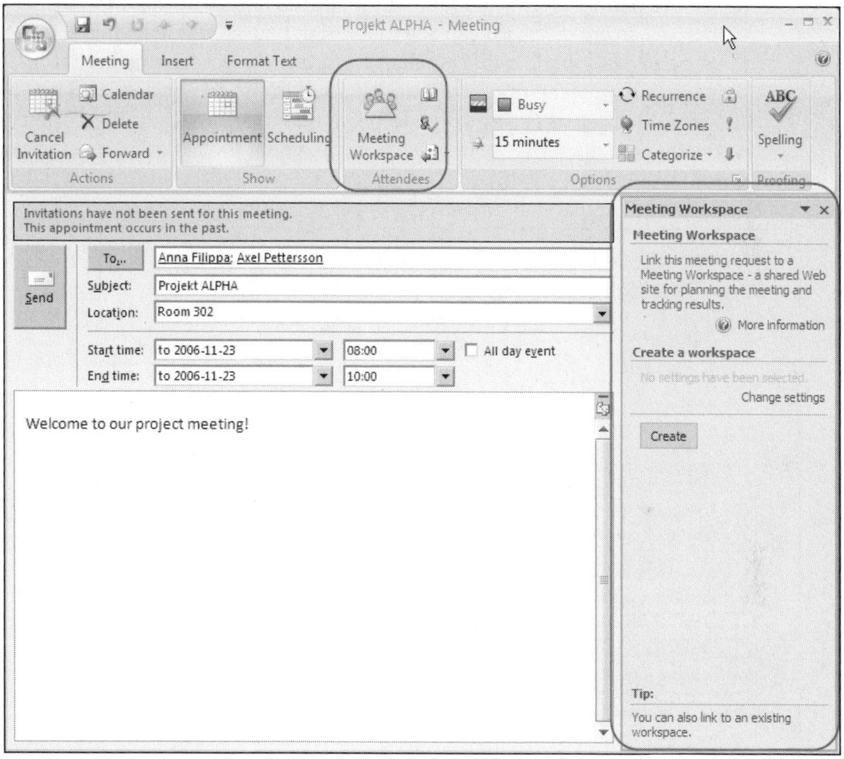

Figure 7-14

5. The default setting is to create a meeting workspace using the Basic Meeting Workspace template in your personal My Site or the current site (if you are the owner of that site). All this is listed in this workspace pane at the right. If all these parameters are okay, click Create, to create the meeting workspace. If not, click the Change Settings link to open a new form, and you will be able to select another web site or enter a URL path. You will also be able to select another meeting site template in this form, if necessary. Note that if the OK button in this form is grayed out, either the selected site is not available or you do not have the permission to create a subsite. If this is the case, you must create the meeting workspace in another location, as described in the following steps:

   a. Pull down the Select a location menu, and choose any of the listed sites. If there are no sites in this menu, then choose Other and enter the URL to the site that will be the parent site for the new meeting workspace. Note that you must have permission to create a site on the location you have selected. For example, enter `http://srv1/sitedirectory/sis` and click OK.

b. If this location is okay, you can now choose the workspace template and language pack. Note that in order to select another language, you must first install that WSS language pack, as described in Chapter 3. For example, select English and Basic Meeting Workspace.

c. Click OK, then Create to create the new workspace. A progress bar is displayed at the top of the pane; this process takes 5–30 seconds, depending on your network. After the workspace is created, you can see that a link has been added in the description of the meeting invitation; its name is taken from the subject for this invitation. Note that the pane gives you some important tips: that all invited attendees will be able to access this site directly after receiving and accepting this meeting invitation. There is also a tip that next step is to open the workspace now, to create the agenda and start adding information to it (see Figure 7-15).

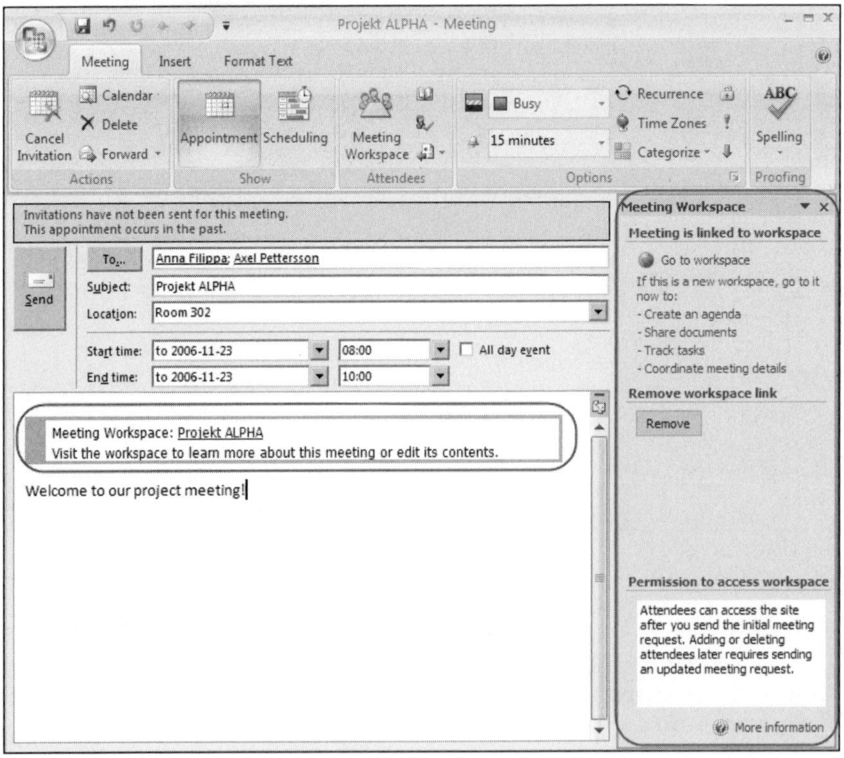

Figure 7-15

6. The invitation is ready, and the workspace and its link have been created. Click Send to send this invitation to all attendees. They will also see this link, and they will automatically be added as Members to this site. This gives them the right to add agenda items, documents, and tasks. However, they will not be able to add new members to the workspace site.

The meeting is now added to the Outlook calendar. If you double-click to open this meeting, it will display the link to this site in its description. You can also right-click this meeting and select View Meeting Workspace, as Figure 7-16 shows.

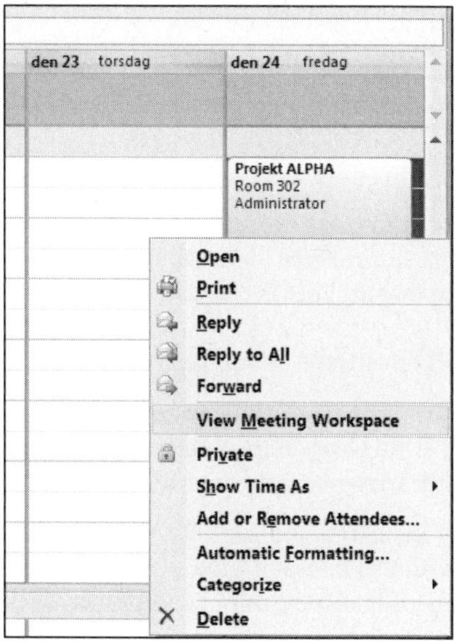

Figure 7-16

Modifying a Meeting Workspace

When you open the new workspace, it displays the four lists: Objectives, Attendees, Agenda, and Document Library. The next logical thing to do is to add information to this workspace, such as the objective and the agenda. Note that you do not need to add attendees, because this list is automatically populated based on the invited users for this meeting. The list also displays each user's status regarding this invitation, for example Accepted, Declined, or No response so far.

Try It Out   **Modifying a Meeting Workspace**

1. Adding an objective is very simple: Click Add new item under the Objectives list, and type in the objective for the meeting.

2. Adding items to the agenda is also very simple. Click Add new item under the Agenda list, and enter the following values:

    a. **Subject:** Enter a short description for this agenda item.

    b. **Owner:** Enter who is responsible for this item.

    c. **Time:** Enter how much time this item will take.

    d. **Notes:** Enter a longer description of this item. Note that you can also attach a file to this item using the Attach File button on the headline.

    e. Click OK to save and close this form. You can now add the next agenda item the same way.

After doing this for a while, you might want a faster way of adding agenda items. The simplest way is to use the Datasheet view, which will display this list in a table view. To do that, follow these steps:

1. On the start page for this workspace, click the Agenda link to open this list on its own page.

2. Click the Actions ➪ Edit in Datasheet button.

3. Enter the values for each item, as if this were an Excel spreadsheet. Note that the user must have Excel 2003 or later installed to have access to the Datasheet view.

4. When done, click Actions ➪ Show in Standard View to see the list in the standard view.

That was an easier method, right? But there are still some things you can do to improve the management of the agenda. For example, you can summarize the total time for this meeting, and you can add a new column that you can use to indicate that an item is completed. Use the following steps to fix these features:

1. Make sure that you still have the Agenda page open. Click Settings ➪ List Settings.

2. To calculate the total time, you need to change the column type for the Time column. In the Columns section, click Time to open its settings. Note that it is defined as Single line of text. SharePoint cannot summarize text columns, so you must change this to a numeric type:

   a. Select Number instead and click OK. This displays a warning: Changing the type of this column may result in a loss of data. Are you sure that you want to change this field from Single line of text to Number? Click OK, and you are taken back to the previous page.

   b. Scroll down to the bottom of this page. Click the view All items (which is the default view for this agenda list). You can now see the configuration settings for this view. Scroll down until you see the Totals section. Expand this section, and change the Total setting for the Time column from None to Sum, using the menu.

   c. Why not change how the list of agenda items is displayed? Expand the Style section, and then select Shaded, then click OK at the bottom of the page. The view will now display the total time for the meeting with each second line shaded.

3. The second feature, to create a check box for each item, is also accomplished using Settings ➪ List Settings. Scroll down to the Columns section again, and click Create column. Note that you can also do this by clicking Settings ➪ Create Column. Enter the following values:

   a. **Column Name:** Done.

   b. **Column Type:** Yes/No (check box).

   c. **Default Value:** No.

   d. Click OK to save and close.

   e. You want this check box at the beginning of each agenda item, so scroll down to the Views section, and click All Items again. In the Columns section, change the Position from Left setting for the Done column from 6 to 1 and click OK.

This enhanced list is now ready to be used. Note that the Done column is the first column on this list. Also note that the total sum for the Time column is displayed on top of the Time column (see Figure 7-17).

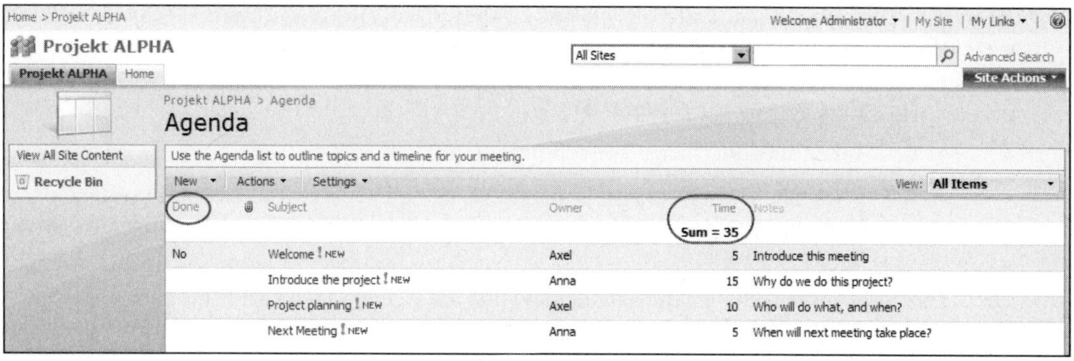

Figure 7-17

The Done column is not that easy to use in the default view. It is much easier to switch to Datasheet view (Actions ⇨ Edit in Datasheet), because you can simply check each item as it is completed. Compare Figure 7-18 to Figure 7-17.

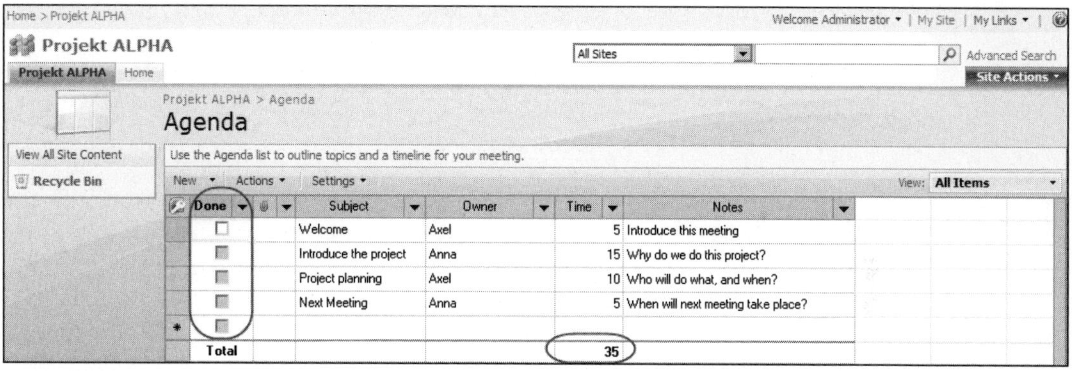

Figure 7-18

Because the Datasheet view is so much easier to see and modify items in, it is the recommended view to use when holding this meeting with the attendees. The smartest thing to do is to create a new view, based on the Datasheet view, and use that view on the start page for this meeting workspace. Use the steps in the following Try It Out to do that.

Try It Out   Create a Datasheet View for the Agenda List

1. Log on as an administrator for the workspace site.

2. Open the Agenda list on its own page.

3. At the far end of the headline row is the View menu; click it and select Create View.

4.   Select Datasheet view, and enter the following values on the web form:

     a.   **View Name:** Table View.

     b.   **First Sort by the column:** ID.

     c.   **Totals section**: change Time column from None to Sum.

     d.   Click OK. The Agenda list is displayed, using the new view. Note that you have the new view listed under Views menu. Click Home at the upper left to open the start page for the workspace.

5.   The next step is to change the default view that the Agenda Web Part list is using: click the arrow to the right of the Agenda Web Part heading, and select Modify Shared Web Part. The configuration pane for the Web Part is displayed.

6.   Use the menu for the Selected View part; change it to the Table View (i.e., the name you supplied in step 4a.). You get a warning that this modification will break any Web Part connections, but this is fine for now. Click OK and then OK again. The new Agenda is displayed using the Datasheet view (see Figure 7-19).

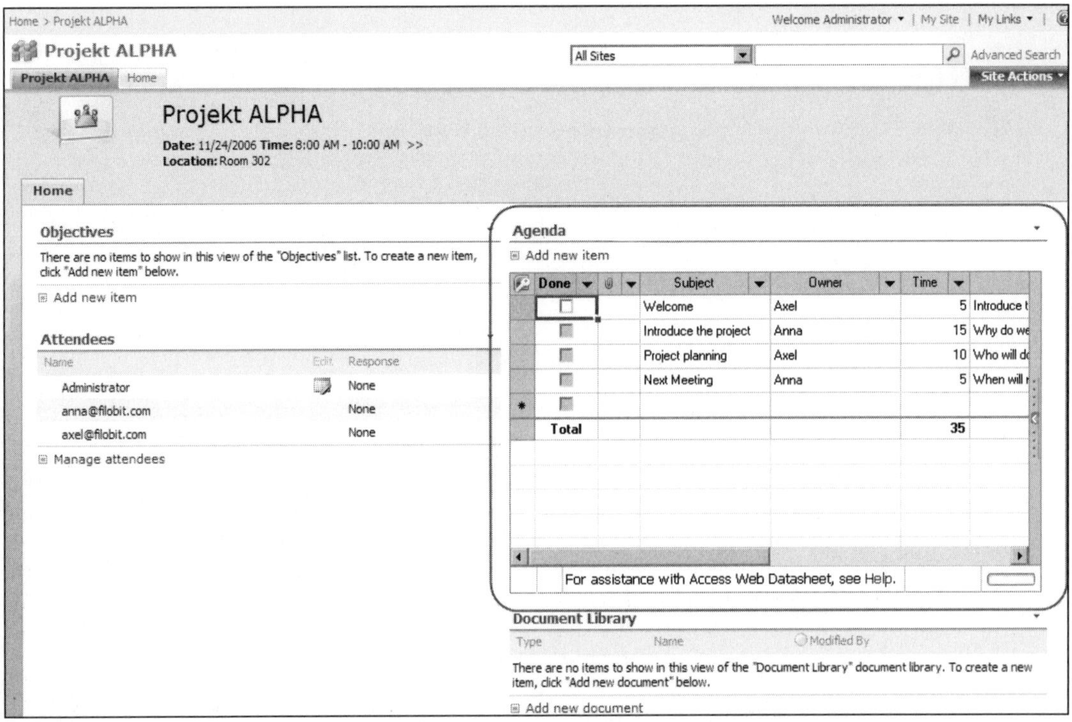

Figure 7-19

The meeting workspace is starting to look good, but some things are still missing. There is no place to add notes or comments from the meeting, and there is no way to store decisions and tasks created during this meeting. You fix this easily by following the steps in the Try It Out below.

Try It Out   Add Extra Features to the Meeting Workspace

1. You can use any of several standard lists for taking notes (for example, Announcements and Discussions), or you can create your own list from scratch. In this example, you will use the Announcements list. Choose Site Actions ➪ Site Settings ➪ Site Libraries and Lists ➪ Create new content. Click on Announcements, then fill in this information:

   a. **Name:** Meeting Comments.

   b. **Description:** Comments from this meeting instance.

   c. **Change items into series items:** No.

   d. Click Create. The new list opens.

2. Click Home to go back to the start page for this workspace. Note that the new list is automatically added to this page to make it easier to use.

This list is a very handy tool for taking notes and comments directly during the meeting. Another way is to write an MS Word file, but the advantage with the Meeting Comments list is that everyone can see these notes directly without the need to open a document.

The other feature that would be nice to have in this meeting workspace is a place to write down tasks assigned to users. This list does not exist, so you must first create it in the same way as you did the Meeting Comments; the difference is that you should select the list type Tasks instead of Announcements. The next step is to configure this list to send e-mail automatically to users assigned a task:

1. Click on the Tasks name, to open this list.

2. Click Settings ➪ Lists Settings, then click the Advanced Settings link.

3. Set Send e-mail when ownership is assigned to Yes.

4. Click OK to save and close. This list will now send e-mail to the user (or group) assigned a task in this list.

Another type of list that is common for meeting workspaces is Decisions. Create it in the same way you did the Task list, but select the list type Decisions instead. If you add many lists to the workspace, you may need to adjust their position on the page:

1. Click on Home for the workspace.

2. Click Site Actions ➪ Edit Page. This page opens in edit mode; this displays all existing Web Parts. Note that each Web Part is stored within a rectangular area, known as a Web Part zone. By default, there are three Web Part zones; Left, Middle, and Right.

3. Locate the Decisions list Web Part. Using the mouse, drag it to the Web Part zone where you want to store it.

4. Locate the Tasks list Web Part; drag it to a Web Part zone.

5. To exit this mode, click Exit Edit Mode

6. Test these two new lists. Click Add new item for the Decision list and for the Tasks list. Make sure they that are listed on the start page for this workspace.

What do you say? Isn't this a very easy, but at the same time powerful, way of organizing all types of information related to meetings, such as meeting comments, agenda, attendees, decisions, and tasks? By adding the lists you need and modifying their columns, you can control what and how information is entered in this workspace, thus making sure nobody forgets about adding important information. It sure beats the traditional meeting minutes!

Managing Workspace Pages

Did you notice that all lists you add to the workspace are immediately displayed on the web page? Compare that to ordinary team sites, where you can choose to add these lists and libraries as links on the Quick Launch bar or not, then later add them as Web Parts to the web page. This choice is not available for workspaces, because they do not have the Quick Launch bar. So for more complex meetings, you may need more than one page for all your lists. This is a very easy task to accomplish with workspaces, but team sites do not have the same functionality. Another difference between workspaces and team sites is that you will automatically create a new list or library when adding list Web Parts in workspaces, whereas in team sites the same operation will create a copy of that list or library. This is demonstrated in the following example.

For example, say that you have a workspace for a project meeting with several lists on the Home page, and you also have a large document library. You discover that this library will make the Home page very long and hard to use, so you decide to create a second page on this workspace and move these documents there, using the steps in the following Try It Out.

Try It Out   **Add a New Page to a Workspace**

1. Open the workspace Home page.

2. Click Site Actions ➪ Add Pages. Now enter these values:

   a. **Page Name:** Add a short name for this page. It will be displayed next to Home. For example, Docs.

   b. Click Add to continue.

3. The new page opens in edit mode, but the problem is that your document library is stored in the Home page and you want to move it to the second page. Because there is no easy method to move or copy a list or library from one page to another in a workspace, you must do it this way:

   a. Drag the Document Library Web Part to the place of your choice on this second page. Its name will be "Document Library1" because this is the second document library created on this workspace and the first was named "Document Library." Remember that adding Web Parts in a workspace will create new libraries instead of copying them, so the new library must have a unique name. This is also clearly stated in the property pane as Create Lists. If the first document library had custom columns, you need to either re-create them in this new document library or create a template from the first library and create this new document library based on that template (if so, click Show All Lists under the Web Part list to see the new template). If you don't do this, you will lose all custom columns when moving the documents to this new library.

   b. Click Exit Edit Mode to leave design mode.

   c. Go back to the Home page and click the title name for the document library. Pull down the View menu, and select the Explorer view. Click any existing document and press Ctrl+A and then Ctrl+C to copy all the documents.

d. Go to the document library on the second page. Click its title name. Switch to the Explorer view. Point the mouse to any free space on that page, and right-click ➪ Paste to paste all files. What you have done now is to copy all the files to the new library.

e. When you are absolutely sure that all the files have been copied to the new document library, go back to the Home page. Click the title of the document library. Choose Settings ➪ Document Library Settings ➪ Delete this document library ➪ OK to execute the delete instruction.

4. Click Home to display this page. Make sure that the old document library is gone. Open the second page. All the files should be visible in this new library, including their custom columns.

> **You can also make a template of the original document library and include all documents, up to 500 MB in total.**

You can move, rename, or delete a page, except for the *Home* page. To move a page, choose Site Actions ➪ Manage Pages. Note that you cannot move the Home page, nor can you move a page to the left of the Home page.

To change the name of an existing page, choose Site Actions ➪ Manage Page; SharePoint will now display the Order action. Click the black menu arrow to display a list with different options, as shown in Figure 7-20. Click Settings and enter the new name for the page.

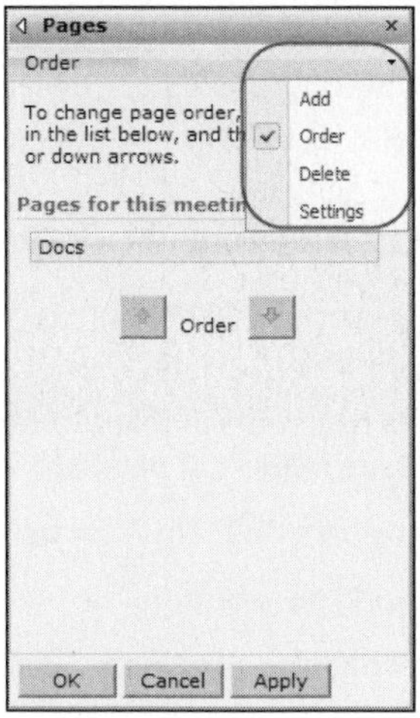

Figure 7-20

Deleting the page also removes all its content. Because there is no way to undo this operation, make sure that you copy the page's lists before you delete it! Use Manage Page and its menu as depicted in Figure 7-20. Then select Delete. This displays a list of all pages except Home. Select the page to be removed, and click the Delete button at the bottom to remove the page from the workspace. Click OK on the warning page.

Managing a Series of Meetings

It is very common to have a series of meetings. For each of these meetings, it is important to have easy access to the information from previous meetings. Using SharePoint's meeting workspaces, this is a breeze. One of my customers complained that their project meetings were almost too complicated to perform, partly due to their constant need to go back to previous meetings to see things like who was responsible for a specific task or when a certain decision was made. After they started to use SharePoint's meeting workspaces, they told me that all this was now much easier; in fact, their meetings were now both fewer and shorter.

The support for a series of meetings in SharePoint is a very strong feature! This can save you a lot of time and energy, compared to using traditional meeting minutes on paper. It makes it possible to go back and forth between the meeting dates and see everything that happened in them. You can even search all the meeting instances for a given text string. This is default with MOSS, but for WSS the SQL Server has to have the Full-Text Indexing feature activated.

Joining an Existing Meeting

After the first meeting workspace has been created as described previously, you can join, or link, new meeting instances to that first workspace. This creates a new page that looks like an individual workspace, but in fact it is a part of the first workspace, cleverly disguised behind smoke and mirrors. "Behind smoke and mirrors" might not be completely true; you will soon see that the workspace gets one enumerated folder for each meeting instance in this series to store the information from that meeting.

For example, say that the first project meeting you created in the previous example will be followed by a number of other meetings related to that project. Now you need to create the second meeting, and you must make sure to link it to the first meeting workspace instead of creating a completely new one. Follow the steps in the Try It Out below to do this.

Try It Out   **Link to an Existing Meeting Workspace**

1. Use the Outlook calendar and create a meeting request (anytime after the first meeting will do fine). Enter the following settings:

   a. Enter all attendees as recipients of this meeting request. Don't forget to add a room reservation on the same request, if needed.

   b. Enter a Subject for this meeting. This will be the instance name of this workspace.

   c. Click the Meeting Workspace button.

   d. Click "You can also link to an existing workspace," located at the bottom of the right pane.

   e. Use the "Link to an existing workspace" pull-down menu in the "Select the workspace" section to select the previous meeting name (Project ALPHA). If you don't see the meeting name, you may have the wrong team site selected. If so, change the site using "Select a location" at the top of this pane.

   f. Click OK and then the Link button to create the second meeting instance in this new series.

   g. Click Send to send this meeting request to all attendees.

2. Right-click the meeting in the calendar, and select View Meeting Workspace to open the workspace. Note that it contains exactly the same lists, libraries, and layout as the first workspace. The reason for this is that it is the same workspace. However, all list content for each meeting instance is stored in a separate subfolder to allow each meeting instance to have its own content.

3. Note that there are now two dates listed in the left pane. To view the content from the first meeting, click the date for that meeting. Using these dates, you can go back and forth to any meeting and view its content. As you later add more meetings to this series, the list of dates will grow.

Managing List Content for a Series of Meetings

The ability to link a series of meetings to the same workspace is a real time-saver. You can easily find any information about an earlier meeting just by clicking a meeting's date. However, sometimes it would be great if the content from one list could be available in any meeting instance. For example, say that you have a list named "Tasks;" it contains a list of actions to be performed, each action's due date, and the name of the person responsible for each action. Assume you have this list on a project meeting workspace; when performing each meeting, you want to see all actions remaining from earlier meetings. To do this, you need to change the list into a "series object," as the next Try It Out describes.

Try It Out   Change a List into a Series Object

1. Open the workspace.

2. Click the name of the list to be converted to a series object (in this example, Tasks).

3. Click Settings ⇨ List Settings, then click Advanced Settings.

4. Set Change items into series items to Yes.

5. Click OK, and then click Home to open the start page for this workspace. Notice that the Task list name has the text (Series Items) added.

6. Test your work by adding an item to the Tasks list. Click Add new item. Add anything you like and click OK. Then select any other meeting date; note that the Tasks list still contains the same items.

In other words, by making a list into "series items," you make it one single list that is shared among all meetings in this series.

This works fine as it is, but sometimes you want to filter the list to prevent it from showing all items. For example, the Tasks list displays all actions, including the ones that have been completed. It would probably be more interesting to see only items that are not completed. This is easily solved by using a view that filters the Status column that the Tasks list contains in this example. The good news is that there already exists such a view for this list, named Active Tasks. You just have to use it as the default view for the Tasks Web Part:

1. Click the arrow to the far right of the Tasks Web Part, and select Modify Shared Web Part.

2. In the Selected View pull-down menu, select Active Tasks. Click OK to refresh the page, and click OK to save and close the Web Part configuration setting.

3. Note that the Tasks list only shows items where Status is not equal to Completed.

Now you have a general idea of how to use lists and views for series of meetings. You have the tools for creating a very powerful and time-saving workspace for meetings.

Tips about Series of Meetings

Adding new meetings to an existing series is easy, but sometimes there is a need to change or manage these meetings. In the following table you get some tips about these situations.

Situation	Comment	Solution
You, the meeting organizer, delete an existing meeting request in Outlook that has an associated workspace.	This will make the specific meeting instance in the workspace an orphan. Its data remains in SharePoint, but there is no connection to Outlook. Note that Outlook 2007 (but not 2003) will open the meeting invitation, and mark it as "Canceled." It will also offer the user to send out an e-mail about this meeting being canceled.	Open the workspace. There is a red exclamation mark next to the orphaned meeting date. Click this exclamation mark, and it displays a menu (see Figure 7-21). You can select the option to Move the workspace's data to another existing meeting instance (overwriting any of its content, so make an empty workspace first; see Figures 7-22 and 7-23); to Keep (data remains in the workspace, but no Outlook appointment is associated); or to Delete (this instance of the workspace and all its data is removed).
You want to remove one meeting instance from a series of meetings.	For example, say that you planned one meeting, but it was canceled, and you don't want to move it.	Use the previous technique: Delete the meeting request in Outlook. Open the workspace and its date will have the red exclamation mark. Use its menu to delete the workspace. Instead of deleting the meeting appointment in Outlook, you can also open its properties and click the Remove button in the Meeting Workspace pane.
You want to connect one meeting instance to a new date.	Say that you have an existing meeting instance with lots of data and that you want to associate it with a new meeting request and a new date.	1. Go to the original meeting request in Outlook. Delete it or remove its workspace link (as described earlier). 2. Create a new meeting request in Outlook. Join the workspace for this series of meetings, but do not add any information to that workspace instance. 3. Open the workspace. Use the menu next to the red exclamation mark for the old meeting date you initially deleted. Select Move and select the new date you just created. This will move all existing information to the new meeting date.

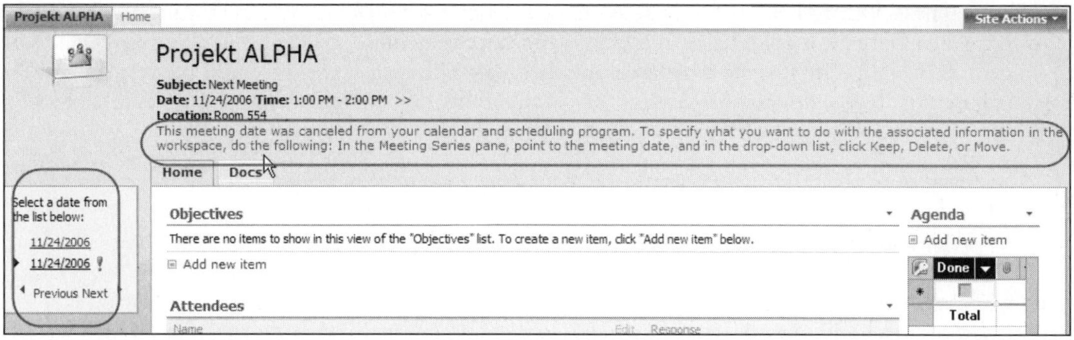

Figure 7-21

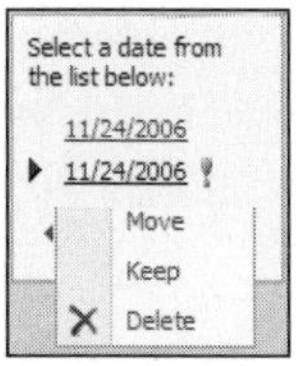

Figure 7-22

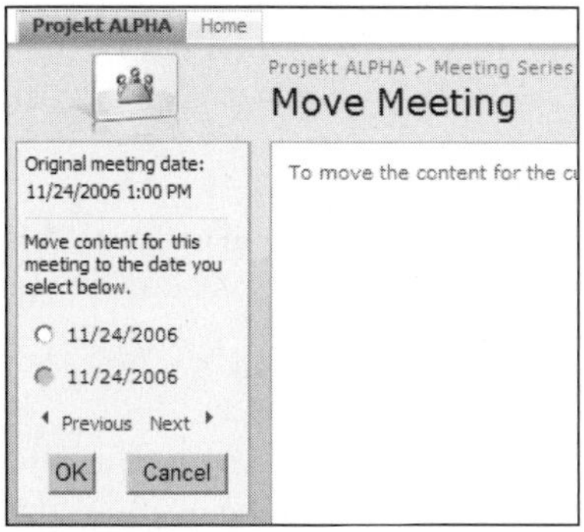

Figure 7-23

Meetings with Other Users

The procedures described in the preceding sections work very well for internal users who have access to your SharePoint environment and have been invited using Outlook's meeting requests. But sometimes you need to allow other users to view the meeting workspace. This section describes the options you have to handle these situations.

Allowing Additional Internal User Access

Sometimes there will be people in your organization who aren't invited to your meetings but who need to access the meeting workspace. The typical example is a manager who wants to know what you do in these meetings. Before you started using meeting workspaces in SharePoint, he got a copy of the meeting minutes. But now, because you don't have these anymore (and frankly, you don't miss them), you must provide him with this information in another way. The easiest way is to add this manager to the list of users with access to this workspace site; making the manager a member of the Visitors SharePoint group is sufficient to enable him to view and copy all the content of this workspace.

> When you have a series of meetings all invited users have Members access (Contributor permissions) to all meeting instances, regardless of when they were invited! There is no way to limit access to just one meeting because the series is sharing the same workspace and, therefore, the same list of users. The same is true when you add additional users; they also have access to all meeting instances. But you can set a unique right for any user to a specific list, or library, using its security settings in Settings ➪ Document Library Settings ➪ Permissions for this document library. You can also set a specific security setting for an individual list item or document, by using its quick menu option: Manage Permissions.

To add an extra user to an existing meeting workspace without making him or her a meeting attendee, follow the steps in the Try It Out below.

Try It Out   Grant Extra Users Access to the Workspace

1. Open the workspace as an administrator.

2. Click Site Actions ➪ Site Settings.

3. Click the People and Groups link.

4. Click the New ➪ Add Users button.

5. Enter the name of the new user to be granted access to this meeting. Grant the user the rights needed (for example, member of the Visitors SharePoint group), enter a message that will be sent to this user and click OK. The user will then get an e-mail with the link to the workspace and a description of the granted permissions.

Another solution would be to manually create meeting minutes from the data in the workspace. One way of making this task easier would be to export the Agenda and Decisions lists to Excel and copy that information into the meeting minutes.

> I have not seen any tool that does this automatically, although it may be possible using MS SQL 2005 Reporting Services.

Allowing External User Access

Another common request is to allow people outside your organization access to the information stored in the meeting workspace. The problem here is that these users do not have access to anything inside your network, because they don't have a network user account. Following are some options to handle this situation:

❑ **Create a user account:** If you make this external person a member of your network, you could grant him or her access the same way as any internal user, as in the previous example about the manager. This solution will be of interest if this a recurring request.

❑ **Create meeting minutes manually:** Again, as the previous section discussed, you can manually create a document with the meeting minutes. This is acceptable for a one-time request with a limited amount of data in the workspace.

❑ **Use MS Office Live Meeting:** This program is designed to allow anyone with an Internet connection to see and participate in any meeting, not only SharePoint's meeting workspaces. One way of using this program is to invite the external user ahead of time to join the Live Meeting. You can also allow a user who has not previously been invited to the Live Meeting session to simply join it at the time it starts by displaying the workspace on the MS Live Meeting panel and sending the user this URL link in an e-mail. Either way, you can give this user real-time access to the meeting and allow him or her to participate and discuss matters like any attendee of this meeting.

The last option may also be of interest for internal users, when they need to attend meetings while working from home or from an Internet café when on vacation.

> **For more information about MS Office Live Meeting, visit** `http://office` `.microsoft.com/en-us/FX010909711033.aspx.`

MS OneNote

Another really exciting application that also integrates with SharePoint is MS OneNote. This is a program for taking notes in a very informal structure, much like when you scribble with a pen and paper. In fact, OneNote is great on any computer, but it is fantastic when used on a Tablet-PC-based laptop, since that will allow you to use a pen to write your notes, including drawings, directly on the screen (see Figure 7-24).

MS OneNote was first released in October 2003, together with the MS Office 2003 suite. At that time, it had some integration features with SharePoint 2003 (i.e., SPS 2003 and WSS 2.0). This integration is enhanced in MS OneNote 2007, and with SharePoint 2007. For example, now you can use OneNote to share a notebook with other OneNote users in real time, by storing the notebook in SharePoint. This is very handy if you are using OneNote to take meeting minutes, and you want the other meeting participants to see, and even change, your notes in real time during the meeting.

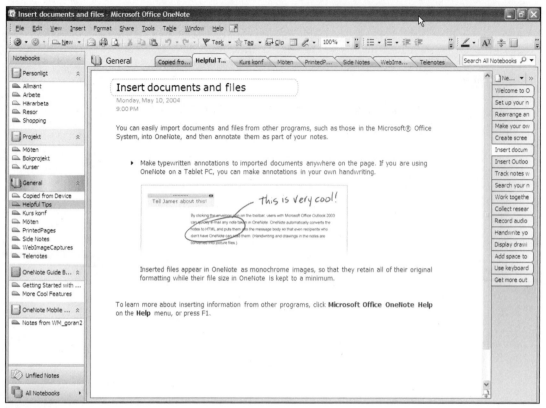

Figure 7-24

Sharing Notebooks with SharePoint Sites

MS OneNote 2007 organizes all its information in one or more notebooks, corresponding to a paper-based notebook. Instead of just using it for your own purposes, you can share a notebook with other OneNote users, so they can see your notes directly, and you can also grant these users permission to add information to your notebook. You could use this for things like:

❑ Meeting minutes

❑ Project discussions

❑ Collecting raw information

❑ Brainstorming meetings

By default, OneNote will store these notebooks on the local file system — My Documents ⇨ My Notebook. To make these notebooks available to others you could store them in a SharePoint library. Besides controlling the access to these notebooks, you can also store extra information about the notebook, such as a project number or the meeting name. Since SharePoint 2007 enables a version history for all types of lists and libraries, this could also be used for the notebooks created by OneNote, thus making it possible to view and even revert to a previous version, if necessary. Also other features of SharePoint lists and libraries, such as being an RSS feed, are available for these notebooks. This is an excellent way to make sure that other users know that the notebook has been changed.

To make it easy to configure OneNote to share a notebook, there is a wizard that guides you through these steps, as described in the Try It Out below.

Try It Out   Share a OneNote Notebook with SharePoint

1. Log on as a user with permission to create a SharePoint library.

2. On the OneNote menu bar, click the Share menu, then select Create Shared Notebook, or click the File menu, then select New ➪ Notebook. This will start a wizard that will guide you through the sharing process.

3. In the New Notebook Wizard you can enter several settings:

    a. **Name:** Enter a name for this notebook, for example Meeting Minutes.

    b. **Color:** Select a color for the notebook icon.

    c. **From Template:** Select a OneNote template, such as Work Notebook.

    d. Click Next to continue this wizard.

4. On the page Who will use this notebook? select Multiple people will share the notebook, then the sub-option: On a server (which is the default setting). Then click Next.

5. On the page Confirm notebook location, in the Path field enter the URL to the SharePoint site containing the library to be used for saving the OneNote notebook. You can also use the Browse button to locate the site.

6. You will now see all available libraries for the site. Select the one where the shared notebook will be stored, for example Shared Documents, then click the Select button.

7. On the Confirm notebook location page, verify that the URL points to the correct library. By default, the wizard will create an e-mail with a link to this location that you can send to the users you want to share this notebook with. Click Create to continue. Note that this process may take several minutes to complete. When it is done, the wizard will open a prepopulated e-mail with the links to this shared notebook. Send this e-mail to all users that you want to share this notebook with.

8. The notebook is now shared. The other users will receive an e-mail that contains the link to the notebook. If they click on the link, their OneNote will start, and connect to that shared notebook. Or the user can start OneNote, click File ➪ Open ➪ Notebook, then enter the URL to the shared notebook manually, and after a short period, the notebook will be displayed, ready to use.

The access to a shared notebook is controlled by the SharePoint permissions set for the document library, and its notebook folder. Make sure that the permissions granted to the shared notebook are correct. There is no other protection, such as a password, and this is not necessary since SharePoint 2007 provides you will all the detailed security settings you will need for this purpose.

> **A change will take a few minutes before it will show up on the other users'
> OneNote. You can force this replication by right-clicking on the shared notebook
> icon, and selecting Sync this Notebook Now.**

MS InfoPath

Another favorite application is MS InfoPath, which was released for the first time in October 2003, along with MS Office 2003. It still looks very much the same in its new version, InfoPath 2007, but under the hood several important things has changed. The main purpose of this application is to create electronic forms, such as expense reports, time cards, vacation forms, and so on. One important new feature in InfoPath 2007 is its ability to create web forms that can be used by SharePoint 2007 and Office 2007; for example, workflow forms and the Document Information Panel displayed by Office 2007 applications, such as Word and Excel 2007. Another very important difference is that SharePoint 2007 can display InfoPath forms as HTML web forms, thus removing the requirement that a user who wants to fill in a form must have MS InfoPath locally installed. This was probably one of the main reasons that InfoPath 2003 was not implemented by customers, although it was great product.

Building InfoPath Forms

An important characteristic of MS InfoPath is its file format: it is completely based on the Extensible Markup Language (XML) standard, which makes the form and its content readable by other applications. SharePoint is one such application. When you save an InfoPath file in a SharePoint library some, or possibly all, of its content will be displayed as columns, so you do not need to open the form to see what's in it. For example, say that you have a time card form that employees use to enter their weekly working hours. Instead of opening each form file to see its content, some of its content is now displayed automatically as columns (see Figure 7-25).

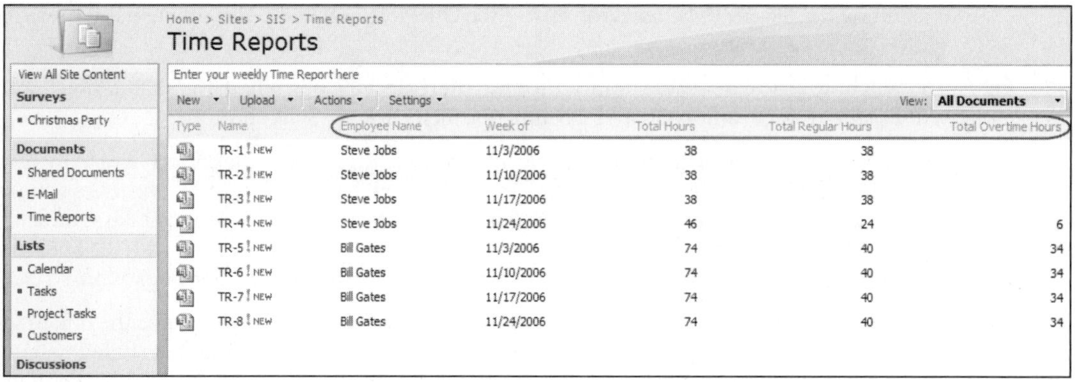
Home > Sites > SIS > Time Reports
Time Reports
View All Site Content
Surveys
Christmas Party
Documents
Shared Documents
E-Mail
Time Reports
Lists
Calendar
Tasks
Project Tasks
Customers
Discussions
Enter your weekly Time Report here
New
Upload
Actions
Settings
View: All Documents
Type
Name
Employee Name
Week of
Total Hours
Total Regular Hours
Total Overtime Hours
TR-1 NEW
Steve Jobs
11/3/2006
38
38
TR-2 NEW
Steve Jobs
11/10/2006
38
38
TR-3 NEW
Steve Jobs
11/17/2006
38
38
TR-4 NEW
Steve Jobs
11/24/2006
46
24
6
TR-5 NEW
Bill Gates
11/3/2006
74
40
34
TR-6 NEW
Bill Gates
11/10/2006
74
40
34
TR-7 NEW
Bill Gates
11/17/2006
74
40
34
TR-8 NEW
Bill Gates
11/24/2006
74
40
34

Figure 7-25

To make this happen, the designer of the InfoPath form must publish the form to SharePoint in a special type of library, called a Forms Library, that stores XML-based documents. When publishing the form, the designer will also decide what information from the form that will be displayed as a column in the library. The beauty of having content displayed as columns is that you can create views for the library, which organize the information in many ways. For example, say that the manager for a team wants to see the time cards organized per employee, while the people in the human resources department want to see them organized by week. And while you are at it, why not make the view summarize the working hours. This way, there is no need to copy these figures to an Excel spreadsheet and create a report from that. The next figure, Figure 7-26, shows you such a view calculating the total hours per week. For example, you can see that for the week of 11/2/2006 there are two time cards and that the total hours for this week is 112, the total regular hours are 78, and total overtime hours are 34.

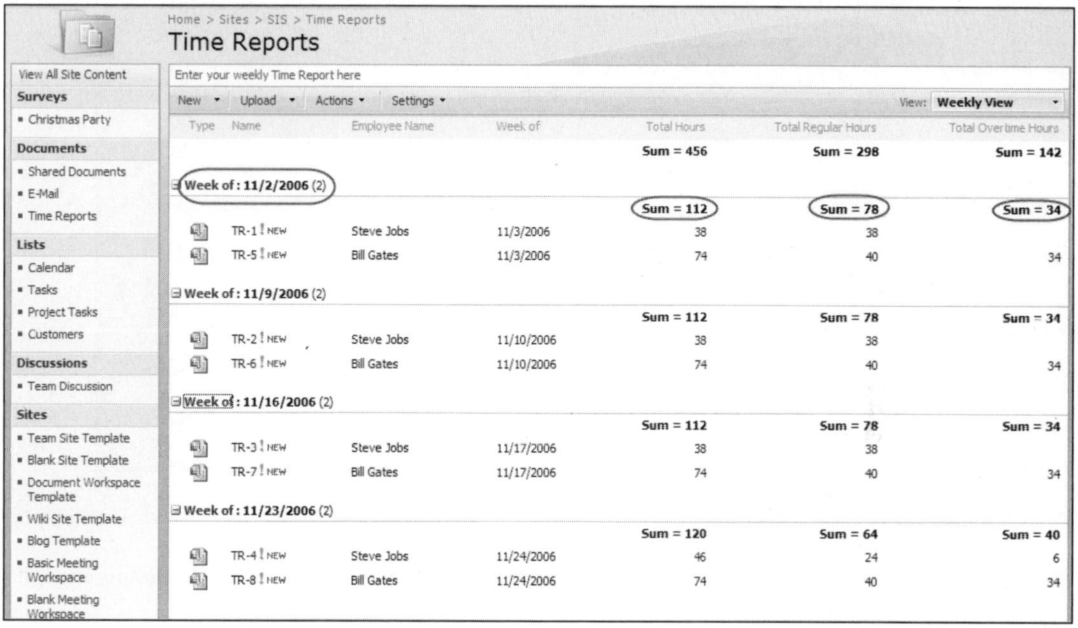

Figure 7-26

To create an InfoPath form, you need the MS InfoPath rich client; you cannot design a form using the web client. You can start from an empty form and add the field controls you need. Or, you can start from a form template that is similar to what you want to do and then customize that template. Let's do another example. Your boss tells you that she needs a very basic form where employees can enter their vacation periods. She also says that she will need a report that shows when employees will be away from the office. Oh, and she wants this by the end of this day. So what do you do? The steps listed in the Try It Out below illustrate one way of doing this.

Try It Out	Create a InfoPath Form

1. Log on with a user account that has permission to create libraries in the site where you want to store the forms.

2. Start InfoPath 2007. It will start by displaying a dialog window named Getting Started. See Figure 7-27. Here, you have several options: you can open an existing form (click the existing form name under Open a form), you can start a form from scratch (Click Design a Form Template), or you can start from a template (click Customize a Sample and select any of the samples in the center pane, or click Form Templates on Office Online, which will display a large number of publically available form templates stored at Microsoft's web site). In this example you will create this form from scratch, so click Design a Form Template, then select Blank and click OK.

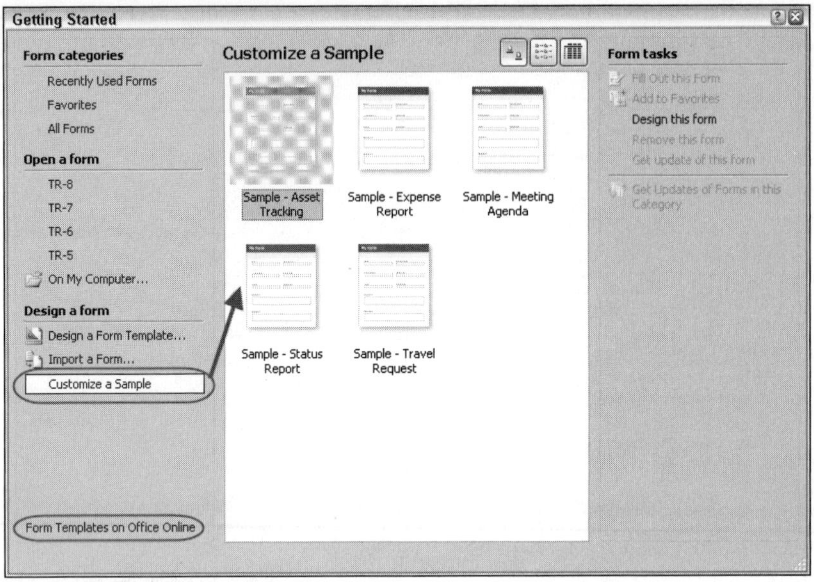

Figure 7-27

3. An empty form window is displayed; at the right you have a Task Pane, displaying Design Tasks. The links in this pane allow you to do a number of things:

❏ **Layout:** Use this link to create tables and regions in the form, which you will use later for storing controls (see below).

❏ **Controls:** This is a toolbox with many different types of controls, such as simple text fields, date fields, and numeric fields, but also more advanced controls for uploading documents to the form, displaying a picture, and creating a hyperlink.

❏ **Data Source:** This is a list of all the data sources for the form, including its field controls. Use this view to quickly get a list of all the data fields and sources.

❏ **Views:** Use this link when you need to create more than one view of a form. For example, the users who fill in the form will see a limited part of the form, whereas the user who manages this form will see everything.

❏ **Design Checker:** Click this link to run a test of your form. If there is any problem, the design checker will tell you what it is.

❏ **Publish Form Template:** This will start the wizard that will help you publish the form, for example, to a SharePoint library.

4. Your vacation form should contain the following types of information: the name of the employee, the start date for the vacation, and the end date, (yes, it's a very simple form). You already have the empty form, so let's start the design:

a. Click Table with Title in the Task Pane, and a headline table will be displayed on the form. Click where it says Click to add a title, and enter the text **Vacation Request**. Then click where it says Click to add form content and enter the text **Enter the dates for your vacation**. By now you should have a nice headline in your form.

b. The next step is to create the table where you will store your text and date controls. Note that this step is just here because it will be easier to get a nice layout. If you want, you can add controls to any part of the form page, not just to a table! First, click anywhere under the headline table to place the cursor there. Press the Enter key once, to get a new line. Now click Three Column Table in the Task Pane. A one-row table with three columns is displayed on the form. Right-click in the first column, then select Table Properties. Switch to the Row tab, and select Automatically set row height, then click OK.

c. Click in the first column: Enter the text **Name**. In the second column, enter **Start Date**, and in the third column, enter **End Date**. Then press the Tab key, and a new row will be created.

d. It is time to add·the field controls. On the Task Pane, click the black arrow to display its menu, then select Controls. Place the cursor in the first column of the second row. Then click on the control Text Box in the Task Pane. Place the cursor in the second column and click Date Picker, then place the cursor in the third column and click the Date Picker again.

e. To make it easier for you later to understand what controls do, give them a descriptive name: Right-click on the text control (second row, first column), then select Text Box Properties, and change the Field name to User_name. Repeat this for the other two controls, and name them Start_Date and End_Date, respectively.

5. The form is now complete. The next step is to save it: Click File ⇨ Save, and click OK if you get a dialog box telling you that you must publish this form before it can be used by others. Enter a folder location, and a name, for example **Vacation Request**, and click Save.

6. It's time to publish this form to a SharePoint library. Before you do this, you should think about where to create this new library. In this example, you will save it in a library named Vacations, stored in the site http://srv1/sitedirectory/sis.

   a. Click on the menu File ⇨ Publish, and a dialog box will be displayed (see Figure 7-28).

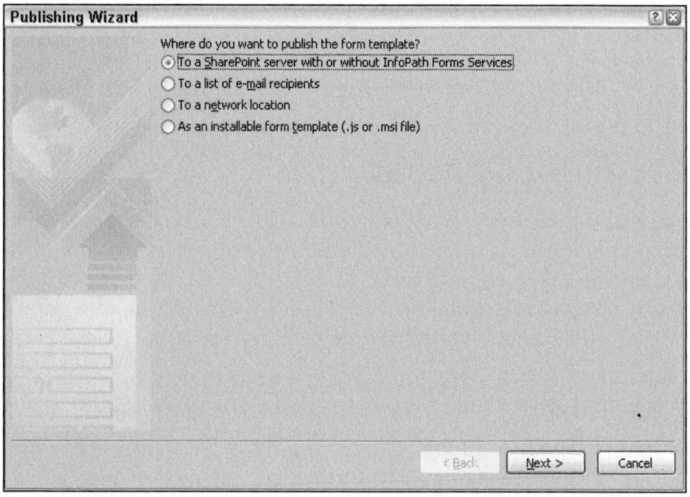

Figure 7-28

b. Make sure that the option To a SharePoint server with or without InfoPath Forms Services is selected, then click Next.

c. Enter the URL to the SharePoint site where the new library will be created, `http://srv1/sitedirectory/sis`, and click Next.

d. A new dialog box is displayed. Select Document Library and click Next.

e. Make sure that the option Create a new document library is selected, and click Next.

f. Next you will enter a name for this new library; in this example, it is called Vacations. You can also enter a description. When you're ready, click Next.

g. The next page is where you define what form content you want displayed as library controls. Click Add, select `User_Name`, and click OK. Then add `Start_Date` and `End_Date` in the same way. You should now see three column names listed. Click Next to continue.

h. You are now almost finished. Click Publish to create the library, and associate the new form with it. The final page in this Publishing Wizard gives you an option to send an e-mail to users you want to have a direct link to this library. You can also choose to open the library directly. Check this last option, and click Close. The new library is displayed.

7. Finally, let's test the new form. Click New, and InfoPath will open the form (see Figure 7-29). Enter a name, plus select a start and end date, then save the form as Form1, and close InfoPath. The new file is now listed in the library, and the columns display the values you set in the form.

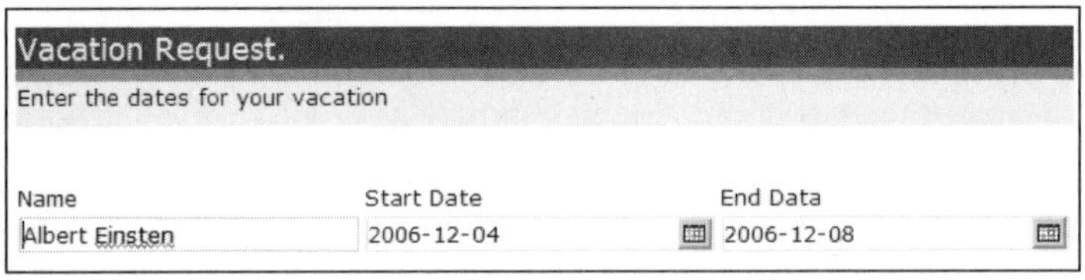

Figure 7-29

Displaying the Form Content

Let's have some fun: Add three more vacation forms to the library, for three other users, but with vacation dates near the first one. You can now test another type of view that is interesting for this type of information, based on dates. The boss, in this example above, wanted a report that showed her when employees have requested vacations. This is easily done by creating a graphical view of the list, based on a Calendar view, or a Gantt schema. Follow the steps in the Try It Out below to create the Calendar view.

Try It Out   Present Forms Data in a Calendar View

1. Open the Vacation library (make sure to log on as a user with permission to create views).

2. Click View: All Documents in the upper right, to display the View menu.

3. Select Create View. On the next page, Choose a view format, select Calendar View.

4. On the Create Calendar View: Vacations page, you will define the new view by entering these values (accept the other default values):

   a. **Name:** Enter a name for the view; for example, Calendar Overview.

   b. **Begin:** Use the menu and select Start Date.

   c. **End:** Select End Date from the menu.

   d. **Month View Title:** Select User Name from the menu.

   e. **Weekly View Title:** Select User Name.

   f. **Daily View Title:** Select User Name.

   g. Then click OK to save and close the new View.

5. The new weekly view should be displayed, and it should look similar to Figure 7-30.

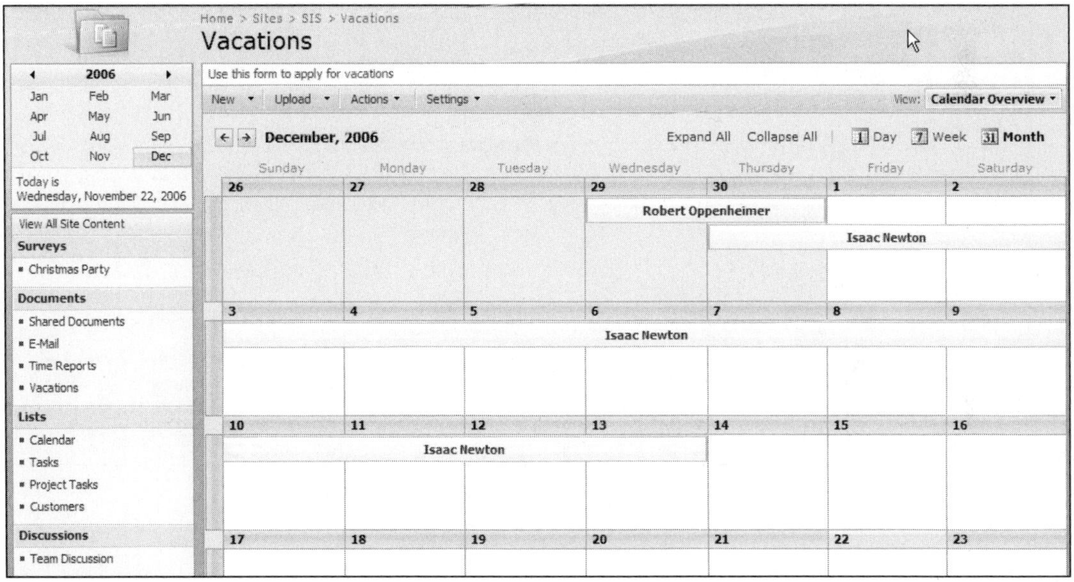

Figure 7-30

Another way to present this vacation form data is to use a Gantt schema, which normally is used to present project activities, but is also excellent for this task, since it gives a better overview than the Calendar view:

Try It Out   Present Forms Data in a Gantt View

1. Open the Vacation library.

2. Click View: All Documents in the upper right, to display the View menu.

3. Select Create View. On the next page: Choose a view format, select Gantt View.

4. On the Create View: Vacations page, enter these values (accept the other default values):

a. **Name:** Enter the name Gantt Overview.

b. **Title:** Use the menu and select User Name.

c. **Start Date:** Select Start Date from the menu.

d. **Due Date:** Select End Date from the menu.

e. Click OK.

5. The same form data as used before is now presented in a Gantt view. It is clearly a better view, and I think your boss will be happy with this. (See Figure 7-31).

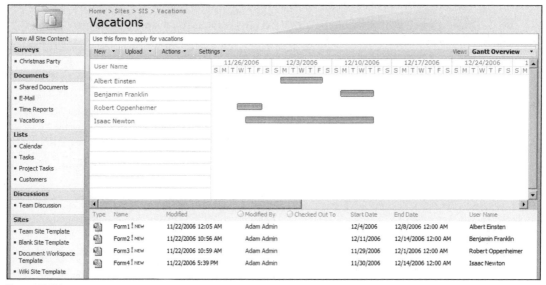

Figure 7-31

The Office Forms Service 2007

If you want to display the form as an HTML web form, you must also have the Office Forms Service 2007, which comes with MOSS 2007 Enterprise Edition. This module can also be purchased separately as an add-on to the MOSS 2007 Standard Edition. This forms service will convert an InfoPath form into HTML, when requested to do so. The great advantage of this is that users do not need to have a local MS InfoPath rich client installed. They just use their web browser to open and fill in the form.

If the Forms Service is properly configured (see more details about this in Chapter 8), you can configure the Forms library to automatically display all new and existing forms as HTML web forms; just follow the steps in the Try It Out below.

Try It Out   **Display Forms as HTML Web Forms**

1. Open the Vacation library.

2. Click Settings ⇨ Form Library Settings, then click Advanced Settings.

3. Set the option Display as a Web page in the Opening browser-enabled documents section. Next click OK, then open the library again.

4. Now try it out. Click New, and the form is displayed as a web page.

Other Applications

There are a lot more Microsoft applications that work closely with SharePoint 2007, but they deserve their own book, so I will only mention them briefly here:

- ❑ **MS Office PerformancePoint Server 2007:** This is the new version of MS Business Scorecard Manager. Its objective is to offer a platform for building web sites that displays information related to Business Intelligence, such as business scorecards, analytics, and planning. This product runs on top of SharePoint 2007 and can be integrated with the other SharePoint web pages. For more information about this product, see `http://office.microsoft.com/en-us/performancepoint/FX101680481033.aspx`.

- ❑ **MS Office Project 2007:** This is a suite of programs that helps users with anything from very simple projects to planning extremely large and complex projects. This product also utilizes SharePoint as its foundation for storing data. For more information about this product, see `http://office.microsoft.com/en-us/project/FX100487771033.aspx`.

- ❑ **MS Office Visio 2007:** This is the perfect tool for creating drawings and flowcharts to visualize complex processes, systems, or information systems. You can create flowcharts that are displayed on a SharePoint page; for example, to visualize a process. The user then clicks on the process step to be performed, and the correct site, library or list opens. For more information about this product, see `http://office.microsoft.com/en-us/visio/FX100487861033.aspx`.

I hope this chapter has convinced you that SharePoint is not just another nice application; it is *the* application that Microsoft is using to make almost all of its products work together in a very smooth and seamless way.

Summary

In this chapter, you learned that:

- ❑ There are a large number of MS Office 2007 editions — make sure to use the right one.

- ❑ Only these editions will have the full integration with SharePoint 2007: Office Professional Plus 2007, Office Enterprise 2007, and Office Ultimate 2007.

❑   With MS Office 2000 and Office XP/2002, you will not have any integration with SharePoint 2007, although you can open and save files in document libraries.

❑   With MS Office 2003, you will have a good integration with SharePoint 2007, but still there are things you cannot do, such as starting workflows, reading the Document Property Panel, and easily comparing document versions, among other things.

❑   The perfect companion for SharePoint 2007 is MS Office 2007 — especially the Professional Pro, Enterprise, and Ultimate Editions.

❑   MS Outlook 2007 has a lot of integration features for use with SharePoint, such as offline storage of documents, two-way synchronization of tasks, a calendar, and contact lists.

❑   RSS feed is a new way of keeping track of changes in SharePoint lists and libraries — but only Outlook 2007 has this functionality built in.

❑   MS Outlook 2003 and 2007, together with SharePoint 2007, are the ultimate tools for optimizing meeting procedures.

❑   Use the Group Policy Templates Office12.adm and Outlk12.adm to configure Outlook and meeting workspaces from a central location.

❑   MS OneNote is a fantastic tool for taking notes — It can be shared in real time with other OneNote users by storing its notebook file on the SharePoint server.

❑   Use MS InfoPath to create any type of form, from the simplest to the extremely advanced that includes code and connects to external data sources. Save these forms to a SharePoint library, and you can expose their content as columns.

❑   There are also a number of other Microsoft applications that directly integrate, or even rely, on SharePoint 2007.

In the next chapter, you will learn more about advanced SharePoint 2007 configurations.

8

Advanced Configurations

So far, you have seen how to configure both WSS and MOSS specific settings. In this chapter, you will learn about more advanced administration, such as how to manage user profiles, import properties from the Active Directory, configure and manage global search and indexing, and more. This chapter is important if you want to master SharePoint's more advanced features. It contains a lot of details, and a lot of step-by-step instructions on how to configure these settings. Note that some of these settings will apply to both pure WSS installations and MOSS farms, while others only apply to MOSS; be sure to read the title of each section carefully.

Managing User Profiles in MOSS

When working in any type of organization, you often need to get more information about a particular user. For example, you may read a document written by a user and need to ask the author for more information, or you may need to send an e-mail to a project manager responsible for developing a solution that is of interest for your own work. So, how do you find more information about people today? Most likely you are doing things like checking the address list in Outlook, looking at the Employee List on an intranet, or contacting the switchboard, asking for the phone number of this person. The most commonly requested information is:

- ❑ **e-mail address**
- ❑ **Phone numbers:** Office phone, mobile phone, and so on.
- ❑ **Organizational information:** What department, group, or team does the user belong to?
- ❑ **Responsibilities:** Who is the manager for this department? Who is the project leader?
- ❑ **Expertise:** Who can I ask about a specific subject?

SharePoint solves this in a much better way! Whenever you see a name listed as a user (for example, the author of a document or the last person modified the Customer address list), simply click the user's name and you will get all publicly available information. Or if you don't see the name listed, you can search for the user. This will save you a lot of time, not to mention the frustration of having to chase around the network resources or find someone with the information needed.

So, where is this information stored? A good guess would be the Active Directory, right? And yes, this is often, but not always, true. Since SharePoint will also work in Windows NT 4 environment, there may not even be a place for storing this type of user-related information. And even if you have an Active Directory environment, you may not be allowed to store new user properties in the AD database; for example, "Personal Interests" or "Skills." Microsoft solved this problem by adding a special database to MOSS for storing user profiles. This database can import information from the Active Directory. Note that this database does not exist in pure WSS environments, regardless of the type of server operating system.

User Profiles in a Windows NT 4 Environment

This configuration is easy to describe. There is nothing stored in the Windows NT 4 user account database that can be imported into the User Profile database! Everything you want to store about users, from their e-mail address to their phone numbers, must be entered manually. SharePoint 2007 does allow you to import user profiles from any LDAP directory or from an existing Business Data Catalog (BDC) connection, so this could be your solution. If not, then every time you make a change, such as adding a new user or giving an existing user a new e-mail address, this must be manually updated in the User Profile database. The procedure for performing this update is exactly the same as that used when running SharePoint in an Active Directory environment, which is described in the next section.

User Profiles in an Active Directory Environment

The most common configuration is to run SharePoint in an Active Directory environment. This enables SharePoint to regularly import information from AD to the User Profile database, typically once every 24 hours. This is only interesting if AD actually contains information worth importing, so there may still be situations in which manual updating may be the preferred solution. In reality, you will often see a mix of these two approaches; that is, some information is imported from AD, and the rest is manually updated. A new feature of SharePoint 2007, which differs from its predecessor, is that it can also import user properties and add these to existing user profiles, using an existing BDC connector.

> You can only use a BDC import to add complementary information to existing user profiles; that is, BDC will not create new user profiles!

SharePoint allows the administrator to control exactly what user properties to import from AD, what properties to be manually edited, and if the user will be allowed to do this editing herself. This last option is very handy for information you may not want to store in Active Directory, for example subject matter expert areas, home phone numbers, or a description of a user.

Configuring the User Profile Import Process

All the settings that control the importing of properties in the User Profile database are accessed through SharePoint's configuration pages for the SSP. To see the options available, follow the steps in the Try It Out below.

Try It Out   Manage the User Profile Database

1. Open SharePoint's Central Administration tool, and click the SSP created by you earlier; typically, this is named `SharedServices1`. You will find it in the Quick Launch bar.

2. Click User profiles and properties (in the User Profile and My Sites section); a new page is displayed, with all the settings related to user profiles (see Figure 8-1).

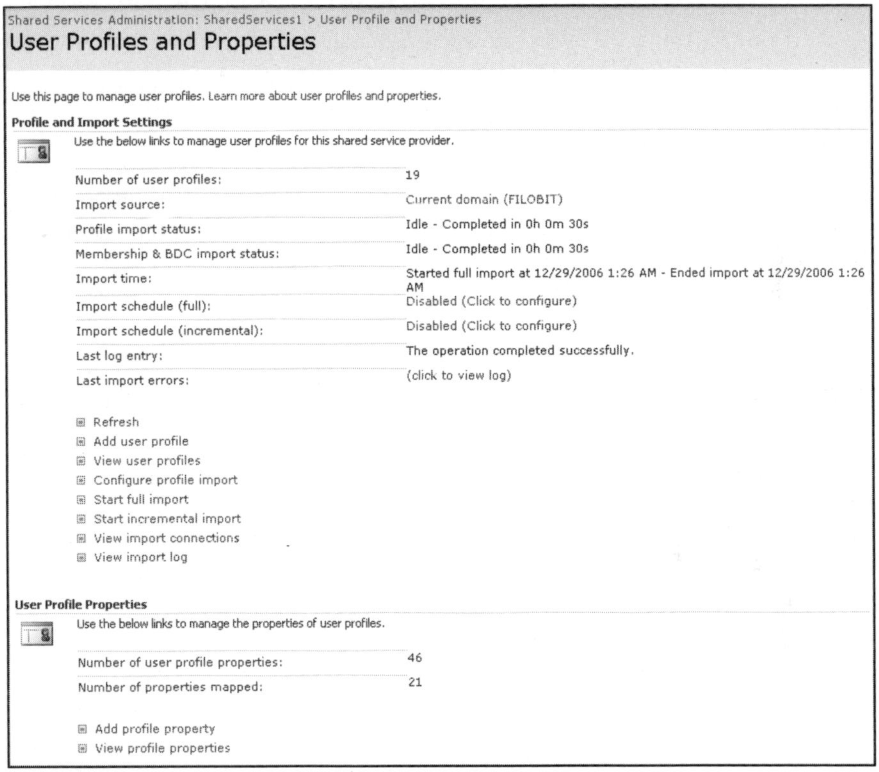

Shared Services Administration: SharedServices1 > User Profile and Properties

User Profiles and Properties

Use this page to manage user profiles. Learn more about user profiles and properties.

Profile and Import Settings

 Use the below links to manage user profiles for this shared service provider.

Number of user profiles:	19
Import source:	Current domain (FILOBIT)
Profile import status:	Idle - Completed in 0h 0m 30s
Membership & BDC import status:	Idle - Completed in 0h 0m 30s
Import time:	Started full import at 12/29/2006 1:26 AM - Ended import at 12/29/2006 1:26 AM
Import schedule (full):	Disabled (Click to configure)
Import schedule (incremental):	Disabled (Click to configure)
Last log entry:	The operation completed successfully.
Last import errors:	(click to view log)

⊞ Refresh
⊞ Add user profile
⊞ View user profiles
⊞ Configure profile import
⊞ Start full import
⊞ Start incremental import
⊞ View import connections
⊞ View import log

User Profile Properties

Use the below links to manage the properties of user profiles.

Number of user profile properties:	46
Number of properties mapped:	21

⊞ Add profile property
⊞ View profile properties

Figure 8-1

In this figure, you can see a lot of interesting things. At the top, you will find a summary of all settings related to the import from Active Directory, such as:

❑ **Number of user profiles:** The current number of profiles. For a newly installed system, you will see a number 0 here. If you see 1, you have probably tested the My Site feature of the portal site.

❑ **Import source:** What Active Directory domain will be imported, if any. Specify Source means this setting is not yet configured. If this is the case, click the Specify Source link to configure the setting, or click Configure user import, as described later in this list.

❑ **Profile import status:** Idle means there is no import process active at the moment.

❑ **Membership & BDC import status:** Idle means there is no import process active at the moment. Here, BDC means Business Data Catalog.

❑ **Import time:** This gives the date and time for the last import.

❑ **Import schedule (full):** This gives the date for the next full import process. Disabled means no schedule is defined. Click this link to configure the setting.

❑ **Import schedule (incremental):** This gives the date for the next incremental import process. Disabled means that no schedule is defined. Click this link to configure the setting.

❑ **Last log entry:** This is the latest status message regarding the import process.

❑ **Last import errors:** Click the Click to view log link to see the latest log messages, including successful imports, errors, and warnings.

Below these links are a number of other links that are self-explanatory. One very important link is the Configure profile import link, which is used to configure the import settings. Click it to open the configuration page. This will open the same page that clicking the Specify Source link in the bulleted list above does. Use this page to define which source to import user profiles from, what account should be used, and the import type and schedule (see Figure 8-2).

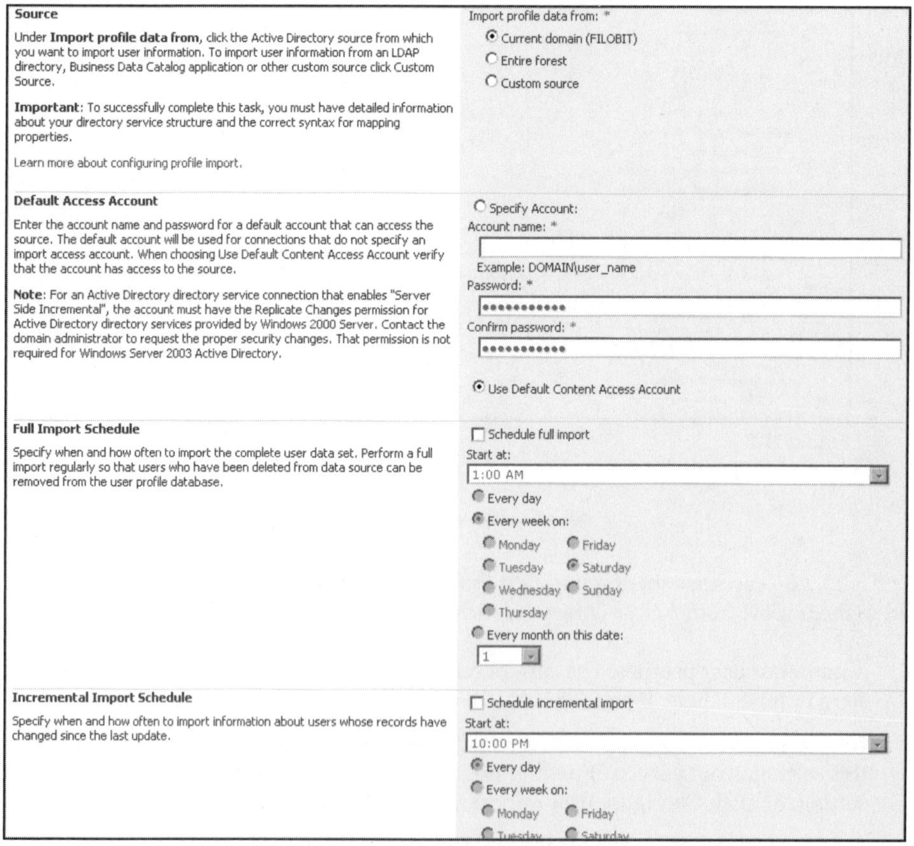

Figure 8-2

Use these setting to configure the import process that fits the needs of your organization. Avoid choosing a time when other activities may run, such as backups or antivirus scanning. In Figure 8-2, the MS Windows domain to be imported is listed as the Current Domain, that is, the same domain that the SharePoint server belongs to. If you have more than one AD domain, and your users belong to any domain other than that of the SharePoint server, you can choose Entire forest.

> **If the DNS name of your AD domain is different from the NetBIOS name, SharePoint may fail to identify the correct domain to be imported. This is common with domains upgraded from NT 4 to AD. To solve this problem, choose Entire Forest even if you just have one domain.**

One consequence of importing the complete domain is that all its user accounts will be imported, including a number of system accounts, such as Guest and IUSR. This may or may not be a problem, depending on the size of your domain and how sensitive you are about having nonstandard users listed in the User Profile database. In reality, these extra accounts do not require that much space and no one will see them, except the SharePoint administrator when looking at this page. Still, you may want to control this import in more detail, especially if you have lots of accounts in your domain that never will be SharePoint users, such as test accounts or multiple organizations.

For example, say that you have an Organizational Unit (OU) in Active Directory named SP2007 that contains SharePoint users. Why not just import that OU? You ask yourself, how hard can it be? What you need to do is to create a Lightweight Directory Access Protocol (LDAP) query filter. For example, the default LDAP filter that SharePoint uses is this:

```
(&(objectCategory=Person)(objectClass=User))
```

This string says that all objects of class Users and the category Person will be imported.

The following Try It Out shows how you do a custom import of the OU SP2007; I'll let you be the judge of how hard it is.

Try It Out   Import a Custom Source from Active Directory

1. Log on as a domain administrator and start the Active Directory Users and Computers tool. Select Advanced features from the View menu.

2. You will need some attribute names in step 5. To get them right-click the OU SP2007, select Properties, and switch to the Object tab. Note the value of the Canonical name of object; in this example, it will be FILOBIT/SP2007. This string tells you the following:

   a. The two domain attributes for this domain, or DC, are com and Filobit.

   b. The name of the OU attribute is SP2007.

3. Start SharePoint's Central Administration tool, then open the SSP instance (typically `SharedServices1`). Click User profiles and properties, then Configure profile import.

4. Select Custom Source and click OK. This will open the View Import Connections page.

5. Click Create New Connection, and enter the following values for this example (see Figure 8-3):

a. **Type:** Active Directory

b. **Domain name:** Filobit.com

c. Select Auto discover domain controller or select a specific DC. If you use the latter approach, be sure to use port 389.

d. **Search base:** First, click the Auto Fill Root Search Base button, then complete the Search base field so that it looks like this: OU=SP2007,DC=FILOBIT,DC=COM.

e. **User filter:** (&(objectCategory=Person)(objectClass=User))

> **You can exclude disabled users by using this filter string instead:**
> (&(objectCategory=person)(objectClass=user)(
> !(userAccountControl:1.2.840.113556.1.4.803:=2)))

f. **Scope:** One level. This will ignore any sub-OU under SP2007.

g. Do not change any of the other values — they are fine for most import scenarios. Click OK to save this connection configuration.

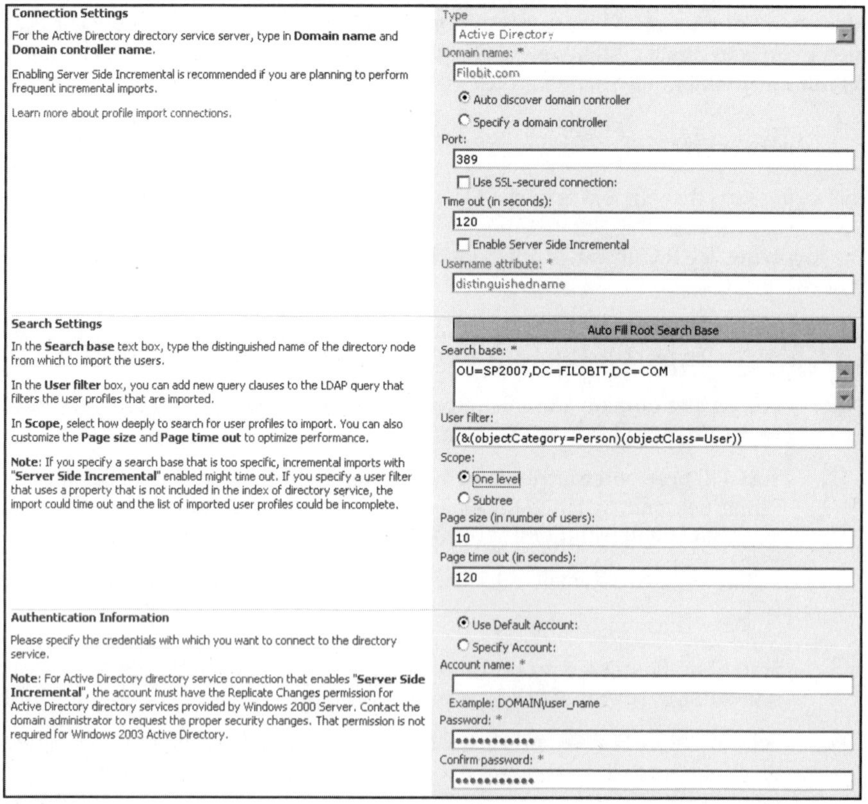

Figure 8-3

6. You are returned to the View Import Connections page again. It is now possible to add other custom import sources, but in this example you are done. If the list contains other import connections, you may have to delete them to make sure that the one you just created is the only one that will be used by the import process.

7. Click User Profile and Properties to return to that page. The Import source is now listed as Custom source.

> **If you want to restore the default AD import connection, select Current Domain as the import source; this will also delete any custom import connections!**

Regardless of whether you configure a custom source or use the default domain setting, the next thing to configure is the schedule for the import, if you did not do it previously. You can also force a full import manually by clicking Start full import. This will immediately start the import. You will see the page get refreshed regularly, and the Profile import status will say Enumerating, then Importing. Wait for it to change to Idle; the import is done. If this is the first time you have performed an import, you will see that the number of profiles has increased.

Click on the View user profiles link to see a list of all the imported user profiles. You can delete any of those users from the user profile or change a profile's imported settings. This will not affect the Active Directory information, since all of this is a one-way import. To view the imported settings, click to the right of a user name to display its quick menu, then select Edit. This displays all the imported information about that user, as shown in Figure 8-4. Since there are a large number of properties, Figure 8-4 only displays some of them.

Note that a yellow disk icon next to any attribute name indicates that the information was imported from the import source, typically Active Directory. You can change it now, but if you do it will be overwritten the next time the import process runs.

All attributes that do not have the disk icon, such as About me and Picture, must be set manually, either by the SharePoint administrator using this page or possibly by the user. This is controlled on another page. But first, if you changed any of these values, click Save and Close now, to return to the View User Profiles page, then click the breadcrumb trail link User Profile and Properties to go back to the first page, as shown in Figure 8-1.

There is more interesting information under the section User Profile Properties on this page. You can see the total number of user profile properties: 46 by default (which is almost twice the number in SPS 2003) and how many of these that are mapped to Active Directory attributes: 21 by default (compared to 14 in SPS 2003). There are two links:

❑ **Add profile property:** Use this link when you need to add more properties to the user profile database. You can configure the new property in many ways, including any mappings to the Active Directory.

❑ **View profile properties:** Use this link to view and modify existing properties; for example, if you want to map an existing property to an Active Directory attribute.

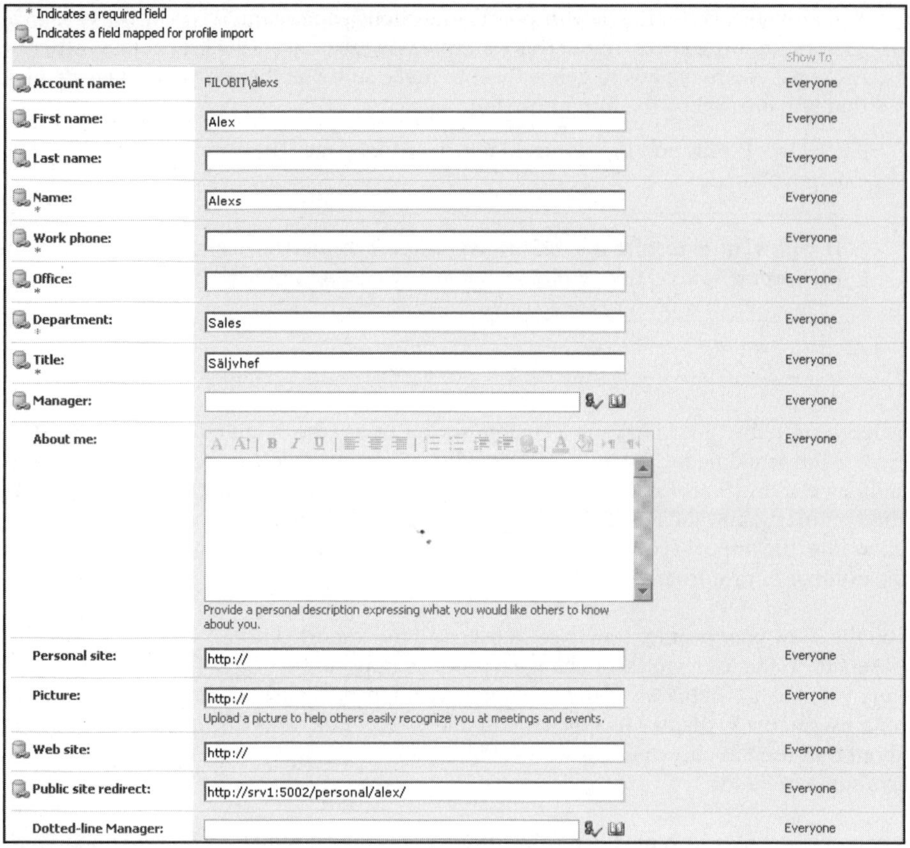

* Indicates a required field
🗊 Indicates a field mapped for profile import

		Show To
🗊 **Account name:**	FILOBIT\alexs	Everyone
🗊 **First name:**	Alex	Everyone
🗊 **Last name:**		Everyone
🗊 **Name:**	Alexs	Everyone
🗊 **Work phone:**		Everyone
🗊 **Office:**		Everyone
🗊 **Department:**	Sales	Everyone
🗊 **Title:**	Säljvhef	Everyone
🗊 **Manager:**		Everyone
About me:	*Provide a personal description expressing what you would like others to know about you.*	Everyone
Personal site:	http://	Everyone
Picture:	http:// *Upload a picture to help others easily recognize you at meetings and events.*	Everyone
🗊 **Web site:**	http://	Everyone
🗊 **Public site redirect:**	http://srv1:5002/personal/alex/	Everyone
Dotted-line Manager:		Everyone

Figure 8-4

The best way of understanding these settings, as usual, is to try an example. Say that you want to add a new property named IQ. You don't want to map this value to any Active Directory attribute, but you want to enable users to set this value by themselves (yes, this is an unrealistic example!). The following Try It Out illustrates how you do this.

Try It Out   Add a New Property to the User Profile

1.   On the User Profile and Properties page, click Add profile property. This opens a web form. Enter the following values (see Figure 8-5):

   a.   **Name:** IQ. The name for this property.

   b.   **Display name:** Brain IQ. The name as displayed to the user.

   c.   **Type:** Integer. Defines what type of information you can store in this property.

   d.   **Description:** "Enter your Brain IQ."

   e.   **Policy Setting:** Choose between Optional, Required, and Disabled. In this example, chose Optional.

f. **Default Privacy Setting:** Define who will see this attribute; chose My Manager. If you also check the option User can override, then users can change this privacy setting in their My Site web site, using the Edit Details link. Leave this unchecked in this example.

g. **In the Edit Settings section:** Select Allow users to edit values for this property.

h. **In the Display Settings section:** Check both Show in the profile properties section of the user's profile page, and Show on the Edit Details page.

i. **In the Search Settings section:** Check Indexed only.

j. **In the Property Import Mapping section:** Select Not mapped.

k. Click OK to save and close this page.

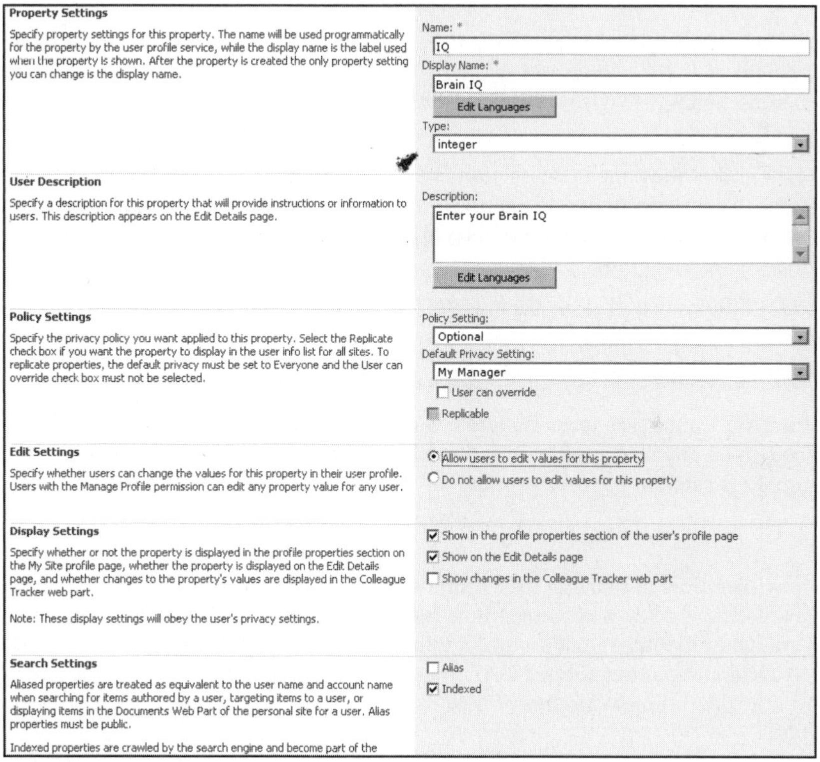

Property Settings

Specify property settings for this property. The name will be used programmatically for the property by the user profile service, while the display name is the label used when the property is shown. After the property is created the only property setting you can change is the display name.

Name: *
IQ

Display Name: *
Brain IQ

[Edit Languages]

Type:
integer

User Description

Specify a description for this property that will provide instructions or information to users. This description appears on the Edit Details page.

Description:
Enter your Brain IQ

[Edit Languages]

Policy Settings

Specify the privacy policy you want applied to this property. Select the Replicate check box if you want the property to display in the user info list for all sites. To replicate properties, the default privacy must be set to Everyone and the User can override check box must not be selected.

Policy Setting:
Optional

Default Privacy Setting:
My Manager

☐ User can override
☐ Replicable

Edit Settings

Specify whether users can change the values for this property in their user profile. Users with the Manage Profile permission can edit any property value for any user.

◉ Allow users to edit values for this property
○ Do not allow users to edit values for this property

Display Settings

Specify whether or not the property is displayed in the profile properties section on the My Site profile page, whether the property is displayed on the Edit Details page, and whether changes to the property's values are displayed in the Colleague Tracker web part.

Note: These display settings will obey the user's privacy settings.

☑ Show in the profile properties section of the user's profile page
☑ Show on the Edit Details page
☐ Show changes in the Colleague Tracker web part

Search Settings

Aliased properties are treated as equivalent to the user name and account name when searching for items authored by a user, targeting items to a user, or displaying items in the Documents Web Part of the personal site for a user. Alias properties must be public.

Indexed properties are crawled by the search engine and become part of the

☐ Alias
☑ Indexed

Figure 8-5

2. You are returned to the User Profiles and Properties page. Click the View profile properties link to verify that the new property is listed (at the end of the page) as Brain IQ and configured in a proper way.

3. To test this value for a user listed in the user profile, click the link User Profiles and Properties to go back to that page (note that Number of user profile properties has increased by one). Click View User Profiles, and edit any user listed there. Enter a value for the Brain IQ property (for example, 120), and click Save and Close. Later, you will see how this value shows up in the My Site page.

To modify an existing property, you use the link View profile properties in the User Profile Properties section on the User Profiles and Properties page. For example, say that you want to map the attribute for the existing user property named "Mobile phone" to the Active Directory property "Mobile." The following Try It Out shows how you do this:

Map a User Property to an AD Attribute

1. Log on as a SharePoint Administrator, and start the Central Administration tool. Click on the Shared Service instance (typically named `SharedService1`) listed in the Quick Launch bar under the Shared Service Administration heading. Next, click User profiles and properties in the User Profiles and My Sites section. At the end of the page, click View profile properties (in the User Profile Properties section). This opens a web form with all existing properties and their settings.

2. Locate the Mobile Phone property, near the end of this page. Use its quick menu to select Edit. This will open the configuration page for the property. Note that there are a lot of settings; for example, settings to define who can see the property, who can edit it, and if it will be searchable or not.

3. At the end of the page is the section Property Import Mapping; you can use that to map a user profile property to Active Directory, or any other existing data connection. Change the Data source field to map to mobile. This will connect the AD property Mobile to the user profile property Mobile Phone.

4. Click OK to save and close the page. Note that the Mobile Phone property is now mapped to mobile.

5. Click the breadcrumb link User Profile and Properties to return to that page.

6. Since you want to see immediately if this works, click Start Full Import. When the process is finished, open any user profile with the mobile property set in AD, then verify that the mobile number is listed in the user profile.

You have now seen how to manage user profiles, and how to add and modify new properties. You have also learned how to do a custom source import of the Active Directory. It was not that hard, was it? Well, if you want to import just the users who belong to a distribution list or something similar, you will need to understand more about LDAP query filters. There are lots of sources with good information about LDAP, including examples of how to do more advanced filtering for SharePoint's custom source imports.

> **Use this link to find more information about custom LDAP queries:**
> http://msdn2.microsoft.com/en-us/library/aa746475.aspx.

Managing Information Targeting with WSS and MOSS

One of the main problems with sharing information among many users is that there will always be a lot of information, but the average user is only interested in parts of that information. A common way of solving this problem is to create specific places for each type of information or interest group, such as local intranets for each department. However, this creates a new problem: Now each user must know where to look, or even worse, information may be stored multiple times, maybe in different versions. This is clearly something to avoid.

MOSS has a solution to this: targeting. Almost every piece of information in a SharePoint site can be targeted for a specific audience. But SharePoint 2007 has other ways of targeting information, which also work in WSS. You can target any of these: audience groups, SharePoint Groups, AD distribution lists, and AD security groups. The following list shows the types of objects that you can control using targeting.

❑   **News:** This list can be configured to only show sales-related news items to the sales team, while the IT staff see only IT-related news, and other users can view both sales and IT news.

❑   **List items and Library items:** All lists and libraries can enable audience targeting. To display a filtered view, you must display these lists and libraries using the Content Query Web Part. For example, you can have an Announcement item filtered for everyone but the Sales team.

❑   **Office Links:** A link displayed in MS Office 2007 Send As or File Open dialog box can be filtered so that it is only available to specific audiences.

❑   **Navigational Links:** The links on the Quick Launch bar can also be targeted. The user will, therefore, only see the links that apply to his or her specific tasks.

❑   **Web Parts:** Almost all Web Parts available to a SharePoint site have an option for targeting. It is usually found in the Web Part configuration section Advanced. Even the Web Parts on the Sites area page, which lists sites, can be targeted for a specific audience, if you need to do this.

More about Audience Groups (MOSS Only)

It is easy to confuse audiences with security. Let's make this very clear: The audience feature is not a security feature. It is a filter that displays or hides information based on membership in audience groups. For example, if you know the URL to a news item that is hidden from you by this audience feature, you can type it manually and still see the news item.

The audience is built on rules that identify users based on properties and memberships. For example, you may have an audience named Sales where all users with the property `Department = Sales` are members. A user can be a member of multiple audience groups; if so, that user will see all information targeted for any of those groups.

You may have as many audience groups as necessary, but when you have a lot of groups, it is easy to get confused. Make sure that you plan your audience groups and take note of why you created those audiences. It is easy to forget that after a while. Audiences are like fresh fruit. It is great to have when it tastes good, but old fruit only attracts flies.

By default there is always one audience group — All site users. As this says, it will contain all users with access to SharePoint. You cannot remove or modify this audience.

Creating Audiences

In a previous section in this chapter, you learned about user profiles; now it is time to use some of this knowledge. The information in the user profile is often used for selecting members for an audience. For example, say you want to create the audience mentioned above: Sales, based on the Department property. If you import the user properties from Active Directory into the user profile, you have the property in two places. So, the big question is which one will SharePoint use when compiling the audience group? The answer this time is the user profile. Actually, most of the time SharePoint will use the properties stored in the user profile database when compiling the rules that define audience groups.

Follow the steps in the Try It Out below to create the Sales audience group, based on the Department property setting in the user profile.

Try It Out   Create an Audience

1. Make sure that you have at least some users in Active Directory with the Department property set to Sales.

2. Make sure that this information has been imported into the user profile, as described earlier.

3. Start SharePoint's Central Administration tool, then open the SSP instance (typically SharedServices1); click Audiences. This will open a page with all settings and management tasks related to audiences. It will list the current status; for example, the number of audiences, when to run the compilation process (i.e., rebuild the audience groups), and any errors encountered.

4. Click the Create Audience link. This opens the first of a series of web forms where you define the audience group. For this example, fill in these values:

    a. **Name: Sales:** This will be the name for this audience. It will be visible anywhere audiences are listed, so give it a descriptive name.

    b. **Description:** "People from the sales department"; make sure to enter a clear description here, so other administrators 12 months from now understand its purpose.

    c. **Owner:** This is an optional setting; the user defined as an owner can modify this Audience.

    d. **Include user who:** Select Satisfy all of the rules. As long as you only have one rule, this setting is not important. But if you want to build a more complex set of rules, you must be very sure if you want "all" or just "any" of the rules. For example, assume that you create two rules: Department=Sales and Department=Finance, and choose the default, "Satisfy all of the rules." Do you really have any user who has both Sales and

`Finance` in their `Department` property? Probably not, so this audience will not find any matching members.

    e. Click OK to open the next web form.

5. The Add Audience Rule page lets you choose between two types of operands: User and Property. Depending on what you select, the rest of this page will adjust to the options available for that particular operand (see Figure 8-6). In this example, you should choose these settings:

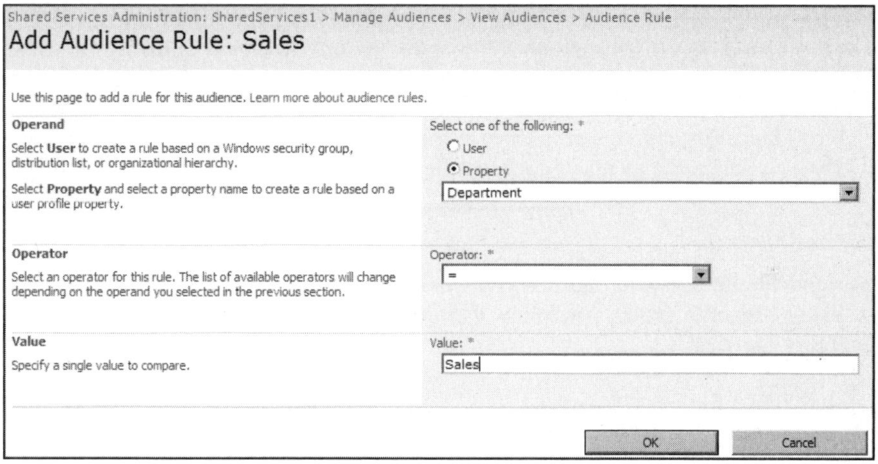

Shared Services Administration: SharedServices1 > Manage Audiences > View Audiences > Audience Rule

Add Audience Rule: Sales

Use this page to add a rule for this audience. Learn more about audience rules.

Operand	Select one of the following: *
Select **User** to create a rule based on a Windows security group, distribution list, or organizational hierarchy.	○ User
	⊙ Property
Select **Property** and select a property name to create a rule based on a user profile property.	Department ▼

| **Operator** | Operator: * |
| Select an operator for this rule. The list of available operators will change depending on the operand you selected in the previous section. | = ▼ |

| **Value** | Value: * |
| Specify a single value to compare. | Sales |

    [OK]   [Cancel]

Figure 8-6

    a. **Operand:** Property

    b. **Property:** Department. All of these are fetched from the user profile. If you have previously completed the example where you create the new user profile property IQ, it will be listed here.

    c. **Operator:** = (the equal sign). The four choices are =, Contains, <>, and Not contains.

    d. **Values:** Sales. This value is not case-sensitive.

> If the property is not always spelled in the same way, such as "Sales" and "Sales Dept" and "Sales Department," choose the Operator "Contains" and set the value to "Sales".

    e. Click OK to save and close this first rule. You will return to a page with the current settings for this audience group. If you need to modify the rule, click on it. If you need to create a second rule, click Add rule. But for this example, you are now done.

> With a brand-new audience, you may be tempted to click the link View membership on this page. Unfortunately, it will tell you that there are no matching users found. The reason, as given, is that this audience is not yet compiled. Instead, first click Compile audience, then click View membership.

6. Click the breadcrumb link Manage Audience at the top of the page to return to start page for audience management.

7. Note that the status says `Uncompiled audiences = 1`. This is a clear indication that you should now compile the audience. This will start a process in SharePoint that will look for all users matching the audience rules. Typically, you will schedule this process, but if you are impatient, you can click Start compilation now, then wait until this process is done (check the Compilation Status). You can also click Refresh sometimes to reduce the adrenaline level.

8. When the Compilation status is idle and the number of Uncompiled audiences is 0, everything is completed. To view the membership of this group, click View audiences to list all existing audiences. Locate Sales; click to the right of its name to open its quick menu, and select View membership. Verify that all the users you expected are here. If not, check the properties in the Active Directory, then the properties in the User Profile, and finally check the rule for this property (use Edit in the menu, or click the View Audience Properties link at the top of the page).

This was rather straightforward, right? If you want to create an audience based on membership in a distribution list or a security group, you follow exactly the same steps as you did above, except for step 5, which will look like this:

5. On the Add Audience Rule page:

    a. **Operand:** User

    b. **Operator:** Member of

    c. **Values:** Filobit\Sales Team (i.e., the complete name for this group)

    d. Click OK to save your work.

So, where did SharePoint go to find the membership of this security group? Remember that the user profile contains nothing about groups, only user accounts. That leaves only a data connection, typically Active Directory, which is the case in this example. So, if you want to create audiences based on groups, you don't need to make sure that the user profile database is up to date.

The other option for the operand User is Reports under. Use this operand if you want to create an audience based on people working for a given person, such as the sales manager. This time, SharePoint will look at the settings in the user profile database, not in Active Directory, so now you must be sure that the profile database has been updated. By default, this property is imported from Active Directory, so the correct way to update these settings is to enter this value in Active Directory, start the import to the user profile database, and then compile the audience. Note that the user account you enter in the Reports under field for the audience rule will automatically be added to the audience. In other words, if you create an audience based on the fact that Anna is the manager, SharePoint will include every user in the profile database with the Reports under setting equal to Anna, including Anna herself.

> If this group contains other groups, they will also be included, as long their group members can be viewed in the current domain. If you have multiple domains, you must use Universal Groups to be sure that SharePoint will see the members in the remote domain.

Applying Audiences (WSS and MOSS)

Now comes the fun part — testing that targeting of information for a given audience actually works. Before you continue with the following Try It Out, make sure that you have at least one audience group besides the default All site users. Note that in some cases you must enable audience filtering, for example when targeting single list items, while in other cases the audience filtering is enabled by default; for example, when targeting a complete Web Part and its content.

Try It Out   Target Information to a Specific Audience

1. In the first example, you create a news item targeted at the Sales audience only. Since news items are pages filed in a list, you must start by enabling audience filtering for the content of that list. Then you can target list items for specific audience groups. Finally, to display the content of the list, you must also enable audience filtering for the Content Query Web Part used to display the content of that list. Sounds complicated perhaps, but hopefully this example will clarify things:

2. Open the SharePoint intranet site; for example, `http://srv1`.

3. Make sure that the list has audience filtering enabled:

    a. Go to the News page on the intranet, and click View All Site Content.

    b. Click Pages (i.e., the list where news files are stored).

    c. Click Settings ⇨ Document Library Settings ⇨ Audience targeting settings.

    d. Enable audience targeting. The Pages list has this enabled by default. Then click OK.

4. Create a news item targeted for a specific audience group:

    a. Click on the News link, click Site Actions ⇨ Create Page.

    b. Enter a Title, and a Description; the URL name will, by default, be the same as the Title. Select a Page Layout of type Article Page (any type will do fine here), and then click Create.

    c. Next, enter the content of this news item. This is defined by the page layout you selected in step f. Add some text in the Page Content control, and possibly a picture.

    d. To define what audience this news item is targeted for, you must edit its properties: Click the menu Page on the toolbar, then select Page settings. Scroll down until you see the section Audience Targeting. Either enter the audience group Sales directly, or click the directory icon to the right of this field, and select Sales, then OK. Go to the end of this web form, and click OK.

    > Before you click the final OK in the previous step, you can click the Check Spelling button to check for any spelling errors. You can also check the spelling in the news item content before publishing it by opening the Tools menu and clicking Spelling.

    e. When you are happy with the content of the news item, click Publish.

5. Enable audience filtering in the Content Query Web Part that displays these news items. Note that the News page has by default two Web Parts for this: one that shows the latest news, including some of its details, and one that shows the last 20 news items.

    a. Click News to make sure that you are looking at the right page on your intranet.

    b. Click Site Actions ➪ Edit Page. This News page opens and is automatically checked out to you (i.e., any modifications you make will not be visible to others until you check the page back in).

    c. Click Edit on the Web Part News Roll Up, then select Modify Shared Web Part. A configuration pane for the Web Part opens to the right. Expand the Query section, and enable the Apply audience filtering setting, then click OK to save and close the page.

> **To display news items that do not have any audience targeting defined, set the checkbox Include items that are not targeted, before you click OK.**

    d. Since the News page is checked out, you must now click Publish on the toolbar to check it in and to approve the modifications to it.

> **If you don't see the news item any longer, you are probably not a member of the audience groups that the news items are targeted for.**

This was one of the most complicated audience targeting procedures you can do in SharePoint 2007, so if you understood this, then the rest will be easy. Just one more comment about targeting news items — the News page has two Web Parts for displaying news, as previously mentioned. If you want both of them to filter items, then you have to enable audience filtering on both, as described in steps 5a–c above. You will learn more about the News page and its news items in Chapter 9.

The next Try It Out is much easier and will teach you to target complete Web Parts. For example, on the intranet's Home page there is a Web Part named "I need to . . . ;" let's show this Web Part to members of the intranet's Owner group, plus the Sales audience group. The problem is that you do not have any audience group for owners yet. But this is really no problem, since SharePoint 2007 allows you to use both SharePoint Groups and AD security groups along with audience groups. "So why do I need audience groups at all?" you ask. Because in some situations you may not have a suitable SharePoint Group, or security group; then an audience group will be the solution for you!

Try It Out   **Target Web Parts to Both an Audience Group and a SharePoint Group**

    1. Open the intranet Home page.

    2. Click Site Actions ➪ Edit Page. This page is now checked out.

    3. On the Web Part "I need to . . . ," click Edit ➪ Modify shared Web Part.

4. In the edit page for the Web Part, expand the Advanced section. At the bottom, you will find the Target Audience field. Click the directory icon (at the right), then do this (see Figure 8-7):

   a. Make sure that the Find field is set to Global Audiences, select Sales, and then click Add. The name is now listed next to the Add button.

   b. Change the Find field to SharePoint Groups, and click the magnifying icon at the end of this line. All SharePoint Groups will now be listed; select the Owners group (i.e., the `<site name> Owners`), and click Add.

   c. Click OK to save and close the page.

5. You are now back at the Web Part configuration pane. The groups are listed in the Target Audiences field. Click OK to save and close this page.

6. Check in and publish the modified Home page by clicking the Publish button on the toolbar. Verify that only members of the Sales audience group and Home Owner SharePoint Group will see the Web Part on this page.

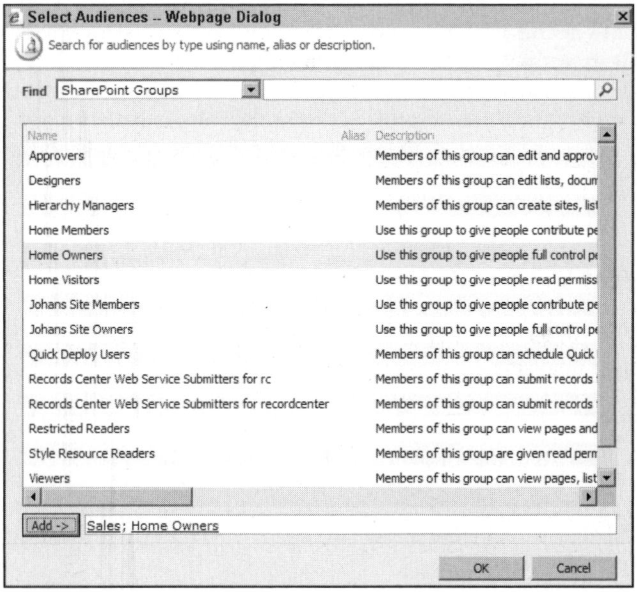

Figure 8-7

So, the natural question now is who can see these targeted news items and the "I need to" Web Part? The answer is: any user who is a member of the Sales audience group or the Home Owner SharePoint Group, but no other users. Do you see how elegant and powerful this feature is? It will help you create a web site that automatically (some would say "automagically") adjusts its content to the current user. This is indeed a very useful feature for an intranet or portal site but will be very valuable in many other types of web sites as well. Remember that Audience groups are exclusive to MOSS, while target filtering using SharePoint Groups and security groups also works on Web Parts, lists, and libraries in pure WSS environments. However, you must enable auditing for these lists or libraries before the Audience property shows up.

> **Remember: Targeting list and library items requires that you present the content of these lists using the Content Query Web Part. Audience filtering will not work with the standard list and library Web Parts.**

But there are more types of objects where you can use the targeting feature of SharePoint 2007 (both WSS and MOSS), using audience groups, SharePoint Groups, distribution groups, and AD security groups:

❑ The File Open and Save As links in the Office 2007 dialog box.

❑ Navigation links in a web site's Quick Launch bar.

❑ Navigational links on users' My Site.

The first of these, links in Office 2007, is very cool, and makes it easy for you as an administrator to control which links will show up in the users MS Office applications, such as MS Word, when opening or saving documents (under the heading My SharePoint Sites). Note that this feature does not work with previous versions of MS Office! For example, say that the Sales team has a web site on `http://srv1/sitedirectory/sales` containing all the quotes and contracts. To make it easy for the salespeople, you can add a link to their MS Office application that points directly to that web site, or even directly to a document library, as described next.

Try It Out   Target Links with MS Office 2007

1. Log on as a SharePoint administrator, and start the Central Administration tool.

2. Open the SSP, typically named `SharedServices1`.

3. Click Published links to Office client applications, in the User Profiles and My Sites section.

4. Click New, then fill in the following web form (see Figure 8-8):

   a. **Type the Web address:** `http://srv1/sitedirectory/sales/Contracts`. This is the URL that will open in MS Office. Note in step c below that you can point to several types of locations.

   b. **Type the description:** Sales Contracts. This text will be presented in the users' Save and Open dialog boxes, under My SharePoint Sites.

   c. **Type:** Document Library. Define what type of location this URL is pointing to; for example, Team Sites, Portal Sites, or Document Library.

   d. **Target Audience:** Sales. As before, you can choose between an audience group (requires MOSS), SharePoint Groups, security groups, and distribution lists.

   e. Click OK to save and close this form.

5. Now you just have to wait up to 24 hours before this link shows up in the users' MS Office applications. To test it, start MS Word 2007, click the Office button ➪ Open, select My SharePoint Sites, and the link will be listed here.

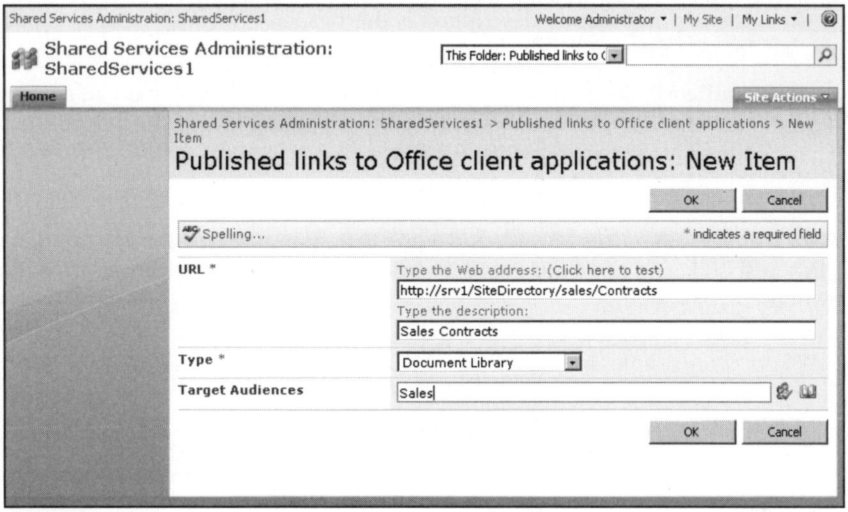

Figure 8-8

The second type of link is a navigation link, displayed on the Quick Launch bar on a web site. These types of links typically point to libraries and lists, in this site, as well as subsites. For example, look at a default WSS team site; what you see in the Quick Launch bar are the links Shared Documents, Calendar, Tasks, and Team Discussions. You can add new links, and they can be targeted, that is, only displayed for users in a specific audience or group. For example, say that you want to add a navigation link on the Sales team site that points to a public web site on the Internet. Then do it as shown in the Try It Out.

Try It Out   Add a Navigation Link to the Quick Launch Bar

1.   Open the web site where you want to add the navigation link; for example, `http://srv1/sitedirectory/sales`.

2.   Click Site Actions ⇨ Site Settings, then click Navigation in the Look and Feel section. Note that to publish a page in MOSS you instead click Site Actions ⇨ Site Settings ⇨ Modify Navigation.

3.   At the end of the next page (see Figure 8-9) is the section Navigation Editing and Sorting. Each link you add is listed under a given heading in the Quick Launch navigation bar. To add a new heading, do this:

    a.   Click Add Heading in the tool bar, and a web form will open.

    b.   **Title:** Market Info. This will be the header line in the Quick Launch bar. You can connect this header to a URL, if necessary. For example, you could add a URL to this header that displays a list of all document libraries. Check one of the default headers to see how it works. If you just want to use the title as a header in the navigation bar, leave the URL field empty. If you pointed to a URL, you can also choose to open that URL in a separate window. In this example, you leave both the URL and "Open link in new window" empty.

    c. **Description:** Enter a description of this header; it will be visible as a tooltip, when you hover a mouse over the header.

    d. **Audience:** Enter the target group for this header. Note that if you plan to add one or more links under this header, they should all use the same Audience definition to make sure that they are consistently filtered.

    e. Click OK to save and close the page.

4. Now that you have a header, let's add a link to it. Mark the new header "Market Info," then click Add Link, and add these values to point to an external web site, which will open in a new window:

    a. **Title:** Financial News. This will be the navigation link.

    b. **URL:** `http://www.financialnews.com`.

    c. Check Open link in new window.

    d. **Description:** Enter a description of this link; it will be visible as a tooltip, when you hover a mouse over the link.

    e. **Audience:** Enter the same target group as for the header.

    f. Click OK to save and close.

5. Click OK to save and close the Site Navigation Settings page.

6. Open the site, and make sure that the new header and its link only show up for users in the targeted group (see Figure 8-10). If not, reopen the navigation page, and edit the Audience definition for these links.

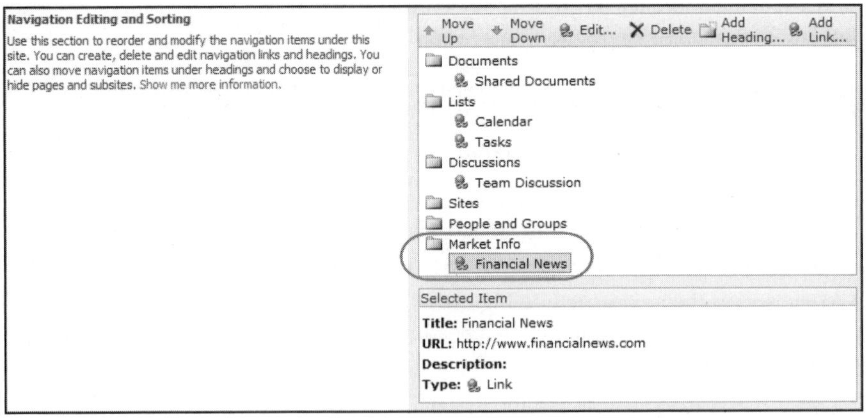

Figure 8-9

Figure 8-10

The third type of targeted link is also a type of navigation link; it will display a link at the top menu of a user's My Site that points to a specific location. For example, instead of using the Web Parts in My Site to display the user's Inbox and Calendar, you can add a menu link that points to the user's Exchange mailbox by Outlook Web Access (OWA), or add a menu link that points to the user's team web site. The same type of targeting as for the previously mentioned links above also applies here: This link can be targeted to an audience group, a SharePoint Group, a distribution list, or a security group.

The example below adds a menu link on My Site that points to the user's OWA but only for users who are members of the Sales audience group. In this example, the URL to the OWA is `http://dcs/exchange`.

Try It Out   **Add a Navigation Link to My Site**

1. Log on as an administrator, then open SharePoint's Central Administration tool.

2. Click on the SSP, typically `SharedServces1`, then click on Personalization site links.

3. Click New, and fill in the following web form (see Figure 8-11).

  a. **Type the Web address:** `http://dcs1/exchange`.

  b. **Type the description:** OWA. This will be displayed on the user's My Site top menu.

  c. **Owner:** Filobit\Administrator. SharePoint will then change this line to just Administrator when the user name is found in the Active Directory. This is the administrative owner for the link.

  d. **Target Audience:** Sales.

  e. Click OK.

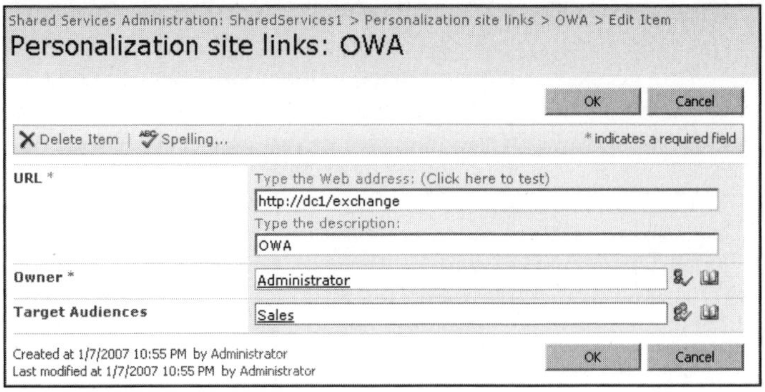

Figure 8-11

Next, log on as a user who is a member of the Sales audience group, and look at My Site. It will now contain a new top menu link named OWA. Click on it, and it will open Outlook Web Access for that user.

> **This works with both Exchange 2003 and Exchange 2007. In OWA 2007, users will also see a link back to My Site.**

Another practical use for this navigational menu link is to create a link that points back to the start page of an intranet. Such a link should typically not be targeted but be displayed for all users. Note that it may take a minute before this menu link shows up on all users' My Sites.

Searching in WSS and MOSS

One of the greatest time savers is search engines. Just look at how often you use MSN Search or Google, just to mention a couple of them. On the Internet, searching is absolutely critical, since you have no idea where information is stored, and there may be new sources one minute from now. That is why you search all the time. This is not really that different from the way you use your internal network. True, the volume of information is much smaller in your network, and you know where at least some of it is stored, since you created it. Still, it does not take much activity within an organization to create so much information that the average user loses track of where things are stored. So, users start looking around to find the file, document or whatever they are looking for. After some minutes, they find it. The question then becomes is this the latest version, or is there a newer version somewhere? Then when they get what they're looking for, they most likely want to be notified if that document gets updated later on. What you need is a solution that helps you:

❑   Find information regardless of where it is stored.

❑   Make sure that it is the latest version.

❑   Send a notification to you when this information is updated.

SharePoint has solutions for the first bulleted item, but there is a great difference between what MOSS is offering and the WSS environment, as the following section will cover in more detail. The second bullet is covered by the built-in version management of documents and list content in both MOSS and WSS, and the third bulleted item is the alert feature, also a built-in feature in MOSS and WSS. So, let's focus on the search functionality.

Searching in WSS

WSS 3.0 has a basic search feature that will allow users to search for content. This is a big change from previous WSS versions, which required WSS to be configured to run on SQL Server 2000, using its Full-Text Indexing engine. Another important change is that WSS 3.0 will search in subsites, while the previous version of WSS only searched in the current site. The following list summarizes the search functionality in WSS, when combined with SQL Server:

❑   Finds information of any type, stored in the current site, or a subsite.

❑   Provides free-text searching in documents, files, and all list content.

SharePoint will create a special Windows SharePoint Services Search (`MSSearch.exe`) in Windows 2003. This service must be running before WSS can use it for indexing and searching. The steps to configure WSS to use this search feature are described in the following Try It Out.

Try It Out   **Activate Search Indexing in WSS**

1.   Log on as an administrator.

2.   Start SharePoint's Central Administrative tool. Switch to the Operations page, then click Services on Server.

3.   Make sure that the correct Server is selected, and then start Windows SharePoint Services Search service, if it's not already started. Fill in this information in the web form:

> If WSS was installed using SQL Express, the Search service may not be listed. If this is the case, select All on the View menu on the toolbar.

    a.   **Service Account:** Enter the service account and its password for the search service; be sure to include the domain name, for example, `filobit\sp_service`.

    b.   **Content Access Account:** Enter the default user account to be used by the search service when searching content sources. You can later configure other user accounts for specific content sources.

    c.   **Search Database:** Enter the SQL server name, plus the Database Name for the index. Use the default database and name, if you don't have a good reason not to.

    d.   **Indexing Schedule:** Enter how often the index process will run. The default is every five minutes.

    e.   Click OK to save and close the page.

> When you create a new web application, make sure to select a search server.

4. When the process is done, all documents and lists are also indexed and ready to be searched within five minutes. Open any WSS team site, and use the search field at the top-right corner of the page. Type a text string that you know exists in any of the lists or inside any documents stored in this team site.

Understanding the Search Feature in WSS

When searching is activated in WSS, there is nothing more to configure. The search engine in WSS is fast and stable; its behavior is controlled by stored procedures in SQL Server. You may find tips on how to optimize these stored procedures, but before you do that you must understand that this will violate the conditions for getting help from Microsoft's support team! It may also create problems when you install the next service pack or upgrade to the next release.

The objects indexed by Full-Text Indexing are these:

❑ **List items:** Such as individual names in a Contact list.

❑ **Documents:** Documents of these types: `.doc`, `.xls`, `.ppt`, `.txt`, and `.html`.

❑ **Lists:** Such as Announcements, and Events.

There are also objects that will not be indexed and therefore not searchable:

❑ Nontext columns in lists — for example, Lookup fields, currency, Yes/No.

❑ Attachments to list items.

❑ Survey lists.

❑ Hidden lists.

The process of reindexing new or modified information is automatic in WSS; the default schedule is to run an incremental indexing process every five minutes. As soon as this process is done, users can search for it.

The search field in the top-right corner of the web page (unless moved) is visible in all team sites. Enter the string you are searching and press Enter or click the icon to the right of the search field. Note that if you enter more than one text string, it will match any object with either or both of the strings; this is called a Boolean OR search. The search engine is using a type of search called FREETEXT; this type of search uses a feature called stemming. For example, if you search for the word Run, it will also match Running and Ran. Therefore, you must enter the complete word. You cannot search for Admin and find Administrator, for example, since Admin is an abbreviation, not a complete word.

> **Stemming only works with certain languages, such as English and German.**

All of these constraints and behaviors are due to the way the stored procedures are defined. If you absolutely must change this, be sure to make a backup of the original stored procedure, and make notes of what you did and why, so that later on anyone can restore or remove this customization, if necessary.

> You may find tips on the Internet about how to enhance the search functionality in WSS, but remember the warnings above about modifying stored procedures in SQL, since Microsoft will not support your system!

Indexing New File Types

You can have the MS Search service in WSS index more file types than it does by default. The most common request is for Adobe's PDF files. What MS Search needs to index any file type is a program that can open that file and read its text. Such a program is called an index filter, or IFilter for short. So, to index PDF files you need an IFilter for PDF. The good news is that this IFilter is free to download from Adobe's web site:

    www.adobe.com/support/downloads/detail.jsp?ftpID=2611

Note that this IFilter is regularly updated; make sure you get the latest version. After you have downloaded this program, install it on the SQL server, if you are using separate WSS and SQL servers.

> This is only true if you are running a pure WSS environment! If you are running a MOSS server, this IFilter must be installed on all SharePoint servers with the Index role.

After the installation, Microsoft recommends in the following Knowledge Base article that all existing PDF files must be reloaded, or updated, in order to be indexed:

    http://support.microsoft.com/kb/927675/en-us

But in many cases it will actually be enough to force a full update in order to index these existing PDF files.

Searching in MOSS

This is one of the strongest features in Office SharePoint Server! It has its own search and index engine, completely independent of the Full-Text Indexing service in SQL Server. In fact, you can activate them both. However, it will be a waste of resources, since the MOSS search and indexing feature works in any web site, including both MOSS sites and WSS sites. A summary of the search features in MOSS are:

❑   Search everywhere in SharePoint — any MOSS site, any team site, and any workspace site.

❑   Can search almost any content source outside SharePoint — file servers, MS Exchange servers, Lotus Notes, and other web servers, including any public web site on the Internet.

❑   With MOSS Enterprise Edition you can use the Business Data Catalog feature to search in external databases and applications, such as Oracle, SAP, and Navision.

❑   Search all MS Office file types by default, plus all neutral file formats, such as TXT, HTML, and so on.

❑ Can be extended to search any file type. All that is needed is an IFilter for each file type.

❑ You can control which file types are to be indexed, even if there is an IFilter installed for them.

❑ The user profile properties will be indexed. You can search for a user with a specific property.

❑ You can set the schedule for full and incremental indexing. You can also force a full indexing anytime.

This indexing and search feature is activated by default for all information stored in SharePoint, both MOSS sites and WSS team sites; there is no special configuration needed to activate this. Since this feature is much more advanced than the full-text search in SQL Server, there is also a lot more configuration you can do; however, this also requires more management. You, as an administrator, must understand how this feature works in MOSS and what you can do to optimize it. This is especially true when a problem arises, such as when the search results are not as expected, or when a content source isn't indexed. The following section will tell you all you need to know for your everyday work as an administrator, and how to extend and adjust this very important feature.

> For an in-depth description of the Search and Indexing feature, see the Microsoft SharePoint Product and Technology 2007 Resource Kit.

The Basics

There are two MOSS services engaged in this feature:

❑ **Indexing:** Responsible for crawling content sources and building index files.

❑ **Searching:** Responsible for finding all information matching the search query by searching the index files.

This is important: All searching is performed against the index files; if they don't contain what the user is looking for, there will not be a match. So, the index files are critical to the success of the search feature of MOSS. In fact, practically all configuration and management is related to the indexing service. The search functionality can be described in its simplest form as a web page where the user defines his or her search query.

The index role can be configured to run on its own MOSS server, or run together with all the other roles, such as the Web service, Excel Services and Forms Services. It performs its indexing tasks following this general workflow:

1. SharePoint stores all configuration settings for the indexing in its database.

2. When activated, the index will look in SharePoint's databases to see what content sources to index, and what type of indexing to perform, such as a full or incremental indexing.

3. The index service will start a program called the Gatherer, which is a program that will try to open the content that should be indexed.

4. For each information type, the Gatherer will need an Index Filter, or IFilter, that knows how to read text inside this particular type of information. For example, to read a MS Word file, an IFilter for .DOC is needed.

5. The Gatherer will receive a stream of Unicode characters from the IFilter. It will now use a small program called a Word Breaker; its job is to convert the stream of Unicode characters into words.

6. However, some words are not interesting to store in the index, such as "the", "a", and numbers; the Gatherer will now compare each word found against a list of Noise Words. This is a text file that contains all words that will be removed from the stream of words.

7. The remaining words are stored in an index file, together with a link to the source. If that word already exists, only the source will be added, so one word can point to multiple sources.

8. If the source was information stored in SharePoint, or a file in the file system, the index will also store the security settings for this source. This will prevent a user from getting search results that he or she is not allowed to open.

Pretty straightforward, if you think about it. But the underlying process is a bit more complex. Fortunately you do not need to dive into these details, unless you have a very good reason to. By default, MOSS will create a single index file. This index file is not stored on the SQL server, as the other information stored in SharePoint is; instead, it is stored in the file system on the server configured to run the Index role in the SharePoint farm. This index file is stored in separate folders in the following location (assuming that you have used the default installation folder):

```
<Drive:>\Program Files\Microsoft Office Servers\12.0\DATA\Office ↵
Server\Applications\<Application GUID>
```

The Application GUID is a unique hexadecimal string that identifies a specific SSP instance, such as ae0cd4fe-ed29-418f-aa0f-eecfd7956b4f. If you have more than one SSP instance created on the same server, you can check the following registry key to see exactly what portal this Application GUID is pointing to:

```
HKEY_Local_Machine/Software/Microsoft/Office ↵
Server/12.0/Search/Applications/<GUID>/CatalogNames
```

The property DisplayName will tell you what SSP instance this is. The number of files and folders stored in each index folder may surprise you, but indexing is a complex process and it shows here. You do not need to configure these files, since everything is managed by SharePoint's administration pages.

The Gatherer process keeps a log of all its activities. These log files are also stored in this folder structure, but the easiest way to view these log entries is to use SharePoint's administrative web pages.

Configuring Searching and Indexing

By default, SharePoint takes care of configuring the search and index feature. Still, there are a lot of things for an administrator to do, especially when you want to extend the information indexed, for example, by adding new content sources and new file types, or by just forcing a full reindexing. To open the start page for all these administrative activities, start SharePoint's Central Administration tool, click the

SSP instance name, (e.g., `SharedServices1`), and then click Search settings. The next page is divided into three sections:

❑ **Crawl Settings (see Figure 8-12):** Contains the status of the index, the number of documents found, and when it was last indexed. It also contains links to the main part of all configuration settings related to search and indexing, such as managing content sources, metadata property mappings, and resetting all crawled content. This section is what you will work with most of the time, when it comes to search and indexing activities, as you will see later in this chapter.

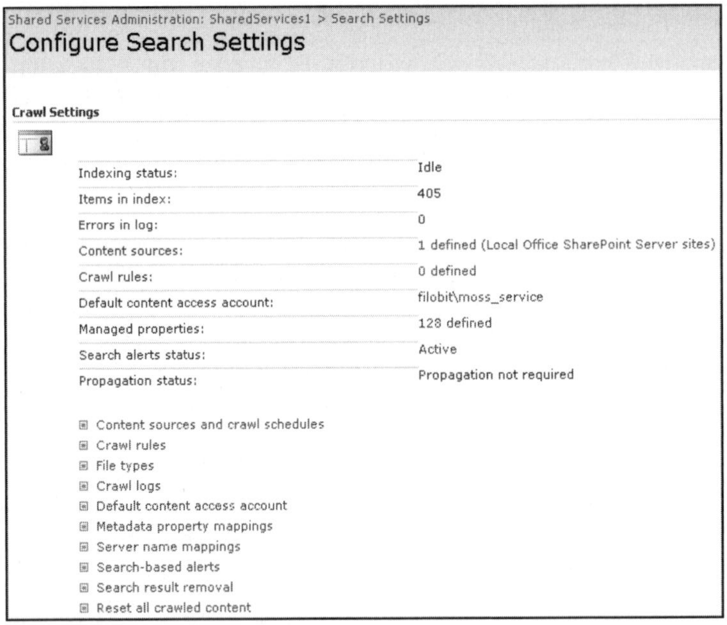

Shared Services Administration: SharedServices1 > Search Settings

Configure Search Settings

Crawl Settings

Indexing status:	Idle
Items in index:	405
Errors in log:	0
Content sources:	1 defined (Local Office SharePoint Server sites)
Crawl rules:	0 defined
Default content access account:	filobit\moss_service
Managed properties:	128 defined
Search alerts status:	Active
Propagation status:	Propagation not required

- ⊞ Content sources and crawl schedules
- ⊞ Crawl rules
- ⊞ File types
- ⊞ Crawl logs
- ⊞ Default content access account
- ⊞ Metadata property mappings
- ⊞ Server name mappings
- ⊞ Search-based alerts
- ⊞ Search result removal
- ⊞ Reset all crawled content

Figure 8-12

❑ **Scopes (see Figure 8-13):** Use this section of the Search settings page when you need to manage existing search scopes or create new ones.

❑ **Authoritative Pages (see Figure 8-13):** Use this section of the Search settings page when you need to define what web site URLs are more important than others, regarding search results. Sites listed here will be listed before other URL sources in the search results, that is, you can control the ranking of search results. There are three levels of authoritative pages: Most, Second, and Third, and it works like this: If you search for the string ABC, and there are two documents containing this word, one in a web page defined as Second-level and one in a Third-level authoritative page, the document stored in the Second-level page will get higher ranking, and therefore be listed above the other document. To define web page URLs as Most, Second, or Third level pages, click the link Specify authoritative pages, and enter the URLs for each level, as depicted in Figure 8-14.

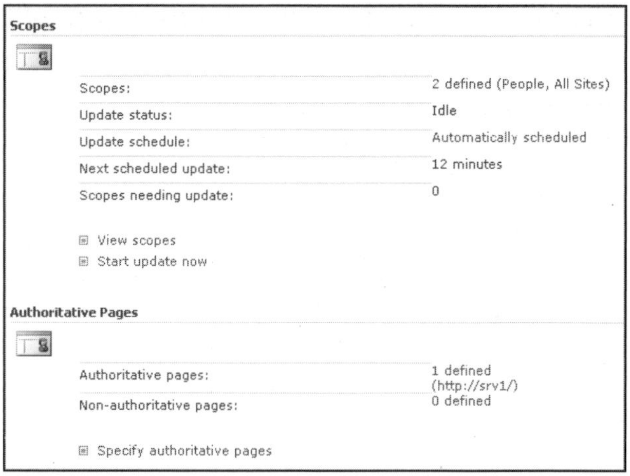

Figure 8-13

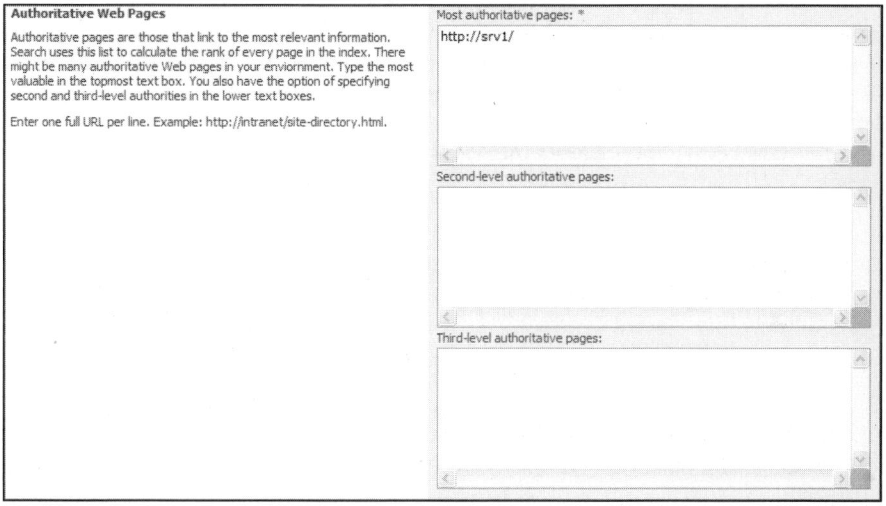

Figure 8-14

Checking Errors and Warnings

With this information in mind, let's work with the indexing feature now. For example, say that you want to check for any error or warning listed in the Crawl Settings section above. Look at the line's Errors in log; if you see something other than 0 here, you may have a problem. To see exactly what error or warning it is, click on the error number, or use the link Crawl Logs. This will open the Crawl Log page, as shown in Figure 8-15.

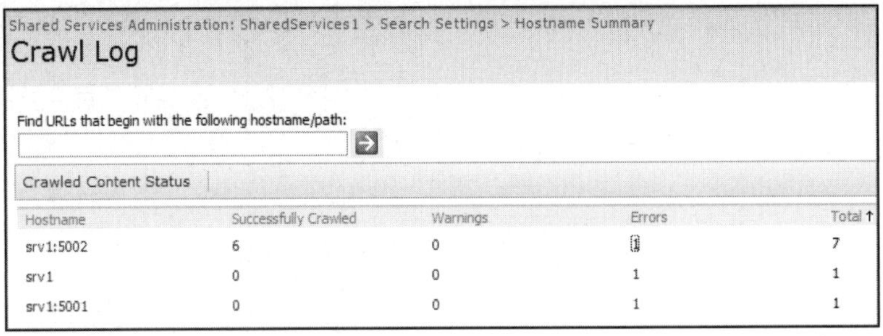

Figure 8-15

A typical error would be that the crawler process failed to connect to a site; for example, an Internet site such as www.microsoft.com. This may be a problem with accessing Internet. Another problem may be a file that is locked by another process. This is usually no problem, since SharePoint will try to index that location next time.

Forcing an Update

Still on the Search settings page, click Content sources and crawl schedules link to open the page where you can see more details about the crawler process (see Figure 8-16). This page will show the current status, and when the next full crawl and the next incremental crawl will take place. If you see None as in Figure 8-16, this means that there is no schedule defined yet. To get more details about a specific content source, such as Local Office SharePoint Server sites, click on its name; this will show the following information:

> The content source Local Office SharePoint Server sites is also known as the Default Content Source. Every time you create a new site collection, its URL is added to this content source.

❏   Name of the content source.

❏   Details, such as type, status, the number of sources it crawls, the last time it was crawled, and errors.

❏   Start addresses, that is, the URL sources that are crawled.

❏   Crawl settings — should only these start addresses be crawled, or should everything under them be crawled as well?

❏   Crawl schedules (full and incremental).

❏   If you want to start a full crawl now.

To force a full or incremental update, use the quick menu for the content source, and select Start Full Crawl or Start Incremental Crawl. You can also start all crawls (for all content sources) by clicking on the line Start all crawls, in the Quick Launch bar. This menu also allows you to stop or pause an active crawl.

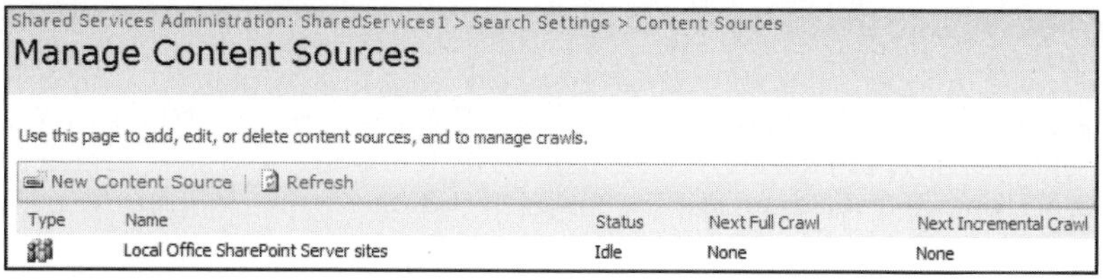

Figure 8-16

Managing the Indexing Schedules

SharePoint uses different indexing schedules for different content sources. You need to know exactly when the index is updated to understand when you can expect updated information to be searchable. These are the default schedules used by MOSS:

❑ SharePoint content — the content in any MOSS and WSS site:

  ❑ **Incremental:** No schedule defined by default.

  ❑ **Full:** No schedule defined by default.

❑ WSS Search — only applied when WSS alone is installed:

  ❑ **Incremental:** Every 5 minutes.

> The WSS Search service is renamed Windows SharePoint Service Help Search when you install MOSS, since then it will only be used to indexing the help system files.

The consequence of this default schedule is that new and updated information on any of the SharePoint sites in a MOSS installation will never be indexed, unless you set a schedule. A WSS-only installation will be indexed every 5 minutes, 24 hours per day. To set the schedule for MOSS indexing, use the Content sources and crawl schedules page, described earlier. To change the WSS Search setting, follow the steps in the Try It Out below.

Try It Out   Define WSS Search Service Indexing Schedule

1. Open Central Administration tool, and switch to the Operations page.

2. Click on Services on Server.

3. Click on the name Windows SharePoint Services Search.

4. Define the indexing schedule (by default every five minutes).

5. Click OK to save and close the page.

Controlling What Files to Index

When the indexing process is running, as described earlier in this chapter, the Gatherer process will open the files found in the content sources. But exactly what file types will it open? This is controlled by a list of file types that you can manage by the link File types on the Configure Search Settings page described earlier. The information in this list shows two things:

❑   What file types the Gatherer will try to open.

❑   If there is any icon defined in SharePoint for this file type.

The last bullet is interesting; if a file type does not have an icon next to it in this list, then this file will not have a specific icon when listed in a document library. Instead, it will have the icon used for unknown file types. This can be modified; later in this chapter you will learn how to add an icon for the PDF file, and the same technique can be used for any file types.

Look at the list "File types." If you are missing one file type, you can add it now by clicking New File Type. But this will not be enough; the Gatherer also needs the specific IFilter for this file type. Some file types actually are managed by the default IFilters and still are not listed here; for example, RTF files. To add the RTF file type, click New File Type, enter **rtf**, and click OK. Note that it is now listed and that the MS WordPad icon was automatically associated with it.

> **You can use this list to temporarily stop indexing a specific file type; just remove it from this list. Then add it when you want to index that file type again.**

Managing Search Scope

SharePoint allows you to limit the search scope, in order to make it easier for users to find the information they are searching for. This is especially handy when the index file contains information from several content sources. For example, if the user knows that the document they are looking for is stored somewhere in the file system, set the search scope to the file system only. This will make the search faster and more focused, and generate less CPU load on the SharePoint server.

By default, there is one single search scope: All Sites. To define new search scopes is a two-step process: first you create the search scope in the Central Administration tool, then you enable this search scope in a site collection. Depending on what scope you want to use, this is easy or may require some planning. For example, say that you want to create a search scope that only matches information in the team site Sales, but no other site. The following Try It Out shows how you do this.

Try It Out   Add a New Search Scope

1.   Open the Central Administration tool, click on the SSP name (e.g., `SharedServices1`), and click on Shared services.

2.   In the section Crawl Setting, click View scopes.

3.   Click New Scope, then enter these values (see Figure 8-17):

   a.   **Title:** Sales Web Only. The name for this scope.

   b.   **Description:** "This search scope only shows results from the Sales team site."

c. **Target Result Page:** Select Use the default Search Results Page. This choice will make sure that search results based on this search scope will use the default result page. If you create a custom result page, then use the other option: Specify a different page for searching this scope, and enter the URL to that `.aspx` file.

d. Click OK to save and close the page.

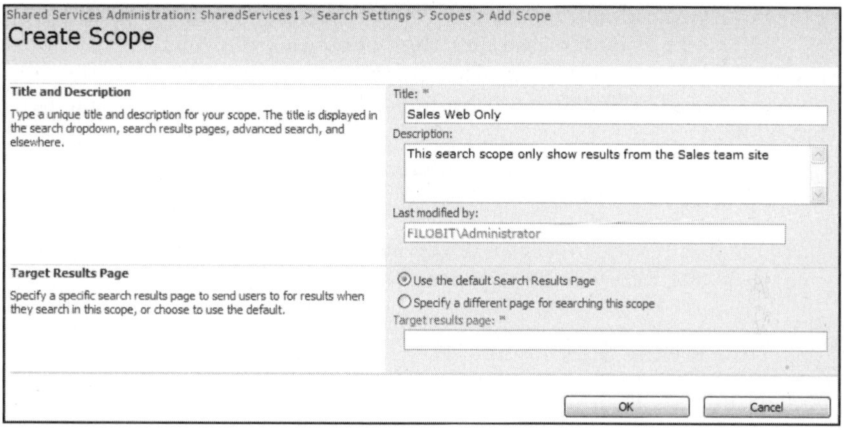

Figure 8-17

4. The new search scope is now listed along with all the others. Look at the Update Status column. It says Empty – Add Rules; this is actually a link to the page where this search scope is defined. Click Add Rules.

a. On the "Add Scope Rule" page, select `"Scope Rule Type"` = `Web Address`. This will expand this page with more settings (see Figure 8-18).

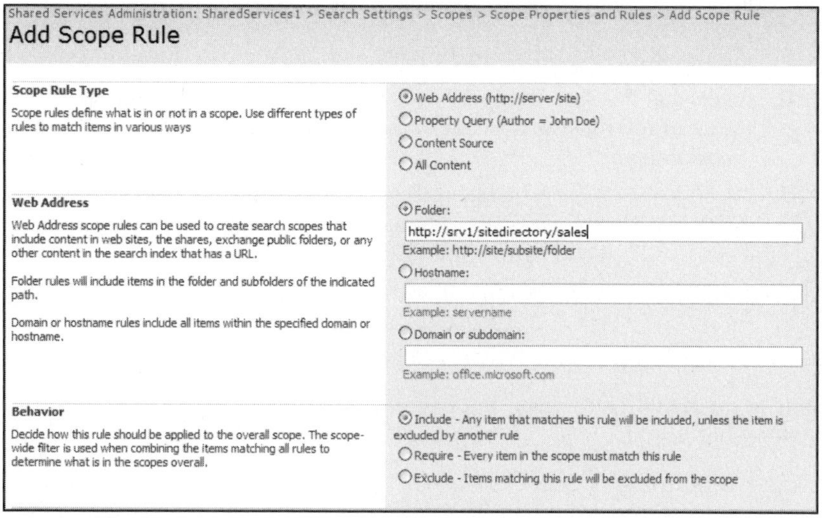

Figure 8-18

   b.   Set Folder to `http://srv1/sitedirectory/sales`. This is the URL to the Sales site.

   c.   Select Include. Any item that matches this rule will be included, unless the item is excluded by another rule.

   d.   Click OK.

5.   Now this search scope has another Update Status message: New Scope – Ready after the next update (start in xx minutes), where "xx" can be anything from 1 to 20 minutes. In other words, this search scope cannot be used until this period has passed. But you can force SharePoint to rebuild the search scope directly: Click Search Settings in the breadcrumb trail at the top of this page, then click Start update now in the Scope section, and wait until the Update status shows Idle.

The global definition of this search scope is now done. The next step is to enable this search scope in a site collection. To do that, follow the steps of our next Try It Out

Try It Out   **Add a New Search Scope**

1.   Open the intranet page; for example, `http://srv1`.

2.   Make sure that the top site in this site collection is open, then click Site Actions ⇨ Site Settings ⇨ Modify All Site Settings.

3.   Click on Search scopes in the Site Collection Administration section. Note that the following View Scopes page lists this new search scope as Unused Scopes. To enable it for the search drop-down menu, do this:

   a.   Click on the link Search Dropdown.

   b.   On the following page, Edit Scope Display Group in the Scopes section and check Sales Web Only (the search scope you created earlier).

   c.   Click OK to save and close the page.

   d.   Note that this search scope is now listed in the display group Search Dropdown. If you want to add this search scope to the Advanced Search page as well, click that link and repeat step b.

4.   Test the new search scope. Open the top site, and note the search dropdown menu at the top right of the page; it will now contain the new search scope. Enter a text string that you know exists in any of the content of the Sales web, and then select the Sales Web Only search scope. The results will now only display content on that site.

There is more to say about search scope, but first you must understand how to add new content sources; more about that shortly.

Managing Crawls of the Site Directory

By default, all sites in a site collection will be indexed. If necessary, you can change which sites are indexed by following the steps in the Try It Out below.

Try It Out   Manage Crawls of Sites

1. Open the site to be managed.

2. Click Site Actions ⇨ Site Settings.

3. Click Search visibility in the Site Administration section.

4. Use the Allow this web to appear in search results setting to enable or disable searching of the site.

5. Click OK to save and close the page.

> In contrast to the previous version of SharePoint, this setting will only apply to the current site, regardless of whether it is a top site or a subsite.

Adding New Content Sources

When installing SharePoint, your organization will have a lot of information stored in your file servers. Some, but most likely not all, of this information will be moved into SharePoint, making it easy to search that content. What should you do with the other files? You probably don't want to delete them; after all, that information may be needed someday. An elegant solution to make this information available to the user is to add this content to SharePoint's index file. This will enable users to search for both old and new information, without requiring them to know exactly where this information is stored.

To add external information to SharePoint's index file, you create new content sources. You may recall from previous sections in this chapter that SharePoint can index almost any source and location, such as SharePoint's own database, any fileserver, MS Exchange folders, Lotus Notes databases, other web applications, and external web applications. The way to make that information searchable is to define a content source that points to that location. This will enable the index engine to crawl that content.

For example, say that you want to index a specific file share: `\\dc1\projects`. The following Try It Out shows you how to do this.

Try It Out   Add a Content Source

1. Open the Central Administration tool, and switch to the SSP instance (e.g., `SharedServices1`).

2. Click Search settings ⇨ Content sources and crawl schedules.

3. On the Manage Content Sources page, click New Content Source, and add this information:

    a. Name = `"Project Files on DC1"`

    b. In the Content Source Type section, select File Shares. This will add more options to this page.

    c.   In the Start Addresses section, enter `\\dc1\projects`. If you want to add more start addresses here to other file locations, add them one per line.

    d.   In the Crawl Settings section, select the folder and all subfolders of each start address if you want the index engine to crawl any subfolder.

    e.   In the Crawl Schedules section, click Create schedule for "Full Crawl" and "Incremental Crawl" to set the schedule for when to crawl this content source.

    f.   In the Start Full Crawl section, check Start full crawl of this content source, if you want the crawler to start indexing the content source immediately.

    g.   Click OK to save and close this page.

> **If the content source contains a large volume of information to be crawled, you must plan when to run a full crawl. One solution is to run incremental crawl only, and then manually force a full crawl when necessary, for example after a restore.**

4.   The new content source is now listed along with the others, on the Manage Content Sources page. If you did not choose to start a full crawl in step 4f above, you can do it now: use the quick menu for the new content source, and select Start Full Crawl. You can safely leave this page; the indexing will continue to run.

If you need to modify an existing content source, click on its name on the Manage Content Source page, and make whatever changes are needed. You can also delete a content source by using its quick menu. This will immediately remove all results from that content source.

> **Before you can add a Lotus Notes database as a content source, you must install a Lotus Notes client on the SharePoint server. The Gatherer will use this client to read the Notes database. Unless this client is installed, there will be no option to install Lotus Notes content sources.**

Adding New File Types

Besides the default file types indexed, you can add almost any other well-known file type. In fact, you can add your own type, if necessary, but this will require that you write some code to do it. There are two things you must do to enable the Gatherer to crawl a new file type:

❑   The file type must be listed in the File types list discussed previously.

❑   There must be an IFilter installed that can read that type of file.

The trick, of course, is to find the IFilter. The good news is that there are lots of sources on the Internet. These IFilters are not specific to the SharePoints index engine, but most will also work for the SQL Server Full-Text Indexing and other MS Search–based engines. The same type of IFilters used for SPS 2003 will also work fine with the MOSS 2007 search engine. Below is a list of the most common IFilters and at least one source. Some are free; others are commercial, but most have a low price:

Table 8.1: Common IFilters

File Type	Download Source	Price
PDF	www.adobe.com/support/ downloads/detail .jsp?ftpID=2611	Free
ZIP	www.citeknet.com	Free
RAR	www.citeknet.com	Free
HLP	www.citeknet.com	Free
CHM	www.citeknet.com	Free
MHT	www.citeknet.com	Free
CAB	www.citeknet.com	Free
EXE	www.citeknet.com	Free
DWF	http://ifiltershop.com	$200 per server
StarOffice	www.ifilter.org	Free for personal use
Inventor	http://ifiltershop.com	$299 per server
SHTML	http://ifiltershop.com	$299 per server
vCard	http://ifiltershop.com	$19 per server
OpenOffice	www.ifilter.org	Free for personal use
MindManager	www.ifiltershop.com	$299 per server
MS Project	www.ifiltershop.com	$299 per server
MS Visio	www.microsoft.com/ downloads	Free
OneNote	Install MS OneNote on the SharePoint server	
Audio/Video files: MP3, WMA, WMV, ASF	www.aimingtech.com	Free for personal use
DWG AutoCad	www.cadcompany.nl	250 Euros

This list is long, and it grows constantly. Remember that each new file type indexed will increase the CPU load and the size of the index files; be sure you really need to search files like MP3s before you add it that type, even if it is cool!

> `www.citeknet.com` **has a very nice (and free) IFilter Explorer. Use it to see all IFilters installed on the server.**

If you need to remove an IFilter, just uninstall it like any other program, using the Add/Remove Programs applet in the Control Panel.

So let's practice all this. In the following example you will add PDF as an indexed file. The download link to the IFilter is listed in the table above, and you know how to add PDF as a file type to be indexed. But in this case, and some others too, there will be one thing missing. Users will not see the familiar PDF icon next to PDF files in SharePoint's document libraries, so you must also download this icon and install it in a proper way. The following Try It Out shows how to do this.

Try It Out   Index PDF Files in MOSS

1. Download the IFilter for PDF as listed in the table above. Install the IFilter on the SharePoint server. If you are running a SharePoint farm, it must be installed on the MOSS server running the Index role!

2. Open the Central Administration tool, and switch to the SSP instance (e.g., `SharedServices1`).

3. Click Search settings ⇨ File types.

4. Click New File Type and enter **pdf**. Click OK to save and close the page. Check that PDF is now listed among the indexed file types. Also note that it does not have any icon. This is a cosmetic, but nevertheless important, problem.

5. Download the file `pdf16.tif` from the Internet; for example, from `http://sharepoint-blog.com/?p=6`. Save the `pdf16.tif` file in the following location on the SharePoint Server: `C:\Program Files\Common Files\Microsoft Shared\web server extensions\12\TEMPLATE\IMAGES`.

   > **Do not change the name — it must be** `PDF16.tif` **or you will not see the icon in every place there is a PDF file!**

6. The next step is to get SharePoint to display this icon for each PDF file. Open the following file with Notepad: `C:\Program Files\Common Files\Microsoft Shared\web server extensions\12\TEMPLATE\XML\DOCICON.XML`.

   > **Make a backup of the original** `DOCICON.XML` **file just to be on the safe side.**

    a. Add the line `<Mapping Key="pdf" Value="pdf16.tif"/>` somewhere in this file, in the section that starts with `<ByExtensions>`. The exact location is not important, but why not add it before the "png" to get it into a nice sorting order?

    b. Save and close the `DOCICON.XML` file.

    c. Open a command prompt, and run `iisreset`.

7. Open the SharePoint administrative page File types again. You should now see that the PDF file type has its well-known icon next to it! If it doesn't, you did something wrong. Everything is done; all new PDF files will now be indexed.

> **Start a full crawl for all content sources where there are PDF files, to ensure that they are indexed.**

Some Tips about Searching

The search and index functionality in MOSS has many features, as you have seen so far, and there are still more things you can do. One common request is to activate wildcard search in MOSS. This is possible, but requires coding; the details are described in the SharePoint Products and Technology Software Development Kit (SPPT SDK). There are also products that enhance the search feature, such as Cartesis 10 (www.cartesis.com), Infosys (www.infosys.com), and Ontolica (www.mondosoft.com). This last section about searching and indexing will describe how to define a specific user account that can be used by the crawler when it opens a specific content source.

You may remember from Chapter 4 that the Default Content Access Account is the user account used by default when the Gatherer crawls external information, such as a file system or an Exchange public folder. If this user account doesn't have at least Read access in these sources, it will generate an access error in the crawl log (see Figure 8-19). If you can use another account with read access granted for this particular source location the crawl process will succeed.

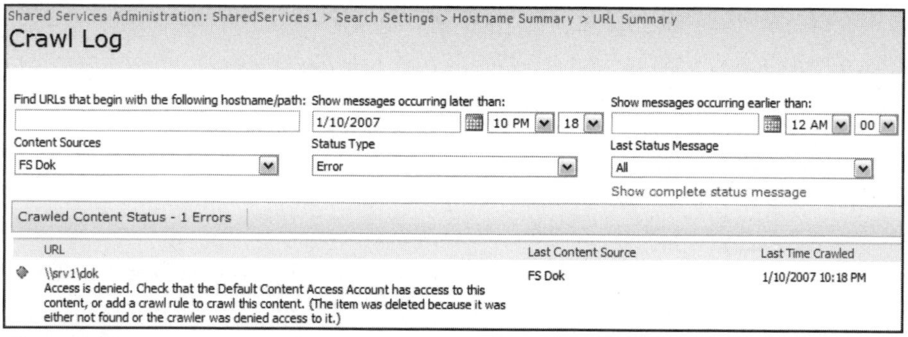

Figure 8-19

> To define the default crawler account, use the Central Administration tool ⇨ SSP ⇨ Search settings ⇨ Default content access account.

To make the content source to use a special account, you must configure Exclude and Include rules for the content index file used by the content source. Follow these steps in the Try It Out below to set up another search account when using advanced search mode.

Try It Out   Configure a Custom Search Access Account

1. Open the Central Administration tool, and switch to the SSP instance (e.g., `SharedServices1`).

2. Click Search settings ⇨ Crawl rules.

3. Click New Crawl Rule, then enter the following (see Figure 8-20):

   a. In the Path section, Enter the start address for the content source; for example, `\\dc1\projects`.

   b. Select the option Include all items in this path.

   c. Select the option Specify a different content access account. Enter the account name and its password twice. Make sure to check Do not allow Basic Authentication (see Figure 8-20).

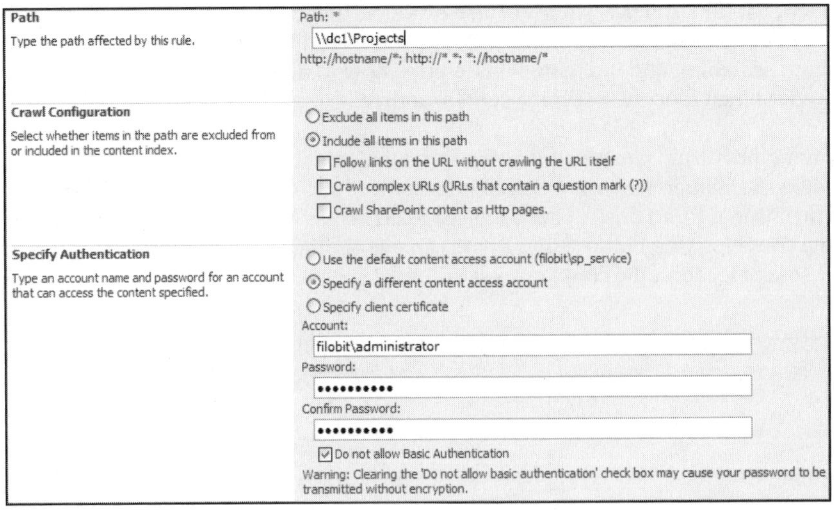

Figure 8-20

   d. Click OK to save the new rule. The new rule will be listed along the other rules.

4. Force a full update of this content source now. When ready, check the crawl logs to make sure that the content source was indexed this time.

With this knowledge about the search and indexing process, you will be able to set up the most common search scenarios, as well as solving most of the problems that arise.

More Advanced Settings for MOSS and WSS

SharePoint 2007 is full of configuration settings, more than this book can cover. You have now seen most of them described in detail, but there are some more that are valuable to understand.

Information Rights Management

This is a separate Microsoft application, also known as Rights Management Server (RMS). Its purpose is to enable users to define the permissions for an MS Office document or an Outlook e-mail in much greater detail than is normally possible. This requires that the RMS server be installed and configured in your network, but not necessarily on the SharePoint server. However, the SharePoint administrator must install the RMS client on the MOSS server in order to activate the IRM features in SharePoint.

> *Download this RMS client with Service Pack 2 from* www.microsoft.com.

When the RMS client is installed, you must configure SharePoint to enable the Information Rights Management feature, as illustrated in the following Try It Out.

Try It Out   **Configure IRM**

1.   Open the Central Administration tool, and switch to the Operations page.

2.   Click Information Rights Management.

3.   Select the RMS server to be used. Typically, you will use the option Use the default RMS server specified in Active Directory.

4.   Click OK to save and close the page.

When this is done, you can configure document libraries to enable IRM permissions, such as Prohibit Save, and Prohibit Printing of Office documents. These permission settings will still be valid even if this document is moved or copied to another location; for example, if it used as an e-mail attachment. This is an important requirement in many situations; for example, for compliance with the Sarbanes-Oxley Act and the Health Insurance Portability and Accountability Act (HIPAA).

Managing Blocked File Types

Since SharePoint will replace your file servers, at least partly, Microsoft has made it possible to prohibit users from uploading all types of files. This is done mainly to ensure that no file type that could carry a virus or Trojan horse can be stored inside SharePoint. But in some situations, this is not acceptable. For example, users may need to store EXE files in a SharePoint document library. The following Try It Out shows how to manage these blocked file types.

Try It Out **Configure Blocked File Types**

1. Open the Central Administration tool, and switch to the Operations page.

2. Click on Blocked file types.

3. On the next page, you will see a list with all the file types that are blocked. Mark the file type you want to unblock, and then press the Delete button on your keyboard.

4. If you want to block another file type, such as `.mp3` or `.avi`, simply add them anywhere in this list. Just make sure that there is only one file type per line.

5. Click OK to save and close this page.

The new settings will be active immediately. Note that if you have blocked a file type, and there are such files already stored in SharePoint, they will still be stored, but you cannot store any new files of this type.

> **Save a copy of all the default blocked file types. Place the cursor anywhere in the list, press Control+A to mark them all, and press Control+C to copy them. Then open Notepad and paste this information in it.**

Managing Diagnostic Logging

An important task for any administrator is to check the health of the system; this is definitely true also for SharePoint 2007. Using the Diagnostic Logging feature in the Central Administration tool allows the administrator to configure what types of errors are stored in the Windows 2003 Event Log, and in SharePoint's own Trace Log. Use the steps in the following Try It Out to configure diagnostic logging.

Try It Out **Configure Diagnostic Logging**

1. Open the Central Administration tool, and switch to the Operations page. Click Diagnostic logging in the Logging and Reporting section.

2. The two first sections on this page allow you to configure if the server will participate in Microsoft's Customer Experience Improvement program, and if error reports should be collected. These two settings are used by Microsoft to understand what may go wrong and help them design a better SharePoint server. If you do not mind, then enable these features.

3. The third section, Event Throttling, is about what level of severity of events you want to store in the Windows event log, and in SharePoint's trace logs, using these settings:

   a. In the Select a category menu, select the type of service or feature to be configured; for example, Backup and Restore.

   b. In the Least critical event to report to the event log menu, chose one of the severity levels: None, Error, Warning, Audit Failure, Audit Success, or Information.

    c. In the Least critical event to report to the trace log menu, chose between None, Unexpected, Monitorable, High, Medium, and Verbose.

4. The fourth section; Trace Log allows you to configure the trace log settings:

    a. In the Path field, enter the file path to the folder where these trace log files will be stored. The default is: `c:\Program Files\Common Files\Microsoft Shared\Web Server Extensions\12\Logs\`.

    b. In the Number of log files setting, define how many of these trace log files to store. When this number is reached, the oldest log files will be deleted.

    c. In the Number of minutes to use a log file setting, define how many minutes a log file will be used. When this number is exceeded, the log file is closed, and a new log file is created.

> **These trace log files will typically be many megabytes in size; you may want to reduce the number of log files to avoid filling up your disk space. You may also want to change the path for these log files to avoid storing them under** `\Program Files`**.**

Summary

In this chapter, you learned that:

❑ User Profiles is a database that contains information about users, such as Department, Phone number, and Skills.

❑ SharePoint can import user accounts from Active Directory, and you can create user profiles in SharePoint, with the user's properties.

❑ SharePoint can also import user accounts from any LDAP-compatible directory, such as Novell NDS.

❑ SharePoint can import user properties from Business Data Catalog sources to existing user profiles.

❑ It is possible to create new user profile properties, either for manual update, or to be mapped to external directory sources, such as Active Directory or LDAP sources.

❑ You can target information, such as news pages, links, documents, and Web Parts, to specific groups of users, known as audiences.

❑ Targeting works with Audience Groups, SharePoint Groups, Distribution Lists, and Security Groups.

❑ You must enable audience targeting in list and libraries before it can be used.

❑ To present a targeted view of list items and documents, you must use the Content Query Web Part.

❑ Use "Publishing links to Office client applications" to target links for the Save and Open options in MS Office.

❑ Use the Navigation option in Site Settings to create targeted navigation links, displayed in the Quick Launch bar.

❑ Use "Personal site links" to create targeted navigation links in users' My Sites.

❑ Searching is now possible also in WSS 3.0.

❑ WSS Search is not dependent on SQL Server Full-Text Indexing, as it was in WSS 2.0.

❑ WSS Search also works with the SQL Express database.

❑ To search for a file type, it must be defined in the File types list, plus a corresponding IFilter must be installed on the SharePoint server responsible for the Indexing service.

❑ MOSS Searching can index content in almost any location, such as in file servers, web servers (both internal and on the Internet), Exchange databases, Lotus Notes databases, and any external database that the SharePoint server has a BDC connection defined for.

❑ By default, MOSS's crawl schedule is not defined, that is, the content in SharePoint will not be indexed; you must configure this schedule manually.

❑ Configure new Content Sources to enable the crawler to index information stored outside SharePoint.

❑ Use Search Scopes to limit the search area; for example, to a specific content source.

❑ By default, all SharePoint sites are indexed.

❑ You can define a specific user account to be used by the crawler when indexing a specific content source.

❑ Enable IRM to achieve a higher level of security for the documents stored in document libraries.

In the next chapter, you will learn more about web content management in MOSS 2007.

Web Content Management

SharePoint 2007 is full of interesting and powerful features, as you have seen in the previous chapters. The administrator has full control over the SharePoint environment, while at the same time users have more power than ever to organize, share, and search for all types of content, such as news, documents and electronic forms. Still there is one very important feature that has only been covered partially in this book so far and that is how to manage the content itself. This chapter will discuss this matter in much greater detail and will help you understand how get the most out of SharePoint's content management features.

This chapter will cover MOSS web content management functionality. This is a very important chapter, since the features discussed here are among those most demanded by the users — and we must never forget that the reason we deploy SharePoint 2007 in the first place is to build a solution that will empower our users. This chapter will also compare the content management functionality between SharePoint 2003 and SharePoint 2007, which will help you find arguments you may need to gain approval to upgrade to the newest version of SharePoint.

Introduction to Content Management

The term *content management* (CM) is very broad, and means different things to different people, but the general meaning is a technical process that supports the management of digital information, during its life cycle. Very often when people talk about content management they mean either or both document management and web content management, and this is also what this chapter will focus on. The type of digital information that is the target for content management is anything that requires some management during its life span, that is, any information that you want to keep for a while, for example:

- ❑ **Standard files:** text files, configuration files, source code, and files created with any type of application, including non-Microsoft applications, such as desktop publishing files, and computer-aided design (CAD) files.

- ❑ **Multimedia files:** Music and audio files (e.g., MP3, WAV), image files (e.g., JPG, GIF, PNG), and video files (e.g., AVI, MPEG).

❑ **Document files:** Files created by MS Word, MS Excel, MS OneNote, MS InfoPath, and similar applications.

❑ **Web content files:** Files, or pages, displayed on a web page, typically an intranet or public web site.

One goal of content management is to make it easier for users to add, update, and delete these types of files. This in turn will make it easier for the users to organize, find, and control how these files are used, during the file's life cycle. The management process can be divided into the following steps:

1. **Create:** For example, when a new MS Word file is created.

2. **Update:** For example, when editing an MS Word file.

3. **Publish:** When a file is made available to other users.

4. **Archive:** For example, when a published file is replaced by a newer version, but you want to keep it in case it will be needed.

5. **Retire:** When the file is removed or deleted.

Exactly who will be responsible for which process step depends on the type of file content and on the organization. In small companies, the same person may be responsible for all steps, but in larger organizations it is usually different people for different steps. The roles for the content management process are usually described as:

❑ **Content Author:** The user that creates and edits the file; for example, the MS Word document.

❑ **Editor:** The user that is responsible for the content itself, for example a user who approves the content, and its looks, and possibly also localizations and translations.

❑ **Publisher:** The user who will be responsible for making this file available to other users; for example, a news item presented on an intranet.

❑ **Administrator:** The user who is responsible for managing permissions for the content; for example, permissions to the MS Word files and the folders they are stored in.

❑ **Consumer:** The user who consumes (views and possibly copies) the content.

These roles relate directly to what SharePoint groups can do, so it will be easy to implement a role-based content management process. SharePoint also supports the technical requirements necessary to implement the content management process. The rest of this chapter will describe how to handle content management in SharePoint 2007.

Why Use Content Management?

The simple answer is: to have control over the content. A more elaborate answer is that content management helps organizations to keep track of all their digital information, such as documents, files, and web content. The more people who consume this digital information, the more important content management becomes. If you are working alone, chances are that you will do fine without content management, although it can help you organize your files in better ways.

Some of the more common challenges of working with digital information without a content management system are:

❑ **No version control:** It is hard at times to be 100 percent sure that the file you are using is the latest version; to be sure, you may have to look in multiple locations to see if there are any other versions of this file.

❑ **No checkout/checkin:** When you need to update a publicly available document or web content, you will most likely copy that information to your local computer, then update its content, and then publish it again. This process cannot prevent another user, unaware of your activity, from updating the same content, so you will have a conflict about which update should be published.

❑ **No approval:** When the author is satisfied with the content, he or she will publish it directly. There is no support for demanding that another person must approve the update before it is published.

❑ **No workflows:** You cannot define a process that triggers on new or updated content. For example when a document's status is changed from Preliminary to Completed, you may want to copy this document to the intranet.

❑ **No policies:** There is no way to say what will happen with a web page or MS Word file during its lifetime. You cannot define a process that will delete a specific document after five years.

Still there are only a few organizations today that have active content management implemented, so obviously you can do without it. Or can you? You can answer this, yourself — just look at how the digital information is managed in your organization. You spend a lot of time making sure that you find the right document and the latest version. You also manually copy documents to the intranet, when necessary, and to be honest: Haven't there been times when you missed something? Of course, you need content management; we all do!

Important CMS Features

The list in the previous section about what you will miss without content management is at the same time a list of what must be included in a content management system — and you need even more. Below is a wish list of features and concepts that a good content management system should have:

❑ **Metadata:** Today, filenames and folders are the only way to describe and organize files and documents. A content management system must allow the user to add properties, also known as metadata, to files and other types of content. This metadata should also be searchable, and able to be used to sort and organize this content.

❑ **Version history:** Whenever content such as a web page or an MS Word document is updated, the previous version should be preserved. This will ensure that you can revert to a previous version, if necessary. You can also see how this content has evolved over time, and what users have updated this content.

❑ **Checkout/checkin:** It must be possible to update publicly available content, without needing to copy the content to another location. To allow a user to update content, without affecting what the consumers (the users with read access) can see, the system must create two copies of the same content: one for the consumers (the latest published version) and one for the content's author. The system must also prohibit another content author from editing the same content, to avoid creating conflicting versions; this is exactly what the *Check Out* process does. When the content author is done updating the content, this new version will now replace the public content, and this is what *Check In* does.

❑ **Approval:** Before updated content becomes public, it sometimes must be approved by a person other than the content's author. For example, when you add a news item to the intranet, your manager must approve its content before it goes public. The system must notify the approver that there is something to approve, typically by e-mail.

❑ **Workflows:** When content or its metadata is updated, you sometimes need to start an activity or a process. For example, every time a new customer is added to a customer list, the sales team should be informed. Another example is that when the metadata "In Stock" for a product list falls below a specific value; a purchase order should automatically be sent to the vendor of that product. These are typical things you can do with workflows: They can trigger a preconfigured process when something happens, such as when a new document is added, or when the document or any of its metadata is updated. A workflow can also be started manually. A typical example is when a content author wants to send an e-mail with requests for comments to her colleagues about an updated document.

❑ **Localizations:** For web content on intranet and public Internet sites, it is sometimes very important that the content can be localized, depending on the person looking at the web page (i.e., a German user should see the information in German, while a Swedish user should see it in Swedish).

❑ **Policies:** Policies define what will happen to content, such as a web page or a document, during its lifetime. For example, every time a document is printed, it can automatically have the text "Only for internal use!" added to it. Another policy example is that all actions regarding a document could be audited, such as when somebody reads, copies, or modifies it. A third policy example is that after a specific time something happens to the content, such as archiving, deleting, or changing metadata.

If your system has support for just some of these features, then it will help your organization to manage your content better. And MS Office SharePoint Server 2007 has support for all of these, and more. For example, to make it easier for an editor or a content author to discover modified or new content pages, news items, or any type of list content, SharePoint lets a user define alerts. This will instruct SharePoint to send an e-mail to the user whenever the content is added, deleted, or modified. Following is an example of how to set up an alert for all changes to the News items list; the result is that any time there is a change to this list, an e-mail is sent to this user.

Try It Out   Create an Alert for News Items

1. Log on as a user with at least permissions to read news items (for example, as a member of the SharePoint group *<Site_Name>* `Visitors`).

2. Open the News tab on the intranet portal.

3. Click View All Site Content in the Quick Launch bar, then click Pages. This is the list that stores all news items by default.

4. Click Actions ➪ Alert Me to open the configuration page for the alert.

   a. **Alert Title**: News Items.

   b. **Send Alerts To**: Enter the recipient's name. By default the user's name will be listed. It is also possible to add more names or distribution groups here.

c. **Change Type**: Select the type of change that will trigger this alert.

d. **Send Alerts for These Changes:** This is an optional filter; for example, you could filter the alerts to trigger only when somebody else is modifying a news item you created.

e. **When to Send Alerts**: Select how often SharePoint will look for these changes: Immediately, Daily, or Weekly. Note that "Immediately" means every five minutes by default. This value can be set with the STSADM tool.

f. Click OK to save and close this alert.

The Alert feature is available in all lists and libraries in SharePoint. You can use it on complete lists, individual documents, or list items. It is a great feature, so make sure to take advantage of it.

Web Content Management

The web content management features for SharePoint Portal Server 2003 were close to nonexistent; it had support for approval, but that's about it. This required content editors for the intranet, extranet, or public Internet site to edit, test, and get the approval of new content on a server other than the production SPS 2003 server. This was clearly not the ideal way to work with web-based content for an organization with high standards. This lack of content management features in SPS 2003 was at the same time a great business opportunity for other vendors, who developed smart add-on products that enhanced the content management features of SPS. Of course, Microsoft was aware of this shortcoming in SPS 2003, and one of their suggested solutions to this was that customers should use their product MS Content Management Server (MS CMS), which had all the standard content management features asked for. There was, to some extent, an integration of the two (for example, content in SPS 2003 could be presented to the MS CSM web site), but they still worked in very different ways, and it was difficult for the IT department to manage both of these products.

With the release of MS Office SharePoint Server 2007, or MOSS, Microsoft has actually integrated the MS CMS product into MOSS, plus added a lot of new features, such as support for workflows. The result is a very advanced but easy-to-use web content management system. Note that this is only true for MOSS 2007. If you choose to go with WSS 3.0 alone, you will not get these content management features. The web content management features are integrated in some (but not all) of the site templates that MOSS comes with; these types of web pages are known as *Publishing Pages*.

Web Content Management in MOSS 2007

As described earlier in this chapter, managing a web site for an intranet or a public Internet site requires more than managing a team web site; the difference is the type and the number of consumers (or audience). If you make a simple mistake on your team site where everyone knows you, then it is embarrassing at most, but if you make a mistake that the world can see, it may be a disaster. So, the need for control is higher for a public web site, including intranet and extranet sites, and this is exactly what you get with MOSS 2007.

Let's see how a web page with support for web content management looks in MOSS 2007. Say that you have created a site based on the MOSS site template Collaboration Portal (which is the typical site template for an intranet, as described in Chapter 6). If you click Site Actions ⇨ Edit Page, you will see something similar to Figure 9-1.

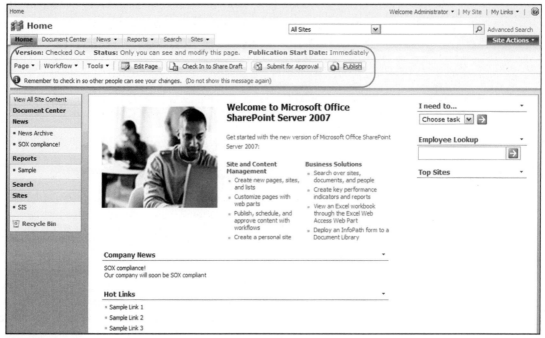

Figure 9-1

A lot of things happened when switching this page to edit mode. Let's analyze it in more detail. Notice the toolbar at the top of this web page; this is typical for a publishing web page with web content management features. At the top of the toolbar appears "Version: Checked Out. Status: Only you can see and modify this page. Publication Start Date: Immediately." In other words, just because you're starting to edit this web page, it was automatically checked out to you, and it is also clear that no one other than you can see the modifications you will make now. It is also clear from this instruction that there is no scheduled publication date, so as soon as this web page is published, its modified content will be immediately visible to all consumers (users).

Depending on the permission you have, you may be able to publish the modified page directly. Since SharePoint 2007 is security-trimmed (only actions you are allowed to make are visible), you can look for the Publish button in the toolbar; if you can see it, then you are allowed to publish your own modifications. In Figure 9-1 this button is visible, so the current user obviously has the necessary permission to publish content. If not, you have two options: Either check it in or submit it for approval. So, the three buttons available to save the modified web page are:

❑ **Publish:** Click this button to publish the modified page.

❑ **Check in to Share Draft:** Click this button if you want to check in the page and possibly give other web authors the opportunity to continue editing the page.

❑ **Submit for Approval:** Click this button if you are done editing this page and you want another user, for example your manager, to approve the new content and make it public.

There are also several menus, with a lot of options that are described later in this chapter. But where is the web page stored? And is the information shown here just one web page? The answer is no! The content of the page (the text, images and Web Parts) is stored in something called a page file. Look at the URL for this page to see the name of this page file; for example, `http://srv1/pages/default.aspx` says that this page file is named "default.aspx", and it is stored in something called "pages." The other file is describing the "chrome lists" for this page (the layout and colors for the Quick Launch bar at the left of this page, including the menus, links and the logotype at the top, which are stored in a separate Master Page file that you will learn more about in Chapter 13).

To see exactly where this `Default.aspx` page is stored, first exit editing mode. If you did not make any modifications, you can discard the checkout information that was automatically generated when you started editing this page.

1. Click the Page menu and then Discard this Check Out. The content management system will now ask you "Do you want to discard this checked-out version?" Click Yes. The web page should now look like it did before.

2. Click the link View All Site Content at the top of the Quick Launch bar; this will display all the lists for this particular publishing site. Note that there is a document library named "Pages," which corresponds to the URL for this page.

3. Click on the name Pages to show all the files in this library. You should now see the `Default.aspx` file listed (see Figure 9-2). Note that the column shows if this page is approved (i.e., published) or not, who made the last modification, if it is checked out, if it has scheduled publishing start and stop dates, and what type of page layout it is built on.

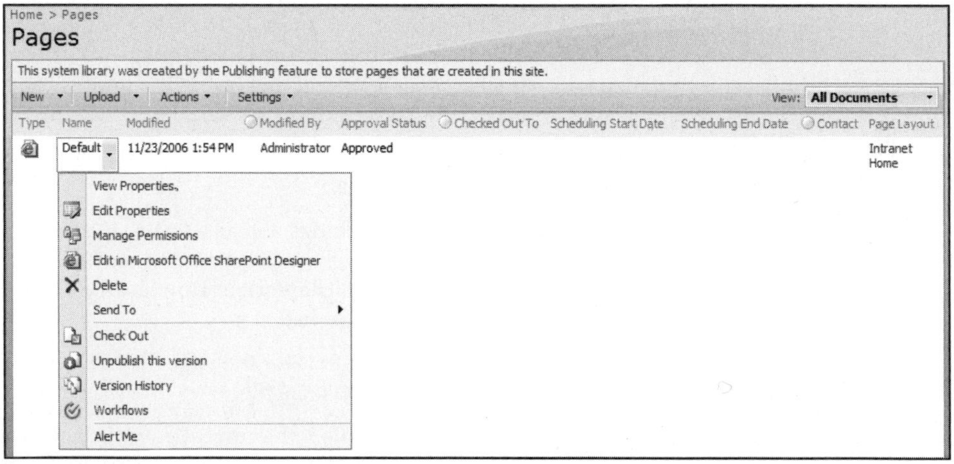

Figure 9-2

If you open the quick menu for this file (click to the immediate right of the filename), you will see a lot of options. Note that some of these will only show up under specific conditions; for example, the option to unpublish a version is only visible when the current page file is published.

❑ **View Properties:** Display all the properties for the web page, including any page images and content, but not Web Parts. You can also see what version it is, when it was initially created, and by whom, and if it is targeted for a specific audience. This property page also lists a number of actions you can take on the web page; for example to edit or delete it, manage its permissions, check its version history, create an alert for this web page, approve any pending modification, and initiate a workflow.

❑ **Edit Properties:** This option is similar to the View Properties option, except that it will allow you to edit parts of the content for the web page, and all its metadata. When you select this option, you must first accept the option to check out the page. Note that there is only a limited set of actions available, such as delete the page, check the spelling, or click OK to save any modification (or click Cancel). Whether you click OK or Cancel, this page will still be checked out, and you must do a checkin, and then click Approve to make it public again.

> If you want to leave editing mode without saving anything, click Cancel, and then select Discard Check Out from the page file's quick menu.

❑ **Manage Permissions:** This option allows you to configure a specific permission for the page file. By default, it will follow the usual way permission inheritance works in SharePoint 2007; that is, this file inherits the permission set on its library, which in turn inherits from the web site. To actually break the inheritance, click Actions ➪ Edit Permissions, and make whatever changes to the permission settings necessary.

❑ **Edit in Microsoft Office SharePoint Designer:** This will allow you to edit the actual page layout, not the content in itself. When selecting this option, you must again accept the option to check out the page file. When SharePoint Designer then starts, it will inform you that you can choose between Edit in Browser, Edit Page Layout, or Cancel. If you select Edit in Browser, then SharePoint Designer will still run, and you scan edit the page in a web browser. If you instead select Edit Page Layout, you will actually open the underlying layout file for this page — and that file will also require you to do a checkout before editing (or select No if you just want to see the content of the Master Page).

❑ **Delete:** Choose this option to delete this web page file.

❑ **Send To:** This options allows you to do one of these things: e-mail a link to this page file; Create Document Workspace, which will create a separate web site, and make a copy of the page file in that site (see more about this feature in the end of this chapter); or Download a Copy. The administrator can also create more links to this Send To list.

❑ **Check Out:** (or Check In, depending on the current status for the page file). This is automatically performed when you select the option to edit the page file.

❑ **Publish a Major Version:** This options is only available if the current page file is in draft mode. Use this option to make it a major version (i.e., going from the draft 7.1 to 8.0), but remember that this page must be approved before it gets published.

❑ **Unpublish this version:** This option is only available when the page file is published. Choose this option if you want to unpublish the current version of this page file. Since this will affect what all users are seeing, a dialog box shows up and asks "Are you sure you want to unpublish this version of the document?" Click OK if you do. The effect is that the page file is converted to a draft, and the last published page is what users will see. For example, if the current published version of the page file is 8.0, and you choose to unpublish it, then it is converted to draft version 7.1, and the version that all users will see is 7.0, since it was the last published version. This type of action can be a real lifesaver if a draft gets approved and published by mistake, and you quickly want to go back to the draft version and continue to modify it.

❑ **Version History:** This option will show a list of all the versions of the page file. It shows when these versions were saved, and by whom, including their size. It will also show what has been modified; for example, page images and page content, (except Web Part content). Each listed version also has a menu (click to the right of the version date) that lists three actions: View (open the page in a web browser), Restore (make this the current major version — for example, if the current version is 8.0 and you select Restore for version 6.0, then 6.0 becomes version 9.0, and 8.0 becomes an old version). The third action listed on the menu is Delete, which removes the version (or really moves it to the Recycle Bin for the site).

❑ **Workflows:** Allows you to start any workflow associated with the document library. By default, there are no workflows for the Pages library, but you could create one with SharePoint Designer; see more about this in Chapter 13.

❑ **Alert me:** Use this option to create a subscription for the page file; for example, if the file is modified by another content author, then SharePoint will send an e-mail to you. See more about this feature earlier in this chapter.

To summarize, the web page displayed on this intranet site is a Publishing Page file named `Default.aspx`, which is stored in a document library named Pages. The layout of the content is defined in a page layout file, and the top menus and Quick Launch bar around the content are defined in a Master Page file. If you have the proper permissions, you can check out the content page file, and modify it. To make the updated version visible to others, you must first publish a major version of that page file and then approve it. There are a lot of actions you can perform on the page file, such as displaying its properties, viewing its version history, and starting workflows. In other words, there are one or two things you need to know before building your intranet, but it is not rocket science.

Editing Web Page Content

The next question is how do you modify the actual page content? Again let's take the home page of the Collaboration Portal intranet site as an example. Open that home page, then click Site Actions ➪ Edit Page to switch the page to edit mode (see Figure 9-1). By default, this page layout has two page content parts and five Web Part zones:

❑ **Page Image:** This part allows you to display an image. The position is defined by the layout file for this page.

❑ **Page Content:** This part allows you to enter HTML formatted text, including pictures and tables. Its position and layout are also defined by the layout file for this page.

❑ **Web Part Zones:** These are the Right Zone, Top Zone, Middle Right Zone, Middle Left Zone and Bottom Zone. Add any type of Web Part to any of these zones. Their position is defined by the layout file for this page.

Later in this chapter you will learn how to edit the layout file, but for now let's see how its content can be modified. To start with, you want to change the image, but before you can do that you should upload some images to the image library of this site, then you can change the image on this home page:

Modify the Page Image Control

1.   All images that will be displayed on any SharePoint web page must reside in a location that all users can read, regardless of where they are located. The smartest place to store them is in an image library in SharePoint itself. By default, you have two image libraries on the Home site of the intranet portal, but you can also create new image libraries when needed. To add one or more image files to the library named Images, do this:

> **a.**   Open the Home page for the intranet, then click View All Site Content. Note that it does not matter if your home page is in edit mode!
>
> **b.**   Click Images. By default, you will only find one single image in a newly installed MOSS server, with the name NewsArticleImage.
>
> **c.**   To upload some more image files to this library, click Upload, and then either click Browse, to upload a single image, or click Upload Multiple Files to display an Explorer view of your file system. Choose whichever method you want, select at least one image file, then click OK, and then OK again, to upload it.
>
> **d.**   The new image file is now copied to the library. However, this is configured to do automatic checkout, so before you can use the image file, you must click Check In (see Figure 9-3).

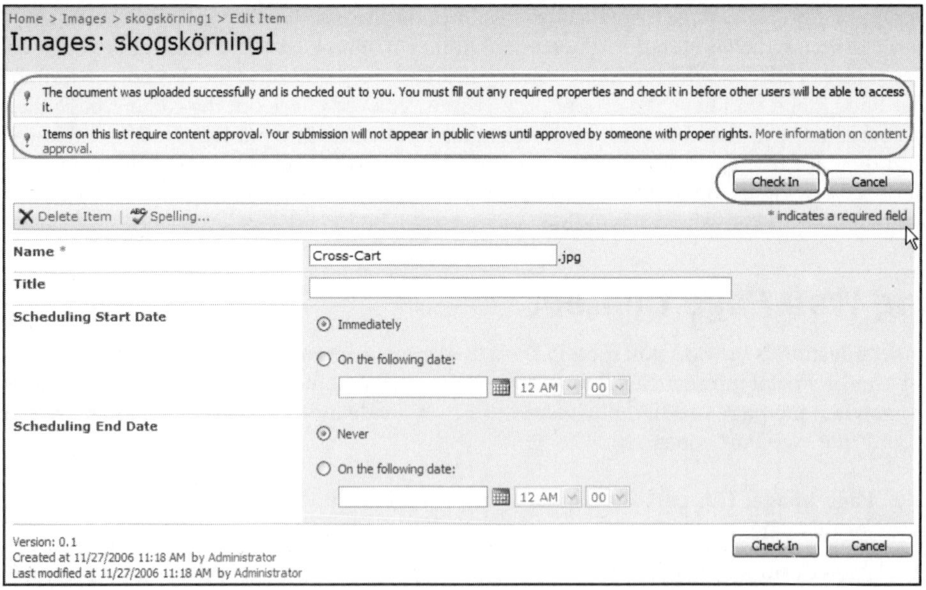

Figure 9-3

e. Next, you must approve it by opening the quick menu for the new file and selecting Publish a Major Version, then click OK.

f. Finally use the quick menu again, select Approve/reject, select Approved, then click OK. Yes, I agree — it was a lot of steps, but this is the price you have to pay for the control that content management gives you. Okay, let's go on. Now, you should see the new image next to the default image file.

2. Click on the Home page again. The page file is still checked out (i.e., you can see the content management buttons and links). Click Edit Page to switch to edit mode.

3. Click the Edit Picture control. This will open a new window where you configure what image to display and its settings (see Figure 9-4).

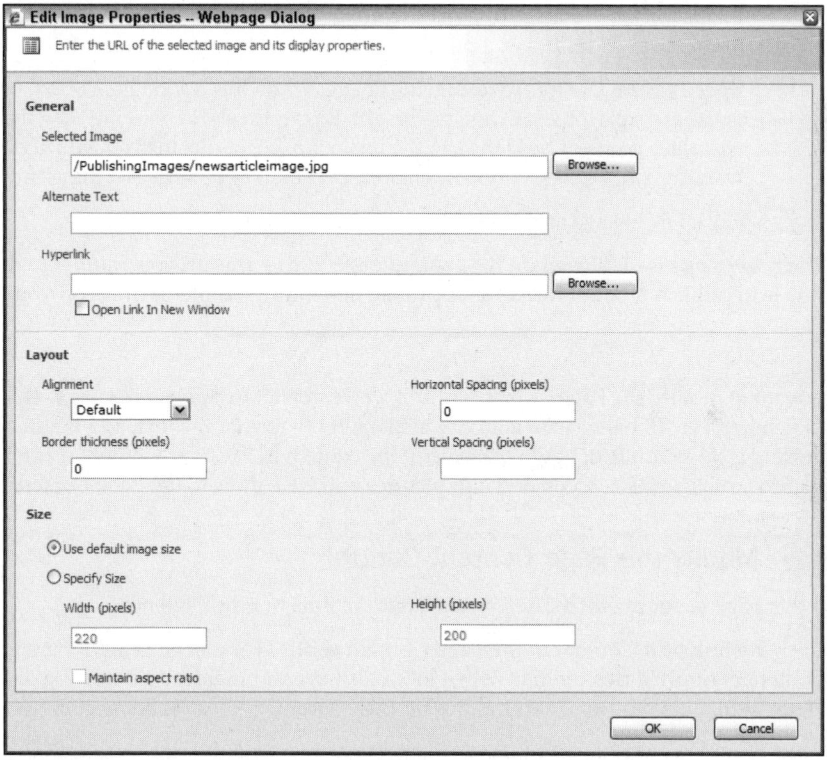

Figure 9-4

a. Selected Image: (Mandatory) If you know the URL of to the image to be displayed, enter it in the field, or better yet click the Browse button to open the image libraries for the current site and for the site collection, and select the image to be displayed, then click OK.

b. Alternate text: (Optional) This is text that will be displayed if you hover a mouse over the image.

    c.   **Hyperlink:** (Optional) Use this field to add an URL link to the image; if a user clicks the image, this link will open. It could be used to open another site or a larger picture. Check Open Link In New Window to open the URL link in a separate window.

    d.   **Alignment:** This setting is not used for images in this page content.

    e.   **Horizontal Spacing:** Set the space in pixels before the image.

    f.   **Border thickness:** Set the border thickness size in pixels; 0 is no border.

    g.   **Vertical Spacing:** Set the space in pixels above the image.

    h.   **Use default image size:** This will display the image in its true size. Note that large pictures may cause the page to look bad, so make sure that the size is okay before accepting this option. Below in the fields Width and Height, you can see the actual size in pixels for the image. A tip is to use image sizes less than 400 to make sure that the rest of this page is visible without the need to scroll the page horizontally.

    i.   **Specify Size:** Use this to rescale the image. When this option is selected, you can enter any value in pixels for width and the height. Be careful about entering both these values manually, since it is very hard to keep the image's aspect ratio; instead, you should set either the width or height, then check Maintain aspect ratio to be sure that the picture looks good.

    j.   Click OK to save and close this window.

4.   The new image is displayed on the content page. If this was all you wanted to do, then the next step is to publish it or submit it for approval, depending on the permission you have.

If you also want to modify the Page Content control, you can wait to publish the page. This Page Content control is a rich-text HTML editor with a lot of functionality to format the text, add tables and pictures, and more. Following is an example of how you can edit the content in the Page Content control add new HTML tables to structure the content, and add pictures and URL links to the Page Content control.

Try It Out   **Modify the Page Content Control**

1.   If this page is not in edit mode yet, click Site Actions ➪ Edit Page now.

2.   Click the link Edit Content in the Page Content control (or just click anywhere inside the Page Content control); a rich toolbar with a lot of buttons and menus will now be displayed (see Figure 9-5). Now you can start modifying this content. Below are some common examples:

Figure 9-5

3. To modify the text, change its format and color:

    a. Place the cursor where you want to start, and type the new text, just as with any standard text editor. For example, change the headline from Welcome to Microsoft Office SharePoint Server 2007 to Welcome to MOSS 2007.

    b. Select the headline Welcome to MOSS 2007, then open the menu Styles and select ArticleTitle. This will format the selected text according to a style defined in a Cascading Style Sheet (CSS) file.

    c. Select any other text, for example the complete sentence beginning with "Get started with," and select the text color icon (an "A" with a color bar under), then select another color for this sentence and click OK.

4. If you look closely at the content in this Page Content control, you can see that there are several tables, each with one or more columns and rows. This is a typical technique used when building HTML-formatted text on a web page to get control over where the content will be displayed. In each table cell you can add text, images, or any type of content supported by the control. For example, say that you want to add a second row to the top cell where the headline is. This is how you would do it:

    a. Place the cursor inside the top cell. A black arrow will be displayed in the top right of this cell. Click on it to open a menu, then select Insert Row Below.

    b. In the new cell, enter the text **Microsoft Web Site**, then mark the text and click the link icon on the toolbar (a globe with some links) to open a new dialog box. In the field Selected URL enter **http://www.microsoft.com**. Then check Open Link In New Window, and enter the tooltip **This is Microsoft's Home Page**. Then click OK to save and close this dialog box.

    c. Hover the mouse over the new text. Note that its tooltip says "This is Microsoft's Home Page" and that the text is underlined, indicating it is an URL link.

> **If you prefer to edit the HTML source directly, select the toolbar icon with a "<>" and a little pen.**

5. To add a picture to the text content, create an empty third row in the top table, just like you did in step 4 above:

    a. Place the cursor in the new cell.

    b. Click the image icon on the toolbar, (a mountain and a sun), and a new dialog box is displayed. Enter the URL to the picture, or click browse to open the image libraries discussed earlier when modifying the Image Page control, and select a picture — for example, the NewsArticleImage — and click OK.

    c. The same type of dialog window as shown in Figure 9-4 will now be displayed. This time, just change the size of the image so that it will not take too much space; select the option Specify Size, set Width to 150, and click OK.

6. To publish all these modifications, click Publish in the content management toolbar. The new home page will look something like Figure 9-6 (depending on what images and modifications you have added).

Figure 9-6

This content page also contains a lot of Web Part zones, and some of them already contain one or more Web Parts. You manage them in the same way you manage Web Parts in any site; there is no specific functionality connected to these Web Parts being placed on a Publishing Page with content management features. Web Parts in general will be covered in Chapter 12, but since the Collaboration Portal site template contains some Web Parts by default, they will be discussed here also. Look at the top of the Home page. It lists three Web Parts, all stored in the Web Part zone named Right Zone:

❑   **I need to:** A Web Part that lists frequently used actions, such as creating news, creating a site, and opening a popular document library. By default this Web Part will only have one action listed: set up MySite.

❑   **Employee Lookup:** Enter an employee name, and SharePoint will search for this user.

❑   **Top Site:** This will list all web sites defined as a "Top Site." Typically, these are commonly used web sites.

So, how do you configure them? To start with, Employee Lookup does not need any configuration. It is just a link to the search site and its People search page. But you must configure the other two Web Parts. The content in these two Web Parts is populated by using the Sites web site. Follow these steps to add a new action to the "I need to" Web Part that will open the Image library and to make the IT web site a Top Site, as listed in this Web Part here.

Try It Out   Modify the Intranet Portal's Web Parts

1.   Log on as a user with administrative permissions to the intranet site (for example, as the administrator).

2.   Open the Sites tab (which is a subsite to the Home site).

3. Click Add Link to Site (in the upper-right corner of the page). This will open a web page where you normally add a link to a web site. This time, you will create a link to an action to be listed in the "I need to" Web Part. Enter the following values (see Figure 9-7).

    a. **Title:** Enter the text for the action you want listed in the "I need to" Web Part (for example, "Open the Image Library").

    b. **Type the Web address:** Enter the URL address (for example, `http://srv1/PublishingImages`). (Note that you do not need to add any description to this URL link; the title above will be enough.)

    c. Check the Top Tasks option.

    d. Click OK.

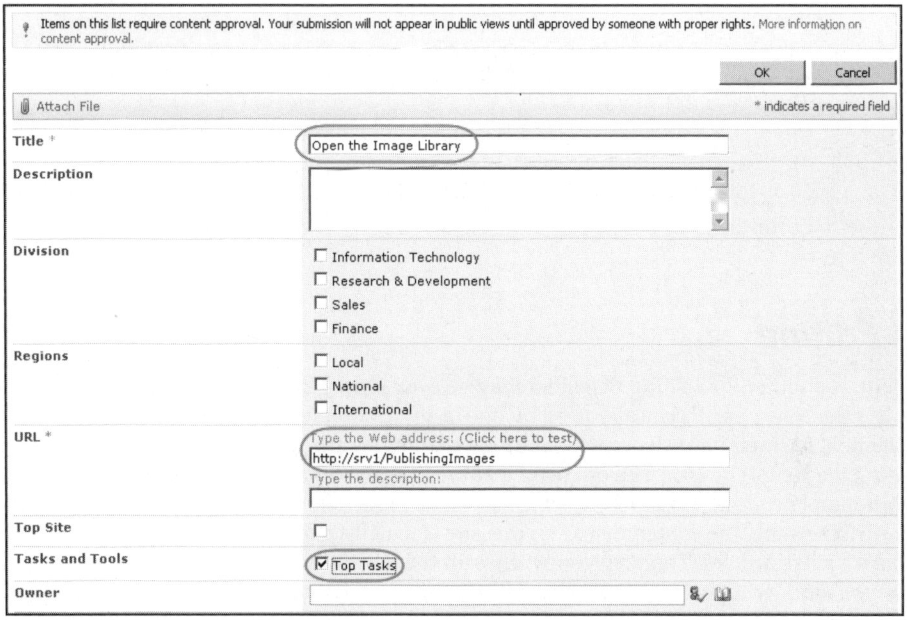

⚡ Items on this list require content approval. Your submission will not appear in public views until approved by someone with proper rights. More information on content approval.	

                                                                         OK   Cancel

🖉 Attach File   * indicates a required field

- **Title** * : Open the Image Library
- **Description:**
- **Division:**
  - ☐ Information Technology
  - ☐ Research & Development
  - ☐ Sales
  - ☐ Finance
- **Regions:**
  - ☐ Local
  - ☐ National
  - ☐ International
- **URL** * : Type the Web address: (Click here to test) — `http://srv1/PublishingImages` — Type the description:
- **Top Site:** ☐
- **Tasks and Tools:** ☑ Top Tasks
- **Owner:**

Figure 9-7

4. Note that this link is not yet active, due to the fact that the list where these links are stored requires approval. The next step is therefore to approve the new link:

    a. On the Sites page, click View All Site Content.

    b. Under the section Lists, click Sites.

    c. Locate the new link Open the Image Library, and open its quick menu (click to the right of its name). Then select Approve/reject.

    d. Select the option Approve; type a comment if needed, and then click OK.

5. The link is now active. Click Home to see if it works. Open the menu for the "I need to" Web Part, and select Open the Image Library, then click the green arrow to the right. The library will now be displayed; if not, you probably entered the wrong URL link.

The next example shows how to make a link to a web site named IT, which is listed as Top Site, and as result have it listed on the Top Site Web Part on the intranet Home page. This is also done using the Sites page.

Try It Out   Define a Top Site

1. Open the Sites page, then click View All Site Content.

2. Click Sites in the Lists section. All existing site links are now listed.

3. Locate the site IT. Open its quick menu, and select Edit Item.

4. At the bottom of this web page, check Top Site and click OK.

5. Again, this modification must be approved before everyone can see this top site. Use the quick menu again, and select Approve/reject, then select the option Approve and click OK.

6. Test that it works: Click Home to open the intranet start page; verify that the link IT now is listed as a Top Site head. Click on IT and that site will open.

A tip is to be restrictive with the number of sites defined as Top Sites. One way to do this is to use permission settings for these links; if a user is not allowed to view (i.e., read) a link, then it will not show up as a Top Site.

News Editing

Let's look at another Publishing Page that may be even more frequently updated than the intranet home page. It is the News page, typically used by one or more content authors to add news items about their organization, partners, and customers. The News page is really a site, and you can either create it manually using the News site template or create it automatically when creating a site collection using the Collaboration Portal site template (in which case, the News site will be located directly under the intranet Home site). The content listed on this site is usually page files based on a specific layout file, suitable for news articles. The way you work with the news site and its news articles is almost identical to how you work with the Home page and its content; the main difference is the layout files used.

Adding News Articles

But there is one important difference: When updating the Home page on the intranet portal, you usually modify its actual page. But to add news you create one new page for each news item. It is really very simple; just click Site Actions ⇨ Create Page, enter a title and a name for the page file, then select any of the page layouts defined as Article Page. Enter the content for the news, according to the article layout you selected; for an example, see Figure 9-8, which shows the Article page with the body only.

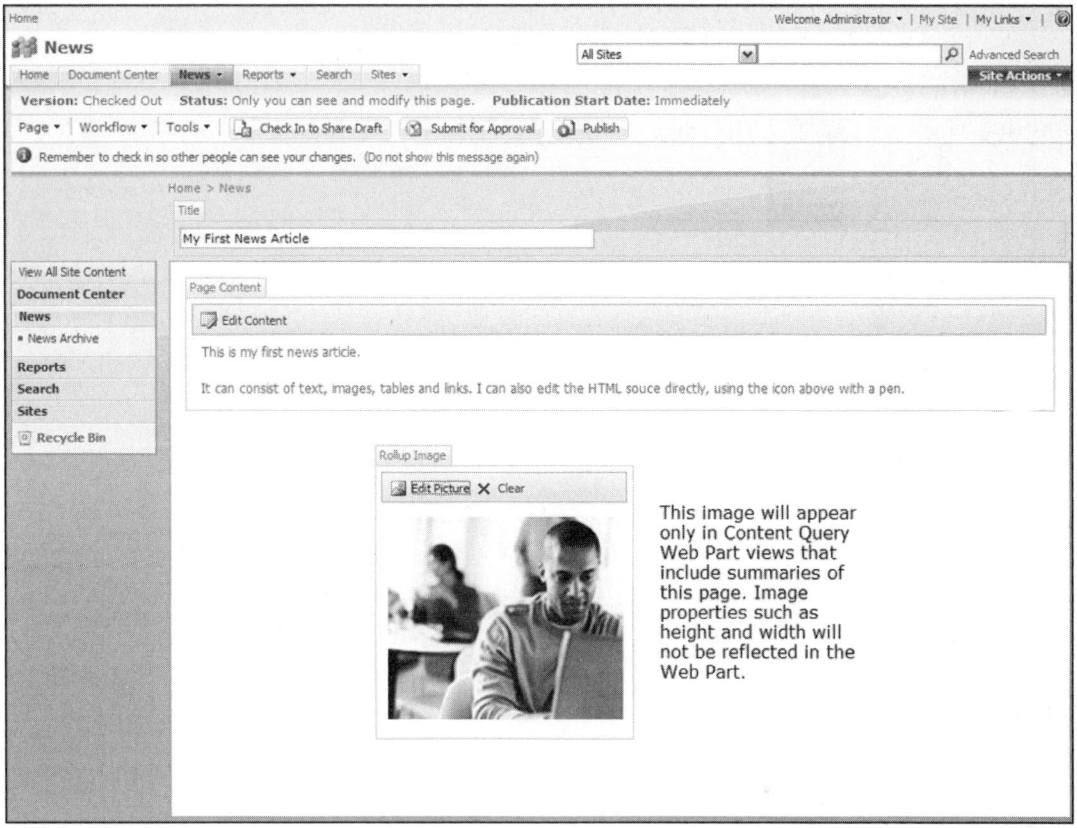

Figure 9-8

As you probably recognize by now, this is a Publishing Page. It is based on the content management features that come with MOSS 2007. To enter the content, do exactly what you did for the intranet Home page described earlier: Click Edit Content and Edit Picture. Then click Publish or Submit for Approval, depending on the permission you have. When published, the news article is displayed in all its splendor. The title of the new page is also listed in the Quick Launch bar, under the News section, and if you hover the mouse over the News navigation tab at the top of the page, the title will be listed there, as well.

So adding news articles is not hard, but what if you want to change how they are presented on the News page? For example, look at the Figure 9-9; it shows three news articles, and two of them have a picture included in the article. The default layout for this News site page is to display the latest news with a picture, title, and description; under that is a list of the 15 of the latest news articles. Switch to edit mode for this News site page by clicking Site Actions ⇨ Edit Page, and you will see that the content on this page is split up into several Web Parts, in particular Recent News and News Roll Up, which both are based on the Content Query Web Part (see Figure 9-10).

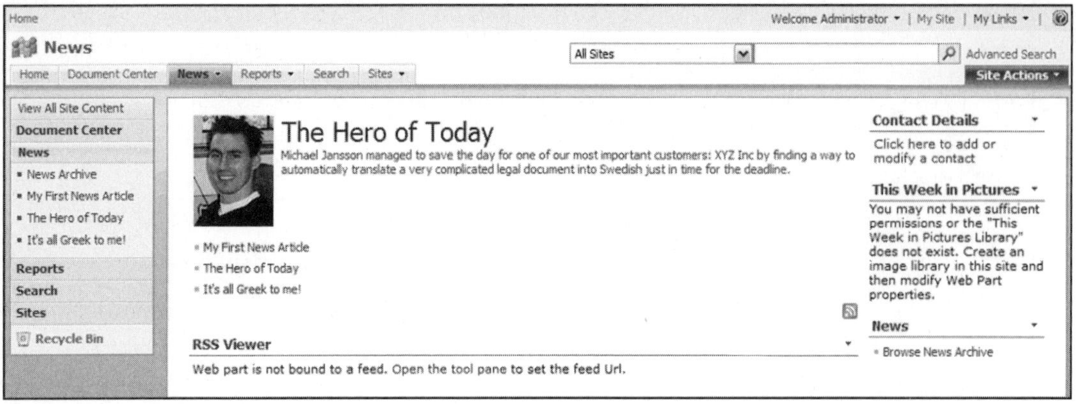

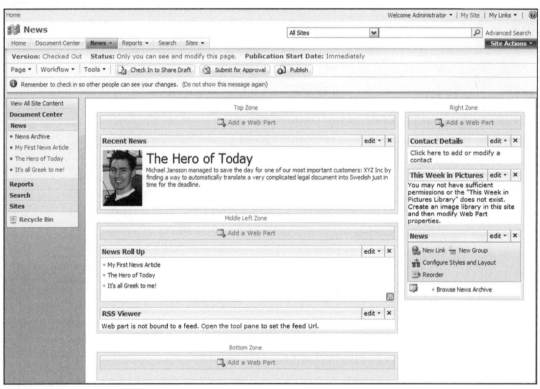

Figure 9-9

Figure 9-10

The images in a news article are used in a special way. For example, the picture displayed on the Recent News Web Part in Figure 9-10 is the rollup image, defined on this news page. Now click the headline, or the picture, and the complete news article is displayed; the picture that is now displayed is the page image. In other words, the content added to a news article is used in the following way (note that some article layouts only use some of these content controls):

❑   **Page Image:** This picture will be displayed when the complete news article is opened.

❑   **Image Caption:** This text is only displayed together with the Page Image, that is, when the complete news article is opened.

❑   **Article Date:** This date is displayed at the top of the complete news article.

❑   **Byline:** This text is displayed at the top-right position of the complete news article.

❑   **Page Content:** This content (text, images, tables and links) is visible only when opening the complete news article.

❑   **Rollup Image:** This picture is visible only when the news item is presented in the Recent News Web Part.

All news articles are stored as page files in a document library named Pages; to display these page files you must open the News site, then click View All Site Content, and then click on Pages in the Document Libraries section. Just like the page files used for the intranet Home site, all these page files are by default under the control of the content management system in SharePoint 2007. You can check out, approve, undelete, view version history, and perform other actions on any of these news page files. To edit an existing news page, use either of these methods:

❑   Open the full news article, then click Site Actions Í Edit Page. The news article is automatically checked out, and you can start editing its content. When done, click Publish to make the new content publically available.

❑   Open the Page library, use the quick menu for the Publishing Page, then select Edit Properties (not Edit with SharePoint Designer, since that will allow you to edit the layout page instead of its content). When done editing, save the page file, then use the quick menu, and select Check-in, then use the quick menu again, and select Approve/reject this time.

Working with Images in MOSS

Do you start to see a pattern regarding how page files are used in MOSS? This is no coincidence, since all document library content is managed in the same way. This pattern is also valid for image libraries, except for the way that image libraries are populated. Since images are often used in news articles and on the Home page of the intranet, you should plan how to make these images available to the content authors. Since each tab on the intranet is a site (Home, News, Document Center, and so on), each of them may contain any number of image libraries. By default, MOSS will create these image libraries when you create a site collection using the Collaboration Portal site template. The purpose of these libraries is to store pictures to be used in Publishing Pages, such as news articles and files.

❑   **Home:** Contains two image libraries — Images, and Site Collection Images.

❑   **News:** Contains one image library — Images (it also contains another image library, for the general storage of pictures).

❑   **Reports:** Contains one image library — Images.

❑   **Sites:** Contains one image library — Images.

The exceptions are the Search and Document Center sites, and the reason is that they are not built upon the Publishing Page site template; in other words, they do not support the content management even though they are built by the MOSS site template. Look at the list above. Notice that each of these sites has one Images library that is supposed to store images to be used locally on that particular site. However, the Home page also contains a library named Site Collection Images. You can use that library to store pictures that you want to be available in any page supporting the content management system (for example, the exact list of sites above).

Although it is possible to add a picture to these image libraries just when you need them, it is much smarter to add all the images you will use before creating news articles and other page files. Just like the document libraries storing pages files, all image libraries are also configured to require checkin and approval before they are visible to everyone — even for pictures included in news articles. The working order for adding content to the intranet page is described in the Try It Out below.

Try It Out   The Working Order for a Publishing Page's Content

1. Locate all the images that the content authors will need when updating a Publishing Page, and news articles.

2. If these images will only be used for news articles, add them to the Image library on the News site:

   a. Open the News page.

   b. Click View All Site Content.

   c. Click Images in the Document Libraries section.

   d. Click Upload. Either choose Browse and add a single image file or click Upload Multiple Files and add one or more files from any file folder (but only one folder at a time).

3. If you instead want to use these images in more than one location, add them to the Site Collection Images library. This library is available on any Publishing Page:

   a. Open the Home page.

   b. Click View All Site Content.

   c. Click Site Collection Images in the Document Libraries section.

   d. Click Upload. Either choose Browse and add a single image file or click Upload Multiple Files and add one or more files from any file folder (but only one folder at a time).

4. Notice that all uploaded images are listed as Draft in the Approval status column. If you look closely at the icon for these image files, you can see that each of them has a green arrow pointing down to the right. This is SharePoint's way of indicating that a file is checked out, that is, in draft mode. Now you must check in one each of these files, like this:

   a. Open the file's quick menu, and select Check-in, then select the option Major version (Publish). This will also list the new version number this file will get. You can add a comment here, if you wish. Click OK.

   b. The file is now waiting to be approved, that is, the column Approval Status now shows Pending. Next, open the file's quick menu again, and select Approve/reject. Then set the option Approved (if you do), and click OK. This image file is now ready to be used.

5. Repeat steps 4a and 4b for each image file uploaded to publish all of them.

6. Create or edit the page file that will include any of these image files, then use the `Page Image` or the `Rollup Image` control to select an image, or edit the `Page Content` control and use its Image button in the toolbar. All of these controls will allow the content author to select an image from these image libraries.

> If you need to add a large number of image files, you can change the Check-out and Approval requirements for the Image library before uploading the files. When done, you should restore the default settings.

Creating News Layouts

The previous discussion has been all about predefined layout files for news articles. They are fine for many types of articles, but sometimes you need to create a new layout. This section tells you more about how to do that. The following table lists the news article layout files that come with MOSS 2007 by default.

Table 9.1: News Article Layout Files

Filename	Page Layout	Description
`PageFromDocLayout.aspx`	"Article page with body only"	Contains only an `Page Content` control.
`ArticleLeft.aspx`	"Article page with image on left"	Contains one `Page Image` and one `Image Caption` control to the left, and a `Page Content` control to the right, plus an article date control, a byline control, and a `Rollup Image` control.
`ArticleRight.aspx`	"Article page with image on right"	Same controls as above, except that the `Page Image` and `Image Caption` controls are located on the right side of the page
`ArticleLinks.aspx`	"Article page with image on left"	Contains a `Page Content` control, and a `Summary Links` control, plus an article date control, a byline control, and a `Rollup Image` control

Remember that even page layout files without a `Page Image` control, such as the `PageFromDocLayout.aspx`, can contain any number of images, since they can be added inside the `Page Content` control (see Figure 9-11).

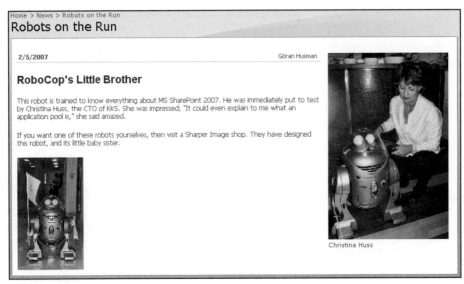

Home > News > Robots on the Run
Robots on the Run

2/5/2007   Göran Husman

RoboCop's Little Brother

This robot is trained to know everything about MS SharePoint 2007. He was immediately put to test by Christina Huss, the CTO of KKS. She was impressed; "It could even explain to me what an application pool is," she said amazed.

If you want one of these robots yourselves, then visit a Sharper Image shop. They have designed this robot, and its little baby sister.

Christina Huss

Figure 9-11

These files are stored in a special gallery for all types of layout files for this site collection, including news articles, intranet Publishing Pages, and Master Page files. To see these files, follow the steps in the next Try It Out.

Try It Out   **Display the Site Collections Layout Gallery**

1. Make sure to log on as an administrator for this site collection.

2. Open the top site for the site collection, for example, `http://srv1`.

3. Click Site Actions ➪ Site Settings ➪ Modify All Site Settings.

4. In the section Galleries, click Master pages and page layouts. Now all files in this Master Page Gallery are displayed; see Figure 9-12, where three of the four Publishing Pages described in the table above are listed (the fourth is further down on this list). Note that you can see if the files are published or in draft status, and who has done the last update of the file and when.

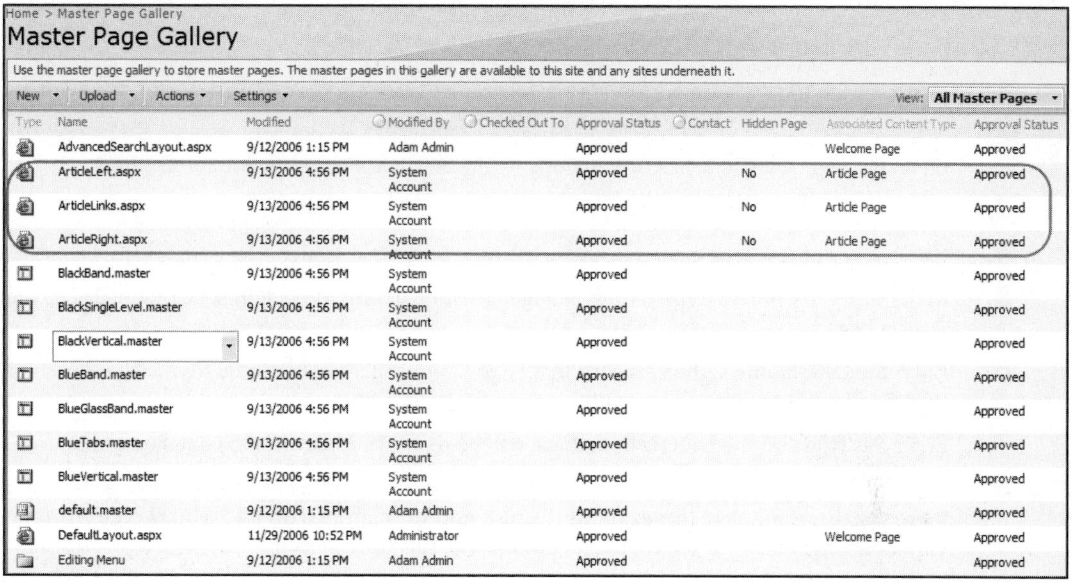

Home > Master Page Gallery

Master Page Gallery

Use the master page gallery to store master pages. The master pages in this gallery are available to this site and any sites underneath it.

New ▾ | Upload ▾ | Actions ▾ | Settings ▾   View: **All Master Pages** ▾

Type	Name	Modified	Modified By	Checked Out To	Approval Status	Contact	Hidden Page	Associated Content Type	Approval Status
	AdvancedSearchLayout.aspx	9/12/2006 1:15 PM	Adam Admin		Approved			Welcome Page	Approved
	ArticleLeft.aspx	9/13/2006 4:56 PM	System Account		Approved		No	Article Page	Approved
	ArticleLinks.aspx	9/13/2006 4:56 PM	System Account		Approved		No	Article Page	Approved
	ArticleRight.aspx	9/13/2006 4:56 PM	System Account		Approved		No	Article Page	Approved
	BlackBand.master	9/13/2006 4:56 PM	System Account		Approved				Approved
	BlackSingleLevel.master	9/13/2006 4:56 PM	System Account		Approved				Approved
	BlackVertical.master	9/13/2006 4:56 PM	System Account		Approved				Approved
	BlueBand.master	9/13/2006 4:56 PM	System Account		Approved				Approved
	BlueGlassBand.master	9/13/2006 4:56 PM	System Account		Approved				Approved
	BlueTabs.master	9/13/2006 4:56 PM	System Account		Approved				Approved
	BlueVertical.master	9/13/2006 4:56 PM	System Account		Approved				Approved
	default.master	9/12/2006 1:15 PM	Adam Admin		Approved				Approved
	DefaultLayout.aspx	11/29/2006 10:52 PM	Administrator		Approved			Welcome Page	Approved
	Editing Menu	9/12/2006 1:15 PM	Adam Admin		Approved				Approved

Figure 9-12

Creating a Page Layout File

You can either edit one of these four default page layout files, and save it under a new name, or you can create a new file from scratch. If you edit one of the existing files, you will automatically get the right type of file, but if you create one from scratch, you must understand how to define it properly so that it will show up as a Publishing Page layout when creating a News page. By default, there are three types of page layout files to choose from when creating a News page:

❑ **Article Page:** This is the page layout that most news articles are built on. The layout files described in the previous table are Article Pages.

❑ **Redirect Page:** This is a special page layout that is used to create Redirect Pages. A user opening this page will automatically be redirected to the URL specified on this page within five seconds.

❑ **Welcome Page:** There are a number of Welcome Pages, and they are most often used to add extra pages to the intranet site, not for news articles, but they can be used for news articles as well.

In other words, when creating a new page layout file for news articles, you will most often create an Article Page. Let's use an example again. Say you need a page layout that allows you to add one page image, page content, one article date control, and one summary link control field. Since there is no such page layout, you must create it. The steps in the Try It Out below tell you how to do this.

Try It Out   **Create a Page Layout File for News Articles**

1. Make sure to log on as an administrator for this site collection; open its top site. (You can also do this from most other web sites based on MOSS templates.)

2. Open the Page Gallery. Click Site Actions ⇨ Site Settings ⇨ Modify All Site Settings.

3. Click Master pages and page layouts. All layout files in the Master Page Gallery are now listed.

4. Click New at the top of the list to create the new page layout file.

5. Make sure the Content Type Group is Page Layout Content Type, and set Content Type Name to Article Page.

6. Enter the URL Name is the name for this Page Layout file; for example, MyFirstLayout. Note that the file will automatically get the `.aspx` file extension.

7. Enter the Title and the Description; these will be displayed later in the page layout list.

8. There is a section for adding Variation Labels. These are used when creating a page layout in more than one language (for example, Danish and Russian). To do that, you need to add these variation labels before creating the layout file. So, this time just click OK.

9. The result is now a new page layout file, stored in the Master pages and page layouts gallery. But the file is empty at the moment. The next step is to add the layout controls to it. Locate the new file (for example, `MyFirstLayout.aspx` file); open its quick menu (click to the right of the page name), and select Edit in Microsoft Office SharePoint Designer.

10. You will now see both the new and empty page layout file, plus its Master Page, showing all the menus, buttons, and Quick Launch items. In the content part of the page, that is, the center of the page, you will see a row named `PlaceHolderMain`; it is this part you want to configure.

11. Mark the `PlaceHolderMain` in the content part; all your control fields must be stored within this `PlaceHolderMain` control. The problem is that it is hard to add a control field and make it stick to a specific place. This is easily solved by creating a table inside `PlaceHolderMain`, then add the control fields to each cell in the table: Click the Table menu and then Insert Table, next set the number of rows = 2 and columns = 2, and then click OK. Note that a consumer of this web page will never see the actual table; it is only used by the designer to add the controls in a specific position. See Figure 9-13.

12. In the toolbox at the right of the SharePoint designer, you will see a number of control fields that you can use in this news page layout. The most commonly used are these grouped by the Content Field. Locate the Article Date and drag it to the top left cell in the `PlaceHolderMain` area. Then drag the Page Image to the second column on the first row. Now drag the Summary Links to the second row, first column, then drag the Page Content control to the second cell in the second row. The layout is now ready (see Figure 9-13).

13. The next step is to save it. In the SharePoint Designer, click File ⇨ Save (or press Control+S on the keyboard).

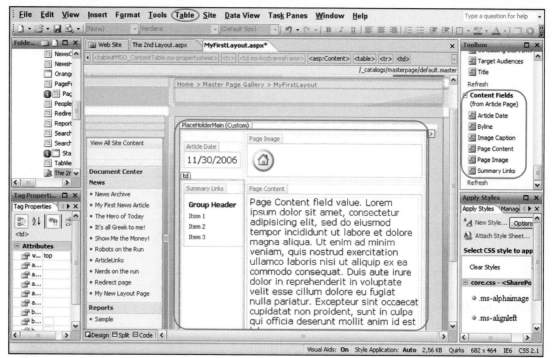

Figure 9-13

14. The next step is to check in, and then approve the file, to make it publically available:

    a. Close the SharePoint Designer.

    b. Open the Master Page Gallery if it is not yet displayed; locate the newly created layout file (MyFirstLayout.aspx), then open its quick menu: select Check In.

    c. Select the option Major Version. If this is the first time you edited this file, the major version will be 1.0.

    d. Locate the MyFirstLayout.aspx file again, then open its quick menu, and select Approve/reject, then click OK. This page layout file is now ready to be used.

15. Let's test the new layout: Open the News page, then click Site Actions ⇨ Edit Page. Enter a page title, and a description, then select the new layout file: (Article Page) My First Layout File and click Create. The result will look like Figure 9-14.

16. Enter some content into each of these seven page controls. The news article must now be checked in, then approved, just like any page file. If you have the permission, click Publish now; if not, click Submit for Approval, and ask the user with Approve permission to approve the page. The new article is now listed on the News page.

Figure 9-14

More about Page Layouts

The editing functionality in SharePoint Designer is very rich, and it will take some time before you master it. Chapter 13 will cover more details about working with SharePoint Designer, but below are some tips that will help you get started with the page layouts for news articles. To start with you can change an existing page layout file, and this will affect both existing news articles and those created from this moment on. For example, say that you need to add Web Part zones to the layout file, thus allowing the content author to add Web Parts later on. None of the default article layouts has this functionality, but it could be very interesting in some cases. For example, say that you once in a while want to create a news article that also contains a list of the latest customers, stored in a Customer list in the News site. In the Try It Out below you will change the page layout of the `MyFirstLayout.aspx` file.

Try It Out	**Edit an Existing Page Layout File**

1. Make sure to log on as an administrator for this site collection, and open its top site. (You can also do this from most other web sites based on MOSS templates.)

2. Open the Page Gallery. Click Site Actions ➪ Site Settings ➪ Modify All Site Settings.

3. Click Master pages and page layouts. All layout files in the Master Page Gallery are now listed.

4. Locate the `MyFirstLayout.aspx` file. Open its quick menu, and select Edit in Microsoft Office SharePoint Designer. A dialog box informs you that this requires the file to be checked out; click OK.

5. SharePoint Designer starts and displays the page layout file. Locate the `PlaceHolderMain` part in the middle of the page. Previously you created a table with two rows and two columns. It is best to create a new row where the new Web Part zone will be stored:

    a. Place the cursor at the beginning of the second row, and you will see a small arrow pointing to the right. Click the left mouse button to select the complete row, then right-click and select Insert ➪ Row Below. Now you have three rows.

    b. Set the cursor in the second column of the third row (because it is widest), then click on the Insert menu on the SharePoint Designer toolbar, and select SharePoint Controls ➪ Web Part Zones. The new zone is created in the table.

6. Save the modified page layout: Click File ➪ Save, then:

    a. Close the SharePoint Designer.

    b. Open the Master Page Gallery, locate the newly modified layout file (`MyFirstLayout.aspx`), then open its quick menu, and select Check In.

    c. Select the option Major Version. The major version will be 2.0, since you have edited this file.

    d. Open the quick menu for `MyFirstLayout.aspx` again, and select Approve/reject, then click OK. This page layout file is now ready to be used.

7. Let's test the new layout: Open the News page and create a new Page file based on the `MyFirstLayout.aspx`, as previously described. Note that it now allows the content author to add any number of Web Parts into the new Web Part zone. Figure 9-15 shows what this looks like when you're editing the page, and Figure 9-16 shows an example where a Web Part displaying a Contact list named Customers has been added. (You will need to create this contact list before you can add it as a Web Part to this page.)

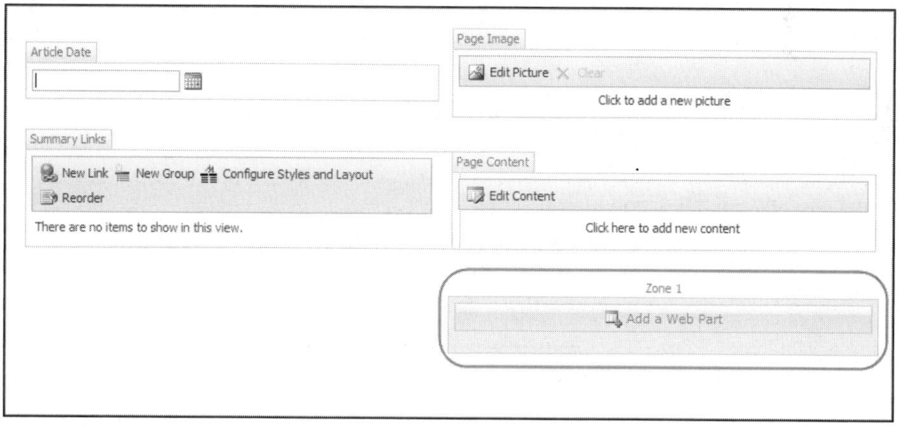

Figure 9-15

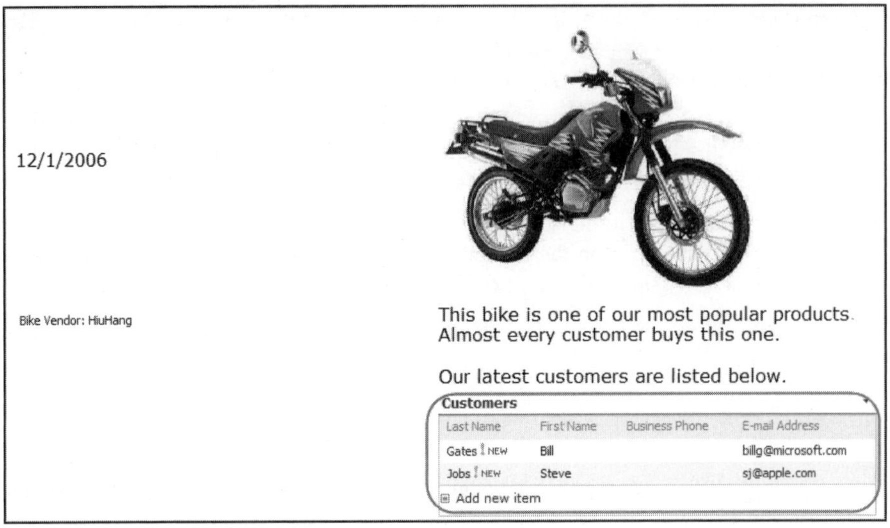

12/1/2006

Bike Vendor: HiuHang

This bike is one of our most popular products. Almost every customer buys this one.

Our latest customers are listed below.

Customers

Last Name	First Name	Business Phone	E-mail Address
Gates ! NEW	Bill		billg@microsoft.com
Jobs ! NEW	Steve		sj@apple.com
⊞ Add new item			

Figure 9-16

If you now edit one of the existing news articles that was built on this page layout file, you will see that the new Web Part zone is displayed. In other words, changing the page layout file will also affect existing news articles. The reason is that when this news article is displayed, SharePoint will open the layout file and fill in the content in its control fields and Web Parts. This also explains why you cannot remove a page layout file as long as there is at least one news article still using it. If you try this, SharePoint will display this error: "This item cannot be deleted because it is still referenced by other pages." If you want to see which news articles use this page layout, follow the steps in the Try It Out below.

Try It Out   Display the Page Layout Used by News Articles

1.   Open the News site.

2.   Click View All Site Content, then click Pages.

3.   Look at the column Page Layout (by default at the far right). This is the page layout file that is used by this news article. You can click OK on the column header Page Layout to sort it, to make it easier to see all news articles used by a specific page layout file.

The content management features in MOSS are very powerful but still easy to use. However, to make the most of web content management, the content authors must take some time to learn how it works. The good news is that it is a lot of fun!

Summary

In this chapter, you learned that:

❑ Web content management, or WCM, gives control over editing and displaying content. This is especially necessary when working with web sites used by many people, such as intranet, extranet, and public Internet sites.

❑ WCM is only available in MOSS 2007, not WSS 3.0

❑ The management process is divided into: Create, Update, Publish, Archive, and Retire content.

❑ Roles used in content managements are: Content Author, Editor, Publisher, Administrator, Consumer.

❑ Important content management features in MOSS 2007: support for Metadata, Version History, Check Out/Check In, Approval, Workflows, Localizations, and Policies.

❑ The previous product MS Content Management Server is now integrated into MOSS 2007.

❑ MOSS web pages that support content management display a number of buttons and menus for editing a page.

❑ Another name for MOSS pages with CM support is Publishing Pages.

❑ All Publishing Pages are stored in a document library, usually named Pages.

❑ The layout of a Publishing Page is controlled by a page layout file.

❑ Page layout files are stored in the Master Page Gallery, which is a library shared for the site collection.

❑ The Master Page Gallery also contains layout files for the Master Page, that is, the look and feel of navigation, top menus, and the logotype.

❑ The primary tool for editing layout files is the MS Office SharePoint Designer.

❑ The page layout file consists of control fields, such as `Page Content` and `Image Content`. It can also contain zero or more Web Part zones.

❑ The `Page Content` control field is a very rich editor — it allows the content author to add text, pictures, links, and tables; it also allows the author to edit the HTML source directly.

❑ The Web Parts "I need to" and "Top Sites" on the intranet start page are configured by adding links to the Sites pages.

❑ Before you start creating news articles and other Publishing Pages, you should add the images you need.

❑ Each MOSS site that supports content management has a local Image library that stores images and pictures that is available for pages created in that site.

❑ The start page of the intranet also has a Site Collection Images library. All images in that library are available in any site supporting content management.

In the next chapter, you will learn more about content management related to files and documents, often referred to as document management.

File and Document Management

Every computer user manages files and documents every day. It is an important and often frustrating task to find the needed file quickly and to be sure that it is the correct version. Every step you can take to make this task easier will be received with applause from your users. If you also can make it just a bit more fun, they will cheer. File and document management is this important! SharePoint can help you make this happen. And this chapter is all about how to help users find their files more quickly and easily.

Traditional File Chaos

To understand what SharePoint can do requires that you analyze how things work traditionally. The following table shows the typical tasks a user performs with files and documents every day:

Table 10.1: Typical Tasks

Common File Tasks	Challenges/Problems
Create a file	Where will this file be stored so it can be found later by me and my colleagues? What name should I give this file so it is clear what it contains?
Update a file	How do I find the file to be updated? How can I save the new version without overwriting the old file? How can I update a public file over a period of days and avoid having someone see the document before it is fully updated? How can several people cooperate when updating a file?
Open a file	How do I find the file? How can I be sure it is the latest version? How can I contact the most recent author if necessary?
Delete a file	How can I be sure that there is no other copy of this file still in existence?

These are the challenges that your users deal with every time they work with a file or document. Face the reality: Users solve these challenges in several ways, and the consequence is that you soon have file chaos. No one is sure where all the files are stored, no one is sure that the file they found is the latest version, and all these files make the backup and restore procedures unnecessarily complicated and time-consuming.

Document Management Systems

There are some great tools for creating documents and files, with MS Office being the premium example. Some of these tools have built-in features for organizing and locating files. This is good, but the problem is that this solution only works within each tool; there is no global solution for managing all types of documents and files. So, the traditional document management solutions may be good to some extent, but they are not enough. That is why all, not some, but all organizations have a more or less chaotic system for managing their files. Even so, users have learned to live with this situation. Can you imagine how much time you would save yourself and your company if you could reduce this file chaos, or even eliminate it altogether?

One partial solution for this file chaos is a document management system, or DMS. These types of products have existed for many years, and people love the idea of them when they read about what they can do. A DMS costs a lot of money, but if all these promises are fulfilled, the improved efficiency and productivity of your users can quickly result in a good ROI (return on investment). While this is a pleasant idea, the reality is not always that positive. What most often happens is that some users love the new DMS and start working with it to its full extent. Others start to use it grudgingly, but after some time they go back to the old routine, which they are more familiar and comfortable with, despite the problems it causes them. And some simply never even start using the new DMS. Period. The result is even worse than before. Now you have some files stored in the old way (usually in a mix of file shares, local disks, and mailbox attachments), while other files are stored in the fancy DMS. And the organization is paying an expensive license every year to keep the DMS working.

What does the manager or other person who is responsible for the DMS purchase do now? That is right, they continue to work with the DMS, to pay its annual fees, and maybe even invest some more in it, trying to make it easier to use. Isn't this strange? At first glance, it might even seem foolish, but that depends on who you are. If you were the person who convinced the CEO that you needed this DMS and that the ROI for this $50,000 per year was no problem, you are now faced with the prospect of either telling the CEO you have problems and most likely get sacked or trying to fix it somehow, while praying to whichever God pleases you that the users will somehow get the idea and start using the system.

How can something like this happen? The basic idea is excellent: Get a system that will help users to manage their documents in a more sophisticated way. So why does it go wrong? The usual reasons are one or more of these:

❑ **The system is too complex to use:** Having too many features makes it hard for the average user to understand how to use it.

❑ **The system is not integrated into MS Office:** If users must produce the document in MS Word and then move to another application for entering document properties and so on, it is easier for users to store the file in the same file system that they have always used.

❑ **The system slows down the users:** If the DMS is slow or requires several extra steps that users must complete, users will see this as an obstacle that has a negative affect on their performance.

❑ **Users are expected to learn the system without training:** This may not be a problem if there are just a few new features to learn that are intuitive and well integrated into MS Office. If not, this is definitely a show-stopper.

❑ **The user refuses to learn anything new, ever!:** This is more common than one first may expect. And the reason for this strange opinion is often fear: fear that he or she will not understand the new system, fear that it will be a more complicated process and take more time than before, and general fear of any type of change, regardless of what it is.

That last bullet is not something to ignore. If you can make such a user to accept the new solution, you can get the results you hope for when investing in this DMS solution. So, try to find these users and use them as indicators of how successful your new DMS solution is.

Traditional File Management Systems

Without a DMS solution, the need to organize files and documents must be solved another way. This organizational need is most often addressed this way:

1. Create a hierarchical folder tree in a file server. The user has a mapped disk drive to that file share.

2. Name each file so it is easy to understand what it contains (for example, "Budget_Q3_2006_V1.XLS").

These two methods have been with us since MS DOS 2.0 was released in 1983, when users for the first time could create hierarchical file structures. It was a great feature at that time, taken from the UNIX operating system, of course. A typical traditional file system looks something like this:

```
C:\Public
        \Projects
                \IT
                        \AD-migration
                        \Exchange
                        \DMS
                \Sales
                        \Marketing
                        \Customers
                                \HM
                                \Ericson
                                \Ford
                        \Products
        \Customers
                \HM
                        \Contracts
                        \Quotes
                        \Products
                \Ericson
                        \Contracts
                        \Quotes
                        \Products
                \Ford
                        \Contracts
                        \Quotes
                        \Products
```

With this hierarchical folder tree, it is very easy to find all project documents for AD migration done by IT and all quotes for Ford. But what if a user wants to see all quotes, regardless of the customer? Then this user must look into three different folders, and if there are 300 customers, the user must look in all 300 Quote folders. In this situation, it is very common for the user to copy these quotes to his local client, just to get them listed together and easier to work with. Now you have the same files in two places. This happens all the time and is one of the major reasons you end up with file chaos.

Why is the folder's structure arranged by customers and then document types? The answer is probably that someone thought that was a great idea when it was created, based on whatever limited criteria he or she was using at the time. If this is not true anymore, you can of course rearrange this structure; it will take some time, but it certainly can be done. But your users must be informed about this change, or they will become very confused when the folder structure has changed. The point here is that a file system is almost static of necessity. The folder structure will stay like this for a long time, even if some people want to change it. This is something you have to accept when using a file system.

What about the filenames, such as "Budget_Q3_2007_V1.XLS"? Is this really a good name? Well, sort of. It is easy to see what type of content it has (Budget), what period it is from (Q3 2007), and what version it is (V1). The problem here is that there is nothing that will force another user to use the same filename format. The next user may call an updated version of that file "2007-Q3_Budget-2.xls". It is still rather easy to guess that this is the second version of the previous file. But the third update gets this name: "Q3-7-3-BG.xls". If these three files are stored in different places, it really starts to get messy. The problem is that you cannot describe the file using anything other than its name. You can of course create a new folder named Budget and then store files with names like "Q3-2007-v1.xls" in it. Imagine that you copy that file to another place now. How will you know it's a budget file in its new location?

Another common problem is keeping track of updates: For example, when a specific file you depend on gets updated by another user, how do you get this information? Or, if there is a new quote sent out to the customer H&M, how will you know this?

As you can see, there are lots of problems and limitations with the traditional file structure as we know it. Fortunately, there are solutions available to address all of this, as you will see in the following sections.

What You Really Need

You need a new method to organize and group files without using folders, something that will be easy to change, or will even change automatically for each user looking at these files. For example, a project manager might want to see project documents presented in one way, but each project member may need to organize this information in another way, maybe even hiding everything but the files the project member works with.

All these problems with filenames could be solved if you were allowed to create your own properties for a file or document, such as Document Type, Year, and Period. Then you could store this information in the properties instead of building it into the actual filename. If the system also could keep track of versions automatically, you would not have this mess anymore either, right?

You also need a mechanism that will tell you when something gets changed. Since each user knows best what files they are interested in, they must be able to define for themselves which files to monitor and how to monitor them. Besides files, users may need to monitor folders as well.

Another common need is to have a feature that will enable a user to update an existing document stored in a shared file resource without any risk that other users may see what they are doing until the work is complete. This method must be able to lock the file for editing by a specific user regardless of whether that person is actively editing the file. If there is more than one user who will update this document during this editorial period, there must be a way that allows several users to collaborate without somebody else seeing what is happening until the work is completed and published.

To summarize the entire situation, what you need are features like these:

❑ A way to organize, sort, and group files, based on file properties.

❑ A file structure that is easy for the user to directly modify at any time.

❑ A way to describe the files other than using the filename.

❑ A way to force all users to follow this new naming standard.

❑ An automatic version history that keeps track of every modification made to the file.

❑ A way to monitor individual files and folders that notifies you when something happens.

❑ A way to lock the editing of a shared file to a specific user, regardless of whether that user is working with the file.

❑ A way to handle the situation where more than one user will edit a shared document during a period. When all of these editorial users are done, this file should be published so that everyone can see it in this shared location.

And all of this must be easy to use and integrate into the MS Office products as much as possible. It must also be fast and reliable. Can it be done, you ask? You bet!

The SharePoint Way

The solutions described in the previous section can be provided with the WSS 3.0 (that is right, the free version of SharePoint). To make the solution complete, you need MS Office 2007, but even with earlier Office versions, you can go a long way. The recommendation is that users who actively update documents have MS Office 2007, or at least MS Office 2003, but users who read and act on these documents can do so with MS Office 2002 or even MS Office 2000.

The features described in this section are available for both MOSS and WSS, meaning that this can be done in any type of site, including intranet portal sites and team sites. But you may remember from previous chapters that collaborating should be done in team sites, so even if you have MOSS installed, you will most likely end up implementing these solutions in a team site.

The basic structure for file and document management is SharePoint's Document Libraries. It provides you with the following built-in features:

❑ **Storing any type of file:** Note that there is a global setting in SharePoint that controls what file types that SharePoint does not allow; see the following section on how to change that setting.

❑ **Built-in version history:** This is disabled by default, but when enabled it automatically keeps track of all updates of each file in the document library. You can choose between a simple version history, just keeping track of the time and date for each version, or a version history, keeping track of both major (1.0, 2.0) and minor (1.1, 1.2) versions.

❑ **Add custom file properties:** You can add any number of columns to a document library to describe properties or any type of information you want about each file.

❑ **Add custom views:** You can create definitions on how to sort and present the files in this document library; these views may be personal or publicly available.

❑ **Built-in file locking:** Using the standard type of checkout/checkin capabilities found in all DMSs, the user can lock a file for any period of time, regardless of whether the file is open or not.

❑ **Create Document Workspace:** This automatically makes a copy of a file and builds a subsite around it. This site, or workspace, can then have one or more users who are allowed to work with this file. When they are done, the new version of the document will be published back to its original location.

❑ **Send notifications when updated:** There are two ways to do this: Use the Alert feature to send an e-mail when a specific document or folder is modified, or make the document library an RSS Feed to MS Outlook 2007, thus sending an RSS posting whenever there is a new document added to the library.

❑ **Undelete:** If a document or folder in the document library is deleted, it can be restored by the user directly, using the built-in undelete feature.

❑ **Workflow:** Create an workflow that triggers when a new document is created or a property is changed. For example, anytime a quote is created, the sales manager will be informed.

❑ **Approval:** You can enforce the rule that all new files and documents must be approved before going public.

❑ **Policies:** Define policies and rules for documents. For examples, all documents older than six months should be converted to a PDF file and moved to another location. Or you can audit every action taken on a document, such as read, edit, or delete but also if the file is moved or copied. (Requires MOSS 2007 Enterprise Edition.)

❑ **Content types:** This is a very advanced feature that allows you to create any number of document templates for a document library, including special workflow settings, property columns, and document policies.

❑ **Item-level security:** Each file and document will inherit the permission setting of its parent, that is, the document library itself, or a folder in the document library. But you can also set the permission for a specific document, if necessary. You can also set permissions to a specific folder in the document library; its setting will be inherited by the documents stored in that folder.

❑ **Fully integrated with Office 2007:** All of these features can be used with the web client interface or an MS Office 2007 application, such as MS Word, MS Excel, or MS PowerPoint.

So there you have it — everything you need to build a solution for more effective document management. And remember that all of this is available not only for MS Office documents but for any file type (for example, PDF files, ASCII text files, and CAD files).

Allowed File Types

There is a global setting that will affect what file types users are allowed to store in any document library. Note that there is no way to control an individual document library in SharePoint 2007. How to view and manage these file types is demonstrated in the Try It Out below.

Try It Out   Manage Disabled File Types

1. Start SharePoint Central Administration, and open the Operations page.

2. Click Blocked file types.

3. On the following page, be sure to check that the Web Application list lists the one used by your intranet or team site.

4. In the example, you will see a list of 81 blocked file types (see Figure 10-1). If a user tries to add a file of any of these file types, he or she will receive this error message: "The following file(s) have been blocked by the administrator: <filename>.<blocked file type>".

5. If you want to enable a blocked file type, just mark that line and press Delete. If you want to block a new file type, add it to a new line. When done, click OK to save and close this page.

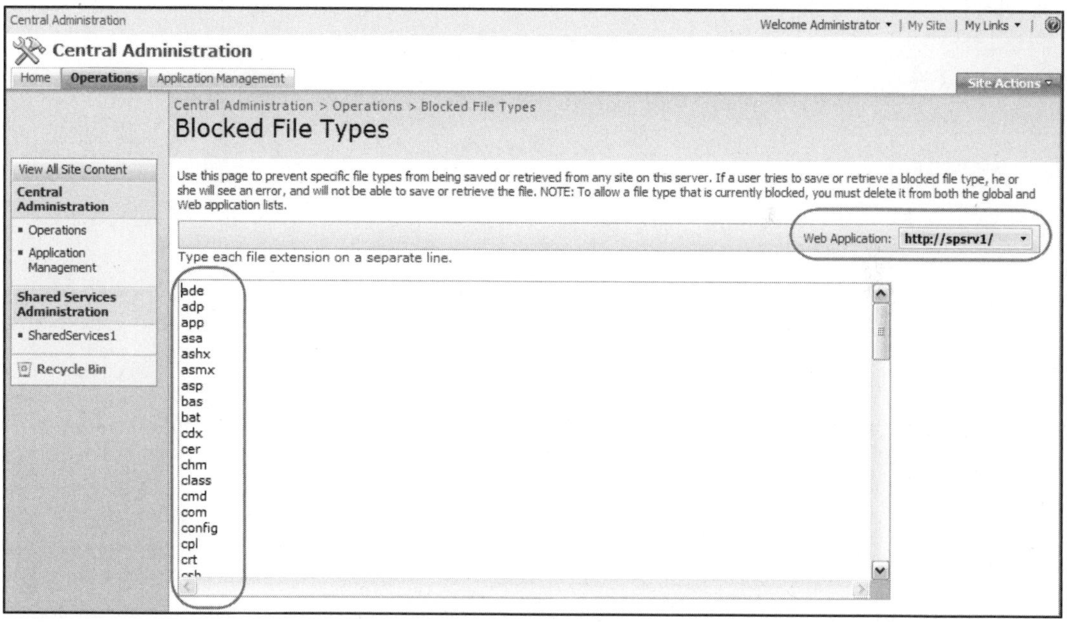

Figure 10-1

The 81 file types that are blocked by default are shown in the following table.

Table 10.2: File Types Blocked By Default

File type	File type	File type	File type
ade	adp	app	asa
ashx	asmx	asp	bas
bat	cdx	cer	chm
class	cmd	com	Config
cpl	crt	csh	dll
exe	fxp	hlp	hta
htr	htw	ida	idc
idq	ins	isp	its
jse	ksh	lnk	mad
maf	mag	mam	maq
mar	mas	mat	mau
mav	maw	mda	mdb
mde	mdt	mdw	mdz
msc	msi	msp	mst
ops	pcd	pif	prf
prg	printer	pst	reg
rem	scf	scr	sct
shb	shs	shtm	shtml
soap	stm	url	vb
vbe	vbs	wsc	wsf
Wsh			

The reason that these file types are blocked is security. They can each be used to activate some sort of malicious action, such as a virus, Trojan horse, or worm. If you want to replace the shared file system with SharePoint's document libraries, you may need to unblock some or all of these file types.

> **Before you unblock these file types, it is strongly recommended you implement a SharePoint-enabled antivirus solution, just as you would do in an ordinary file system.**

Creating Document Libraries

To start with, you need a document library. Contrary to previous SharePoint versions, you can use all of these document management features on any document library, regardless of whether it is a MOSS site, or a WSS team site. However, since a team site is most commonly used for file and document management, this is what you will use in the examples below. Several site templates, such as Team Sites, already contain one document library named "Shared Documents." Either you start with this or you create a new one, using the steps in the following Try It Out.

Try It Out   Create a New Document Library

1. Go to the site where the new document library will be created.

2. Click the link Site Actions ⇨ Create at the top of this page.

3. To create a standard document library, click Document Library in the Libraries section, and enter its properties in the following page (see Figure 10-2):

    a. **Name:** Enter a name for this document library that is unique in this site.

    b. **Description:** Enter a description of this document library.

    c. **Navigation:** Select Yes if you want this document library to be listed in the left pane of this team site; this pane is referred to as the Quick Launch bar. If you select No, you can find it by clicking the link Documents and Lists on the team site. You can also add it as a Web Part to display its content directly to the team.

    d. **Document Version History:** Select Yes to activate version history for all documents in this library or No to only save the latest version of each document. You can later change this setting for existing libraries. Note that if you activate the version history here, it will default into the simple version history that stores the date and time for each version. If you want to keep track of major and minor versions, then you must later open the configuration page for this document library and change the version settings.

    e. **Document Template:** Select the document that will be used as a template when a user clicks the New Document button on the document library page.

    f. Click Create to close this page and create the document library.

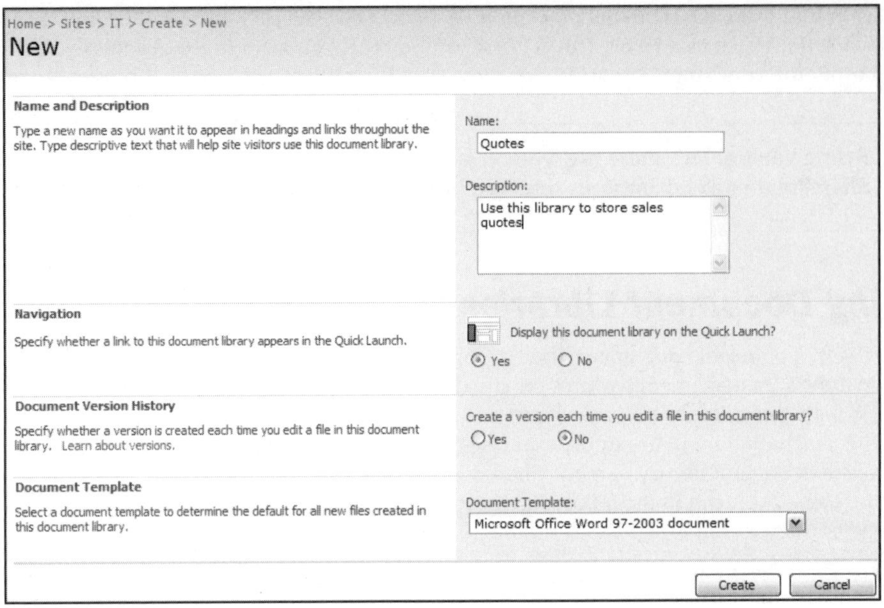

Figure 10-2

By default, a document library can only contain one single document template. However, using SharePoint's feature Content Types you can add multiple document templates, as described later in this chapter. The available default templates are listed here and allow the creator of this library to choose between the old file format, used in MS Office 97-2003, and the new format introduced in MS Office 2007. Note that the selected template file will be stored in the subfolder Forms in the document library. To create a new document based on this template, the user clicks New in the document library.

❏ **None:** Use this option if you want no template at all, for this document library.

❏ **Microsoft Office Word 97-2003 document:** Create a MS Word file based on the file format used by Word 97-2003, and the content of the file `Template.doc`. You can edit `Template.doc` if you want all new files to start with a specific content.

❏ **Microsoft Office Excel 97-2003 spreadsheet:** Create a spreadsheet file based on the file format used by MS Excel 97-2003, and the content of the file `Template.xls`. Edit `Template.xls` if you want all new files to start with a specific content.

❏ **Microsoft Office PowerPoint 97-2003 presentation:** Create a PPT file based on the file format used by PowerPoint 97-2003, and the content of the file `Template.pot`. Edit `Template.pot` if you want all new files to start with a specific content.

❏ **Microsoft Office Word:** Create a MS Word file based on the file format used by Word 2007, and the content of the file `Template.docx`. You can edit `Template.docx` if you want all new files to start with a specific content.

❏ **Microsoft Office Excel spreadsheet:** Create a spreadsheet file based on the file format used by MS Excel 2007, and the content of the file `Template.xlsx`. Edit `Template.xlsx` if you want all new files to start with a specific content.

❏ **Microsoft Office PowerPoint presentation:** Create a PPT file based on the file format used by PowerPoint 2007, and the content of the file `Template.potx`. Edit `Template.potx` if you want all new files to start with a specific content.

❏ **Microsoft Office OneNote section:** Create a MS OneNote file based on the content of `Template.one`. Edit `Template.one` if you want all new files to start with a specific content.

❏ **Microsoft Office SharePoint Designer Web page:** Starts the SharePoint Designer tool, and opens the file `Template.htm`. Edit `Template.htm` if you want all new files to start with a specific content.

❏ **Basic page:** Create a new basic web page in this site. Note that all extra web pages for a SharePoint site will be stored as files in a document library. This page will have the Content Editor Web Part added to allow you to enter information on this page in rich-text format, including tables and pictures.

❏ **Web Part Page:** Click New Documents to create a new Web Part page with a specific layout in this site. Just like basic pages, these Web Part pages must be stored in a document library.

The last two options, Basic page and Web Part Page, may need some extra clarification. All team sites consist of one single Web Part page named Home. You can create additional pages for the team site, both standard HTML pages and Web Part pages; these extra pages are stored as files in a document library in this team site. To actually display a page on the site, the user must open its page file. In order to make it easier for the user to see what extra pages exist and open them, you can use either of these methods, on the Home page for the team site:

❏ Change the navigation settings for this site to show pages (if possible, depending on the site template), or add a link to each page to the Quick Launch bar.

❏ Display these page files on the start page for this site by using the Web Part for that document library. Make sure to give these page files descriptive names so that the user understands what they are used for.

❏ Use the Links Web Part, and create links to these page files. Use descriptive link titles so that the user understands what the pages are used for.

> Note that the extra pages will not be displayed in a tab view. You can use page layers and tab buttons to create this view, as described in Chapter 13.

A relevant question now is "How many document libraries do I need?" And the answer is: Start with one single library and use it for everything until one of the following scenarios happens:

❏ **You need to activate version history for some, but not all, files:** Since this feature is set per library, not per file, you must create a separate document library for each set of files, unless you don't mind having version history active even for those files that don't really use it. The price will be that more disk space is required on the SQL Server.

❏ **You need content approval for some, but not all, files:** This feature is also set per library. If only some of the files need this feature, create a separate document library for them.

❏ **The number of files is more than 2,500 per folder:** To ensure optimum performance, no folder in a document library should contain more than 2,500 files, and the total number of files should be less than 3,000,000.

Note that one document library can host more than three million files, as long as they are divided into a number of folders. When you exceed this number, you must divide them into several libraries to ensure the optimum performance when listing and updating the files. After all, SharePoint is a web application.

Understanding Columns and Views

The most common mistake when moving from a file system to SharePoint is to create one document library for each main file share structure; for example, in the file system depicted earlier in this chapter, you would end up with one library named "Projects" and another named "Customers." That might sound like a good idea, since it will resemble the old environment. But you should first test if you can store *all* files in *one* library and then use columns and views to sort them into Projects and Customers, to mimic the old file structure. To do this, you need to create custom columns for the document library, and then build views that use these columns to sort and filter the list of files. The biggest advantage of using views, instead of a folder structure, is that views are dynamic and easy to create and modify. You can have more than one view for presenting and sorting files, to meet different needs, depending on what the user wants to see.

Document Library Columns

This feature makes it possible to describe the file's content without using the filename. Actually, when you start using these columns, you may even start to wonder why you need filenames at all. When you add columns to a document library, you have a number of types to choose from. It is important to use the correct column type, since it will affect what you can to with the column, especially when creating views. The following table displays all the default column types and how to use them:

Column Type	Description	Examples
Single line of text	Allows the author to enter one text line with up to 255 characters.	Can be used for short descriptions or comments.
Multiple lines of text	Allows the author to enter up to 1,000 lines of text of 80 characters each.	Can be used for longer descriptions.
Choice	Allows the author to select from more than 100 predefined choices.	Create a list of Document Types, such as "Info, Quote, Contract," or Customers, such as "Ericson, H&M, Ford."
Number	Allows the author to enter a number with or without decimals or in percent.	Enter the number of products in stock, the weight of a patient, a zip code, and so on.
Currency	Allows the author to enter a number that will be treated as currency. You can define what format is to be used.	Use for prices, income, net results, and so on.

Column Type	Description	Examples
Date and Time	Allows the author to enter a date and optional a time value.	Use for contract dates, defining time periods, birth dates, and so on.
Lookup	The value displayed in this field will come from another list or library on this site.	Use for displaying a list of all members for the site, a customer name retrieved from a Customer Contact list, or a Product list on the site.
Yes/No	The author can select Yes or No.	Use it for binary options, such as "This document is public," or "Quote is active."
Person or Group	Allows the author to choose a user or a group, from Active Directory or a given SharePoint group.	Use this to pick out a user that responsible for a document.
Hyperlink	The author can enter an HTML URL address; this address can be displayed as a link or formatted as a picture.	Use this to add links to external information, or to display pictures of products or people.
Calculated	This field is automatically filled with a calculated value. The author will not enter anything in this field. You can use mathematical formulas and logical operators.	Calculate the total sum based on two other "Number" columns, or the date 30 days from now.
Business data	This field will be populated with data retrieved from an external data source.	Get the customer list from an external customer database, or list the products available in a specific segment.

The column type `Calculated` is similar to a calculated cell value in MS Excel. For example, say that you have two columns named "Price" and "Pieces" and you want a third column that calculates the total sum based on Price × Pieces. A reference to another column is defined by entering the name within `[ ]`; for example, `[Price]` and `[Pieces]`. The formula would then be:

```
[Price]*[Pieces]
```

Another example would be to display text based on a given limit. For example, if the value in the column Sales is higher than Expenses, you want a third column to display "Nice business"; if not, it should display "You are losing money!" The formula for this will look like:

```
IF([Sales]>[Expenses],"Nice business","You are losing money!")
```

The result would then look like Figure 10-3.

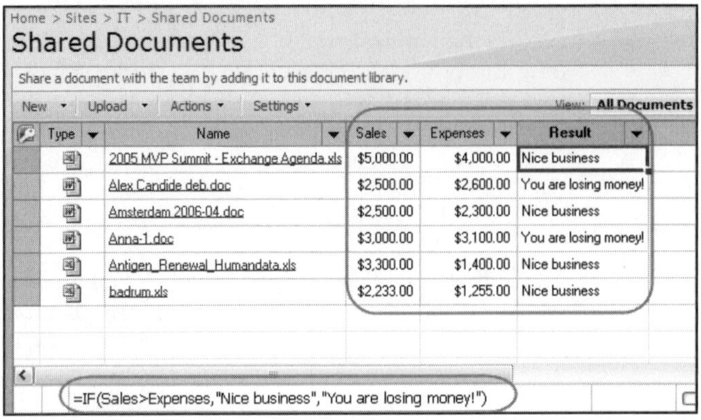

Figure 10-3

You can find a lot more information about calculated columns using the Help window and opening the link Formulas and functions (see Figure 10-4).

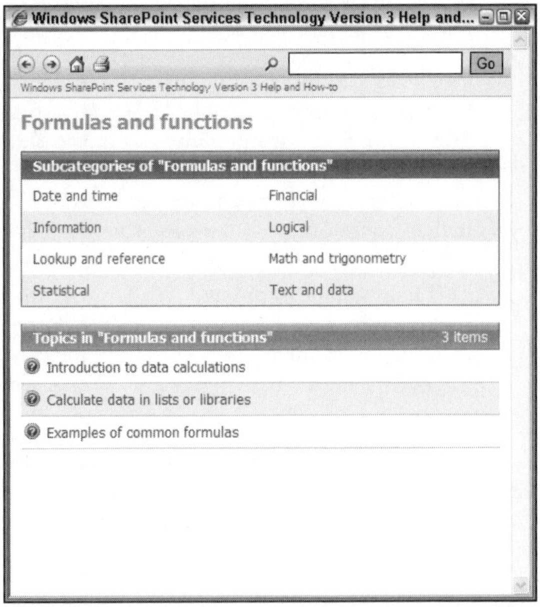

Figure 10-4

As usual, examples are the best way of demonstrating how to work with columns in document libraries. Say that you have a list of files and you need describe the document type (Quote, Order, and Contract) and security class (Public, Internal only, and Secret) for each of these files. Instead of creating files with names such as Quote_Internal_Ford.doc, you want to do it the SharePoint way. The following examples and descriptions assume that you are working with a WSS site based on the Team Site template.

Try It Out | Create Columns for Document Libraries

1. Log on as a user with Designer or Owner rights for the site.

2. Click the document library name (for example, Shared Documents), to display its content along with all the features available for that document library.

3. Click the menu Settings ➪ Create Column. A new web form opens where you can configure this column. (see Figure 10-5). Enter these settings:

    a. **Column name:** Doc Type. This will be a column for storing the document types.

    b. **The type of information in this column is:** Choice.

    c. **Description:** "This column is used to describe the document type."

    d. **Type each choice on a separate line:** Enter the following values; make sure to enter one choice per row: Quote; Order; Contract.

    e. **Display choices using:** Drop-Down Menu.

    f. **Allow "Fill-in" choices**: No.

    g. **Default value:** Clear this text box; you don't need a default value this time.

    h. Click OK to save this web form. The first column is now done!

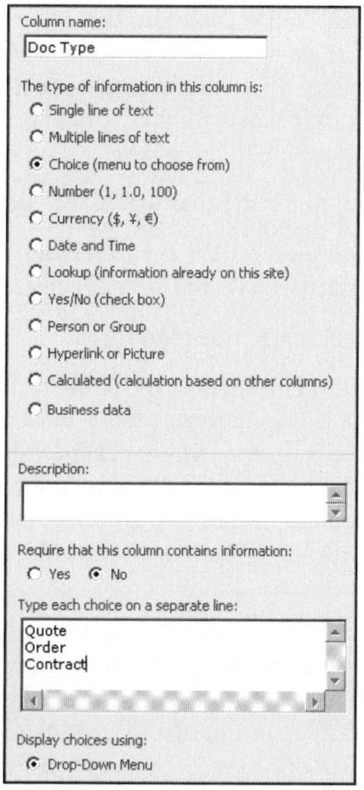

Figure 10-5

4. You need a second column as well; click Settings ⇨ Create Column again, then enter these values:

   a. **Column Name:** Security Class.

   b. **The type of information in this column is:** Choice.

   c. **Description:** "This column is used to define the security class for this document."

   d. **Type each choice on a separate line:** Public; Internal only; Secret.

   e. **Default value:** Clear this box.

   f. Click OK to save this web form. The second column is now done!

5. To see all created columns click Settings ⇨ Document Library Settings. All existing columns are listed in the section Columns. To modify or delete a column, click its name to open its configuration. To add a column click Create column at the end of the section; this is an alternative way to create a column as opposed to the method used in step 3 above.

6. Near the top of the page, click on the breadcrumb trail with the library name, for example Shared Documents, to return. Note that the two new columns are listed to the far-right side of the header line. All new columns will show up like this, but you can easily change their position, as you will see in just a few minutes.

7. It is time to add some documents to see how this works. Click on Upload and a web form is displayed. Next click Upload Multiple Files to display a window similar to Windows Explorer. Select the folder and the files to be uploaded, then click OK. You will get a dialog box, asking you if you want to upload these files; click Yes. The selected files are uploaded; the document library then opens again. Since you did not configure any default values for the two new columns, none of the uploaded files will have any value for those columns. To set these columns do this:

   a. Open the quick menu for the first uploaded file, and select Edit Properties.

   b. Use the pull-down menu for the column Doc Type and set its value to Contract. Then set the column Security Class to Internal only.

   c. Click OK to save and close this page.

8. If you want to update a number of files at the same time, also known as "bulk update," you can use another, faster method: Click Actions ⇨ Edit in Datasheet. This will open a view of the document library that looks much like an MS Excel spreadsheet, but it is in fact an ActiveX component, so the client must have MS Excel 2007 installed locally in order to use it. Now you can change any cell modifiable value, such as the Name, Doc Type, and Security Class. To return to the standard view, click Actions ⇨ Show in Standard View.

> When updating these new property settings using Edit in Datasheet, you may sometimes get a question that says: "You have pending changes or unresolved conflicts and errors. Do you want to wait for this operation to complete?" Click Yes if this happens. The reason that this happens is that the Datasheet is an ActiveX component that does its synchronization in short intervals; if you are too fast when switching back to the standard view, it might have not automatically synchronized the modifications yet.

9. The Datasheet view is also perfect when you want to change the order of columns, and to hide, edit, or delete a column. Use the description below to move the columns Doc Type and Security Class more to the left in this document library. There are even more actions available in the Datasheet view. Click Actions ⇨ Edit in Datasheet. Then select any of these operations:

❑ **Move a column:** Click on the column header, and you will see an icon with four arrows; keep the left mouse button down and drag the column to a new position, then release it.

❑ **Edit a column:** Right-click on the column header to be modified, then select Edit/Delete Column; the configuration page for this column is now displayed, and you can change the settings for this column.

❑ **Delete a column:** Right-click on the column header, then select Edit/Delete Column; at the end of the configuration page for this column, click Delete.

❑ **Add a column:** Right-click on any part of the table, and select Add Column, then enter the settings for this new column.

❑ **Open a document:** Right-click on any cell for this document row, and select Document ⇨ Open Document. The document will open in read-only mode.

❑ **Edit a document:** Right-click on any cell for this document row, and select Document ⇨ Edit Document.

❑ **Check out document:** Right-click on any cell for this document row, and select Document ⇨ Check Out Document (or Check In Document if the document was previously checked out).

❑ **Discuss the document:** Right-click on any cell for this document row, and select Discuss. The document is opened in a web browser, and the Discussion pane is presented where you can add your comments about the document. Note that this does not change the actual content of the document; all discussions are stored in a separate location in the SQL database, but are linked to this document.

> **Note that web discussions will only be available for documents that are opened in a web browser, not in full clients such as MS Word.**

❑ **Create an alert:** Right-click on any cell for this document row, and select Alert Me.

❑ **Copy or move cell content:** mark the cell, right-click, and select Copy or Move, then mark the destination cell, right-click and select Paste.

> **To learn more about all the functionality the Datasheet offers, right-click on any cell and select Help.**

The method in step 7 above is fine if you just want to change the properties for a single document; the second method in step 8 is very handy when you want to modify several documents' properties at the same time. Use whatever method you find convenient.

This is fun, don't you agree? It is so easy to add a new column if there is a need to keep track of a new property. Now try some more: Say that you want to list the person who is responsible for each document. You also want to display the company name that each file is connected with. Now, (and this is very nice), if you already have a contact list that contains all the company names, you can use that list in this document library.

To make this exercise more fun, before you continue, add some company names to the Contact list for this site: In the Quick Launch bar, click Contacts to view this list. To add a contact, click the New button. On the following web form, enter at least the Last Name and the Company name, then click OK. Now add some more contacts with other company names. When you're ready, continue with these steps:

1. Click the Shared Documents link to open a new page with the library.

2. Let's start by adding a column with the person responsible for a given document: Click Settings ➪ Create Column. On the web form enter these settings (accept the other default settings):

   a. **Column Name:** Responsible.

   b. **The type of information in this column is:** Person or Group. Instead of adding a choice list of possible document managers that you need to update regularly, you can do a lookup on the Active Directory.

   c. **Description:** "Enter the user responsible for this document."

   d. **Allow selection of:** People Only.

   e. **Choose from:** All Users.

   f. **Show field:** Name (with picture).

   g. Click OK to save and close this page. Your column is done.

3. The next and final column will retrieve its content from the Contact list. What you need is just the company name for each customer. Click Settings ➪ Create Column. On the web form enter these settings (as shown in Figure 10-6):

   a. **Column Name:** Company.

   b. **The type of information in this column is:** Lookup.

   c. **Description:** "This column gets its value from the Contact list."

   d. **Get information from:** Contacts (the name for this list).

   e. **In this column:** Company.

   f. Click OK to save and close this page. Your new column is done.

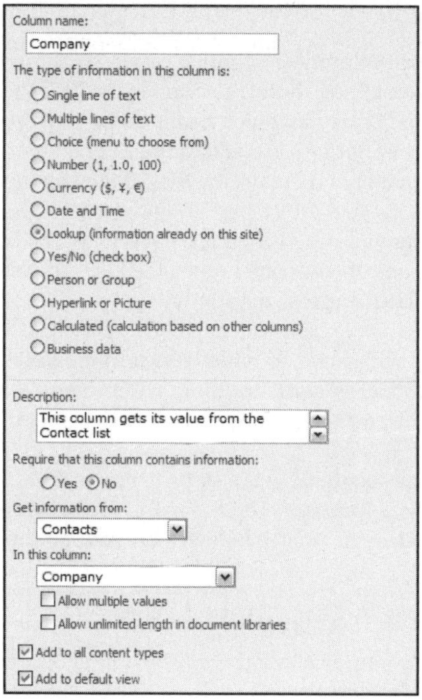

Column name:

Company

The type of information in this column is:

○ Single line of text
○ Multiple lines of text
○ Choice (menu to choose from)
○ Number (1, 1.0, 100)
○ Currency ($, ¥, €)
○ Date and Time
◉ Lookup (information already on this site)
○ Yes/No (check box)
○ Person or Group
○ Hyperlink or Picture
○ Calculated (calculation based on other columns)
○ Business data

Description:

This column gets its value from the
Contact list

Require that this column contains information:
○ Yes ◉ No

Get information from:
Contacts

In this column:
Company

☐ Allow multiple values
☐ Allow unlimited length in document libraries

☑ Add to all content types
☑ Add to default view

Figure 10-6

4.   You have the two new columns now. Let's see how they work: Switch to the Datasheet view (Actions ⇨ Edit in Datasheet View), the edit the following columns for the document in the library:

    a.   In the Responsible column, use its dropdown menu (note that it lists all users in this Active Directory environment), and select any name.

    b.   Then use the Company dropdown menu, and note that it will contain the names in the Contacts folder; select any company name in this list.

    c.   Repeat steps a and b until at least five documents have a value for these columns, to prepare for the next exercise. Then go back to the standard view: Actions ⇨ Show in Standard View. Note that in standard view, a picture of the Responsible user will be displayed, since you selected the option to show the field Name (with picture) in step 2f above.

As you have seen, adding new columns is very easy and makes it much easier to understand what a specific file is used for. To sort the list of documents, click on the column names. For example, if you want to sort the files based on document types, click the Doc Type name; click one more time if you want to reverse the sort order. Even though the column feature is very nice, it will be hard to find what you are looking for when the list contains hundreds or even thousands of files. What you need is a way of grouping and filtering the filenames.

Working with Views

A document library with custom columns is so much easier to use than a standard file system. But you can also use these columns to do something more; they can be the base for sorting, grouping, and filtering the files presented in the document library. SharePoint calls this a view. You can create a view that only displays documents where the Security Class is equal to Secret or a view that groups all documents and files based on company, or a view that only displays the files of which you are the Responsible person.

A document library can have any number of views. Each view can be either public or personal. Note that views are not security definitions; if someone knows the URL address for another user's personal view, he can use it by typing in the URL address manually.

The real beauty with columns will show up when you start creating views. Note that end users are supposed to create their own views, after some training, without any assistance from the administrator or a web developer. Views are an important feature and a key to achieving effective document management.

Now it's time for some exercises again. Use the steps to create the views mentioned above. Remember that they are dependent on the columns made in the previous examples, so if you have created other columns, you will have to replace the names below with your column names.

Try It Out　　**Create Views in Document Libraries**

1.　Log on as an administrator or a member of the SharePoint group "Designer," and open the same web site as in previous exercises.

2.　Open the document library where the new views will be created (in this example, Shared Documents).

3.　At the far end of the toolbar, you will see a menu named View showing the current view, most likely named All Documents. Open this menu, and select Create View.

4.　You will select one out of five available types of views: Standard View, Datasheet View, Calendar View, Gantt View or the Access View. In this example, select Standard View.

5.　Now you see a web form asking about how this view is to be configured. The first example is to create a view that only displays a document where the Company column is equal to Microsoft:

　　a.　**Name:** Microsoft Documents. This is just a label for this view.

　　b.　**Make this the default view:** No (the default value).

　　c.　**View Audience:** Create a Public view (the default value). A personal view will only be visible for the user who created it.

　　d.　**Columns:** Check each column to be displayed in this view. You can also change the order by using the Position from Left option.

　　e.　**Sort:** Name (for use in forms). This setting will present all documents in the list sorted by the filename.

　　f.　**Filter:** In the "Show the items when column" section, set Company equal to Microsoft. Note that this will automatically set the filter option "Show items only when the following is true." Now you have created a filtered list. Click OK at the end of this page to close and store this page.

6. The content for this document library is now displayed, but only documents that match the filter criteria, that is, where the Company name equals Microsoft.

7. Look at the view menu on the toolbar. You will see the name for this new view listed. Open its menu and select All Documents, and you will see all the documents again.

8. The next example shows how to create another view that will group all files based on Company name, you use the view menu again, and select Create View, then select the Standard View, and Enter these values:

    a. **Name:** Companies.

    b. **View Audience:** "Create a Public view."

    c. **Columns:** Define the columns you want to display and in what order.

    d. **Sort:** Name (for use in forms).

    e. Expand the section Group by and then set First group by column: Company. Note that the setting "By default, show groupings" is set to Collapsed. This will show only the group names by default, not the individual documents for each group.

    f. Click OK.

9. The document library is displayed again, but this time only showing groups of companies (see Figure 10-7). Note that the numbers in parentheses indicate how many files match the company name. If there are documents without any value in the Company column, then they are all grouped under the headline Company. For example, in the Figure 10-7 there are six documents without a Company setting.

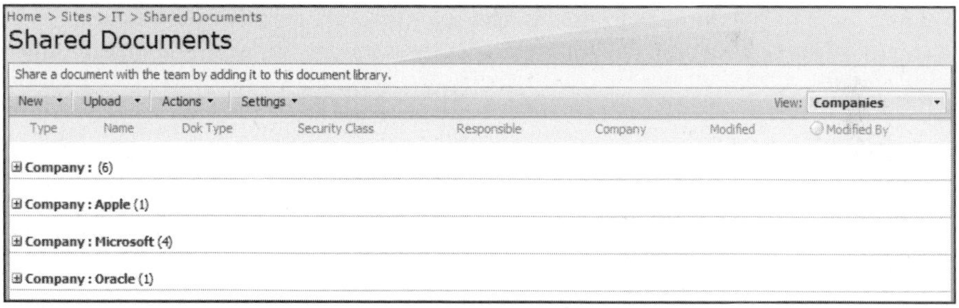

Figure 10-7

10. To create a third view that only lists documents where you are the Responsible person is almost as easy; the only difference is that you must in some way tell the view who you are. SharePoint has a special variable for this: [Me]. Note that these variables are translated into your local language if you install anything other than U.S. English. Create a new view as described above, based on the Standard View, then enter these values:

    a. **Name:** My Documents.

    b. **View Audience:** Create a Public view.

    c. **Columns:** Define what columns to display and in what order.

    d. **Sort:** Name (for use in forms).

  e. **Filter:** Set "Show the items when column" Responsible is equal to [Me]. (Note that you have to enter [Me] manually).

  f. Expand the Totals section: Set the column Name to Count. This will calculate and display the number of files over the Name column.

  g. Click OK; only documents where your name is listed as Responsible will be listed in the library.

It should be clear to you now that views are easy to create, yet very powerful. The variations are almost endless. You can also combine multiple columns (for example, if you need a view that lists all *public* files that you are *responsible* for). It is also possible to display more advanced calculations. For example, say that you have one column that displays the date when a contract ends. You want a view that lists all documents with fewer than 30 days to the end of the contract. This is not possible to define with just a view, but you can use a little trick: Create an extra column that contains the date 30 days before the end of the contract and then use both of these columns when creating the filter criteria for this view.

Try It Out **List Documents with Less Than 30 Days to a Date**

 1. Open the Document Library; click Settings ➪ Create Column, then enter:

  a. **Name:** End Date.

  b. **Type:** Date and Time.

  c. Click OK.

 2. Enter the end dates for each file in this new column. Make sure that some have dates more than 30 days away and some have dates less than 30 days away, to make the search results more interesting.

 3. Click Settings ➪ Create Column, and enter these settings:

  a. **Name:** 30 Days.

  b. **Type:** Calculated. Use the formula "=[End Date]-30" and set the returning data type to Date and Time.

  c. Click OK.

 4. Now you have the two values you need for this view. The next step is to create the view that compares today's date with these limits. SharePoint has the special keyword [Today] that you will use in this example; it allows you to compare dates with the current date. If the current date is within the limits defined in step 2 and 4 above, this document should be listed; if not, do not list it. Create a new Standard View with these settings:

  a. **Name:** Check these documents.

  b. **View Audience:** Create a Public view.

  c. **Columns:** Define what columns to display and in what order.

  d. **Sort:** Name (for use in forms).

  e. **Filter:** "30 Days" is less than or equal to [Today] and "End Date" is greater than [Today].

  f. Click OK.

Working with Alerts

One of the really cool features in SharePoint is alerts. An alert is your own private servant that checks all documents and other information types. If something you are interested in changes, you will get an e-mail from SharePoint. This is known as an alert, and it works with both MOSS and WSS. Here are the most common types of alerts:

❑ **A single file:** Sends you an e-mail if a specific file is changed.

❑ **A complete folder:** Checks a folder; if it is modified or if a file is added, modified, or removed, you are notified.

❑ **A list item:** Checks a specific list item in any type of list; if the item is modified, you are notified.

❑ **A complete list:** Checks a specific list; if the list is updated, for example if a list item is added or modified, you get an e-mail.

❑ **A news item:** Lets SharePoint's alerts govern the News list on an intranet; when something happens to this list, you get an e-mail.

❑ **Search query:** Gives you the option when creating a search query (under the Action section) to define a persistent SQL query, meaning that your search query can be saved and used again later.

> **SharePoint 2007 also allows you to send updates as RSS Feeds, as a complement to or replacement for alerts; see Chapter 7 for more information about RSS.**

A common question when discussing SharePoint alerts is how to add an alert for somebody else or for a group. This was not possible in SharePoint 2003, unless you added special Web Parts. But in SharePoint 2007 this feature is built in.

In the following example you add an alert for a single file and for a complete document library.

Try It Out   **Add Alerts to Files and Document Libraries**

1. Log on as a member of the SharePoint group Designer or as a Site owner.

2. Open the site and click on the document library to view its content.

3. To add an alert:

   ❑ **For a separate file:** Use the quick menu for any file; select Alert Me.

   ❑ **For a document library:** Click Actions ➪ Alert Me.

4. The default e-mail address will be your own. If you want to create an alert for other users or groups, simply enter their names in the Users field. You can also click on the little user directory icon and search for users and groups.

5. In the Change Type section, select what type of change you want to trigger an alert. The default is All changes.

6. In the Send Alerts for These Changes section, select the type of filter to be used for the alert; the default is Anything changes. Here you can also set the rule that the alert must only trigger when a document is displayed in a specific view.

7. Define how often you want SharePoint to check for modifications. The recommended frequency is Send a daily summary. This will group all alerts into one e-mail message per day. If you select the option to send an e-mail immediately, the e-mail will show up within five minutes after the change. You can also select an option to get one alert message once every week.

8. Click OK to save and close the web form.

9. A summary of the alerts are listed in two places. Note that they do not show the same information:

    a. **All alerts for a specific team site:** Click Site Actions ➪ Site Settings ➪ User Alerts. This page can also be used by the site owner to delete alerts for a specific user.

    b. **All alerts for a user, in both the portal site and any team site:** In Outlook 2003 and 2007 the user will see these views by opening the menu Tools ➪ Rules and the Alerts ➪ Manage Alerts tab. Note that this is the only way for a user to display a total summary of all alerts!

The alert feature is available almost everywhere in SharePoint, both in MOSS sites and in every WSS site. Learn how to use them. They can save you a lot of time and ensure that you know about important changes.

Checking Out and Checking In

So far you have learned how to work with custom columns and views, as well as alerts. Now you will look more closely at how the actual document is updated. When you open a MS Office document stored in a file share, it automatically opens in edit mode, even if your intention is only to read it. If someone else tries to open the same document while you have it open in edit mode, it will not work, since you have locked it. The other user can use a copy of that document or wait for you to close the document (also closing edit mode). It would have been better if documents were automatically opened in read-only mode instead of edit mode. SharePoint does this, and you actually must use the document's quick menu to select Edit in Microsoft Office Word or whatever file type you are opening.

Assume that the user Anna needs to update a specific document that is stored on a public file share; she knows that it will take more time than she has available today, so what do she do? One solution is to copy the file to her local computer and update this file locally. The problem with this very common solution is that someone else, let's say Thomas, may start modifying the original file, unaware that Anna is updating a copy of this file. When Anna is done with her editing, she copies the file back to the original storage. What will happen if the original file has been updated by Thomas during this time, without Anna knowing this? Well, Anna's file will overwrite Thomas's version, without any warning.

A much better approach is to lock the file so that only one person can edit the document. This is a standard feature of all SharePoint's sites, including the free WSS team sites. It is called checking out when a user locks the editing process on a file; from that point on only that user is able to update that document.

When that user is done, he or she performs a check in, which saves the current version and removes the editing lock. The file is now available for others to edit.

So what happens when a user checks out a file? It actually splits in two separate versions: one that the content author sees and works with and another that other users see, which is the same as the most recent public version. When the author later checks in the file, that version replaces the previous public version and becomes the new public version. What happens with the previous version depends on the setting for version history. If version history is activated, the file is saved but hidden; if version history is not activated, the file is overwritten.

When a user checks out a file, her name will be listed in the default column Checked Out To that all document libraries have. If another user tries to open that file in edit mode, she will be warned that this file has been checked out by the first user, but SharePoint will offer the user the option to open the file in read-only mode. There is no way that a checked-out file can be edited by more than a single user.

When a user opens any MS Office files, such as Word and Excel files in the normal way, without any previous checkout process, this also works as if the file were checked out. In other words, SharePoint does a silent and implicit checkout when opening any Office document; when the document is later saved and closed, a silent checkin occurs. No listing is created in the Checked Out To column, but the process works the same way as before, except that it only works as long as the user has the document open in her MS Office application. This feature will work with MS Office 2000 or later.

Try It Out — Check Out and Check In Documents

1. Go to any document library where you have at least Contributor permissions, such as the SharePoint group Members (i.e., where you can add, delete, and modify files).

2. In this example, choose an existing MS Excel file. Use its quick menu and select Check out. Note that your name now is listed in the Checked Out To column (as in Figure 10-8), regardless of whether you have the file opened in MS Office or not.

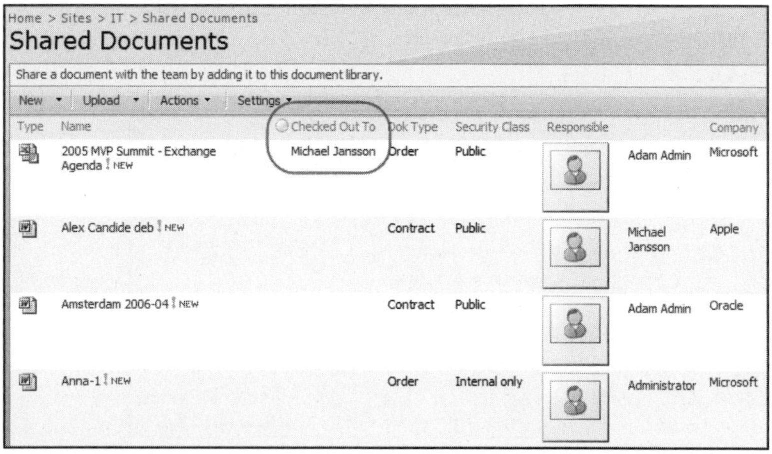

Figure 10-8

3. Log on as another user. Try to open the same document, using its quick menu and Edit in Microsoft Office Excel. You will get a warning that this document is checked out by another user (see Figure 10-9). Close that warning and the MS Office program again.

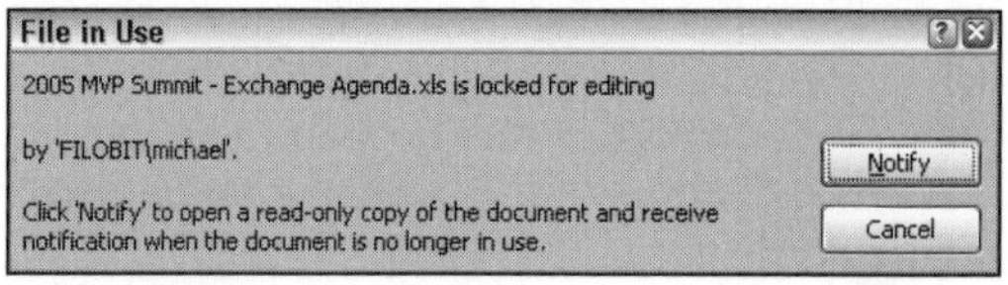

Figure 10-9

4. Go back to your first account. Try to edit the same document, and it will work just fine. Do some modifications and then close down MS Excel. What happens next, depends if the library has version history activated or not.

    a. **No Version History:** This is the default setting for all libraries. First, you will be asked if you want to save the modification or not; click Yes. Next, you will be informed that other users cannot see your modification unless you select the option to check in the document (see Figure 10-10); click Yes. Finally, you will get a chance to enter a comment about this version. This information will then be listed in the version history. You can also choose to keep the document checked out after saving it.

    b. **Version History Activated:** First, you will be asked if you want to save the modification or not; click Yes. Next, you will be asked if you want to check in a minor (draft) version, or a major (published) version; you can also enter a comment about this version (see Figure 10-11). Select the option to check-in a major version.

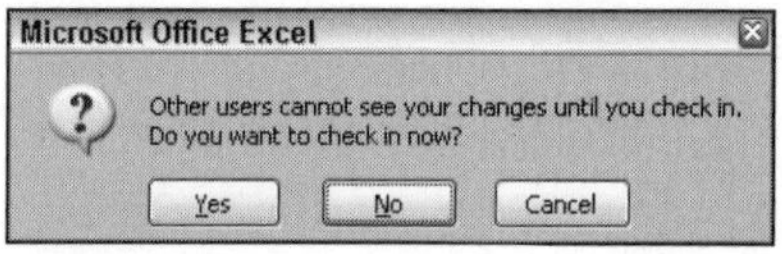

Figure 10-10

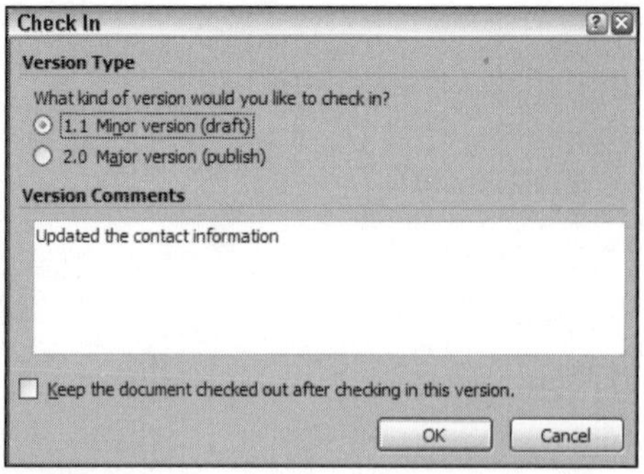

Figure 10-11

5.   The column Checked Out To is now empty, since the file is no longer checked out. If instead of checking in the file, you chose to keep the file checked out, the file would be closed and your name would still be listed in the Checked Out To column. That is perfectly fine if you want to go home for the night and continue to edit the file the next day.

A commonly asked question is whether the administrator can break or undo a checkout lock made by somebody else. The answer is Yes! The administrator simply goes to the same document library, uses the Quick Launch bar, and selects either Check in to keep whatever the author has saved so far or Discard Check Out to revert the document to its last public version. If the administrator chooses to check in the document, SharePoint will display the following warning depicted in Figure 10-12.

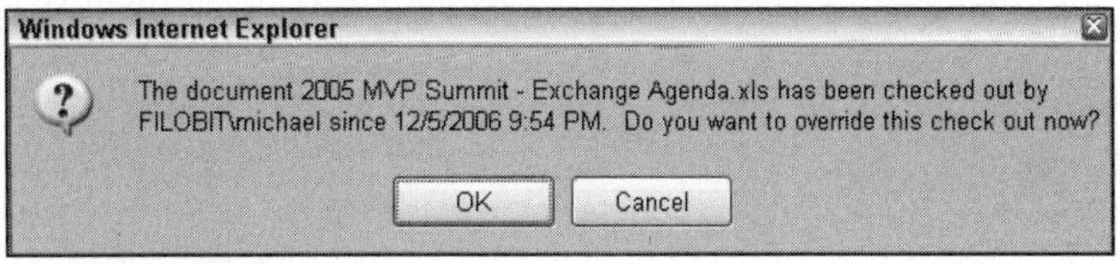

Windows Internet Explorer

? The document 2005 MVP Summit - Exchange Agenda.xls has been checked out by FILOBIT\michael since 12/5/2006 9:54 PM. Do you want to override this check out now?

OK   Cancel

Figure 10-12

Document Version History

By default SharePoint will not store previous versions of any document. It is possible to activate the version history feature for most types of lists and document libraries, XML libraries, and picture libraries. This is a big improvement over the previous SharePoint 2003 version, where only libraries had version history.

The reason that version history is disabled by default is that it requires disk and CPU resources. However, the load is much less with SharePoint 2007 than with SharePoint 2003. Now SharePoint only stores the delta, that is, the information updated, not complete documents as in previous SharePoint version. If you have version history active and later revert back to no version management, it will in effect delete all prior versions of all documents except the latest version.

There are two types of version history in SharePoint 2007: one that only stores public, also known as major, versions (i.e., 1, 2 and 3), and another type that keeps track of both draft (1.1, 1.2) and major versions (1.0, 2.0). Choose the one that suits your needs best; you will probably need a mix of all three types for all your document libraries.

Try It Out   Enable Version History

1.   Log on as an owner of a site.

2.   Click on the document library, for example Shared Documents, to view its content.

3.   Click Settings ➪ Document Library Settings. If you do not see this option, then your account does not have permission to change the settings for this library!

4.   Click on the link Version settings. In the section Document Version History, you can choose the type of version history for this library: No versioning, Create major versions, or Create major

and minor (draft) versions. Note that here you can also set the number of versions to store. Another related setting is in the Draft Item Security: If you selected Create major and minor (draft) versions above, you can define who will see the draft versions:

❑ **Any users who can read items:** Choose this option if all users should be able to read draft versions.

❑ **Only users who can edit items:** Choose this option to limit the group of users who will see draft versions to authors only, (i.e., not users with only Read access).

❑ **Only users who can approve items (and the author of the item):** Choose this option when nobody except the author and the user with Approve permission should be able to see the draft version. Note that this option is only available if you activate the Require content approval for submitted items option is set to Yes, at the top of this web form!

5. Click OK and then the breadcrumb trail Shared Documents at the top of this page.

Regardless of the type of version history you selected, it is now active, but only for the current library! If you have more document libraries and want a version history of them all, you must enable this for all of these libraries. Test it now:

1. Edit any MS Office document in the list and then save and close this file.

2. Use the file's quick menu and select Version History. Depending on the type of version history you selected, you will now see the following:

❑ **Only Major Versions:** The list shows that the current version is 2.0.

❑ **Major and Draft Versions:** The list shows that the is version 1.1, that is, this is a draft version, not a major (published) version. To make this the published version, go back to the previous page, and open the quick menu for the file again. This time, select Publish a Major Version, enter a version comment, then click OK. Next, open the version history again, and the current version is now 2.0.

3. If you changed an existing file once, you should now see a list of two files, but with different version numbers, times and dates, plus the name of the user who modified the file. You can also see information about what was changed in a specific version. These versions also have a quick menu. You can use it to view, restore, or delete any of the previous versions (see Figure 10-13). If you choose to restore a previous version, the current version will simply be the second newest version, so if you want to undo this restore, you can restore the second newest version. In other words, using the preceding example, you now have three versions, where 1.0 and 3.0 are identical.

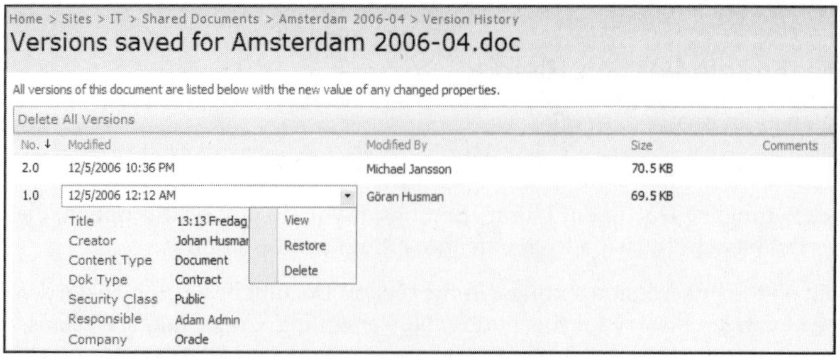

Figure 10-13

Content Types and Document Templates

One of the most requested features in the previous version of SharePoint was to be able to add more than one document template for any given document library. By default, a document library would only offer one type of document template; for example, an empty MS Word document.

Microsoft's solution was to create functionality beyond simple document templates. Why? Because many users will eventually need it, even though this need might not seem obvious at first glance. For example, say that you want to have two document templates in a document library, one Sales Quote and one Contract. The content of these templates looks different, of course. Each template most likely needs different properties, or metadata. For example, the Sales Quote needs to keep track of the due date for this quote, while the Contract stores the period that it is valid (the start and end dates). The Sales Quote also has an attached workflow, so every time a new quote is created, the sales manager will get an e-mail, while the Contract has a workflow that will inform the user responsible for this contract when there is one month left in the period. There may even be more differences between these types of documents, and if you have more than two templates, the differences will be even greater. This is why Microsoft did not just call their solution a "document template," but instead a "content type."

Content Types Overview

The solution Microsoft created for SharePoint 2007 works for both WSS and MOSS and allows an administrator to create any number of content types, each with different settings, such as:

❑ **Document Template:** The precreated content of the document; for example, with document headers, footers, contact information, and so on.

❑ **Columns:** You can define any number of specific columns for storing metadata about the type of documents. Whenever an author creates a document based on a content type, these columns will be visible.

❑ **Workflows:** A content type can have one or more workflows associated with it. You can also create a workflow that starts automatically every time an author creates or modifies a new document, based on the content type.

❑ **Property Pane:** You can customize the property page displayed in MS Office 2007 when working with documents based on a content type. You can also define if the property pane should be visible or not in MS Office 2007.

❑ **Policies:** You can define a number of document policies that will affect a document based on a specific content type. These policies will follow the document through its lifetime.

In other words, content types make it very easy to use documents in a process-oriented manner, not just as individual files. This is also the reason SharePoint 2007 can be used to comply with many governmental regulations, like the Sarbanes-Oxley Act (SOX) or the Health Insurance Portability and Accountability Act (HIPAA), which define how an organization should manage any type of information.

A content type can inherit its setting from a parent content type. For example, say that you have three types of sales quotes; each of them has a specific document template, but all of them have the same columns and workflows. If so, you could create a content type for the master sales quote, and the three other content types that inherit the settings from the master quote, except the document template. If you later decide to change the workflow on the master quote, the change will be inherited by all three sales quotes automatically. Working in this way, you will have a much better control over these quotes, and it will be easy to change and update them later on.

All content types you create must inherit from one of the base content types, for example a Document content type. These base content types come with SharePoint, and you can see all of them if you follow the steps in the Try It Out below.

Try It Out   List the Default Content Types

1. Log on as an administrator, and open the top site for the site collection; for example, http://srv1.

2. Click Site Actions ➪ Site Settings ➪ Modify All Site Settings.

3. In the Galleries section, click Site Content Types. The complete list of content types for the site collection is displayed (see Figure 10-14).

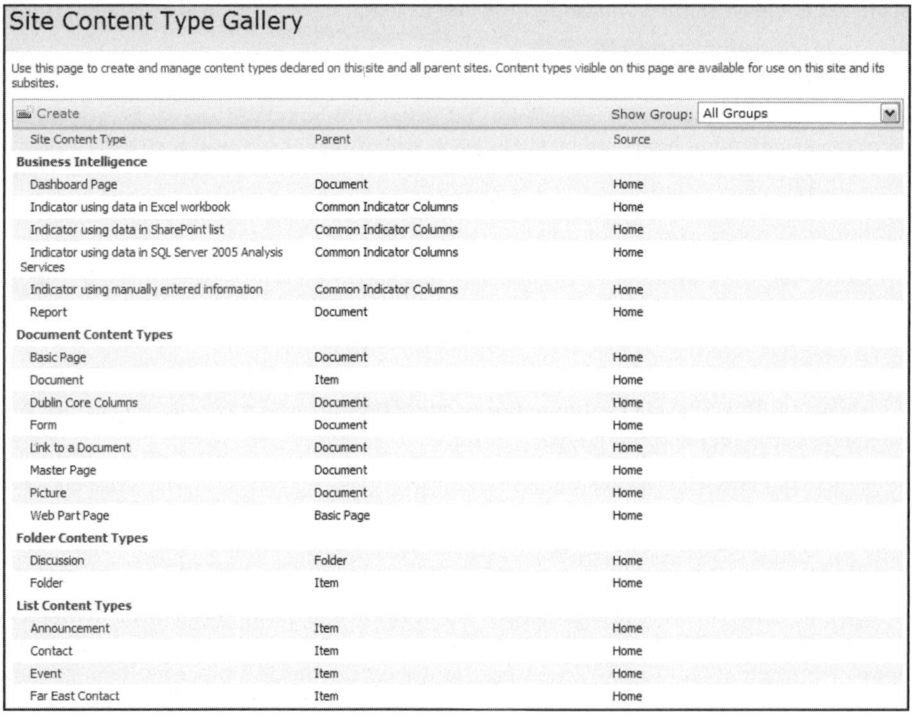

Site Content Type Gallery

Use this page to create and manage content types declared on this site and all parent sites. Content types visible on this page are available for use on this site and its subsites.

📖 Create   Show Group: | All Groups   ▼ |

Site Content Type	Parent	Source
Business Intelligence		
Dashboard Page	Document	Home
Indicator using data in Excel workbook	Common Indicator Columns	Home
Indicator using data in SharePoint list	Common Indicator Columns	Home
Indicator using data in SQL Server 2005 Analysis Services	Common Indicator Columns	Home
Indicator using manually entered information	Common Indicator Columns	Home
Report	Document	Home
Document Content Types		
Basic Page	Document	Home
Document	Item	Home
Dublin Core Columns	Document	Home
Form	Document	Home
Link to a Document	Document	Home
Master Page	Document	Home
Picture	Document	Home
Web Part Page	Basic Page	Home
Folder Content Types		
Discussion	Folder	Home
Folder	Item	Home
List Content Types		
Announcement	Item	Home
Contact	Item	Home
Event	Item	Home
Far East Contact	Item	Home

Figure 10-14

Each site content type is grouped into sections, such as Business Intelligence, Document Content Types, and so on, to make it easier for you to find the right one. When you create new content sources, you can store them in existing groups or create new groups. For each content type this list will display its parent content type, and the Source column shows what SharePoint site the content source belongs to. Note that a content source can have one site as the source, while still be used in subsites of that site.

Creating Content Types

You can create a new content type, whenever you need it, but very often you have a document template already that you want to use for the new content type. For example, you may have a Sales Quote in a MS Word template that you have been using for a while, and now you want to use it in a site content type. The following Try It Out shows how to do this.

| Try It Out | Create a Content Type |

1. Log on as an administrator.

2. Locate the current MS Word file used as a template for Sales Quotes, and make sure that it is formatted properly. In this example, assume that this file is named `Quote-Template.doc` and is stored on the file server at `\\FS1\Templates`.

3. Open the top site for the site collection; for example, `http://srv1`.

4. Click Site Actions ⇨ Site Settings ⇨ Modify All Site Settings.

5. In the Galleries section, click Site Content Types.

6. Click Create on the toolbar for this page, then enter the following (see Figure 10-15):

   a. **Name:** Sales Quotes. This will be visible to the authors later on.

   b. **Description:** "Use this template to create Sales Quotes." This will be visible to the authors later on.

   c. **Select parent content type from:** Document Content Type.

   d. **Parent Content Type:** Document.

   e. **Put this site content type into:** New Group: Filobit. This will save this content type in its own group on the site content type listing, which makes it easier for the administrator to locate it later.

   f. Click OK.

7. The content type is now created, but it has no specific settings, besides the settings it inherited from its parent, the "Document" type, which is just one column named Title. This column, along with all of the configuration available for this content type is now displayed on a web form. The next step is to start configuring this content type; click Advanced settings, and do this:

   a. Select the option Upload a new document template, then click Browse.

   b. Locate the document template file you want to use for this content type; in this example it was `\\FS1\Template\Quote-Template.doc`. Then click Open.

   c. The other options on this page are okay, so do not change them. Click OK to save this setting and copy the listed file into SharePoint (you can then change or move the original template file without anything happening to the content source).

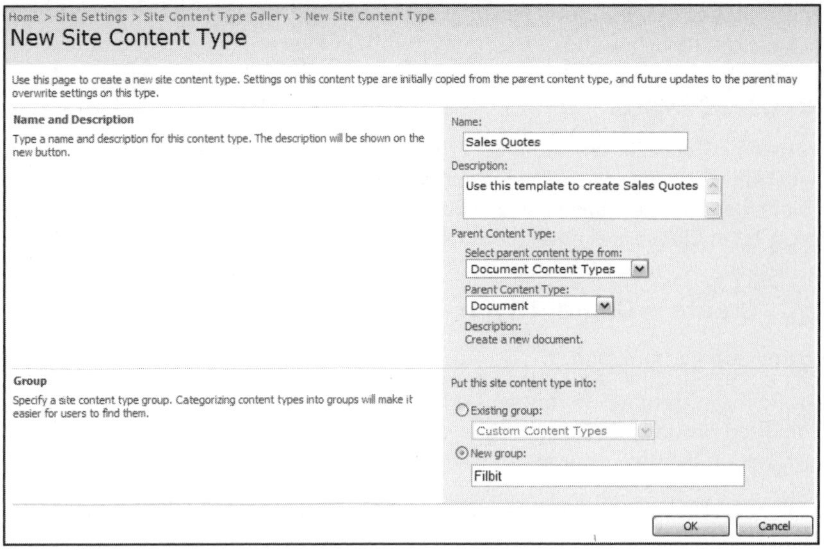

Home > Site Settings > Site Content Type Gallery > New Site Content Type

New Site Content Type

Use this page to create a new site content type. Settings on this content type are initially copied from the parent content type, and future updates to the parent may overwrite settings on this type.

Name and Description

Type a name and description for this content type. The description will be shown on the new button.

Name:
Sales Quotes

Description:
Use this template to create Sales Quotes

Parent Content Type:

Select parent content type from:
Document Content Types

Parent Content Type:
Document

Description:
Create a new document.

Group

Specify a site content type group. Categorizing content types into groups will make it easier for users to find them.

Put this site content type into:
○ Existing group:
Custom Content Types
● New group:
Filbit

OK   Cancel

Figure 10-15

8. You are taken back to the general configuration page for the content type. Next, you can modify any of these settings for the content type (but in this example, you will not change any of these):

❑ Click Workflow settings to change or update any workflows.

❑ Click Delete this site content type, if you want to remove it. Make sure not to click this link unless you really want to remove the content type.

❑ Click Document Information Panel settings, if you want to add or update the property pane displayed in MS Office 2007 applications, such as MS Word 2007. This pane will display the columns associated with the document. On that page is also an option to always display the property pane in MS Office 2007.

❑ Click Information management policy settings, if you need to define policies for the document based on this content type.

❑ Click Manage document conversion for this content type, if you want to define how a document based on the content type can be converted to other file types, such as converting an MS InfoPath form to a PNG image, or a Word document to a PDF file. Note that this requires that you have installed the support for creating PDF files, as well as activated the conversion feature for this web application (see Chapter 5).

9. Let's add a new column for Sales Quotes that stores the last date for the quote:

a. Still on the configuration page for this content type, click Add from new site column, then enter the following values.

b. **Column name:** Last Date.

c. **The type of information in this column is:** Date and Time.

d. **Put this site column into:** New group: Filobit.

e. Date and Time Format: Date Only.

    f.   Default value: Today's Date.

    g.   Update all content types inheriting from this type? Yes.

    h.   Click OK to create this column and return to the previous web form. The new column is now visible in the Columns section.

The content type is now configured and ready to be used. Since it is created in the top site for this site collection, it can be used in any of its sites. Let's test it and add it to the document library in the IT site created before.

Try It Out   **Apply a Content Type to a Document Library**

1. Log on as an administrator, then open the site, containing the document library where this content type should be added; for example, `http://srv1/sitedirectory/it`.

2. Click on the Shared Document to open it.

3. Click Settings ➪ Document Library Settings.

4. Click Advanced settings, then set the option Allow management of content types to Yes, then click OK. You will be returned to the configuration page for the document library.

5. Note that you now see a new section on this configuration page: Content Types. Click Add from existing site content types.

6. Open the menu for "Select site content types from" to Filobit; the content type Sales Quote you created before will now be listed.

7. Click Add to move the Sales Content to the Content types to add pane, then click OK. Again, you are returned to the configuration page for this document library. Note that the Sales Quote is now listed as a new content type, along with the default Document content type.

8. Click Shared Documents on the breadcrumb trail to leave this configuration page and display the content of the document library.

9. Click on the black arrow next to the New button to display its menu; it will now display Sales Quotes as an option (see Figure 10-16). Select Sales Quotes, and MS Word will open with the document template associated with this content type. Enter some values in the document, and save it. The default location will be the current document library.

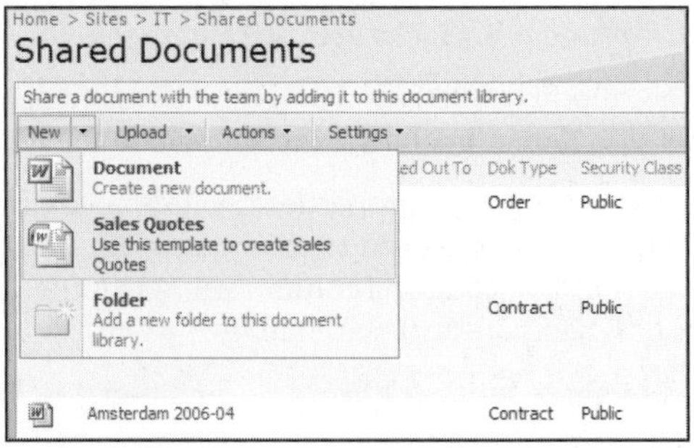

Figure 10-16

What if you need to change the settings for this site content type; for example, to modify its document template or add more columns? This is really where content types shine. Just open the content type where it was created (usually at the top site), as previously described, then change any setting, including uploading a new document template. Make sure to set the option Update all content types inheriting from this type to Yes, and all document libraries associated with that content type will be updated.

> Note that existing documents in the library will not be affected by the modified document template. But other settings, such as new columns or policies, will affect existing documents as well.

Document Management with MS Office

So far you have worked exclusively with a web browser, typically MS Internet Explorer. A user of MS Office 2007 will also find a lot of SharePoint-related features integrated into products like MS Word, MS Excel, and MS PowerPoint. The integration will make it possible for a user who works a lot with MS Office products to view and set SharePoint information without having to switch to a web browser. Using any edition of Office 2007, you can do the following SharePoint-related tasks:

- ❑ **Check Out/Check In:** Lock and unlock editing for a file.

- ❑ **View version history:** Display a list of all previous versions, including all comments. You can also view, restore, and delete previous versions.

- ❑ **View Workflow Tasks:** View or start workflows defined for the document library where the document is stored. This requires MS Office Professional Plus or higher editions.

- ❑ **Manage Alerts:** Set an alert for the current document.

- ❑ **Manage other files in the library:** Set alerts and delete and open other files. You can also add new documents and create folders in the current library.

- ❑ **Manage Document Workspace:** Create or delete a workspace for the current document; see more about workspaces later in this chapter.

- ❑ **View membership:** See what members have access to a team site, and if they are online, add new members, edit their Site Group membership, and remove members.

- ❑ **Manage Tasks:** View, modify, delete, and add new tasks, and create alerts for a task. This information will be stored in a task list on the site where the document library is stored. For more information about working with Tasks lists, see Chapter 7.

- ❑ **Manage Links:** View, modify, delete, and add new URL links; and create alerts for a link. This information will be stored in a link list on the site where the document library is stored.

- ❑ **Manage Document Properties:** All properties (including column settings) for the document are available here and may be changed and used in the Office document (for example, in a document header or footer). If you change a column value in Office, this will be replicated back to the document library when you store the changes.

- ❑ **Manage the team site:** From within Office, you can open this site, change its title, and open its site settings.

A subset of these features will be available for users of MS Office 2003, but none of these features is available for earlier versions! It is therefore important that at least the users who produce documents have MS Office 2007 in order to have an optimal working environment.

To see how all these features work, some examples follow. Use the steps in the following Try It Out to get familiar with this MS Office integration.

Try It Out   MS Office 2007 Integration

1. Log on as a user with at least contributor rights, (for example a user with membership of the SharePoint group Members) to a team site. Open any of its document libraries. Use the quick menu for a MS Office document (for example, an MS Word file), and select Edit in Microsoft Office Word.

2. Depending on what SharePoint feature you want to use, you will use different buttons in MS Office. For example to use MS Word 2007 and display the document management panel for the current document, start a workflow, check out the document, or view the version history, click the Office Button ➪ Server (see Figure 10-17).

Figure 10-17

3. To work with the other files in this document library or create tasks in the SharePoint task list, manage members of this site, manage links, or create Document Workspaces, click the Office button, then select Server ➪ Document Management Information (see Figure 10-18).

Figure 10-18

4. Click on the leftmost icon on the Document Management Information pane. It will display important status information about this document, such as if someone has checked out the document. The number under the icon indicates the number of current status information messages.

5. Click on the user icon (second from the left). The number under the icon indicates how many users and groups have access to this library. You will also see the names of these users and groups and their current online status, if you are using a local MS Live Communication Server in your network or the public MSN instant messaging service. Point the mouse to any of these users; a quick menu is available that allows you to manage that user, assuming that you have administrative rights on that team site to do so. You will see more information about those users, such as calendar status, phone numbers, mail addresses, and other Outlook properties. At the bottom of this pane tab is a button to add new members and to send e-mail to all members. This last feature is very handy when you want to inform all users about an important update and you do not know if everyone has created an alert for this document.

6. Click on the task icon (third from the left). The number indicates the total number of tasks in this list. Note that some of these may have been added directly to the task list on the team site. Using the links at the bottom of this tab, you can add new tasks and request alerts about tasks. If there are any existing tasks, they will be listed. Point to a task to see all its details; use its quick menu to edit, delete, or create an alert for that particular task. If a task is completed, check the check box in front of the task and this information will directly be updated on the team site. Use tasks when working with documents as a reminder or to delegate things to do to other members. This is much better than sending an e-mail to team members when delegating tasks.

7. Click on the document icon (second from the right); the number indicates the total number of documents in this library. Below this the documents are listed, unless the number is too great; if so, you will see a link to open the list in a browser instead. The reason for this is to avoid downloading a lot of information to the MS Office program. There is a dropdown menu for sorting this document list, based, for example, on creation date or filename. Every document listed has a quick menu that can be used to open or delete it, or to create an alert for that specific document. At the bottom of this tab are links for adding new documents, adding folders to the library, and creating an alert for the current document.

8. Click on the link icon (rightmost). The number indicates the current number of URL links available in the linked list in the team site. The actual URL links are listed below it; use the Sort by menu to change the sort order for the list. For each URL, there is a quick menu that can be used to edit or delete that link, and to create an alert for that particular link. At the bottom, you will find buttons for creating new links and managing alerts for the links.

9. At the top of the Document Management Information panel is a link to the site the document is stored in; click it to open the site.

One very handy feature is the propagation of document properties from columns in SharePoint's document library to MS Office document properties. This makes it possible to view and display those properties inside the content of a document. For example, say that you have a column in the document library that defines the customer name for a document. You can use that information to display the customer name in the document header, or anywhere in the document, by following the steps in the Try It Out below.

Try It Out   Display Properties inside Office Documents

1. Open an MS Office document in edit mode from any document library, which has a custom column, such as the Doc Type column you created in a previous example.

2. Set the cursor in the document, where you want this information to be displayed; for example in a document header. A tip is to type a label in front of this column value to describe the property to be displayed.

3. Select the ribbon Insert, and then click Text ⇨ Quick Parts ⇨ Document Properties. Here are list all the SharePoint columns that have been propagated into document properties; locate a property to add, and select it. The property is now displayed in the document. Note that Word documents, by default, have a number of properties, such as Author and Customer. If you have created a column with the same name, you will find two properties with the same name. For example, if you created the column Customer, you will find both the first Customer (which is the standard property found in all Word documents) and a second Customer property, which is your column.

> If the Quick Part's "Document Properties" is grayed out, save this document and try again.

4. There are two ways to change the value of a column property from within MS Office applications: Either you change the value in the document information panel, or you change the Quick Part added to the document itself. Either way, this will update the column value in the document library.

This last feature for displaying column settings inside an MS Office document is very handy when using document headers or other structured documents. Instead of adding values such as document type, customer name, or project number manually in the document, you can create columns for the document library and then expose them in the document, which will make it much easier for the user to both view and set the values.

More about Datasheet Views

Earlier in this chapter you saw how any list or library could be displayed using a Datasheet view, based on MS Access 2007. This Datasheet view actually has more features besides those previously explained. For example, you can print a list using MS Exchange or create a report using MS Access. This is particularly important, since the print capabilities in any web application, including SharePoint, are not too impressive.

There is a cleverly hidden button at the far-right side of the Datasheet view. It looks like a part of the right frame. Click on it, and a task pane will be displayed (see Figure 10-19). Another way of displaying this pane is to click the menu Actions ⇨ Tasks. Note that Datasheet view must be displayed to find the Tasks option on the Actions menu.

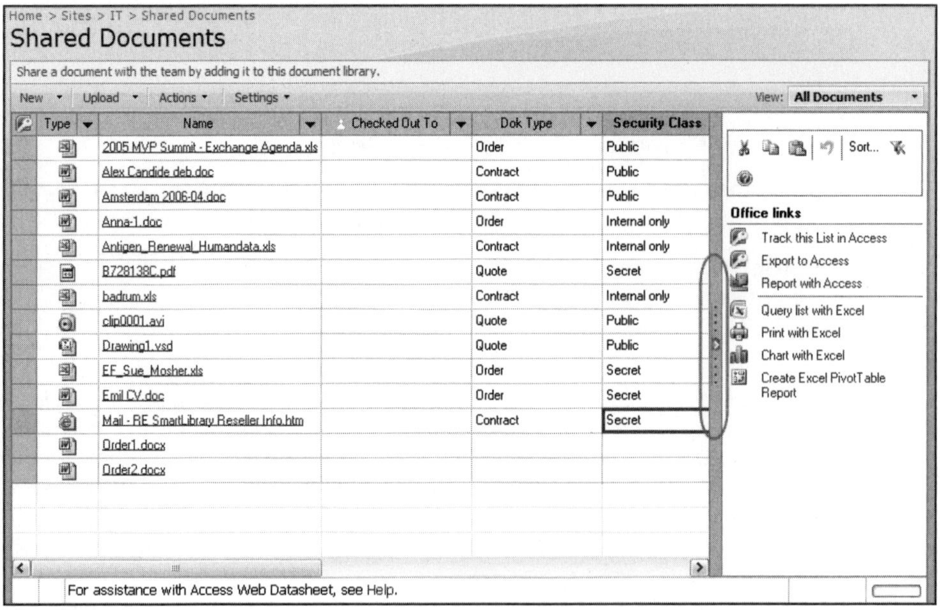

Figure 10-19

Using this task pane, a user can activate these features:

❑ **Track this List in Access:** You can link this list to an Access database and use it to create reports or work with its data with all the features of MS Access. If the content in the list is modified, then the Access database will automatically be updated. If you modify a value in the Access database, then the content of the list in SharePoint is updated. This is also a way to take the list offline, since all of the actual content of the list is copied to the Access database, not only the columns displayed in the current view. You can use one Access database for several lists, or you can create a separate database for each list, whatever suits your needs.

❑ **Export to Access:** This is simply a way to copy all the content of the current list to an Access database table. It will not have the two-way synchronization feature that the previous option had. Use this option when you simply want to take a snapshot of the current values in this list, possibly for calculating or reporting purposes.

❑ **Report with Access:** The content of this SharePoint list is copied to Access, and a default report is created. You can then modify this report; for example, removing columns, changing the order of columns, changing the logotype, and using Access AutoFormat feature to create a better-looking report (see Figure 10-20).

❑ **Query list with Excel:** Use this option to copy the list content to an Excel spreadsheet. By default, Excel will warn you about opening this data connection. To continue, you must select Enable. The result is a formatted table in Excel. You can now use this content with all the features of Excel, such as calculating, sorting, building a diagram, and printing. Note that this option will not replicate any local modifications in the spreadsheet back to the SharePoint list, as in SharePoint 2003. To modify list content outside SharePoint, you should use the option Track this List in Access instead.

❑ **Print with Excel:** Since SharePoint is a web application is has poor printing functionality. Use MS Excel if you want better control of the print process for the list content, such as the formatting, fonts, and colors. By default, Excel will warn you about opening this data connection; you must click Enable to continue.

❑ **Chart with Excel:** If you have columns with numerical or date format you can use these values in MS Excel to create charts, such as histograms and pie charts. Also here Excel, by default, warns you about opening a data connection. Select Enable to continue, then select the columns to be used for the diagram and the type of diagram; you will see the resulting diagram.

❑ **Create Excel Pivot Table Report:** Use the column properties to create a dynamic summary of these cell values; this is typically used for pivot tables. Also here Excel warns about the data connection; click Enable to continue.

❑ At the top of this task pane, you will also find buttons for actions like sorting, cutting, copying and pasting documents or columns.

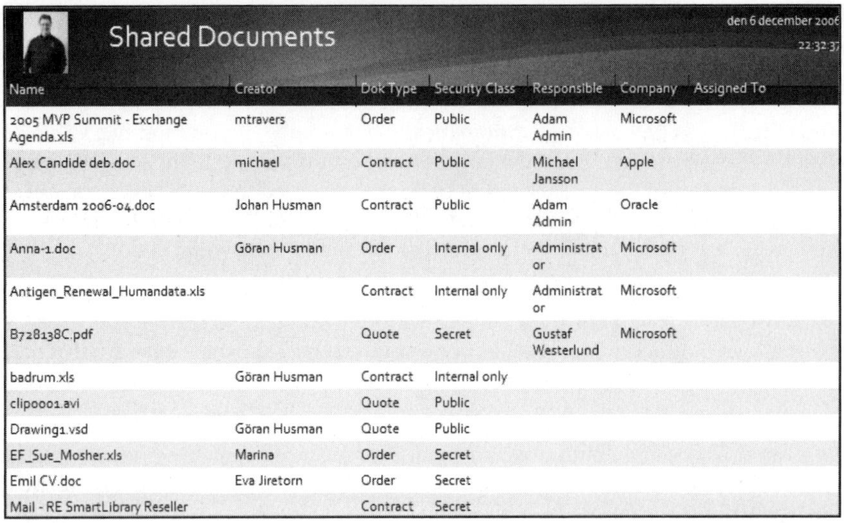

Name	Creator	Dok Type	Security Class	Responsible	Company	Assigned To
2005 MVP Summit - Exchange Agenda.xls	mtravers	Order	Public	Adam Admin	Microsoft	
Alex Candide deb.doc	michael	Contract	Public	Michael Jansson	Apple	
Amsterdam 2006-04.doc	Johan Husman	Contract	Public	Adam Admin	Oracle	
Anna-1.doc	Göran Husman	Order	Internal only	Administrator	Microsoft	
Antigen_Renewal_Humandata.xls		Contract	Internal only	Administrator	Microsoft	
B728138C.pdf		Quote	Secret	Gustaf Westerlund	Microsoft	
badrum.xls	Göran Husman	Contract	Internal only			
clip0001.avi		Quote	Public			
Drawing1.vsd	Göran Husman	Quote	Public			
EF_Sue_Mosher.xls	Marina	Order	Secret			
Emil CV.doc	Eva Jiretorn	Order	Secret			
Mail - RE SmartLibrary Reseller		Contract	Secret			

Figure 10-20

Managing List Access

Each document list will, by default, inherit the security settings of the SharePoint site. In other words, if Axel is a member of the SharePoint group Member for the site, and therefore has Contributor permissions, he will also be a contributor for any document library and list in the team site. You can break the inherited permissions, when necessary, so Axel in this example gets other permissions specifically on a library. This is true, regardless of whether the site is a WSS site or a MOSS site, contrary to how it worked in SharePoint 2003, where only WSS sites allowed you to configure different permissions for a list or library.

Not only will SharePoint 2007 allow you to set specific permissions for each list and library in a site, but you can also set specific permissions on folders within a library, and even individual documents and list items. This is also new, compared to SharePoint 2003, and opens up a lot of opportunities to set whatever security definitions needed on the content of a site.

Another possibility for controlling the permissions for individual document items is to use Microsoft's Information Rights Management (IRM) client, which is supported by both Office 2003 and Office 2007 applications. This functionality is also known as the Rights Management Service (RMS) and allows you to define security settings such as:

❑ Axel can read the document, but only Anna can modify it.

❑ This document cannot be printed by Axel, but can be printed by Anna.

❑ This document will cease to exist on Friday at 5 P.M. for both Axel and Anna.

And all of these security settings will be valid regardless of how a user gets a copy of the document, whether it is by the file system, as an e-mail attachment, or by a document library in SharePoint. If you want to know more about IRM and RMS, look at this page: www.microsoft.com/rms.

Individual Permission Settings

To show how the individual permissions work in SharePoint 2007, here is an example. Remember that SharePoint groups are always connected to a permission level; for example, the group Members is connected to the permission Contribute, and the group Visitors is connected to the permission Read. Still, it is possible to grant an individual user a specific permission level instead of using SharePoint groups. For example, say that you have two users named Anna and Axel, who both have been granted the Contribute permission level on the site IT. By default, this will also give them Contributor permission to all the content in that site, including any list or library. There is a document library on the site named Shared Documents. The owner of the IT site wants to restrict the security settings for Axel to Read permission only. The following Try It Out shows how the owner can do this.

> **Try It Out**   **Set Individual Permissions for a Library**
>
> 1. Open the Shared Documents library using an account with administrative rights for the site.
>
> 2. Click Settings ➪ Document Library Settings.
>
> 3. Click Permissions for this document library. This will list all the permissions inherited from the site itself. Note that the list is grayed out, which is a clear indication that you cannot change the current settings. To change these settings, you must break the inheritance, using the following procedure:
>
>   a. Click Actions ➪ Edit Permissions.
>
>   b. This will display a dialog box that informs you that this will break the inheritance; click OK.
>
>   c. Now all inherited permissions are editable, including the Contributor permission of Axel and Anna. For example, if you want to remove the SharePoint group Restricted Readers from this list, check its check box, and select the menu Actions ➪ Remove User Permissions, and on the following dialog box, select OK to accept to remove that group.
>
>   d. To change Axel's permission level from Contribute to Read, click his name. On the web form that appears you will see the current permission for Axel; uncheck Contribute and check Read, then click OK.
>
>   e. The editable list of users and groups, and their permission settings, is displayed again. Since you do not need to make any more modifications, click the Shared Documents breadcrumb link at the top of the page.
>
> 4. Test the new permissions; log on as Axel and make sure that he cannot add, delete, or modify any document in the Shared Documents library.

There is an extra challenge if both Axel and Anna are members of a SharePoint group, such as the site's Members group, since there is no way to deny a permission in SharePoint to a specific group member, as there is in the Windows file system. If this is the case, then you could either create another

SharePoint group and move Axel to that group, or if the Members group is small, you could remove that group from the Shared Documents library and then add each individual member with the permissions they should have here.

If for any reason want to revert back to using the inherited permissions for this document library, you can open the Permissions for the document library page again (see steps 2 and 3 above), then open the menu Actions ⇨ Inherit Permissions, and click OK on the dialog box that pops up, asking you if you really want to revert back to inherited permissions. Note that every change to this permission list is then lost and cannot be restored, so make sure that you really want to revert to inherited permissions!

Another similar task is setting specific permissions on a single document or list item. For example, say that Anna should not have any permissions at all, to the document Proposal.doc. Anna has the Contributor permission level to the site and therefore to the Shared Documents library where Proposal.doc is stored. To meet the new security requirements, the owner of the site now must perform the process described in the following Try It Out.

Try It Out   Set Individual Permissions for a Document

1.   Open the Shared Documents library using an account with administrative rights for the site.

2.   Locate the document to be changed (such as Proposal.doc). Use its quick menu to select Manage Permissions. You will see the list of inherited permissions.

3.   The list of permissions is inherited from its parent, that is, the folder it is stored in, if any, or the document library. Note that if the library inherits permissions from the site, then the permissions for the document will be the same! The next step is to break the inheritance. Click Actions ⇨ Edit Permissions, then click OK in the dialog box that appears to accept the stopping of the inheritance of permissions from its parent (the library).

4.   In this case, Anna is listed as a contributor; check her name and click Actions ⇨ Remove User Permissions. In the dialog box that appears, click OK to confirm that you want to remove the user.

5.   Test this: Log on as Anna, and open that Shared Document library. Notice that Anna will not even see that the document Proposal.doc exists, since she has no access at all.

As before, this example was based on the fact that Anna was granted permissions as an individual user. If, instead, she was given permissions as a result of her membership in a SharePoint group, then you would have to solve this problem differently! Either Anna must be removed from that SharePoint group, or the group itself must be removed, and then all other users in that group must be given permissions either individually or by creating a new SharePoint group with the corresponding permissions to the site. All of this is necessary because SharePoint does not support a Deny Permission feature.

A task related to creating item-level security, such as individual document permissions, is to set permissions on a folder in a library. Normally, you should avoid creating folders in libraries and instead use columns, together with views, to sort and organize content. But there is one good reason to create a folder: For example, say that you have a document library where new documents are added every day. You have set the permissions, so they match your security requirements. But now and then a document is added that should have unique permissions. You could solve this problem by using the steps above, but if there are too many documents that need this unique permission, it is better to create a folder in this library, then set these unique permissions on that folder and make sure that those specific documents are stored in that folder. Since the inheritance mechanism works through documents inheriting permissions from their parent, in this case the folder, it will work just fine, and it will be much easier to manage those documents. To create a folder in a library, open the library, then open the menu next to the Add button, and select New Folder.

Allowing Access to a Single List

Sometimes you need to set a security setting in a way other than through inheritance from the site permissions. For example, a user named Beatrice who works in another department may need Read access to certain documents but should not be able to read anything else on the site. This is managed as shown in the following Try It Out.

Try It Out   Allow Access to a Single Library Only

1. Open the document library using an account with administrative rights for the site.

2. Open the menu Settings ⇨ Document Library Settings.

3. Click Permissions for the document library; the inherited permissions are displayed.

4. Click Actions ⇨ Edit Permissions, and accept the option to create unique permissions (i.e., stop the inheritance of permissions from its parent).

5. Click Add, and enter the following information:

    a. **Users/Group:** In this field, enter the name to add, in this example Beatrice. You can also click the address book icon and search for the user. If you add more than one name, use a semicolon between the names.

    b. **Give user permissions directly:** Set the permission for the users entered in step a, above, in this example Read.

    c. To make sure that Beatrice is informed about the new permission, check the Send welcome mail to the new user check box, and enter the mail message to be sent. Note that you do not have to add the type of permission (Read, in this example), or the link to the library, since SharePoint will add this automatically to the e-mail.

    d. click OK to save and close the form. The e-mail message will be sent immediately.

6. The permission list for the document library is again presented; note that Beatrice's name is now listed, along with her permission.

The preceding example was about adding the user Beatrice as a reader to a library, but she should not get access to anything else on the team site. This goal is certainly accomplished using the preceding steps, but how will Beatrice be able to see a list inside a SharePoint site that she has no access to? SharePoint solves this by adding this user to the site's permission list, with Limited Access (see Figure 10-21). This will allow her to read the specific library but nothing else on the site. The exact same technique will work if you need to grant a user or group access permissions to a folder or an individual list or library item.

In SharePoint 2003, the permission Limited Access was called Guest.

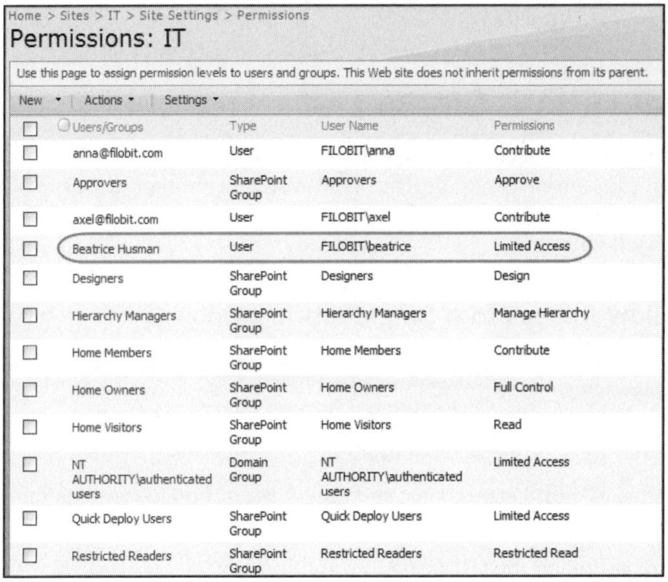

Home > Sites > IT > Site Settings > Permissions

Permissions: IT

Use this page to assign permission levels to users and groups. This Web site does not inherit permissions from its parent.

New ▾ | Actions ▾ | Settings ▾

Users/Groups	Type	User Name	Permissions
anna@filobit.com	User	FILOBIT\anna	Contribute
Approvers	SharePoint Group	Approvers	Approve
axel@filobit.com	User	FILOBIT\axel	Contribute
Beatrice Husman	User	FILOBIT\beatrice	Limited Access
Designers	SharePoint Group	Designers	Design
Hierarchy Managers	SharePoint Group	Hierarchy Managers	Manage Hierarchy
Home Members	SharePoint Group	Home Members	Contribute
Home Owners	SharePoint Group	Home Owners	Full Control
Home Visitors	SharePoint Group	Home Visitors	Read
NT AUTHORITY\authenticated users	Domain Group	NT AUTHORITY\authenticated users	Limited Access
Quick Deploy Users	SharePoint Group	Quick Deploy Users	Limited Access
Restricted Readers	SharePoint Group	Restricted Readers	Restricted Read

Figure 10-21

Managing Document Workflow

For some types of documents, the author is not allowed to publish the document by herself. If this is the case, you must configure the document library to activate Content Approval. The effect is that every added or modified document is hidden until a user with Manage Lists rights approves it. Even if the author has this right, the document must be approved in a separate step.

Try It Out   Activate Content Approval in a Document Library

1. Log on as an administrator for the team site where the document library is stored.

2. Open the document library.

3. Open the menu Settings ➪ Document Library Settings.

4. Click on Versioning settings

5. Select Yes for the option Require content approval for submitted items?

6. Click OK to save and close the page.

7. Click on the document library name in the breadcrumb trail near the top of the page to open the library.

The approval process is now activated. Log on as a user who is a member of the SharePoint Members group. This group does not have the Approve permission, so every update from these members will need to be approved by a user with this right (for example, the Owners group, and the site administrator).

> Note that even if a user with Approve permission adds or modifies a document, it must still be approved. This was not the case in SharePoint 2003.

Try It Out   **Test the Content Approval Process**

1. Log on as a member of the SharePoint group Members.

2. Update any existing document. Note that the document is now listed as "Draft" in the column Approved Status. This column was automatically added to the document view when you activated the Content Approval feature. You can specify if the draft version will be visible to everyone or not:

    a. Click Settings ⇨ Document Library Settings on the library.

    b. Click Versioning Settings. In the section Who should see draft items in this document library?, you can choose between three options; if you choose Any user who can read items, then every user with at least Read permission can see and open documents with the pending approval status.

3. The next step in this example is to publish the document. This will change the document's status from "Draft" to "Pending." Open the quick menu for the same document, then select "Publish a major version." You have the option to enter a comment, then click OK.

4. A user with the Approve permission must now check the modification. When the content approval process is activated for a document library, you will find that it gains two new document views: Approve/Reject Items and My Submissions. The first of these two views is not available unless you have Approval permission; the second view will list all documents that you have submitted to this document library and show their status. When a user with the Approve permission uses the view Approve/Reject Items, he or she will see all documents awaiting approval or that have been denied approval (see Figure 10-22). Make sure to select the view Approve/Reject Items before you continue with the next step.

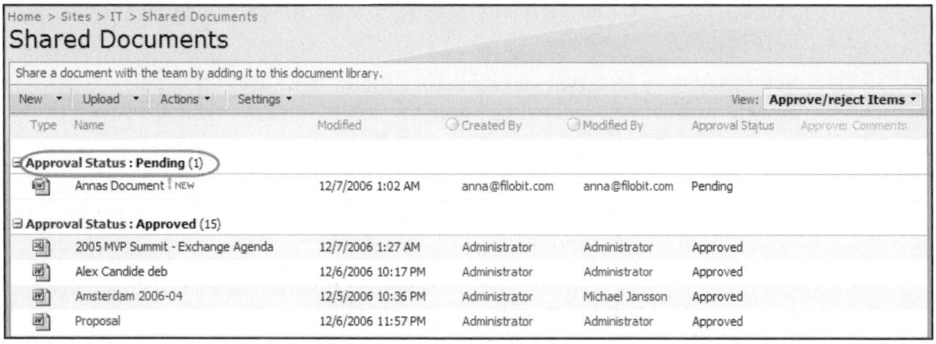

Type	Name	Modified	Created By	Modified By	Approval Status	Approver Comments
	Approval Status : Pending (1)					
	Annas Document NEW	12/7/2006 1:02 AM	anna@filobit.com	anna@filobit.com	Pending	
	Approval Status : Approved (15)					
	2005 MVP Summit - Exchange Agenda	12/7/2006 1:27 AM	Administrator	Administrator	Approved	
	Alex Candide deb	12/6/2006 10:17 PM	Administrator	Administrator	Approved	
	Amsterdam 2006-04	12/5/2006 10:36 PM	Administrator	Michael Jansson	Approved	
	Proposal	12/6/2006 11:57 PM	Administrator	Administrator	Approved	

Figure 10-22

5. Before you approve or reject the modification, you should view the document. Open the document in a normal way, and read both its content and its column settings. To approve or reject it, use the quick menu for the document and select Approve/reject. This will open a web form where you choose to approve or reject the document; you can also enter a description that will be stored along with the document.

> When the document is approved, it will be public; if it is rejected, the document continues to be hidden. SharePoint 2007 will not inform the author about the result of the approval process, but you can create a workflow that does this.

To summarize this process: The content approval process is very handy for some types of documents where a specific user, such as a manager, must approve a document before it goes public. The problem with this process in SharePoint 2007 is that, by default, neither the user who must approve or reject the modification nor the author receives an e-mail saying what is going on! Luckily, this is easily addressed by adding a workflow process to the document library, as shown in the following Try It Out.

Try It Out   Add an Approval Workflow

1. Log on as a site administrator.

2. Click on the document library to which you want to add the workflow.

3. Click the menu Settings ⇨ Document Library Settings.

4. Click Workflow settings.

5. If this is a MOSS installation, you will find a ready-made workflow named Approval. If you are running WSS 3.0 alone, then you must first create a workflow, using either SharePoint Designer, or Visual Studio .NET. In this example, we assume the Approval workflow exists, so the next step is to configure it:

    a. Select the Approval workflow.

    b. **Type a unique name for the workflow:** Approving Docs.

    c. **Select a task list:** Tasks. This list will keep track of approval tasks and who they are assigned to.

    d. **Select a history list:** Workflow History (new). This list will log all actions related to the workflow. This will make it possible for you to later see who approved or rejected a specific document.

    e. Check Start this workflow when a new item is created, and Start this workflow when an item is changed. This will ensure that both newly created documents and modified documents in the document library will trigger the approval workflow process.

    f. Click Next. A new web form opens where you will define settings for the approval workflow. In this example, assume that the user Filobit\Administrator will be the sole approver.

g. In the Approvers field, enter **Filobit\administrator**, and click the Check Names button to perform the name completion. Verify that the name is underlined, which indicates that the name has been identified. If not, check your spelling.

h. In the Type a message to include with your request field, enter: Dear Admin, please approve this document.

i. In the Give each person the following amount of time to finish their task (serial) field, set the duration to 2 Days.

j. Check the Update the approval status (use this workflow to control content approval) option.

k. Click OK.

6. On the next page, you will see the name of your workflow process listed, that is Approving Docs. The process is now active.

7. Test the workflow:

a. Let a user with the Contributor permission level add or update a document in the document library.

b. Verify that the document is listed as Pending in the Approval Status column and that the new column Approving Docs is listed as In Progress for the document.

c. Then open the administrator's Outlook program. Wait for an e-mail that tells you to approve this modified document; there is a link to open the document, and also to approve or reject the document. Approve the document now.

d. Open Anna's Outlook mailbox. You will find two messages; one that states that the workflow process has started and one that informs Anna about the outcome, that the document was approved by the administrator in this example.

e. In the document library, verify that the document now is approved and that the workflow Approving Docs is completed.

Working with Document Workspaces

When you are working alone and updating a public document, you will be fine with the checkout feature that the document library offers. But what do you do when you are working collaboratively with one or more other people, or when you need input from two other colleagues during the development of an updated version of a document? This is clearly not something that can be addressed with the checkout procedure. This is what you use Document Workspaces for. A Document Workspace is a team site that initially contains only one thing: a document copied from another site, usually the parent site.

To create a Document Workspace, you have two options:

❑ Use the quick menu for the document and select Send To ➪ Create Document Workspace.

❑ Inside MS Office 2007, display the Document Management pane by clicking the Office button and selecting Server ➪ Document Management Information, Then click its fourth icon from the left, the documents tab, to display the documents in this library. Locate the current document (it will be marked with a different color), then select Create Document Workspace from its menu.

When creating a Document Workspace, a copy of this document will be stored in the new workspace. Initially, only the user who created the workspace will have access, so the next step is often to add one or more users to this workspace. Note that even in a Document Workspace the same rules apply; only one user at a time can update a document. If necessary, you can also use the checkout/checkin feature in the workspace.

Why do you need a new site for just one document? Well, it is simple. If the document is so important that you need several people to be able to update it, you will most likely want to have your own private playground for this work. This workspace will also allow the group to share ideas, links, tasks, and maybe other supporting documents by storing all this information in the workspace.

When the document update is done, it should be copied back to the original location. This is taken care of by SharePoint's feature "Publish back to source location." Use the steps in the following Try It Out to create a workspace, update the copy of the document, and finally publish it back to the source location.

Try It Out   **Work with Document Workspaces**

1. Log on as an owner of the site containing the library with the document you want to create a Document Workspace for. You must be an owner in order to be able to create the workspace. If you want to enable authors to create Document Workspaces, you must either make them members of the Owner site group or add the right Create Subsites to the SharePoint group Members.

2. Open the document for editing in MS Word (assuming that it's a Word file).

3. In the Document Information pane, on the documents tab, locate the currently open document (it will be listed) and using its quick menu, select Create Document Workspace. Accept the option to create it, when asked. Word now automatically switches to the document copy stored in the workspace. The workspace's name is based on the document's title.

4. Add some more users to the workspace. In the Members Web Part, click on Add new user. Enter the user's name (user account or e-mail address) and set the site group membership. Accept the option to send an e-mail to this user, stating his new rights and where to go to start collaborating on the document. Click OK when you're ready. If you don't send this e-mail to users, you must give them the URL to the workspace in another way. Otherwise, they won't know where to find the workspace.

5. Use the standard procedure to open, edit, and close the document, using the user accounts that are granted permissions to the workspace. At some point, when you are done with all the editing, it is time to send the updated version back to its original location.

6. You can either use the Document Information pane/Document tab in MS Office and the quick menu for this document to select Publish back to source location, or go to the Document Workspace, use the quick menu in the document library for the document, and select Send To ⇨ Publish to Source Location. If you choose to do this from within MS Word, then Word will close the version of the document stored in the workspace and open the same document stored in the source location.

Note that the Document Workspace will still remain after you have copied the document back to its source location. The reason for this is that you may later be interested in going back to the workspace to see what users were active in developing the new version and view the other information used during that development.

Using SharePoint as a File Share

So far, you have used the web client to view and open documents. But SharePoint can display its information just like any file share, using either the traditional file share (for example F:) or by your defining a web folder. The main difference between these two options is that file shares only allow you to use one character for this share, while web folders allow you to type a name, including blank spaces. This is much easier to read and understand, but not all programs understand how to use a web folder. You have to test this to see whether web folders work in your environment. All recent MS Office products understand web folders.

To create a traditional file share link to a document library, you do follow the process in the next Try It Out.

Try It Out   **Create a File Share Link to a Document Library**

1. Assume that you have a document library named Shared Documents in the team site `http://srv1/sitedirectory/it`. You want to access that library using the F: disk label. Start Windows Explorer.

2. Click Tools ⇨ Map Network Drive.

3. Set the `Drive = F`.

4. Enter the following address:

    `\\srv1\sitedirectory\it\shared documents`

Now you will find F: listed in Window Explorer and any program that has an Open and Save feature. Note that this will only work directly for Windows XP clients; if you do this on a Windows 2003 server, including the SharePoint server itself, it will fail. The reason is that Windows XP has a service running that is needed for this functionality, while Windows 2003 does not.

Just open the Start ⇨ Administrative Tools ⇨ Services, locate the service WebClient, open its properties, and switch to Manual or Automatic, click Apply to activate the setting, and finally click Start.

The second method is to use web folders. This works the same way, except that you can have a longer and better description of what the link is pointing to. Follow the steps in the Try It Out below to create the web folder.

> **SharePoint 2007 has a new feature that opens a document library in a temporary Windows Explorer view directly. Open any document library, click Actions ⇨ Open with Windows Explorer. The instructions below are for creating a permanent Explorer view for a library.**

Try It Out   Create a Web Folder to a Document Library

Assuming that you are using the same document library and team site as in the last Try It Out, do this:

1. Start Windows Explorer.

2. Click Tools ⇨ Map Network Drive.

3. Click Sign up for online storage or connect to a network server. This link is on the same page as the one used in step 4 in the previous set of steps.

4. The Add Network Place Wizard will start up. Click Next. On the next page, make sure that "Choose another network location" is selected, and click Next again.

5. Type the following network address:

    ```
    http://srv1/sitedirectory/it/shared documents
    ```

6. Type a descriptive name for the web folder, such as Shared Documents on IT, then click Next.

7. Click Finish. Your new web folder is now created.

8. Test it: Start MS Word, click the Office button, select Open, and select My Network Places, and your new web folder should be listed. Click on it and you will see all Word files in the folder.

Both the traditional disk label and the newer web folders can be used directly from Windows Explorer (for example, to copy files from the file system into a SharePoint document library or to copy files from one library to another).

> **Note that when you copy or move files using web folders or disk labels, only the latest version of the document is copied or moved, not previous versions. However, if you open and update files using the web folders or disk labels, the version history is updated, exactly as when using the web client interface.**

SharePoint will automatically create web folders for any document library that you have stored documents in. They are seldom cleverly named, so to give them better names or just check where they point to, right-click on the web folder and select Properties. There, you will see the URL address, and you can enter another name for the link.

For each document library, there is a system folder named Forms that contains .aspx files for default views, the default document template, and some specific web forms. It also contains all custom views created by users. When using Windows Explorer you will see this Forms folder. Normally, users will not be able to delete or modify any of its files, but just to be safe, you should instruct your users to avoid changing anything in that folder or deleting that folder itself.

Summary

In this chapter you learned that:

❑ The traditional file system is not enough anymore. It is much too easy to create file chaos, where few, if any, have control of the information stored.

❑ Traditional document management systems, DMSs, are often very advanced and hard to use, which may be an obstacle when implementing a DMS in an organization.

❑ Traditional DMSs are not always so well integrated into MS Office.

❑ SharePoint enables you to create new columns for document libraries that contain metadata or properties for documents.

❑ Using SharePoint's view, documents can be sorted, presented, and grouped in a large number of ways, based on the column settings for the document library.

❑ By default SharePoint does not allow all file types to be stored in a document library, but that is easy to fix. However, be sure to protect your document library with SharePoint-enabled antivirus solutions.

❑ Each document library may have individual permission settings. All settings will be valid for all documents in that library.

❑ SharePoint allows unique permission settings for libraries and lists, plus folders and individual list items and documents.

❑ Create alerts when you want to be notified that a specific document or a folder has been updated.

❑ To keep track of changes in lists and libraries, you can also choose to configure them to be RSS feeds, then use Outlook 2007 as an RSS client.

❑ You can lock a file for editing by using Check Out; this will remain active until the user does a check in.

❑ An administrator can break an active checkout.

❑ SharePoint supports version history. However, by default it is disabled; when activated it will store any number of versions for all documents in a folder.

❑ SharePoint 2007 only stores the changes, not the complete document, when the document is updated.

❑ Using MS Office 2007, a user will have access to a lot of SharePoint specific features, such as Check Out/Check In, version history, document properties, workflows, and undelete functionality.

❑ Use Access Datasheet for fast editing of document properties and for managing columns and their position on the page. This requires that the local client have MS Access 2007 installed.

❑ SharePoint supports content approval but will not send e-mail to the person who should approve any modification. Solve this by using workflows.

❑ A Document Workspace is a team site that contains a copy of a document; this copy can be updated by several users. When done, you will publish this document back to its source location.

❑ Create network drives, such as F:, or web folders, such as Shared Documents on IT to make it possible to view information in SharePoint as a file share.

In the next chapter, you will learn more about building intranets and extranets, using SharePoint 2007.

Intranet and Internet Sites

The previous chapters have covered all the details about how to install SharePoint, how to do important configuration settings, and how to create sites for your users. This chapter will focus on two specific types of web sites: a public Internet site, and an intranet portal site. Typically, the first type of site is used for exposing content to external users, such as partners, or even anonymous users on the Internet; the other type is used to publish information for internal users within an organization. Some of the information in this chapter has been discussed previously in other chapters, but here you will see how all that information is used for building these two specific types of sites. The purpose of this chapter is to give you a realistic example with a complete step-by-step description on how to set up and configure these types of sites.

This chapter also compares how to build these sites using WSS alone and using MOSS. This is both a technical issue and a financial matter: If you want to use MOSS for these types of sites, then you must purchase the appropriate type of SharePoint 2007 client access license (CAL). If you instead will use a WSS environment, there are no SharePoint CALs; instead, you must make sure to have the proper Windows Server 2003 client access license model.

Analyzing the Needs

When building a software solution you need to know two things: What is the current situation, and what is your objective? To answer that you must analyze what you have today and the needs of your users. The more time and energy you put into this analysis, the greater the chance that you will do the right thing and avoid costly mistakes. A golden rule when analyzing this is to ask the right people, check the answers, if possible, and never accept a vague answer, like "I think we have enough free disk for your new SharePoint server." If you are even the slightest bit unsure about some answers, make sure to start a thorough investigation to get the truth. This does not necessarily mean that you have to do everything yourself; it could also mean that you delegate tasks to reliable people.

Another golden rule when you start designing the SharePoint environment is KISS — Keep it simple, stupid! If you can make it with just one SharePoint server, then do so; if the intranet will work with just one SharePoint group, then use one; if one document library will be enough for storing all documents, then use one library. Every time you add more servers, more SharePoint groups and more document libraries, you also add to the complexity of the SharePoint solution. And more complexity means more time spent on administration and management, plus a more complex environment to analyze if something goes wrong. So please, remember KISS. It will make your life easier, both when implementing the solution and when managing it.

Building an Intranet Using WSS or MOSS?

The boss comes to you and tells you that the company needs an intranet, and fast! You need to get something up and running within one week, if possible without spending any money. So, your mission is to build an intranet, and you start wondering what to do next. There are some questions you should get answered before you start, like the ones in the following table.

Question	People to Ask	Comment
Do you need an intranet for the whole organization?	Top management; people responsible for managing organizational wide information	For a company requiring just a basic intranet, WSS may be sufficient. But if the requirements are greater, MOSS will fill your needs much better.
Do you need a local intranet for your department or teams?	Middle management; team leaders	WSS may be a good choice if the department or team is working with the same type of information.
Do you want to be able to search for information stored both inside and outside SharePoint?	All types of users	Only MOSS offers global search functionality.
Is searching inside SharePoint sites enough for your needs?	All types of users	This is a complementary question to the previous one; if the answer is yes, then you could fulfill this need by using WSS and its search capability.
Is there a need to share and display Excel spreadsheets and diagrams, using a web browser?	Groups working with Excel	If yes, this need requires the Excel Services in MOSS Enterprise edition.
Is there a need to present InfoPath forms, using a web browser?	General managers, HR managers, sales managers	This requires the Forms Service, which comes with MOSS Enterprise edition.
Do you need a way of presenting more information than just the email address and phone number for some or all of your users?	Middle management, team leaders, project leaders	MOSS has its My Site feature that presents much more information about users than the typical "employee list."
Is there a need to present information stored in external line-of-business systems?	General managers, HR managers, sales managers	This requires the BDC feature in MOSS Enterprise Edition.

If the answers to these questions indicate that WSS will be sufficient, then by all means go on and build the intranet using Windows SharePoint Services. It will indeed be a very good platform for sharing information within your organization. With the new search capabilities in WSS 3.0, this intranet will also offer some basic search features.

But if you need more than WSS 3.0 will provide, don't hesitate to go with MS Office SharePoint Server 2007; its list of features is remarkable and will give you the best intranet and collaboration environment that Microsoft can offer today. If you are unsure what to choose, why not use the free MOSS 2007 evaluation copy that will work for 180 days? It will give you a fair chance to see what MOSS can do for your users.

Analyzing an Intranet

The intranet as we know it has been around for more than 10 years now. But let's look at what an intranet really is; here are some common definitions:

❑   An intranet is a web application for sharing information that only internal users can access.

❑   An intranet is a secure web-based environment where local users can access information.

❑   An intranet is a web-based solution for sharing news, links, and documents with internal users.

An elderly definition states that an intranet is a TCP/IP-based local network, but this type of definition is not what is discussed in this book. The general consensus today is that an intranet is a web site where the local users will find the information they need, much like an internal company newspaper. Now stop for a while, and think again. Is this really what your user needs? Both yes and no! Who is asking for this intranet? Everyone, you say. This is true, but when I try to ask my clients this question, I often find out that:

❑   Management wants to publish information about the company and its activities.

❑   The users want to find information related to their work.

One of the reasons management wants to publish information is to ease the burden on some internal groups. If the intranet contains all the news and links to all local policy standards, handbooks, and forms, then it is up to the user to find it: "How do I apply for a vacation?" "Look at the intranet!" After a while, the users do indeed learn how to find the information they need. If you have an intranet in your organization today, how many of your users have this site as the start page for their web browser? How many of the users are checking the intranet every day, or at least once per week? I don't know the exact answer in your case, but the traditional intranets I have seen provide depressing answers — maybe 20 percent, if you are lucky. How can this be? Hint: Look at what the users are using as the default start page for their browsers (usually a search site, such as Google, or a news site on the Internet — and by the way, what site are you using?) Why is this? Because it gives the user what they want — interesting information that is updated frequently! This is something you should have in mind when designing your intranet. If you don't, well, why bother to build it at all?

If the intranet contains information that the users are interested in, you don't need to force them to check the intranet. But to be fair, all types of intranets cannot be all that interesting, at least not for all users; in these cases it would be great if the user could be notified whenever there is something new and interesting. Another important piece of intranets is pictures. Compare a typical intranet to some popular news web sites; did you notice how important the pictures are to make the articles more interesting? Your intranet should learn from these news web sites. To summarize it, an intranet should contain the following things to be interesting to your users:

❑ Company news that relates to the current user, with pictures when possible.

❑ External news from a web site the current user are interested in.

❑ Information related to the user's personal tasks and interests, such as:

    ❑ Forms for notifying the reception desk about absences and meetings.

    ❑ Fill-in time cards or vacation forms.

    ❑ Today's menu at the local restaurant.

    ❑ The weather forecast for the users' local area.

❑ Information related to the users' work, such as documents, contacts, and project information.

❑ Information about coworkers, such as their e-mail, phone numbers, responsibilities, and pictures.

One could argue whether or not information such as external news and weather forecasts should be listed on the intranet, but in my experience this type of information is important if you want to make this site so interesting that users may even voluntarily use it as the start page on their web browsers. In the next section, you will try to follow these rules when building an intranet using a WSS environment.

Available Web Parts

When you build intranet and Internet web sites, you must know what tools that are available, that is, what Web Parts, and what type of functionality you can use for building your solution. One of the main differences between WSS and MOSS is the Web Parts available; the list below shows these Web Parts.

Default Web Parts	WSS 3.0	MOSS Enterprise
Content Editor Web Part	Yes	Yes
Form Web Part	Yes	Yes
Image Web Part	Yes	Yes
Page Viewer Web Part	Yes	Yes
Relevant Documents	Yes	Yes
Site Users	Yes	Yes
User Tasks	Yes	Yes
XML Web Part	Yes	Yes
Contact Details	No	Yes
Business Data Actions	No	Yes
Business Data Item	No	Yes

Default Web Parts	WSS 3.0	MOSS Enterprise
Business Data Item Builder	No	Yes
Business Data List	No	Yes
Business Data Related List	No	Yes
Excel Web Access	No	Yes
IView Web Part	No	Yes
WSRP Consumer Web Part	No	Yes
Site Aggregator	No	Yes
Key Performance Indicators	No	Yes
KPI Details	No	Yes
Content Query Web Parts	No	Yes
I need to…	No	Yes
RSS Viewer	No	Yes
Summary Link Web Part	No	Yes
Table of Contents Web Part	No	Yes
This Week in Pictures	No	Yes
Business Data Catalog Filter	No	Yes
Choice Filter	No	Yes
Current User Filter	No	Yes
Date Filter	No	Yes
Filter Actions	No	Yes
Page Field Filter	No	Yes
Query String (URL) Filter	No	Yes
SharePoint List Filter	No	Yes
SQL Server 2005 Analysis Services Filter	No	Yes
Text Filter	No	Yes

Continued

Default Web Parts	WSS 3.0	MOSS Enterprise
My Calendar	No	Yes
My Contacts	No	Yes
My Inbox	No	Yes
My Mail Folder	No	Yes
My Tasks	No	Yes
Advanced Search Box	No	Yes
People Search Box	No	Yes
People Search Core Results	No	Yes
Search Action Links	No	Yes
Search Best Bets	No	Yes
Search Box	No	Yes
Search Core Results	No	Yes
Search High Confidence Results	No	Yes
Search Paging	No	Yes
Search Statistics	No	Yes
Search Summary	No	Yes
Categories	No	Yes
Sites in Categories	No	Yes
Top Sites	No	Yes

It is easy to see that MOSS provides a lot more Web Parts than WSS, so building an advanced web solution, such as an intranet portal or a public Internet site, is much easier with MOSS than with WSS.

An Intranet Based on WSS

The team sites in Windows SharePoint Services are really meant to be a place for collaboration. But this does not stop you from using them as a simple intranet. You have the basic features available for building an intranet, such as:

❑   A news list — text only, no pictures — but you can add an extra column for pictures.

❏ A Web Part you can use as a RSS feed reader to display news items from an Internet news web site.

❏ A list of links that point to important locations inside SharePoint and other locations, including a file.

❏ A Page Viewer Web Part to display the content of any public Internet site.

❏ Lists for storing documents, contacts, and tasks related to specific projects or activities.

❏ A list of employees, including e-mail addresses, phone numbers, and pictures.

❏ A Web Part for displaying a picture.

These are just some of the tools for building the intranet. You could also find more advanced Web Parts on the Internet; some are free, and others are commercial products. One problem in a pure WSS environment is that you cannot filter any information in a list — either you see the list content or you don't. WSS has no feature similar to the audience targeting that exists in SPS. So, you must think hard before you create one intranet for all users in your organization. One way to solve this problem is to create a top site that is the start of this WSS-based intranet, containing more general information, and from that follow links to local intranets for departments, teams, and similar groups.

The General Features of the Intranet

To make it easier for you to understand how to build an intranet here's an example: Your job is to create a WSS-based intranet for a company named Filobit with 80 users. This company has these departments: Sales, HR, Finance, and IT. There is also an important group named "Board of Directors." All of these groups also need a place to share internal information, beside the intranet web site. Finally, it is important that the Finance department and the Board of Directors team have their own security.

First, you analyze the current situation in your organization:

❏ You have a fresh WSS site, built on the clean site template, which does not have any lists in the beginning.

❏ Today, users save some documents in the common file share "P:" and some on their local disk.

❏ Common calendar and contact lists are stored in MS Outlook's public folders.

❏ Important news about the company and its customers is distributed by e-mail.

❏ Information about coworkers is found in MS Outlook's global address list.

Next, you summarize the objectives for the new intranet, based on the analysis you did in your organization:

❏ There should be one start page on the intranet that displays this info:

❏ Common news with pictures for the company and its customers.

❏ Links to often requested information, such as company policies, HR documents, and local intranets.

❏ A list of external news from the Internet news site: http://www.usatoday.com.

❏ A weather forecast function using an RSS feed.

❏ A list of employees, including their data and pictures.

❑ Each of the IT, Sales, and HR departments needs its own local intranet, with the following content:

 ❑ Local news for the department.

 ❑ Local list of customer and vendor contacts.

 ❑ Links to folders, documents, and team sites used by the local department.

❑ The two Board of Directors and Finance groups also need their own team sites, but the access permission to these sites must be set so that the only people who can view or modify that information are the ones who are supposed to be able to do so.

So now you know you starting point, and you also know where to go, that is, the objectives for the intranet site. Make sure to keep an eye on the objectives during this implementation to make sure not to miss any important features.

Building an Intranet Using WSS

To build an intranet using WSS, following the example discussed above, start with a top site created using the Blank Site template with the URL address `http://srv1`. Then follow the steps in the Try It Out below to create the intranet.

Try It Out   **Create a Basic Intranet**

1. Log on as the administrator to the existing site `http://srv1`.

2. Create a list of pictures to be used in the News listing:

 a. Click Site Actions ➪ Create ➪ Picture Library.

 b. **Name:** Pictures for News.

 c. **Display this picture library on the Quick Launch:** No.

 d. **Create a version each time you edit a file in this picture library:** No.

 e. Click Create.

 f. The new picture library is displayed. Click Upload and add all the pictures you will need for the next news items. Make sure to use small sizes, since these pictures will be displayed in their actual size!

3. The next step is to create a list for displaying the three latest news items, including pictures; make sure that the picture is displayed to the left of the news article.

 a. Click Site Actions ➪ Create ➪ Announcement.

 b. **Name:** Company News.

 c. Choose not to display this announcement list on the Quick Launch.

 d. Click OK to save and close the page.

 e. Click Settings ➪ List Settings.

> If you just want to create a new column, you can also click Settings ➪ Create Column instead of following step 3e. However, you will also change the view, so opening the site settings for this list is more effective.

f.   In the Columns section, click Create column. Give it the Column name Picture; set the Type to Hyperlink or Picture, set Format URL to Picture, and click OK.

g.   In the Views section, click All Items and change the Position from Left to 1 for the column Picture, to 2 for the Title, and to 3 for the Body. Clear all other rows in the Display column. Go down to the section Item Limit; set the Number of items to display to 3 and select Limit the total number of items returned to the specified amount. Click OK.

h.   Open the Home page for this team site; click Site Actions ⇨ Edit Page. In the "Left" Web Part zone, click Add a Web Part; select Company News, and click Add — the news list is now displayed on the Home page.

i.   Since you have modified the All Items view, you must configure this Web Part to use the updated view: Click edit ⇨ Modify Shared Web Part on the Company News Web Part. In the configuration pane for the Web Part, change Selected View to All Items, and then click OK.

j.   All modifications of this list are now completed; click Exit Edit Mode in the top right of this page.

k.   Click the link Add new announcement to add one news item, including a body and a URL to one of the pictures you added in step 2f above.

> The easiest way of copying the URL to any of these pictures is to open the picture library in a separate web browser, click a picture to display it, then right-click on the picture and select Copy Shortcut, as in Figure 11-1.

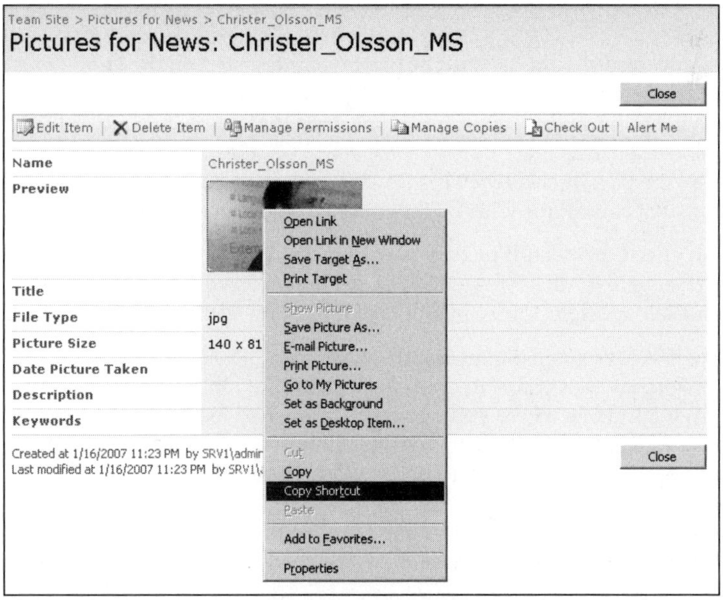

Figure 11-1

After adding at least three items, with or without news, you should have a news list that looks similar to Figure 11-2.

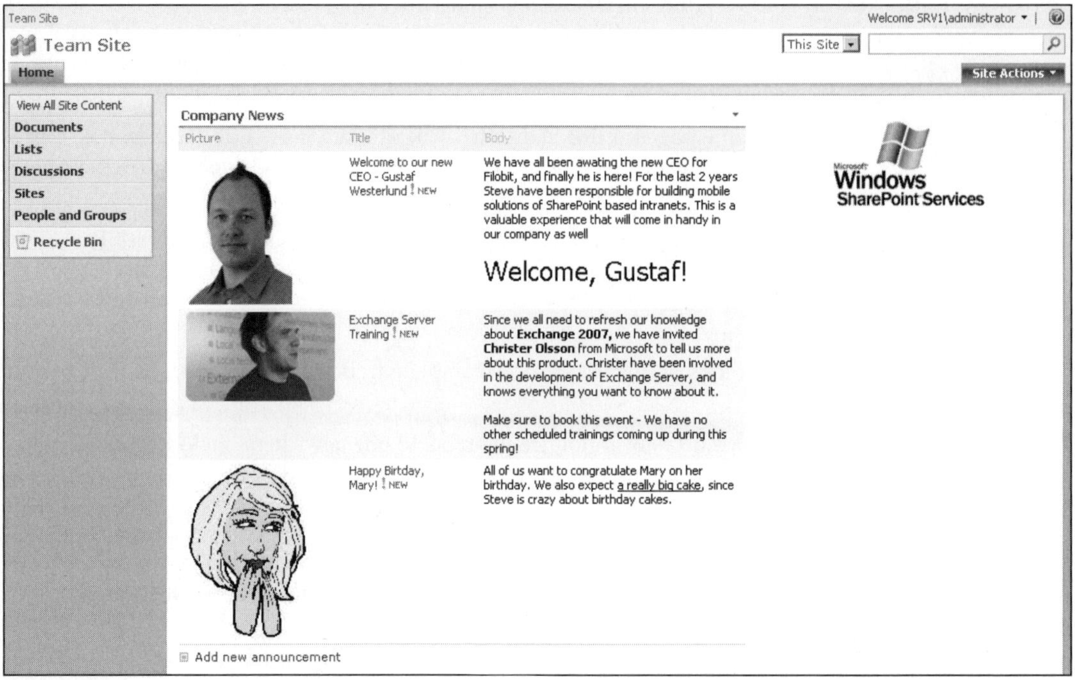

Figure 11-2

4. The intranet also should have the current weather listed on the Home page. Previously Microsoft offered a free Web Part named MSNBC Weather — this Web Part does not work any more. What you can do is configure a RSS feed that points to a publicly available weather forecast web site, such as the `http://www.weather.com/weather/rss/subscription`. Use any free RSS Web Part, such as the FeedReader from `www.smilinggoat.net`, or configure the XML Web Part that comes free with WSS to operate as a RSS feed reader, as described in step 6.

5. You don't need the default picture Web Part displaying the WSS Logo at the top right of this page. To remove it, click Site Actions ➪ Edit Page, use the quick menu for this Site Image Web Part, and select Delete. (You can still take it back by adding it from the Web Part site gallery).

6. To make this page more interesting for your users, add an RSS feed for the latest news from the web version of USA Today. To do that, click Site Actions ➪ Edit Page and click Add a Web Part in the Web Part zone where you want to add the RSS feed, for example the zone "Left;" then check the XML Web Part and click Add. Click on the link open the tool pane in this XML Web Part, and enter the following URL in the XML Link field:
    `http://rssfeeds.usatoday.com/usatodaycomWorld-Topstories`. Expand the Appearance section and set the Title to **USA Today**. Then click XLS Editor and paste the code below to make the Web Part understand RSS feeds. Click OK to save and close the Web Part.

```
<?xml version="1.0" encoding="UTF-8" ?>
<xsl:stylesheet version="1.0" xmlns:xsl="http://www.w3.org/1999/XSL/Transform">
```

```
<xsl:template match="/">
<html>
<body>
<xsl:for-each select="rss">
<xsl:for-each select="channel">
<xsl:for-each select="item">
<xsl:for-each select="title">
<a>
<xsl:attribute name="href">
<xsl:value-of select="../link" />
</xsl:attribute>
<B>
<span style="color:navy; font-family:Tahoma; font-size:8pt; font-style:normal;">
<xsl:apply-templates />
</span>
</B>
</a>
</xsl:for-each>
<br />
<xsl:for-each select="pubDate">
<span style="font-family:Tahoma; font-size:8pt;font-style:italic;">
...
<xsl:apply-templates />
</span>
</xsl:for-each>
<br />
</xsl:for-each>
</xsl:for-each>
</xsl:for-each>
</body>
</html>
</xsl:template>
</xsl:stylesheet>
```

> When setting up an RSS feed, it is always a good idea to check the policies and requirements of the provider. For example, to review *USA Today*'s policies, go to http://asp.usatoday.com/marketing/rss/index.aspx.

7. Next, you want to make a list of all employees. This list must be searchable by last name. Start by creating a contact list; add all employees, and then display the Web Part for the list:

   a. Open the Home page, then click Site Actions ⇨ Create.

   b. In the Communications section: Click the Contact list, give it the name Employees, and click OK.

   c. Click New, and add each employee to this list.

   d. Add this list to the Home page: Open the Home page, then click Site Actions ⇨ Edit Page. In the Web Part zone "Left," click Add a Web Part and select Employees, then click Add. The new Web Part is added to the top of the Web Part zone; use the mouse to drag it to the end of the zone.

8. Make it possible to display only employees with specific last names. Use the Form Web Part for this:

    a. Click Add a Web Part and add the Form Web Part directly above the Employees list.

    b. Using the edit menu for the Forms Web Part, select Connections ➪ Provide Form Values To ➪ Employees.

    c. Set the column to T1, then click Next.

    d. Set the column to Last Name, then click Finish.

    e. Use the Edit menu once again on the Form Web Part, and select Modify Shared Web Part to open its tool pane. Expand the Appearance section, and change the Title to Search for Last Name. Then click OK to close the tool pane.

    f. To exit from design mode, click Exit Edit Mode. Test the Form Web Part by entering a last name you know exists, and clicking Go — the Employees list below will now only display the names that match your search string.

The page now has some basic features that a simple intranet usually has. It should look something like Figure 11-3.

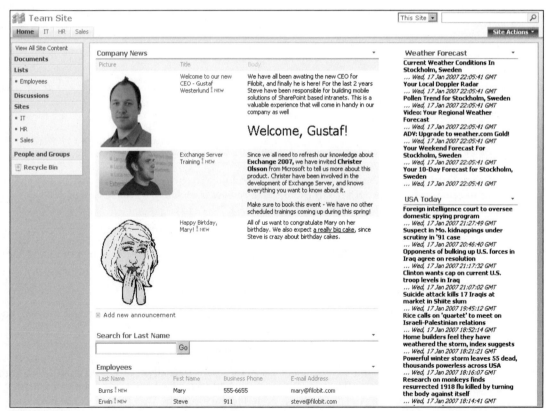

Figure 11-3

Creating Local Departments and Team Intranets

It is time to create the local intranets for the departments and the teams. Remember that two of them require their own security settings. Since the current intranet is the top site in this site collection, it will also control all the subsites under it, such as the administrative settings and templates for lists and sites. If the Finance and the Board of Directors groups must have their own settings, you must create a new site collection for each for them. The other local intranets for HR, IT, and Sales can be located under the current intranet site, so let's start by creating the last three site collections.

Try It Out   **Create a Local Intranet**

1.   Log on as the administrator and open the `http://srv1` site collection (i.e., the top site).

2.   Click Site Actions ➪ Create and select Sites and Workspaces in the Web Pages section.

3.   Now, enter these values to create the intranet for IT department, using the standard Team Site template (accept the other default values on this page):

    a.   **Title:** IT.

    b.   **Description:** Intranet for IT.

    c.   **URL:** it — so the total address will be `http://srv1/it`.

    d.   **Select a template:** Team Site.

    e.   **User Permissions:** Use unique permissions.

    f.   Click Create.

4.   Since you chose to create unique permissions, this will bring you a new form where you define the SharePoint groups for the site. By default, you will have three groups: Visitors, IT Members, and IT Owners. Grant users access to the IT site by adding them to the appropriate group:

    a.   Change the section Visitors to this Site to the option Create a new group. This will ensure that nobody from the top site will have access to the site unless specifically given the right. Then add the user names or security group names in the field below the IT Visitor group name. Note that there is a link named Add all authenticated users that you can use in case you want to allow every user who logs on to this Activity Directory domain Read access.

    b.   In the Members of this Site section, add the users or security groups that should have contributor rights to the site. Typically, these are users that read, add, and modify list content and documents.

    c.   In the Owners of This Site section, add the users that you want to give full administrative access to this site. These users can access everything on this site, and change security settings, create new lists, and libraries, and so on.

    d.   Click OK to save and close this page.

The new IT site is now displayed. If you look at the URL `http://srv1/it`, it is clear that IT is a subsite directly under the top site. Click the breadcrumb trail Team Site near the top of the page to go back the top site.

5. Repeat steps 2, 3, and 4, and add two subsites as local intranets for the HR and Sales departments, respectively. When all this is completed, you will have three subsites under the top-level intranet site.

6. WSS 3.0 will, by default, add three tabs on the top navigation bar, for the top site and each subsite. Since SharePoint 2007 is security trimmed, a user must have at least read access to see the tab for a specific subsite; that is, users with no access to the HR subsite will not see its tab on the top navigation bar. These sites are also listed in the Quick Launch bar, under the heading Sites; just click on any of them to open that subsite.

Creating Top-Level Local Intranets

Now, you have two more local intranets to create for the Finance and the Board of Directors teams. These must be separate site collections in order to have their own security settings and management settings that are local for a site collection. Both of these intranets require a more elaborate design, and instead of doing this design from scratch, it would be great to use a site template somebody else has created. Microsoft has 40 very nice WSS site templates, known as "the Fab 40," that you can download for free; they will have been released by the time you read this book. They would have been excellent to use for the two new site collections in the example, but as of this writing they have not yet been released. Instead you will use some of the default site templates.

> **Use this link to download the "Fab 40" site templates:** www.microsoft.com/technet/windowsserver/sharepoint/wssapps/v3templates.mspx.

Try It Out   **Create Finance and Board of Directors Intranets**

1. Start the SharePoint Central Administration tool, then switch to the Application Management page. The first site collection to be used is a web site for the Finance team, based on the Team Site template.

2. Click Create site collection in the SharePoint Site Management section, and then enter these values:

    a. **Title:** Finance.

    b. **Description:** Welcome to the Finance team.

    c. **URL:** Add "finance" (the complete URL is then http://srv1/sites/finance).

    d. In the Template Selection section: select Team Site.

If you have installed language packs, select the language first, then select the site template.

    e. In the Primary Site Collection Administrator section, enter the user account that should be the administrator for this complete site collection.

    f. For this site you do not need a quota template. Leave the default setting, No Quota.

    g. In the Site Categories section, set Finance for the Division.

    h. Click OK, then OK again. You are now back on the Application Management page.

3. Next, you will create a site for the Board of Directors group. Most of their information is meeting minutes, so they want a simple top site that will be the parent of multiple meeting workspaces. For this top site, you will use the site template Blank Site. Click Create site collection in the SharePoint Site Management section, then enter these values:

    a. **Title:** Board of Directors.

    b. **Description:** "Welcome to the Board of Directors web site."

    c. **URL:** Add "bod" (the complete URL is then `http://srv1/sites/bod`).

    d. In the Template Selection section: select Blank Site.

If you have installed language packs, then select the language first, then select the site template.

    e. In the Primary Site Collection Administrator section, enter the user account that should be the administrator for this complete site collection.

    f. For this site you do not need a quota template, so leave the default setting, No Quota.

    g. Click OK, then OK again. You are now back on the Application Management page.

4. Time to adjust the design of these site collections; make sure that you are logged on as the administrator for the Finance site collection. Start by opening `http://srv1/sites/finance`, then:

    a. **Replace the WSS image:** Click Site Actions ➪ Edit Page. On the Site Image Web Part, click Edit ➪ Modify shared Web Part. In the Image Link field, enter the URL to another picture that is related to the Finance team; for example, their logotype.

> You can use a picture in Pictures for News stored in the `http://srv1` **top site. When you're ready, click OK.**

    b. **Change the Calendar Web Part to a monthly view:** Click edit on the Web Part, then click Modify Shared Web Part. Change the Selected View to Calendar, and click OK save your work.

    c. **Add a Web Part that displays a Internet web site with financial information, such as** `money.cnn.com/market/news`: While this page is still in edit mode, click Add a Web Part in the "Left" Web Part zone, then add the Page Viewer Web Part. Next, drag the Web Part to the bottom of the Web Part zone. Click the link "open the tool pane" in the text body of the Web Part. Enter the following URL in the Link field: `http://money.cnn.com/data/us_markets`. Expand the Appearance section in the tool pane, and change the Title to US Markets. Finally, change the Height to 600 pixels. Click OK to save and close the tool pane.

> **Make sure to follow whatever policy the public Internet site has regarding using their web site!**

> **d.** **Define a link to go back to the main intranet site:** Click Site Actions ➪ Site Settings ➪ Portal site connection in the Site Collection Administration section, then select Connect to portal site and enter the Portal Web Address, `http://srv1`, and the Portal Name, **Intranet**. Then click OK.
>
> **e.** Click Exit Edit Mode at the top right of the page. The Finance web site should look similar to Figure 11-4.

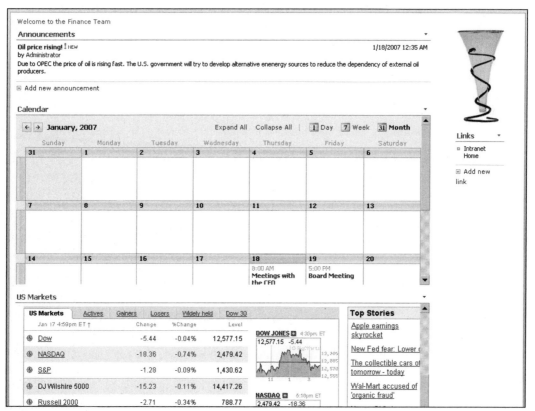

Figure 11-4

5. Your next task is to adjust the Board of Directors web site. It will mostly be used to navigate to subsites with meeting workspaces. It was built using the Blank Site template, so there is nothing on the page. Log on as the administrator for that site collection, then open `http://srv1/sites/bod`, and do this:

> **a.** **Replace the WSS image:** Click Site Actions ➪ Edit Page. On the Site Image Web Part, click Edit ➪ Modify shared Web Part. In the Image Link field, enter the URL to another picture that is related to the board of directors. When ready, click OK.
>
> **b.** **Add a document library:** Click Site Actions ➪ Create ➪ Document Library. Give the library the name Document Archive, select the option Create a version each time you edit a file in this document library. Then click Create.

c. **Place the Document Archive library on the Home page of the web site:** Go to the Home page, then click Site Actions ➪ Edit Page. In the "Left" Web Part zone, click Add a Web Part and add the Document Archive library.

d. **Change the color by selecting a new Site Theme for the web site:** Click Site Actions ➪ Site Settings ➪ Site Theme, then select a nice theme, for example "Obsidian" and click Apply.

e. **Still on the Site Settings page, define a link to go back to the main intranet site:** Click Portal site connection in the Site Collection Administration section, then select Connect to portal site and enter the Portal Web Address, `http://srv1`, and the Portal Name, **Intranet**. Click OK. The site should like something like Figure 11-5.

Figure 11-5

6. Almost done! You only have to add links from the company intranet to the two new local intranets. Go to `http://srv1`, then:

a. Click Site Actions ➪ Site Settings ➪ Top Link Bar.

b. Click New Link. Enter `http://srv1/sites/finance` in the Type the Web address field, type **Finance** as the Description, then click OK.

    c.   Click New Link again, and enter the web address `http://srv1/sites/bod`, then the description **BoD**. Click OK. The new navigation bar on the top site will look like the one in Figure 11-6.

Figure 11-6

The next logical step would be to configure the user access list for the Finance and Board of Directors sites and then educate the users of these two groups about how to start adding information to their site. Note that these site collections may grow whenever there is a need to add subsites for projects, activities, and meetings for these teams. Since Finance and Board of Directors are separate site collections, no user outside the group will have access to their content.

An Intranet Based on MOSS

In the previous section, you saw that a simple but useful an intranet could be based on WSS can be. However, you were forced to make several adjustments just to make the lists suitable for containing news. There was no way to target news items for specific groups of users; they saw either everything or nothing.

If you have a MOSS installation, then it contains a ton more features than WSS, such as global search capability, many more Web Parts, and advanced site templates. You really get something for your money when you invest in MOSS. Even though WSS 3.0 is very good, the difference between WSS 3.0 and MOSS 2007 is even greater than the difference between WSS 2.0 and SPS 2003. The options when building an intranet portal using MOSS are almost endless, so this section of the book will only describe the basic steps to show you how to build a complete intranet from scratch. As stated before, much of the information in this chapter is discussed in several other chapters as well, but here you will see it in context. Hopefully, it will appear more logical here, and you will understand how and why certain steps must be performed, and in what order.

The General Features of the Intranet

This section uses the same example as above for WSS — to build one company-wide intranet and then several local intranets for HR, IT, and so on. Comparing these two case studies will give you a better understanding of the differences between WSS and MOSS. As before, you will do this by following an example. In this case, the manager of your company, Filobit, wants you to create an intranet with support for web content management on its Publishing Pages. It must have advanced searching, a news section, and a list of all sites and workspaces, such as departmental web sites, project web sites, and meeting workspaces. The intranet should also have a diagram displaying the current sales statistics, using a MS Excel file. Users must be able to send copies of documents to a shared document archive.

This time, we will skip features like advanced document management, forms management of MS InfoPath files, and building a custom workflow solution to keep the example easier for you to follow. These topics are discussed in other chapters of this book. Note that the suggested solution in this example does not use any third-party products; everything is based on the standard features and Web Parts of MOSS 2007 Enterprise Edition.

Building the Intranet

In this example, assume that MOSS 2007 Enterprise Edition is installed and configured, but there is no site collection for the intranet created yet. Now follow the steps in the Try It Out below.

Try It Out   **Create the Site Collection for the Intranet**

1. Start the SharePoint Central Administration tool, then switch to the Application Management page. The first site collection to be used for this intranet is based on the Collaboration Portal site template.

2. Click Create site collection in the SharePoint Site Management section, then enter these values:

   a. **Web Application:** `http://srv1` (if you need to change the web application, click on the current URL and then click Change Web Application).

   b. **Title:** Home.

   c. **Description:** Welcome to Filobit's Intranet.

   d. **URL:** Accept the default, `http://srv1/` in this example.

   e. **Template Selection:** Switch to the Publishing tab, then select Collaboration Portal.

   f. **Primary Site Collection Administrator:** Enter the name of the user who will be the main administrator for this site collection. In this example, enter **Filobit\administrator**. You may also want to add another site collection administrator here, but in this example you can leave this field now.

   g. **Quota Template:** Accept the default, No Quota, (i.e., there is no size limit for this site collection).

   h. Click OK to save and start creating this site collection.

When the process is completed, you will have a new site collection with the following characteristics (see Figure 11-7):

❑ A top site named Home.

❑ Five subsites named Document Center, News, Reports, Search, and Sites.

❑ All of the sites are based on MOSS site templates, so they have more functionality than ordinary WSS sites.

❑ Some of these sites display "Publishing Pages;" that is, the content of the pages must be checked in and sometimes even approved before going public. These pages also support a version history, so it is easy to back to a previous version of the page.

Figure 11-7

Web Content Management

This intranet will use web content management to control the process of adding content to its pages. In many other content management systems, you use a separate server for developing new content (sometimes called a "stage server"), or other content management systems force the web content authors to use a separate application for creating and adding content. With MOSS 2007, you add and edit web content directly on the production server, using only a web browser such as Internet Explorer. To assist web content authors, SharePoint offers a number of features to control the editing process, such as:

❑ Automatic checkout when you start editing a page; for example, the start page of the intranet.

❑ Automatic version history tracking, with major and minor version numbers.

❑ Capability to revert to a previous version of the a page.

❑ Modifications must be published to be made public.

❑ Draft versions can start workflows; for example, to send an e-mail asking another web content author to check a new version of a page.

❑ Capability to force all modifications to be approved before being published.

❑ Capability to define when the page will be displayed, and when it will be removed.

❑ Spellchecking of content.

❑ Previewing of the modified page in a new window.

❑ Capability to compare text changes between versions.

All of these features will ensure that even an organization with very high content management requirements will find that MOSS is a very attractive solution, both for the web content authors and for administrators.

When you open a site based on a MOSS template, it will display a page file of type `.aspx`. This page is usually stored in the current site's page library. This is a new type of library, not found in SharePoint 2003, and its purpose is to be a repository for web page files. This page library can contain any number of pages, but the web site will only display one of them, at any given time. For example, look at the Home site in your intranet; its URL is `http://srv1/pages/default.aspx`. Let's divide the URL into its single parts:

❑ `http://srv1` is the URL to the Home site (i.e., the top site in the site).

❑ `/pages` is the name of the page library.

❑ `Default.aspx` is the current page displayed for the site.

So let's look at this page library. Click View All Site Content at the top of the Quick Launch navigation bar; this will display all the lists and libraries in this Home site. Click on Pages (in the Document Libraries section), and you will find the `Default.aspx` page mentioned above. Since this page library is like any other document library, you work with its files in the same way; for example, if you want to modify the `Default.aspx` file, click with the mouse just to the right of this file, to open its quick menu (see Figure 11-8). Then click Edit Properties. Now you must click OK to accept the option to check out the page file before it can be modified.

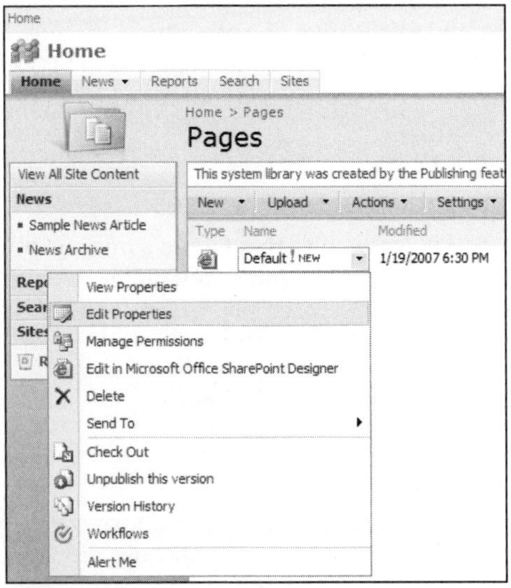

Figure 11-8

The form displayed now has all the content you previously saw on the Home page for this intranet, plus a number of properties you did not see, such as Target Audience, Contact Name, and Contact Picture. Now edit the content of the page. Click anywhere inside the Page Content area, for example, change the headline color to red, then click OK. Now go back to the Home page again. Note that the page is now checked out, and you will see a number of buttons on the editing toolbar. Since this modification (i.e., the red headline) has not yet been checked in, or published, only you can see the new look of this page. Now you can choose any of these actions:

❑ **Discard the modification:** Click the toolbar buttons Page ➪ Discard Check Out.

❑ **Continue to edit the page:** Click the Edit Page button.

❑ **Check in, but do not publish the modified page:** Click the Check in to Share Draft button. This allows another web content author to continue to edit the page.

❑ **Publish the modified page:** Click the Publish button. Any user with Read access to the site can now see the modified page.

In this example, discard the modifications, and click OK to confirm the operation. The original content of this page is now displayed again. You can actually start editing a content page much more easily than by using the procedure described above. Simply click Site Actions ➪ Edit Page, and once again, the `Default.aspx` page file is automatically checked out and is ready to be edited. Now discard the modifications again (even if you did not do anything): Click Page ➪ Discard Check Out, and click OK to accept this.

Let's test this with another page. Click on the News tab on the top bar, then click Site Actions ➪ Edit Page. The page will be checked out, and its content will be editable. Be sure to discard the checkout of this page. Obviously, this is also a Publishing Page. In fact, all of these MOSS sites in this intranet are Publishing Pages, thanks to the site template it was built on: the Collaboration Portal site template. It is safe to say that Filobit's new intranet will fulfill the requirements for web content management.

Did you note that there is more information on the Home site than defined in the `Default.aspx` file, such as menus, logotypes, and navigation links? It is clear that the Home site must display more than just the `Default.aspx` page, and this is true! The other type of information on this page is stored in a Master Page; this is a new type of layout file that did not exist in SPS 2003. It comes with the new ASP.NET 2.0 environment, and defines the exact layout for a SharePoint site. You will learn more about Master Pages in Chapters 12 and 13.

The News Site

Another requirement from your manager was that Filobit's intranet must support news items. Luckily, the Collaboration Portal site template comes with a News site, ready to be used. Its news items are built on pages very similar to the page files discussed in previous section. So, let's create a news item to see how this works.

Try It Out   Create News Items

1. Open the News site in the intranet.

2. Click Site Actions ➪ Create Page. This will open a form where you define the content of the news items. For example, to create a news item about dinosaurs you would make these entries:

   a. **Title:** The Death of Dinosaurs. This will be the headline of the news item.

b. **Description:** "All of them were killed when a giant meteorite hit the Earth 65 million years ago." This will be the beginning of the news item.

c. **URL name:** This will, by default, be the same as the title, but without space characters. Accept this name, unless you have a good reason not to.

d. **Page Layout:** In this section, you choose what type of layout file to use for the news item. By default, there are four Article Page layouts, but you can easily create new ones when needed. To do this, you will need SharePoint Designer (see Chapter 13). In this example, choose the Article page with image on left.

e. Click Create. After a few seconds the chosen article layout file is checked out and opened in edit mode (see Figure 11-9). This layout file consists of a number of web controls, such as a `Page Image`, `Page Content`, and a `Rollup Image`.

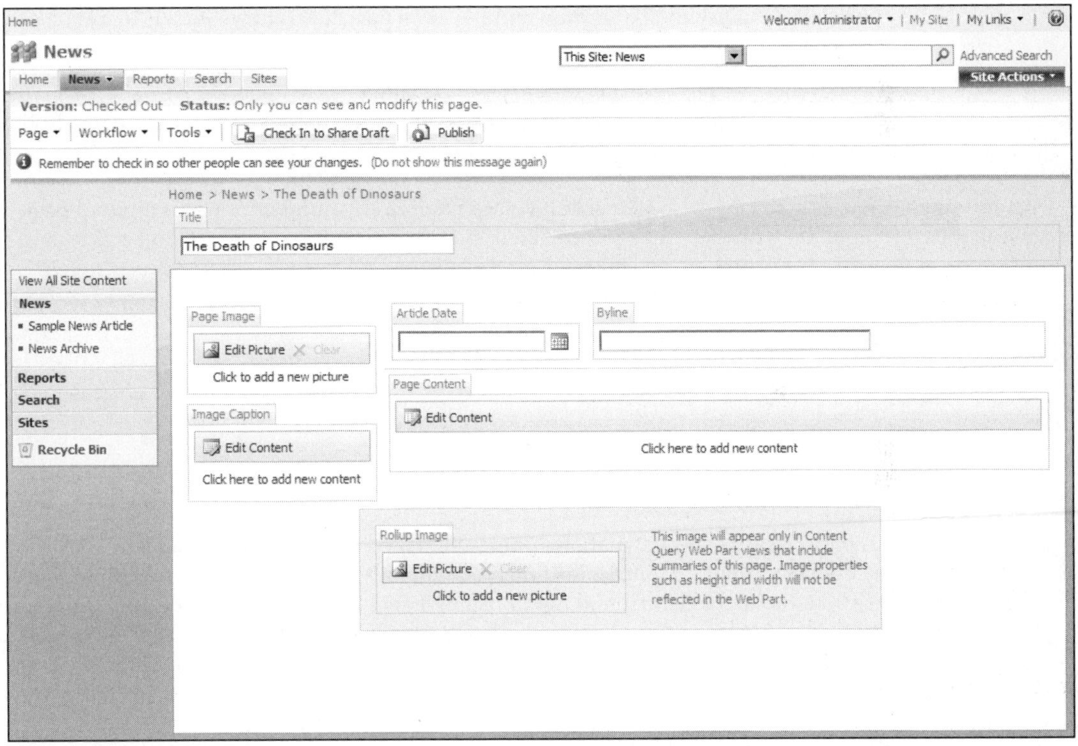

Figure 11-9

f. In the `Page Image` control, click Edit Picture. In the next form, click Browse and select a picture of your choice.

> You can choose between two image libraries: one in the current News site and one called Site Collection Images. If you don't find the picture you want, select the image library and then click Upload to add the picture of your choice. Then click the Refresh button to see the uploaded picture.

g. In the Image Caption control, type the text you want to appear under the image.

h. In the `Article Date` control, click its calendar icon and select the date when this article was published (or simply any date you want to set as the article date).

i. In the `Byline` control, enter the name of the author of the article.

j. Click inside the `Page Content` control, and type or paste the article. Note that you can use a rich set of formatting controls, including editing in raw HTML format, creating tables, and inserting images.

k. In the Rollup Image control, click Edit Picture and add a picture in the same way as described in step f. This picture will be shown when the news item is displayed using a rollup Web Part, as you will see later. It can be another picture than in step f or the same picture.

l. Click the Publish toolbar button and the main part of this news item is displayed; that is, all the information except the Rollup Image and the Description will be displayed.

m. Next, click on the News tab on the top navigation bar to open the News site with its default view. Now this news item is listed at the top of that page, but only the Rollup Image, the Title, and its Description are shown.

As you can see, it is easy to add news items, and you can define any number of preconfigured page layout files for these. But where are they stored? Well, click on a news item to see its full article, and then look at the URL. For example, the Dinosaur article has the URL `http://srv1/News/Pages/TheDeathOfDinosaurs.aspx`, which tells you this:

❑ `http://srv1` is the URL of the top site the site collection.

❑ `/News` is the part of the URL that points to the News web site (a subsite under `http://srv1`).

❑ `/Pages` is the page library that stores the news items.

❑ `TheDeathOfDinosaurs.aspx` is the name of the page file for the news item.

So, let's open that page library and see what other news item it contains. On the News site, click View All Site Contents. In the Document Libraries section, you will find Pages, which is a page library exactly like the one you saw before in the description of Publishing Pages on the intranet. The only difference is what it is used for. The page files in this library are all news items, except two: `Default.aspx` is the content page for the News site, and `newsarchive.aspx` is a special file that operates similarly to a page library; it will contain all news items, including archived (i.e., hidden) news items. For example, you can create a news item that will be visible from today and one week from now. After that the news item is removed from the standard news lists. But if you open the News archive, it will still be listed there.

If you need to modify an existing news item, you have two options: edit the news page directly or edit the page file in the page library. Both options are described here.

Try It Out   Modify News Items

1. Open the News item directly in the News site, and then click Site Actions ➪ Edit Page.

2. Modify the News item.

3. Click Publish.

The second option is to edit the page file using the Page library on the News site:

1. Open the News site.

2. Click View All Site Content ➪ Pages to open the page library.

3. Open the quick menu for the news item, and select Edit Properties. Click OK to accept the option to check out the file.

4. Modify the news item.

5. Click OK to save and close the page.

6. Open the quick menu for the file again. Select Check In, and select the option to check in a major version.

You may ask yourself "How do I specify when a news item should be archived?" This feature is referred to as "item scheduling" and is actually not enabled by default; you must enable it as shown in the following Try It Out.

Try It Out   Enable the Scheduling of News Items

1. Open the News site in the intranet.

2. Click View All Site Content ➪ Pages to open the page library.

3. Click Settings ➪ Document Library Settings. In the General Settings section, you will find Manage item scheduling. Open it and you will see that in order to enable the scheduling of news items, you must first activate both major and minor version history, and content approval. Click the Back button on your web browser to step back to the previous page.

> If you click either OK or Cancel here, you will be taken to the general Site Settings page for the News site, which is not what you want! If this happens, start all over with step 1 again.

4. Click Version settings, then continue with:

    a. Select Yes in the Content Approval section.

    b. Verify that the Document Version History section is configured for major and minor versions.

    c. Click OK to save and close the page.

5. Now click the Manage item scheduling link.

    a. Check Enable scheduling of items in this list.

    b. Click OK to save and close the page.

You are taken to the general Site Settings page for the News site — scheduling is now enabled. Test this by creating a news item. Open the News site, then click Site Actions ➪ Create Page. Enter the Title and Description, and click Create. Note that at the top is a new link: Publication Start Date: Immediately (see

Figure 11-10). Click that link to open a configuration page where you define the scheduling of the news item (as depicted in Figure 11-11).

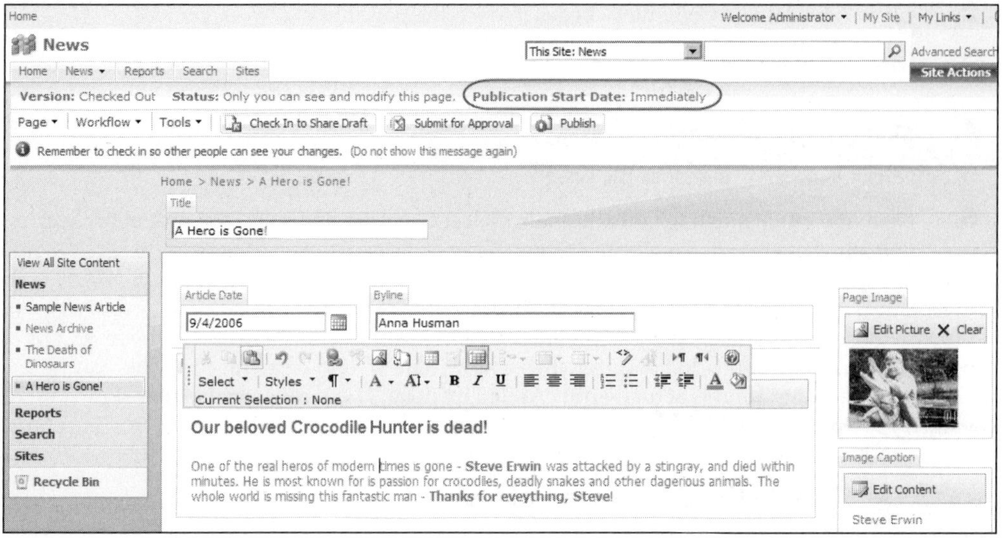

Figure 11-10

Figure 11-11

Note that the Schedule section on this page contains an option to send an e-mail to the contact person for the news item some time before the article is archived; the contact person is set on the same page. This is a very handy feature that ensures that important articles are not removed without the contact person knowing about it; for example, this contact person may decide that the archival of this news item should be postponed.

The Site Directory

Another feature that the Filobit manager in this example asked for was that all sites, subsites, and workspaces be easy for the user to find. A very good solution is to create a Site Directory (a directory that shows all the sites in the SharePoint environment). Since this may include many thousands of sites, there must be an easy way to organize all these sites. Compare this to a file system: Instead of storing all files in one folder, you create a folder structure. With SharePoint's site directory, you have the same option: You can define any number of categories, such as Department, Project Type, and Customer, and then assign these categories to links pointing to the sites.

An example will illustrate this better: You talk with the people who will create sites in the new intranet, such as project leaders, team managers, and department managers, and you determine that the sites can be divided into three categories:

❑ **Division:** Filobit consists of these divisions: Sales, IT, Finance, and HR. The last division will be used for sites like the Board of Directors site.

❑ **Project Type:** There are three types of projects in Filobit: Internal, External, and Other.

❑ **Site Type:** There are four types of sites: Intranet, Project, Meeting, and Other.

With MOSS comes a special web site for managing the site directory; its name is Sites, which is both good and bad. It's good because it describes exactly what it is used for, and bad because it is very easy sometimes to get confused, since the term "site" is used both to refer to a type of object and as the name for several objects. For example, try to understand this: "The Site site stores site links in the Sites list!" Maybe a better name for this site would be the Site Directory.

The Site Directory consists of links to SharePoint sites; these links are stored in the list called "Sites." On the Sites page is a button named Add Link to Site, which you can use to add new site links. Another way of adding site links is to open the list (View All Site Content ➪ Sites) and click New; this last method is also used to modify or delete existing site links.

> The Sites list requires approval of any modified site link. In other words, when adding a new site link or editing an existing site link, it must be approved before the users can see the modification.

To manage all the categories available for these site links, you must open the settings for the Sites list, as described below. Note that if you later change any existing categories, all existing site links that belong to that category will then lose the setting. In other words, make sure to evaluate what categories you need, before you start adding site links, unless you are prepared to modify all existing site links!

Your job as a SharePoint administrator is to create a Site Directory with the categories described below. At this stage there are no other sites, beside the one created automatically by the Collaboration Portal site template. Soon you will create new sites, and before that you need to adjust the site categories. The following Try It Out shows how you do this.

Try It Out   **Configure Site Directory Categories**

1. Open the Sites site in the intranet. It contains already three categories: Division, Region, and "Tasks and Tools."

2. Click View All Site Content.

3. Click Sites in the Lists section. This will open the list where all site links are stored.

4. Click Settings ⇨ List Settings. The configuration page for the list is displayed. Look in the Columns section; it shows both properties, such as Title and URL, and the three default categories: Division, Region, and "Tasks and Tools."

5. Start by modifying the Division category. Click on its name to open its configuration form:

   a. In the section Additional Column Settings, replace the text Information Technology with **IT**.

   b. Then replace Research & Development with **HR**.

   c. At the bottom of the list, add **Management**.

   d. Click OK to save and close the form.

6. Next step is to remove the default category Region. Click on its name, click the Delete button at the bottom of the form, then click OK to delete the column.

7. Add the Project Type category. In the Columns section, click Create column, then enter these settings:

   a. **Column name:** Project Type.

   b. **Type:** Choice. The form is rebuilt to allow you define the options for this choice.

   c. **Description:** "Enter the project type."

   d. **Type each choice on a separate line:** Delete all current lines in this field, then enter these values, one per line: Internal, External, Other.

   e. Clear the Default value field.

   f. Click OK.

8. **Add the Site Type category:** In the Columns section, click Create column, then enter these settings:

   a. **Column name:** Site Type.

   b. **Type:** Choice. The form is rebuilt to allow you define the options for this choice

   c. **Description:** "Enter the site type."

    d.   **Type each choice on a separate line:** Delete all current lines in this field, then enter these values, one per line: Intranet, Project, Meeting, and Other.

    e.   Clear the Default value field.

    f.   Click OK.

9.   Click on the top navigation tab Sites. Note that it now shows the updated categories (see Figure 11-12).

The site categories are now ready to be used.

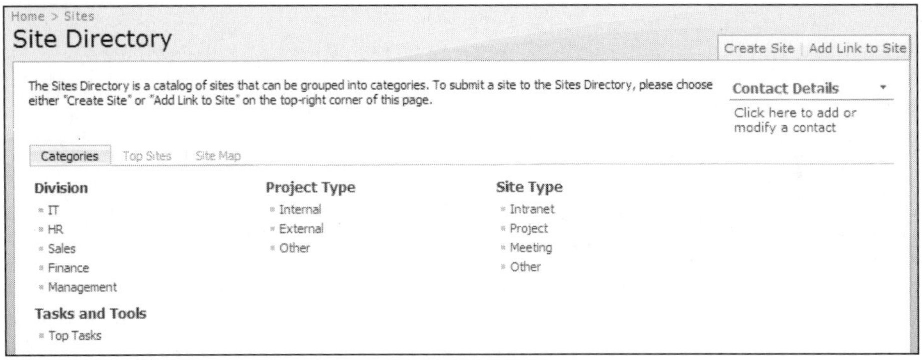

Figure 11-12

Displaying an Excel Diagram on the Intranet

The next step in this example is to display an MS Excel diagram, showing the latest sales figures. With MOSS 2007 Enterprise Edition comes Excel Services, which enable you to display any Excel spreadsheet or diagram in HTML format (users do not need an MS Excel client to view this information). In order to use Excel Services to display Excel files, the SharePoint administrator must configure at least one setting: the trusted file location where these Excel file are stored. Excel Services are a part of the Shared Service Provider module, so all configuration settings for Excel Services are located in the SSP instance, typically named `SharedService1`.

To display this file you will use a special Web Part, named Excel Web Access; it will display any Excel file, in HTML format. If you have ever used Outlook Web Access to view your Exchange mailbox using a web browser, you get the idea. In both cases, you can use a web browser to view content instead of using a full client, such as MS Excel or MS Outlook.

> **You must use the new Excel 2007 format (`.xlsx`) to use Excel Services. If you use the old `.xls` format, you will get an error saying "Unable to Load Workbook" (see Figure 11-13).**

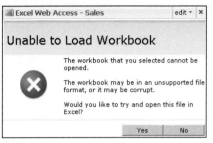

Figure 11-13

In this example, the sales figures and the diagram you need to display will be saved in the `Sales.xlsx` file, stored in the document library Sales Info, which belongs to the Document Center site. This document library does not exist yet, so you must create it. Then you must publish the `Sales.xlsx` file to that document library, using Excel services. Follow the steps in the Try It Out below to configure the Excel services, and to display the diagram using the Excel Web Access Web Part.

Try It Out   Use Excel Services to Display an Excel File

1. Open the intranet: Go to `http://srv1/` and click on the top navigation tab Document Center (note that its full URL is `http://srv1/docs`; that is, this is a subsite directly located under the top site).

2. Click Site Actions ⇨ Create, and then click Document Library in the Libraries section. Then enter this value:

    a. **Name:** Sales Info.

    b. Click Create.

3. Open the `Sale.xlsx` file in the file system (or create it from scratch now):

    a. If the diagram does not exist yet, create it now. A tip is to create an embedded chart on a spreadsheet page instead of creating a separate chart page in Excel. This way, you can control its size, which makes it easier later to display this diagram in the Excel Web Access Web Part. Click on the diagram, and note its name; for example, Chart 1.

    b. In Excel, click the Office button, then Publish ⇨ Excel Services. Navigate to the document library Sales Info. Before you click Save, perform the next step.

    > You must use MS Excel 2007, which comes with MS Office Professional Plus, Enterprise, or Ultimate edition in order to publish to Excel Services. See Chapter 1 for more details about the different MS Office 2007 editions.

    c. Click Excel Services Options. On the Show tab, use the menu to select Items in the Workbook, then check the chart name; for example, Chart 1. Click OK to close the page.

    d. The selected diagram will now open in a web browser. This Excel file is now ready to be used in SharePoint.

4. The next step is to configure Excel Services. Open the SharePoint Central Administration tool, and then open the SSP instance, typically `SharedServices1`.

   a. In the Excel Services Settings section, click Trusted file locations.

   b. Click Add Trusted File Location, and a web form will be displayed where you define a number of settings related to Excel files and their locations. In this example, you only add a simple path. In the Address field, type `http://srv1/docs/Sales Info`, which is the URL to the document library where the Excel file is stored.

   c. Click OK.

5. The final step is to display the Excel diagram, using the Excel Web Access Web Part. Open the intranet site (`http://srv1`), then click Site Actions ⇨ Edit Page.

6. Select the Web Part zone where you want to display the Excel diagram, for example Top Zone, then click Add a Web Part.

7. If necessary, expand the section All Web Parts, then check mark the Excel Web Access Web Part, located in the Business Data section. Click Add. After a few seconds, the new Web Part will be visible. Configure the Web Part like this:

   a. On the Excel Web Access Web Part, click Edit ⇨ Modify Shared Web Part (or click the link Click here to open the tool pane in the text body of this Web Part). The tool pane will open.

   b. In the Workbook Display section, click the button at the far right of the Workbook field, then double-click on the Document Center site, and select Sales Info. Select `Sales.xlsx`, and click OK to add the URL to the document.

   c. This Web Part does not rescale the Excel file to match the size of the Web Part window, so adjust the Rows and Columns fields to match the size of the diagram. Note that you may have to test these settings to make the diagram display properly.

   d. If you want to define a special title for this Web Part, you do it like this: Uncheck the options "Autogenerate Web Part Title" and "Autogenerate Web Part Title URL," then expand the Appearance section and enter the name you want in the Title field.

   e. If you have more than one sheet in the Excel spreadsheet, you may want to prohibit the users from seeing anything besides the first sheet. To do that, uncheck Workbook Navigation in the Navigation and Interactivity section.

   f. Click OK to save and close the tool pane. After a few seconds, the Excel file is displayed in the Excel Web Access Web Part. If it looks good, then you are done; if not, open the tool pane for the Web Part and change its settings.

8. Click Publish on the toolbar. This page now shows the Sales diagram; it should look similar to Figure 11-14.

9. Test the new diagram: Edit the `Sales.xlsx` file in the Sales Info document library, and make some changes that will affect the diagram, then save and close the Excel file. Now open the page with the Excel Web Access Web Part. Click Update ⇨ Reload Workbook on the Web Part toolbar to make sure that it shows the latest information.

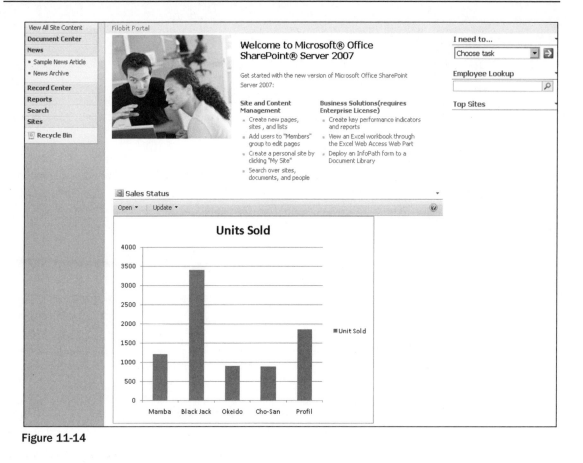

Figure 11-14

Creating Departmental Intranets

As described in the example, this intranet must have three local intranets for the departments IT, HR, and Sales. Since the security requirements are moderate, you can create subsites in the current site collection for these departmental intranets, as described in the following Try It Out.

Try It Out   Create Departmental Intranets

1. Open the intranet (`http://srv1/`, and click on the top navigation tab Sites (note that its full URL is `http://srv1/SiteDirectory`; that is, this is a subsite directly located under the top site).

2. Create the first departmental intranet site for IT:

   a. Click Create Site in the upper right of the Sites page, and enter the following settings.

   b. **Title:** IT.

   c. **Description:** "Local Intranet for the IT Department."

    d.   **URL name:** IT. (the complete URL will then be `http://srv1/SiteDirectory/it`).

    e.   **Select a template:** Team Site.

    f.   **User Permissions:** Select the option Use unique permissions.

    g.   Accept the default Use the top link bar from the parent site.

    h.   Check the option List this new site in the site directory, and select Division: IT, and Site Type: Intranet.

    i.   Click Create. The site will be created.

    j.   Since you requested unique permissions, the next step is defining the permissions for the site. Select the option Create a new group for "Visitors to This Site" and accept the default "IT Visitors." Next you should add users and groups to the three groups on the page, as required by your organization. In this example you will skip this for now; click OK to save and close the permissions page.

    k.   The new site is displayed; if it looks good, then it is time to create the next site.

3.   Create the departmental intranet site for HR:

    a.   Click Create Site in the upper right of the Sites page, and enter the following settings.

    b.   **Title:** HR.

    c.   **Description:** "Local Intranet for the HR Department."

    d.   **URL name:** HR (the complete URL will then be `http://srv1/SiteDirectory/HR`).

    e.   Select a template: Team Site.

    f.   **User Permissions:** Select the option Use unique permissions.

    g.   Accept the default Use the top link bar from the parent site.

    h.   Check the option List this new site in the site directory, and select Division: HR, and Site Type: Intranet.

    i.   Click Create. The site will be created.

    j.   Define the permissions for the site. Select the option Create a new group for "Visitors to This Site" and accept the default "HR Visitors." Click OK to save and close the permissions page.

4.   Finally, create the departmental intranet site for Sales:

    a.   Click Create Site in the upper right of the Sites page, and enter the following settings.

    b.   **Title:** Sales.

    c.   **Description:** "Local Intranet for the Sales Department."

    d.   **URL name:** Sales (the complete URL will then be `http://srv1/SiteDirectory/Sales`).

    e.   **Select a template:** Team Site.

    f.   **User Permissions:** Select the option Use unique permissions.

    g.   Accept the default Use the top link bar from the parent site.

> **h.** Check the option List this new site in the site directory, and select Division: Sales, and Site Type: Intranet.
>
> **i.** Click Create.
>
> **j.** Define the permissions for this site. Select the option Create a new group for "Visitors to This Site" and accept the default "Sales Visitors." Click OK to save and close the permissions page.

All three new sites are now created and ready to be used; time to continue with the configuration of the intranet.

Publishing Documents to a Document Archive

Your manager in this example requested that the intranet have a shared document archive that users can use to upload important documents they want to share with others. This is a standard feature in SharePoint. You simply create one ordinary document library in a suitable site and configure its permissions, if necessary. Then you configure individual document libraries in subsites, project sites, and the like to show an upload link to the document archive. Whenever a user uploads a document to the archive, a copy of that document is stored in the archive, but it contains a link back to the original document. If the original document is modified, that author will be reminded that there is a copy in the archive, and he or she can choose to update that archived copy. A user that looks at the properties for the files in the archive can see that the document is a copy, and where the original file is stored.

One important reason to use a separate document library as an archive instead of allowing users to read the original files is permissions. For example, say that you have three subsites; users in these subsites create a lot of documents, and some of them should be publically available. Instead of opening these subsites and/or their document libraries to all users, you can copy documents to the public document archive. That archive can have any permission setting that your organization needs, without your needing to worry about the permissions on the original documents and their libraries. But this creates a new challenge: How do you make sure that the copies in the archive are updated? SharePoint solves this problem by creating a link back from the copied document to the original version, as described in the previous paragraph.

In the Filobit example, you will first select a document library to be used as the document archive. Then you will modify the document libraries in the subsites IT, HR, and Sales to contain a upload link to that document archive, as described in the Try It Out below.

Try It Out   Configure a Shared Document Archive

> **1.** Open the site `http://srv1/docs` (i.e., the Document Center).
>
> **2.** Click on Documents, and note its URL: `http://srv1/docs/Documents`. This will be the new document archive for Filobit. In a real-world scenario, you should now update the permissions to the document library, but in this example you will accept the default settings; that is, anyone who is a member of the Visitor SharePoint group will be able to open documents in the archive.

3.   Add a link to this document archive to some of the document libraries:

    a.   Open the IT site, `http://srv1/SiteDirectory/it`.

    b.   Click on Shared Documents in the Quick Launch bar.

    c.   Click Settings ⇨ Document Library Settings ⇨ Advanced settings.

    d.   In the Custom Sent to Destination section, enter Destination name: Document archive and the URL: `http://srv1/Docs/Documents`.

    e.   Click OK.

4.   Repeat steps a–e above for the HR and Sales subsites.

5.   Test this:

    a.   Open the IT site (`http://srv1/SiteDirectory/it`), and add any document to the Shared Documents library.

    b.   In the quick menu for the document, select Send To ⇨ Document Archive.

    c.   The following form shows the filename and the URL to the archive; accept the settings. Change the option in the Update section to Yes. This will ensure that an author who updates this document will be notified that there is a copy of the document in the archive and that the copy can also be updated.

    d.   A new dialog window named Copy Progress opens. Click OK to copy the file to the archive. When the process is completed, click Done.

    e.   Open the document archive (`http://srv1/docs/documents`). Verify that it contains a copy of the document.

    f.   Open the quick menu for the copy. Note that it has the option Go to Source Item. Select this option to open the properties of the original document, and possibly also the document itself.

    g.   Open the quick menu again for the copy in the archive, then select View Properties. It will show the link back to the original document (see Figure 11-15).

Figure 11-15

Creating New Site Collections

The intranet, as requested by your manager in this example, is now almost complete. But you need to do some more things. Since the Finance department and the Board of Directors group requested much higher security, you decide that they will each get a separate site collection. Doing this means that there is no way a user, or even an administrator from the first site collection, will have access to either of these two sites. You may remember from earlier discussions about security in Chapters 3 and 5 that each site collection is similar to an isolated island. Its settings only affect the sites in that site collection, and never a site in another site collection.

The quick steps to create the site collections for the Finance and Board of Directors groups are listed below. Instead of creating these new top sites using the WSS Team Site template, you will use the MOSS site templates Document Center and Report Center. These templates are identical to the subsites with the same name in the main intranet site (http://srv1).

Try It Out   Create Finance and Board of Directors Intranets

1. Start the SharePoint Central Administration tool, then switch to the Application Management page. The first new site collection to be used is a web site for the Finance team, based on the Report Center template.

2. Click Create site collection in the SharePoint Site Management section, then enter these values:

   a. **Title:** Finance.

   b. **Description:** "Welcome to the Finance team."

   c. **URL:** Add "finance" (the complete URL is then http://srv1/sites/finance).

   d. In the Template Selection section, on the Enterprise tab, select Report Center.

   > **If you have installed language packs, select the language first, then select the site template.**

   e. In the Primary Site Collection Administrator section, enter the user account that should be the administrator for the complete site collection (use Filobit\Administrator in this example to be sure that you can manage that site collection).

   f. In the Site Categories section, select Division: Finance and a Site Type of Intranet.

   g. For this site you do not need a quota template; leave the default setting, No Quota.

   h. Click OK, then OK again. You are taken back to the Application Management page.

3. Next, you will create a site for the Board of Directors group. Most of their information is meeting minutes and documents, so they want a suitably designed top site that will be the parent of multiple meeting workspaces. For this top site you will use the site template Document Center. Click Create site collection, in the SharePoint Site Management section, then enter these values:

   a. **Title:** Board of Directors.

   b. **Description:** "Welcome to the Board of Directors web site."

   c. **URL:** Add "bod" (the complete URL is then http://srv1/sites/bod).

    d. In the Template Selection section, on the Enterprise tab, select Document Center.

> **If you have installed language packs, select the language first, then select the site template.**

    e. In the Primary Site Collection Administrator section, enter the user account that should be the administrator for the complete site collection.

    f. Check the option List this new site in the site directory, and select Division: Board of Directors, and Site Type: Intranet.

    g. For this site you do not need a quota template; accept the default setting, No Quota.

    h. Click OK, then OK again. You are taken back to the Application Management page.

4. Finally, you must add a link on these new site collections that points back to the main intranet site. Start by opening the Finance site, then continue with the following steps:

    a. Click Site Actions ⇨ Site Settings ⇨ Portal site connection (in the Site Collection Administration section).

    b. Select the option Connect to portal site, then enter the Portal Web Address: `http://srv1` and Portal Name: Filobit Home.

    c. Click OK to save and close the page.

5. Repeat steps a–c above for the site Board of Directors site (`http://srv1/sites/bod`).

Intranet Summary

Building a new intranet using MOSS was a lot easier than doing so with WSS, since MOSS contains much richer functionality, such as web content management, advanced News features, a configurable site directory, and features such as Excel Services and more advanced site templates. After building these sites and configuring these features, the next steps could be these:

❑ Adjust the design by adding new Master Pages and page layout files for news items and the like.

❑ Add more Web Parts; for example, use the RSS Feed Web Part that comes with MOSS to present information stored in external web sites, instead of adding code to the XML Web Part to make it work as an RSS Feed client.

❑ Analyze which users should have access to specific sites, libraries, and items, then implement that using SharePoint groups and/or AD security groups.

❑ Start investigating how InfoPath forms could assist your organization to work in a more process-oriented way.

❑ Analyze what content types your organization needs.

❑ Prepare yourself for constant change. Listen to your users; try to understand what their needs are, and help them find solutions based on the standard features of SharePoint. When that is not enough, look at the vast market of third-party products and solutions for SharePoint.

Building Internet Sites

When building a Internet web site you face the same questions and use the same toolbox of features as when building an intranet. The main differences relate to protecting the Internet web site and making sure that anonymous users do not see more than they are allowed to see. Note that an Internet site is not the same as an extranet site. The latter is used by external partners, customers, and other groups of users who need to access information on your network. In order to control a user accessing the extranet, you require them to log on. In other words, they must have a user account in your IT environment that can be validated by SharePoint, or to be more exact, by the Internet Information Service (IIS) that is governing the SharePoint application.

An Internet site (with a capital I, since it is a proper name!) is a site that people can access without any authentication process; that is, they log on automatically as anonymous users. SharePoint 2007 can offer anonymous access in these situations:

❑   When you create a new site collection in an existing SharePoint environment and use it as a public Internet site.

❑   When you use a subsite in an existing site collection for the public Internet site.

❑   When you install a separate WSS or MOSS server for the public Internet site.

There are two main questions you should ask when building a public Internet site: How will users access the site, and should you use WSS 3.0 or MOSS 2007 to build it? These questions are discussed below.

Accessing the Web Site from the Internet

You could install the SharePoint server on the local internet and then open the firewall for anonymous access using port 80. But this is *a very bad idea*! Do not do this; it will only be a matter of hours before your complete network is invaded by nasty applications such as Trojan horses, viruses, and applications that send spam to the world, using your internal mail server. Besides that all information on that network must then be considered public, regardless or whether or not it is "secured" by file system permissions, and hacking tools are vast in number and free! Even "script-kiddies" (young computer nerds with no expertise in hacking and breaking applications) will be able to use these hacking tools as long as they can find a way into your internal network. So you get the message? Do not open any anonymous connection from the Internet into your internal network. Period.

A better idea, but still not good enough, is to place the SharePoint server directly in the Demilitarized Zone (DMZ), that is, a network segment directly connected to your firewall, typically used for servers open for public access, such as Exchange front-end servers, and in this case an intranet. The reason that this is not a good idea is that the SharePoint server will be open to attacks, such as denial-of-service (DoS) attacks, or totally hacked. Maybe you think this is not as serious; then think about all the public Internet sites where the content has been modified in a way that is not flattering to the organization that owns the Internet site. Even if you can accept the possibility of losing the server, you surely do not want anyone to make a fool out of you by changing your public web site.

The best idea is to use a firewall that works as an application proxy server; that is, "pretends" to be an internal server, such as a SharePoint site. It works like this (see Figure 11-16).

1. The External user opens the Internet site. The URL will point to the network firewall.

2. The network firewall checks to see if the URL is open for anonymous access. If so, a connection is established between the external user's web browser and the application proxy server, which pretends to be a SharePoint server.

3. When the external user requests information from the SharePoint server, such as the opening of a web page, the application server will contact the internal SharePoint server, asking for that information.

4. The internal SharePoint server will send the requested information to the application server, which passes it on to the external user.

Under no circumstances will the external user get a connection to anything except the application proxy server.

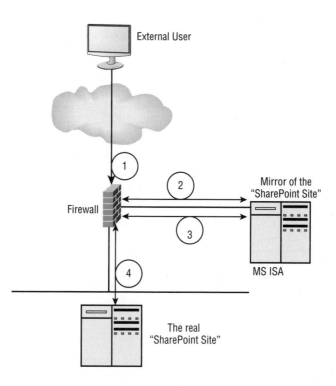

Figure 11-16

Microsoft has a great product for this type of operation: MS Internet Security and Acceleration Server 2006 (MS ISA 2006). It comes with configuration wizards for pretending to be a SharePoint site, and many other applications, such as an Exchange server. In fact, MS ISA 2006 is a very good firewall as well as an application proxy server, so in most situations you will in fact be able to replace the old firewall with the MS ISA server, making your Internet connection both very safe and easy to manage. It also allows you to use a different URL on the Internet than the URL used when connecting to the web site from the internal network. Another very handy feature in MS ISA is that you expose just a part of the internal SharePoint environment, thus prohibiting that external Internet users from gaining access to more sites and information than you want them to.

You may ask yourself what will happen if somebody hacks the MS ISA server? The answer is: almost nothing! The worst that can happen is that you have to reinstall the MS ISA server, and during that time all connections to and from the Internet are down (the faster you can replace the MS ISA server, the faster your connections to the Internet get up and running again). Since the MS ISA server does not contain any actual content besides cached pages (and you can define how long they will be cached, if at all), there is no risk that somebody can change the content on your Internet site. Make sure to back up the MS ISA server whenever you change its configuration settings.

WSS or MOSS for Internet Sites?

This answer to this question is similar to the one in the intranet site discussion: It depends on the features you need and how much money you are willing to spend on the solution. You have already seen that MOSS contains a great web content management functionality, which really will be needed for a serious Internet web site. But for a small organization, with simple needs, WSS will do just fine. Since WSS now also comes with a search and index engine, such an Internet site will also offer search features. Some of the pros and cons of these products are listed in the table below.

Feature	WSS 3.0	MOSS Enterprise
Web content management	No — everything you change will immediately be visible to the external users on the Internet.	Yes — there is full support for page layout files, version history, approval control, workflows and more. You will not need any staging or test server.
Searching	Yes — but only for information in a SharePoint site open to anonymous access.	Yes — in any source location that SharePoint has access to and that is open to anonymous access.
Support for Master Pages	Yes	Yes
Support for Excel Services	No	Yes
Support for InfoPath Services	No	Yes
Support for displaying information in external databases, such as Navision, Oracle, and the like	No	Yes
Price	Free	Not free (contact your license partner to find your price).

Again, the main reason for selecting MOSS for a public Internet site is usually its advanced web content management. In the following sections, you see how to install both WSS and MOSS as a public Internet site.

Using WSS for Internet Sites

In this example, you will create an Internet site on your existing SharePoint server. First, you will create a new IIS web site named `Internet-site`, using the TCP port 8080, since the default port 80 is already taken by another web application. Another solution would be to use TCP port 80 for this new IIS web site as well and give it a Host Header name to distinguish these two web applications. If you do so, do not forget to create an Alias record in the DNS server for your network. You will use this IIS web site to create a new web application (i.e., an extended IIS web site). Then you will create a site collection, using the WSS site template named Blog. You will then open that site to anonymous access to allow any user access to the site. The following Try It Out shows how you do this.

Try It Out   Use WSS for an Internet Site

1. Start the SharePoint Central Administration tool, and then switch to the Application Management page.

2. Click Create or extend Web application, then do this:

   a. Click Create a new Web application.

   b. In the IIS Web Site section, select the option Create a new Web site, and set the description to Internet-Site and the TCP port to 8080.

   c. In the Application Pool section, select the option to create a new application pool, named Internet-Site, using a security account that is different from the other web applications, just to be safe. Note that you can also use the same security account that you use for other web applications, but the security level is then slightly reduced, compared to using a separate account.

   d. Click OK to save and close the form.

3. Go back to the Application Management page. Click Create site collection in the SharePoint Site Management section, then enter these values:

   a. **Web Application:** `http://srv1:8080`.

   b. **Title:** My Blog.

   c. **Select a template:** Blog.

   d. **Primary Site Collection Administrator:** Filobit\administrator. You would here normally enter the owner of this blog site, but in this example you will use the administrator in order to see how this works.

   e. Click OK to save and close the form.

4. The Blog site is now created. The next step is to open it to anonymous access. You must use the SharePoint Central Administration tool for this. Open the Application Management page, then click Authentication Providers in the Application Security section. Continue with this:

   a. Select the Web Application `http://srv1:8080`.

   b. Click on Zone "Default."

      c.   Check Enable anonymous access in the Anonymous Access section.

      d.   Click Save.

5.   It is now possible to enable anonymous access to the Blog site, but so far, this site only allows authenticated users. Test it by opening `http://srv1:8080`. You will see that it lists the current user's name at the top.

6.   To enable anonymous access to the site:

      a.   Click Site Actions ➪ Site Settings ➪ Advanced Permissions. This opens the Site Permission page for the site collection.

      b.   Click Settings ➪ Anonymous Access. On the next page you will decide how much of the site you want to open to anonymous access (see Figure 11-17). Select Entire Web site and click OK.

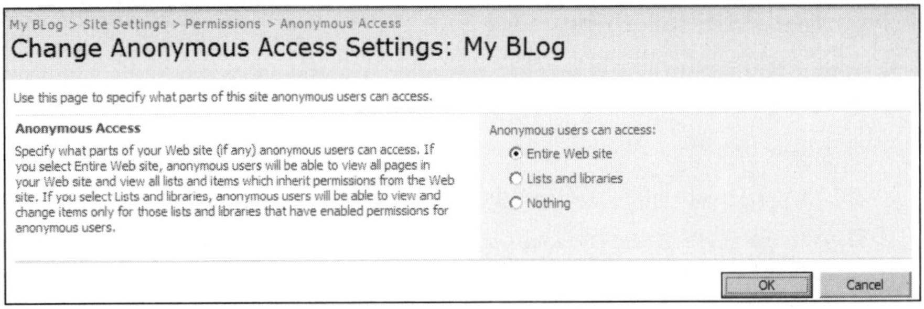

My BLog > Site Settings > Permissions > Anonymous Access

Change Anonymous Access Settings: My BLog

Use this page to specify what parts of this site anonymous users can access.

Anonymous Access

Specify what parts of your Web site (if any) anonymous users can access. If you select Entire Web site, anonymous users will be able to view all pages in your Web site and view all lists and items which inherit permissions from the Web site. If you select Lists and libraries, anonymous users will be able to view and change items only for those lists and libraries that have enabled permissions for anonymous users.

Anonymous users can access:
- ⦿ Entire Web site
- ○ Lists and libraries
- ○ Nothing

[OK]   [Cancel]

Figure 11-17

7.   Finally, start a new web client, and open `http://srv1:8080` again — this time, you will see a Sign in link instead of the current user name; that is, you are now accessing the site as an anonymous user. The only permission an anonymous user has is Read access. Since you opened the complete web site to anonymous access, this will also include Read permission to all list and libraries in the web site, and all subsites you later create that inherit permissions from this site.

8.   Click Sign in at the top right of the web page. You will be automatically authenticated, since you are doing this from the internal network. If you, instead, tried signing in from the Internet, you would have entered your logon credentials in a normal fashion. After you have signed in, you will be able to add content to and modify the settings on this page, just like normal.

The next step is to allow external users to access this site from the Internet. Exactly how to do this depends on what solution you choose, as described earlier in the section "Accessing the Web Site from the Internet." I do remind you that one of the best ways is to use an MS ISA 2006 server.

Using MOSS for an Internet Site

The method to create a public Internet site using a MOSS server is very similar to that using a WSS server, as described in the previous section. The only real difference is the site template you use. MOSS comes with a starting template for anonymous Internet sites, named the Publishing Portal and located on the Publishing tab for site templates.

In this example, you will once again create an Internet site on your existing SharePoint server. To make this example shorter, you will use the same web application as in the WSS example above. To do that you have to delete the WSS site collection first, then you will create a new site collection, using the MOSS site template named Publishing Portal. You will then open that site to anonymous access to allow any user access to it. The following Try It Out shows how you do this.

Try It Out   Use MOSS for an Internet Site

1. Start the SharePoint Central Administration tool, then switch to the Application Management page.

2. In this example, you will first remove the old WSS site collection so that you can create a MOSS site instead, using the same web application:

    a. Click Delete Site Collection.

    b. Click No Selection, and select Change Site Collection.

    c. Then change the Web Application to http://srv1:8080, select the only existing site collection (i.e., the Blog site you created earlier), and click OK.

3. Go back to the Application Management page. Click Create site collection in the SharePoint Site Management section, then enter these values:

    a. **Web Application:** http://srv1:8080.

    b. **Title:** Filobit Home Page.

    c. **Description:** "Welcome to Filobit's Home Page."

    d. **Select a template:** Publishing Portal (on the Publishing tab).

    e. **Primary Site Collection Administrator:** Filobit\administrator. You would here normally enter the owner of this Internet site, but in this example you will use the administrator in order to see how this works.

    f. Click OK to save and close the form.

4. The Publishing Portal web site is now created. The next step is to open it to anonymous access. You already enabled anonymous access for this Web Application in the previous example (step 4) with WSS, so you do not have to repeat those steps here.

5. It is now possible to enable anonymous access to the Publishing Portal site, but so far, this site only allows authenticated users. Test it by opening http://srv1:8080, and you will see that it will list the current user's name at the top. Note that the content of this page contains a lot of tips, for example how to open this site for anonymous access, change the Master Page, and set up multilingual support (see Figure 11-18).

My Site | My Links ▾ | Welcome FILOBIT\administrator ▾ | Site Actions ▾

Filobit Home Page

Press Releases   Search [   ] →

Enable anonymous access
You must enable anonymous access on the site collection for the forms authentication
logon page to work from Office SharePoint Server. Contact your administrator to have
anonymous access enabled in Central Administration and IIS.

Manage navigation
Change the navigation links in this site.

Go to master page gallery
Change the page layouts and master page of this site collection.

Manage site content and structure
Reorganize content and structure in this site collection.

Set up multilingual support
Use the variations feature to manage multi-lingual sites and pages.

Add users to the Approvers and Members groups
Users in the Approvers group can publish pages, images, and documents in this site. Users
in the Members group can create and edit pages, and they can upload images and
documents, but they cannot publish the pages, images, or documents. Workflow is enabled
in the Pages library, and content approval is enabled in the Documents and Images
libraries.

Figure 11-18

6. To enable anonymous access to this top site:

   a. Click Site Actions ⇨ Site Settings ⇨ People and Groups.

   b. Click Site Permissions in the Quick Launch bar.

   c. Click Settings ⇨ Anonymous Access. On the next page, you will decide how much of
   the site you want to open to anonymous access (see Figure 11-17). Select Entire Web site
   and click OK.

7. Finally, start a new web client, and open `http://srv1:8080` again. This time, you will see a
   Sign in link instead of the current user's name; that is, you are now accessing the site as an
   anonymous user. As described in the previous example, an anonymous user will only have
   Read permission to this site, all its lists, and all subsites you later create that inherit permissions
   from this site.

8. Click Sign in at the top right of the web page. You will be automatically authenticated, since you
   are doing this from the internal network. If you, instead, tried this from the Internet, you would
   have entered your logon credentials in a normal fashion. After you have signed in, you will be
   able to add content to and modify the settings on this page, just like normal.

The next step is the same as for the WSS Internet site: Set up the network to allow external users to
access the site from the Internet. Exactly how to do this depends on what solution you choose, as

described earlier in the section "Accessing the Web Site from the Internet." As before, I recommend that you use an MS ISA 2006 server for this purpose.

Summary

In this chapter you learned:

❑ Follow the KISS design rule: "Keep it simple, stupid!"

❑ Use WSS to build simple intranets that do not require advanced features like web content management, Global searching, Excel Services and Forms Service.

❑ Use MOSS to make an advanced intranets with web content management.

❑ Try to find out what the intranet will be used for — do not simply create a copy of the old intranet, but try to see what features in SharePoint that will help users work more easily and faster.

❑ MOSS Enterprise Edition has 57 Web Parts by default, WSS has 8.

❑ WSS does not have a RSS Feed Web Part, but you can configure the XML Web Part for this purpose.

❑ Use the same site collection for all sites in your intranet, unless you have a good reason to create a new site collection, such as a demand for separate security settings.

❑ The Web Content Management System (WCMS) in MOSS allows web content authors to update the production server directly, while still being able to use version history, workflows, and so on.

❑ WCMS in MOSS is built on MS Content Management Server (MCMS), and has been extended with a lot of new features, such as workflows.

❑ The News site in MOSS allows content authors to create news items with the same control as any web page, using WCMS.

❑ The scheduling of News items is not enabled by default. It requires that the document library have Content Approval and Major and Minor Version history enabled.

❑ The Site directory in MOSS makes it easy for a user to locate a specific web site, regardless of the type (i.e., top site, subsite, meeting workspace, etc.).

❑ Before you can use Excel Services, you must define a trusted location where these spreadsheet files will be stored.

❑ You must use the new Excel 2007 file format in order to present files using Excel Services.

❑ Enable links from any document library to a document archive. This will create a copy of the document in the archive.

❑ Building public Internet sites is very similar to building an intranet site. Make sure that you know what you will use it for before you start.

❑ WSS can be used for public Internet sites, but it will lack the WCMS feature as well as other MOSS features.

❑ Use MOSS for Internet sites when you need full control of their content.

❑ Plan very carefully how external users will access your public Internet site from the Internet.

❑ Best practice is to use an application proxy server that will act as the Internet site, instead of allowing external users to access the site directly.

❑ Best practice is to use a separate web application for the Internet site, if you want to use the same SharePoint server for both intranet and Internet sites.

In the next chapter, you learn more about designing SharePoint sites.

Customizing SharePoint 2007

In this chapter, you learn how to configure and manage the MS Office SharePoint Server 2007. You may recall from previous chapters that MOSS is an optional add-on to the WSS platform. It will enable you to build more advanced sites, such as portals, intranets and Internet sites, along with the WSS team sites. MOSS will also make it easier for users to navigate between sites and sharing information within the whole organization. The objectives for a portal site are different than for the team sites, thus new functionality is needed: You could say that the portal site is the place where a few people create and manage information directed to many, whereas the team sites are the places where a group of people create and manage information that is directed to the other members of this group.

MOSS Site Templates

When adding MOSS to WSS, you get basically three things: more advanced site templates, more Web Parts, and more features such as global searching, User Profiles, and My Site. Contrary to previous versions of SharePoint, there is no difference in the basic code between a WSS site and a MOSS site; the difference is in the functionality available in that sit. For example, when creating an Internet-facing web site, you need control over its content, as when an author adds content to this site and a manager has to read and approve this content before it goes public. You may also need to keep track of the version history, so you can see how a specific web page looked like before, and possibly revert to that version. All of this, and more, comes with MOSS site templates. This kind of control is usually not necessary when creating web sites for sharing information within a group or project. In fact, it will only be an annoyance, since all group members will have an easy way of updating the information on the team web site; this is what you use WSS site templates for.

In the following table, you can see the most important differences between site templates for WSS and MOSS.

Functionality	MOSS Site Templates	WSS Site Templates
Adding/Modifying Content on Web Page	Full web content management: Whenever the page is opened in Edit mode, the page is automatically checked out.	No web content management: All editing on this page will immediately be available for all user who can access the page.
Approval of modifications	Active by default: Before a modified page goes public, a user with Approval permission must approve the page.	No approval procedure
Support for Workflows	Yes. For example, a modified page can start a workflow to ask one or more users for comments about this page.	No
Version History	Yes. Every time a page is updated and approved, a new major version is created. You can list and look at previous versions, and revert to any of them.	No
Master Pages for configuring the look and feel of top menus, logos and the navigation bar	Yes	Yes

This chapter focuses on the MOSS and how it works. To follow the instructions in this chapter, you will need at least one portal site, such as the Collaboration Portal. Use the instructions in Chapter 4 to create this portal site.

Changing the Look and Feel of the Portal Site

It is easy to create a new portal site, but most organizations want to customize its look and feel; this is sometimes referred to as *branding*. Some of this customization is very easy to do, whereas other modifications require extensive knowledge of HyperText Markup Language (HTML) and general web design expertise. This chapter gives you the basic information needed to change the design of the portal.

Chapter 13 teaches you more about how to use MS SharePoint Designer 2007 for customizing both portal and team sites. Look at Figure 12-1 to see how the default portal intranet site looks when based on the Collaboration Portal site template.

Figure 12-1

Before you can modify any part of SharePoint, you must have the proper permissions, which means being a SharePoint Administrator or a member of the Web Designer site group. In Chapter 3, you learned how to add users to SharePoint groups in WSS. In MOSS you use the same technique, which is described in the "Managing Access to the Portal Site" section in Chapter 5.

Modifying the Portal Site

The easiest parts to customize in a portal are things like the logotype, the portal name, and the description. You can do this with a web browser on any computer, as long as you have the proper permission. You need to be a SharePoint administrator or a member of the Web Designer site group to perform modifications of this type. The following table explains the things you can easily customize.

It is the logo file that most organizations want to replace. As previously described, you should avoid very large pictures, because they will reduce the available area for the rest of the page. It is okay to use animated GIF pictures, but you should really make sure that they look good, not only fun the first time one sees it.

Object	Displayed	Comment
Portal site name	At the top of every web page and the Site Settings administration page on the portal site.	Limited to 80 Unicode characters such as a, b, c and å, ö, ü, except for these: \ / : * ? " < >	.
Portal site description	Not displayed.	Only visible to users who are allowed to use the Site Settings page. Limited to 200 Unicode characters.
Logo file	At the top of every web page on the portal site.	By default: `titlegraphic.gif` File formats: GIF, BMP, JPEG, and PNG (TIFF is not supported). The default logo type is 225w x 26h pixels with a 96 dpi resolution. Use any reasonable size; the banner will adjust itself, but avoid pictures more than 50 pixels in height, because this will make the banner too dominant on the page.
Logo Description: This is the Logo alternative (alt) text.	ALT text is displayed when you hover the mouse over this logotype.	Enter the text in the Logo Description; the system will then use this as the ALT.

> You can find lots of free animated GIF images on the Internet. Use your favorite search engine and look for "animated GIF."

To modify any of these three properties, follow the steps in the Try It Out below.

Try It Out   Modify the Portal Site Properties

1. Log on as a web designer or administrator to any computer with access to the intranet site.

2. Open the Home page for the intranet; for example, `http://srv1`.

3. Click Site Actions ⇨ Site Settings ⇨ Modify All Site Settings, and then click Title, description and icon in the Look and Feel section.

4. On the next page, you can see the Title and Description, and the Logo URL and Description. Change them according to your needs.

> **The default URL is** `/_layouts/images/titlegraphics.gif`**; this points to the folder:** `C:\Program Files\Common Files\Microsoft Shared\web server extensions\12\Template\images`**. You can add your own logo files there.**
>
> **If you have more than one SharePoint 2007 server running the web service, make sure that all of them have a local copy of the logo file.**

5.   Click OK to save and close the page. Any changes to the portal name or logo will become effective immediately.

Note that the default path to the logo file is `/_layouts/images`. This is a virtual IIS directory that in turn points to a physical file location on the MOSS server. To see where it points to, follow the steps in the Try It Out below.

Try It Out   **View the Virtual Directory Folder Location**

1.   Log on to the MOSS server as an administrator.

2.   Open the Internet Information Service Manager.

3.   Expand the node `Web Sites/Default Web Site/_layouts` (if your MOSS portal site is using another virtual IIS web server, make sure to use that virtual server instead of the Default Web Site).

4.   Right-click the "images" virtual directory, and select Properties.

5.   On the Virtual Directory tab, look at the Local path. It will point to this file location: `<disk>:\Program Files\Common Files\Microsoft Shared\Web Server Extensions\12\template\images`.

6.   Change nothing. Click Cancel to close the dialog box.

If you want to replace the default logo with your own logo file, Microsoft recommends that you create a new subfolder under the `images` folder. For example, assume that you want to use the custom logo file `My_Logo.gif`. Create the new subfolder `Custom` and put the `My_Logo.gif` there. Then set the Location of the logo file to `/_layouts/images/custom/My_Logo.gif`.

> **If you want to revert to the default logo file, simply clear the logo URL field; SharePoint will then show the default logo. (However, this will not restore the text on the icon field.)**

The folder path you found in step 5 is part of a large folder structure used by MOSS for storing all files that describe how the portal site looks and behaves. It also contains the files for the WSS team sites. Note that all other content, such as documents, files, and other information that users create inside SharePoint, is not stored there. It is all stored in a content database in the SQL Server used by SharePoint. Use Windows Explorer and navigate to this path:

```
<disk>:\Program Files\Common Files\Microsoft Shared\Web Server ↵
Extensions\12\template
```

> **Microsoft internally calls this file structure the "12-hive," since it is full of nested folders; this is also the starting point of all SharePoint folders and files.**

SharePoint's Folder Tree

SharePoint keeps a number of files in these folders, most commonly ASP.NET files (.aspx) and XML files (.xml). These files describe exactly how a given web page will look, including its icons, links, and lists. For example, if you wanted to move the logo on the Home page to the far right instead of its current left position, you would modify the .aspx file for that particular page. Most of these files can be modified with an editor, such as Notepad, but you should think twice before changing them. Some of them can be replaced when you apply the next service pack, and improper modifications may corrupt the portal site. In the following table is an explanation of the most interesting folders under the Template folder for the U.S. English version of SharePoint (1033) and what is inside them. Note that for all site templates listed below the Template ID is also listed; this ID is used when SharePoint code and applications need to refer to a specific site template.

> **Note that customizing the Master Page used by this site is the preferred way of customizing the logo, as described later in this chapter. The description here is just to help you understand how the files work in this folder structure.**

ID	\Template Folders	Comments
0	\Global	The global template
1	\Site Templates\STS	Team Site, Blank Site, Document Workspace
2	\Site Templates\MPS	Basic Meeting Workspace, Blank Meeting Workspace, Decision Meeting Workspace, Social Meeting Workspace, Multipage Meeting Workspace
3	\Site Templates\CENTRALADMIN	SharePoint Central Administration
4	\Site Templates\Wiki	Wiki site
7	\Site Templates\BDR	Document Center

ID	\Template Folders	Comments
9	\Site Templates\Blog	Blog site
20	\Site Templates\SPS	(Obsolete) The Home page of the SharePoint Portal Server site, including its lists and configuration settings.
21	\Site Templates\SPSPERS	My Site
22	\Site Templates\SPSMSITE	Personalization Site
30	\Site Templates\SPSTOC	(OBSOLETE) - Contents area Template
31	\Site Templates\SPSTOPIC	(OBSOLETE) - Topic area template
32	\Site Templates\SPSNEWS	(OBSOLETE) - News area template
33	\Site Templates\SPSNHOME	(SubWebOnly) - News Home template
34	\Site Templates\SPSSITES	Site Directory area template
36	\Site Templates\SPSCOMMU	(OBSOLETE) - Community area template
38	\Site Templates\SPSREPORTCENTER	Report Center Site
39	\Site Templates\PUBLISHING	Publishing and Team Collaboration Site
40	\Site Templates\OSRV	Shared Services Administration Site
50	\Site Templates\SRCHCEN	Search Center
51	\Site Templates\PROFILES	Profiles
53	\Site Templates\BLANKINTERNET	Publishing Site, Press Releases Site
54	\Site Templates\SPSMSITEHOST	My Site Host

ID	\Template Folders	Comments
90	\Site Templates\ SRCHCENTERLITE	Search Center Lite
14483	\Site Templates\offile	Records Repository
	\ADMIN	Contains all .aspx files used by SharePoint Central Administration. Avoid modifying these pages.
	\IMAGES	Contains all icons and images used by SharePoint for its portal site and team sites. Create a sub-folder under Images if you want to add your own pictures. Avoid modifying this folder.
	\LAYOUTS\1033	Contains all pages required for standard site administration. Do not modify these files.
	\LAYOUTS\1033\STYLES	Contains Cascading Style Sheets (CSS) that control how the portal area pages will look.
	\LAYOUTS\1033\IMAGES	Contains the images used by MOSS and WSS in the administration pages.
	\SQL	Contains SQL scripts that are used when creating configuration and content databases. Do not change these files.
	\XML	Contains configuration files. The DOCICON.XML file is used when you need to map icons to new document file types.

MS Office SharePoint Server 2007 is available in more than 20 different languages. After the installation you cannot change the language of the portal site, but you can install extra language template packs for the team sites (i.e., the WSS part of this SharePoint installation). There are more than 30 different language template packs for WSS, which you can download for free from www.microsoft.com, and you can install any number of of these on a WSS or MOSS server. This will make it possible to create WSS sites, such as team sites, with different languages, but again, the MOSS sites will not be affected by these language packs. If you install any of these optional language templates for WSS, you will find corresponding Locale Identifier (LCID) folders in the Template and Layouts folder. For example, if you add the Swedish template pack, it adds the new folder 1053.

The complete LCID table is not so easy to find, but in the following table you will find all the locales currently supported by Microsoft.

LCID	Locale	LCID	Locale
5121	Algeria	6145	Morocco
11274	Argentina	5129	New Zealand
3081	Australia	19466	Nicaragua
15361	Bahrain	1044	Norway
16394	Bolivia	8193	Oman
1046	Brazil	1056	Pakistan
3084	Canada1	6154	Panama
4105	Canada2	15370	Paraguay
13322	Chile	2052	Peoples Republic of China
9226	Colombia	10250	Peru
5130	Costa Rica	1045	Poland
1029	Czech Republic	16385	Qatar
1030	Denmark	1049	Russia
7178	Dominican Republic	1025	Saudi Arabia
12298	Ecuador	4100	Sinagapore
3073	Egypt	1051	Slovakia
17418	El Salvador	1060	Slovenia
-2	European Union1	7177	South Africa
-1	European Union2	1053	Sweden
4106	Guatemala	2055	Switzerland
18442	Honduras	10241	Syria

LCID	Locale	LCID	Locale
3076	Hong Kong SAR	1028	Taiwan
1038	Hungary	1054	Thailand
1081	India	7169	Tunisia
1065	Iran	1055	Turkey
2049	Iraq	14337	UAE
1037	Israel	2057	United Kingdom
1041	Japan	1033	United States
11265	Jordan	14346	Uruguay
1042	Korea	8202	Venezuela
13313	Kuwait	1066	Vietnam
12289	Lebanon	9217	Yemen
4097	Libya	8193	Oman
2058	Mexico		

> Go to `http://www.microsoft.com` **and search for "Windows SharePoint Services 3.0 Language Template Pack" to download, and then add new language templates for the WSS team sites.**

Branding a SharePoint Site

All the files and folders mentioned in the previous section are the key to understanding how and what to modify when branding a SharePoint web site. So, now start with a common request: modifying the layout of the top navigation menu, and the Quick Launch bar. In SPS 2003 you had to edit the actual `.aspx` files, used by the different SPS area pages, such as `Template\1033\SPS\Default.aspx`. The problems with this method were these:

❑ You needed to understand how these aspx files work. Changing the wrong setting could mean that the portal did not work at all.

❑ Any changes you did on one area page in SPS, for example the Home page, had to be repeated on all other area pages.

❑ Applying a service pack or hotfix on the SPS server could overwrite your modifications, then you needed to redo the modifications again.

These problems are now history, since SharePoint 2007 (both WSS and MOSS) use a special layout file, referred to as a Master Page, for controlling how the top navigation, links, logotype, and Quick Launch navigation will look and feel like (see Figure 12-2). These parts of a web page are also sometimes referred to as the *chrome*.

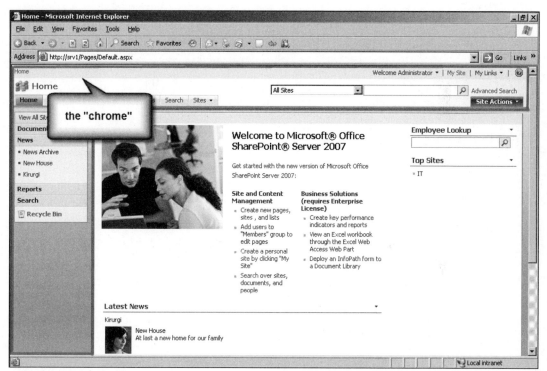

Figure 12-2

MOSS comes with a number of preconfigured Master Pages, ready to be used in your SharePoint environment. But there are actually two types of Master Pages:

❑ **Site Master Pages:** Used by publishing pages (i.e., web sites based on a MOSS site template).

❑ **System Master Pages:** Used by all forms, views, and Web Part pages (i.e., sites based on WSS site templates).

In other words, before you can change the master page for a web site, you must know if this is a WSS site or a MOSS site. If you pick the wrong master page type, nothing will change.

> **Administrative pages in SharePoint, such as Site Settings, will not be affected by the Master Pages.**

The table below shows you the default Master Pages you get in a MOSS 2007 environment; note that the same Master Page file can be used as both a Site Master Page, and a System Master Page. For example, if you want to apply the `BlueTabs.master` file on both MOSS sites and WSS site, then set both the Site Master Page and System Master Page to `BlueTabs.master`.

Master Page	Comments
`Default.master`	The default master page you get in a newly created SharePoint environment.
`BlueBand.master`	Provides a top navigation band and a vertical navigation section, and presents them with a blue color scheme.
`BlackBand.master`	Same layout as `BlueBand.master` but with a black color scheme.
`BlueGlassBand`	Same layout as `BlueBand.master` but with a blue glass color scheme.
`BlueVertical.master`	Provides top navigation by using tabs and a vertical navigation section, and presents them by using a blue color scheme.
`BlackVertical.master`	Same as `BlueVertical.master` but with a black color scheme.
`BlueTabs.master`	Provides top navigation by using tabs and a vertical navigation section, and presents them with a blue color scheme.
`OrangeSingleLevel.master`	Provides a top navigation bar that shows a single level of navigation and a vertical navigation section that does not include flyouts, and presents them with an orange color scheme.
`BlackSingleLevel.master`	Same as `OrangeSingleLevel.master` but with a black color scheme.

Let's try an example: Your boss comes to you and says that the structure of your MOSS environment is good, but he demands a new look and feel. After showing the boss the different master pages listed above, you decide that you will apply the `BlueTabs.master` to both MOSS and WSS sites. Below are the steps to do this.

Try It Out   **Apply a Different Master Page**

1. Log on as the administrator to the existing MOSS site `http://srv1`.

2. Click Site Actions ⇨ Site Settings ⇨ Modify All Site Settings.

3. Click Master page in the Look and Feel section.

4. A new page opens where you set the Site Master Page and the System Master Page (see Figure 12-3).

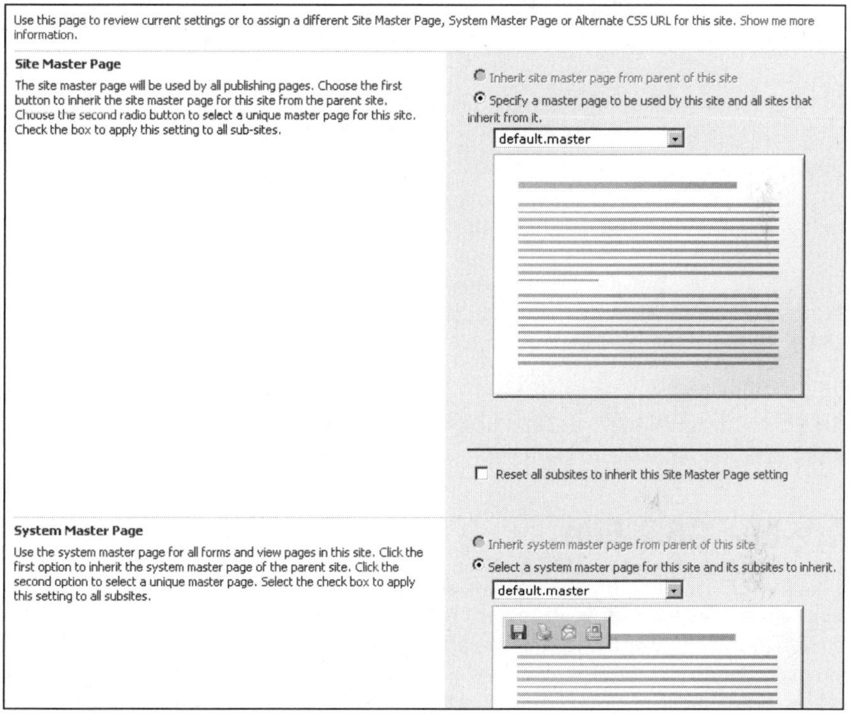

Figure 12-3

5. Change the Site Master Page to `BlueTabs.master`. Then change the System Master Page to the same Master Page.

6. Click OK to save and close the page.

7. Open the top site. It will now have a new look and feel (see Figure 12-4, and compare it with Figure 12-1). Then open a WSS site; it will have the same look and feel.

Figure 12-4

Using SharePoint Designer 2007, you can design new master pages. You will learn more about this in Chapter 13.

Changing the CSS File

The look of a web page, including its color, fonts, and font size, can be set directly in the code. But this would make a complex web application very hard to adjust. For example, if you wanted to change all text that uses Times New Roman to Arial on all web pages, this would require you to manually edit every web page. A much smarter way is to use labels for each part of the web page, like the header, text block, and tables, then define what colors, fonts, and size are to be used for each part in a separate file. This is called a style sheet. If you later want to change the header from blue to green, you identify the label for the header and change its color settings in the style sheet.

SharePoint is indeed a complex web application with lots of pages, and it uses style sheets to control the appearance of these pages. SharePoint actually uses several style sheets, which are read one after another, and the settings in the last style sheet have precedence over any other setting for the same object. This is called a Cascading Style Sheet, or CSS. Every Master Page has multiple CSS files associated with it, to control its appearance. Below is a list with some of the more common CSS files used by MOSS:

❏   Core.css

❏   Controls.css

❏   PageLayouts.css

❑ rca.css

❑ Band.css

❑ Vertical.css

❑ Tabs.css

Most CSS files for simple web applications are rather short, but not SharePoint's CSS files. Some of them may contain more than 1,000 lines of definitions, and it is hard to understand exactly what each line does without some help. If you want to change just parts of the web page, you can add your own custom CSS files or you can change the original CSS files. Note that if you apply a new service pack or a hotfix for SharePoint, it may overwrite these standard CSS files, so it is safer to add your own custom CSS file.

> **Shane Perran, a SharePoint MVP, has created a nice simple example of what you can do with a custom CSS file; you will use his demo in the following example. Read more on his blog:** www.graphicalwonder.com/?p=642.

Try It Out   Add a Page Curl

In this example, you create a custom CSS file that will add a page curl to the top-left corner of every web page. You will start with an empty CSS file with the name Pagecurl.CSS and add the code to it that will display an image file named Pagecurl.gif. Both of these two files will be stored in a new document library named Custom-CSS that you will create in the subsite http://srv1/SiteDirectory. Finally, you will configure the Alternate CSS URL setting to show this custom CSS file. This file will override the default CSS settings. Follow these steps:

1. Log on as a SharePoint administrator, and open the site http://srv1/SiteDirectory.

2. Click Site Actions ➪ View All Site Content ➪ Create ➪ Document Library. Then enter these settings:

   a. **Name:** Custom-CSS.

   b. **Display this document library on the Quick Launch?** No.

   c. Click Create. You now have a place to store the two files you need for this example.

3. Open Notepad (or your favorite editor, including SharePoint Designer) and create a file with this content:

```
/* Add a Page Curl to each SharePoint Page */
.ms-bodyareacell
{
background-image:url("http://srv1/SiteDirectory/custom-css/Pagecurl.gif");
background-repeat:no-repeat;
background-position:top left;
/* padding should be a few pixels more than the Pagecurl image height */
padding:30px;
}
```

4. Save the file as `pagecurl.css` in the `Custom-CSS` document library you created in step 2 above. For example, you can save this file to the file system and then use the Upload button on the document library page.

5. You need to upload the `Pagecurl.gif` file that the CSS file refers to: Get a copy of that file from this URL: `www.graphicalwonder.com/pagecurl.gif` and store it in the `Custom-CSS` document library. This library now contains both the CSS file and the GIF file for this example.

6. Time to apply your custom CSS file. Go to the site where you want to apply this CSS file, for example: `http://srv1/sitedirectory`.

7. Click Site Actions ➪ Site Settings ➪ Modify All Site Settings. Click Master Pages in the Look and Feel section.

8. At the bottom of the following form, select the option: Specify a CSS file to be used by this publishing site and all sites that inherit from it. Then enter the URL `/SiteDirectory/Custom-CSS/Pagecurl.css`; click OK. Look at Figure 12-5 (before) and Figure 12-6 (after) to see the difference.

> Change the color of the gif image to get a nice impression of a curled page.

Figure 12-5

Figure 12-6

9. You can also add a background color to this part of the page; simply add the command `Background-color` anywhere within the curly brackets. The complete code then looks like this:

```
/* Add a Page Curl to each SharePoint Page */
.ms-bodyareacell
{
background-image:url("http://srv1/SiteDirectory/custom-css/Pagecurl.gif");
background-repeat:no-repeat;
background-position:top left;
/* padding should be a few pixels more than the Pagecurl image height */
padding:30px;
/* Set the background color for the .ms-bodyareacell to Green */
background-color:green;
}
```

How do you know how to define the color green? And what if you want to use another color? The answer to that is to learn how to define colors using the standard Cascading Style Sheets Level 2 (CSS2) color codes. You can learn a lot more about this in any HTML development book, but you get a quick summary in the following table, which shows the ways to define a standard green color. Use whatever method you want; the point is that you have a number of options for defining a specific color, and some of them give you much more control over the exact color tone, if this is needed. For example, change the background color from "green" to "#ebf3ff" and the frame will be blue like the top row with the global breadcrumb link.

Method	Example	Explanation
HTML 4.0 color names	Green	Use the HTML 4.0 standard names, like Black, Red, Green, Olive, Yellow, and so on.
RGB 3 digits	#080	The first character is Red, the next is Green, and the next is Blue, with hexadecimal values between 0 and F.
RGB 6 digits	#008000	The first two characters are Red, the next two are Green, and the last two are Blue, with hexadecimal values between 00 and FF.
RGB Triples	rgb(0,128,0)	The first number is Red, the next is Green, and the last is Blue, with decimal values between 0 and 255.
RGB Triples	rgb(0%,50%,0%)	Same as above, but with values between 0 and 100%.

> **You will find more information about color setting on this site:** www.w3.org/ TR/REC-html40/types.html#idx-color.

The need for creating CSS files in SharePoint 2007 is not as great as in SharePoint 2003. Now, you do most of the customization by modifying a Master Page file, as you will learn in Chapter 13.

Managing the SharePoint Sites

If you created an intranet based on the MOSS site template Collaboration Portal, you now have one top site and five subsites. Each of these subsites inherits the same look and feel as the top site, since they all use the same Master Page file. The Collaboration Portal was introduced in Chapter 6, but the following is a quick summary to remind you about the structure of this portal to prepare you for the examples that follow. Note that in several cases the URL of these subsites is different from the sites' display name:

- ❑ **Home:** http://srv1 — the start page and top-level site for the portal.

- ❑ **Document Center:** http://srv1/docs — this is a subsite of the top site.

- ❑ **News:** http://srv1/news — a subsite that is used to list news and information.

- ❑ **Reports:** http://srv1/reports — a subsite for reports and KPI lists.

- ❑ **Search:** http://srv1/SearchCenter — this is a subsite used when searching for content and people.

- ❑ **Sites:** http://srv1/SiteDirectory — a subarea that can list all subsites in the site collection.

Few organizations implementing MOSS are completely satisfied with the default portal site. But the good news is that all of these sites and pages can be changed in almost any way you want. And most changes do not require anything other than the web client browser (and the permission to do it, of course). Now look more closely at these area pages and what you can do with them.

The Home Page

The home site of the intranet is a kind of welcome page for the intranet. It should contain important content, such as the latest news about the company and its associates, plus frequently requested information such as links to popular sites and to frequently used actions, such as adding a news item. You can adjust the Home page in many ways, for example, to display news lists from several local intranet sites. Since the Home page is also the top site of its site collection, it affects the navigation in subsites, as you will see later in this section.

News Listings

Let's start with the Web Part "News" displayed at the bottom of this Home page. It shows three sample links, but none of them is related to a news item, so you probably want to change that immediately. This News Web Part is in fact a Summary Link Web Part, and it is used to display links to other locations, such as subsites, document libraries, or even external web sites on the Internet. First, you will change the name of this Web Part to something more appropriate, such as Important Links, and then you will add a Content Query Web Part to display the news items in the News site.

Try It Out **Modify the News List on the Home page**

1. Log on as a SharePoint administrator.

2. Open the Home page using a web browser.

3. Click Site Actions ➪ Edit Page. Since this Home page is a publishing page (named `Default.aspx`), SharePoint will now check out this page.

4. Click edit ➪ Modify Shared Web Part on the News Web Part.

5. Expand the Appearance section, then enter a better name for this Web Part in the Title field, for example Important Links.

6. Click OK. The modification of this Web Part is now completed. Next step is to adjust the links in this Web Part to show something of interest to your users.

7. Click the edit button to the left of the link named Sample Link 2 (see Figure 12-7), and select Edit. Change the link so that it points to the subsite `http://srv1/SiteDirectory/it` (see Figure 12-8):

   a. Select the option Create a link to an item.

   b. **Title:** IT Department.

   c. **Description:** "This is the local intranet site for IT."

   d. **Link URL:** `/SiteDirectory/it`. This is a relative link, (i.e., you do not need to enter the full URL address, including `http://srv1`).

   e. **Style:** Bulleted Title. This will only show the title, not the description of the link. If you also want to show the description, change this style to Title and Description.

   f. Click OK to save and close the page.

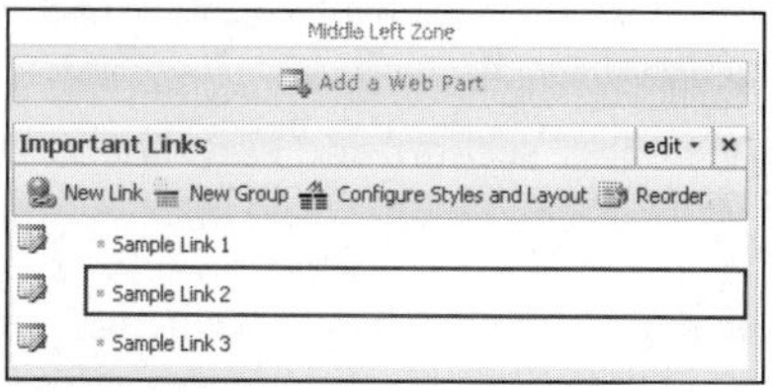

Figure 12-7

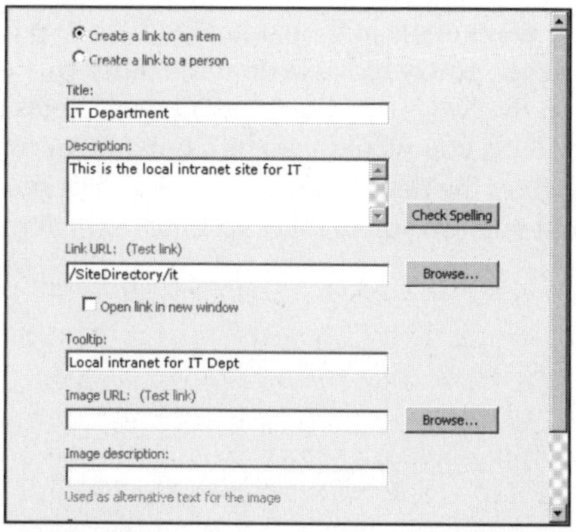

Figure 12-8

8. Change the second link to point to an MS Word file, for example using the URL `/SiteDirectory/it/shared documents/Policy_statements.doc`.

9. Change the third link to point to a user, such as the Administrator, using these settings:

    a. Select the option Create a link to a person. The form is now modified.

    b. Enter the person's name, (i.e., `Filobit\Administrator`), and click the check button to the right or click the Browse button.

    c. Change the Title to Administrator.

    d. **Description:** "Your friend in the IT world."

    e. **Link URL:** Note that this URL is automatically filled in and points to the person's My Site.

    f. Select the option "Open link in new window."

    g. **Style:** Bulleted Title.

    h. Click OK to save and close the page.

10. In the Middle Left Zone, you will now add a Content Query Web Part and display the latest news from the News site. Click Add a Web Part, check the Content Query Web Part, and select Add. Then do this to display the news items:

    a. On the new Content Query Web Part, click edit ⇨ Modify Shared Web Part.

    b. Expand the Query section. This is where you define the content source to be displayed in the Web Part. Select Show items from the following list, click Browse, and select Pages Library in the News site. Then click OK.

    c. Make sure that the List Type is Pages Library.

    d. Expand the Presentation section, and change Item limit to 5. This will limit the number of news item in this list to 5.

    e. Expand the Appearance section, and enter the Title as Latest news.

    f. Click OK to save and close the page.

11. At the top toolbar of the page, click Publish to save and publish the modified home page. The page will look similar to Figure 12-9.

Using the Content Query Web Part, you can create any number of News lists in any site, including WSS sites, and still show all of these news items in the same Web Part. Typically, the Home page is used as a front page, much like a newspaper. You could also do it the other way around: Create a new site column named Dept on the Page list on the News site, then add all news items to the list, and enter the department for which the item is targeted. Then you would use the Content Query Web Part on each departmental site and configure the Web Part to filter the news list based on the Dept site column. This way, all news items are stored in one single list, and you can still display specific news items for each department.

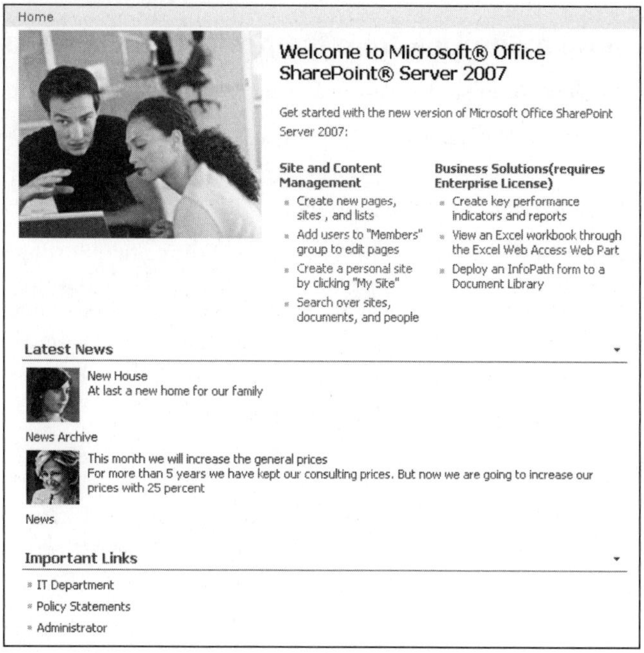

Figure 12-9

Hiding Subsites and Site Links

Sometimes you may need to hide subsites, at least from some of the users. For example, if you install an intranet based on the Collaboration Portal site template mentioned above, you will have five subsites. Instead of deleting the ones you don't need now, you can hide them, then later when needed they can be displayed again. This can be done in two ways:

❑ **Permissions:** Remove the Read permission to this subsite for all users. The drawback is that this will force you to break the permission inheritance. Not a big deal, since the inheritance can be reestablished later again.

❑ **Navigations:** You can hide this subsite from the navigation (i.e., the top navigation tabs and the Quick Launch bar). The drawback is that anyone who knows the URL will be able to open the subsite anyhow. In some cases this is not a problem, then again in others it may be a real security problem.

You have already learned to break permission inheritance for a site (see Chapter 3) but to change the navigation settings follow the steps in the Try It Out below.

Try It Out   **Remove a Site Link from the Navigation Elements**

1. Log on as the Site Administrator.

2. Open the top site. For example, `http://srv1`.

3. Click Site Actions ➪ Site Settings ➪ Modify Navigation. This will open the configuration page for the navigation part of the MOSS intranet.

4. Hide the Document Center site: In the Navigation Editing and Sorting section, select the Document Center in the Global Navigation and click the Hide button; the text now indicates that the link is hidden. Will this be enough? No! So far you have only removed the link on the top navigation bar, but the Quick Launch bar still shows the Document Center. So, you must also hide the link Document Center in the Current Navigation section (see Figure 12-10).

5. Click OK. Both references to the subsite are removed.

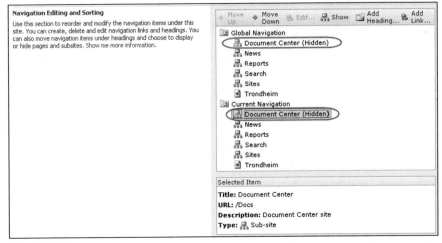

Figure 12-10

From this, you can see that the Global Navigation element controls the top navigation bar, while Current Navigation controls the Quick Launch bar, usually located to the left of the page. This can help you address another common request, which is to avoid using the Quick Launch bar to show links to all sites under the Site Directory while still showing these sites in the Sites dropdown menu. To illustrate this, say that you have 15 subsites created directly under the Sites subsite (i.e., `http://srv1/SiteDirectory` in the example environment). You may remember from Chapter 8 that these sites can be displayed in a dropdown menu by hovering the mouse over the "Sites" tab at the top bar navigation. But you may not want these sites to be listed in the Quick Launch bar, since this will make the Quick Launch long and clumsy (see Figure 12-11).

Figure 12-11

Solve this problem by hiding the Sites link in Current Navigation as shown in the following Try It Out.

Try It Out   **Hide Sites Link on the Quick Launch Bar**

1. Log on as the Site Administrator.

2. Open the top site (for example, `http://srv1`).

3. Click Site Actions ⇨ Site Settings ⇨ Modify Navigation.

4. In the Navigation Editing and Sorting section, select the Sites link in Current Navigation, and click the Hide button; the text now indicates that the link is hidden.

5. Click OK. The list of site links is now gone from the Quick Launch bar. Hover the mouse over the top menu Sites, and it will still display the list of sites (see Figure 12-12).

> If you don't see this dropdown list, click Site Actions ⇨ Site Settings ⇨ Modify Navigation, and make sure that you have checked the option Show subsites.

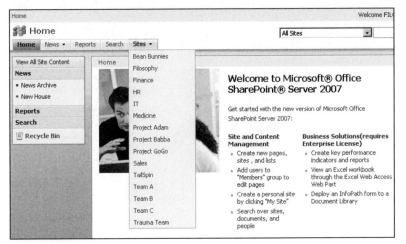

Figure 12-12

WSS Pages

WSS sites may be configured to show or hide links to other locations, such as sites, libraries, and external Internet sites. In the previous version of SharePoint, there was no tree view of subsites, so you either wrote your own tree view Web Part or bought it from a third-party vendor; for example, from http://sharepoint.advis.ch. This is no longer necessary, since WSS now comes with its built-in tree view Web Part. There is nothing to install, simply select to display it. Since it will show the same type of information as the Quick Launch bar, it is a good idea to hide that bar at the same time. The following Try It Out shows you how to do it.

Try It Out   Change to a Tree View Navigation in WSS

1. Open any WSS site as a Site Owner; for example, http://srv1/sitedirectory/it.

2. Click Site Actions ➪ Site Settings.

3. Under the Look and Feel heading, click Tree view.

4. Check Enable Tree View, and uncheck Enable Quick Launch.

5. Click OK.

That's it. Open the site, and it will display a tree view of its lists and libraries, plus all subsites under the site. Compare Figure 12-13 showing the Quick Launch bar and Figure 12-14 with the tree view to see the difference.

Figure 12-13

Figure 12-14

But to be fair, the Quick Launch bar can also be configured to show subsites, as described in the Try It Out below; it is up to your users to decide which version looks best.

Try It Out   **Show Subsites in the Quick Launch Bar**

1. Open the WSS site as a Site Owner.

2. Click Site Actions ➪ Site Settings.

3. Under the Look and Feel heading, click Tree view.

4. Uncheck Enable Tree View, and check Enable Quick Launch.

5. Click OK.

6. Under the Look and Feel heading, click Navigation.

7. In the Subsites and Pages section, check Show Subsites and click OK.

Now look at the site again (see Figure 12-15); the subsites are listed at the bottom of the Quick Launch bar.

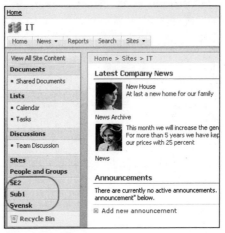

Figure 12-15

Another solution is to change the top menu bar navigation elements. By default, the top menu bar shows the same navigation links as all sites, including the top site. You can change it to only show the current site and all its subsites. If you use the same site as depicted in Figure 12-15, you can make it look like Figure 12-16 by following the steps in the Try It Out below.

Try It Out   Show Subsites in the Top Menu Bar

1.   Open the WSS site as a Site Owner.

2.   Click Site Actions ➪ Site Settings.

3.   Click Navigation in the Look and Feel section.

4.   In the Global Navigation section, select the option Display the navigation items below the current site.

5.   Click OK.

Figure 12-16

This navigation setting will not be affected by whether you select the tree view or the Quick Launch view. Note that although the global navigation is replaced, there is still a breadcrumb link at the top left of the page so that users can easily go back to the top site. As you can see, there are a lot of interesting options regarding the navigation links; make sure to play with them all to see how they work. This will ensure that you can find the type of navigation elements your users ask for, without the need for custom development or third-party products.

Managing Links

In previous chapters, several times you have seen seen the list of links you can create in any site, and earlier in this chapter you saw how the Summary Link Web Part works. The simplest type of link list is the one that comes with WSS, but that one can be used for more than you may think. All the links in the previous examples have been to web pages and other lists or libraries in SharePoint, but you can link to other types of content as well. For example, you can create a link that will open a specific document or a file folder or even an e-mail with a preconfigured recipient and subject. In other words, links in SharePoint are more powerful than you may at first believe. The table below shows examples of the links you can create:.

Type of link	Example
Files	`\\Server1\share1\example.txt` links to a specific file. `\\server1\share\public` links to a folder.
Mailto	`mailto:Diana@filobit.com` creates an e-mail addressed to Diana. `mailto:Diana@filobit.com?subject=Book me for this training` creates an e-mail addressed to Diana with a given subject.
HTTP	`http://www.microsoft.com` links to a web page. `http://MOSSrv2/doc/quote.doc` links to a Word file.
HTTP to Person	`http://srv1:5002/person/carmela` will open the public view of the user Carmela's My Site

For example, say that you have a list of links, named Links. Now you want to add more advanced links to this list, as described in the table above. The following Try It Out shows how you do it.

Try It Out   Create Advanced Links

1. Open any site with a list of links.

2. Click on the list to open it.

3. Click New; in the following form enter these values to create a link to the file share `\\FS1\Projects`:

   a. **URL:** `\\FS1\Projects`.

   b. **Type the Description:** "Open Projects file share."

   c. Click OK.

4. If you want to create a link that will open an e-mail preconfigured with the recipient Carmela@filobit.com and with the subject "Order more cars," then click New and press Enter:

    a. **URL:** `Mailto:Carmela@filobit.com?subject=Send more cars.`

    b. **Type the Description:** "Order cars from Carmela."

    c. Click OK.

> **If you remove any of the sources, the link will be broken. However, you will not notice this until you try to open it. Some tools are available on the Internet that will help you check for broken links and sometimes even try to repair them.**

Creating Site Definitions

Up to now, all sites and subsites you have created are based on the same type of site; the only difference between them is the site template used when you created the site. With SharePoint 2007, you can use Master Pages for customizing the look and feel of the site, and there is seldom a need to change the actual code that is the base definition of a site. This was not the case in SharePoint 2003; almost all changes, besides the modifications you could do with just a web client, required that you customize the site definition files. Still today there may be a need to create a customized site definition with, for example, a specific set of list settings, layout, and color. One way of doing these customizations is to use SharePoint Designer, but by doing so, you will "unghost" the site. This requires some explanation: When you create a WSS site, all its content is stored in content database in your SQL server, but the code that rules how the site looks and how it behaves is stored in the file system of the SharePoint server, or to be more specific in this folder:

```
C:\Program Files\Common Files\Microsoft Shared\web server
extensions\12\TEMPLATE\SiteTemplates\sts
```

So if you have 100 WSS sites, all of them will use the files in this "sts" folder, but they will display different content. These are known as "ghosted" sites, that is, they look like they are a part of the content database, along with the actual site content, but they are not. If you modify one of these sites with SharePoint Designer, then SharePoint must store the complete site definition and the content in the database; thus, the site is "unghosted," and any modifications of the files in the "sts" folder will no longer affect this particular site. So if you modify all 100 of these sites with SharePoint Designer, then you will have 100 unghosted sites. This will have some consequences:

❑ **Performance:** It takes longer time for SharePoint to read an unghosted site, since all the files plus the content are stored in the SQL Server database.

❑ **Disk requirements:** Storing 100 site definitions files instead of using one shared site definition will require more disk space.

❑ **Flexibility:** If you want to modify all unghosted sites, then you must change all of them, one by one, but modifying 100 ghosted sites is very easy: just change the common set of site definition files.

These consequences may at first look like a very serious problem that may prohibit you from using SharePoint Designer, but in reality it is not a problem in most installations. The performance decrease will only be visible in larger installations, you will not see any noticeable difference in a SharePoint installation with less than 5,000 to 10,000 users. The increased disk requirements will also be barely noticeable, unless you have thousands of unghosted sites. The last consequence, flexibility, will only be a problem if you need to modify a lot of sites after they are created, and this modification is not something you can do with a Master Page file. So most of the time, unghosting a site is a theoretical problem, not a practical one.

> If you want to revert an unghosted to a ghosted site, open the Site Settings for the site and select "Reset to site definition."

Still, there are situations when you want to avoid unghosting — the solution is then to create your own site definition. This required a lot of work in previous versions of SharePoint, but now it is a rather easy task, depending on what modifications you want to make. You have two options for changing a site definition, while still retaining a ghosted site:

❑ **Create new definition files:** Either you start from scratch and create these files one by one, or you copy an existing site definition and modify it.

❑ **Copy a site definition and change it in Visual Studio 2005:** If you are a .NET developer, you may instead copy an existing site definition, and modify it, then create a new site definition.

In the example below you will use the first method, that is, create a new site definition by copying an existing site definition. If you want to use the Visual Studio 2005 method, then look at `msdn.microsoft.com` for more information.

> Open this URL to find another good description of how to build a site definition using Visual Studio:
> `http://weblogs.asp.net/soever/archive/2006/11/11/SharePoint-`
> `Solution-Generator-_2D00_-part-1_3A00_-create-a-site-definition-`
> `from-an-existing-site.aspx.`

In the following example you will create a site definition with two extra Web Part zones for all WSS 3.0 sites. By default, all WSS team sites (i.e., not Meeting or Document Workspaces, nor blog or Wiki sites), have two Web Part zones: Left Zone and Right Zone. In this example you will add a Top Zone and a Bottom Zone as well; both span the complete page width. Just follow the steps in the Try It Out below.

Try It Out   Create a WSS Site Definition

1. Log on as an administrator.

2. Use the Windows Explorer, and navigate to `C:\Program Files\Common Files\Microsoft Shared\web server extensions\12\TEMPLATE` (assuming that SharePoint is installed on the C: drive).

3. Copy `SiteTemplate\sts` to `SiteTemplate\stsdemo`.

4. Open the file `siteTemplate\stsdemo\Default.aspx` with Notepad. Now you must add the code in the two shaded sections in the code below at the end of that file:

```
<asp:Content ContentPlaceHolderId="PlaceHolderMain" runat="server">
<table cellspacing="0" border="0" width="100%">
        <tr>
        <td class="ms-pagebreadcrumb">
            <asp:SiteMapPath SiteMapProvider="SPContentMapProvider" ↵
id="ContentMap" SkipLinkText="" NodeStyle-CssClass="ms-sitemapdirectional" ↵
runat="server"/>
        </td>
        </tr>
        <tr>
        <td class="ms-webpartpagedescription"><SharePoint:ProjectProperty ↵
Property="Description" runat="server"/></td>
        </tr>
        <tr>

        <td>
        <table width="100%" cellpadding="0" cellspacing="0" style="padding: 5px 10px ↵
10px 10px;">

        <tr>
        <td valign="top" width="100%" colspan="3">
        <WebPartPages:WebPartZone runat="server" FrameType="TitleBarOnly" ID="Top" ↵
Title="loc:Top" />
        </td>
        </tr>

        <tr>
            <td valign="top" width="70%">
            <WebPartPages:WebPartZone runat="server" FrameType="TitleBarOnly" ↵
ID="Left" Title="loc:Left" />
             
            </td>
            <td> </td>
            <td valign="top" width="30%">
            <WebPartPages:WebPartZone runat="server" FrameType="TitleBarOnly" ↵
ID="Right" Title="loc:Right" />
             
            </td>
            <td> </td>
            </tr>

        <tr>
        <td valign="top" width="100%" colspan="3">
            <WebPartPages:WebPartZone runat="server" FrameType="TitleBarOnly" ↵
ID="Bottom" Title="loc:Bottom" />
        </td>
        </tr>

    </table>
    </td>
  </tr>
  </table>
</asp:Content>
```

5. Save the modified `Default.aspx` file.

6. The final step is to register this new site template in SharePoint, to make it available for users when creating new sites:

    a. Open the folder `12\TEMPLATE\1033\XML`.

    b. Copy the file `WEBTEMP.XML` and save it as `webtempstsdemo.xml`. Note that the text "stsdemo" inserted just before the `.XML` part must be identical to the name of the new site definition folder you created in step 3 above!

    c. Open the file `webtempstsdemo.xml` with Notepad and replace all its content with:

```
<?xml version="1.0" encoding="utf-8"?>
<! - _lcid="1033" _version="12.0.4518" _dal="1" - >
<! - _LocalBinding - >
<Templates xmlns:ows="Microsoft SharePoint">
<Template Name="stsdemo" ID="1001">
    <Configuration ID="0" Title="Team Site w 4 Zones" Hidden="FALSE" ↵
ImageUrl="/_layouts/images/blankprev.png" Description="A Team Site with 4 ↵
zones." DisplayCategory="Custom" AllowGlobalFeatureAssociations="False" >
    </Configuration>
  </Template>
</Templates>
```

7. Save and close the `webtempstsdemo.xml` file.

8. Open a command prompt and run: `iisreset`.

9. Open SharePoint, and create a new WSS site. You will find this new site definition in the template selection part, in the Custom tab (see also Figure 12-17).

If you get an error when opening SharePoint after the `iisrest`, then something is wrong in your configuration files above. Read the instructions again and correct any errors.

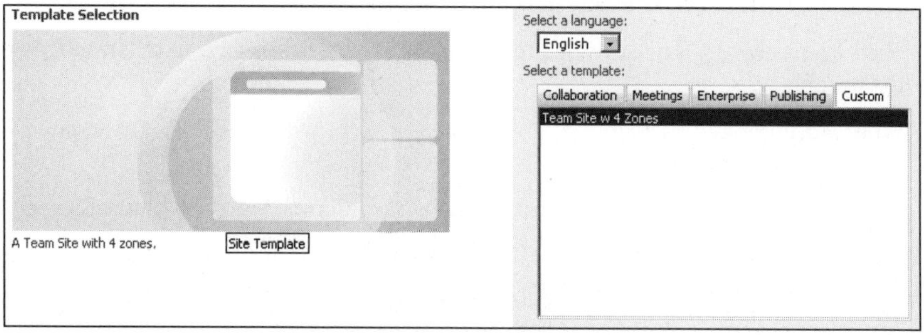

Figure 12-17

This was a very simple modification, and you can do a lot more with this site definition, for example:

❑   Modify the default lists and libraries on the web site: Change the `stsdemo\xml\onet.xml` file.

❑   Modify the default Web Parts displayed on the site: Change the `stsdemo\xml\onet.xml` file.

❑   Modify the two standard Web Part zones: By default the Left Zone is configured to use 70 percent of the page width, and the Right Zone, 30 percent; change that by editing the `stsdemo\default.aspx` file.

Since this is a custom site definition, it will not be overwritten by any service pack that you may apply later on the SharePoint server. You own this site definition, and you take the responsibility for it; make sure to make a backup of it. If you have multiple SharePoint servers running as web servers (i.e., accept incoming users connections to SharePoint sites), then make sure that all of them have the same set of modifications.

Summary

In this chapter you learned that:

❑   MOSS site templates are more advanced than WSS site templates.

❑   It is possible to change a number of settings on the portal using only a web client, such as Internet Explorer.

❑   SharePoint stores all its site templates, also known as site definitions, in the 12 hive (i.e., `<disk>:\Program Files\Common Files\Microsoft Shared\Web Server ↵ Extensions\12\template\Site Templates`).

❑   The 12 hive also contains all the configuration files, such as images, layout files, styles, and `.aspx` code files.

❑   Download free Windows SharePoint Services 3.0 Language Template Packs when you want to create WSS sites in other languages than the default one.

❑   SharePoint uses LCID — Locale Identifier codes — when referring to language-specific features in SharePoint.

❑   When adding new WSS language template packs, new LCID folders are created in several places in the 12 hive.

❑   The chrome of a page is the navigation parts, top menus, logo and Quick Launch bar.

❑   SharePoint 2007 uses the ASP.NET 2.0 feature called Master Pages to control the chrome.

❑   Add a custom Cascading Style Sheets (CSS) file if you want to modify some parts of the page without modifying the default CSS files.

❑   Instead of deleting default subsites in the intranet, you can hide them from the navigation and Quick Launch bar. You can also set permissions and remove read access from users who should not be able to see a specific site.

❑   Use the Content Query Web Part to display information in other sites, such as lists and libraries.

- ❑ Use the tree view instead of the Quick Launch bar if you want a hierarchical tree view of a site and its current subsites.

- ❑ Use links to open file folders, files, or create Outlook e-mail messages.

- ❑ Create custom site definitions when you need to have full control over a site's look and feel.

- ❑ "Ghosted" sites are sites that use a shared site definition stored in the file system.

- ❑ "Unghosted" sites are sites that are stored completely in the SQL database, both the site definition and its content.

- ❑ Avoid modifying a site with SharePoint Designer if you don't want unghosted sites.

- ❑ Reset an unghosted site to ghosted by using the command "Reset to site definition" on the Site Settings page for the site.

In the next chapter, you will learn more about the SharePoint Designer and how to create Master Pages and page layout files.

SharePoint Designer 2007

SharePoint is built to allow an ordinary user with the proper permissions to easily change the layout of sites without any extra tool besides the web browser. This feature is very important since it makes it possible for nondevelopers to quickly adjust a portal site or a team site to their own needs. No web designer or administrator is required for this task. The key to this functionality is the use of Web Parts and their Web Part zones in SharePoint web pages; just add any new Web Part needed to the preferred location on the page. In order to allow this, SharePoint has specially constructed Web Part pages, also known as Smart Pages, and every MOSS site and WSS site is built upon such Web Part pages.

However, sometimes it may be necessary to do more modifications than are possible using a web browser; this is where SharePoint Designer 2007 comes in. This program was especially designed with SharePoint 2007 in mind and has a lot of features for enhancing the look and feel of SharePoint sites. No other design tools for web sites have this functionality, so even if you today prefer other design tools, you will need to use SharePoint Designer when it comes to SharePoint.

When SharePoint 2003 was released, it requested FrontPage 2003 for this type of customization. SharePoint Designer 2007 is the next generation of FrontPage and now contains a lot more functionality that did not exist in FrontPage, such as Master Pages and page layout files. FrontPage simply does not understand how SharePoint 2007 works, so you should avoid customizing SharePoint 2007 with FrontPage 2003. If you are serious about getting the most out of SharePoint 2007, then you need to understand SharePoint Designer. This chapter will help you understand how to use this tool for customizing any type of MOSS 2007 or WSS 3.0 site.

Why SharePoint Designer 2007?

The big question is of course why you need SharePoint Designer. What does it allow you to do that cannot be done using a web browser? The answer is: A lot! In fact, most of the things you can do with the web browser, such as adding and managing Web Parts, can also be done in SharePoint Designer, and more. Here is a quick list of things that SharePoint Designer allows you to do with SharePoint 2007 web sites:

❑   Manage Master Page files.

❑   Manage page layout files.

❑ Create workflows for SharePoint lists and libraries.

❑ Add new Web Part zones.

❑ Add some special Web Parts.

❑ More advanced formatting of lists.

❑ Add extra links in the Quick Launch bar, and the title bar.

❑ Add buttons and tabs.

❑ Add background pictures.

❑ Create new site themes.

❑ Install special SharePoint packages.

❑ Back up and restore individual team sites.

And there is more. Note that only SharePoint Designer 2007 has this SharePoint 2007 integration. SharePoint Designer 2007 is not only the recommended web design tool for SharePoint 2007, but it will also work with the previous versions of SharePoint 2003. Therefore, if you have a mixed SharePoint 2007 and 2003 server environment, you will only need one single design tool. SharePoint Designer 2007 is also enhanced in many ways over FrontPage and offers more functionality, while still being easy to work with.

Even though SharePoint Designer 2007 (from now on, referred to as SPD) is a general design tool for standard web sites, it has special features when editing a SharePoint site. You will need to have some basic understanding of SharePoint Designer in order to start using it with SharePoint. The sections below describe the basic features of SharePoint Designer and to work with them. Later on you will see detailed steps on how to add and modify the site with SharePoint Designer.

Opening Sites with SharePoint Designer

SharePoint Designer is like all other editors; either you open an existing file and modify it or you create a file from scratch. However, when using SPD for editing SharePoint sites, you don't normally start by creating a site. It is much easier to create the SharePoint site the normal way, then open it in SPD and start editing. You have several options to open an existing SharePoint site, depending on whether it is a MOSS site or a WSS site:

❑ **Any site type:** Start SPD with Start ➪ All Programs ➪ Microsoft Office ➪ Microsoft Office SharePoint Designer 2007, and connect it to a SharePoint site by selecting File ➪ Open Site and entering the URL to that site; then open the content page you want to see, usually **Default.aspx.**

❑ **Master Pages & page layouts:** Open the page library in SharePoint 2007, then in the page files quick menu: select Edit in Microsoft Office SharePoint Designer.

❑ **WSS Site:** Open the site you want to modify in Internet Explorer (IE), and then select Edit with MS Office SharePoint Designer. In IE 6 you find this option under the File menu; in IE 7 it is under the Page menu.

> The Edit option is, by default, disabled in IE 7. Enable it by selecting the menu options Tools ➪ Internet Options, switch to Advanced tab, and disable "Disable script debugging (Internet Explorer)."

The last method is of course easiest, since you don't have to enter the site URL, but it requires that SharePoint Designer be the default web editor on your computer. Either way, SharePoint Designer will load the SharePoint site and display its content, showing much more detail than even design mode using Internet Explorer (see Figure 13-1 for an example of how a WSS site looks).

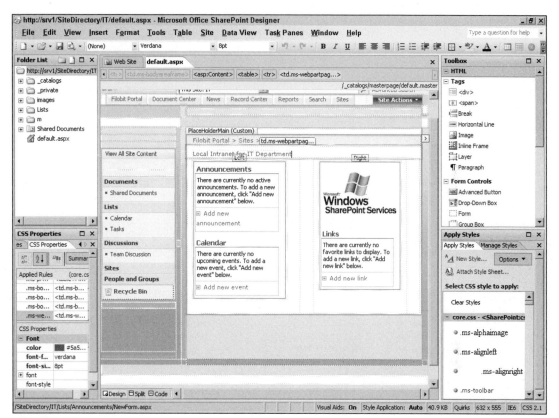

Figure 13-1

SharePoint Designer's Display Modes

When working with a design tool such as SharePoint Designer, you will sometimes need to see the code behind a page, and sometimes see the page layout. SPD fulfills this need by having several display modes that will present different types of content. Whenever necessary, you can switch between these display modes. Look at the bottom line of Figure 13-1; it lists these displays options:

❑ **Design:** Shows the graphical presentation of the current site in real time. It will also show the content of many Web Parts and lists. Figure 13-1 uses this mode to display the IT team site.

❑ **Code:** Will show the code behind the page.

❑ **Split:** Will show both the graphical design and the code behind. If you select an object in the graphical part, SPD will highlight the code for that object. For example, look at Figure 13-2 where the Web Part displaying the WSS logo is selected and its code is automatically marked.

Press F12 to open a preview window. This will save and then display the page as it will be shown when opened in a web browser.

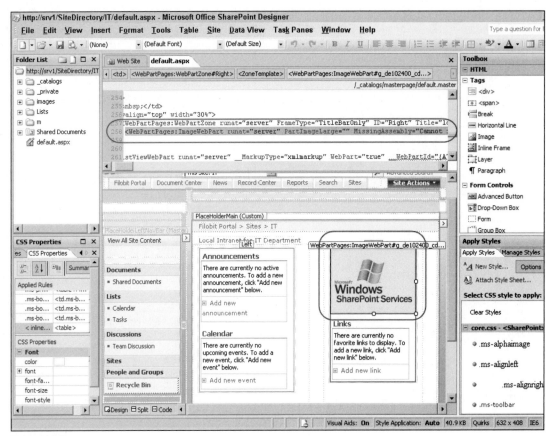

Figure 13-2

The two most useful modes are *design* and *split*. Design mode is very handy when you want to see exactly what part of this page you are working with, but the code part in the split mode gives you control of the exact location when managing objects on the page, while you still see the graphical representation of the page.

Modifying the Site

Use the menus and toolbar buttons to add, delete, and modify the SharePoint site. For example, if you want to add a Web Part you select the Web Part zone in the design mode and click on the menu Insert ⇨ SharePoint Controls ⇨ Web Part.

By default, SPD will display a number of panes on both sides of the page; these contain different information, such as Folder list, CSS properties, Tool box, and Styles. You can close any one of these or add new panes, such as a list of available Web Parts. If you open more than one site, web page, or layout file, they will be displayed as tabs at the top of the SPD window. If any of these tabs shows an asterisk (*) the page is modified but not saved. To close any of the tabbed pages, open it and click the X at the far right of the tab bar.

You can also modify the code directly. For example, if you want to display a frame around the content part of a page, search for the text PlaceHolderMain using Edit ➪ Find (or press Ctrl+F) and change the border property from 0 to 10 in the line under PlaceHolderMain; the result will immediately be displayed in the Design window.

If you know HTML and ASP.NET programming, you will have full control of this page. However, you must also understand how SharePoint's object model works in order to make changes. To add your own code, use the code or split display mode.

Saving Your Work

When working with a SharePoint site, it is only a copy; that is, you can make and test whatever modifications you want on the site, but they will not be stored in SharePoint unless you save the changes in one of these ways:

❑   Select File ➪ Save (or click the Save button on the toolbar).

❑   Press the F12 key. It will save the current modification and display the result using Internet Explorer.

Depending on the type of modification, when saving a SharePoint page, you may see a Site Definition Page Warning dialog box (see Figure 13-3), telling you that this site will now be customized, which is also known as "unghosted;" more about this later in this chapter. If you want to save the modified page then you must click Yes.

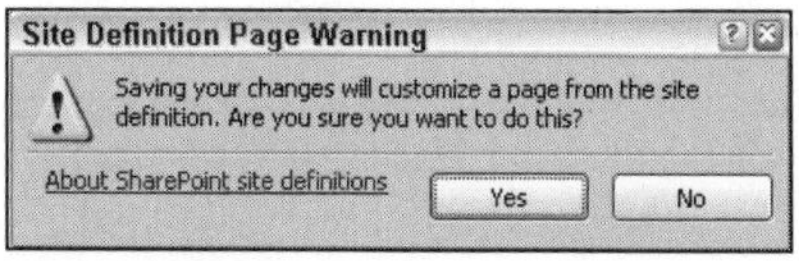

Figure 13-3

> As long as you don't close SharePoint Designer, you can undo any changes and then save the site. This way, you can restore a site from a modification that you happened to save but don't want to keep anymore.

Differences between MOSS and WSS Sites

When using SharePoint Designer for editing SharePoint, you must be aware that there is a difference between MOSS sites and WSS sites. The big difference when it comes to customization is that MOSS sites are built using Publishing Pages, that is, the content of each MOSS site is stored in a Page file, which in turn is built upon a layout file; these Page files and layout files are stored in page libraries in the MOSS site. The content of all WSS sites, on the other hand, is built upon a shared `Default.aspx` file, stored in the file system (see Chapter 12 for more about site definitions). This file contains the page layout, but the actual content is stored along with the site in the content database. That is why a MOSS site must be treated differently than a WSS site when customizing with SharePoint Designer:

❑ **Master Pages:** Define the chrome of the site (the top menus, and Quick Launch bar, plus bread-crumb links, logotypes, fonts, and colors for this part of the page); see Figure 13-4. All Master Pages are stored in a "Master pages and page layout" gallery, accessible only from the top site in a site collection (In the "Galleries" on the Site Actions ➪ Site Settings ➪ Modify All Site Settings page). Both WSS and MOSS use Master Pages.

❑ **MOSS Publishing Pages:** Contain the content displayed on the site. They are stored as page files in the local site (Open the site: click View All Site Content ➪ Pages). Each of these page files is associated with a special type of content type called a "layout file," see below. Normally you do not change the content of a Publishing Page by using SPD; instead, use Site Actions ➪ Edit Page in the web browser.

❑ **MOSS Layout Files:** A content type that is stored in the "Master pages and page layout" gallery (see Master Pages above). The layout file governs how the content will be displayed, for example where the text body and images will be located on the content page.

❑ **WSS Sites Content Pages:** To change the layout of this page, either change the shared `Default.aspx` file, stored on the SharePoint server's file system (see the section about site definitions in Chapter 12) or use SharePoint Designer to change the layout. But this will also "ung-host" this page (see next section for more information about this).

Figure 13-4

In other words: if you need to customize the look and feel of a SharePoint site, you must know if it is a MOSS site, or a WSS site. You must also understand that the chrome of a site is governed by Master Pages. For example if you need to customize the look of an intranet based on MOSS sites, you customize the Master Page file regarding chrome features like navigation, and top menus, and you will customize the page layout files when you need to change the way the content of this MOSS site looks.

Customizing a WSS site is almost the same: Modify the Master Page for the chrome features, and open the WSS site in SharePoint Designer when you need to modify the layout of the content part of the site. An alternative is to create a new site definition instead of modifying the layout of the site.

Ghosting and Unghosting

As described in Chapter 12, all SharePoint sites are defined by one or more files stored in the file system on the SharePoint server, such as `Default.aspx`. For example, all WSS team sites are built upon this file:

```
\Program Files\Common Files\Microsoft Shared\Web Server ↵
Extensions\12\TEMPLATE\Site templates\STS\Default.aspx
```

Even if you have 300 team sites, all of them will be built on this `Default.aspx` file. This makes it fast to open team sites, and it also saves a lot of space, since there is just one copy of the site definition. This is called "ghosting."

When you modify any team site by using SPD, SharePoint must store the complete site definition, including all its content, in the SQL database; the site now is "unghosted." The consequences of unghosting SharePoint sites are that it will require more space in the database and it will take slightly longer to load such a site, compared to a ghosted site. But in reality you must have thousands of SharePoint sites and/or a lot of users before anyone will ever notice any difference. I have never met a SharePoint administrator who actually had any real performance problem because of unghosting, so do not hesitate to use SharePoint Designer for editing these SharePoint sites.

There is one important thing about unghosted sites that may prohibit you from using SPD in some situations: An unghosted site will no longer be connected to the original site definition. If that site definition is modified, it will not affect unghosted sites, since they store their individual site definition. For example, say you have 2,000 WSS sites, all ghosted, and you want to change the configuration of the Web Part zones used by these sites. Simply edit the site definition stored in the file system of the SharePoint server, and all 2,000 sites are updated. This will not happen if those 2,000 sites are unghosted. In that case, you need to update them individually. In other words, if you believe that you may need to change the content layout for multiple WSS sites sometime in the future, then you should consider creating a new site definition for those WSS sites.

If you need to prohibit anyone from modifying SharePoint team sites with SharePoint Designer 2007 you can edit the `Onet.xml` file in the STS\XML structure as shown in the following Try It Out.

Try It Out   Prohibit the Use of SharePoint Designer to Edit SharePoint Sites

1. Log on to the SharePoint server, as an administrator.

2. Navigate to this folder:

```
\Program Files\Common Files\Microsoft Shared\Web Server ↵
Extensions\12\TEMPLATE\Site Templates\STS\XML\Onet.xml
```

3. Edit `Onet.xml` with Notepad.

4. Locate a line near the top that begins with:

```
<Project Title="$Resources:onet_TeamWebSite
```

5. Add the following text: `DisableWebDesignFeatures="wdfopensite"` near the end of that line, just after the text Microsoft SharePoint. The complete line then looks like this:

```
<Project Title="$Resources:onet_TeamWebSite;" Revision="2" ↵
ListDir="$Resources:core,lists_Folder;" xmlns:ows="Microsoft SharePoint"; ↵
DisableWebDesignFeatures="wdfopensite"><!-- _locID@Title="camlidonet1" ↵
_locComment="{StringCategory=HTX}" -->
```

6. Reset IIS with Start ➪ Run: **IISRESET**.

7. Test your work by opening any team site in SharePoint Designer. It will display a dialog stating that SharePoint Designer cannot edit the site (see Figure 13-5).

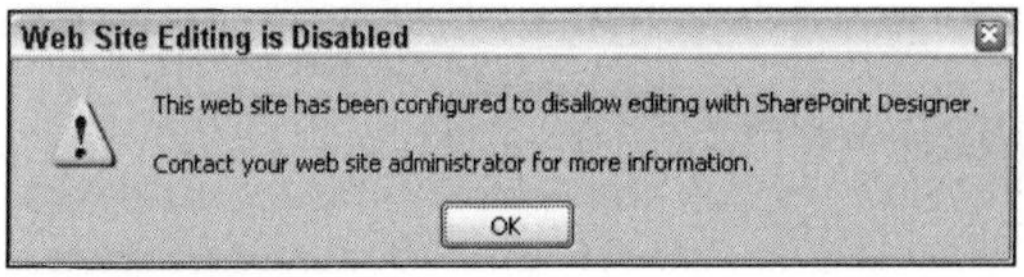

Figure 13-5

Basic Design

Using SharePoint Designer for editing SharePoint sites allows you to do almost anything. To give you an idea of what you can do, this section describes often requested modifications that are easy to make. Remember to keep SharePoint Designer open while testing these modifications; if anything goes wrong you can use the undo feature in SharePoint Designer and then save the file again.

Adding Text Outside Web Parts

There are a lot of Web Parts for displaying text on a SharePoint site, but sometimes you need to add a text block without relying on a Web Part; for example, you may want to add an instruction at the top of the site where there is no Web Part zone.

Try It Out   **Add Text to Any Part of a Site Page**

1. Log on as a user with web design permissions (for example, a site Owner, or the Site Collection Administrator).

2. Open the site to be modified in SharePoint Designer.

3. Make sure that SPD is using Design view.

4. Place the cursor where you want to enter the new text block, for example next to the site description.

> **You can create a new table row or column for this text; select a table cell near where you want the text, right-click, and select Insert.**

5. Enter the text.

6. Press F12 to save and view it (see Figure 13-6). If it does not look good, go back to SharePoint Designer, use the Undo feature under the Edit menu, and save the page again.

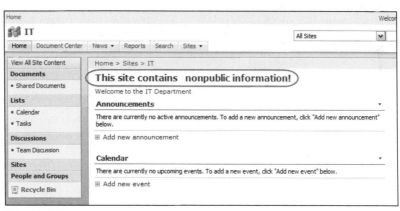

Figure 13-6

Add a Background Picture

Since team sites use Master Pages or site themes for controlling the style of the page, you cannot add a background picture to the whole page, but you can add it to a table or cell on a page. For example, say that you want to add a photo as a background picture to a Web Part zone in a team site, right-click a free part of the cell where that Web Part zone is stored and edit the cell:

Try It Out   **Add a Background Picture to a Web Part Zone**

1. Open the site to be modified in SharePoint Designer as previously described.

2. Right-click anywhere in the cell where the Web Part zone is stored; select Cell properties.

3. Check Use background picture, and enter or browse to the picture.

4. Click Save. You will then be asked if you want to customize a page from the site definition; answer Yes.

5. Next, you will be asked to save these embedded files: click OK. Note that embedded files will be visible in the Folder List pane to the left in SPD. If the picture needs to be adjusted, right-click on the picture and select Picture.

> **To add a background picture to all Web Part zones, select Table properties in step 2 above.**

Interactive Buttons

Many SharePoint customers ask for a button on the site page that performs an action or open another page. This is very easy to do with SharePoint Designer, and you have a lot of different looks for these buttons, so you will most likely find just the right button for your site.

Try It Out   Add Interactive Buttons

1. Open the site to be modified in SharePoint Designer as previously described.

2. Place the cursor where you want the button. Note that you cannot place the button inside a Web Part zone! If you need more space, right-click on a table cell, and select Insert to add a new row, column, or cell.

3. Click menu Insert ⇨ Interactive Button, then:

   a. Use the Buttons field to select the type of button you want. There is a preview of these buttons above this field.

   b. **Text:** Enter the text for the button; for example, Create Site.

   c. **Link:** Enter the link to be activated for this button; for example, `http://srv1/ SiteDirectory/it/_layouts/newsbweb.aspx` to create subsites under the IT site.

   d. Click OK to save and close. Note that first time you save a button, SPD will ask if you want to embed the button images; click OK.

4. Save the modified page. Then test the new button to make sure that it works as expected. See Figure 13-7, which has three different types of buttons added.

> **If you add a button with rounded corners on a shaded background, you will see the default white background color for the button's picture. If this happens, right-click on the button and select Button Properties, switch to the Image tab, and either change the background color or make the button a GIF image so that it can use a transparent background.**

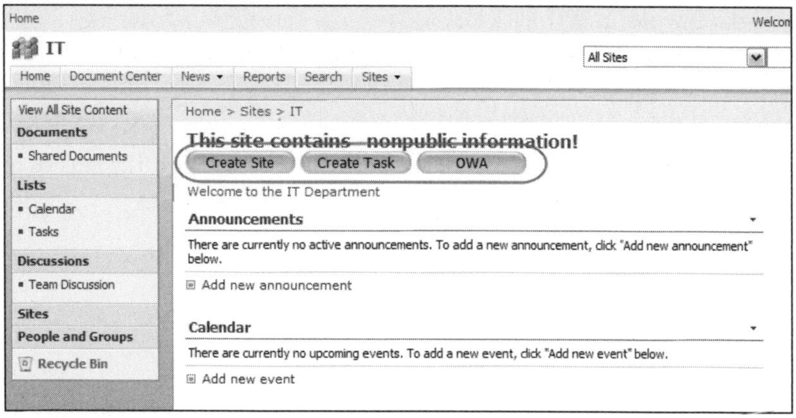

Figure 13-7

Copying Complete Sites

You may recall that any team site may be stored as a site template. This is a very handy way of creating templates for sites, including content if necessary. The problem with that technique is that you can only store 500 MB of content. But using SharePoint Designer you can save a complete site, including all its content, in a backup file, then restore it anywhere, including other SharePoint environments. This is very handy if you have a test environment and need to copy sites from that environment to the production server.

The technique for copying and moving sites with SharePoint Designer is to back up the site to the file system, then move those files to the destination server and restore them with SharePoint Designer. But before you can do a restore, an empty site must exist where SPD can restore the files. So, how do you create an empty site? Use the STSADM tool, mentioned in many previous chapters. It has a special command for creating an empty site. In the following example, you will make a backup of the WSS site IT, using SPD, then restore those files to another site in another site collection on the server. These steps can also be used to copy a site to any SharePoint environment.

Try It Out   Copy a Site to Another Site Collection with SPD

1. Log on as an administrator.

2. Open the WSS site to be copied in SharePoint Designer.

3. In SPD, select the menus options Site ➪ Administration ➪ Backup Web Site.

4. Choose if you want to include subsites, as well. Click OK, then enter the path where the backup files will be saved, and give the backup file a name. Note that the file type will be Content Migration Package (cmp). Click OK to start the backup process; wait for it to complete, then click OK.

5. The next step is to create an empty site, that is, a site without a site template. You must use the STSADM tool for this. Open a new command window, and type this command to create an empty site with the URL http://srv1/sites/sc2/abc:

```
Stsadm -o createweb -url http://srv1/sites/sc2/abc
```

6. Open the new site in SPD: click File ⇨ Open Site and enter or browse to `http://srv1/sites/sc2/abc`. It will be empty, except for some default folders.

7. Click Site ⇨ Administration ⇨ Restore Web Site, then browse to the `cmp` file you created in step 4; open that file and click OK to start restoring the site.

8. Open the new site in a web browser, and verify that it is correct. The next step is to define the permission settings for the site, since these settings are not restored.

Managing Web Part Zones

You already know that a Web Part must be stored in a Web Part zone. But sometimes you need to add a Web Part to another part of the page. A common example is when you want to add a site tree Web Part to the Quick Launch bar in a team site. To do that you need to create a new Web Part zone. Only SharePoint Designer allows you to create such a zone; no other third-party web design tool knows how do this.

Try It Out   Create a New Web Part Zone

1. Log on as an administrator

2. Go to the page you want to add the Web Part zone; for example, `http://srv1/SiteDirectory/it`.

3. Open this page with SharePoint Designer.

4. Place the cursor where the new zone will be; for example to create the zone in the Quick Launch bar, go to the last action line in that bar, then press Space to get a new row in the Quick Launch bar.

5. Click the menu options Insert ⇨ SharePoint Controls ⇨ Web Part Zone. The new zone is added to this location.

6. The next step is adding a Web Part. Use the link on the new zone. Click it to insert a Web Part, and select the Web Part from the Web Part pane on the right of the SPD window. If you need to configure the Web Part, right-click on it and select Web Part Properties.

7. When all the Web Parts you need are added, save this page in SharePoint Designer. Then open it in a web browser and make sure that it works as expected.

8. To delete a Web Part zone, select it by clicking its name, then press the Delete key.

Note that you can create any number of Web Part zones, and they will be resized automatically when you add new Web Parts to them.

> When editing Web Part properties from within SPD, you will not see some properties, such as the current view for lists or libraries. To change the view, open this page in the web browser and edit the Web Part properties there.

Retrieving a Site Summary

Since SharePoint Designer knows how SharePoint works, it can also present a lot of information for a given portal or team site, such as a list of all files, all links, and all pictures. It can run a test to see what pages are slow to load and much more.

Try It Out **Create a Site Summary**

1. Open the site in SharePoint Designer.

2. Click the menu Site ➪ Reports and select:

    a. **Site Summary:** A summary of the current site (see Figure 13-8).

    b. **Files:** Lists all files, new files, old files, and so on.

    c. **Shared Content:** Master pages, style sheets, themes, dynamic web templates, and so on.

    d. **Problems:** Unlinked files, slow pages, hyperlinks, and component errors.

    e. **Usage:** Displays statistics about the site; it requires that you have activated logging (SharePoint Central Administration ➪ Operations ➪ Usage analysis processing).

One analysis that this site summary can perform is to test the speed with which your pages load. For example, if you link a lot of external information to your SharePoint pages, you must make sure that it does not take too long to open those pages. Control this by using the Site Summary that displays slow pages, or use Problems ➪ Slow Pages to test how long your pages take to load. Note that this page allows you to set the limit in seconds to define what a "slow page" really is.

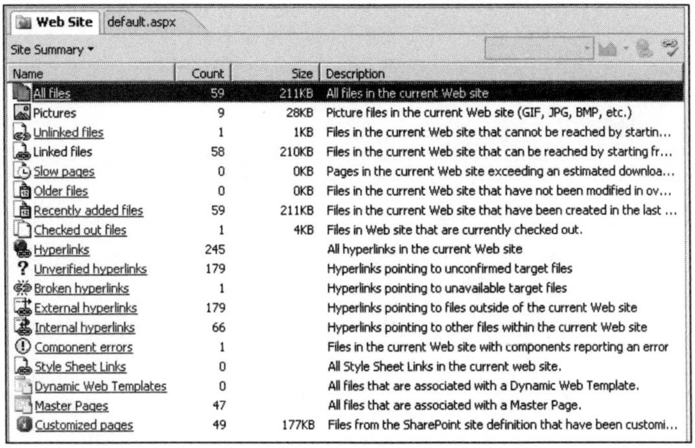

Figure 13-8

Extended Design

The previous section described several modifications that are easy to do on any SharePoint site page. In this section, you will see more advanced modifications that SharePoint Designer allows you to do.

Managing Site Themes

The look and feel of a SharePoint site is completely controlled by its Master Page, which uses Cascading Style Sheets (CSS) to define how the site looks. But WSS sites also have another technique called site themes to define what fonts, sizes, and colors are to be used by different parts of a page. By using pre-configured site themes, a team site owner can easily change its look and feel directly using the web browser. Using the link Site Actions ⇨ Site Settings, and click on Site theme in the Look and Feel section the site owner can select between 18 different themes. Note that some of them are especially high contrast themes for visually impaired users, and these are hard to see for people with normal eyesight.

Using SharePoint Designer Themes

Site themes are just another way of using CSS files in WSS site, which was introduced in previous versions of SharePoint. Today when WSS 3.0 can use Master Pages, themes may be less essential, but still only site themes change the color setting for the complete page, while Master Pages affect just the site chrome, that is, the navigation, Quick Launch, and logotypes of the page. You must decide if you want to use Master Pages or site themes for a site. If you select anything other than the Default Master page, it will have precedence over the site theme setting on the content page, that is, the Home page for the site, and the list and library views. But the Site Setting pages and other administrative pages will still be affected by the site theme — probably something you may want to avoid. You may want to create your own theme; this is easily done with SharePoint Designer, since these themes in SharePoint are indeed SharePoint Designer themes.

> In FrontPage 2003 (the predecessor of SPD) you could manage Site Themes directly. This feature has been removed, since you now can modify the style of each visual element of a page.

Adding New SharePoint Themes

You can add your own site themes to WSS; this will make it possible to apply that theme to new sites without the need to use SharePoint Designer. Even though this chapter is about SharePoint Designer, this section provides an interesting discussion of SharePoint themes in general.

All of the preconfigured themes in SharePoint are stored in the file system on the SharePoint server. Each theme consists of a number of CSS and GIF files. Instead of creating all of the elements from scratch for your new theme, you can copy an existing theme folder and modify its files as necessary.

Try It Out   Create New Standard SharePoint Themes

1. Log on to the SharePoint server as an administrator.

2. Open this folder:

```
C:\Program Files\Common Files\Microsoft Shared\web server ↵
extensions\12\TEMPLATE\THEMES
```

3. Note that it contains a number of folders, each with a name that matches one of the themes listed in the team site's administrative page. Start by copying one of these folders, for example VINTAGE, and paste it into the same THEMES folder. Rename the new folder using capital letters only; for example, DEMO.

4. Open the new folder; locate the INF file with the same name as the folder you copied, in this example VINTAGE.INF. Rename it to match your folder exactly: DEMO.INF.

5. Edit the DEMO.INF with Notepad. Change the Title to the same name as your folder; note that you don't have to use capital letters here. When finished, save the file.

```
[info]
title=Demo
```

6. Next, open this file in Notepad:

```
C:\Program Files\Common Files\Microsoft Shared\web server ↵
extensions\12\TEMPLATE\LAYOUTS\1033\SPTHEMES.XML
```

7. Each theme has a section in this XML file; for example, the theme VINTAGE:

```
<Templates>
  <TemplateID>Vintage</TemplateID>
  <DisplayName>Vintage</DisplayName>
  <Description>Description</Description>
  <Thumbnail>../images/thvintage.png</Thumbnail>
  <Preview>../images/thvintage.gif</Preview>
</Templates>
```

8. Copy this section and paste it back. Then edit the copied section to match the name of your theme. The TemplateID must match your folder name but must include small letters! You also need to change the DisplayName and the Description field, since they are displayed in SharePoint's theme list.

```
<Templates>
  <TemplateID>demo</TemplateID>
  <DisplayName>Demo</DisplayName>
  <Description>My Demo Theme</Description>
  <Thumbnail>../images/thice.png</Thumbnail>
  <Preview>../images/thice.gif</Preview>
</Templates>
```

9. The new theme is now active. Open the list of Themes to check that it is there (Site Actions ➪ Site Settings ➪ Site theme); make sure to refresh the cache in your web browser (Ctrl+F5) or else you may get an error stating that this theme already exists.

10. Next step is to change this theme so that is does not look the same as the one you copied. Open the THEME.CSS file in your newly created Theme folder. Change whatever element you need in this CSS file, then save the file.

> **In order to see the modification you must: a) first select another theme, then b) apply your new theme, and then c) refresh the browser (Ctrl+F5).**

It is not so easy to understand the `Theme.css` file and what elements to modify to get a specific result. Luckily there are some good resources that describe what each element does:

❑ This article by Microsoft describes each locator and an image of each object so you easier can see what it does: `http://msdn2.microsoft.com/en-us/library/ms438349.aspx`.

❑ The SharePoint MVP Shane Perran not only offers a good explanation of how to create your own theme, but also offers a package of free themes, which all contains descriptive comments so that you will understand what it does. This is an excellent tool to learn the fine art of creating themes: `www.graphicalwonder.com` and search for "themes."

Adding Pages to SharePoint

You may have noticed that each WSS site only consists of one single Web Part page; the other pages for displaying a document library and lists are, in fact, also Web Part pages and can be modified with a standard web browser. Sometimes you may need one or more extra pages, perhaps because there is too much information to be displayed on this site. In MOSS sites, it is very easy: simply add a new Publishing Page, and then configure the navigation settings to display this page on the top navigation bar. In WSS this is harder, since it does not have the feature for Publishing Pages and page libraries, and therefore WSS pages will not be listed in the top navigation bar.

WSS allows you to create two types of pages: basic HTML pages and Web Part pages, either through the browser or by using SharePoint Designer. This section describes how to add an extra page of each type to the Home page of a WSS team site. Each page, regardless of type, must be stored as a file in a document library on this site. The trick is not to create these extra pages, but to make them easily and seamlessly integrated in the Home page.

> In SharePoint 2003, you had to use FrontPage to create navigation tabs to any extra pages. In SharePoint 2007, you can simply change the navigation settings, so you don't need SPD for this. However, in some situations there may be a need to create custom tabs on a WSS site. Both methods are described in the following section.

Adding Web Part Pages

This type of page is exactly like the Home page of a team site; it has one or more Web Part zones, which you add Web Parts to. This type of page will also display the same header and menus as the Home page.

In this example, you will use a web browser to add one new Web Part page to the following team site: `http://srv1/SiteDirectory/it`. The new page will also have some Web Parts added to it. At this stage, you will just create the page; later on you will create buttons to make the page easer to use for the user.

Try It Out   Create a New Web Part Page within the Browser

1. Open the IT team site in a web browser.

2. Start by creating a new document library for storing the page files: Click Site Actions ➪ Create ➪ Document Library, and create a library named WSS-pages.

3. Next, create a Web Part page: select Site Actions ➪ Create ➪ Web Part Page, then enter these settings:

    a. **Name:** WP-Page.

    b. **Choose a Layout Template:** Header, Footer, 3 Columns.

    c. **Document Library:** WSS-pages. This is where this file will be stored.

    d. Click Create.

4. The new page opens. Add some Web Parts, for example Site Users and Shared Documents.

5. Click IT to open to the default start page for the team site.

The big question now, of course, is how to display it again. The answer is as simple as it is surprising: Open the WSS-page library, and click on the WP-Page file. This was easy but not intuitive, right? You will soon see some ways to make this more intuitive.

Adding Standard HTML Pages

Now let's create the other type of pages. The difference here is how the page behaves; it will not contain any Web Part zones, so you cannot add Web Parts to it. But it will contain a Content Editor server control that allows you to enter most types of HTML-formatted information, such as text, images and links. With SPD you can also add any other type of HTML tags and form controls to the Content Editor, such as an IFrame.

In this example, you will create a basic web page in the same document library as previous page:

Try It Out   Create a Basic Web Page

1. Open the team site in a web browser.

2. Click Site Actions ➪ Create and select Basic Page in the Web Pages section.

3. Enter a name for the page, then use the menu next to Document Library to change its name to WSS-pages. Then click Create.

4. The new page is displayed, and its Content Editor is opened. Now, you can start adding information to the Content Editor. Click Save when you're ready (see Figure 13-9 for an example).

5. Option: If you open the basic page in SPD, you can then add more HTML tags and forms controls to it than the default tools in the Content Editor offer. When you save it, SharePoint will inform you that the page will now be unghosted; click Yes to save it.

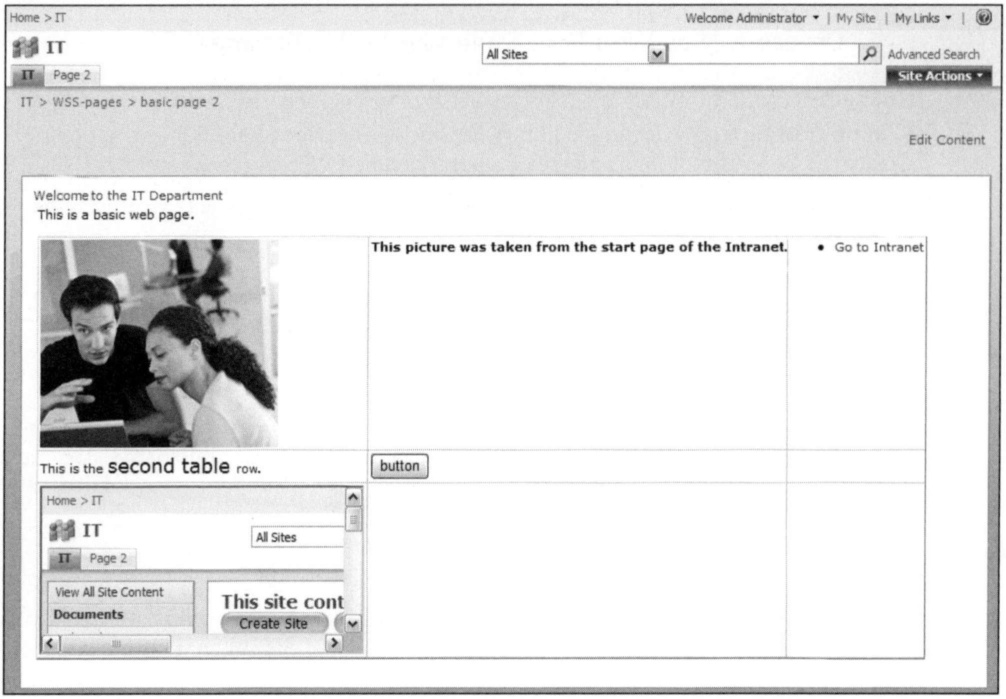

Figure 13-9

Making Pages Easier to Open

Creating extra pages both is easy and opens up interesting opportunities. As stated before, the challenge is to make them work seamlessly with the rest of this team site. There are several options available:

❑ **Create a link in a list:** Requires that you create a SharePoint list of links. This is very easy, but may not be the most intuitive way of opening these added pages.

❑ **Create a link in the Quick Launch bar:** Requires that you change the navigation for the WSS site: Click Site Actions ➪ Site Settings ➪ Navigation, and add the link in the section Navigation Editing and Sorting. The result is easy for the user to use and understand.

❑ **Create a button linked to the page:** Requires SharePoint Designer; this option is also easy to use and may be a very intuitive, since you can design the buttons to make them more recognizable and attractive.

❑ **Create a list of tabs, version 1:** You can add a tab to the global top navigation bar of the WSS site, as described below. But to do that you must create a unique set of navigation tabs for the site. That is, the site will only show its own navigation tabs, not the global Home, Document Center, and News tabs. This is really an advantage, since users will understand better that the new set of tabs points to pages related to the particular WSS site.

❑ **Create a list of tabs, version 2:** Instead of using the built-in navigation tabs you can create buttons shaped as tabs and place them near each other to give the impression of a number of tabs instead of pages. The best result will be when using Web Part pages, since they also use the same top header and color as the Home page. This technique is described in the following Try It Out.

Try It Out   Create Navigation Tabs to Pages

1. In this example, you will customize the standard navigation tabs for the WSS site that contains multiple pages. Start by open the site in a web browser.

2. Click Site Actions ➪ Site Settings ➪ Navigation (in the Look and Feel section). Note that there is an option for showing pages but it is grayed out, since it only works for Publishing Pages, that is, pages in MOSS sites.

3. You must configure the WSS site to show customized navigation elements: In the Global Navigation section, select the option Display the navigation items below the current site.

4. The previous step will display the new heading Global Navigation in the Navigation Editing and Sorting section. Select Global Navigation, and then click Add Link. Then enter these values:

   a. **Title:** Enter the tab title — try to keep it short but descriptive.

   b. **URL:** Enter the full URL to the page. You can use Browse to select the page URL, or enter the URL manually.

   c. **Open link in new windows:** Optional.

   d. **Description:** Optional; this information will show up as a tooltip when the user hovers the mouse over this tab (see Figure 13-10).

   e. **Audience:** Optional; use it to target this page for specific groups of users.

   f. Click OK.

5. Go back to the navigation settings (see Figure 13-11). Add any extra links you need, then click OK to save and close the page.

6. Open the WSS site and inspect the new navigation tabs (see Figure 13-10).

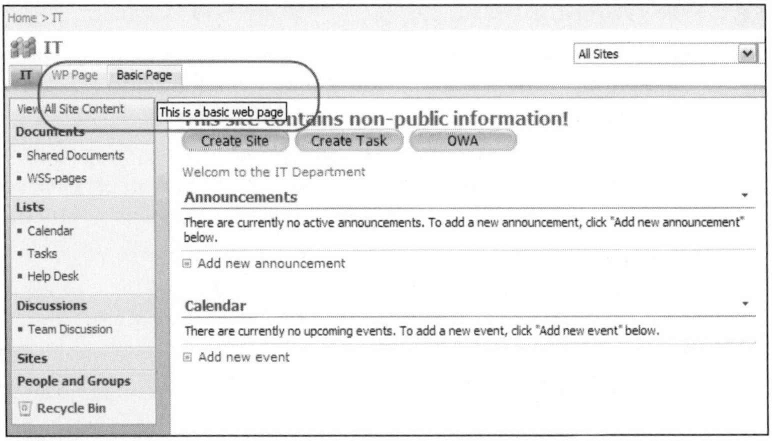

Figure 13-10

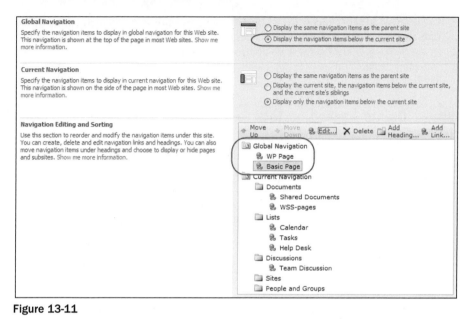

Figure 13-11

The second version adds tab buttons to give the impression that this is a Pages view. The advantage compared to the first version is that the global navigation function is still intact. The drawback is that this approach requires some extra steps. The challenge here is that you must add the tab buttons on all pages, and in the same position, to make it seamlessly integrate with the team page. This can be tricky at times, but if you are careful it will be very nice. Instead of adding single tab buttons on each page, you can create a layer that contains the tab buttons, then copy this layer onto each page. The following Try It Out shows one way of doing this.

Try It Out **Create Tab Buttons**

1. Open the site's start page, `Default.aspx`, with SharePoint Designer.

2. Use the Insert menu to select HTML ⇨ Layer. Locate the layer where you want the tab buttons to go, for example just under the top menu. You may need to adjust the size of the layer to fit all the buttons you will add.

> If the Layer option is grayed out, you have located a part of the page that does not allow you to create a layer. If so, go to the top of the code for the page and try again.

3. Make sure that the cursor is inside the layer, then add the first tab button:

    a. Click Insert ⇨ Interactive button.

    b. Select the tab button you prefer; note that there are several types and colors to choose from. In this example, use Glass Tab 1.

    c.   **Text:** Home. Since you will add this layer to several pages, you should also have a button that takes you back to the Home page. This is especially important to get a consistent view of these navigation tabs.

    d.   **URL:** Click Browse and select `Default.aspx`, which is the Home page for the team site.

    e.   Click OK to save this button.

4.   Add the second button next to the first one. Instead of creating the button from scratch, select the existing one; right-click and select Copy.

    a.   Place the cursor directly to the right of the first tab button.

    b.   Right-click and select Paste.

    c.   Double-click on the new button. Its configuration pane opens.

    d.   Change the Text to whatever you want to call the second page.

    e.   Click Browse for the URL field; open the document library `WSS-pages`, where these added page files are stored, and select the second page.

    f.   Click OK to save and close the page.

5.   If you have more pages, add a tab button for each of them to the layer in the same way.

6.   When you are done, adjust the position and size of the layer so that it will look good on every page, and then save the page. Click OK to save the images for the buttons, but do not close SharePoint Designer yet.

7.   Right-click on the frame around the layer and select Copy; you will now paste the layer into all the other pages:

    a.   Open the second page in SharePoint Designer.

    b.   Select the menu options Edit ⇨ Paste. This will place the layer in the same location as on the first page.

    c.   Save the page.

    d.   Repeat steps a–c for all the pages added to this team site.

8.   Make sure that you have saved all modifications in SharePoint Designer. Open the team site with a browser; click on one of the tab buttons. It should open that page, which should also contain the same buttons. Make sure that it works and that it looks good. See Figure 13-12, where the second page is displayed with its three buttons.

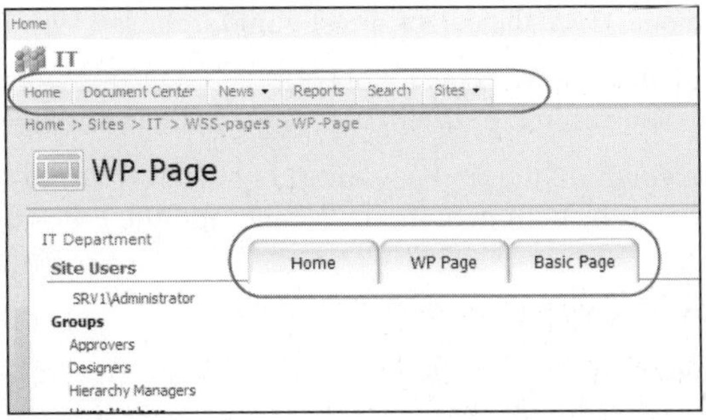

Figure 13-12

If you choose to add tab buttons to these pages, you may want to remove the text Home from the start page for this team site to make that page look better; use SharePoint Designer to do this.

Data Sources and Data Views

A very common request is to make content in one site available in another site. Most SharePoint installations uses team sites for managing projects, and after some time there is a need for a shared view of tasks as different sites emerge. Another similar request is to have one team site that displays the document libraries in other sites. Finally, a third request may be to display content in an external database, for example a product database on an MS SQL server.

There are several ways to meet these needs: MOSS Standard Edition comes with the Content Query Web Part, (see Chapter 8), which is very good for displaying content in lists and libraries in other sites. MOSS Enterprise Edition also adds the Business Data Catalog, which is a very flexible and advanced feature that allows SharePoint to view, update, and search in almost any type of external data source, such as MS SQL databases, Oracle databases, or a SAP system. However, there are two other Web Parts that also can be used to meet these needs: Data Source and Data view; these two Web Parts are only available when using SharePoint Designer 2007:

❑ **Data Source:** Defines what source to read.

❑ **Data view:** Defines how this source will be displayed.

Both of these are integrated in the same package in SharePoint Designer: the Data View package. These are not standard Web Parts and cannot be installed in a Web Part zone; you must add them to another part of the page. In the following example, you will see how to display a document library in another team site and how to display a table in an external MS SQL database.

Displaying Content in Other Sites

The first example will use the team site `http://srv1/SiteDirectory/sales` to display a document library stored in `http://srv1/SiteDirectory/it`. This example can easily be extended to display any type of list, and it works for both MOSS and WSS environments.

Try It Out   **Display Content in Another Site**

1. Log on as an administrator.

2. Open the team site `http://srv1/SiteDirectory/sales` in SharePoint Designer.

3. Using Design mode, place the cursor directly under the left Web Part zone.

4. Select the menu options Data View ➪ Insert Data View. This will open the Task Pane and display all the data sources in the current team site, as shown in Figure 13-13.

5. The data source you need (i.e., `http://srv1/SiteDirectory/it`) is not listed. Click Connect to another library at the bottom of the Task Pane, and then click the Add button and enter the following:

   a. **Display Name:** IT Team Site.

   b. **Location:** `http://srv1/SiteDirectory/it`.

   c. Click OK twice. Note that the Data Source Library pane now lists IT Team Site.

Figure 13-13

6. Expand the IT Team Site (click on its plus sign); all lists and libraries in this site are now listed. Expand SharePoint Libraries; you will see the Shared Documents library. Add this library to the page like this:

   a. Place the cursor where you want the new list to be displayed.

   b. Click on the name Shared Documents. A menu is presented.

   c. Click Show Data. The columns for the document library are displayed in the Data Sources Details pane.

   d. Select all the properties you want to display in the new list, then click the Insert Selected Fields button to open that menu and chose Multiple Item View. Note that to select more than one property you must hold down the Ctrl key.

   e. Verify that the content is displayed. If you are happy with this view, then save the page in SharePoint Designer.

7. You can also change the view of table, for example what columns to display, the sort order and formatting. This is similar to creating views for any SharePoint list but is more powerful. Following are some of the things you can do, starting with how to display more columns. Note that it is a bit tricky, so make sure to follow these instructions exactly.

   a. Continue with SPD working on the same page as in the previous step. If you want to display more columns on the Data View list, you must first create a new empty column and then insert a Data Source column. Place the cursor at the top of the column you want to move to the right; when you see a black arrow pointing down, you are in the right position. (It is easiest if the list is not currently selected.) Right-click and select Insert ⇨ Column to the left (or right); a new column is displayed in the table.

   b. Set the cursor inside the new column for any of the data rows. Make sure not to set the cursor in the title row! Note that the column is very narrow, since it does not contain any data yet. It is actually easier to use the arrows on the keyboard to place the cursor in this cell than it is to use the mouse.

    c.   In the Current Data Source pane, right-click the column to be added. Select Insert as <Text/Number/Currency>. (Choose whatever type is appropriate for this column.)

    d.   Place the cursor in the title row for the column; type a name for the column.

8.   Another thing you probably want to do is to create a link to these documents, so they can be opened. By default, only their names will be displayed, but you cannot click on them to open them, as you can in a normal document library. You will need to include the property URL Path in the list, then you can replace the existing URL column with the same content but with hyperlinks:

    a.   Right-click the URL path for the first document in the list (but not the title row).

    b.   Select Format item as ⇨ Hyperlink. You will be prompted as to whether you trust this environment. Click Yes, then you can edit the hyperlink. Just accept the default and click OK.

9.   Another way to do this is to make the document names hyperlinks. Clicking a name first opens the web form for the document, where the user can open the actual document.

    a.   Select any of the existing filenames.

    b.   Right-click, and select Format Item as ⇨ Hyperlink to ⇨ Display Form.

10.   To change the sort order and group items, you can do this:

    a.   Click anywhere on the new list; at the top right part of the list an arrow pointing to the right is displayed. Click on the arrow to open the Common Data View Tasks menu (see Figure 13-14).

    b.   Click Sort and Group in the menu.

    c.   Select the column to sort by; click Add. If necessary add more columns. Check Show group header if you want to group the list items based on the added column.

    d.   Click OK to save and close the page.

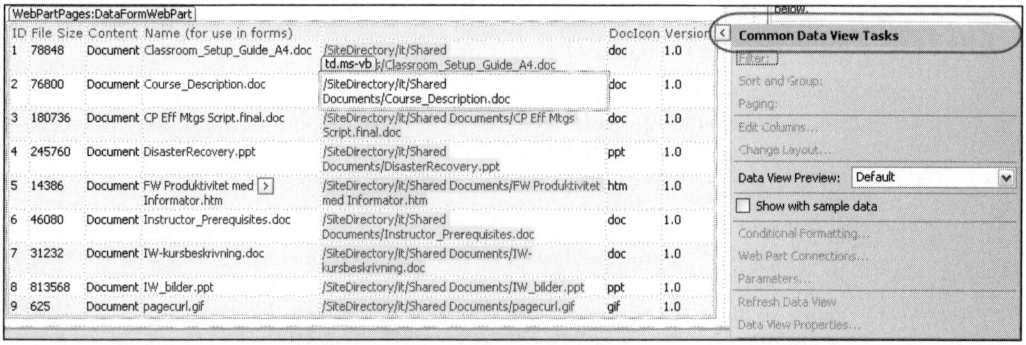

Figure 13-14

You can do a lot more, such as conditional formatting, filtering, and changing the layout for the list, using the Common Data Views Tasks menu, but these examples will give you the general idea of how to use and customize this list.

Displaying External Information

The second use for the Data view is to display content in sources outside SharePoint., and it is capable of connecting to many type of sources, such as:

- ❑   MS SQL Databases
- ❑   XML files
- ❑   Web Services

In this example, you will connect to the demo database Northwind that is included by default in all MS SQL databases. By coincidence this database is stored on the same SQL server that SharePoint uses, but you can use these steps to connect to any database. You will display the Products table on the same team site as in the previous example.

Try It Out   Display Content in an External Database

1.   Log on as an administrator.

2.   Open the `http://srv1/SiteDirectory/sales` site, then open `Default.aspx` in SharePoint Designer.

3.   Select the menu options Data View ➪ Manage Data Sources. This will open the Data Source Library pane and display all the data sources in the current team site. Look at the listing under this site name; it will show you all the sources available for this team site, that is, lists and libraries, plus database connections, XML files, Business Data Catalogs, server-side scripts, and XML Web services.

4.   Expand the database connections:

a.   Click Connect to a database. A dialog box opens.

b.   Click Configure Database Connection.

c.   Enter the server Name for the SQL database, and select the Provider Name. You must also define what user account to use when reading this information. You could also choose Single Sign-on authentication, if you have configured Single Sign-On in SharePoint. This is a separate database that stores user accounts and passwords for accessing databases and information outside SharePoint. Click Next to continue. You may receive a warning that the user name will be stored as clear text in the data connection string. Click OK to continue.

d.   All databases on the MS SQL server are listed; select Northwind. A list of all tables for that database appears. Select Products and click Next.

e.   A list of options for filtering and formatting the table is displayed. Don't change anything now, just click OK.

f.   In the Data Source Library, under Database Connections, you will see Products on Northwind. Click on this, and add data in the same way as described in the previous example on how to show content in other sites.

As you can see, the Data Source and Data view offer a number of ways to present information stored in other SharePoint sites, as well as external data sources. If you need more control and functionality, you should use the Business Data Catalog Web Part, but remember that this is only available for MOSS Enterprise installations.

Master Pages and Layout Pages

So far in this chapter you have seen how to customize SharePoint pages in general, both MOSS and WSS pages. In reality, many of these customizations are used on WSS pages, since MOSS has a smarter way to control the look and feel of both the chrome and the content of a web page. In SharePoint 2003, you customized WSS 2.0 in a different way than SPS 2003. The differences are much smaller in SharePoint 2007, although there are some: Both MOSS 2007 and WSS 3.0 use Master Pages to control the chrome of the page, while only MOSS uses page layout files to govern the look and feel of the page content. Instead, WSS pages are configured directly, either by customizing the site definition files or by editing the page using SharePoint Designer, as previously described in this chapter.

Master Pages

A Master Page file consists of a style definition and one or more CSS files. The style definition controls, for example, the position and layout of the navigation and Quick Launch bar, while the CSS file controls the font types, sizes, and colors for the text. One SharePoint page can only be associated with one specific Master Page; different pages can have different Master Pages. Each site collection has a library with all the Master Pages available for this SharePoint page, known as the Master Pages and Page Layouts Gallery. As this name implies, this library also contains page layout files, but for now, let's focus on the Master Pages. To list these Master Pages, use the steps in the following Try It Out.

Try It Out   Display Existing Master Pages

1. Log on as a site administrator, and open the top site of a site collection.

2. Click Site Actions ⇨ Site Settings ⇨ Modify All Site Settings.

3. In the Gallery section, click Master pages and page layouts to open the list with all existing Master Pages (see Figure 13-15).

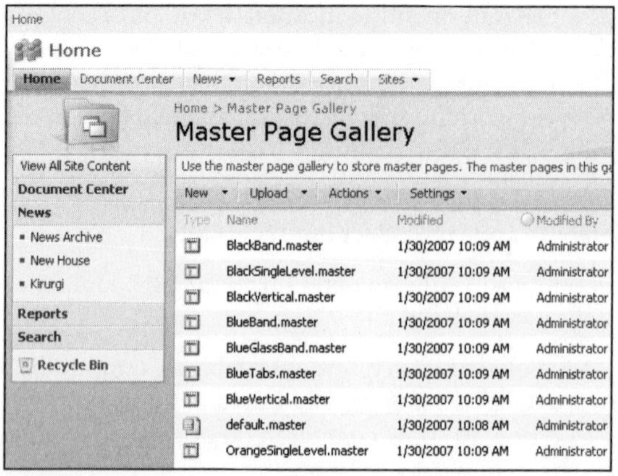

Figure 13-15

One of these Master Pages is `default.master`. You should normally avoid customizing the default Master Page, since it is the base for all default SharePoint pages, and it also has a special feature: Only WSS sites that are configured to use `default.master` can use site themes. However, if you want to apply a customization that will affect all existing site pages, as well as all new pages that will be created later, then you should consider modifying the `Default.master page` file; a typical example is when you want to replace the default logo with your company logo. Remember to make a backup copy of the original `default.master`, just in case you need to revert to it.

When customizing a Master Page, you either copy an existing Master Page and save it with a new name or create a new one from scratch. As usual, it is easier to start by editing an existing file, as long as you only want to make minor modifications. In the example below you will copy `Default.master` and save it as `Demo.master`.

Try It Out   Replace the Page Logo on a Master Page

1. Log on as a site collection administrator, and open the top site in a site collection.

2. Open the Master Page Gallery: click Site Actions ⇨ Site Settings ⇨ Modify All Site Settings, then click Master pages and page layouts.

3. Open an Explorer view of the library to make it easier to copy the original Master Page: Click Actions ⇨ Open with Windows Explorer.

4. Right-click on the `Default.master` file and select Copy, then right-click on any free space in the window, right-click, and select Paste. Rename the copied file (usually named "`Default(2).master`") to `Demo.master`, then close this Explorer view window.

5. Locate the new `Demo.master` in the list; open its quick menu and select Edit in Microsoft Office SharePoint Designer. Click OK when you are prompted if you want to check out this file. Now SPD will open with the `Demo.master` page (see Figure 13-16). Note that this page only shows the chrome of this page. The marked section in the center of this page, PlaceHolderMain, is where the page content later will be displayed, but that part is not customized using Master Pages.

6. The page is now ready to be customized; for example, change the logotype like this:

    a. Upload the logo to an image library that all users can access, such as the Image library on the top site. In this example, assume that you have a file named `MyLogo.png` in this image library. Note that the URL for this library is `http://srv1/PublishingImages`.

    b. Select the logo at the top left of this Master Page.

    c. Click Split (at the bottom of the SPD window) to view both the graphic Design view, and the code; note that the part in the code that is marked has a property named `"LogoImageURL="/_layouts/images/titlegraphic.gif`. Replace this line of code:

```
<SharePoint:SiteLogoImage id="onetidHeadbnnr0" ↵
LogoImageUrl="/_layouts/images/titlegraphi.gif" runat="server"/>
```

    with this line:

```
<asp:Image runat="server" id="Logo" ImageUrl="/PublishingImages/MyLogo.gif"/>
```

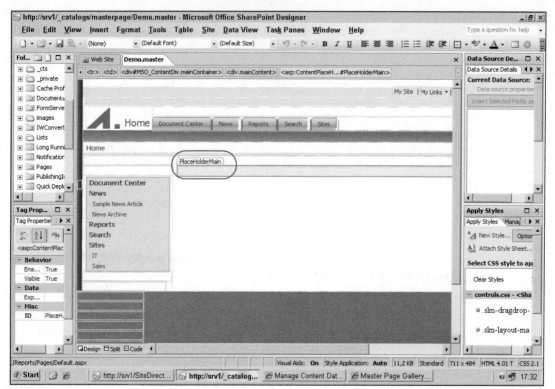

Figure 13-16

    d.   Save the modified Master Page, then click Edit ➪ Check In. In the next form, select the option Publish a major version (you can also add a comment), and click OK. After a few seconds, you will see a new dialog box. Click Yes to modify the approval status; this will open a SharePoint page where you can approve this modified Master Page. Open the quick menu for the Master Page, select Approve/reject, and approve the modified Master Page. Now the page is ready to be used.

7.   Now apply this Master Page to SharePoint. You can choose if you want to apply the Master Page to a single site or to all subsites as well. Note that you should also apply the Master Page as a System Master Page to ensure that the site has the same look and feel when opening non-publishing pages such as document libraries and lists.

    a.   Go to the top site, then click Site Actions ➪ Site Settings ➪ Modify All Site Settings.

    b.   Click Master page in the Look and Feel Gallery. This is the place to select which Master Page is to be used by the site.

    c. In the Site Master Page section, select your new Master Page (`Demo.master`). Then check the option Reset all subsites to inherit the Site Master Page setting.

    d. Click OK.

8. Verify that all sites now display the new logo.

> When changing the Master Page, only content pages will be updated; that is, Site Settings and other configuration pages will not be affected by the new Master Page.

Next, you will add a copyright statement to the bottom of all pages, using the `Demo.master` page file. This is simply a matter of adding a short code segment to the file; it will be visible on all SharePoint pages connected to the Master Page.

Try It Out   Add a Copyright Statement to a Master Page

1. Log on as a site collection administrator, and open the top site in a site collection.

2. Locate the same `Demo.master` page file in the Master pages and page layouts gallery, then use its quick menu to start editing the file in SharePoint Designer. (Accept the option to check out the file).

3. Switch to Code view, then search for the PlaceHolderMain. This is the place where SharePoint will later put the actual page content.

4. Add a new table row under the PlaceHolderMain segment; that is, add the last three lines in the code segment below:

```
<tr>
    <td class='ms-bodyareaframe' valign="top" height="100%">
      <A name="mainContent"></A>
      <asp:ContentPlaceHolder id="PlaceHolderPageDescription" runat="server"/>
      <asp:ContentPlaceHolder id="PlaceHolderMain" runat="server">
      </asp:ContentPlaceHolder>
    </td>
</tr>

<tr>
  <td colspan="2">Copyright 2007 - Filobit Corporation</td>
</tr>
```

5. Save the page, check it in, and approve it. Open a SharePoint site based on `Demo.master`, and notice that it now has both a new company logo and a copyright statement (see Figure 13-17).

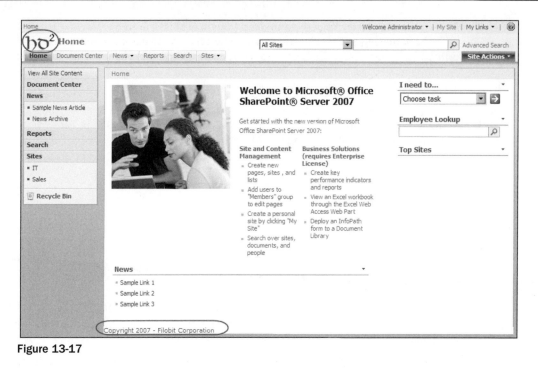

Figure 13-17

Layout Pages

Look at the start page for the intranet; by default, it shows a picture, a text segment, plus several Web Parts, such as "I need to" and Employee Lookup. Click Site Actions ⇨ Edit Page. It is now clear that this type of page consists of more content parts, such as Page Image and Page Content, than the WSS pages you customized earlier in this chapter. The reason is that this is a Publishing Page, which only comes with MOSS sites. But how do you control the layout of this page? For example, what if you wanted to display the image to the right instead of to the left? This is where page layout files come in. You saw in the previous section about Master Pages that there is one common gallery named Master Pages and Page Layouts; this library contains the page layout files, besides the Master Pages.

This is how it works: The content of this page is stored in a page file; the layout of this page is controlled by a layout file. In other words, there are two file types involved here. Let's look at where these files are stored.

Try It Out   **Locate the Content Page and the Layout Page**

1. First, discard the checkout of the page you just performed above: click Page ⇨ Discard Check Out and then click OK.

2. Next, click View All Site Content and open the Pages library. This is where all the Publishing Pages are stored for the site (each MOSS site has its own page library).

3. This library will by default only contain one single page file: `Default.aspx` (the file type is not displayed, but if you hover the mouse over the file, you can see the complete filename in the status menu below). Open the quick menu for the file, then select View properties.

4. At the bottom of the property page, it says that the content type used by this page is the Welcome page (see Figure 13-18). This is a special content type associated with Publishing Pages, typically used as a start page for an intranet. If you edit this page, you could in fact change the content type, but for now, click Close.

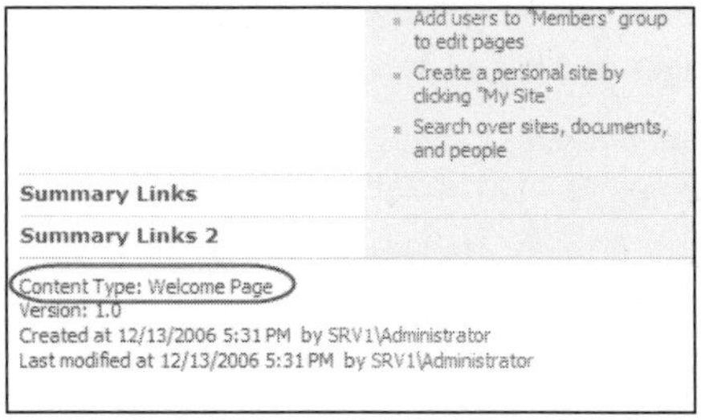

Figure 13-18

5. Let's look at another MOSS site that also uses Publishing Pages: Switch to the News web site, then click Sample News Article to open it.

6. This is also a Publishing Page. Click View All Site Content ⇨ Pages, and you will find a page file named Article1; view its properties and you can see that this page is connected to the content type Article Page. Then close the properties.

7. There are different content types for different Publishing Pages. Now try this: Open the News site again, then click Site Actions ⇨ Create Page. Look at the Page Layout section; it contains multiple layouts all based on either Article Page, Welcome Page, or Redirect Page. So what you can do is to create new layout pages for news articles, based on the content type Article Page. You will do that in just a few seconds.

8. First, let's look at where these layout files are stored; for example, "Article page with body only":

    a. Click Site Actions ⇨ Site Settings ⇨ Modify All Site Settings and then open Master pages and page layouts; all files with an Associated Content Type equal to Article Page is what you are looking for (see Figure 13-19).

    b. Open the properties for the file `PageFromDocLayout.aspx`, and you will see that the title for this layout file is "Article page with body only."

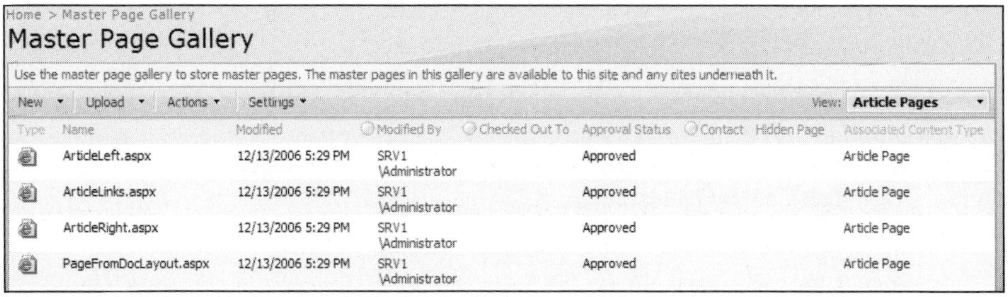

Figure 13-19

So now you know where the content pages (i.e., the Publishing Pages) are stored and where the layout pages are stored, and that there is a content type associated with each layout. The next example shows you how to customize an existing layout file and how to create a new layout file from scratch.

Try It Out   Customize an Existing Layout File

1. Open the Master Pages and Page Layouts Gallery, as described earlier.

2. Locate the `PageFromDocLayout.aspx` file; open its quick menu and select Edit in Microsoft Office SharePoint Designer, then accept to check out the file.

3. This layout file is now open in edit mode in SPD. To make it easier for you, SPD also loads the associated Master Page, but in read-only mode (see Figure 13-20). Note that this layout page consists of two controls only: the Page Content and the Rollup Image. Let's add a Byline control to this page:

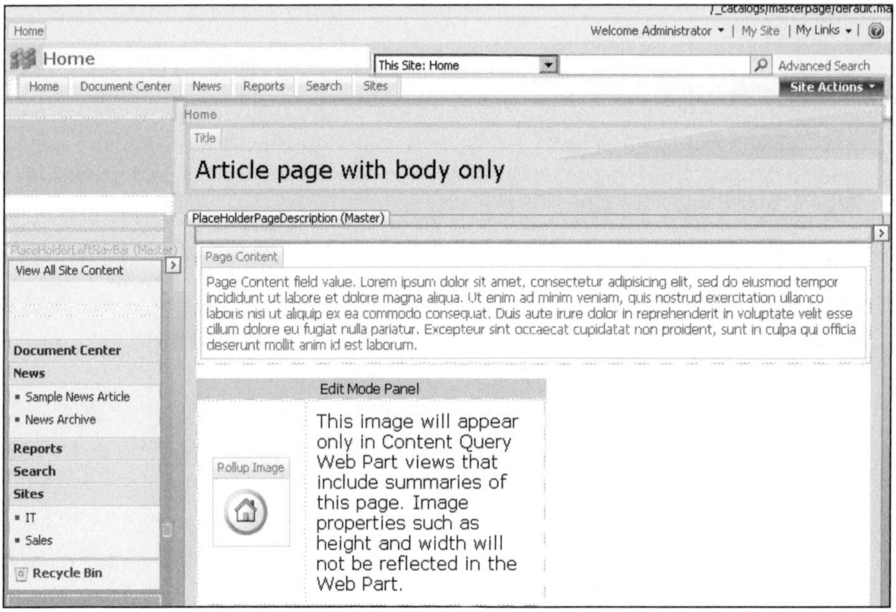

Figure 13-20

a. Place the cursor to the left of the Page Content control (it may be easier using the arrow keys on the keyboard).

b. From the Toolbox pane at the top right of the page, expand SharePoint Controls and then Content Fields.

c. Right-click on the Byline control and select Insert.

d. Save this page; check it in and publish it, then approve this page.

4. Now open the News site again, and create a news article: Click Site Actions ➪ Create Page and select the layout "Article page with body only." Enter a title and a description, then click Create. The layout page is now displayed, and it also contains the new Byline control you added. Enter some text in the page content control, and enter your name in the Byline, then click Publish. Verify that the article has the correct layout; if not, edit the layout again.

Finally, let's look at how you create a new layout file from scratch. In the following example, you will create a layout file named `My Layout.aspx`, associated with the content type Article Page.

Try It Out Create a New Layout File

1. Open the Master Pages and Page Layouts Gallery, as described earlier.

2. Click New and then enter these values:

    a. **Content Type Group:** Page Layout Content Types.

    b. **Content Type Name:** Article Page.

    c. **URL Name:** MyLayout.

    d. **Title:** "My Layout."

    e. **Description:** "This is a demo layout."

    f. Click OK to save and close the page layout.

3. The new layout file is stored along with the other page layouts. By default, it will be checked out. Open its quick menu, and select Edit in Microsoft Office SharePoint Designer.

4. The empty page layout file opens in SPD. Now add the controls you want for this layout; open the Toolbox pane, and expand SharePoint Controls ➪ Content Fields. As usual with HTML-formatted pages, it is easiest to create a table to get control over where these content fields will be located. Click the menu options Table ➪ Insert Table. Then drag the content fields to this table.

5. When you're done, save the page layout, check it in, and publish it, then approve it.

6. Open the News site and create a new news article, based on My Layout; enter a title and a description, and click Create (see Figure 13-21). Finally, add some content to this page to verify that the layout works as expected.

As you can see, it is easy to start customizing both Master Pages and page layout files. But you can do a lot more than these simple examples demonstrate. Microsoft has some excellent articles written by Patrick Tisseghem regarding customizing layout files that are a good start for your new career as a design freak — check out these articles:

```
http://msdn2.microsoft.com/en-us/office/aa830818.aspx
http://msdn2.microsoft.com/en-us/office/aa830815.aspx
http://msdn2.microsoft.com/en-us/office/aa830817.aspx
```

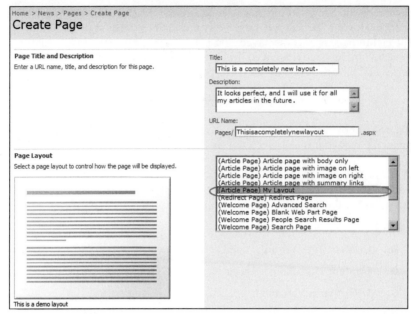

Figure 13-21

Summary

In this chapter you learned that:

- ❑ A Smart Page is another name for a Web Part page in SharePoint.

- ❑ More advanced customization requires MS SharePoint Designer.

- ❑ Only SharePoint Designer 2007 knows how SharePoint works; no other web designer tool has the features required to customize SharePoint 2007.

- ❑ Ghosted sites are the default way that site definitions work. All the settings and the layout for every page in all SharePoint sites are based on a set of files stored on the SharePoint server's file system.

- ❑ Unghosted sites are produced when a page is customized by SharePoint Designer; in this case, SharePoint must store the page in the database. The site definition on the file system is no longer used for the page. Instead, everything is stored in the content database.

- ❑ Use the DisableWebDesignFeatures keyword in the Onet.xml file to prohibit a site page from being edited by SharePoint Designer.

- ❑ Examples of basic customization with SharePoint Designer are things like adding extra text, extra buttons, and extra links on a team site.

❑ SharePoint Designer allows you to install complete site packages of unlimited size. This is a very handy way of copying a large site to another SharePoint environment.

❑ Using SharePoint Designer's Report feature, you will get a summary of a given SharePoint site, including a list of broken links and pages that are slow to open.

❑ SharePoint Designer allows you to customize an existing theme in great detail. You can also create new themes.

❑ SharePoint Designer's Data Source and Data view are very powerful tools; they allows even WSS to display content stored in other SharePoint sites and in external sources, such as SQL databases, XML files, and Web services.

❑ The formatting features of Data view are much more advanced than the views available for lists and libraries in SharePoint.

❑ Master Pages are used by both MOSS sites and WSS sites.

❑ WSS sites can still use site themes for controlling the fonts and colors of a site.

❑ Publishing Pages are associated with a content type, such as Article Page.

❑ The layout of Publishing Pages is controlled by page layout files.

❑ All layout files, including Master Pages and Page Layout files, are stored in the Master Page and Page Layouts Gallery, hosted by the top site in a site collection.

In the next and last chapter, you will learn more about backup and restore procedures for SharePoint and how you can move content between different SharePoint environments.

14

Backup and Restore

By now I am sure you agree that SharePoint 2007 is a great product and a fantastic tool for managing information for your organization, regardless of what type of tasks or activities you may have. When a SharePoint project goes from being a test installation into a production environment, it will suddenly contain important information that constantly grows every day. Sooner than you might expect, SharePoint will be a mission-critical application in your environment. How can you protect it? By making backups, of course! As the old SharePoint geek joke goes: "What do you call a SharePoint administrator who does not make backups?" The answer: "Unemployed!"

This chapter tells you how to keep your job as a SharePoint administrator. It starts by describing what information you need to protect and then lists all available options. You will learn how to perform backup and restore procedures. You will also read about other options, such as MS SQL backups and third-party backup tools.

Just remember this: If you do not regularly verify that your backup solution works (that it actually is possible to actually restore data), you can save a lot of time and effort by skipping the backup process completely; the result will be the same. During my 29 years in the computer business, I have seen a large number of backup solutions that do not work when you actually need them! A lot of IT administrators seem to think that it is enough to get some sort of backup solution, manage to get it running (at least one time), and then just relax and be happy. In my experience as a consultant hired by customers to help them deal with disasters, the number of restore failures is close to 50 percent, for many reasons, such as wrongly configured backup procedures, hardware problems, and media problems. Please make sure you don't join this group. Restore the data and make sure that you can read it; you will be surprised how often it will fail the first time you try to restore it. By performing these fire drills regularly, you and your team will gain experience in how to perform a quick restore that actually works; this will help you all sleep better at night, and it will help you retain your jobs.

What Data Should You Protect?

This is a good question to start with. What data do you need to back up in order to be sure that you can survive a catastrophic situation? The answer is that the information that relates to

SharePoint is stored in a lot of places, not only the databases as one may at first assume. This section will describe what you need to know in order to protect the SharePoint environment. There is one golden rule when it comes to SharePoint backups:

> **Rule #1: What you back up is what you can restore!**

In other words, if you make a backup of a site, you will be able to restore that site, and nothing but that site. For example, you will not be able to restore a list or a single document in that site. The consequence is that you will most likely develop a strategy consisting of several backup procedures that all work together, in order to make it possible to restore whatever data has been lost.

The SharePoint Database

All information in all SharePoint sites is stored in the SQL database, including data, configurations, and customizations. SharePoint will use the types of databases in the following table, depending on whether you are using MOSS or WSS.

Database	Content
Content Databases (MOSS and WSS)	All documents, news, links, contacts, calendars, and so on. All Web Parts and their settings. All customization of sites done with SharePoint Designer.
Config Database (MOSS and WSS)	All team site names and their configuration properties. All site collections. All portal sites, including portal areas. All general configuration settings of the SharePoint server.
SSP Content Database (MOSS Only)	Excel service settings, Audience groups, User Profile database with all user properties entered manually or imported from AD, LDAP, or BDC sources. Indexing and search settings.
My Site Content Database (MOSS Only)	All content stored in the personal part of users' My Sites.

Note that SharePoint may have more than one content database, so make sure that all of these databases will be backed up by your procedure, if you perform pure SQL-based backup procedures instead of using any of the special backup tools that exist for SharePoint.

> **Rule #2: Make sure that all of SharePoint's databases are backed up.**

SharePoint Files

If all your databases are backed up, you will be able to restore all data and configurations, as listed in the table in the previous section. But in the event of a total server disaster, you will still lose SharePoint information, since some of it is stored in the file system on the SharePoint server. You may recall from Chapter 4 that there are different types of SharePoint servers, with different roles:

❑ **Front-End Server:** A SharePoint server responsible for one or more roles; see the following table.

❑ **Back-End Server:** The server running the MS SQL database (SQL Express or MS SQL Server).

If you are using separate front-end and back-end servers, you will have to take steps to back up both of them, since both contain vital SharePoint information. The previous section described the information stored on the back-end server (the SQL server). The front-end sever may also contain information regarding what role it has in the SharePoint farm, as listed in the following table.

Front-End Role	Data Stored in the File System of This Server
Web	General SharePoint binary files
	Default site definitions, CSS files and WSS themes
	Customized site definitions
	Customized CSS files
	Customized WSS themes
	Customized Web Part files
	Customized IIS Metabase settings, including virtual servers
Search	General SharePoint binary files
	Copy of Index files (used by the search engine)
Index	General SharePoint binary files
	Index files generated by the crawler process
Excel Services	General SharePoint binary files
Central Administration	General SharePoint binary files

> **In a Single-Server or Small Farm scenario all these roles run on the same SharePoint server.**

The conclusion is that the SharePoint server running the Web role is very important, if you have customized your environment. If this information is lost, you will have to redo all branding and customization, and this requires that all these changes have been documented. (I am still waiting to see a SharePoint environment that is completely documented, including the IIS settings. Promise me that you will take the first approach, okay?)

If the Search server crashes, there is no real worry; just reinstall the SharePoint binaries, and the index files will be copied from the Index server again.

If the Index server crashes, it may be a problem, depending on how important the search process is for your users. The solution if there is no backup is to rescan all data sources. This may take a long time, if there is a large data volume, and during this time users cannot trust that the search results they get are complete, since all data may not yet have been crawled.

If the server running Excel Services or Central Administration crashes, just reinstall the SharePoint binaries; there is no specific data stored on this server.

> **Rule #3: Make sure to back up the file system and the IIS Metabase on the front-end servers.**

Backup Options

As you should understand from the previous sections, you should think carefully about how to design your backup plan. It is may be more complicated than you at first may expect, especially if you want to have multiple options for the restore process. Still, it is a very easy and manageable task when you know how to do it and what tools to use. SharePoint comes with several tools that you can use for backing up the most important SharePoint information:

- ❏ **STSADM:** Will do backup and restore complete site collections, plus single subsites.

- ❏ **SharePoint Central Administration's backup tool:** Will do backup and restore of complete SharePoint environment or single web applications

> **SMIGRATE, which was used in SharePoint 2003 for backing up single sites, has now been replaced by new commands in the STSADM tool.**

You should learn to use these two tools, since they are focused on different backup scenarios, but remember that they will only serve to back up SharePoint data in the SQL database, plus in the case of the Backup feature in the Central Administration tool also the index files. Besides these tools that come with SharePoint, there are also several commercial backup solutions for both WSS and MOSS; at the end of this chapter you will learn more about some of these.

Moving and Copying Information

Sometimes you need to move or copy information, such as a site, a list or a single document. For example, say that you are developing a team site on a test server and after determining that it works as expected, you want to move it to the production environment. Another example is when you want to restore a single document that was accidentally deleted. There are several methods to do that, and almost all of them use these backup and restore procedures.

The exceptions are when you want to move or copy a list or library, a list item, or a single document between two sites. In this case, you have these options:

❑ Move/Copy single documents, for example, a MS Word file. Use any of these methods:

  ❑ Using the Explorer View, you can right-click a document and select Copy, then open the destination library in an Explorer View and select Paste.

  ❑ Use web folders mapped to each library, then copy and paste between those folders like any standard file folders.

  ❑ Open the document in MS Word, then save it in the destination library.

> **Rule #4: You can only copy the latest version of a document, not its complete version history.**

❑ Move/Copy single list items, for example a customer contact:

  ❑ Open the Contact list using the Datasheet view, right-click the contact and select Save, then open the destination list in the Datasheet view, right-click, and select Paste.

  ❑ Open the Contact list using the Datasheet view, right-click the contact, and select Save, then open the destination list in the Datasheet view, right-click on the last line (marked with an asterisk), and select Paste.

❑ Move/Copy a complete library, for example a document library:

  ❑ To another site in the *same site collection*: Click Modify settings and columns for the library to be moved, then select Save document library as template, and give it a name and a description, make sure to check Include Content, and click OK. Open site to which the library will be copied; click Create in the top menu bar, select the template, and give it a new name.

  ❑ To *another site collection*: Click Modify settings and columns for the library to be moved, select Save document library as template, give it a name and a description, make sure to check Include Content, and click OK. On the following page, click on the link List Template Gallery, then click the template name for the list, and select Save. Next, open the top-level site for the site collection the list will be copied to: Click Site Settings ➪ Go to Site Administration ➪ Manage List Template Gallery and click Upload Template. Select the previously saved file, and click Save and Close. Then go to the site where you want to place the library and click Create. Your copied library is listed in the Document Library section.

  ❑ Moving a library with more than 500 MB of content: Save the library as a template as described above, but do not check Include Content. Continue to import that template into the other site collection. Now use the previous technique to move single documents and move (or copy) all documents from the old library to the new one.

> **Rule #5: A template for a list or library can only contain up to 500 MB of content.**

❏ Move/Copy a complete list, for example a Task list:

    ❏ For lists with less than 500 MB of content, use either of the first two options for moving and copying a complete library.

    ❏ Moving a list with *more than 500 MB* of content: Create a view that shows all the columns you want to move with the list, and then open the list using that new view. Click the Actions button, and click Export to Spreadsheet. In Excel save the list as an Excel file. Go to the site where you want to place the list. Click Create in the top menu, and then select Import Spreadsheet. Give the new list a name, and enter saved file in the File Location and click Import. In Excel, use the Range Type "List Range," and for the Select Range field pick the only option available, then click Import. The complete list, including column definitions, will be copied. Note that this method will not copy any special views; you will have to recreate them (or save the list as an empty template and create the new list using that template, then use Excel to export and import the list content).

Rule #6: Use Excel for moving or copying lists greater than 500 MB.

There are also third-party tools that may help you move single documents and lists; for example, DocAve from AvePoint (`www.avepoint.com`) and SPManager from NSE (`www.tnse.com`); later in this chapter more information is provided about these tools.

Backup with STSADM

The same tool as you have seen described several times in this book when discussing site templates and Web Parts can also be used for backup and restore procedures. It is a fast and "full-fidelity" procedure; that is, it will exactly restore the sites you backed up, including security settings and personal site views. This tool has some limitations and behaviors you must be aware of, such as:

❏ It can back up and restore a complete farm, a single site collection, or a single site.

❏ The result will be stored as a file. STSADM cannot write to other backup media.

❏ It must be executed on the SharePoint server.

❏ You must be a SharePoint server administrator to run STSADM.

❏ This is a command-line tool. There is no graphical user interface included for this tool.

There is a free graphical interface for STSADM 2007; see the section "Tools for STSADM" later in this chapter.

This is the premier tool for all backup scenarios in SharePoint 2007, for both WSS 3.0 and MOSS 2007 installations. You should invest some time learning how to use this tool and make sure that you understand how to both back up and restore data. Since it has more than 170 operations (or commands), it is almost impossible to remember all the arguments each operation requires, but the tool referred to above will make it much easier.

Preparing for STSADM

STSADM.EXE is stored away deep down in the file system, or to be exact in this folder:

```
C:\Program Files\Common Files\Microsoft Shared\web server extensions\12\BIN
```

As described in Chapter 2, you should add the file path to this folder to the system path variable to avoid having to type the long path above every time you need to run STSADM. This is how to add the path to STSADM to the PATH system variable:

Try It Out   Update the PATH System Variable

1.   Start Windows Explorer, and navigate to the path for the STSADM as given above. Right-click on the file path in the Address field, and select Copy.

2.   Click Start to see the Windows Start menu.

3.   Right-click on My Computer, and select Properties.

4.   Switch to the Advanced tab, and click on the Environment Variables button.

5.   In the lower pane named System Variables, locate PATH and click Edit.

6.   Go to the end of the current list in Variable value (use the END key or the right arrow on the keyboard). Type in a semicolon (;) as a separator, and paste the path you copied in step 1 above. Then click OK three times to save this modification and close all dialog boxes.

Test it by opening a command window (Start ⇨ Run and type **Cmd**); type **STSADM** in this command window. If you get a long list of options, then you did it right. If not, repeat these steps and make sure to do it exactly as described.

Running the STSADM Backup

Remember that this tool can back up complete farms, single site collections, or single sites. Let us start with an example of how to back up the site collection for the IT department with the following URL to the top-level site: http://srv1/sites/it. You then follow the steps in the Try It Out.

Try It Out   Back Up Site Collections with STSADM

1.   Log on to the SharePoint server as the administrator.

2.   Locate a file folder where the backup file generated by STSADM will be stored; in this example, you use C:\Bkup. Note that in a real-world scenario you would more likely save the backup files to another computer instead of the local disk, as in this example!

3.   Open a command window and run the following command; remember that the URL points to the top site of the IT site collection:

```
Stsadm -o Backup -url http://srv1/sites/it -filename c:\bkup\wss-back.bak
```

4.   When the backup is completed, you will find the file wss-back.bak in the folder C:\bkup.

Tools for STSADM

There is a great add-on for STSADM 2007 that gives a graphical user interface on top of STSADM, which will make it much easier to use it, especially for an inexperienced SharePoint administrator. The name of this tool is Stsadmwin.exe, and it is free. You can download a copy from this URL: http://blogs.msdn.com/ronalus/archive/2007/01/04/stsadmwin-has-an-2007-version.aspx. (Note that the download link is located at the end of the article.) Using the graphical Stsadmwin 2007 tool for doing the same type of backup as described above will look like the following figure. Just select the Backup operation and the list of command switches shows "URL," "Filename," and "Overwrite;" enter the values for the command switches, and click either Submit to execute this command or Compose to see the complete command string, as depicted in Figure 14-1.

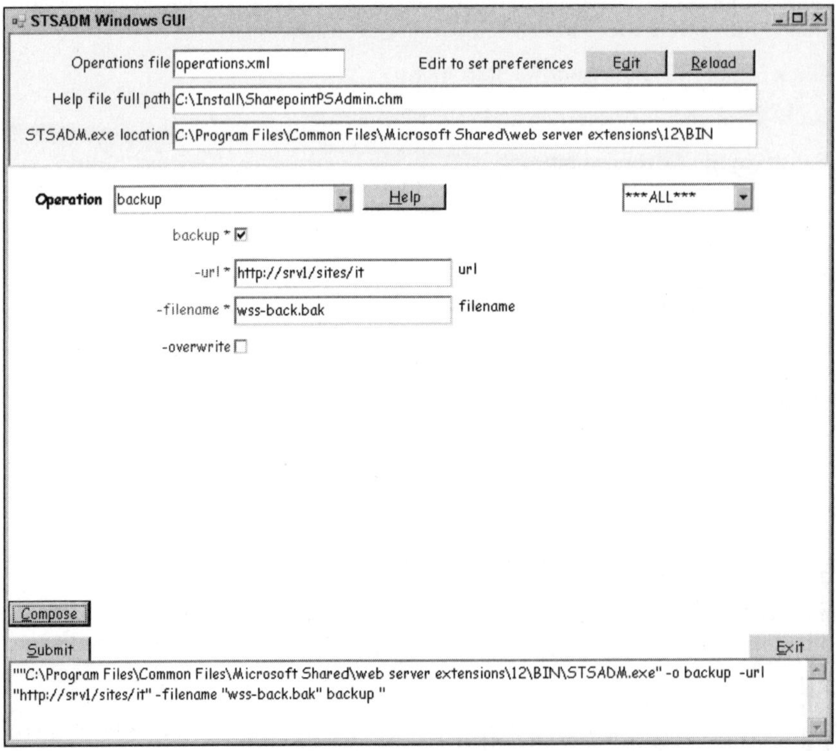

Figure 14-1

This tool is also an excellent way of learning all the commands of STSADM; just select an Operation, and you will see its command switches. Play with this tool, and you will be surprised how much STSADM can do for you. In fact, all you can do with the SharePoint Administrative Tool can be done with STSADM; it even has some commands not available in SharePoint Central Administration, such as Backup and Restore, plus Export and Import! If you have been working with STSADM in SharePoint 2003, you will find that it now contains no less than 173 commands, as listed in the following table.

Command	Command	Command
activatefeature	creategroup	email
activateformtemplate	createsite	enablecmsurlredirect
addalternatedomain	createsiteinnewdb	enablessc
addcontentdb	createssp	enumalternatedomains
adddataconnectionfile	createweb	enumcontentdbs
add-ecsfiletrustedlocation	databaserepair	?enumdataconnectionfile dependants
add-ecssafedataprovider	deactivatefeature	enumdataconnectionfiles
?add-ecstrusteddata connectionlibrary	deactivateformtemplate	enumdeployments
add-ecsuserdefinedfunction	deleteadminvs	enumexemptuseragents
addexemptuseragent	deletealternatedomain	enumformtemplates
addpath	deletecmsmigrationprofile	enumgroups
addpermissionpolicy	deleteconfigdb	enumroles
addsolution	deletecontentdb	enumservices
addtemplate	deletegroup	enumsites
adduser	deletepath	enumsolutions
addwppack	deletepermissionpolicy	enumssp
addzoneurl	deletesite	enumssptimerjobs
?allowuserformwebservice proxy	deletesolution	enumsubwebs
allowwebserviceproxy	deletessp	enumtemplates
associatewebapp	deletessptimerjob	enumusers
authentication	deletetemplate	enumwppacks
backup	deleteuser	enumzoneurls
backuphistory	deleteweb	execadmsvcjobs
binddrservice	deletewppack	export
blockedfilelist	deletezoneurl	extendvs
canceldeployment	deploywppack	extendvsinwebfarm
changepermissionpolicy	deploysolution	forcedeletelist
copyappbincontent	disablessc	formtemplatequiescestatus
createadminvs	displaysolution	getadminport
createcmsmigrationprofile	editcmsmigrationprofile	?getdataconnectionfile property
	editcontentdeploymentpath	
	editssp	

Command	Command	Command
getformsserviceproperty	?remove-ecstrusteddata connectionlibrary	setholdschedule
getformtemplateproperty	?remove-ecsuserdefined function	setlogginglevel
getproperty		setpolicyschedule
getsitedirectoryscanschedule	removeexemptuseragent	setproperty
getsitelock	removeformtemplate	setrecordsrepositoryschedule
geturlzone	removesolutiondeploymentlock	setsearchandprocessschedule
import	renameserver	setsharedwebserviceauthn
installfeature	renameweb	setsitedirectoryscanschedule
listlogginglevels	restore	setsitelock
?listregisteredsecurity trimmers	restoressp	setsspport
localupgradestatus	retractsolution	setworkflowconfig
managepermissionpolicylevel	retractwppack	siteowner
migrateuser	runcmsmigrationprofile	spsearch
osearch	runcontentdeploymentjob	spsearchdiacriticsensitive
osearchdiacriticsensitive	scanforfeatures	sync
preparetomove	setadminport	syncsolution
profilechangelog	setapppassword	unextendvs
profiledeletehandler	?setbulkworkflowtask processingschedule	uninstallfeature
provisionservices	setconfigdb	unquiescefarm
quiescefarm	?setcontentdeploymentjob schedule	unquiesceformtemplate
quiescefarmstatus		unregistersecuritytrimmer
quiesceformtemplate	?setdataconnectionfile property	unregisterwsswriter
reconvertallformtemplates	setdefaultssp	updateaccountpassword
refreshdms	set-ecsexternaldata	updatealerttemplates
refreshsitedms	set-ecsloadbalancing	updatefarmcredentials
registersecuritytrimmer	set-ecsmemoryutilization	upgrade
registerwsswriter	set-ecssecurity	upgradeformtemplate
removedataconnectionfile	set-ecssessionmanagement	upgradesolution
removedrservice	set-ecsworkbookcache	upgradetargetwebapplication
?remove-ecsfiletrustedloca-tion	setformsserviceproperty	uploadformtemplate
remove-ecssafedataprovider	setformtemplateproperty	userrole
		verifyformtemplate

As you can see, STSADM is a very powerful tool that can assist you in most types of administrative tasks, not just backup and restore scenarios. To learn more about this tool, you can search www .microsoft.com for "stsadm 2007;" two good articles to start with are listed below:

❑ www.microsoft.com/technet/technetmag/issues/2007/01/CommandPrompt/ default.aspx

❑ http://technet2.microsoft.com/Office/en-us/library/ab9653b9-de50-4407-8025-1c415bc67c041033.mspx?mfr=true

And it does not stop here — you can actually create custom commands for STSADM 2007, since it is extensible! For example, you can add a custom command that enumerates all tasks in a Task list, or a command that lists all checked out documents in a document library. You must use Visual Studio .NET for developing these custom commands.

> **A good article about creating custom commands is this:** www.johnholliday.net/ archive/2006/11/04/Extending-STSADM-with-Custom-Commands.aspx.

Backing Up a Single Site

The new version of STSADM even replaces the old Smigrate, which previously was the preferred way of backing up a single site or copying sites between SharePoint servers. The new commands in STSADM are Export for backing up a single site and the Import for restoring the site. Below is a summary of what this new set of commands can do:

❑ It can back up and restore single sites.

❑ It can back up any site including its subsites. It does not have to be the top-level site in the site collection.

❑ It can restore the site permissions (something the old Smigrate could not do).

❑ The result will be stored as a file.

❑ It must be executed on a SharePoint server with a Central Administration tool installed.

❑ You must be the site administrator to run this command.

❑ This is a command line tool. You can schedule it using Windows Tasks.

This is a great tool when you need to make a backup of a single site; for example, when you want to move or copy a site to another SharePoint environment, or to move a site from one site collection to another in the same SharePoint server. In the following example, you will make a backup of a subsite with the URL http://srv1/sitedirectory/it and save the backup file as "it.bak" to the c:\bkup folder. Then you will restore this site to another URL location (http://srv1/sitedirectory/sales/it) and retain the same user permission settings.

Try It Out   **Back Up a Single Site with STSADM**

1. Log on to the SharePoint server as the administrator.

2. Open a command window and run the following command:

```
Stsadm -o export -url http://srv1/sitedirectory/it -includeusersecurity ↵
-filename c:\bkup\it.bak
```

3. Open the c:\bkup folder and verify that your backup file is there, along with a log file.

4. Next, restore this file to the URL http://srv1/sitedirectory/sales/it:

```
Stsadm -o import -url http://srv1/sitedirectory/sales/it ↵
-includeusersecurity -filename c:\bkup\it.bak
```

5. Log on to the new site and verify that it works and that it has the same user permissions.

Backing Up a Complete Farm

This version of STSADM 2007 can back up a complete farm, including index files. This is sometimes referred to as a "catastrophic backup and restore" procedure. This type of process is a backup of all the SharePoint databases on the SQL Server, plus all the files that are related to the indexing system. However, this backup process will not cover IIS configuration settings, modified site definition files, or other direct modifications of the files related to SharePoint are stored in the file system. Be sure to run a complete backup of these other files and IIS configurations (such as the Metabase) as well.

When running a complete farm backup, you can select either a full backup or an incremental backup (i.e., only changes). This type of backup is a replacement for the backup process described later in this chapter in the section Backup with the Central Administration Tool. In fact, each time you run this backup process, it will be listed in the Central Administration tool under the Backup and restore history page. Following is a step-by-step instruction on how to perform a full backup of a SharePoint farm and save these backup files to the c:\bkup folder, plus how to check the status of this process in the SharePoint Central Administration tool.

Try It Out   **Back Up a Complete Farm with STSADM**

1. Log on to the SharePoint server as the administrator.

2. Open a command window and run the following command:

```
Stsadm -o backup directory c:\bkup -backupmethod full
```

3. Open the c:\bkup folder and verify that it contains a newly created folder starting with "SPBR" and an index number.

4. Open SharePoint Central Administration, and switch to the Operations page; click "Backup and restore history" in the Backup and Restore section. The backup process you started in step 2 should be listed here.

> When running this backup process, you will see a lot of details listed. To stop STADM from showing these details, add the command switch "-o quiet" at the end of step 2.

Scheduling the Backup Process

For scheduled backup procedures you need to run STSADM, since the backup procedure in SharePoints Central Administration tool cannot be scheduled. For example, say that you want to schedule a backup job of the complete SharePoint farm at 04:00 am every day, saving these files to the location \\srv2\bkup, and without listing any details. The following Try It Out shows how to configure that.

Try It Out   **Schedule Backup Procedures with STSADM**

1. Log on to the SharePoint server as the administrator.

2. Open Windows Scheduler: Starts ➪ All Programs ➪ Accessories ➪ System Tools ➪ Scheduled Tasks, then enter these settings:

   a. Click File ➪ New ➪ Scheduled Task.

   b. Enter a name for this task, for example, **MOSS Backup**.

   c. Double-click on this new task to open and configure it (see Figure 14-2).

   d. **Run:** `stsadm -o backup directory \\srv2\bkup -backupmethod full -quiet`.

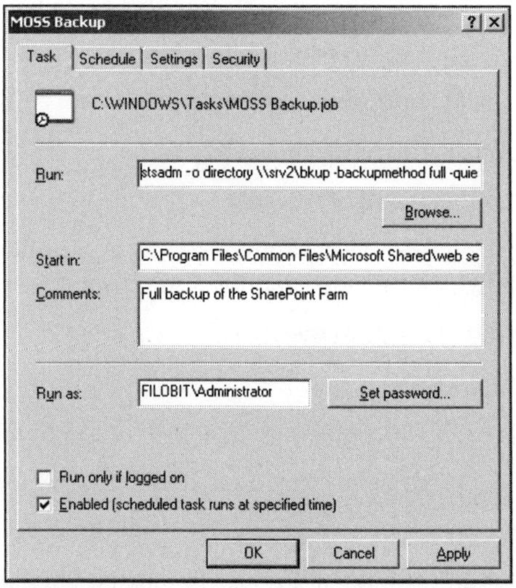

Figure 14-2

e. **Start In:** `C:\Program Files\Common Files\Microsoft Shared\web server extensions\12\bin`.

f. Switch to the Schedule tab, then enter 04.00 am as the daily start time.

g. Click OK to save and close the scheduled task.

h. **Test this scheduled task:** Right-click on the Moss Backup task, and select Run. Then wait for a short period, and then look in the `\\srv2\bkup` folder to see if there is a newly created folder starting with the letters "SPBR;" if so, the scheduled task works fine.

> This backup process will also truncate the transaction log files in MS SQL Server, which was not the case in SharePoint 2003. This will eliminate the risk of filling the disk on the SQL server with transaction log files.

Backup with the Central Administration Tool

SharePoint Central Administration comes with a graphical user interface for backup and restore operations. Its focus is to create complete backups of SharePoint's farms (portal sites), including all WSS sites, personal sites, and workspaces. This backup process does exactly the same thing as running STSADM with the `Directory` switch; it also will back up the index files, created by the crawler process, and truncate the SQL Server transaction log files. The features and limitations of this backup procedure are:

❑ Can back up complete SharePoint environment, including all MOSS and WSS sites.

❑ Can back up single web applications, but not specific site collections or sites.

❑ Can make full backups or incremental backups.

❑ Must be executed on the SharePoint server.

❑ The Windows SharePoint Services Administrative Service must be running on all SharePoint servers (note that Single Server installations don't have this service started by default).

❑ Requires Administrative rights to the SharePoint server.

❑ This is a full-fidelity backup tool.

❑ Must save the backup files to a file share that ends in "$" or an IP address.

❑ This backup procedure cannot be scheduled. Use STSADM for scheduled backups

This process (along with its `STSADM -o backup Directory` counterpart) is the most complete backup utility that ships with SharePoint; it will make a backup of all the database files in the MS SQL server and the index files. The only thing it does not back up is any customizations of SharePoint files such as site definitions, CSS files, and XML files stored on the SharePoint servers file system, plus modifications of the virtual IIS web servers, such as SSL certificates.

Making Backups with SharePoint Central Administration

This graphical interface can be used for running backups and restore procedures. You can select what to back up by selecting the components listed in the left pane of the backup window. It will display a number of objects that you can select to back up, such as the complete farm or a specific web application. For example, say you want to make a complete backup of the SharePoint farm, including all MOSS sites, all WSS sites, and the index files. The following Try It Out shows how you do it.

Try It Out   **Run a Complete Backup Using the Central Administration Backup Process**

1. Log on to the SharePoint server as the full SharePoint administrator.

2. Start the SharePoint Central Administration tool.

3. Switch to the Operations tab.

4. In the Backup and Restore section, click Perform a backup.

5. This is step 1 (of 2): Select what to back up. In this example check Farm; note that all options are now marked. Then click Continue to Backup Options (see Figure 14-3).

6. This is step 2: On this page, you define the type of backup (Full or Incremental) and the location where to store the backup files. In this example, select a Full backup and save these files in the \\srv2\bkup folder. Also note that the size of the data to be backed up is listed on this page (see Figure 14-4).

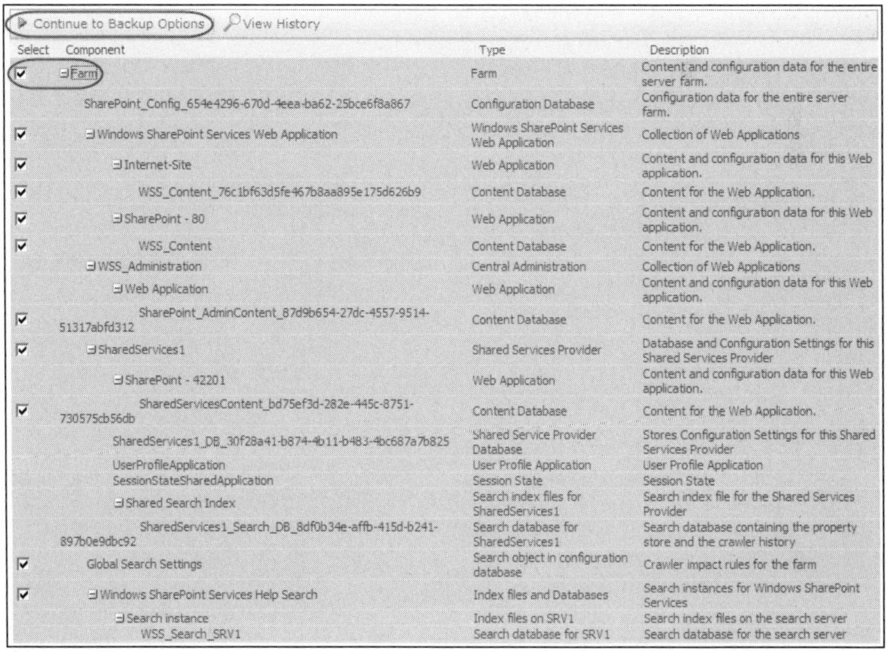

Figure 14-3

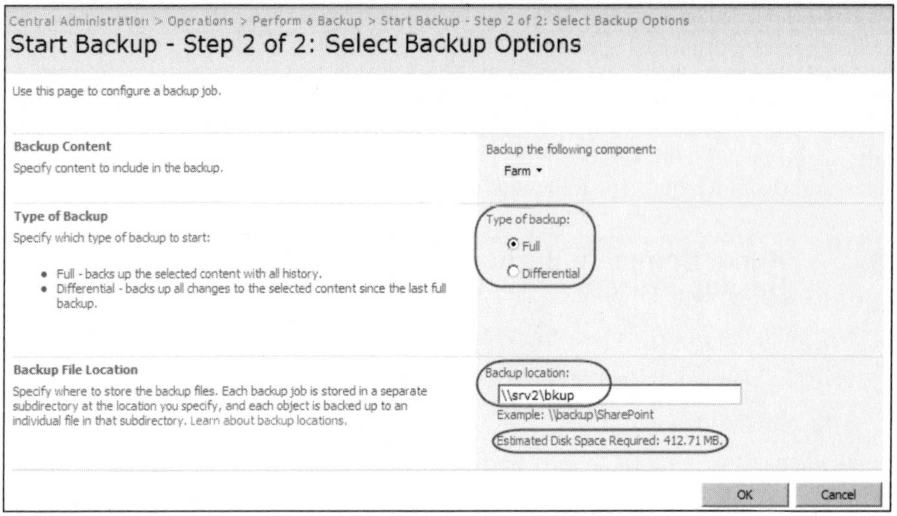

Figure 14-4

7. Click OK to start the backup process. This will open the Backup and Restore Status page. This page can also be opened from the Operations page and the link Backup and Restore job status.

8. When the backup is completed, you can find the backup files in the `\\srv2\bkup` folder in this example. Open that folder and you will see one file named `spbrtoc.xml`. This is a file that contains the information needed to later do a restore; make sure not to lose this file! If you open this file, it will look something like this:

```xml
<?xml version="1.0" encoding="utf-8"?>
<SPBackupRestoreHistory>
    <SPHistoryObject>
        <SPId>75e3ad46-a64e-4941-a132-be05c21107c4</SPId>
        <SPRequestedBy>FILOBIT\Administrator</SPRequestedBy>
        <SPBackupMethod>Full</SPBackupMethod>
        <SPRestoreMethod>None</SPRestoreMethod>
        <SPStartTime>02/07/2007 21:11:18</SPStartTime>
        <SPFinishTime>02/07/2007 21:17:49</SPFinishTime>
        <SPIsBackup>True</SPIsBackup>
        <SPBackupDirectory>\\srv2\bkup\spbr0000\</SPBackupDirectory>
        <SPDirectoryName>spbr0000</SPDirectoryName>
        <SPDirectoryNumber>0</SPDirectoryNumber>
        <SPTopComponent>Farm</SPTopComponent>
        <SPTopComponentId>26cfc071-9b35-478c-82d7-794dd892ef4e</SPTopComponentId>
        <SPWarningCount>0</SPWarningCount>
        <SPErrorCount>0</SPErrorCount>
    </SPHistoryObject>
</SPBackupRestoreHistory>
```

9. The line above that begins with `SPBackupDirectory` points to the location for the backup files, usually a subfolder under the folder where the `spbrtoc.xml` file is stored. If you look in that folder, you will see something similar to this:

```
2007-02-07   22:11            2,280 00000000.bak
2007-02-07   22:11            1,548 00000001.bak
2007-02-07   22:11           19,728 00000002.bak
2007-02-07   22:11           79,014 00000003.bak
2007-02-07   22:11            1,893 00000004.bak
2007-02-07   22:11           78,970 00000005.bak
2007-02-07   22:11            1,896 00000006.bak
2007-02-07   22:11           15,540 00000007.bak
2007-02-07   22:11           56,160 00000008.bak
2007-02-07   22:11            2,095 00000009.bak
2007-02-07   22:11            2,552 0000000A.bak
2007-02-07   22:11           76,326 0000000B.bak
2007-02-07   22:11            1,896 0000000C.bak
2007-02-07   22:11            1,061 0000000D.bak
2007-02-07   22:11            1,081 0000000E.bak
2007-02-07   22:11            1,809 0000000F.bak
2007-02-07   22:11            1,174 00000010.bak
2007-02-07   22:11            2,250 00000011.bak
2007-02-07   22:11            1,049 00000012.bak
2007-02-07   22:11              256 00000013.bak
2007-02-07   22:11        8,279,552 00000014.bak
2007-02-07   22:11            1,118 00000015.bak
2007-02-07   22:11       15,038,976 00000016.bak
2007-02-07   22:11            1,118 00000017.bak
2007-02-07   22:12       61,150,720 00000018.bak
2007-02-07   22:12               55 00000019.bak
2007-02-07   22:13       60,269,056 0000001A.bak
2007-02-07   22:13            1,118 0000001B.bak
2007-02-07   22:13       12,213,760 0000001C.bak
2007-02-07   22:13        7,824,896 0000001D.bak
2007-02-07   22:15       30,389,760 0000001E.bak
2007-02-07   22:16       38,995,456 0000001F.bak
2007-02-07   22:15   <DIR>          82a09d6d-9f0c-49ab-9bc0-1ab725539374
2007-02-07   22:35                0 backupfiles.txt
2007-02-07   22:13   <DIR>          c3c6fa07-3c9f-446a-a579-88e82f559808
2007-02-07   22:17           52,950 spbackup.log
2007-02-07   22:17           42,455 spbackup.xml
```

These are the files that contain the actual data that has been backed up. The file named spbackup.xml is known as the "Manifest file." It is vital for the restore process, since it contains information about how these files relate to each other; make sure not to change this file in any way! It contains the definition of the objects that have been backed up and where this information will be restored in a future restore process.

Restore Procedures

Now you know how to make backups of the SharePoint data; you also know that some information like custom site definitions, CSS files, and XML files are not covered by the standard backup tools that SharePoint provides. These files need to be backed up with the usual file backup procedures; for example, the Windows Backup tool that comes free with Windows 2003 Server, also known as NTBackup.

But the big question is how to restore data from these backups in case of a disaster. The answer to that question depends on what you need to restore, and what type of backup you have. Remember the first golden rule (what you back up is what you can restore); so if you only run an STSADM backup of site collections, then all you can restore is a site collection; that is, you cannot restore just one specific site or library from that backup set. If this is what you need to do, then you must first restore to a temporary location and then move the data to the production environment.

The following sections describe how to restore different types of data, such as single documents, a site collection, or a complete portal server. Remember that all these descriptions are based on the backup tools that come with SharePoint; later on in this chapter you will learn more about what third-party backup tools can do.

Restoring a Single Item

At long last is the Recycle Bin back in SharePoint. It was introduced in SharePoint Portal Server 2001, and then disappeared in SharePoint Portal Server 2003, and now it is back again; we are all grateful for that! The absolute most common cause for a restore operation in the previous SharePoint version was that a user deleted a document and then wanted it back again. Now this is a breeze, since even the user himself can do this undelete operation of single items, thanks to the Recycle Bin feature available in all sites, both MOSS and WSS. You do not have to activate anything to make this Recycle Bin work; it is enabled by default and works like this:

❑ When a list item, such as a contact, or a library item, such as a document, is deleted, it is copied to the Recycle Bin.

❑ If a complete list or library is deleted, it is copied to the Recycle Bin.

❑ A user can open the Recycle Bin and restore the object.

❑ The deleted object will stay in the Recycle Bin for 30 days by default.

❑ After 30 days, the object is moved from the site's Recycle Bin to a site collection Recycle Bin.

❑ Only the Site Administrator can restore objects from the site collection Recycle Bin.

> **Note that the Recycle Bin cannot restore deleted sites or site collections.**

You can configure how long SharePoint will store deleted items in the Recycle Bin; this setting is set per web application. That is, if there are multiple site collections using the same web application, they will all have the same Recycle Bin settings.

Try It Out   Configure the Recycle Bin

1.   Log on as the SharePoint administrator, and start SharePoint Central Administration.

2.   Switch to the Application Management page.

3.   In the SharePoint Web Application Management section, click Web application general settings.

4.   On the next page, enter the following values (see also Figure 14-5).

a.   At the top, make sure that you are looking at the right web application; if not, click on its URL, and select Change Web Application.

b.   At the end of this page is the Recycle Bin section. Configure the option Recycle Bin status: (Default: On). This setting controls whether the Recycle Bin feature is available or not on the web application, and therefore its site collections.

c.   Use the Delete items in the Recycle Bin to define how long items will stay in the Recycle Bin that the user can use (Default: 30 days).

d.   Use the Second Stage Recycle Bin to define how long deleted items will stay in the site collection's Recycle Bin that only the administrator can use (Default: 50 percent of the disk quota for the web application. For example, if you have allotted 1000 MB of space for the web application, SharePoint will add 50 percent more (i.e., 500 MB) to that quota (a total quota of 1500 MB) to be used for the second-level Recycle Bin. When this limit is exceeded, the oldest items will be removed from the second stage Recycle Bin.

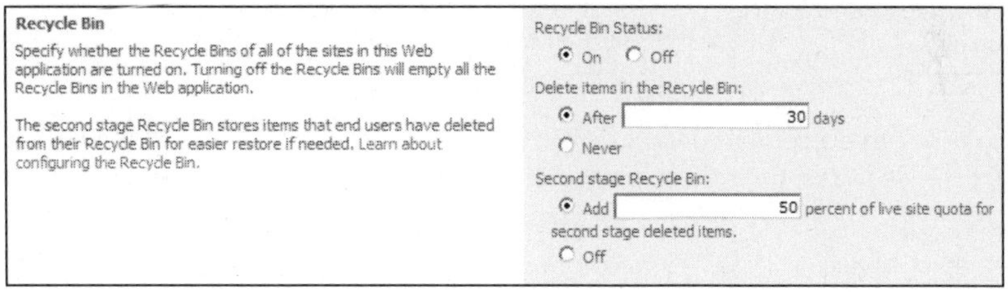

Figure 14-5

To recover items, the user simply opens the Recycle Bin, using the link in the Quick Launch bar, then selects the item to be restored and clicks Restore Selection. To recover items that have been removed from the first stage Recycle Bin, you must be a site collection administrator. The following example describes how to restore items from the second stage Recycle Bin.

Try It Out   Recover Items from the Second Stage Recycle Bin

1.   Log on as the site collection administrator, and open the top site in the site collection where the item is to be restored.

2.   Click Site Actions ⇨ Site Settings ⇨ Modify All Site Settings (or just Site Actions ⇨ Site Settings for a WSS site), then click Recycle bin in the Site Collection Administration section.

3.   All deleted items will now be listed; select the one to restore, and click the Restore Selection button. Note that the Quick Launch bar at the left also has a link for displaying items that the user has manually selected to be removed from a first stage Recycle Bin. If you don't find the item you are looking for in the first list, click the link Deleted from end user Recycle Bin.

> **Rule #7: By using the Recycle Bin any item, including a previous version, can be restored.**

What happens if you need to restore a single document or a list after they have been deleted from the Recycle Bin, and all you have is a backup of the complete site collection? If this is the case, you can restore the site collection as a new site collection on the production server and then move the data the same way as described earlier in this chapter. The big advantage of this restore technique is that you do not need a dedicated restore server. Follow the steps in the next Try It Out for this type of restore process.

Try It Out   **Restore a Single Document from an STSADM Backup**

1. Find the latest backup file containing the document. In this example, the file is stored in the backup for the site collection IT: `C:\Bkup\it.bak`.

2. Since the backup file contains a complete site collection, you most likely don't want to restore this information back to the original location, since that would overwrite a lot of data. But you can restore it to another site collection on the same SharePoint server. Before you can do that restore, you must first create a new content database for this new site collection: Open a command prompt window and enter the following command (on one line).

```
STSADM.exe -o createsiteinnewdb -url "http://srv1/sites/Restore" -ownerlogin ↵
"filobit\administrator" -owneremail administrator@filobit.com
```

3. You now have a content database for restoring any site collection to the URL address above. The next step is to run the restore procedure: Open a command prompt and type (on one line):

```
STSADM -o restore -url http://srv1/sites/restore ↵
-filename c:\bkup\it.bak -overwrite
```

4. The temporary site collection is now active and has the exact same settings as the original site collection. Use a web browser to open the site in this collection where the document is stored, locate the missing document and copy it to the production site, as described in the earlier section in this chapter "Moving and Copying Information".

> If you cannot open the newly restored site collection, then open a command window and run an `iisreset`.

5. When the document is restored to the production environment, this temporary site collection can safely be deleted, if needed. A quick way to do this is to use STSADM (see below). Just make sure to delete the right site collection! Note that you don't need to delete this site collection; you can still restore new site collections to it, as long as you use the switch `-overwrite` to overwrite it in step 3.

```
STSADM -o deletesite -url http://srv1/sites/restore
```

Next time you need to restore a site collection you don't have to create a content database first; that is, you can omit step 2 above. This process can be used to restore any site collection in the future.

What if you only have a backup set created with the Central Administration tool and need to restore a single document? This requires a separate server; there is no way to restore that information to a temporary location on the production server, as you could for STSADM backups. Use the following steps to restore a single document from a backup made in SharePoint Central Administration.

Try It Out   **Restore a Single Document from a Backup Made with SharePoint Central Administration**

1. Find a temporary server that you can use as a temporary SharePoint server. Note that you can use MS Virtual PC or VM-Ware when creating this server; it does not have to be a physical server.

2. Install the same SharePoint release, including service packs, as on the production server. You can use a local SQL Server in this temporary environment, regardless of how the production server is configured. Make sure to install the MS SQL Server Client Tools and apply the same MS SQL Server service packs as in the production environment.

> The temporary server doesn't need to have the same name as the production server!

3. Locate the latest backup files, in this example in C:\Bkup.

4. Start SharePoint Central Administration and switch to the Operations page, then select the link Restore from backup in the Backup and Restore section.

5. The restore process consists of four steps:

    a. Enter the backup location; for example, \\srv2\bkup. Click OK.

    b. You will see a list of all previous backup instances stored in that backup location (see Figure 14-6). Select the backup instance, and click Continue Restore Process.

Central Administration > Operations > Backup and Restore History

Restore from Backup - Step 2 of 4: Select Backup to Restore

Use this page to manage the history logs for backup and restore operations.

Results 1-1 of 1 jobs.

| ⊘ Continue Restore Process | 🗀 Change Directory |

Select	Type	Method	Top Component	Start Time	Finish Time	Failure Message	Requested By	Backup ID	Directory
⊙	Backup	Full	Farm	2/7/2007 10:11 PM	2/7/2007 10:17 PM		FILOBIT\Administrator	75e3ad46-a64e-4941-a132-be05c21107c4	\\srv1\bkup\spbr000

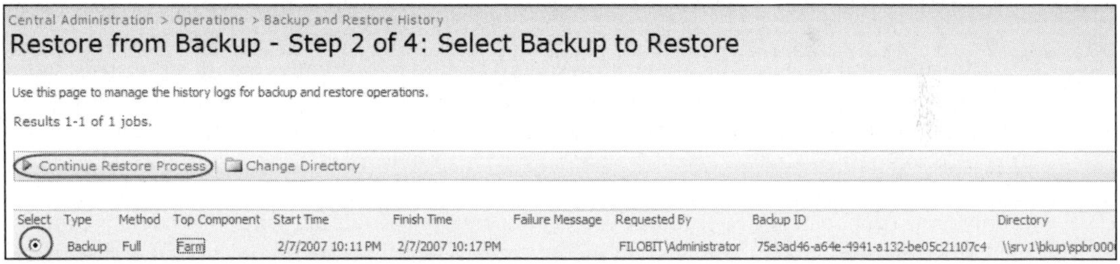

Figure 14-6

    c. Select what to restore from the selected backup instance, for example, the complete farm, then click Continue Restore Process.

    d. Configure how to restore this data, for example do you want to use the same configuration, or do you want to define a new configuration, that is new web applications, databases, and service accounts? This is where you would enter a new SQL Server name, database names, and service accounts, If you have an image of the production environment in a virtual server, such as MS Virtual Server, then you can select Same Configuration, since the restore process will only overwrite the server in your virtual environment. Click OK to start the restore process.

6. When the restore process is completed, open the temporary SharePoint server, locate the file to be restored, and move it using the steps listed earlier in the section "Moving and Copying Information" in this chapter.

All these examples describe how to restore a single document. Use the same steps when restoring single list items, or a single list or library.

Restoring a Single Site

When you want to restore a single site, you will follow almost the same steps as when restoring single items. The only difference is that you can restore items directly to the production server, if you have made a backup of individual sites using STSADM and its export operation. If not, you must restore the site to a temporary storage location and then move it. All scenarios are described below.

For example, say that you accidentally deleted the subsite Projects in the IT site collection; its URL was `http://srv1/sites/it/projects`. You must now restore that site, including all its content. Depending on what type of backup you have available, you will follow different steps, as listed below.

Try It Out   Restore a Single Site Using the STSADM Import Method

1. Locate the backup file for the site, in this example `C:\Bkup\projects.bak`.

2. Open a command prompt window, and enter the following command:

```
Stsadm -o import -url http://srv1/sites/it/projects -filename C:\bkup\projects.bak
```

3. Open the restored site with a web browser; make sure to manually update all security settings. The site is now restored and ready to be used.

If you only have backup of site collections, you cannot restore a single site, since the backup contains a complete site collection. In this case, you must first create a temporary site collection, then use STSADM export method to back up the site to be restored, and finally use the method above.

Try It Out   Restore a Single Site Using STSADM Backups

1. Find the latest backup set containing the site to be restored. In this example this site is stored in the backup for the site collection IT: `C:\Bkup\it.bak`.

2. As described before, a site collection needs a new content database before it can be restored. If you have not done so before, open a command prompt and enter the following command. This will create a content database and associate it with the site collection `http://srv1/sites/restore`.

```
STSADM.exe -o createsiteinnewdb -url "http://srv1/sites/Restore" -ownerlogin ↵
"contoso\administrator" -owneremail administrator@contoso.com
```

3. You now have a content database for restoring any site collection to the URL address above. Next step is to run the restore procedure: Open a command prompt and type (on one line):

```
STSADM -o restore -url http://srv1/sites/restore -filename ↵
c:\bkup\it.bak -overwrite
```

4. The temporary site collection is now active and has the exact same settings as the original site collection. The next step is to make a backup of the single site to be restored. Open a command prompt and type:

```
STSADM -o export -url http://srv1/sites/restore/projects -filename ↵
c:\bkup\projects.bak
```

5. Now you have a backup of the single site Projects. Follow the steps for restoring a single site using an STSADM import operation to copy it back to the production environment.

Finally, if all you have is a backup made by SharePoint Central Administration, you need to follow a similar procedure to the last example. First, restore the backup to a temporary SharePoint server, next make a backup with STSADM's export operation of the single site to be restored, and then restore that site to the production environment, as shown in the following Try It Out.

| Try It Out | Restore a Single Site Using Central Administration Backups |

1. Find a temporary server that you can use as a temporary SharePoint server. Note that you can use MS Virtual PC or VM-Ware when creating this server; it does not have to be a physical server. In this example, the server is named restore-srv.

2. Install the same SharePoint release, including service packs, as the production server. You can use a local SQL server in this temporary environment, regardless of how the production server is configured. Make sure to apply the same MS SQL Server service pack as in the production environment.

3. Locate the latest backup files, in this example in \\srv2\Bkup.

4. Start SharePoint Central Administration, and switch to the Operations page, then select the link Restore from backup, in the Backup and Restore section.

5. The restore process consists of four steps:

   a. Enter the backup location; for example, \\srv2\bkup. Click OK.

   b. You will see a list of all previous backup instances stored in that backup location; select the backup instance, and click Continue Restore Process.

   c. Select what to restore from the selected backup instance, for example, the complete farm, then click Continue Restore Process.

   d. In the final step, you configure how to restore the data; for example, do you want to use the same configuration, or do you want to define a new configuration (i.e., new web applications, databases, and service accounts) ?This is where you would enter a new SQL Server name, database names, and service accounts. If you have an image of the production environment in a virtual server, such as MS Virtual Server, then you can select Same Configuration, since the restore process will only overwrite the server in your virtual environment. Click OK to start the restore process.

6. When the restore process is completed, open the temporary SharePoint server. Locate the file to be restored, and move it using the steps listed earlier in the section "Moving and Copying Information" in this chapter.

7. Open a command prompt and run the following command to make a backup of the site to be restored:

```
STSADM -o export -url http://restore-srv/sites/it/projects -filename ↵
c:\bkup\projects.bak
```

8. Now you have a backup of the single site Projects. Follow the steps described earlier for restoring a single site using an STSADM import operation to copy it back to the production environment.

Restoring a Single Site Collection

If you have to restore a complete site collection, you will need a backup made by STSADM or SharePoint Central Administration's backup process. For example, say that you accidentally delete the complete site collection `http://srv1/sites/it`. You must now restore it. Depending on what type of backup files you have available, you will follow one of these procedures.

Try It Out — Recover a Site Collection Using STSADM

1. Find the latest backup set containing the site to be restored. In this example, this site is stored in the backup for the site collection IT: `C:\Bkup\it.bak`.

2. Since you need to restore the complete site collection, you can do this directly on the production server. Open a command prompt and enter:

```
STSADM -o restore -url http://srv1/sites/it -filename c:\bkup\it.bak -overwrite
```

That was simple, since the backup set contained exactly what you needed to restore. If you only have a backup made with SharePoint Central Administration, you first need to restore to a temporary server and then make a backup of that site collection, and finally restore that site collection to the production server.

Try It Out — Recover a Site Collection Using MOSSBACKUP

1. Find a server that you can use as a temporary SharePoint server. Note that you can use MS Virtual PC or VM-Ware when creating this server; it does not have to be a physical server. In this example the server is named `restore-srv`.

2. Install the same SharePoint release, including service packs, as on the production server. You can use a local SQL server in this temporary environment, regardless of how the production server is configured. Make sure to install the MS SQL Server Client Tools and apply the same MS SQL Server service packs as in the production environment.

3. Locate the latest backup files, in this example in `C:\Bkup`.

4.   Start SharePoint Central Administration, and switch to the Operations page, then select the link Restore from backup, in the Backup and Restore section.

5.   The restore process consists of four steps:

   a.   Enter the backup location; for example, `\\srv2\bkup`. Click OK.

   b.   You will see a list of all previous backup instances stored in that backup location; select the backup instance, and click Continue Restore Process.

   c.   Select what to restore from the selected backup instance; for example, the complete farm, and then click Continue Restore Process.

   d.   Configure how to restore this data; for example, do you want to use the same configuration, or do you want to define a new configuration (i.e., new web applications, databases, and service accounts. This is where you would enter a new SQL Server name, database names, and service accounts). If you have an image of the production environment in a virtual server, such as MS Virtual Server, then you can select Same Configuration, since the restore process will only overwrite the server in your virtual environment. Click OK to start the restore process.

6.   When the restore process is completed, open the temporary SharePoint server, and locate the site collection to be restored. Then open a command prompt and run the following command to make a backup of the site to be restored:

```
STSADM -o backup -url http://restore-srv/sites/it/ -filename c:\bkup\it.bak
```

7.   Now you have a backup of the site collection IT. Since you need to restore a complete site collection, you can do this directly on the production server. Open a command prompt, and enter:

```
STSADM -o restore -url http://srv1/sites/it -filename c:\bkup\it.bak -overwrite
```

Restoring a Complete Portal Server

The final scenario is when you have lost a complete MOSS portal site and need to get it back fast. This requires that you have a backup set of the complete farm made by SharePoint Central Administration. Using other tools such as the MS SQL Server backup utility or third-party backup solutions for SharePoint will also do, and they are described later on in this chapter.

For example, say that you have a portal with the URL `http://srv1`. It contains a large number of site collections and subsites as well. Something happens, and the portal gets corrupted beyond repair. Now, you must restore the complete SharePoint environment. Luckily, you have a full backup made with SharePoint Central Administration last night; now restore the farm by following the steps in the Try It Out below.

Try It Out   Restore a Complete SharePoint Environment Using MOSSBACKUP

1.   Install the same SharePoint release, including service packs, on the same server. Make sure to install the MS SQL Server Client Tools and apply the same MS SQL Server service packs as in the production environment.

2. Locate the latest backup files, in this example in \\srv2\Bkup.

3. Start SharePoint Central Administration and switch to the Operations page, then select the link Restore from backup in the Backup and Restore section.

4. The restore process consists of four steps:

   a. Enter the backup location; for example, \\srv2\bkup. Click OK.

   b. You will see a list of all previous backup instances stored in that backup location; select the backup instance, and click Continue Restore Process.

   c. Select the option to restore the complete farm, then click Continue Restore Process.

   d. Select the option Same Configuration. Click OK to start the restore process. Note that this process may take many hours, or even days, to complete, depending on the volume of data to be restored. As a general rule, it takes about 4 to 5 times longer to perform a restore than to make a backup.

5. Open the restored portal server and make sure that it works.

Making a Backup Plan

A backup plan is very important and something you should make before using SharePoint in a production environment. Exactly how this plan should look varies, depending on a lot of parameters, such as:

❑ What SharePoint edition are you using — WSS alone or MOSS including WSS?

❑ How important is the data stored in SharePoint?

❑ What sites will be most important to protect?

❑ How often are the sites updated?

The description you get here is just general guidelines that you can follow to make your own backup plan. And remember the initial statement in this chapter. If you don't regularly verify that the backups are working, you cannot be sure that your backup plan is working. It is very important that you run fire drills now and then, to see that you actually can restore data. I suggest that you do a test every month and verify that you and your fellow SharePoint administrators can do a restore of:

❑ A single document

❑ A single site

❑ A site collection

❑ The complete portal environment (if you are running MOSS)

Use the following guidelines to write your own backup plan:

1. Document your SharePoint environment, including:

   a. The name of the SharePoint Server(s).

   b. The name of the MS SQL server.

   c.   The URL for the SharePoint environment.

   d.   The IIS Settings, i.e.virtual server and application pool settings.

   e.   The Search and Index Settings (if using MOSS).

   f.   The Audience groups (if using MOSS).

   g.   Any customization of the User Profile settings (if using MOSS).

   h.   The security settings for the portal site areas (if using MOSS).

   i.   All customization of portal sites (if using MOSS).

   j.   A list of all web applications, site collections, and their owners.

   k.   Any nondefault configuration settings of SharePoint.

   l.   A list of all added Web Parts, including where you found them.

   m.   A description of all modified SharePoint files, such as ASPX, CSS, and XML files.

2.   Decide if and when to run the STSADM export operation to protect important sites (like your boss's site) to make it very easy and fast to restore single sites and single items.

3.   Decide if and when to run STSADM to make it easier to restore site collections, sites and single items.

4.   Decide how often to run a full backup using SharePoint Central Administration.

5.   Decide where to store the backup files, if you should overwrite them every time, or what to do with them.

6.   Decide how often to run a file backup on the SharePoint server, including a System State backup that also covers the IIS Metabase. This will make it possible to recover from a complete disk crash.

7.   Document the restore procedures and who is responsible, including their contact information.

8.   Document the fire drills: what to test, how often, and by whom.

I am sure you can think of more things to describe in this backup plan. Just remember that this is a "living" document; it needs to be constantly updated. For example, when you add new Web Part, change any configuration settings, or create new site collections. The perfect place to store this backup plan is, of course, in SharePoint, but this is not a good idea, since you will need it in case of a SharePoint disaster. Make sure to have not one but at least two copies of this backup plan in different locations in case of fire, flooding, or similar disasters.

Third-Party Backup Tools

There are alternatives for the backup tools that come with SharePoint; both specific SharePoint backup utilities, and SharePoint agents for general backup applications. They will often make it easier to do backups and in some cases make it possible to restore things that SharePoint cannot do, such as restoring a specific version of a document.

The purpose of this section is to give you a general overview of these third-party tools to make you aware that they exist and how they can be an alternative to SharePoint's own tools. This is not a complete list of everything that is available, so please do not get upset if I don't mention your favorite tool. As of this writing, only the backup tools from AvePoint are available for SharePoint 2007, but the other tools will most likely be released sometime during 2007, so they are mentioned here as well.

General Backup Agents

Practically all popular backup applications available today know how to back up SharePoint sites besides the file system, MS Exchange, and other applications. Mostly you will need to purchase a special "SharePoint 2007 Agent" to enable these applications to back up and restore SharePoint information. Below is a table with the most common backup tools and their SharePoint add-ons.

Backup Program	SharePoint Add-On	Comment
Veritas BackupExec	For WSS and MOSS 2007	Can restore single items, sites, site collections, and portal sites.
Veritas NetBackup	For WSS and MOSS 2007	Can restore single sites, site collections, and portal sites.
Commvaults Galaxy	For WSS and MOSS 2007	Can restore sites, site collections, portal sites, and individual documents.
Brightstore ArcServe	For WSS and MOSS 2007	Can restore sites, site collections, and portal sites.

Note that there are only two of these general backup products that allow you to restore individual documents, but no version history, web discussions, or lists or list items. To get this type of functionality, you need to look at backup tools specifically designed for SharePoint, such as DocAve.

MS SQL Backup Tools

Since SharePoint uses MS SQL for data storage, it is only natural to think about using the standard backup tools for MS SQL for SharePoint backups as well. And this is definitely true; you can use these SQL tools for SharePoint data. But there are some things you need to be aware of:

❑ Both MS SQL 2000 Server and SQL 2005 Server come with backup tools, but not MS SQL Server 2005 Express Edition; if you use this, you will therefore need a special tool for backups of SharePoint databases.

❑ When using SQL backup tools, you must restore a complete database in case of data loss. In other words, you cannot restore a single site or site collection. Only a complete restore is possible with these tools.

❑ SQL backup tools do not back up files on the SharePoint server, such as the Search and Index files; you will still need to use another backup tool as a complement.

❑ When using SharePoint's standard tools for backups you don't need to use SQL backup tools. All SharePoint data in the SQL database will be secured by SharePoint's own tool. And it works for MS SQL Express databases, too.

It is easy to resolve the first issue above: There are several excellent tools on the market that can be used for backing up MS SQL Server 2005 Express Edition databases, such as Simego's SQL Admin Studio (`http://simego.co.uk`).

The remaining issues in the previous list are harder to resolve. I recommend that you combine any SQL-based backup tool with one or more of the SharePoint tools, such as STSADM, to make it possible to restore single items, lists, or sites when necessary. Today, hardware is most often very reliable and there is very seldom a disk crash. Almost all recovery situations are about restoring single documents, lists, or sometimes complete lists. And the SQL Backup tool will not help you with that. The biggest advantage with SQL backups is that it will back up all data in the SQL server, including SharePoint's databases. So, it is convenient when doing backups, but it is not the best solution when it is time for a restore.

AvePoint Tools

One of the first vendors that developed backup solutions specifically for SharePoint was AvePoint (`www.avepoint.com`). They were also first with a backup solution for SharePoint 2007 and with migration tools for moving content from SharePoint 2003 servers to SharePoint 2007. Their main product, DocAve, is today one of the most popular tools due to its very advanced restore options, and it is often recommended by Microsoft as the solution for organizations that require a way to recover single documents, including the complete version history. Note that DocAve by itself is not a substitute for a complete SharePoint backup. Its objective is to offer the administrator the capability to restore the following objects to their original location or to another SharePoint farm:

- ❑ Restore a single document, including all its previous versions and web discussions.
- ❑ Restore a specific version of a document instead of all versions.
- ❑ Restore a single list item.
- ❑ Restore a single list or library.
- ❑ Restore a single site.
- ❑ Restore a single personal site.
- ❑ Restore a single portal area.

The current version of DocAve is not backing up the complete SharePoint structure, so you will still need to use a tool like SharePoint Central Administration backups, a SQL backup tool, or DocAve's own SharePoint Disaster Recovery tool. However, since DocAve will protect all data, it will most likely be enough to run tools like MOSSBACKUP once per week or even once per month, depending on how often you change the structure of your SharePoint environment. The SharePoint Disaster Recovery tool will replicate the complete SharePoint environment to another server. If a total disaster happens, you simply rebuild the basic structure on the old server, and press the Recover button and all data will be replicated back to that server again.

There is also a very handy complement to DocAve called TrashBin, which allows a user to undelete any document, list item, or list directly from within the site, without any assistance from the administrator. TrashBin will use the backups made by DocAve, which gives the user the same type of restore options as the administrator (i.e., all the options listed above). Compare that to other "undelete" tools, which cannot restore documents deleted from the file system or by using the Explorer View. This is no problem for TrashBin.

NSE Tools

Another company that focuses on SharePoint backups is NSE (www.nse.com) with their product SPManager. It is also a complete backup solution for SharePoint 2003 environments. During 2007, NSE will release an upgraded version of SPManager that works with SharePoint 2007, both WSS and MOSS. It has been around for several years now and is easy to use for both backup and restore tasks. The main features of SPManager are these:

❑ Restores single documents.

❑ Restores single list items.

❑ Restores Web Parts.

❑ Restores single sites.

❑ Restores complete SharePoint environments.

All these restore operations can be performed against the original SharePoint server or on another SharePoint server. This tool can also be used as a migration tool or when you need to create a test environment of your production server.

Summary

In this chapter you learned that:

❑ **Rule #1:** What you back up is what you can restore.

❑ **Rule #2:** Make sure that all of SharePoint's databases are backed up.

❑ **Rule #3:** Make sure to back up the file system and the IIS Metabase on the front-end servers.

❑ **Rule #4:** You can only copy the latest version of a document, not its complete version history.

❑ **Rule #5:** A template for a list or library can only contain up to 500 MB of content.

❑ **Rule #6:** Use Excel for moving or copying lists greater than 500 MB.

❑ **Rule #7:** Using the Recycle Bin any item, including previous version, can be restored.

❑ SharePoint's new Recycle Bin will also restore complete lists or libraries within the configured time limits.

❑ STSADM can back up and restore single sites, site collections, and complete SharePoint farms.

❑ STSADM is a full-fidelity backup tool. All settings, including users and rights will be restored.

❑ Use stsadmwin 2007 for a graphical user interface for STSADM.

❑ SMIGRATE has been replaced by the new STSADM operations "export" and "import."

❑ The backup procedure in SharePoint Central Administration will back up the complete MOSS farm, including all WSS team sites.

❑ Running STSADM -Domain performs the same type of backup process as in Central Administration.

❑   The backup procedure in SharePoint Central Administration performs a full-fidelity backup. It will restore every content database in the SQL database and all index files, plus truncate the SQL Server transaction log files.

❑   The backup procedure in SharePoint Central Administration does not have a command interface; use `STSADM -Directory` instead.

❑   Use Windows' built-in Scheduled Tasks to schedule STSADM backups.

❑   Make sure to devise a Backup Plan, also known as a Disaster Recovery Plan.

❑   Do fire drills to make sure that the backups are working and that you know how to do a restore.

❑   For easier recovery procedures and a way to restore single items, including the version history, look at third-party backup tools like DocAve that focus on SharePoint.

Index